Reviews for

The Natural Death Handbook

'What could be more healthy than bringing society's last taboo
out of the closet?'
The Observer

'Excellent'
*The British Holistic Medical
Association Newsletter*

'Investigating Natural Death is a cheering experience and I
would recommend it to anyone facing bereavement'
Midweek

'Inspiring'
Church Times

'Strongly recommended for its scope, interest and practicality'
Network

'Full of amazing advice and information'
Sunday Independent

'I'd advise anyone interested to get hold of a copy of *The
Natural Death Handbook*, altogether a very good thing'
Green magazine

The Natural Death Centre is especially grateful to John Bradfield and the A. B. Welfare and Wildlife Trust – the Centre largely relies on the Trust for sound information on law and ecology (although the Trust is not responsible for any errors or shortcomings within the text).

Thanks are also due to: Mike Jarvis, Billy Magner, Johanna Taylor, Nick Temple and Jana Hirsch for their help in preparing this present edition; Susan Morris for her invaluable contributions to Chapter 3; solicitor Desmond Banks for advice on wills and probate; Enid France for her contribution to Advance Directives; landscape architect Andy Clayden for his contribution to Chapter 9; and all those who have suggested improvements including Jane Feinmann, Christianne Heal, Andrew Herxheimer, Gina Mackenzie, Yvonne Malik, Steve Small, and Tony Walter.

THE NATURAL DEATH HANDBOOK

Edited by Stephanie Wienrich and Josefine Speyer
of The Natural Death Centre

RIDER

LONDON · SYDNEY · AUCKLAND · JOHANNESBURG

5 7 9 10 8 6

First published in 1993 by Rider, an imprint of Ebury Publishing
This edition published by Rider in 2003

Ebury Publishing is a Random House Group company

The Natural Death Centre
6 Blackstock Mews
Blackstock Road
London N4 2BT
Tel: 020 7359; Fax: 020 7354 3831
Email: ndc@alberyfoundation.org; Web: www.naturaldeath.org.uk

All royalties from this book are going to The Natural Death Centre, a charitable project, towards its work in supporting those dying and advising on funerals. The Centre is grateful to all the many people and publishers who freely contributed items and it apologetic to any whom it failed to trace or acknowledge.

The Random House Group Limited Reg. No. 954009

Addresses for companies within the Random House Group can be found at
www.rbooks.co.uk

A CIP catalogue record for this book is available from the British Library
The Random House Group Limited supports The Forest Stewardship
Council (FSC), the leading international forest certification organisation.
All our titles that are printed on Greenpeace approved FSC certified paper carry the
FSC logo. Our paper procurement policy can be found at
www.rbooks.co.uk/environment

Mixed Sources
Product group from well-managed
forests and other controlled sources
www.fsc.org   Cert no. TT-COC-2139
© 1996 Forest Stewardship Council

Printed in the UK by CPI Mackays, Chatham, ME5 8TD

ISBN 9781844132263

Copies are available at special rates for bulk orders. Contact the sales development team on 020 7840 8487 for more information.

To buy books by your favourite authors and register for offers, visit www.rbooks.co.uk

Formal disclaimer: Neither the publisher nor The Natural Death Handbook can accept responsibility for any action taken as a result of reading this book; the reader would be wise to get a second opinion or to consult professional advisers. Please send all comments and updates to the NDC as the above address.

CONTENTS

Chapter 1

The Natural Death Movement

The idea that launched the Natural Death Centre

The Natural Death Centre is a charitable educational project, founded in 1991 by three psychotherapists – husband and wife Nicholas Albery and Josefine Speyer, and Christianne Heal. For Josefine and Nicholas, the idea for the Centre grew from the experience of the birth of their son. As Nicholas described it:

> Back in 1975, Josefine was pregnant and I'd taken a long spell off work to help her fulfil a cherished fantasy of travelling by horse and cart. With our horse Patience (on £2 a week rent from the Heavy Horse Preservation Society) and our converted manure tip cart, we meandered our way through the wilder parts of Wales, looking for a cottage for the winter and the birth. Josefine was adamant that she wanted to be at home for the birth. As she put it: 'I'm not ill, why should I go into hospital?' At last we found a place by the river Teifi and a doctor who was willing to come to the farm cottage – 'I don't mind if you give birth on a haystack, I'll come wherever you want,' he told Josefine.

In the event they were very lucky:

> It was a short, almost painfree and ecstatic labour for Josefine, and all the preparation helped – the raspberry leaf tea, the natural birth books and classes, the visualisations and breathing exercises – and the doctor and midwife were like guests in our home for this Leboyer-style birth of low lights and quiet.

In 1988, Nicholas Albery's father died at home. This death triggered in Nicholas a realisation of the need for a natural death movement to parallel the natural childbirth movement, and to spread the tenets of good hospice care to home care for those dying of all causes, not just cancer. As Nicholas put it:

> It wouldn't suit everybody, but why shouldn't those families who wanted it be fully supported by the NHS in looking after the dying person at home, with adequate financial and other help for carers? Wouldn't more people, if it were possible, prefer to die at home amongst friends rather than in the anonymity of a big and noisy hospital? As with birth, could preparation, exercises and rituals help reduce the anxieties that people feel about dying? Could dying at least for a lucky few become as easy and as ecstatic a process as our experience of birth? Granted that no one can be certain what happens after death, could it be that preparation matters, as the Tibetans argue, to

enable the soul at the point of death to merge fearlessly with that bright light reported by many who have recovered from Near-Death Experiences? I remembered how a friend's mother insisted on being given her travelling rug to die with; could the process of dying be the labour pains of the soul, with sometimes the same feeling of expectation and transition as at birth?

Just as many people want to experience birth as consciously as possible, so some people want to face death with minds as unclouded as their circumstances permit. It is here that the analogy between birth and death breaks down somewhat, for drugs are more likely to be necessary to relieve pain for the dying, if only because dying can be a much more drawn-out labour than giving birth.

Aldous Huxley sat by his wife Maria at her death, urging her with hypnotic repetition to 'go towards the light'. Perhaps many people would like a Huxley-type figure sitting by them as they go. Perhaps there could be a new profession of 'Midwives for the Dying', people skilled in holistic care of the dying person's practical, emotional and spiritual needs (and the needs of the family), and more intent on creating a calm and supportive atmosphere than on high-tech medical interventions to prolong life to the utmost. There is a need for such skills in modern life, for as Huxley wrote: 'The living can do a great deal to make the passage easier for the dying, to raise the most purely physiological act of human existence to the level of awareness and perhaps even of spirituality.'

As the baby boomer generation reaches late middle-age, so the natural death movement will inevitably become a force in health politics, bringing about a redirection of NHS and other resources towards home care and proper provision for carers. The Natural Death Centre aims to be in the vanguard of such changes. In 1994 it founded the Befriending Network, now an independent charity, which trains volunteers who visit the home of someone who is dying, sit with them and assist the carer. Christianne Heal offers Living With Dying workshops for the general public on preparing for dying. Josefine Speyer, who helped develop the training programme for the Befriending Network, provides individual counselling for those who are anxious or bereaved. She offers workshops for nurses, doctors and others concerned with looking after people who are dying, and workshops for the public on the theme of 'Accepting Death and Living Fully'.

At present, dying mostly happens 'off stage', as it were, in care homes and hospitals, and many people are superstitious enough to believe that the less they think about the subject the longer they will live. Sixty per cent of the UK adult population have not even taken the first step of writing a will, thus potentially leaving additional problems for their survivors. The Centre wants to make death and dying an unexceptional topic for daily meditation and conversation, and to that end has hosted a series of seminars and workshops on subjects ranging from care for those who are dying to family-organised funerals. It also organises a National Day of the Dead celebration in April each year, inspired by the Mexican Day of the Dead festivities – a day for remembering our friends and relatives who have died and a day to contemplate our own mortality.

Once a family has looked after someone dying at home, they are more likely to want to take care of the dead body themselves too. The Centre found itself submerged in mail from families wanting ecologically-sound and inexpensive funerals, often without using funeral directors. A great deal of research later, the material for the funeral chapters in this book was assembled. Chapters Four to Six cover not only on how to organise a funeral without using a funeral director, at a fraction of the normal cost, but also detail who are the best professionals to approach, should you want some help.

The Centre now acts as a consumers' association, giving an in-depth consumer's perspective on, and awards to, the funeral trade. It also perforce has had to campaign on behalf of the public with the National Association of Funeral Directors and the Office of Fair Trading, to try to ensure, for instance, that itemised price breakdowns on funerals are available to the public and that coffins and other funeral items are sold to those people who want to organise a funeral themselves. The kind of changes in policy that still seem necessary are outlined in the chapter 'The Politics of Dying' which also includes a Declaration of Rights for the person dying at home.

The Natural Death Centre in 1994 launched an Association of Natural Burial Grounds, in an attempt to ensure that every locality should have its own natural burial ground, where a tree is planted instead of having a headstone. Ten years later, more than 180 such grounds exist in the UK (see Chapter 6 for a complete list). The UK movement has inspired other countries to take similar initiatives (New Zealand, Canada, the US and Italy, to name but a few).

The Centre is financed on a shoestring. Ninety per cent of its income comes from the sale of publications. For the rest it survives thanks to members of the public who very kindly become Friends of the Natural Death Centre (contact the centre for details on this). This book too requires your assistance if it is to become ever more useful in future editions – if you have a recommendation, update, correction, tip or experience you are willing to share with others, please send it in.

The purpose of this book is also to introduce readers to the great pioneers of the natural death movement and to the ideas in their writings. The very best books on the subject are marked ✪✪✪ in the Resources chapter. Update leaflets for this book are available from the Centre for six first class stamps (or a £2 cheque). These updates and most of the Centre's books (although not the present volume) are accessible via the Centre's website (www.naturaldeath.org.uk).

Nicholas Albery, writer, social inventor and the real powerhouse behind the Natural Death Centre, died suddenly in a car collision in June 2001. He is greatly missed not only by his family, friends and colleagues, but by the many people who benefited from his research, campaigning and advice over the years. As sociologist Tony Walter put it in an email to the Centre just after he heard the news of Nicholas' untimely death: 'His ability to disseminate creative and practical ideas – without at the same time promoting himself – was remarkable. ... We have lost a wonderful engineer of social change.'

In Nicholas' memory, the Nicholas Albery Foundation (charity no. 1091396) was set up to foster this spirit of social invention and ideas dissemination. The Natural Death Centre is just one of the many projects of the Foundation, see www.alberyfoundation.org for more information.

The wider movement

What have others had to say about the need for a natural death movement? Douglas Harding has emphasised our resistance to thinking about our own mortality:

The cult of youth-at-all-costs

Our current resistance to such an investigation, to any candour or realism concerning our own mortality, can scarcely be exaggerated. Witness the popular cult of youth-at-all-costs in the worlds of advertising and fashion. Witness those communities of old folk dedicated to being 'as young as you feel' and to avoiding all reminders of old age, sickness, and death. Witness the newspeak and double-talk of '70 years young' in place of '70 years old' and 'elderly person' or 'senior citizen' in place of 'old man', 'old woman'. Witness the funerary nonsense so tellingly described in Evelyn Waugh's *The Loved One*. Witness cryonics – the freezing of the newly dead for revival when technology is further developed, thus giving effect to the view that 'death is an imposition on the human race, and no longer acceptable'. Witness the cultists who seriously maintain that death is unnecessary and unnatural, and we can choose to live as long as we wish. How unlike the veneration of old age and the preoccupation with death and the hereafter which are such marked features of some great cultures! And again, what a contrast with the *memento mori* (remember you must die) of earlier centuries of our own civilisation – its human skulls carved on tombstones and displayed on mantelpieces, its countless engravings and paintings confronting the living with the grim spectacle of Death the Reaper and the imagined sequel!

> *Reproduced by permission of Penguin Books Ltd from*
> The Little Book of Life and Death *by D. E. Harding.*
> *For fuller details of all main book references*
> *see the booklist in the Resources chapter.*

Ivan Illich in 1975 wrote about the torments inflicted on the dying in some hospitals:

The medicalisation of society

Today, the man best protected against setting the stage for his own dying is the sick person in critical condition. Society, acting through the medical system, decides when and after what indignities and mutilations he shall die. The medicalisation of society has brought the epoch of natural death to an end.

> *From* Medical Nemesis: The Expropriation of Health
> *by Ivan Illich, Calder & Boyars Ltd, 1975.*

The isolation of the dying and the bereaved in a centralised society that has lost almost all sense of neighbourhood has been highlighted by Tony Walter:

Neighbours no longer share the loss

Because the elderly person who has died may well not have been widely known by the friends of those left behind, the grief of the bereaved is not shared. When someone dies in Ambridge, or in an African village, or in a police unit, an entire community feels the loss: everyone knew the person and everyone to some degree mourns the loss. But when most old people in Britain die today, only a few close relatives are still in touch to feel the loss.

Nor is this true only when the deceased is elderly. In a relatively isolated nuclear family in which outsiders have played little if any role in child care, the death of a child may be a uniquely isolating experience. Contrast this account by Miller after the destruction of the primary school in Aberfan: 'One bereaved mother told me that when she lost her child the company she sought was not that of other bereaved mothers but of her neighbours. They might not have lost a child themselves, but she realised they had lost her child. It was the neighbours who had helped to bring him up, who had minded him when she went out, had watched him grow and had taken pride in his achievements. In a very real sense they shared her grief.' Usually though, friends and neighbours may be sympathetic, but they do not know the child well enough truly to share the loss. Friends in their thirties or younger may never have experienced any close bereavement.

So the bereaved today often are isolated, and may well report being treated as lepers.

From 'Modern Death: Taboo or Not Taboo?' by Tony Walter,
Sociology, *Vol. 25, No. 2.*

Tony Walter shares the Natural Death Centre's perception that the green movement and the natural birth movement will tend to lead to the acceptance of death and dying as natural processes to be shared with our family and friends:

Natural childbirth leads to natural death

The Green movement surely must lead to a more realistic acceptance of the fact that human beings are natural creatures who must die. This movement has prompted all of us to question our technological hubris; we all know now that we are part of a delicate natural system; we are less able to split a heroic, rational soul from an inconvenient body.

This new attitude surely underlies the natural childbirth movement. Giving birth may be painful, but it is part of the natural human experience, and many women would not wish it anaesthetised away. Nor do they want to be socially isolated; they want to share this miracle of nature with their partners and their other children.

Death is also a natural part of being human, and therefore I do not wish to be drugged into oblivion: I want the pain to be controlled, but I would like to be conscious and in control as far as is possible. And I would like to share this unrepeatable and important event with my partner and my children.

From Funerals and How to Improve Them *by Tony Walter.*

Tony Walter pointed out in a letter to the Natural Death Centre that 'natural' does not necessarily mean adopting the practices of pre-technological societies:

The diversity of non-Western, pre-modern death practices is astonishing – many segregate the dying, the Hopi have as many taboos as we do, and the ceremonies of most hunter gatherer societies are as 'thin' as are our own. Not many traditional societies see death as 'natural'.

The historian Roy Porter has shown convincingly that it was doctors in the late 18th century who introduced the idea that death is a natural event, which then eased out older notions of death as ordained by God and as a spiritual passage.

I'm inclined to agree with Arney and Bergen in 'Medicine and the Management of Living' (Chicago, UP, 1984) that it's doctors, not a consumer revolt, that first pushed the demedicalisation, ie naturalisation, of death. Would it all have happened without medics such as Kübler-Ross, Saunders, Parkes and Jolly?

There are, moreover, many kinds of natural death. It is just as much a part of nature to die abruptly or in agony, through accidents or violence or illness, as it is to die with ease and dignity. But even in such circumstances, to feel prepared for any eventuality may help. Gandhi was assassinated, but his instant reaction to the bullets was to chant the name of God. He was prepared, in his own way. As Jung appreciated:

Death as a goal in old age

Willy-nilly, the ageing person prepares himself for death. Thoughts of death pile up to an astonishing degree as the years increase. That is why I think that nature herself is always preparing for the end. Objectively it is a matter of indifference what the individual consciousness may think about it. But subjectively it makes an enormous difference whether consciousness keeps in step with the psyche or whether it clings to opinions of which the heart knows nothing. It is just as neurotic in old age not to focus upon the goal of death as it is in youth to repress fantasies which have to do with the future.

From 'The Soul and Death' by C. G. Jung in The Collected Works, series XX, vol. viii, translated by R. F. C. Hull, Princeton University Press, 1969.

Many people ask: Is it not morbid to think about death and dying earlier in life? No, it is necessary, for preparing for dying is half a lifetime's work. The main preparation is that which the Dalai Lama advises: 'For most of us ordinary people who lead busy lives, what is important is to develop a kind, generous heart to others. If we can do that and live accordingly, we will be able to die peacefully.' And for those who have the opportunity and the necessary circumstances, he adds, there are higher spiritual preparations available through religious and yogic practices. But above all, an awareness of death can sweeten every remaining living moment. Yeats is not the only poet to warn:

'Begin the preparation for your death'

Get all the gold and silver that you can,
Satisfy ambition, animate
The trivial days and ram them with the sun ...

But then:

No longer in Lethean foliage caught
Begin the preparation for your death
And from the fortieth winter by that thought
Test every work of intellect or faith,
And everything that your own hands have wrought,
And call those works extravagance of breath
That are not suited for such men as come
Proud, open eyed and laughing to the tomb.
From 'Vacillation' by W. B. Yeats.

Ageing to Yeats was a growing of the soul:

An aged man is but a paltry thing,
A tattered coat upon a stick, unless
Soul clap its hands and sing, and louder sing
For every tatter in its mortal dress.
From 'Sailing to Byzantium'.

To adopt this new outlook, we have first to rid ourselves of a great deal of cultural conditioning. Paula Hendrick has surveyed the natural death movement from an American perspective and concludes that our technological mastery of nature and our focus on personal autonomy and self-development have made it very hard for us to accept the inevitability of death:

Natural dying – an American perspective

In the world of nature, death provides a service because it makes room in an ecological niche for a young one. People are part of nature, too, and when people die, they make room for more people. In a time of population explosion, it would be useful to be able to die without making too much of a fuss about it. But we humans, particularly in the affluent cultures of the first world, face the final journey of life with a load of weighty baggage. We avoid talk of death, and we dread the realities of the ageing process.

We as individuals don't necessarily create and lug around this excess baggage on our own. Something pervasive in our society moulds our collective choices. Michael Ignatieff, writing in 'The New Republic', offers this explanation: 'Cultures that live by the values of self-realisation and self-mastery are not especially good at dying, at submitting to those experiences where freedom ends and biological fate begins. Why should they be? Their strong side is Promethean ambition: the defiance and transcendence of fate, the material and social limit. Their weak side is submitting to the inevitable.'

We have become victims of the health care system that our cultural values have created. The dying process has been transformed into a series of wrenching choices. A woman, getting along pretty well after a stroke at age 80 – some confusion, but lots of independence and zest for life – develops increasing heart problems. She has no family support, just a few friends who do the best they can. The doctor recommends a pacemaker. She says no but he persuades her. There are complications during surgery. Now she's totally disorientated and can barely walk even with assistance. Her pacemaker keeps her going.

Out of the apparently needless suffering of countless people has grown a strong movement towards patients' rights and natural death – that is, death with a minimum of medical intervention. Advances are continually – albeit slowly – being made in legislation and public education. The Patient Self-Determination Act, which went into effect in the USA in 1991, requires health care facilities to inform patients of their rights to refuse treatment and to formulate advance directives such as a living will or health care proxy. Difficult moral dilemmas are also being debated on the topic of 'aid-in-dying' or physician-assisted suicide. The goals of the broader 'natural death movement' are to guarantee choice for individuals and to bring about a large-scale cultural shift. An article in The Economist of London describes such a large scale shift this way: 'To civilise death, to bring it home and make it no longer a source of dread, is one of the great challenges of the age ... Gradually, dying may come to hold again the place it used to occupy in the midst of life: not a terror but a mystery so deep that man would no more wish to cheat himself of it than to cheat himself of life.'

Excerpted from In Context *magazine No. 31 (w: www.context.org).*

Fasting as death approaches

The Natural Death Centre gathers research on the theme of fasting as death approaches. The Hindus who go to die in Benaras in India, for instance, consider ceasing to eat as a natural part of preparing to die – not as a form of passive euthanasia or as a way of accelerating death.

There are examples of pioneering Westerners following a similar path. 'We rarely if ever,' writes Scott Nearing's wife, 'used doctors, pills or hospitals. Yet Scott lived to a hale and hearty 100 and died when he decided to – by fasting for a month and a half at the very end.'

Scott's dying, as Helen describes it, was like nature itself:

Scott Nearing – 'death like a leaf falling from a tree'

He did more than his share of mental and physical work up to his last years. At 98 he said, 'Well at least I can still split and carry in the wood.' And when he was close to the end, lying in our living room, his one regret at leaving this Earth plane was on watching me lug in the wood for our kitchen stove, 'I wish I could help with that,' he said. He was a help unto the end.

A month or two before he died he was sitting at table with us at a meal. Watching us eat he said, 'I think I won't eat anymore.' 'Alright,' said I. 'I understand. I think I would do that too. Animals know when to stop. They go off in a corner and leave off food.'

So I put Scott on juices: carrot juice, apple juice, banana juice, pineapple, grape – any kind. I kept him full of liquids as often as he was thirsty. He got weaker, of course, and he was as gaunt and thin as Gandhi. Came a day he said, 'I think I'll go on water. Nothing more.' From then on, for about ten days, he only had water. He was bed-ridden and had little strength but spoke with me daily. In the morning of August 24th, 1983, two weeks before his 100th birthday, when it seems he was slipping away, I sat beside him on his bed.

We were quiet together; no interruptions, no doctors or hospitals. I said, 'It's alright, Scott. Go right along. You've lived a good life and are finished with things here. Go on and up – up into the light. We love you and let you go. It's alright.'

In a soft voice, with no quiver or pain or disturbance he said, 'All...right,' and breathed slower and slower and slower till there was no movement any more and he was gone out of his body as easily as a leaf drops from the tree in autumn, slowly twisting and falling to the ground.

Excerpted from In Context *magazine No. 31 (w: www.context.org).*

Caroline Walker, a nutritionist dying of cancer, also decided to stop eating for the weeks before she died:

Caroline Walker – a gentle death by fasting

Caroline was exasperated rather than fascinated by her illness. We did learn a lot, though; enough to make another book. For example, when a doctor says you have cancer he (it's usually a he) will no doubt go on to say what will become of you. Our advice is take note, say thank you, shop around, and take your own decisions. After all, if a builder says you have dry rot, you do not immediately take his word for it, sign his estimate without looking at the small print, shut your eyes and resign yourself to the pickaxes. (No disrespect intended, to doctors or builders.)

There again, just as there are societies to encourage home births, there should be societies for home deaths. Being looked after at home is more trouble, of course, just as home cooking takes more time. But dying in hospital as most people do now, stuck full of tubes in white rooms, surrounded by sufferers and strangers, with those you love kept at the end of a telephone, is a sad and bad ending. Caroline thought being sent to hospital to die is like being put in a skip. (Again, no disrespect to builders or doctors.)

At home in August, Caroline finished planting our garden, with seeds and bulbs identified with little flags, so I would know what to expect the next spring and summer. She gave two interviews: one at the beginning of the month, for the Guardian, on her sense of death, as we ate lunch; the other from her bed, at the end of the month, for 'The Food Programme', on the meaning of her work.

Our home filled with family and friends and flowers. Pain was the only uncertainty. The surgeons had warned me that obstruction caused by the cancer would eventually be horribly painful. Not so; Dr Anne Naysmith, consultant at our local community hospital, a woman about Caroline's age, disagreed; and with a careful cocktail of drugs, Caroline rested at home, and took responsibility for her death, simply by stopping eating, two weeks before she died. Around midnight as her last day began, she foresaw her death. How was it – what did the thought feel like? 'Oh, lovely,' she said; and we laughed. And it was lovely to be with her when she died.

From The Good Fight *by Geoffrey Cannon.*

That was how Caroline's husband Geoffrey Cannon saw her death.

She was resting after a long conversation in which she described what it was like to die. As she spoke, I could forget her gaunt and fleshless body. I'd known her as the campaigning nutritionist, attacking the food industry and the Government.

The ultimate irony was that Caroline was dying from cancer of the colon. Despite her emaciation, her spirit was still strong. Her campaign now was to urge us to come to terms with death in general. We are all so afraid of death, she said. [...]

She derived most comfort from the regular presence of a healer, Julian Leech. 'I love seeing him. Not because I think he's going to come up with a miracle cure but because he's so relaxing to talk to. He's used to being with people who are dying and he has tremendous respect for the process, with no rejection or fear.'

'I have to live with it. Why can't other people? I know they find it difficult and disgusting, but whoever said that life was easy? Or that dying was a piece of cake? What do they want? Tinsel and gift-wrapping?' These are the people who said 'Poor you' and bought their way out with flowers. Caroline didn't feel poor. She was consumed by pain, which made her sometimes tense and fractious, but she was not poor. She did not want an Enid Blyton attitude to death. Indeed, she felt she had to be viciously blunt in imposing her death on the world. 'Dying is an alien state. You have to make the effort to communicate otherwise you are totally cut off. And you have to help others come to terms. Although I wasted much precious energy trying to prop up other people, I slowly learned who was important and who wasn't.'

Caroline has shone some light on the mystifying business of dying. She has been brave enough to expose her fear and other people's. We cling to life, avoiding thoughts of death until the very end. Surely that's too late?

From the Guardian *(September 7th 1988).*

These stories reinforce the accumulating medical evidence that fasting is not necessarily such a terrible way to die. The debate on euthanasia, in Chapter 11, brings in the wider implications of fasting near death.

Near-Death Experiences

Near-Death Experiences (NDEs) are another theme on which the Natural Death Centre gathers research, believing that such experiences can often help people reconcile themselves to their mortality.

While many people who have had NDEs are convinced about what has happened to them and the transformations that have occurred in their lives, many sceptics are equally convinced that the whole phenomenon has nothing to do with life after death, or God, or infinity, but is explicable in simple mechanistic, that is, neurological terms.

Thus Dr Robert Buckman views the sense of peace and tranquillity in an NDE as being caused by substances produced in the brain called endorphins, which are somewhat like painkillers. The 19th century explorer, David Livingstone, felt calm, peaceful and painless whilst being crushed across the chest in a lion's jaws. It led him to believe that 'death agonies' may appear so to the onlooker, but may be experienced differently by the patient, protected by a bodily defence mechanism switched on at the approach of death.

Dr Susan Blackmore, a psychologist, explains the common NDE vision of a long tunnel with a bright light at the end, as the retina at the back of the eye becoming starved of oxygen, with nerve cells beginning to fire at random. There are more nerve cells in the most sensitive part, the fovea, so a bright spot that could look like the end of a tunnel is seen.

Her explanation is linked to the most common physiological explanation for NDEs, which is that the brain is in receipt of insufficient oxygen (cerebral anoxia). Or that NDEs are the result of temporal lobe seizure. This can produce similar effects to those of some NDEs, without necessarily accounting for the complete range of near-death phenomena. Whereas temporal lobe seizure causes distorted perceptions of the immediate environment, this is not always the case with NDEs.

Whatever the truth of the matter, to know that nature has evolved a way of allowing dying humans to feel blissful can only be reassuring, even for the sceptic who dismisses the visions and feelings as delusionary. The term 'Near-Death Experience' is in some cases a misnomer – a seemingly almost identical experience is accessed by people during 'peak' experiences, by mystics and by others who have not as yet suffered physical harm – such as those falling from a mountain, who have their NDE before hitting the ground, when they have been no more damaged than a free-fall parachutist. The difference between the person falling from the mountain and the parachutist is one of expectation of harm and thus degree of shock; and this seems the essence of many experiences of heightened consciousness. The trigger is any severe jolt to our normal consciousness, whether or not physically damaging, which brings about a change of perspective and releases us into a world of rich and strange magic.

In the end it may come down to a choice. Do you see consciousness as being contained and confined to the brain? The Horizon Foundation in Southampton has commissioned a largescale study, set to involve 25 hospitals, with the aim of further investigating this dichotomy.

Could NDEs prove existence of the soul?

A pilot project at the city's general hospital, led by Dr Sam Parnia, Senior Research Fellow at the University of Southampton, suggested that a small proportion (11 per cent) of patients who had a cardiac arrest and survived reported some kind of unusual experience while they were clinically brain dead (with no pulse, no respiration and fixed dilated pupils).

None of the patients had a history of psychiatric problems or expressed a strong religious belief and it did not appear likely that any drugs administered during resuscitation had caused the experiences.

Dr Parnia argues that this suggests that consciousness and the mind may continue to exist after the brain has ceased to function and the body has been declared clinically dead: 'Some of those people are able to recall specific details of the resuscitation attempts, so in other words a form of consciousness has had to have been present for them to come back and tell us what was happening to them. ... This may therefore imply that the mind is a separate entity to the brain.'

The Horizon Research Foundation
(e: info@horizon-research.co.uk).

Return to nature

A final thread running through this book is an almost pagan wish to return to the world of nature. This is sometimes expressed by those who are dying as a preference for being outdoors or to be surrounded by plants and flowers. In the following instance, it concerns a woman's wish for a natural burial:

Joy's burial

My mum Joy's love and concern for the world (her greenness) came through in her funeral much more than a snapshot of the props and mechanics of the event would suggest. It is the feel of the event that is important, not the outward appearance.

For my mum, being green was more than about cycling and recycling tins, and more than organic gardening and protesting about globalisation. It was all those things too but at bottom it was a spiritual matter: striving to live in harmony with the world, naturally and non-invasively; a love of the natural in all of its guises.

Funerals too are spiritual matters, the ceremony that poses the big questions. A ritual designed to help us understand our place in life and in the world.

My mum's green funeral whilst in accordance with her wishes was not for her benefit. It was for the benefit of us left behind, an opportunity for us to say our goodbyes, make our peace, to reflect and consider.

Mum chose a wonderful spot in a private area overlooking the hills and under a large shady oak tree. Her choosing of a place rather then being allocated an anonymous plot made it personal and underlined that she had faced up to and accepted her death.

Sun and rain alternated, all things grow, die and regenerate.

This ceremony was free. Everyone who wanted to could say what they wanted to, when they wanted. During periods of silence the speeches were made by the birds and the wind in the trees. Strong words were spoken by the people who knew and cared for my mum and what she believed in.

People cried, people hugged each other and they even smiled. My mother's love of nature, of life, came through in her choice of funeral. It turned what could have been a sterile necessity of an occasion into a life-affirming event.

There will be no headstone, solid and inflexible, one is not needed. The changing woodland about my mother will, as the seasons unfold, provide a far more fitting memorial.

My mum is buried under an oak tree. With time her body will return to the earth she loved and will nourish that tree and the environment around. Her spirit lives with us who were privileged to know her.

The oak occupies a special place in the lore of birth, death and regeneration. Diana the goddess of fertility and of the wood was personified in the oak. Some cultures would bury an effigy of death under the oak in order to banish it. My mum's funeral was a celebration of life, and I see it as being in that way a banishment of the force of negativity. A point to move forward from.

My mother's funeral was a celebration of her life and of life itself. From what I see respect and love of life is really what being green is all about.

Ian Ross-Bain, from After Life *(NDC, 2002; see Resources).*

May this present Handbook on improving the quality of all aspects of dying prove a useful contribution to the contemplation of this magnificent and awe-inspiring subject. Above all, may it allow people to 'die in character' as Elisabeth Kübler-Ross puts it. Dr Buckman in his book on how to support a dying person is rightly adamant on this point:

It should be your objective as friend and supporter – as it is my objective when I'm looking after dying patients – to help your friend let go of life *in his own way*. It may not be your way, and it may not be the way you read about in a book or magazine, but it's his way and consistent with the way he's lived his life. You can and should help your friend achieve that.

From I Don't Know What To Say – How to Help and Support Someone who is Dying *by Dr Robert Buckman.*

Chapter 2

PREPARING FOR DYING

Preparing for dying is really preparing for living. Yet dying is an emotional subject, tied up with grief. It brings up painful feelings, so most people try to avoid the subject. The superstitious feel that talking about dying will somehow cause death or bring it on prematurely, whereas in actuality, the sooner the subject is raised, the better prepared you will be when the time inevitably comes. Ignorance breeds fear. The more we ignore death the more frightening it becomes when we are faced with it. By looking at our own death and preparing for it, we can learn to make friends with death. As it becomes a reality, life takes on a new dimension, as if switching from 2D to 3D.

> *'To begin depriving death of its greatest advantage over us, let us adopt a way clean contrary to that common one; let us deprive death of its strangeness, let us frequent it, let us get used to it. Let us have nothing more often on mind than death ... We do not know where death awaits us: so let us wait for it everywhere. To practise death is to practise freedom. A man who has learned how to die has unlearnt how to be a slave.'*
>
> Michel de Montaigne, French philosopher (1533-1592).

It is becoming more and more common for people to grow up without experiencing the death of someone close or without seeing a dead body. For these reasons and more, many people find discussing issues around dying and grieving like entering unknown territory. In addition, the rituals traditionally used around death may convey little or no meaning. This is why the natural death movement suggests we treat death similarly to the way the natural birth movement treats birth: we inform ourselves, we make choices, and we discuss these choices. We are consciously involved with what is going on. We do not necessarily hand over to the 'professionals'. We create our own personal rituals.

Facing the reality of our own eventual death

Preparing for dying is a healthy, practical and even therapeutic thing to do – because we all die. Most of us get an inkling of our own mortality when we start having children or as part of the ageing process, when people close to us are ill or dying, or when we ourselves get sick. If you have not taken the opportunity to prepare for dying whilst you were healthy and well, *now* is a very good time. Thinking and talking about death in a practical sort of way helps to break the taboo about death that still exists in many families. It may bring you closer together, and it will certainly allow you to be creative and prepare things that you may wish to leave behind for your loved ones.

Learning to make friends with cancer, learning to make friends with the possibility of an early and perhaps painful death, has taught me a great deal about making friends with myself, as I am, and a great deal about making friends with life, as it is. I know that there are a lot of things I can't change. I can't force life to make sense, or to be fair. This growing acceptance of life as it is … has brought me a kind of peace.

Ken Wilber, author of *Grace and Grit* (see Resources).

Don't wait for the doctors to tell you that you are dying. If you are a patient in hospital you may think that the medical professionals will tell you all you need to know or all there is to know about the state of your illness and if you are dying, but be aware that this is not necessarily so. Doctors have particular ways of dealing with giving 'bad news' and there is a high chance that if you do not ask the right questions you will not be offered the information you need. Doctors think that if the patient wants to know something, they will ask, but most patients expect that the doctor will tell them anyway.

Professor Lesley Fallowfield, director of the Psychosocial Oncology Group at the University of Sussex, is working to introduce better communication skills training for doctors:

> Doctors have difficulty being honest with patients when the news is very bad ... They often underestimate the information needs of their patients, and may censor the information in the belief that they are being kind ... Failure to give adequate information about a patient's true prognosis or what lies ahead can leave patients isolated and scared.

Palliative Medicine, 16, 4, July 2002.

Patients would benefit greatly if doctors and nurses prepared for their own dying. In doing so they would face their own fears and concerns around dying and have more awareness and a better understanding of what is involved. As Thich Nhat Hanh, the Vietnamese Buddhist monk and teacher, says: 'If you can free yourself from the fear of dying, then you will be very helpful to accompany the people who are dying; you inspire faith, confidence and peace in them.'

The Janki Foundation for Global Health Care (see Resources) is one of many organisations that believes the psychological and spiritual needs of doctors and nurses need to be addressed. 'The aim is to help doctors in a consultation to "be themselves in that space with someone else",' says Dr Craig Brown, a GP and healer who practises in Rustington, Sussex, and who has put together a training package ('Values in Health Care, a Spiritual Approach'), funded by the Foundation: 'We are taught in medical school that getting involved with patients will be emotionally exhausting – but the opposite is true. By learning the skills to be openly caring, doctors can protect themselves against burn-out and regain their role as an integral part of the healing process,' he says.

For those who are dying the healing process is not concerned with the healing of the body but of the spirit. Hope does not mean hoping for a cure, but for quality of life until the very end of their life; making the most of the time left. Lawrence LeShan makes this point in his inspiring book, *Cancer as a Turning Point*:

All of us need to understand before death the meaning of our lives ... We cannot really say goodbye to something without knowing what it was ... The essence of the task of the Dying Time is to see the whole of our lives as a pattern and a symphony ... It calls for forgiving and accepting ourselves, so that at the end we are real to ourselves ... This time then becomes the last adventure.

Cancer as a Turning Point *by Lawrence LeShan (see Resources).*

Of course, you don't have to wait until you are on your deathbed to start reviewing your life. Life review is an integral part of dealing with change, and becomes particularly important at times of major life crises. We look back in order to reflect and find meaning, to make peace with ourselves and how we have lived, to forgive ourselves and others and to look ahead to the future.

What follows is an extract from a structured exercise used by Natural Death Centre director Josefine Speyer as part of her training course, 'Accepting Death and Living Fully'. Participants fill in a questionnaire at home and then discuss it in pairs as part of the course. You may use this exercise to conduct your own life review or develop your own version. You may do it on your own, or with one other person or a small group in order to support each other with what the questions bring up. Leave out those questions which you find too difficult. This exercise can also be used with a dying person, either in an unstructured way, by focusing on a particular question or questions and allowing the person to speak freely, as part of a reflective conversation; or, in a more structured way, by taking them through the exercise, writing down their answers and creating a 'lifeline' for them.

Life Review Exercise

For this exercise you will need a large piece of paper, a notebook and pen for your written answers, and a red and a blue colour pen.

Looking back

1. Start off the exercise by drawing your lifeline: On a big piece of paper draw a line, marking one end with zero or 'birth' and the other end with the age you are now. Now mark on this line, in chronological order, all the important events of your life with dates and keywords of the event.

2. What were your dreams as a child, as a young adult and later in life? Make a list of them in your notebook and describe if necessary.

Reflecting on the past

3. What were the best times, when you were happy and felt life was good and exciting? Mark these times as events or periods with a red pen on your lifeline. What age were you? What else was happening at those times? What were the particular ingredients that made this a happy time for you? Write a few key words on your life line and write about these in your notebook.

4. Describe a significant happy memory from your childhood. Allow yourself to be as detailed as you like.

5. Remember times when you were unhappy in your life, perhaps you were suffering or struggling in some way. Mark the event or period with a blue pen

on your lifeline. Write in your notebook what the circumstances were. What happened? Did you learn something or did something positive come out of these difficult times for you?

6. Who were the most important people and influences in your life and why?

7. Is there anything you feel you need to forgive yourself for or others?

8. Overall, looking back at your life, was it a good life? Do you have a sense of satisfaction, fulfilment and gratitude? Why?

9. What were some of the most important things in your life?

Looking ahead

10. Consider your age and situation now, what are your priorities at this time and stage of your life? Mention three aspects or tasks.

11. What are the important aspects or tasks you want to bring to completion before you die?

12. How do you need to live now so that you can die without regrets?

13. Do you have a religious or spiritual outlook? Describe it. How can it support you in your dying?

14. Have you created your 'death file'? (see page 23)

15. Having completed this exercise to the best of your ability, how do you feel?

From 'Accepting Death and Living Fully' (see Resources).

Live this year as though it were your last

Inspired by Stephen Levine's book, *A Year to Live: How to live this year as though it were your last* (currently out of print, alas), a group of nine friends – including an engineer, a nurse, a mother, and an artist – met one weekend in January 2002 to decide how they could effectively prepare for death and stop putting off their lives. They looked at their diaries to see how they had used their time in the previous year, and then asked themselves, 'If I knew for sure that I only had one year to live, what would be my actual priorities?' They also shared their knowledge of death, wrote their obituaries, designed their farewell parties, mused on their ideal death and ideal funeral, and considered Wills and Advance Directives. Combining their responses with an assessment of how they had spent the last year, they wrote recommendations to themselves for a wiser and more meaningful approach for the coming year and decided to keep a journal to record their experiences. They agreed to meet for a mid-year picnic to talk about how they were getting on and then to meet again at the end of the year. After the process, one member of the group reported back:

> Like many people I had tried to ignore death. That is no longer the case. It is no longer something I cannot contemplate. I have started to tidy my life so as not to leave a mess behind and have now got a Will which reflects my wishes ... I am not treating this year as if it were my last. Rather, I am trying to make changes in the way I live, so as to be able to die at any time knowing that I have done my best to be true to what I know – and to be OK with that.

Caroline Sherwood, who organised the aforementioned group, runs regular retreats on this theme – see 'Courses' under Resources for more details.

Recording a video message

Another practical and fun first-step could be to make a videotaped message to be played after your death. Natural Death Centre founder Nicholas Albery recorded such a message with filmmaker Thom Osborn (see Memorial Messages under Resources) in 1998, in one take. He spoke about what he believed the afterlife would be like and what he felt was important in life, passing on bits of wisdom and advice, while avoiding speaking of his regrets (with the exception of mentioning 'Don't send your children to public school!'). The candid video meant a lot to his family and friends when he died suddenly three years later, and it was played repeatedly at his memorial. A video message, like any home movie, can also be a great way for any future grandchildren or great-grandchildren to get to know more about you. As Josefine Speyer, Nicholas Albery's widow says, 'It is a good idea to make your video now, not least because you will never again be as young as you are today ...'

If you own or could borrow a video camera, you may consider doing this exercise yourself (try to avoid the Oscar speech list of thanks!). If not, or if you would like some support, the Natural Death Centre runs occasional workshops with Thom Osborn and others to help people discuss the concept and practise speaking to the camera. The workshop in itself, in getting participants to think about their own mortality, tends to be a useful, even therapeutic exercise – regardless of whether or not individual participants actually go on to make a video. These workshops are usually held on the National Day of the Dead, an annual event which is inspired by the Mexican 'El Dia de los Muertes':

Mexican Day of the Dead

That a festival to do with the dead should be a joyous occasion perhaps strikes those of us from other cultures with our different perceptions as something hard to come to terms with. The Day of the Dead is just that: a festival of welcome for the souls of the dead which the living prepare and delight in. The souls return each year to enjoy for a few brief hours the pleasures they once knew in life.

In the urban setting of Mexico City and other large towns the celebration is seen at its most exuberant, with figures of skulls and skeletons everywhere. These mimic the living and disport themselves in a mocking modern dance of death. It is not surprising that so colourful an event should have become a tourist event.

Not far away from the tourist routes there is, however, another Mexico. In the rural areas, in every village or small town, the Day of the Dead is celebrated beyond the glare of flashbulbs. Each household prepares its offering of food and drink for the dead to be set out on a table among flowers and candles. The blue smoke of burning copal incense sanctifies the ceremony, just as it has done for centuries. Outside the peace is shattered by the explosions of the rockets set off to mark the fulfilment of an obligation deeply felt. The whole company of the living and the dead share in the flowering and fruiting of the land which both have cultivated.

The Day of the Dead is essentially a private or family feast. It has a public aspect at community level, but the core of the celebration takes place within the family home. It is a time of family reunion not only for the living but also the dead, who, for a few brief hours each year, return to be with their relatives in this world.

From The Skeleton At The Feast *by Elizabeth Carmichael*
& Chloë Sayer, British Museum Press (out of print).

UK Day of the Dead

Traditionally of course the Day of the Dead is celebrated on October 31st, the eve of All Saints' Day. However, the Natural Death Centre holds its Day of the Dead in blushing springtime rather than gloomy autumn, when the burgeoning of life all around us seems to help us in our endeavours to remember the dead and to contemplate our own mortality.

Spring offers us a metaphor for hope and perseverance. The Chinese public holiday of 'Qingming', an annual family gathering at ancestral gravesides, normally falls on April 4th or 5th. In the early days, having a coffin display in the Centre's garden, amongst the daffodils, on an invariably sunny day, certainly imbued the event with a peculiarly British sense of the bizarre.

The UK event is now held annually on one Sunday in April. Each year has a different theme, and past events have included: an art exhibition; death-related poetry, music and theatre; a coffin-making workshop; a lunchtime debate on euthanasia; an evening dinner discussion on Near-Death Experiences; a co-ordinated open day at natural burial grounds; and video workshops as mentioned above. These practices enable us to commemorate and celebrate our loved ones, and keep our own sense of death in perspective, by giving death and the dead a time as well as a place.

Ready to go

A photographer who frequently has overseas assignments in remote parts of the world, always keeps a packed bag by his front door in readiness for his next journey. A 'ready packed bag' in the case of dying would mean to be prepared on many levels: emotionally, psychologically, spiritually and practically. It would also mean keeping an up-to-date death file, which would include everything those we leave behind might need to deal with our affairs after we die. After all we could be 'out of the door' suddenly, unexpectedly. Or, in the case of a stroke, for instance, we could have little or no energy for 'packing' as it were. 'See you tomorrow, or in the next life!' is another way of saying that life is very unpredictable and being in readiness is always an advantage.

A death file

This idea was written about by Richard Reoch in his book *Dying Well* (see Resources). The idea is that you keep together in a file a copy of your will, Advance Directive, Death Plan and Advance Funeral Wishes (see section on advance statements later in this chapter), an address list of all the people to be invited to your funeral, along with any letters, tape recorded or videoed messages for loved ones, plus a memorial book for your children, if you have any. (If you have young children you might also write special letters or cards in anticipation of birthdays or key milestones in their lives.)

It is also worth including a dossier of information that will be helpful for your survivors, including perhaps this book and the guide 'What to do after a death' (see Resources), along with the following details:

Your birth and marriage certificates and NHS medical card (or at least its number); address and phone number of the local register office (for registering a death, under 'R' in the phone book); your full name (exactly as on birth or marriage certificate); maiden name if a married woman; date and place of birth; home address; (last) occupation; full name and occupation of the husband if applicable (and in Scotland, the names and occupations of the spouse, male or female, and of all previous spouses and of the deceased's father; and whether the parents are alive); your NHS number; date of birth of your spouse; information about state or war pensions and allowances. Plus the addresses, telephone numbers, account numbers, etc for: your bank; landlord; building society; credit cards; standing orders; mortgage; house insurance; council rent department; Benefits office; local gas, electricity, water and telephone offices; TV licence; life insurance; hire purchase agreements; debts or loans; car and driving licence details; passport office; share certificate details (or the originals of these); premium bonds; pension details; your doctor; solicitor; accountant; stockbroker; local inspector of taxes and your tax district and tax district reference number; your employers and professional associations; and your main clients. Do you have an organ donor card? Does anybody know? By contrast, is the idea against your wishes?

You will need to update this death file regularly.

Making your will

There is one obvious and sensible preparation for death: make a will. Only about one in three adults in Britain has a will. This may not matter so much for single people without children, but it can lead to unnecessary financial hardship for many families. If you die without a will (intestate), the intestacy rules dictate who receives your estate (the total of your house and its contents, car, various insurance policies and savings accounts may well come to more than you realise). The rules will also decide who should manage the affairs of your estate. It is important to realise that unmarried partners may have no claim on the estate (unless a dependant, but this could be expensive to establish; both the Law Commission and the Law Society are critical of the current law and advocate new legislation. In the meantime, as the Law Commissioner for England and Wales notes: 'Far too many unmarried couples still believe that they come under the protective wing of "common law marriage". Not only should they be disabused of this impression, but the desirability of executing a declaration of trust to give effect to their real intentions needs to be proclaimed loud and clear.'). Even a legal wife or husband may have to sell the home to pay the other automatic beneficiaries. Of particular importance in the case of divorced or separated parents, the rules will determine who the legal guardians of your children will be; with a will you can name the person you would like to act as your children's guardian.

The standard way to get a will drawn up is to consult a solicitor (this would be likely to cost from about £45). It is worth familiarising yourself with the procedure before you visit a solicitor as this could save you time, money and possible confusion. There are six simple steps to take before you make a will:

(1) List **all the items you have to leave** – house and contents, car, savings accounts, etc, and their rough value.

(2) Consider **who you would like to provide for** and in what way. (Write down the full names, including middle names, and the addresses of all such people and the dates of birth of all children to be named in the will.)

(3) Consider **whether you would like to leave money or property 'in trust'** for children or grandchildren until they are grown up and at what age you think they should inherit your gift.

(4) Decide **who you would like to receive your sentimental belongings**. These may be of little financial value but you can pass them on to someone you know who will appreciate them.

(5) Consider **whether you would like to leave some money to charity** (bequests to charities are not liable to inheritance tax).

(6) **Choose one or more executors** to wind up your affairs. The executors can be spouses or members of the family or friends, although it is as well to get their agreement in advance. If, in the event, they find the task too onerous, as they well may, they can always ask a solicitor to take over.

As a postscript to the above, if you must appoint a professional executor, choose a (cheap and specialist) solicitor rather than a bank, as the latter tends to charge far more, as evidenced by the following letter:

My father, unknown to the rest of the family, had a new will drawn up naming his bank as executor ... When the quite modest estate was finally settled, a fee in excess of £3,000 had been deducted by the bank, without any explanation, for, as far as I can make out, writing one letter. When I challenged this sum they suggested it was a 'responsibility payment'.

The moral is: never let a bank anywhere near a will.

From a letter to the Times, *October 19th 2002.*

Find a solicitor prepared to forego the standard 'charging clause' in the will – replace this with a statement as to the maximum amount of money chargeable to the beneficiaries for the administration of the estate. Bear in mind that the solicitor will not be under any obligation to take on the task of being the executor when the time comes.

Here is an example of a will for a married man with two children who is concerned to minimise long-term liability to inheritance tax, and with several other unusual features (check their relevance to you with your legal adviser):

Will for a married man with two children

WILL of Donald Roland Winterton of [full address], made this fourteenth day of April 2003.

1. I revoke all previous Wills and Codicils made by me. I appoint as my executors my brother Arthur Winterton of [full address & telephone number] and my sister Alice Maples of [full address & telephone number] – or if either or both of them is unable or unwilling to act my friend Alan Beam of [full address & telephone number] is to be an executor.

2. My funeral wishes are that I be buried in a natural burial ground with a tree planted by the grave instead of having a headstone and I would like my executors to contact an information source such as The Natural Death Centre (tel 020 7359 8391) to find out the nearest or most suitable such ground after my death.

3. If my wife Rosemary dies before me or does not survive me for thirty days I appoint my sister Alice Maples and her husband Michael Maples as the guardians to the age of eighteen of my son Arthur my daughter Mary and any other children I may have.

4. I give the following bequests free from all taxes and duties payable on or by reference to my death. These bequests and legacies are to lapse automatically if the recipient dies before me or if a total of six letters or telephone calls in any particular case fails to trace him or her within six months of the first attempt to do so. No advertisement or any other means need be used.

(a) my painting by Emily Young to my friend Amelia Hart of [full address & telephone number]

(b) such motorbike as I may own at my death to my nephew Joseph Lawlor of [full address & telephone number].

5. I give the following further legacies free from all taxes and duties payable on or by reference to my death:

(a) £1000 to each of my executors who proves my will

(b) £1000 to my secretary [full address & telephone number]

(c) £2000 to the Nicholas Albery Foundation, 6 Blackstock Mews, Blackstock Road, London N4 2BT (tel 020 7359 8391) Registered Charity Number 1091396 for the benefit of their project The Natural Death Centre. I declare that the receipt of the charity's treasurer or other person professing to be the duly authorised officer shall be a full and sufficient discharge to my executors.

6. I give free from all taxes and duties payable on or by reference to my death all my interest in the property at [full address] to my executors as trustees. They are to sell everything not in the form of cash but they may postpone the sale of anything as long as they like. They are to invest or apply what is left in any type of property just as if it were their own money. They may borrow money from institutions in advance of probate if the money is needed to pay the Inland Revenue with the loan to be repaid in due course as my assets become available.

7. My trustees may give to the guardians of my children any part of what is left to enable them to acquire property as needed for my children or to apply for my children's benefit.

8. My trustees are to divide the trust fund (including any income from it) between such of my children as reach the age of eighteen – if more than one then in shares as near to equal as is reasonably practicable. My children are my son Arthur (born 3/1/1986) my daughter Mary (born 28/7/1978) and any other children I may have in future. The trustees may apply the actual assets rather than cash if they think fit without requiring the consent of any other person. Each of these children is to have a contingent rather than vested interest in my estate until he or she has attained the age of eighteen.

9. If any child of mine dies before me or dies under the age of eighteen leaving children who do reach that age then my trustees are to divide as equally as is reasonably practicable between these grandchildren the share of my estate which their parent would have received if that parent had lived long enough.

10. If my trustees think it proper they may at any time apply for the maintenance education or benefit of any beneficiary under the provisions of the two previous paragraphs any part of the capital of the property to which he or she would have become entitled on reaching eighteen.

11. After the executors have paid my debts any taxes and duties payable on my death and the expenses of my funeral and of administering my estate I give to my wife the whole of the rest of my estate including the contents and furniture at the said [address of aforementioned property].

12. The receipt of the guardian or any person professing to be the proper officer of any school college or other education establishment which any of the children are attending at that time shall be a full and sufficient discharge to my trustees in respect of that beneficiary.

13. Any person contesting this will or attempting to set aside any part of it before any court is to be denied any benefit from my estate.

Signed by Donald Roland Winterton
in our presence and then by us in his:
Signature

First witness:	Second witness:
Signature	Signature
Name	Name
Address	Address
Occupation	Occupation

Some points about this will:

• On the whole a will can be written in plain English. Avoid any possible ambiguities of meaning.

• In the passages above where it descends into legal gobbledegook it is for a reason, so beware if you make significant changes in such wordings. Beware generally, and seek legal approval of your will if in any doubt. A very useful guide, used in designing the above will, is the Which? book, *Wills and Probate* (see Resources).

- Always revoke previous wills even if you have never made any.
- Note the absence of commas in the text, except in the addresses, an absence which some lawyers think helps guard against the need for judicial interpretation of the comma's meaning and against fraudulent alteration of a will (in the days of handwritten wills, a comma could easily be added). If the will goes over one side of paper, continue on the back of the paper. If further pages are needed, these should be numbered and you and the witnesses should sign at the bottom of each sheet.
- Those appointed as guardians for children can also be executors of the will, unless you think there could be a conflict of interest – for instance the possibility of the trustees enriching themselves; or, on the contrary, of the trustees not taking enough, through being too diffident to recoup expenses.
- New natural burial grounds are opening all the time and some may be closer or more appropriate than any currently available, so this document allows for future developments.
- Inheritance tax was described by Roy Jenkins as 'a voluntary tax, paid only by those who distrust their heirs more than they dislike the Inland Revenue'. The tax raised about £2.5 billion in 2002-2003. There is no inheritance tax payable when the spouse inherits, but when the spouse in turn dies, then the tax is payable on net assets over £255,000 (the current figure, which alters regularly). To avoid this in advance, the will (above) gives a house to the children, and the contents, furniture, cash, etc, to the spouse. This would obviously only be appropriate in a case where the children are to be trusted not to evict or harass the spouse and where the house and the rest of the estate are of substantial value.
- Phone numbers and dates of birth are not normally put in a will, with all such details on separate sheets put with the will. But, as long as the details are correct, what harm can it do? Do not, however, fasten information sheets or anything else to the will itself, whether by pins, staples or paperclips.
- The reference to bequests lapsing if the beneficiaries are not readily traceable is to prevent the executors having to go to enormous lengths to find beneficiaries – as sometimes happens, especially when a person has lived to a grand old age and lost contact with those remembered in the will.
- A will such as this containing several vital technicalities and creating a 'trust for sale' for the children (which avoids various legal pitfalls and needs careful wording) should at the very least be checked by a solicitor. One way to do this for free is through one of the house insurance schemes which includes a free 24-hour medical, domestic and legal advice service (eg Frizzell, ☎ 0800 748748).
- The children have a 'contingent' interest – ie contingent in this case upon each reaching the age of eighteen. If the child dies earlier, then that gift will lapse (unless there are children of that child), and the gift will go to the other children. A vested interest on the other hand would have formed part of the child's estate.
- Denying any part of the estate to those contesting your will may not stand up in court, but it could put them off trying – or it could make lawyers rich interpreting the clause! Another way to reduce the risk of dependants from previous relationships contesting the will is to insert a clause that says: 'I have

reviewed my obligations to [...] and consider that I have already made adequate and proper provision'.

• John Bradfield, author of 'Green Burial', suggests that if you are asking for something unusual in your will, which your beneficiaries could obstruct, such as a garden burial, you could make all gifts to them in the will conditional on the request being carried out.

• Neither the witnesses nor their spouses should benefit from your will, or they will forfeit any provision made for them. Ideally, witnesses should be traceable after your death, in case there is a dispute as to the will's validity. Desmond Banks, a solicitor in Notting Hill and one of the Natural Death Centre's honorary consultants, suggests that the testator and witnesses should all use the same pen if possible, to help demonstrate that the testator signed the will in the presence of both witnesses and that they then signed in the presence of the testator.

The following points are worth noting about wills in general:

A will could be left in a safe place in the house, along with your other main papers. This would be simpler and quicker than leaving it with a solicitor or depositing it at the bank. Tell your executors, your spouse and your children where you have left it and consider giving them copies (note on the copies who has the original and where; and write at the bottom of the copies: 'We certify that this is a true copy of the original', with signatures from the testator and the witnesses).

If your circumstances are such that the will is not certain to be found, you may like to phone the deposit of wills section at the Probate Registry (☎ 020 7947 7022). They will send you an envelope and a form. You then send them the will and a fee of £15. If it is known that there is a will and it cannot be found, those handling your affairs may be required to write to every solicitor in the region, and the bill for this can mount up.

A will is automatically negated by marriage (unless made in anticipation of marriage), so make another one at this time. It is as well to make another one too if you divorce.

Tax can sometimes be saved within two years after death by the beneficiaries of the will entering into a deed to vary its terms.

To repeat: be careful in your use of words in your will. Do not write for instance, 'I give all my money to ...', if what you really mean is, 'I give everything I own to ...'.

Avoid inadvertently giving your spouse a mere 'life interest' in your property (where the person is only able to get income from the house and no capital). You could make this mistake by specifying what is to happen to the property after the spouse's death. Such considerations should be left for the spouse's own will to deal with.

In Scotland, your spouse and children have rights to one third or more of your estate (other than lands or buildings) whatever your will may say to the contrary.

If a person has property abroad, a will should also be made in that country.

Many more such interesting points are raised in the Which? book mentioned above.

Typing errors in a will are best avoided. If retained and corrected, they must be signed with your signature and that of your witnesses in the margin. To make small changes in a will, one way is to add a codicil, with two new witnesses signing at the end, using the same legal formula as in the main will ('Signed by ... in our presence and then ...'). Part of a sample codicil might read:

This is the first codicil to the will made this fourteenth day of April 2003 of me Donald Roland Winterton of 26 Oxford Gardens, London W10.

(1) I revoke the bequest of £1000 to Janet Simmonds.

(2) In all other respects I confirm my will.

But normally it is safer to make an entire new will rather than to attempt to draft your own codicil.

If you want to find a solicitor or will-writing company to draw up your will, you could ask friends for personal recommendations or phone around for the cheapest and best. The Institute for Cancer Research (☎ 020 7352 8133) runs a scheme under which solicitors write wills for people over 50 without charge to the individual. The Institute pays the solicitor for the work in the hope that the individual will mention the Institute in the will, but there is no obligation to do this. Age Concern (☎ 020 8765 7527 or see Resources), offers a will-making service based on a questionnaire for £55 (£75 for a couple; £35 for a single codicil). If you or your child suffers from a physical or mental handicap or if you are over 70 and of very modest means with low savings (eg less than £1,000), you may be able to get a will drafted for free under the Legal Help scheme via a law centre, advice centre or by some solicitors.

Inheritance tax information is available from the Capital Taxes Office: Ferrers House, PO Box 38, Castle Meadow Road, Nottingham NG2 1BB (☎ 0845 3020900; **w**: www.inlandrevenue.gov.uk/cto).

A reminder: if you are married and if your total estate after debts is likely to be worth over the inheritance tax limit (currently £255,000) then it may be worth taking measures to reduce this figure, such as leaving the first £255,000 of your estate directly to your children and not to your spouse – so that your children will not be hit by the tax when your spouse dies. There are ways to set up trusts and to take out life insurance so as to reduce inheritance tax liability. One of the cleverest for a couple seems to be a life assurance investment bond, owned by one partner, who leaves it in trust for the children. It stays in force as long as one of the couple remains alive. The owner may draw income from the bond whilst alive, and the trustees can lend money to the partner after the owner's death (from an article by financial planner Colin McLachland who used to work for the accountancy firm BDO Stoy Hayward, ☎ 01292 263 277, which may refund to the client some of the high initial commission charges for such products). Another method is the Loan Plan which uses the inheritance tax-free band twice. The deceased spouse's assets pass to the surviving spouse who, in return, gives an IOU to the trust. The trust can make loans to the surviving spouse until his or her death, at which point the IOU is repaid and the assets pass to the children. For more information about the Loan Plan, contact the accountants Speechly Bircham (☎ 020 7427 6400; **w**: www.speechlys.com).

A final warning from the Which? book:

Pitfalls of DIY wills

The one thing worse than not making a will at all is making a mess of making a will. Many lawyers would say that they can make more money out of poor home-made wills than they do out of drawing up wills for clients. There is probably some truth in this. There are many ways in which people who prepare and sign their own will can go wrong. This can, later, lead to long and expensive court cases to resolve the matter, with enormous legal costs for the lawyers. This can reduce by staggering amounts the size of the estate to which the beneficiaries are entitled.

A will is a technical legal document; it is not surprising that some laymen go astray when they try to make a will unaided. If you have any doubts, you should seek a solicitor's advice.

From Wills and Probate *(Which? Books, see Resources).*

Enduring Power of Attorney

At the same time as making a will, it is a good idea to fill in a form entitled 'Enduring Power of Attorney' (EPA helpline ☎ 0845 330 2963; **e**: andrew.howse@guardianship.gsi.gov.uk; **w**: www.publictrust.gov.uk/Enduring.html). This enables you to nominate one or more people to represent you at some future stage should you become mentally incapable of handling your financial affairs. Your form would only be officially registered with the Public Guardianship Office if and when required. Filling in such a form in advance could save your relatives up to £1,000 a year or more, as otherwise a receiver would have to be appointed by the court. It could also place a friend between you and any local authority trying to extract money from your account to pay for the cost of your care in a residential home.

Scotland introduced an expanded 'Continuing Power of Attorney' (CPA) – which allows you to choose a person to look after not only your financial affairs but also your health care and personal welfare – as part of the Adults with Incapacity (Scotland) Act 2000. The act also appointed a new regulator for the affairs of incapable adults. This 'Public Guardian' keeps a public register of Attorneys, and is able to investigate any complaints about their conduct. It is hoped that similar legislation will soon be brought forward in England and Wales.

Protecting your assets from community care charges

Yet again leading the way, Scotland has introduced free longterm nursing and personal care for the elderly, regardless of means. Elsewhere in the UK, however, every year tens of thousands of people have to sell their homes to cover care home fees. For providing care at home, a local authority is allowed to make a 'reasonable' charge, but for providing this care in a care home there is a national means test. If you have over £19,500 in assets (levels are current for

England and Northern Ireland only), you will normally pay in full (subject to assistance with the negligible 'registered nurse element' of care which is now being paid for by the NHS); if you have less than £19,500 the local authority will start to help; and if you have less than £12,000 the local authority will pay in full, but you will still be expected to contribute from your income.

If your care home stay is classified as temporary (up to 52 weeks, possibly longer), the value of your home will be disregarded when calculating fees. For a permanent stay, its value will be disregarded for the first 12 weeks after you enter into care. However, it may be disregarded for longer – at the local authority's discretion – if the house is also lived in by your partner, by a relative who is incapacitated or over 60, or by a carer.

You may of course want to pay your full contribution, in which case no preparation is required, but be aware that the current average cost of nursing home care is about £21,000 per year. If you do want to shelter your assets, you should get advice from an organisation such as Carers UK (☎ 0808 8087777) or a specialist solicitor. However, if you start taking active measures, you may wish to instruct a non-specialist solicitor, as this person's actions are less likely to be construed by the local authority as avoidance tactics than the use of schemes that have been marketed with this is mind. (If the local authority can show that 'deliberate deprivation' did occur, it can force you to pay, however long ago you gave it all away.) Some simple tips include:

• Have a good and legitimate reason for giving away your assets.

• Do so as far ahead as possible.

• Spouses need to consider opening separate bank accounts, so that less remains in the account for assessment once you have begun paying charges.

• Joint owners of houses will be better protected if they sever any joint tenancy and create a tenancy in common.

• Consider adding the names of those family members living with you to the title deeds of the house, so reducing value of your interest for assessment purposes.

• Your children or heirs may prefer to club together to pay your care fees, rather than lose the house.

• Insurance policies are best written in trust, so that the proceeds will not be regarded as your capital.

• Your pension may be used to fund care fees, leaving your dependants in hardship. Options available include taking the maximum lump sum you can, so you can use this money to ensure your spouse's financial security, having the benefits transferred to another person, or going for a deferred annuity or phased retirement, so leaving funds in place for the future.

• Beware that if you give your house away to a relative, this person may die without making provision for you, or may go bankrupt or go through an expensive divorce – or he or she may lose their own entitlement to state benefits. It should also be someone you trust absolutely.

Age Concern (see Resources) do a good downloadable factsheet on the intricacies of care charges.

Simplifying your affairs before death

Anyone who has looked into the complexities of probate (the administration of your estate after death) will know that you can greatly simplify matters before death, and especially if death is imminent, by dividing your assets among the relevant beneficiaries (it should be more enjoyable too, making these gifts whilst still alive). Assets given to the spouse are not liable to inheritance tax (although they may be when the spouse comes to die); nor are small gifts of up to £250 per recipient; nor are gifts up to £3,000 in total per year (you may also be allowed a further £3,000 if your previous year's allowance was not used; and a marriage gift can be up to £5,000 to your own child); nor are assets liable that are given away more than seven years before death (such assets attract a proportion of the tax between three and seven years). If the family home is given to the children, however, the recipients must take up 'genuine possession of the gifted asset' and the donor may either have to vacate the house or take a lease and pay rent, so as not to be benefiting from the gift (although a donor can return to the house 'if effectively forced to due to unexpected hardship arising after the gift' was made). Note too that children who are given a house which is not their principal residence may pay out more as capital gains tax when they sell the house than they would have if they had simply paid inheritance tax instead.

If no precautions are taken, a spouse can be left with access to very little money, as death tends to freeze (non-joint) bank accounts: so, if death is near, it is as well either to take money out of the bank or to open joint bank or building society accounts. Probate on stocks and shares is excessively complicated: again, if death is imminent, it might be as well to cash them in, or to transfer them into the name of one's spouse (Con40 stock transfer forms are obtainable for £4 each from OyezStraker, see Resources). In fact your executors may be able to avoid the whole problem of probate altogether if you leave behind you only cash and 'personal effects' (car, furniture, etc), having previously disposed of house, shares, bank accounts, pension arrears, etc.

If you need to maintain a personal store of money in your own name until your death, consider post office National Savings Investments. Up to £5,000 in any of these can be handed over to the appropriate relative after death simply by that person filling in form DNS 904 from the post office and sending this in with the death certificate.

Although banks and building societies are now able to transfer funds directly to the Inland Revenue from the deceased's accounts before probate is granted, not all banks or branches have the procedures in place, so it is worth checking beforehand and perhaps moving your account if it seems they might be particularly obstructive. (See also Chapter 4 on payment of inheritance tax.)

If you can keep the total net worth of your estate (including any jointly owned property) at your death below £100,000 (the current figure, not to be confused with the £255,000 inheritance tax figure), your executors can avoid the Inland Revenue rules demanding a full account of the estate.

If you are taking out life insurance, make sure that it is 'written in trust', so that your beneficiaries can get the money out without waiting for probate.

Advance statements

The Natural Death Centre recommends that all competent adults prepare three advance statements: an Advance Directive appertaining to health care, a Death Plan, and an Advance Funeral Wishes form.

Advance Directives

Any competent adult has a legal right to give or withhold consent to medical treatment. However, once he or she becomes 'incompetent' or unconscious, treatment may be given without his or her consent, 'in the best interests of the patient'. An Advance Directive (AD, also known as a Living Will) is a written document designed to give doctors treatment preferences in the event of the maker becoming incompetent. An AD is considered legally effective as regards refusal of medical treatment *if* it applies to the circumstances that have arisen. The main threat to an AD's effectiveness is that while it will mostly be made in advance of need (as its name implies), an AD made *other* than in response to a known condition is open to challenge as to whether the patient would have wanted it applied in the circumstances that have arisen.

The following AD (which is also available as part of a pack of advance statements from the Centre, see Resources) looks long but is self-explanatory and easy to complete. It is less likely that the medical profession would challenge this particular version because it shows that the maker has thought through and discussed with their loved ones the various treatment options and the conditions under which they might be offered. Furthermore, it gives the named proxies specific guidance on the level of tolerability of various conditions that may arise. Incidentally, where it gives a '___ months' option, it is advisable not to go beyond 13 months (a year is needed for a persistent vegetative state determination), but you may use a shorter period with some other concerns.

Proxy decision-making, while not yet officially recognised in England, is supported by the Law Commission and the BMA. It perhaps goes without saying that your appointed representatives should be people whom you trust absolutely, especially if they would benefit financially from your death. (In fact, their credibility is less likely to be challenged if they are *not* beneficiaries.)

Advanced Health Care Directive

The original of this instrument was developed for use in the USA by Norman L. Cantor, Professor of Law at Rutgers University School of Law, Newark, NJ, USA. With his kind permission it has been adapted for use in the UK by Enid France of the University of Sussex. Professor Cantor takes no responsibility for the changes made by Ms France.

The following material is designed to guide my medical treatment after I have become incompetent – that is, unable to understand the nature and consequences of important medical decisions, or incapable of communicating. My objectives are to inform medical professionals providing my care of my treatment preferences and to appoint a decision maker on my behalf (to be known as my health care representative) and to instruct that decision maker concerning the level of deterioration that would warrant ending life-sustaining medical intervention. I authorise my doctor to make full disclosure of my condition to my named health care representatives. I assume that comfort care (care intended to keep me pain free, clean, and comfortable) will always be provided.

Part I: Designation of a Health Care Representative
A. Primary Designation

I,_____, hereby designate the following individual as my health care representative to act on my behalf, in the event of my incompetence, with respect to any and all health care decisions. These include decisions to provide, withhold, or withdraw life-sustaining measures, to hire and fire health care providers, or to transfer my care to another physician or institution.

Primary Health Care Representative:
Name: _____
Address _____
Telephone(s) _____

B. Alternate Designation(s) (*naming of alternate(s) is recommended, but not required*)

In the event the individual named above is unavailable, or is unable or unwilling to serve as my health care representative, I hereby designate the following individual(s) to act as alternate(s):

First Alternate:
Name:
Address:
Telephone:

Second Alternate:
Name:
Address:
Telephone:

C. Consultation

To the extent feasible in the circumstances, I direct my health care representative to confer with the following individuals prior to making any health care decisions on my behalf. These individuals may provide advice to be considered by the health care representative, but they shall not have veto power over the health care representative's decisions. (Check all that apply, and provide names and telephone numbers if not specified above):

a)   Family member(s): (Give names and contact numbers)

_____

b)   My physician(s), general practitioner(s) or doctor(s):

_____

c) My solicitor: _____

d) My priest or other minister: _____

e) Others: _____

Part II: General Instructions for Care
To inform those responsible for my care, I declare that there are circumstances in which I would not want my life to be prolonged by further medical treatment. In such circumstances (as described below), life-sustaining measures should not be initiated and, if they have been initiated, they should be discontinued. I recognise that this is likely to hasten my death.

If I become stricken with a serious illness or condition, with no reasonable expectation of cure or recovery to a competent state, I do not want life-sustaining treatment to be provided or continued after my health care representative determines that the burdens of my continued existence outweigh the benefits or that my condition has permanently deteriorated to a point of intolerable indignity. In making these judgments, I want my health care representative to consider my suffering and my diminished quality of life, with particular attention to the elements of indignity noted in my values profile in Part III. In the event my wishes are not clear, or if a situation arises that I did not anticipate, my health care representative is authorised to use his/her best judgment about what I would want done, keeping in mind my conceptions of indignity sketched in Part III.

Part III: Values Profile Introduction
Like many people, I am concerned about medical prolongation of my life upon reaching an intolerably deteriorated condition. Below I have given my reactions to various factors which many people consider important in shaping post-competence medical care. I have indicated my level of concern about each of these factors by placing my initials next to the statement that reflects my feelings.

A. Pain and Suffering
1.   In my post-competency (or incommunicative) state, I am concerned about extreme pain and would expect to receive pain medication to make me as comfortable as possible. My attitude toward being in a permanent condition in which pain can be controlled only by substances that leave me unconscious all or most of the time:

____ intolerable; I prefer to be allowed to die, even if that means withholding or withdrawal of artificial nutrition and hydration in my unconscious condition

____ intolerable; I prefer to be allowed to die, but I want artificial nutrition and hydration

____ a very negative factor, to be weighed with other factors in determining intolerable indignity

____ unimportant; I prefer that I be kept alive even if pain medication leaves me unconscious

2.   My attitude toward being in a permanent condition in which pain or suffering can be controlled only by substances that leave me disoriented and confused all or most of the time:

____ intolerable; I prefer to be allowed to die, even if that means withholding or withdrawal of artificial nutrition and hydration in my disoriented condition

_____ intolerable; I prefer to be allowed to die, but I want artificial nutrition and hydration

_____ a very negative factor, to be weighed with other factors in determining intolerable indignity

_____ unimportant; I prefer that I be kept alive even if pain medication leaves me disoriented

B. **Mental Incapacity**

1.   In my post-competency (or incommunicative) state, I am concerned about the level of my mental deterioration to the following extent:

_____ a very critical factor

_____ important, but not determinative by itself; a factor to be weighed with other factors in determining intolerable indignity

_____ unimportant

2.   My attitude toward a permanently unconscious state, confirmed by up-to-date medical tests, showing no hope of ever regaining consciousness:

_____ intolerable; I prefer death

_____ tolerable

_____ tolerable, so long as insurance or other non-family sources are paying the bills

3.   My reaction to profound dementia to the point where I can no longer recognise my loved ones and interact with them in a coherent fashion:

_____ intolerable; I prefer death

_____ a very negative factor, to be weighed with other factors in determining intolerable indignity

_____ tolerable

4.   My reaction to dementia to the point where I can no longer read and understand written material such as a newspaper:

_____ intolerable; I prefer death

_____ a very negative factor, to be weighed with other factors in determining intolerable indignity

_____ tolerable

5.   My reaction to moderate dementia (such as Alzheimer's disease) characterized by frequent confusion and loss of short-term memory, though I am still able to experience pleasant feelings and emotions and to interact with people:

_____ intolerable; I prefer to be allowed to die, even if this means non-treatment of curable conditions such as pneumonia or infections

_____ a very negative factor, to be weighed with other factors in determining intolerable indignity

_____ tolerable

C. **Physical Immobility**

1.   In my incompetent state, I am concerned about physical immobility to the following extent:

___ important
___ unimportant

2.   My reaction to being permanently bed-ridden:
___ intolerable; I prefer death
___ a very negative factor, to be weighed with other factors in determining intolerable indignity
___ tolerable

3.   My reaction to being non-ambulatory, meaning that I can leave my bed but can only move around if others transport me in a wheelchair:
___ intolerable; I prefer death
___ a very negative factor, to be weighed with other factors in determining intolerable indignity
___ tolerable

D. Physical Helplessness

1.   In my incompetent state, I am concerned about my independence and ability to tend to my own physical needs to the following extent:
___ important
___ unimportant

2.   My reaction to being incapable of feeding myself:
___ intolerable; I prefer death
___ a very negative factor, to be weighed with other factors in determining intolerable indignity
___ tolerable

3.   My reaction to being incapable of dressing myself:
___ intolerable; I prefer death
___ a very negative factor, to be weighed with other factors in determining intolerable indignity
___ tolerable

4.   My reaction to being bladder incontinent:
___ intolerable; I prefer death
___ a very negative factor, to be weighed with other factors in determining intolerable indignity
___ tolerable

5.   My reaction to being bowel incontinent:
___ intolerable; I prefer death
___ a very negative factor, to be weighed with other factors in determining intolerable indignity
___ tolerable

E. Interests of Loved Ones

1.   In my incompetent state, the emotional and financial burdens imposed on my loved ones are of concern to the following extent:
___ a critical factor
___ an important factor, depending on degree of burden
___ unimportant

2.   My reaction to emotional strain posed for my spouse or other loved

ones surrounding me during my incompetency:

___ an important factor

___ a somewhat important factor

___ unimportant; although I care about my loved ones, I want my treatment decisions to be based on my own circumstances

3.   My reaction to a heavy financial burden being imposed on my spouse or other loved ones:

___ an important factor

___ a somewhat important factor

___ unimportant; although I care about my loved ones, I want my treatment decisions to be based on my own circumstances

4.   My reaction to my assets being depleted by heavy medical expenses for my care:

___ an important factor

___ unimportant

F. Living Arrangements

1.   In my incompetent state I am concerned about my living arrangements to the following extent:

___ not important; I want my care to be determined by my personal condition rather than the surroundings

___ some living arrangements would be intolerable (if so, proceed to the next question)

2.   I would find any of the following living arrangements intolerable, so that if there were no alternative I would prefer cessation or withdrawal of life-sustaining medical care (initial all that apply):

___ living at home, but with need for full-time help

___ living permanently in the home of one of my children or other relative

___ living permanently in a nursing home or other long-term care facility

___ being confined to a hospital with little or no hope of ever leaving

G. Types of Medical Intervention

1.   My attitude toward artificially-provided nutrition, such as feeding tubes or intravenous infusion:

___ intolerable on other than a short-term basis (__ months); I prefer death

___ a very negative factor, to be weighed with other factors in determining intolerable indignity

___ tolerable, to be provided at all times, regardless of my condition

2.   My attitude toward artificially-provided hydration: [see note below]

___ intolerable on other than a short-term basis (__ months); I prefer death

___ a very negative factor, to be weighed with other factors in determining intolerable indignity

___ tolerable, to be provided at all times, regardless of my condition

3.   My attitude toward having my bladder drained by a catheter:

___ intolerable on other than a short-term basis (__ months); I prefer death

___ a very negative factor, to be weighed with other factors in determining intolerable indignity

___ tolerable, to be provided at all times, regardless of my condition

4.   My attitude toward having my bowels cleared by an enema:

___ intolerable on other than a short-term basis (__ months); I prefer death

___ a very negative factor, to be weighed with other factors in determining intolerable indignity

___ tolerable, to be provided at all times, regardless of my condition

5.   I understand decisions as to all types of medical intervention will be governed by my instructions as indicated in this document. However, I feel an especially strong aversion to certain form(s) of intervention. (*Indicate here any special aversions, such as a blood transfusion, or CPR*)

---

6.   My attitude toward hand- or spoon-feeding in the event that I have reached a level of deterioration that I have defined as intolerably undignified:

___ I wish to receive oral nutrition only so long as I am willingly taking what is offered, and I do not want to be force-fed or to receive artificial nutrition or hydration in the event I am resisting oral nutrition

___ I wish to receive oral nutrition only so long as I am willingly taking what is offered, but I would expect artificial nutrition or hydration in the event I am resisting oral nutrition

7.   My attitude toward respiratory assistance should I have problems breathing (you may initial more than one response):

___ I wish to receive oxygen to ease my breathing

___ If I lose the capacity to breathe independently, I wish to be maintained on a ventilator only until the conclusion is reached that I will not regain the capacity to breathe independently, at which time I wish the ventilator removed

___ If I lose the capacity to breathe independently, I wish to be maintained on a ventilator

Part IV: Signature and Witnesses
A. Signature

By writing this directive, I intend to ease the burdens of decision making on those entrusted with my health care decisions. I understand the purpose and effect of this document and sign it knowingly, voluntarily, and after careful deliberation.

Signed this _____ day of _____ , 20 _____

Printed Name:_____

Address: _____

Signature: _____

B. Signature of Witnesses (two required)

I declare that the person who signed this document, or asked another to sign this document on his or her behalf, did so in my presence, that he or she is personally known to me, and that he or she appears to be of sound mind and free of duress or undue influence. I am 18 years of age or older and am not designated by this or any other document as the person's health care representative, nor as an alternate health care representative.

1st Witness's Printed Name _____

Address _____

_____

Signature _____

2nd Witness's Printed Name _____

Address _____

_____

Signature _____

C. Signature of Health Care Representatives and Alternates (*optional, but strongly encouraged*)

I have read this document and agree to act as health care representative, or as an alternate health care representative.

Signature of Primary Health Care Representative:

Signature of First Alternate:

Signature of Second Alternate:

D. Periodic Review

You may cancel or change this document at any time. You should review it every so often. Each time you review it, place your initials and the date below and initial and date any changed treatment preferences in the body of the document:

NOTE: If you change an alternate health care representative, cross out the designation above and place your full signature and date next to that deletion and complete the following:

I substitute _____ as my 1st 2nd health care representative.

Address _____

My Signature: _____

Date: _____

Witness No.1 Signature   Witness No. 2 Signature

Signature of substitute (if possible) _____

If you change your designated primary care representative, complete the following page. It is **NOT** necessary to complete the following page IF your original primary representative has become incapacitated. Your 1st alternate will become primary, your 2nd alternate will move up, and you can name a new 2nd alternate above.

GIVE A COPY OF THIS DOCUMENT TO EACH OF YOUR NAMED HEALTH CARE REPRESENTATIVES AND YOUR DOCTOR(S). BE SURE YOUR DOCTOR UPDATES HIS/HER RECORDS AS TO WHO SHOULD BE NOTIFIED SHOULD YOU BECOME INCOMPETENT OR INCOMMUNICATIVE.

Re: Artificial Hydration: It is STRONGLY recommended that you select the same option for artificial hydration as you selected for artificial nutrition. Continuation of artificial hydration after termination of artificial nutrition simply prolongs the dying process and can have adverse effects.

Designation of New Primary Health Care Representative
(Make a copy of this page before using it so if you want to make another change, you have a copy of this page to use.)

I, _____ , hereby amend my advance health care directive dated _____ , this _____ day of _____ , 20_____ .

I hereby name _____ as my primary health care representative.

Address _____

Telephone(s) _____

Signature of Witnesses (two required)

_____

I declare that the person who signed this document, or asked another to sign this document on his or her behalf, did so in my presence, that he or she is personally known to me, and that he or she appears to be of sound mind and free of duress or undue influence. I am 18 years of age or older and am not designated by this or any other document as the person's health care representative, nor as an alternate health care representative.

1st Witness's Printed Name _____

Address _____

Signature _____

2nd Witness's Printed Name _____

Address _____

Signature _____

Signature of Named Representative: _____

GIVE A COPY OF THIS PAGE TO ANY DOCTORS TREATING YOU AND GIVE IT, PLUS A **FULL** COPY OF YOUR PREVIOUSLY SIGNED ADVANCED DIRECTIVE, TO YOUR NEWLY NAMED HEALTH CARE REPRESENTATIVE. **ALSO**, YOU SHOULD NOTIFY PREVIOUSLY NAMED HEALTH CARE REPRESENTATIVES OF THIS CHANGE.

A Death Plan

A Death Plan is analogous to a birth plan. Of course no one can be sure how they will die or whether such a plan will be of any relevance in the event, and they may change their minds when the time comes; but nevertheless, a death plan may help friends and relatives to know one's orientation and wishes.

Some families have found the following sample Death Plan helpful. It was designed by the Natural Death Centre and has been commended by Age Concern as an 'important step in the deprofessionalisation of death'. An A4 copy of this form comes as part of the Natural Death Centre's set of Advance Statements as mentioned above. This form can be photocopied for personal use. Simply strike out those bits that don't apply, or write your own Plan, using this one as a guide.

Death Plan

(1) If my condition is terminal I would like to be told the full details / plus implications of treatment and non-treatment / a summary / not to be told at all / other [specify].

(2) If possible, I would / would not like the doctor to tell me a guess as to how much time I might have left, the best and worst cases, and the average.

(3) I imagine I would / would not like every effort to be made to find alternative medicine and approaches / latest medical breakthroughs that might give me a miraculous last-minute remission.

(4) I have / have not made an Advance Directive, specifying how much high-tech medical intervention I wish for when dying and whether or not I wish to be force fed [if yes, the location of this Advance Directive].

(5) I imagine that I will / will not choose to fast as death approaches.

(6) If possible, when I am dying I would like to be cared for at [location, whether hospital, hospice, at home, indoors, outdoors, etc].

(7) I would like to be surrounded by [flowers, nature, photos, etc].

(8) My next of kin is [name, address, phone number].

(9) If I go into hospital / when I die, what I would like to happen to my pets is _____

(10) I would / would not like for close relatives / friends / everyone to be told that I am terminally ill.

(11) Those friends or relatives who I would most like to be involved in my nursing care are _____

(12) I would like _____ to be able to sleep in the same room / bed as me.

(13) I may change my mind, but I imagine I would / would not like visitors when near the end. The ones I would particularly like to visit me include _____ [give addresses and phone numbers if necessary].

(14) I would / would not like to be left as alone as possible when dying.

(15) I imagine that I would / would not like to discuss the fact that I am dying with these visitors, and would / would not like to make explicit the possibility that these are final goodbyes.

(16) My religion / spiritual practice / philosophy is mainly _____ and therefore for my dying I would like _____

(17) Depending on my medical condition and feelings at the time, the kind of ministrations I might appreciate when dying include:

(18) Music. My favourite pieces would be [specific music or broad range].

(19) Live singing, chanting, hymns, psalms, particular prayers or texts, etc [as specific as desired].

(20) Physical contact [eg hand held].

(21) Massage.

(22) Aromatherapy [or other such approaches].

(23) The person(s) I would most like to be there at the moment of my death is / are _____

(24) I would like to be as conscious / unconscious as possible as I die, and would like pain control prescribed accordingly. The drugs I imagine I might appreciate include _____ [specific, or class of drugs].

(25) For the moment of my death I would / would not like all life support machinery and monitors disconnected from my body.

Signed by:
Name
Signature
Date

This signing is witnessed by the two undersigned, neither of whom stand to benefit from the signatory's Will:
Name of first witness
Signature
Witness's occupation and address
Name of second witness
Signature
Witness's occupation and address

Advance Funeral Wishes

'Everyone knew it wasn't the done thing to plan your own funeral,' said Christianne, 'but most of us put plenty of effort into organising weddings and christening parties, so why did funeral parties have to be such thrown-together, dismal affairs?' Thus prompted, ideas for imaginative send-offs flowed thick and fast. Bridget wanted a pub crawl for all her friends, followed by a short service at a harbour during which her body would be thrown into the sea. Peter wanted a funeral al fresco, preferably on a hillside, with a ragtime band playing his favourite melodies. Monica said she would like a green funeral, with her body buried in a biodegradable bag rather than a tree-wasting coffin. Christianne suggested that anyone with ideas of how they'd want their funeral to be conducted ought to write them down and leave them with a close family member. 'Families have enough to think about after a death without spending hours trying to imagine what the dead person would or wouldn't have wanted at their funeral.'

From an article by Joanna Moorhead in the *Guardian* (1990). See Resources for details of Christianne Heal's 'Living with Dying' courses.

Almost half of those interviewed in a recent UK survey said they regretted that they had not known what a friend or relative had wanted for their funeral, and yet 60 per cent of people in the same survey had not discussed their own funeral arrangements. Given that there is no law that says you must have a religious funeral, hire a funeral director or have a cremation, but you can have all of this if you want, what do you really want?

Funeral wishes, whether in a will or as described in the Advance Funeral Wishes form below, are not legally binding after death. However, the following may stimulate you to think of the kind of funeral you would like and, if you fill it in and leave it with your will and next of kin, it will be a helpful guide for those you leave behind. In addition, discussing your wishes with your family or friends – those who would be actually be carrying out your wishes after you die – will also help you to consider *their* wishes and perhaps integrate them into your plans in some way.

Where sample prices are given, these are 2003 prices. This form also comes as part of the Natural Death Centre Advance Statements pack (see Resources).

(1) I have / have not written a will [location] which expresses / does not express my funeral wishes. [If there is such a will] Please treat this present document as expanding on the wishes expressed in that will, with the will taking legal precedence if relevant.

(2) My next of kin is [name, address, phone numbers].

(3) With this will / this present document is also added all potentially needed information [see list under Death File above] plus any deeds to a grave.

(4) I have / do not have any preferences about what happens to my body. [If no preferences] I leave it all entirely to the discretion of [name, address, phone numbers].

(5) I do / do not wish to donate my body / my organs [specify which and to whom, if relevant].

(6) If possible, I wish my body left undisturbed after my death for [length of time].

(7) Nurses attending the death normally lay out the body, but I would like it very much if _____ could also assist / do this instead.

(8) If a postmortem after my death requires the consent of my next of kin, I would like them to give it / not to give it.

(9) I would / would not like my body to be brought back to my home after death / to remain at home until the funeral if I die at home / to remain in the hospital or other establishment's mortuary if possible / to go to a funeral director offering a refrigeration service.

(10) I do / do not wish for my body to be embalmed [sea burial is not permitted for embalmed bodies and natural burial grounds prefer that bodies are not embalmed].

(11) I have / do not have a prepaid funeral plan / funeral insurance scheme [if so, please give details and make sure your next of kin are aware of the existence of this plan. Some of what follows may then not be relevant in your case].

(12) The friend(s) or relative(s) I wish to be mainly responsible for arranging my funeral is / are _____

(13) I would prefer for the above-named to arrange it with / without using a funeral director.

(14) If a funeral director is used, I would like it to be _____ / I would like someone to phone around for the cheapest / most suitable funeral director / phone the Natural Death Centre (☎ 020 7359 8391) to see if they have a recommendation for a helpful funeral director locally.

(15) In general terms, I would like the expenditure on my funeral to be no more than £ ____

(16) I would like to be cremated / buried [for burial options see (26) below] / other [specify].

(17) I already have my coffin/ shroud / other [specify] in store waiting [location] / I would like a coffin made by [specify] / I would like a cardboard / chipboard / pine / bamboo / willow coffin / ecopod / body bag / shroud / other [see Chapter 5 for full range of containers & current prices].

(18) I would like my body to be transported to the relevant place in our / a friend's estate car / van [give details where relevant] / I would like a large estate car / small van to be hired for the occasion / I would like a funeral director to be asked to supply a hearse with / without following cars / I would like a horse-drawn hearse [from about £450] / other transport [specify].

(19) I would ideally like _____ as the bearers of my coffin.

(20) I would / would not like flowers brought to my funeral / one flower per person / donation instead to _____

(21) I would / would not like my death and funeral announced in the following publications _____

(22) I would / would not like a funeral service.

If to be cremated:

(23) I would like my funeral service [if having one] to take place at a church / other venue [specify] before my body is delivered to the crematorium [state what if anything is to happen at the crematorium and who is to attend there] / I would like the funeral service to take place at the crematorium.

(24) After cremation, what I would ideally like done with my ashes is

_____

(25) [If an urn to be used] The kind of urn I would most like is home-made by _____ / standard container / wooden / bamboo / other.

If to be buried:

(26) I do / do not have a burial place reserved / in mind [details if so]. I would like to be buried in a churchyard / cemetery / natural burial ground [the Natural Death Centre has a list of UK sites] / on private land [give details] / at sea [sea burial can be difficult and very expensive to arrange.]

(27) If allowed, I would / would not like [names] to help dig / fill my grave

If having a funeral service:

(28) Amongst those I would most like invited who might otherwise be neglected are _____ [names and addresses and phone numbers].

(29) The kind of numbers I would like at my funeral service are ._____.
I see it as ideally a very small family affair / family and friends / all comers.
(30) I would like a funeral service to take account of the fact that my religion
/ spiritual belief / philosophy is _____
(31) I would like the service led by _____ [relative / friend
/ named or duty minister / officiant / celebrant / other; plus contact details].
(32) The form of service I would like is _____
(33) The kind of music, hymns, psalms, songs etc I would like include
_____ [be as specific as you like] played by / sung by _____
(34) The kind of texts / poems I would like include _____
read by _____
(35) If possible I would like a main address about my life given by
_____ or by _____
(36) At this service / at some later occasion [specify] I would / would not like
my friends to have a chance to speak up about me.
(37) I would / would not like an open coffin [assuming body is relatively
presentable].
(38) Other rituals I would like to see at this time include _____
[eg single flowers placed in coffin by family and friends].
(39) I have / have not left a last written / audio / video message for my family
or friends [if yes, location], and wish for this to be read aloud / played at the
funeral service / some other occasion [specify].

Party or gathering after funeral
(40) I would / would not like a party / gathering after the funeral.
(41) [Assuming one is wanted] In general terms, I would like the expenditure
on the post-funeral gathering to be no more than £ ____
(42) The form I would like this gathering to take is ._____
[indoors / outdoors / location / food / drinks / etc].
(43) The rituals I would most like it to include are _____

Memorial service
(44) I would / would not like a memorial service __ months after the funeral.
(45) The form I would like this memorial gathering to take is
_____
(46) The rituals I would most like it to include are _____
(47) Those who may not have come to the funeral that I would like invited
to the memorial service include _____
(48) I would like the funeral / memorial service announced in the following
media _____

Commemoration
(49) I would / would not like a tree / flowers [specify species] planted on / near
grave / other location [specify] in memory of me.
(50) Memorial objects or ways of commemoration I would ideally like
include: entry in memorial book / plaque / headstone [suggest wording of
epitaph] / bench / endowment [details].
(51) I would / would not like there if possible to be a ritual or remembrance

on the anniversaries of my death. Ideally the form this could take would be

---

(52) Amongst things left unsaid to particular people that I would like to say now are: _____

(53) I shall find out for sure in due course, but as a matter of interest, I do / do not believe in an afterlife, which I visualise as _____

Signed by:
    Name
    Signature
    Date
Witnessed by the two undersigned who do not stand to benefit from the signatory's Will:
    Names
    Signatures
    Witnesses' occupations and addresses

One Belgian man decided to have a dress rehearsal of his own funeral:
Jos Thys, from Westerlo in Belgium, had always been curious about what his funeral would be like. So, for his 68th birthday, his six children invited 250 guests to a funeral reception. There was no church service or visit to the cemetery, but all the mourners wore black, sent flowers and cards, and had lunch together – in traditional Belgian funeral style. Mr Thys said he got the idea years ago, at his best friend's funeral, when it struck him that it was a pity his friend could not be there. 'I always wanted to know how people would think about me and would speak about me at my funeral. Some people would have found it sinister, but I was so pleased to share it with my friends – and I heard no gossiping at all. I am still in good health, but in case something happens to me, my children are prepared now. They spent the last three days trying to find the addresses of long-lost friends and family. If I die suddenly, it will be easy to inform them.'
    From a news story on www.ananova.com (February 27th 2003).

Involving children in preparing for dying

Sixty Year 10 and 11 pupils from Leicestershire attended a mock funeral in the parish church of Evington. The minister of St Denys Church, Reverend Steve Heygate, came up with the idea as a way of giving the children a gentle introduction, in the hope that they would be more prepared when a death occurred. The funeral was based on the Reverend's own mother's funeral; afterwards there was a discussion on funerals of other religions.
    News story from the *Funeral Director Monthly*, March 2002.

How do we speak to children about dying? How can we help children to prepare for the death of someone close to them? How can we help children who are dying prepare for their own death? What assumptions do we make about children's ability to understand what is going on?

Children are incredibly sensitive to the feelings and states of mind of adults around them. Young children especially will assume that what is going on is somehow due to their own doing. So if the parent is unhappy, sad or angry, a young child might believe that it has done something to cause it. They might think that their own angry thoughts are responsible for the illness or dying of their parent or sibling for instance. It is therefore extremely important to speak to children about what is going on. Grieving starts as soon as the child realises someone is very ill and they might die.

The Acorns Children's Hospice Trust (see Resources), which has years of experience helping bereaved children individually, in groups and in advising schools, says, 'Listening carefully to children's questions and answering them is one of the most important foundations for helping children to understand death.' You might find it helpful to bear the following points in mind when answering children's questions on any issues around dying or death:

- consider the age and developmental level of the child
- listen carefully to exactly what is being asked
- think about any unspoken contexts within a question
- clarify any areas of confusion or misunderstanding
- reply to questions in straightforward, easily understood language, avoiding the use of clichés, euphemisms or rehearsed answers
- strive to give answers that help dispel fantasy and encourage reality
- make distinctions between physical remains and 'spiritual' aspects of death
- acknowledge that we don't have all the answers.

Adults can offer help and support to a child by giving the child their undivided attention, by not interrupting when they are talking, by allowing the child to express their feelings in any way they wish, as long as they do not endanger themselves or anyone else, and by helping the child to have some control over what is happening. The following story shows how this might be done:

The three questions

Little Arya's mother was seriously ill in hospital. On the only occasion when the child had visited her there, he had been so terrified by all the equipment around the bedside that he had never been able to go back. Now she was near death and the parents asked a counsellor to assist them by talking to the little boy. The counsellor asked Arya three questions. 'Do you realise your mother is dying?'

'What does that mean?' replied Arya. 'It means she will not be coming home. She will not be able to look after you any more. She will not be able to do any of the things with you that she used to. You will never see her again.' The little boy was silent. The counsellor was silent too for some time. Then he asked his second question:

'What does that feel like to you?'

'Very sad,' said Arya. 'Very lonely.' The counsellor was silent for a long time. Then he asked his third question:

'What do you want to do about that?'

After a while, the boy described to the counsellor exactly how he would like to say goodbye to his mother, what he wanted to do at her funeral and how he would like to remember her in the years ahead. As a result of these three questions and the ensuing unconditional silences, the boy's responses emerged with precision and honesty. His innate ability to be direct and creative had been unlocked.

You may already be asking yourself the fourth question: 'Shouldn't we try to do that for everyone and not only for our children?' Whenever there is a death in the family the three questions are a way forward. They go straight to the heart of the matter, enabling us to acknowledge the reality of death in terms of our own experience, giving us permission to feel the emotional impact of the event and allowing us to express ourselves in a meaningful way.

From page 168 of Dying Well *by Richard Reoch (see Resources).*

I didn't know what to say ...

What do you say when someone tells you that a loved one of theirs is dying – or that they themselves are dying? Caught between a feeling that there's nothing we can really do to help and a fear of upsetting the person by touching their pain, we might gloss over the subject. However, if you have done some of the exercises suggested in this chapter, you may find yourself feeling more at ease and you may realise that the best thing you can do is simply to ask the person how they are and listen with compassion. Most people will appreciate the invitation to talk freely without interruption, as much or as little as they feel able to; some might just want to give you the facts. Simply be open to whatever they want to say – it will usually be fine just to nod and let what they say resonate in you. Hold back from giving advice or trying to make it 'better'. Instead, let the person tell you what they feel and need. They will want to feel that you care. Dying means grieving, so Chapter 10, which looks at issues around bereavement, could also be useful in this respect.

Being afraid to let go

Sometimes you will find that people hold onto life and are afraid to let go or die, because they have not come to terms with what they have been and done. And when a person dies harbouring guilt and bad feelings towards others, those who survive him suffer more deeply in their grief. Sometimes people ask me: 'Isn't it too late to heal the pain of the past? Hasn't there been too much suffering between me and my dying friend or relative for healing to be possible?' It is my belief, and has been my experience, that it is never too late ... The moment of death has a grandeur, solemnity, and finality that can make people re-examine all their attitudes, and be more open and ready to forgive, when before they could not bear to. Even at the very end of life, a mistake of a life can be undone.

From *The Tibetan Book of Living and Dying*, by Sogyal Rinpoche
(see Resources for details).

Unfinished business

> *If I live my life 'finishing business' by keeping myself up to date and clear in my relationships, living from the deepest truth of myself, working to dissolving the barriers to love in my life – how much more easy my death might be.*
>
> Caroline Sherwood (see under Courses in Resources).

The following exercise may facilitate understanding and forgiveness in a situation where there is conflict. You can do it by yourself, and the person with whom you have the conflict need never know, yet it will still work. It is especially useful in preparing for dying – for the person dying or for a relative or carer.

Usually unfinished business is the result of blocked communication; when we have been wounded, we often become very defensive, always arguing from a position of being in the right and blindly refusing to see the other person's point of view. This is not only unhelpful, it freezes any possibility of real exchange.

So when you do this exercise, begin it with the strong motivation that you are bringing up all your negative thoughts and feelings and try to understand them, to work with them and resolve them, and finally now to let go of them. Then visualise in front of you the person with whom you have the problem. See this person in your mind's eye exactly as he or she has always looked to you. Consider now that a real change has taken place, so the person is far more open and receptive to what you have to say, more willing than ever before to share honestly, and resolve the problem between you. Visualise vividly the person in this new state of openness. This will also help you to feel more open to him or her. Then really feel, deep in your heart, what it is you most need to say to that person. Tell him or her what the problem is, tell the person all your feelings, your difficulties, your hurt, your regret. Tell him or her what you have not felt safe, or comfortable enough, to say before. Search yourself and see if there is anything else you need to say to the person, any other hurt feelings or regrets from the past that you have been holding back or have never aired. Again, each time after you have stated your feelings, write a response by the other person, writing down just what ever comes into your mind. Continue this dialogue until you really feel there is nothing more you are holding back, or nothing more that needs to be said.

To see if you are truly ready to conclude the dialogue, ask yourself deeply if you are now able to let go of the past wholeheartedly, ... , satisfied by the insight and healing that this written dialogue has given you, to forgive this person, or to feel that he or she would forgive you. When you feel that you have accomplished this, remember to express any last feelings of love or appreciation you may have been holding back, and say goodbye. Visualise the person turning away and leaving now; and even though you must let go of him or her, remember that you can keep his or her love, and the warm memories of the best aspects of your relationship, always in your heart.

From The Tibetan Book of Living and Dying, *by Sogyal Rinpoche*
(see Resources for details).

Dealing with anxiety

If someone who is ill or dying is in a state of great anxiety, this may make those caring for him or her feel helpless or anxious too. Anxiety can also aggravate pain. Effective pain control is important and should be readily available. However, knowing a simple technique such as co-meditation, can be of great help to both the ill person and the person practising the co-meditation with them. Co-meditation originates from the Tibetan Buddhist tradition and has been widely publicised by the American psychotherapist Richard Boerstler. He describes the technique in detail in his book *Letting Go* (see Resources). The following is a brief summary of his instructions:

Lie the person down with the co-meditator sitting close by. The room should be quiet and the couple should be left undisturbed for the duration of the exercise. Begin with a muscle relaxation. The co-meditator says: 'The toes and feet are relaxing ... The calves are relaxing,' moving slowly up the body, giving the message to all parts of the body to relax, including the muscles of the face and the brow. Then, watching the person's outbreath, the co-meditator breathes out together. Making an 'ahhh' sound, the co-meditator emphasises the person's outbreath, without trying to change it in any way. Then, instead of the sound, the co-meditator counts aloud each breath and in doing so visualises the number disappearing over the horizon. This can also be done silently. Through breathing together, with the ill or dying person feeling held by the gentle presence of the co-meditator, anxiety will be reduced and the mind calmed.

Sacred Dying

The moment of death is a threshold. We are leaving behind this life and this body and entering into something new or unknown. During the last weeks or days of life, what feels unresolved may cause great pain to a person dying and make it difficult for them to let go. There may also be fear of what happens after death. The American theologian Megory Anderson is a true midwife for the dying. Her remarkable book, *Sacred Dying*, suggests ways of helping someone find forgiveness and peace:

After someone lets go of the many concerns she has, there is often a feeling of lightness or cleansing. When Cheryl was in the last days of her breast cancer, her husband and teenage daughter were with her. They spent a long time talking, letting go of all the hurt and pain that had been a part of their lives together. Afterward, the daughter picked up a wash cloth and began washing her mother's face. It was more than just wiping away tears and making her mother comfortable. Over and over again, the daughter repeated the phrase, 'It's alright, Mummy, it's alright.' The act of cleansing and the assurance of her mantra-like words, let Cheryl relax into a needed peacefulness ...

Family stories can provide the same bond. Draw on times when love was present; draw on the emotions and tenderness of love. Now is the perfect time to bring in rituals of faith traditions. They represent community and tradition as well as formal connection with the divine. For example, Christians can break the bread of the Eucharist. Jews can put on the prayer shawl and recite family prayers.

People need and want to die with a clear conscience, with a feeling that the burdens of this life are past, and with a knowledge that their wishes will be granted. It is important to give them the opportunity to do that in a sacred setting. Take your cue from the patient. Be respectful of what he needs most. Speak what he needs to hear. Provide an opportunity for the divine to heal and restore, and then reassure the loved one that you also love and forgive him and will do everything you can do to carry on his legacy.

From Sacred Dying *by Megory Anderson (see Resources).*

A legacy for others

What you give to others is not merely what you possess; what you leave behind is not solely what you have accomplished. At every moment of your life and in the period of your dying you shape the future of others. You do this in many ways, but the most powerful and the most pervasive is the impact that you make upon other people's understanding of themselves and their underlying attitudes towards life. One of the greatest legacies you can leave them is the impact of your own preparation for death, your own understanding of it and the manner of your dying.

From p.138 of *Dying Well* by Richard Reoch (see Resources).

In preparing for dying we not only help ourselves, we can help others by bringing about an urgently needed change in our society. By reintroducing death as a natural part of life, we can begin to live more fully, more truly connected to ourselves, to each other and our environment. Death has much to offer us and we have much to learn. The practical implications are many and various. We may become more truly humane in how we structure our lives and our expectations, embracing anxiety, sadness, anger, helplessness and dependency as very real and valuable aspects of our condition, not something to hide and be ashamed of. It is when these aspects have to be hidden that they most create havoc in our lives; it is what death represents, and is hidden away for, that causes it to become a destructive power. And it is in the embracing of death that life becomes truly what it can be.

Chapter 3

PRACTICAL CARE AT HOME

If asked, most people would say, 'I want to die at home, in my own bed and surrounded by my family'. In actuality, home deaths account for less than a quarter of UK deaths. The majority die in hospital and a small minority in a hospice. The possibility of a home death tends to depend upon the following factors: the type of illness; a stated preference for a home death; being aged under 65; family support; access to a palliative care nurse; and availability of the necessary equipment.

Those with cancer are more likely to die at home because there is usually a defined dying stage. With other illnesses, such as advanced lung disease, regular hospital admissions (eg to treat chest infections) will be needed during the last few years. A common scenario is that on one such occasion treatment is ineffective and the patient dies. Heart and renal disease tend to follow a similar pattern, which leaves little opportunity to anticipate the death and therefore arrange for transfer home.

Research shows that if a person persists in stating a preference to die at home, then the likelihood of success increases because the medical team and the family have the opportunity to prepare for it. Incidentally, it is not uncommon for people close to death to reverse their decision, so it is important to keep the communication lines open.

Those who are under the age of 65 when dying are more likely to die at home. Greater family support and more youthful, healthy carers are the key factor. The more support someone has from family and friends generally then the more likely they are to be able to die at home. Family and friends fulfil a practical caring role whilst offering valuable emotional support. They can also act on behalf of the dying person to access medical and nursing support. The Natural Death Centre highlighted this point many years ago and set up the Befriending Network of volunteers to support those caring for someone dying at home (see Resources for further information).

The role of the palliative care nurse

If the patient is cared for by a palliative care nurse then a home death is, on average, 50 per cent more likely. The most obvious reason is that if a palliative care nurse has been assigned then it has been formally recognised that the person has an advanced illness and may soon die. The nurse's expertise can also help in identifying the dying stage and help in accessing increased resources such as district nurses for extra nursing support, Marie Curie cancer nurses for night care, or respite care in a hospice to allow carers to rest. The nurse can also make choices about medication to make symptom control at home more feasible. Practical and medical needs can be anticipated, reducing the likelihood of a crisis admission to hospital and sudden death away from home.

The palliative care nurse's role is analogous to that of the midwife at a natural birth. However, whilst care from a midwife is generally automatic, palliative care is offered to only half of cancer patients and only rarely to non-cancer patients. Palliative care services have now acknowledged the need to move away from their cancer-focused approach to embrace all of those who are dying, regardless of the cause. However, limited resources and an increasingly specialist focus on symptom control means that progress has been slow. Further progress will also depend on a cultural attitude-shift towards accepting death as a natural and inevitable event. Aggressive treatments which extend life at all costs should be reconsidered within a context of informed choice and patient and family needs.

Who can get a palliative care nurse?

The modern hospice movement aims to provide support and health care to patients who are dying or those with advanced, incurable illness. The emphasis is on holistic care for the patients and their family and friends, plus bereavement support. Since 1987 the hospice movement has been recognised as an independent medical speciality known as palliative medicine. Palliative care is practised by nurses and doctors within hospices, hospice day-centres, in people's own homes and in hospitals, and by other professional groups throughout the NHS.

Ninety-six per cent of a typical palliative care nurse's caseload consists of cancer patients, although 75 per cent of the population die of other causes. It is not that all these others lack palliative care needs, but that they are not referred to palliative care teams. This is partly because palliative care nurse practice evolved from Macmillan nurses, and money donated to Macmillan Cancer Relief is directed to the care of people with cancer. However, most specialist services now accept patients regardless of their diagnosis. *Any* dying person can insist on seeing a palliative care nurse. However, although the need will be acknowledged, eligibility ultimately depends upon the dying person fitting into the criteria of that particular palliative care team.

> **!**
> If the doctor or GP refuses to let you see a palliative care nurse, it could be that he or she does not fully understand the nurse's role. Try contacting your local palliative care nurse through your local hospice if you are at home, or via the hospital switchboard if you are in hospital or being seen as an outpatient. Alternatively, the Hospice Information Service (☎ 0208 778 9252) holds a directory of all palliative care services in the UK.

To satisfy a person's wish for a home death, the person who is ill (and their carers) need to know when the time of death is approaching. The aim of the following section is to help make this information more accessible.

'How long have I got?'

Clinicians caring for patients with terminal cancer need to be aware of their tendency to overestimate survival, as it may affect patients' prospects for achieving a good death.

'A systematic review of physicians' survival predictions
in terminally ill cancer patients' (*BMJ* 2003;327:195).

This is the question that everyone asks and no one answers. Health professionals tend to say that prognoses are difficult to make as there are so many physical and medical factors involved, meaning that most answers are nothing more than good guesses. Patients themselves, however, often know that they are dying as they understand their own bodies and can feel when a change occurs which is different to previous ones. As with professionals, though, patients can be wrong.

Discussion of death is often avoided by doctors until close to the end – when the patient is clearly rapidly deteriorating with no obvious reversible cause – and even then the talk may be indirect and euphemistic. They may say: 'the patient has more advancing disease' or is 'not responding to treatment', or they may ask about the patent's or family's wishes about cardio-pulmonary resuscitation. You can help your doctors by making sure at the outset, that they have a copy of your Advance Directive and your Death Plan amongst your medical notes. This offers a clear indication that you are prepared to talk about dying. But in spite of this, in most cases the onus will still be on the patient to bring up the subject.

> **!** Ask specific questions, eg 'What symptoms of this lung illness may be a sign of my dying?' Ask the doctor or nurse to make an educated guess of a number of years, months or weeks. The closer the patient is to death, the more accurate the answer is likely to be.

Sometimes dying is a long, drawn-out process, the body slowly deteriorating over a number of months. Extensive research shows that life expectancy for people dying from heart, lung and renal disease is more unpredictable than for those with cancer. The diagnosis of these conditions may not begin with 'bad news', and the patient could be treated for many years with a chronic condition. At other times a patient decides to stop aggressive treatment, choosing relative quality of life until they die. However, in all cases there are some key indicators which professionals consider when they are trying to establish life expectancy. These include the person's energy levels and their ability to walk and wash and dress themselves. Loss of appetite and looking thin and facially-drawn can also be a sign. The fact that the person may be requiring ever stronger doses of painkillers such as morphine does not necessarily indicate that death is near. Neither is there any evidence to suggest that their use speeds the dying process.

As a very rough guide: if someone is deteriorating monthly, they may have months to live; if deteriorating weekly, they may have weeks to live. However, within this decline there will be many fluctuations, and sudden deterioration cannot be excluded.

Where is the best place to die?

> The specialist told my husband that he had liver cancer and nothing could
> be done for him. He died ten weeks later. I regret that the specialist told my
> husband without asking me to be present and that he was so blunt about it.
> A friend advised me to get in touch with Macmillan nurses. My GP told me
> they would not be needed yet and did not seem to know where they were
> based. I then rang a cancer charity who told me that they were in the same
> hospital where the specialist was based. I got in touch and from that time
> their support was invaluable. They are in fact not just nurses but specialists
> in the treatment of cancer, and also counsellors. The nurse who called at
> the house regularly soon realised that my husband was in far more pain
> than he would admit to the doctor and arranged for him to have increased
> painkillers. When later he was given drugs to combat sickness and consti-
> pation, she was able to tell me whether the way he reacted to them was
> normal. The doctors appear not to want to recognise that these nurses can
> help the patients and families more than they can.
>
> We had the choice whether to keep my husband at home or whether he
> should go to hospital. He was always very attached to his house and family
> and although we never talked to him about it, I was sure he would wish to
> stay at home, as we were able to carry on as if he had an illness from which
> he might recover. I was able to sleep in the same bed with him right until
> the day he died.
>
> From a letter to the Natural Death Centre.

The best place to die is where the patient can get the best support possible. For
many people this can be made available at their home, but it needs planning and
discussion. Other options are a residential home, if the person has months or
years to live, or a hospice, if less than a month to live. Hospice care is also
available for periods of respite care and symptom control during the patient's last
year. In practice, though, over 95 per cent of patients in a hospice have cancer.

Usually people spend most of the last year of life at home, although only about
one in four actually die at home. A typical scenario is that someone who is being
cared for at home becomes increasingly ill and needs to go to hospital for medical
care. Subsequently it becomes clear that the patient is not improving (the doctor
might begin to talk about the patient 'not responding to treatment'). This is the
trigger to discuss either continuing with invasive treatments or trying to get
home. It could also be worth discussing with the palliative care nurse the
possibility of transfer to a hospice, which is much less formal than a hospital and
is more able to accommodate the family. If it is not practical to go home from
hospital, the hospital environment could be made as homely as possible.

> **!** Many parents fear that children will become too upset if they know
> someone they love is dying. However, if they are not involved, they may
> sense the tension in the house and feel even more insecure. Chapters 2 and
> 10 suggest ways of talking to children about death and dying.

What help might be needed at home?

Services at home are theoretically meant to be based on what a patient and carer needs rather than on what the service can offer. In reality, however, unless you state a 'need' you may not be offered a service. Your palliative care nurse is able to act as your advocate and help you make decisions about services from which you could immediately benefit, and anticipate services which you may need in the future. It is often difficult for the dying person to identify themselves as being 'disabled' or the carer to acknowledge that help is needed.

How to get help

Each area of the UK has its own guidelines and criteria for what is available through a Community Care Assessment (an appointed social worker as a gatekeeper to access home-helps, carers, meals on wheels, and so on), and the local Community Health Services (GP, palliative care or district nurse). The following sections should be recognised as a general guide only, as provision differs throughout the country.

> **!** Ask the health or social care professional who is assessing the patient's needs for a 'care package' and ask whether there is a palliative care programme. Some areas offer increased services if someone has less than three months to live or has an advanced illness which needs a lot of nursing, rather than social, support.

Four examples of different care packages follow:

1) Example of a care package for a patient in the last six months of life who is housebound but mobile from room to room and lives with a carer who is well

The patient is likely to need a visit from a palliative care nurse every two to three weeks, or less, for support and symptom control. He or she is probably eligible for Attendance Allowance and Disability Living Allowance as the illness is terminal (see Finance section). It is presumed that the carer is doing the shopping, cleaning, and laundry.

Useful equipment

• Commode for the night-time (available from the district nurse).

• Telephone with memory facilities to store emergency numbers and the carer's mobile.

• Bath aid such as a bath lift (available from the occupational therapist).

• Blue Disabled Car Badge. If the patient or the carer drives a car, and the patient has been granted top-rate Disability Living Allowance or Attendance Allowance, they are eligible to apply for a Blue Disabled Badge and possibly a Taxi Card (black cab, £1 per journey in London and some other areas of the country). (See Finance section.)

• Wheelchair (available through the occupational therapist, although there is often a waiting list; or hired privately from the Red Cross).

2) Example of a care package for a patient in the last six months of life, who is housebound but mobile from room to room and lives alone.

• Palliative care nurse visits, as above.

• Carer from social services to visit at least twice a week for shopping, cleaning and laundry.

• Meals on wheels – if required

• Hospice therapy day centre: weekly visits (arranged by the palliative care nurse) to access medical and nursing review as well as complementary therapies.

• Finance – it would be useful to have a benefits review.

Useful equipment

• Emergency call bell: a panic button worn like a necklace to alert the 24hr call-centre staff who will phone either friends, family or an ambulance, as appropriate (available via social services and some private companies).

• Commode for the night-time (available via the district nurse).

• Bath aid (available via the occupational therapist). A plastic chair for the shower is helpful.

• Kitchen aids: for example an approved stool to perch on whilst making snacks in the kitchen, or a wheeled-trolley to take food and drinks from the kitchen to the lounge (available via the occupational therapist).

• Transport assistance: Taxi card or Dial-a-ride (see Finances section). Local Age Concern can sometimes organise day trips out, with assistance.

3) Example of a care package for someone in the last six months of life, who is housebound, can only move from bed to chair with assistance, and lives alone

Choose to base the 'bedroom' in a large room with a good view from the window, such as the lounge. If the patient attends a day centre, a weekly bath may be offered there. A designated washing-up bowl can be used for a strip wash.

• Carer for personal care (from social services). Usually three home visits a day: in the morning to help with getting up, washing, dressing, toilet assistance and preparing breakfast; early afternoon for toilet assistance and to prepare a sandwich for supper; and late afternoon for toilet assistance and to prepare a drink.

• Meals on Wheels (arranged via social services) delivered seven days a week at lunchtime.

• District nurse visits daily, usually in the morning, give medications, and assess pressure areas, constipation, etc.

• Palliative care nurse may still visit only every two to three weeks if the patient is reasonably well symptom controlled. The district nurse will liaise with the palliative care nurse as necessary.

• Hospice therapy day centre once a week may be available if there is adequate wheelchair access to the street.

Useful equipment

• Emergency call bell (available via social services).
• Hospital bed, pressure-relief mattress, incontinence pads, commode, pressure-relief seat cushion (all available from the district nurse).
• Dosset box for daily pills (available from the district nurse).
• Bed table: hospital type (available from the occupational therapist).
• Transport: an ambulance can be arranged for out-patients appointments.
• Keys to access the home: carers, nurses and approved visitors will need keys for the front door.

4) Example of a care-package for a patient at home, who is bed-bound, in the last week or two of life, and lives alone

A patient who is so ill ideally needs someone with them 24 hours a day, not necessarily for nursing but just to be there. If the patient lives alone, this is the time for a family member or friend to put their own life on hold and move in, or for each member to cover a few days. A campbed or armchair in the dying person's room is often used by carers, and they should make sure they get some sleep at night. During the day when normal household chores need to be done, a mobile baby intercom (available from Mothercare or Argos) can be useful. The patient is probably sleeping on and off for most of the day and night, so the main task is just being there, rather than actually nursing.

• District nurse would need to attend at least once a day (more as necessary) to give a bed bath, check medications, assess incontinence management, etc.
• Marie Curie cancer night nurse (for patients with cancer) to cover a night shift, 10pm-7am, to give the family a break. (Available through the palliative care nurse, but limited in many areas.)
• Palliative care nurse will probably telephone daily with a view to visiting as necessary.
• GP will likely visit to review.

Useful equipment

• Hospital bed and a pressure relief mattress (available from the district nurse). Sometimes electric bed-headrests are available.
• Urinary catheter for passing urine, or incontinence pads, may be needed (available from, and supervised by, the district nurse).
• Protective sheet for the mattress is adequate, as the patient is more likely to be constipated than have diarrhoea.
• Mouth sponges for regular mouth care (available from the district nurse).
• Syringe-driver: the patient will probably be unable to take tablets at some point, so a small battery-operated syringe-driver pump may be set up and supervised by the district nurse.
• Medicines for symptom control for the dying, prescribed by the GP (see 'First Aid box for the dying' in the Symptoms section).

Health Services available (through NHS and other care)

Person	What help is offered	How to contact
General Practitioner (GP)	24-hour medical care at home	GP surgery, deputising GP out of hours
Hospital Doctor	Illness-specific medical care in hospital or out-patient clinic.	referral through GP
Palliative Care Nurse (Macmillan Nurse)	Clinical nurse specialist who cares for people with advanced illness or who are dying. Focuses on quality of life, support for the family. Specialist in pain and symptom control. Usually available at home, hospital, and hospices.	referral through hospital team, GP, district nurse
District Nurse (Community Nurse)	Qualified nurse directing the nursing care at home. Able to dress wounds, assists with medications, advice on broad areas of symptom control, and provide equipment such as hospital bed, pressure relief mattress, and commode.	referral through hospital team, GP
Marie Curie Nurse	Qualified nurse with cancer experience. Can provide several night / day shifts in the last few weeks of life, to give the family a break.	referral through palliative care or district nurse. Primarily for people with cancer
Other Clinical Nurse Specialists	Specialist nurses for particular illnesses, eg heart disease, Parkinson's, Motor Neurone Disease and dementia. Specialist nurses in specific cancers and particular symptoms, eg incontinence, stoma care, respiratory problems.	referral through hospital team or GP. Limited availability. Tend to be based in hospitals.
Carer for personal care	Daily help, eg with getting up in the morning, washing, dressing, and toilet assistance.	referral through social services
Occupational Therapist	Assesses patient's needs for equipment and aids, eg wheelchairs, bathing aids. Can help patient decide where best in the house to be based.	referral through hospital team, social services, district or palliative care nurse
Physiotherapist	General assessment of mobility. Provides walking aids, eg Zimmer frames. Able to teach carers about safer moving and lifting at home.	referral though hospital team, GP, district or palliative care nurse
Dietician	Nutritional advice and supplement drinks.	referral through the hospital team, GP

Practical help at home

Person / organisation	What help is offered	How to contact
Social worker/care manager via Social Services	Assessment of Community Care Package needed. Care package such as personal carers, home help, meals on wheels, emergency call bell, and benefits.	referral by GP, district nurse, hospital nurse
Home helps	Generally provide home visits for cleaning, laundry and shopping.	referral through Social Services
Meals on Wheels	A hot midday meal delivered daily, or a weekly delivered supply of frozen meals.	referral through Social Services
Emergency Call Bell Alarms	There are many kinds of emergency call bells; some are provided by social services, some by private firms.	referral through Social Services
Local Volunteer Groups	Help may include a Befriending Service, complementary therapies, gardening, DIY jobs in the house, day trips out.	ask your local palliative care nurse about volunteer services through the local hospice, also Citizens Advice Bureau; local volunteer bureau, library & Age Concern for info.

> **!** If you feel the patient needs more help than social services are offering, contact your district or palliative care nurse who should know and understand well the services in your area. It may be that you are already receiving the maximum support available, but they can act as an advocate to negotiate for more. Your local Carers' Centre may also be able to help.

Carer Support

Person / organisation	What help is offered
Social Worker	Able to undertake independent 'carers assessment' of carers needs – see Carers UK booklet on 'How do I get help? Carers' assessments made clear'.
Local Carers Centre	Most offer carer advice about eligibility to services, finances, and some offer support groups.
Carers UK / Carers Online (see Resources)	National carers charity providing advice and a whole range of booklets, which are comprehensive and easy to follow. Booklets include: 'Coming out of Hospital', 'Taking a Break', 'When Caring becomes a Crisis', 'Making Life Easier', 'How do I get Help', 'Residential and Nursing Home care', 'Getting help to adapt your Home', 'Benefits', 'Looking after Someone Else's Money', and many more.
Palliative care nurse	The Palliative care nurse is also there to support carers, including bereavement support where necessary.
GP	The GP is there to help with the carer's own health and emotional needs.
Literature (see Resources)	The Natural Death Centre, Carers UK and Age Concern all provide suggested reading lists. Cruse Bereavement Care also has a suggested reading list, which includes stories of how individuals coped after their loved one died and years of caring ended.

Support for the carer

Becoming a carer for someone you love may be something that happens naturally over time as the dying person becomes less able to cope with daily tasks. However, while some people will adapt fairly easily to this new role, others will find it difficult to come to terms with. Feelings of resentment and frustration are common, along with feelings of love and a sense of achievement. In order to care for someone else it is essential to acknowledge your own needs. Jane Brotchie writes in 'Help at Hand – The home carer's survival guide':

> If you have very high expectations of being patient and loving every second of the day, it can be upsetting to feel angry and frustrated. But feeling guilty about it will not help – that simply turns the anger on yourself and sooner or later you will start feeling depressed.
>
> Anger may also be a reaction to loss – witnessing the suffering of someone you are close to can make you feel angry at the injustice of it all. Or it may be a reaction to the anger expressed by the person you look after: carers often bear the brunt of that anger and frustration.

> **!** Do not use holiday leave from work: ask your GP to sign you off sick due to the stress of someone dying instead. The palliative care nurse may be able to write a supporting letter.

Asking for support – offering support

The daily routine of coping with an illness or caring for someone who is dying can be exhausting and there may be little time for the usual socialising. At a time when you most need to be connected to the community, you may find yourself isolated. You may, of course, have chosen to isolate yourself; if you are not very good at reaching out and asking for help, this could be an opportunity to break the habit. Others can help by reaching out and offering support. Here is a list of the kind of support which friends, relatives or neighbours might be able to offer, and which the carer or ill person might find useful:

- People to phone when you need a shoulder to cry on or a listening ear
- An email group to whom you write, to keep them in touch with developments
- People living nearby who would enjoy cooking for you
- People who are able to give you a massage, shiatsu, reflexology or cranial osteopathy at your home
- Someone who will help you with your paperwork
- Someone who will go for a walk with you
- Someone to look after the garden, mow the lawn etc
- Someone to take the dog for a walk
- Someone to look after the children: play with them, take them to the park, swimming, to a piano lesson or pick them up from school
- Someone to organise a visit to the ballet, a concert or the cinema, or rent and watch a video with you at home
- Someone who will offer to do some shopping or cleaning for you or just do the washing up and take the rubbish out

• Someone who has time to chat and have a cup of tea with you

• Someone who co-ordinates support during the final weeks or days (see Support Plan below).

If you offer support, ask yourself what you want to offer, and make a suggestion. Visit, phone or email the person and tell them you want to offer support. Ask what they would most want from you, being realistic about your own needs and how much time you have to give. If you find that something you have agreed to do is too much for you after all, say so as soon as you realise this. It is very important to be reliable and to be honest.

If you need support, make your own list and talk to your friends and family about it; maybe together you can draw up a 'support plan'. If you have a befriending service in your area, your palliative care nurse or your GP may be able to put you in touch with them. The Befriending Network, which is active in Oxford and Oxfordshire and in some parts of London, has excellent volunteers who are especially trained to offer support to people with a life-threatening illness, or who are dying, at home. The Buddhist Hospice Trust also has volunteer befrienders (for non-Buddhists and Buddhists alike), and the Terrence Higgins Trust provides a befriending service to people with AIDS. Some hospices have local befriending schemes (for all of these see Resources).

Volunteers or family and friends can offer invaluable support which may improve the quality of life for the ill person and the carer. One woman carer says:

> I have three or four friends who I can phone up and talk to when I feel very low or lonely or hopeless. I always ask them first how they are, and check that they have a moment to talk to me. Often I want them just to listen. It is so comforting to know they are there at the other end of the line, silent maybe, whilst I cry or we are both lost for words. I phone them regularly, so they not only get my bad moments. I have a few such friends I can rely on, so I spread the burden amongst them and it also means someone is usually available when I need to talk.

A support plan for the dying person and their carer

A support plan is a chart which lists when people are visiting and if they are coming to do a specific thing (eg cut the lawn, do the ironing, walk the dog). Supporters can book themselves in, and the ill person and their carer will then know when someone is coming and for how long, so not too many are there at any one time. This chart would also include all hospital appointments and visits from the palliative care nurse, home-help, professional carer or volunteers.

! If the dying person has a last wish to visit somewhere special, there may be practical issues to be addressed, especially if this involves flying abroad. Your palliative care nurse can advise you but, as a general rule, if the patient is feeling quite weak, then a holiday within the UK is more advisable. Plan for it sooner rather than later. If it is unrealistic to go on holiday, try to bring the place to the patient through reminiscing, with photographs etc. The British Lung Foundation (☎ 020 7831 5831), Cancer BACUP, Age Concern and Carers UK all do useful factsheets on travel (see Resources).

Finance and benefits

Person / organisation	What help is offered
Hospital Benefits Adviser / Welfare Rights Officer. Citizens Advice Bureau.	There are many benefits for the sick and disabled. If you are not used to the Benefit System, ask for a Benefit Assessment. The hospital Benefits Adviser is experienced in helping people who are ill and advising on issues such as employment and finance.
Palliative care nurse	Disability Living Allowance (under age 65) and Attendance Allowance (over 65) are non-means-tested benefits paid to people with a prognosis of less than six months rather than claiming under disability criteria which is more complicated. However, as it is so difficult to estimate prognosis ask your palliative care nurse if you can apply immediately. The nurse is able to complete the medical report (DS1500) and advise on how to complete the forms – see Carers UK booklet 'Disability Living Allowance and Attendance Allowance'.
Palliative care nurse/ Macmillan nurse	Macmillan Cancer Relief provides means-tested grants for essential items for people with cancer; for example help with bedding, clothes, heating. See 'Patient grants' leaflet from Macmillan(see resources). Other illness-specific charities, such as the Terrence Higgins Trust (HIV) and the Motor Neurone Disease Association have similar grants, as do some local church communities.
Benefit Enquiry Line	Tel: 0800 882 200 for Benefits Agency advice and leaflets – 'Sick and disabled' (SD1), 'Caring for Someone' (SD4)
Age Concern literature (see Resources)	The fact sheets are actually very comprehensive booklets, and include useful titles such as: 'A brief guide to money benefits' (fact sheet 18), 'Attendance Allowance and Disability Living Allowance' (no. 34), 'Legal arrangements for managing financial affairs' (no. 22), 'Paying for help at home and local authority charges' (no. 46).
Carers UK literature (see Resources)	Booklets include: 'Benefits, what's available and how to get them', 'Direct payments for carers', 'Invalid Care Allowance and the carer premium', 'Dealing with someone else's money', 'Council tax'.
Cancer BACUP (see Resources)	Fact sheet on financial issues. Provides practical information on managing finances when diagnosed with a life-threatening illness. Includes issues such as debt management, employment rights, and cashing in life insurance polices.

! Never presume you are not eligible, some benefits are not means tested.

Complementary therapies

Therapies such as counselling, massage, aromatherapy, reflexology, cranial osteopathy, acupuncture, acupressure, healing, hypnotherapy, art, music and creative writing or meditation may be used alongside conventional treatments.

The British Complementary Medicine Association (listed under Resources) may help guides you through the maze of therapies and therapists available, and there is a directory of therapies on the website: www.macmillan.org.uk

Aromatherapy and massage

Massage has been used for thousands of years to aid the sick and the dying. Essential oils extracted from plants, and chosen for their relaxation and medicinal properties, are available in many healthfood shops, or by mailorder from:

• Neal's Yard Remedies (☎ 0161 831 7875; **w**: www.nealsyardremedies.com): oils, pre-prepared balms and much more. They have outlets all over Britain and you can order by mailorder.

• Potions & Possibilities Aromatherapy Company (**w**: www.potions.co.uk): oils and balms for relaxation, fatigue, pain relief, etc. Aromatherapist Julie Foster may be able to suggest specific essential oils (**e**: julie@potions.co.uk).

A list of oils is included in the section on Symptoms, and suggested ways of using them is included in the section on Medicines for the dying. Consult an aromatherapist for advice.

Art therapy

Image-making consists not only of painting or drawing, but also of collage or three-dimensional work, photography, poetry or creative writing. It can be used as a tool of exploration or it can be recreational and fun. Art therapists are professionally trained, working either in NHS hospitals, hospices or in private practice.

The artist Michele Angelo Petrone painted his way through Hodgkin's disease and exhibited his work 'The Emotional Cancer Journey' throughout Europe. He says about the pictures: 'I didn't know then, that these images were actually depicting the emotional events of this journey of illness.' Michele has since recovered and now devotes much of his time to promoting the expressive arts as a tool for communication and understanding for people affected by serious illness and dying. To this end, he founded the MAP Foundation (see Resources).

Music therapy

Hearing is the first sense to be developed and it is the last sense to go. Music has the ability to stimulate, soothe, comfort and to carry one along. We can be cradled by music. Music therapy is increasingly used in palliative care in America and Germany and now also in Britain. To find out more visit the website of the Association of Professional Music Therapists (**w**: www.apmt.org.uk).

How to get free complementary therapies

Hospitals and cancer units often have counselling, massage, reflexology, aromatherapy, music or art therapy available. Most hospices and hospice day therapy centres offer a range of complementary therapies and creative arts. A hospice aromatherapist may be able to advise on the use of essential oils at home.

Symptoms in the last few months of life

An overview of several studies provides a list of the most common symptoms, which occur in the last few months of life. The studies were based predominately on cancer patients, but many symptoms are also commonly seen in patients dying from other illnesses. The symptoms are in order of decreasing incidence:

- Loss of appetite
- Sleepless nights
- Immobility
- Malaise/Fatigue
- Mouth infections (eg thrush)
- Cough
- Breathlessness
- Pain
- Pressure sores
- Constipation
- Nausea
- Oedema (eg swollen legs)
- Confusion
- Incontinence
- Vomiting
- Non-healing wounds

As the illness progresses, there will be good days and bad days, and symptoms can vary between people and between illnesses. Never presume the symptoms are due to the illness and cannot be relieved – many symptoms can be reduced or relieved with help from the GP or palliative care nurse. Cancer BACUP also provide information booklets on managing these symptoms (see Resources).

Loss of appetite

People who are ill often have little or no appetite. Even if they were able to eat large meals they would still lose weight because of the illness. The focus is therefore on the enjoyment rather than the quantity of food. Smaller, more frequent meals are better than large meals, as are foods that are easy to eat, such as soups or milk-based puddings.

Nourishing supplement drinks, such as Ensure and Fortisip are available on prescription through the GP or dietician. Complan and Build-up are available from the chemist. Taste changes are common: try experimenting with different tastes, as bitter tastes such as crème caramel, Marmite and citrus flavours are often better tolerated. Bland food does not tend to alter in flavour.

Artificial feeding – feeding by a tube through the nose into the stomach – is rarely used when a patient is dying; it is unlikely to extend life and can cause other problems.

Mouth care

People can develop occasional mouth irritations. The GP can prescribe medicines for mouth ulcers (Bonjela), fungal infections (Nystatin), false saliva spray for a dry mouth (Glandasone), and also antiseptic mouthwashes. Tincture of propolis is a wonderful natural remedy for mouth ulcers, available over the counter from chemists or health food shops. In the last few months of life the gums may recede a little so dentures may become loose fitting and need denture fixative. Otherwise, just choose not to wear them.

Fatigue

Tiredness is one of the most common symptoms in the last year of life. The person chats only for a few minutes at a time and catnaps more during the day. As the pace of life slows down, try to focus on simple activities such as sitting in the garden or the park. If the person wants to do something that you know will be exhausting, try not to be too overprotective; if the person is completely exhausted after such an activity they can spend the following day in bed. Later on, offer short activities which do not expend too much energy and where the enjoyment is maximised, such as watching a video or film on TV together, listening to music or talking books, or the carer reading aloud snippets from a book or newspaper. Essential oils such as lime and bergamot may help reduce fatigue and lift spirits.

Decreased mobility

When the patient becomes weaker, decisions need to be made as to whether he or she can manage at home. The patient may be less agile, have difficulty getting in and out of the bath and managing stairs. Then it is perhaps better to have the bed downstairs where the person is surrounded by normal home activity.

Keep everything as normal as possible. If the pet usually sleeps on the bed, let it. It is a way of maintaining a feeling of reality which is comforting when someone is drifting in and out of consciousness. The bed should be accessible on both sides to facilitate moving and turning the patient and the making of the bed, as well as bed-bathing, etc. If possible, a chair by the bed that is easy to transfer into is initially good for morale – the patient can spend the periodic half-hour sitting – which is also useful for the bed-maker. Later on, the chair can be used by visiting family.

From Elizabeth Lawlor's letter to the Natural Death Centre.

A commode can be obtained from the district nurse, and a dedicated washing-up bowl can be used for bed baths.

A hospital bed may be preferred and is better for the carers if lifting is involved. The district nurse will be able to advise on this and can also provide a pressure relief mattress – a large air-filled ripple mattress with segments which slowly inflate or deflate to alter the pressure. Up to six pillows are usually required as a backrest.

If you are using your own bed, then a waterproof towelling mattress protector (available from major department-stores, about £25 for a double), is useful, and for sofa/chair protection use a small square quilted mattress protector (£15 from Mothercare). Both are machine washable and quick-dry. Unfortunately the NHS does not provide such protectors but can provide disposable incontinence pads.

> **!**
> • Rehearse with the nurse what to do in certain scenarios, for example, after a fall, or on not being able to get out of the bath.

Pain

Pain is often the most feared symptom, when in fact one in four patients with advanced cancer has no pain, and most pains can be reduced or relieved. Pain is natural, but that does not mean that the patient should suffer. It is the body's warning that something is wrong; but a dying person knows that their body is not working, so the message serves no purpose. If there is pain, there are likely to be multiple causes such as constipation or arthritis. Your palliative care nurse should be an expert on pain control. Essential oils such as camomile may also help by soothing anxiety and aiding sleep. Heat from a warm hot-water bottle over the pain site, combined with a gentle massage, can be very relaxing.

> **!**
> • Cannabis, though illegal in the UK, has been known to have therapeutic benefits for pain and nausea control. Palliative care nurses are able to advise on the prescribing of Nabilone (a synthetic cannabinoid) for nausea.

Richard Boerstler advocates a meditative Tibetan-inspired breathing technique (see also 'Dealing with anxiety' in Chapter 2). The carer copies the dying person's breathing pattern, making the sound 'ah' on the out-breath, strung out as 'aaaahhhh'. The patient may like to make the same sound at least for the first few breaths, or prefer just to listen. This technique focuses on the out-breath to release tension and calm the mind.

Stephen Levine offers a guided pain meditation in his book *Who Dies?* (see Resources). The carer or a visitor could read aloud the following to the patient, or record it on a tape, quietly and slowly, spacing out the directions:

Bring your attention to the area of sensation that has been uncomfortable.

Let your attention come wholly to that area. Let the awareness be present, moment to moment, to receive the sensations generated there.

Allow the discomfort to be felt.

Moment to moment new sensations seem to arise.

Does the flesh cramp against the pain? Feel how the body tends to grasp it in a fist, tries to close it off.

Begin to allow the body to open all around that sensation.

Don't push away the pain. Just let it be there. Feel how the body tries to isolate it. Tries to close it off. Picture that fist. Feel how the body is clenched in resistance.

Feel how the body holds each new sensation.

Begin gradually to open that closedness around sensation. Open. Soften. All around the sensation. Allow the fist, moment to moment, to open. To give space to the sensation.

Let go of the pain. Why hold on a moment longer?

Open. Soften all around the sensation. Let the fist of resistance begin to loosen. To open.

The palm of that fist softening. The fingers beginning to loosen their grip. Opening. All around the sensation.

The fist loosening. Gradually opening. Moment to moment, letting go of the pain. Release the fear that surrounds it.

Notice any fear that has accumulated around the pain. Allow the fear to melt. Let tension dissolve, so that the sensation can softly radiate out as they will. Don't try to capture the pain. Let it float free. No longer held in the grasp of resistance. Softening. Opening all around the sensation.

The fist opening. The fingers, one by one, loosening their grip.

The sensation no longer encapsulated in resistance. Opening.

Let the pain soften. Let go of the resistance that tries to smother the experience. Allow each sensation to come fully into consciousness. No holding. No pushing away. The pain beginning to float free in the body.

All grasping relinquished. Just awareness and sensation meeting moment to moment. Received gently by the softening flesh.

The fist opened into a soft, spacious palm. The fingers loose. The fist dissolved back into the soft open flesh. No tension. No holding.

Let the body be soft and open. Let the sensation float free. Easy. Gently.

Softening, opening all around the pain.

Just sensation. Floating free in the soft, open body.

Pressure sores

If someone lies or sits in one position for a long time, the skin over the bony parts, such as the heels, and bottom of the spine can become reddened and break down, causing pressure sores. The aim is to reduce the tenderness before it happens.

Changing position every few hours and keeping the skin clean and moisturised helps. The district nurse can provide pressure-relieving mattresses and seat cushions, which reduce the frequency of position changes. If the skin does redden and break down, a nurse should be consulted as soon as possible.

Constipation

Constipation, rather than diarrhoea, is a common symptom in the last year of life. It is one of the more common causes of pain in people with advanced cancer. Severe constipation can cause distressing symptoms such as nausea, vomiting, abdominal pain and even confusion. Constipation is caused by the disease itself, immobility, a low-fibre diet, reduced fluids, as well as painkillers.

If the patient feels very weak, drinking a lot and a high-fibre diet would be inappropriate. For this reason most people in the last year of life are on daily laxatives and occasionally need enemas from the district nurse. If painkillers are increased, it is likely that the laxative dose will need to be increased. The rule of thumb is: if the bowels have not been opened three to four days, there is likely to be a need for suppositories or an enema. Some patients gain relief by eating certain foods, such as prunes or apricots

First aid box for the dying

If it is planned for the person to die at home, it is useful to obtain in advance a range of medicines for injection prescribed by the GP (see the middle column below). Then, if the patient deteriorates rapidly with increasing symptoms there is a basic pack of injectable medicines for the GP or nurse to use. The aim of medicines at this stage is comfort.

As the patient will probably be no longer eating or drinking they will be unable to take medication orally. The nurse or doctor can set up a syringe-driver-pump containing comfort-medicines, which the nurse can renew every 24 hours.

A range of essential oils may also help (third column). Use up to six drops per application on tissues for smelling or in a burner or a few drops in the water for a bed bath. For a gentle massage add two drops to a tablespoonful of sweet almond oil or a moisturiser for the hands, feet or back.

Symptom	Injections	Essential Oils
Pain	Diamorphine	Lavender, Rosemary, Camomile, Geranium
Breathlessness	Diamorphine, Midazolam	Frankincense, Eucalyptus, Lime
Chestiness / Death Rattle	Glycopyronium	Frankincense, Eucalyptus, Geranium
Nausea / Vomiting	Metoclopramide, Levomepromazine (Nozinam)	Peppermint, Ginger, Camomile
Agitation	Midazolam, Levomepromazine	Frankincense, Lavender, Geranium, Camomile

The last few days

In the last few days of life the body is slowly winding down, the organs are failing, and the dying person is withdrawing from the world. It is not possible to predict exactly when someone will die, but there are often signs that death is close. The final stages of dying are usually peaceful.

> **!**
> • Now is the time to re-look at the 'Death Plan' and 'Advance Funeral Wishes' forms, if these have been made (see Chapter 2), to clarify wishes immediately before and after death.

Consciousness and communicating with the dying

In the last few days most people slip in and out of a coma and become increasingly drowsy, often sleeping for most of the day and night. Some people describe this drifting in and out of a coma as being like waking up in the morning and trying to get your bearings, but knowing you are safe. People who are dying often experience varying degrees of consciousness, but if they were not confused previously, they are unlikely to be so when dying. They may be able to hear and understand what is being said, but be unable to respond. If the patient is conscious of pain, they will still communicate by grimacing or tensing.

Try communicating through other senses: holding the person's hand whilst gently massaging in hand-cream, or carefully massaging the feet, can be immensely soothing.

Use familiar smells to communicate a sense of safety. For example, a spouse's perfume sprayed onto the bed linen, and the use of familiar washing powder for the laundry. Use essential oils such as lavender, geranium, and frankincense in a burner or vaporiser to promote a sense of calm. Play the dying person's favourite music quietly.

The aim is to promote a sense of calm, but equally, to keep the surroundings as normal as possible. If you want time on your own with the patient, then say so. This may be your last chance to say things, even if the patient can't respond. Many people talk to the patient of loving them, and reassuring them that the family will be able to cope after they have gone so it is all right to let go.

This time is very precious and often involves the family sitting vigil around the bed, or just being with the patient. It is difficult to predict exactly when a person will die, so if the dying process takes more than a few days you must make sure to take care of yourself. You need to rest, to sleep, to eat, and to get out for at least a breath of fresh air. Some families organise a rota of 'sitting shifts'.

> **!**
> Jackie Carpenter kept a daily journal during the last three weeks of her partner's life. Ian Daycock was an engineer and environmentalist who founded the educational charity, Energy 21. Jackie's letters provide a poignant insight into the day-to-day practicality of caring for someone who is dying at home (see in Resources the book *Progressive Endings*).

Vision-like experiences

People who are dying occasionally have vision-like experiences where they mumble in their sleep as if talking to their ancestors. It is not unusual to hear the patient calling out names of loved ones who have died. This can also happen in the weeks before death when the dying person recalls vivid dreams, for example, of seeing their grandparents again. These can be pre-death premonitions, and are usually quite comforting (see Resources for Raymond Moody's book *Life after Loss*, which discusses 'death coincidences').

Agitation

Some people in the last few days of life, during the process of transition, get agitated or confused and then become peaceful again before they die. There are many causes for such agitation (eg abnormal chemicals in the blood, constipation, infection or a rush of adrenaline). At this stage it is not appropriate to investigate and to treat the causes. Simply aim for comfort and symptom control. The exception is urinary retention (see below). Sometimes just sitting with the patient, holding their hand, telling them they are safe and that you are with them will settle them again. Silence may also help; try not to react to every movement. Circulating air such as a light breeze from a fan or window helps to prevent claustrophobia. The patient may need a mild sedative to induce sleep. Try to make the room as relaxing as possible, with dimmed lights and familiar sounds and smells. The essential oils frankincense, sandalwood, lavender and geranium may help. Co-meditation practice may have a calming effect (see Chapter 2).

> During the last five days before my mother died of primary liver cancer, my father, sister, and I were with her day and night at the Rudolph Steiner hospital. My mother was mostly peaceful and no longer had the energy to speak. Periodically she became agitated: she would be looking at us with anxious eyes, struggling to breathe, wanting to sit up. We would call for the nurse to give her a homeopathic remedy to ease her breathing. With our support my mother sat up in bed, looking at my father who spoke to her softly, saying 'You are my angel, you always will be my angel, I love you.' This calmed her very much. One time he added to this: 'Soon you will be my guardian angel!' and she smiled. One time she had a fantastic rush of energy, sitting up in bed almost without our help. We understood that she wanted to look at the trees outside the window. She sat at the edge of her bed, taking in the view. She loved trees with a passion, all her life, and was now seeing them one last time. Her moments of agitation seemed to me to resemble contractions during childbirth, or the stations of the cross, a kind of labour. The labour of letting go.
>
> *From a letter to the Natural Death Centre*

Eating and drinking

In the last few days of life most people will have stopped eating and drinking. Terminal dehydration is very different from dehydration in someone who is well; it is a very natural and normal part of the body winding down. The dying person will not feel hungry or thirsty, though their mouth will be dry. The nurse can provide sponges for moistening the mouth. Use lip balm as the lips may become dry and cracked.

> **!** When moistening the mouth sponge you could use the patient's favourite drink instead of mouthwash, though not alcohol as this will dry the mouth further. Gently cleaning the teeth with a baby toothbrush may help to freshen the mouth.

Urine and bowels

In the last few days of life many people develop mild kidney failure, pass less urine, and may be incontinent a couple of times a day. Normally this is managed with pads and some skin protection cream. However if the person becomes agitated and has not passed urine for 24 hours, their bladder will probably be retaining urine, which is painful. The district nurse can assess the situation and insert a catheter if necessary.

Most dying people are constipated but if the constipation is severe, liquid diarrhoea may leak out several times a day. If this is the case the dying person is usually too weak for an enema, so aim to comfort only with incontinence pads and creams. Drops of peppermint oil on the pad will help deodorise any smells.

Breathing

In the last few days of life as the body becomes weaker, fluid can build up in the air passages, as breathing becomes shallower, and the dying person may sound chesty as if needing to clear the throat. As they slip into a coma they are unaware of this so do not feel any distress.

In the last day or two the breathing slowly fades. It is often irregular, with pauses of up to 30 seconds. The breathing becomes shallower. This is known as 'cheyne stoking', and a clear sign that someone could die within a few hours (or possibly a few days). The patient might appear to be groaning or moaning, but this is a natural part of the lungs winding down and unlikely to indicate distress. Similarly the patient may move the shoulders up and down to expand the lungs mechanically, though they are not fighting for breath. These are all normal physiological changes. Frankincense, geranium and eucalyptus essential oils may help calm the breathing.

Most patients look and are very peaceful at this stage, but if you think they are distressed, ask the nurse to reassess the situation. Carers also need to acknowledge that they may be projecting their own distress onto the dying person.

Decreasing circulation

During the last few days of life as the body is winding down the circulation decreases. Often the extremities (the hands, feet, nose and ears) feel cold to touch and the skin can become mottled and blue.

The hands occasionally swell a little. Try raising the hands up on a pillow so gravity can reduce some of the swelling. Rings on fingers may aggravate the situation, consider removing them. If a bit of washing up liquid does not help loosen them, ask the nurse.

The moment of death

Television often portrays the moment of death as someone saying their farewells and then dying. In reality a patient may not have spoken for hours or days, and is probably slipping in and out of consciousness. Nevertheless, there is a sense of release, as consciousness leaves the body. This can be experienced by those vigiling, in a powerful way; it has a solemnity.

In the last few minutes the breathing becomes particularly shallow and irregular, and then stops. There may be another small breath a minute or so later. Then the face muscles relax, the jaw often drops and the eyes become less clear. The hands, feet, and nose will feel cold, but this will probably have been increasingly so for several days. The face may feel clammy to touch. The moment of death is usually very peaceful; let it take place in a peaceful environment, so that everyone present can take in the moment, which may be like the after-ring of a bell, echoing on. There is no rush to do anything, only to be present with peace and gratitude.

What to do after the person has just died

Take note of the time of when the death occurred. Then, the best thing may be just to sit and be there with the person who has died. Some feel a great sense of sacredness and peace and wish to meditate or pray for the person. Some feel relieved or sad; some cry. Some may sense that this is an important, exquisite time; a transition, and may wish to say farewell, and silently pay tribute to the person who has just died. Others may have planned a ritual but when the time comes find that they feel drained of all emotion, often simply from sheer exhaustion, and just want to leave.

If the patient has died at home, and it is an expected death, then call the GP. If it is during the night you may prefer to wait until morning for the family GP to visit you at home. The GP will confirm the death and issue you with a Confirmation of Death Certificate and details of how to register the death at the registry office (which is often at the Town Hall).

If you would prefer the body to be lying straight, this needs to be done in the first four to six hours before rigor mortis sets in. Just lay the body flat and straight, with one small pillow behind the head. If you wish, close the eyes; if they will not stay closed, wet a wad of tissues to place over them.

Freshen the mouth with mouth-sponges. If the person wore dentures, then replace them, though denture-fixative may be needed (a little jam or toothpaste will do) as the gums will have receded slightly in the last few weeks. To hold the mouth closed, roll up a towel tightly and wedge it between the chin and chest. If it will not stay closed you could place a scarf under the chin and tie the ends on top of the head.

If the person has died in hospital or a hospice, the nurses will explain what to do next. Do not feel rushed to leave the body if you would prefer to stay.

After death and before the funeral

The time just after death – and the hours and days following – is time to take in what has happened, to sit and be with the body, if possible, or with the person in mind. Megory Anderson, in her book *Sacred Dying* (see Resources), suggests both simple and elaborate rituals for this unique time. These may involve all the people who were close to the person who has died or only a few. Simple suggestions include: sit with the body; burn a sandalwood joss stick (believed to carry the soul heavenward); use prayer or chanting; hold hands in a circle around the body in silent meditation; play music; have a toast with the person's favourite drink. The hours after death have the potential to be a time of great peace and coming together.

There are also other, more practical things to be done. These could include: laying out the body and anointing it with oils; dressing the body; keeping the body at home for a time; organising the funeral yourself with help from family and friends; and planning the funeral or memorial service.

Washing and laying out the body

Laying out the body means washing the body and putting on clean clothes. Some people would rather do this themselves, as they perceive it as a last act of love. As a general rule if you have been closely involved with washing and intimate-care when the person was dying, then this may be a natural progression. However, if you have not been so closely involved, you may find it a shock to see the body, as it may be much thinner. You do not have to lay out the body, you could ask the nurse or a funeral director to do it.

Laying out a body is just like giving a bed bath: wash the body with soap and water, then with a clean cloth, dry it, and, if appropriate, shave the face. It does, however, take two people. Some choose to add some water of special significance to the bed bath (eg holy water), or essential oils. To reduce bacteria and odours, use an anti-bacterial soap (liquid handwash) and then rinse the soap off with salt water, or add some drops of tea tree oil. Put a little moisturiser on the face. Nails could be trimmed and cleaned.

As you may be coming into contact with body fluids like urine, faeces and possibly blood (from the stomach contents) the precautions are the same as when someone is alive. You could still be at risk of infections such as MRSA, hepatitis, and HIV, and should wear rubber gloves. A nurse will be able to advise further.

When you roll the body onto its side to wash the back, sometimes fluid from the stomach will come out of the mouth – it can be up to a litre and offensive smelling. When you turn the body, place a thick folded towel over the face in anticipation. Someone who has died from an abdominal cancer is more likely to leak such fluid. When you turn the body for the first time you are putting pressure on the lungs and there may be a groan as the air from the lungs is expelled. This is quite normal and nothing to worry about.

If the patient has a urinary catheter, ask the nurse or the GP to remove it when they come to write the death certificate. Otherwise, cut the ends off furthest away from the body so the balloon holding it inside deflates, and pull gently. Hold onto the catheter as, very rarely, a vacuum sucks it back into the body. Use an incontinence pad as more urine can follow. Gently press on the lower abdomen over the bladder to help empty it.

Some people talk of packing orifices with cotton wool to reduce the risk of body fluid leakage, but this is rarely practised now. An incontinence pad for possible urine or diarrhoea is usually adequate. Any diarrhoea that does leak may be of a black tar-like consistency which is normal. A few drops of peppermint oil and lavender oil on the incontinence pad will help reduce odours. However if there was a lot of liquid from the stomach when you turned the body it may be worth packing five or more cotton wool balls down the throat using a pair of tweezers. Put some oil such as lavender on the first cotton wool ball to grease the throat and act as a plug and to retract fluid. Cover any wounds with cotton wool and then masking tape.

Jewellery, such as a wedding ring, is often removed from the body. Washing up liquid rubbed on the finger will help loosen the ring, but if you have difficulty you may need to reduce the width of the finger. Hold the hand vertically and take a reel of cotton thread and, starting from the finger tips, slowly and tightly rap the thread evenly down the finger with increasing pressure until all the finger is completely wrapped with cotton. This will hopefully have compressed any fluid out of the finger and you will be able to slide the ring over the cotton. If still unable to remove it, then consult a funeral director (see Chapter 7 for recommended funeral directors).

Dressing the body

If you are organising the funeral yourself then this is the best time to dress the body for the final time. Otherwise you can choose to take the chosen clothes to the funeral director, if you prefer them to do it, and dress the body in a nightdress or pyjamas in the meantime.

The choice of the final outfit may feel as symbolic as that chosen for other rites of passage such as a christening or wedding. Natural colours, to signify the return of the body to the earth, or light colours symbolic of the passage of the body and soul, may be chosen. Or a shroud (a white high-necked linen nightdress with long sleeves) may be preferred. Alternatively, the person might have earlier expressed a wish to be dressed in particular clothes, or you could choose their favourite ones. It is easier to put the clothes on when there is no rigor mortis (either in the first four to six hours after death or after a couple of days). If the limbs, particularly the arms, have stiffened again, try gently bending them at the joints with increasing pressure to reduce some of the lactic acid. However, if the chosen garment is too fiddly, you may need to cut it completely down the back in order to slide each side on separately.

After the body is prepared some choose to make the room feel more special, for instance by replacing everyday objects with symbolic objects or photographs. The body may also be anointed (see the section on oils below).

What happens to the body after death?

From the moment of death you will start to notice changes which are all quite normal. As the heart is no longer working, the blood begins to settle in the lower extremities and the skin will look blotchy.

Different cell types can live for a while after someone has died. Nerve cells in the brain are particularly vulnerable to oxygen deprivation and will die within three to five minutes after death. Even up to about ten minutes after death you might notice occasional tiny electrical twitches, such as eyelashes moving slightly, but this is normal and nothing to worry about.

As the blood drains away the face will begin to look pale and quite waxy in appearance, and the fingernails and fingers often become dark blue. The body can take a few hours to become cold. Rigor mortis, or stiffness due to the build-up of lactic acid as the muscles are no longer being fed, usually starts within four to six hours after death and lasts for about two days.

Hair and nails do not continue to grow after death; any apparent growth is due to the skin drying out and retracting.

Not everyone decomposes at the same rate. The colder and dryer the body is kept, the slower the decomposition will be. People who die from abdominal diseases, or who are larger, will generally decay faster. As a general rule, within a day or two the body will start to smell. After a few days the bacteria in the bowel multiply and the body organs begin to break down. Putrefaction usually begins after a week or two – earlier if the body is not cold-stored. The chest and abdomen will have a greenish tinge because of enzymes, and the body can inflate slightly due to gas. In mortuary conditions putrefaction can be delayed for a few weeks.

Why choose to keep the body at home?

If the person has died at home, it would be only natural to want to keep the body at home for a day or so after death. Some religions believe it best to leave the body undisturbed for several days after death to allow the complete departure of the soul; others emphasise the importance of allowing family members and relatives to visit the body. The first 24 hours after a death are often particularly revered – a night vigil may be held over the body, for instance, and a window opened to allow the soul to depart. You could of course also hold a vigil at the mortuary or funeral home, though there will often be time restrictions (the funeral directors listed in Chapter 7 may be more accommodating). If one of the purposes of a vigil is to bid the soul a 'good journey', a vigil could be held without the body at a significant place and with objects symbolising a journey, such as food and water.

It may be wise for the body may be taken into cold storage either until the day before the funeral, when it can be brought back home in the coffin, or at least for a few days in between. Local funeral directors may agree, for a fee, to store the body in their refrigerators even if you are not using any of their other services. If the person died at the hospital or hospice you be may able to leave the body there until the funeral. With prior arrangement your local municipal mortuary attached to the hospital might also be able to help. Avoid embalming if you can, especially if a natural burial is planned.

How to keep the body at home

Even if the person died in hospital, as long as you have registered the death you can arrange to take the body home from the mortuary. The coroner may insist on a postmortem if the death has occurred in unexpected or suspicious circumstances and with certain notifiable diseases. However, this is rare for an expected death at home. If you are planning to keep the body at home, discussing this in advance with the doctor or nurse may help you to anticipate any problems.

The length of time you can keep the body at home really depends on how quickly the body starts to decay and any odour becomes offensive. It may be a good idea after 24 hours to put the body in a coffin, seal the lid and keep it cool.

To keep a body cool:

• Choose the coolest room, turn the heating off, close the curtains to reduce the heat from sunlight, and open the windows to reduce odour.

• Use several fans.

• Wrapped ice cubes can be placed by the body (but not touching it, as they will burn the skin). It is most important to keep the trunk cool and dry as this is the main source of bacteria.

For more than 48 hours, or in summer, or with a large body at any time, the following additional cooling systems would ideally be standing by to be used no later than 24 hours after death:

• Portable air conditioning unit (£100 per week): great at reducing the odour and takes the temperature down to 16 degrees even on a summer's day (a mortuary fridge is about five degrees).

• Dry ice: sometimes used by funeral directors when their equipment breaks down. From £25 for 10kg (approx. one day's supply), eg from BOC Hackney Ltd, 59 Eastway, London E9 5NS (☎ 020 8985 5544). Wear gloves and keep the room well-ventilated (see www.dryiceinfo.com).

• A contingency plan: what to do if putrefaction occurs early (though in reality this happens to less than one in 300 bodies).

Reducing odours

• Sealing the coffin lid prevents release of odour.

• Use several deodorising air freshener gels, which actually deodorise rather than just mask the smell, also joss sticks.

• Wood shavings in the base of the coffin smell fresh and natural. Ask your local carpenter to save some up for you (you will need at least a dustbin-liner full). (Please note sawdust is not suitable for cremation, according to FBCA regulations – see Chapter 4 for more information.)

• Essential oils massaged into the skin or dripped around the body, or used in a vaporiser. Try a mixture of rosemary, lavender and peppermint or cedarwood, myrrh and lemongrass.

• Bruised or burned herbs, or flowers – but not directly on the skin as this can promote bacterial growth. John Gerrard in his 16th century herbal wrote:

'The flowers steeped in oil and set in the sun are good to anoint the body that is grown cold.'

Herbs and essential oils for used around the body and in the coffin

 • **Cedarwood**: associated with the preparation of bodies since Egyptian times when oil was used for embalming. On a practical level it repels insects.

 • **Cloves:** commonly lain in the folds of the shroud because of their pungent aromatic smell.

 • **Frankincense**: often used in rituals and worshipping around the body as it facilitates meditation.

 • **Lavender**: traditionally used around the body for its strong perfume and antiseptic properties.

 • **Lemon grass**: strong, pungent and uplifting scent

 • **Myrrh**: an aromatic incense for fragrancing the room or as an antifungal balm around the body.

 • **Peppermint**: a powerful deodorising oil used around the body.

 • **Rosemary**: antiseptic properties. Associated with memory.

 • **Sandalwood**: widely used in India and known as the oil of divinity. It is believed to carry prayers and spirits heavenward and is often used to perfume the bodies of the dead.

 • **Vervain**: also known as the holy herb. Said to have grown on the hill of Calvary where Christ was crucified and used to staunch the flow of blood from his wounds. Also known as 'holy salve'.

Removing a pacemaker

If the body is to be cremated and has a pacemaker, then it is essential for it to be removed (a doctor, funeral director or mortician could do this), otherwise it will explode in the cremator and cause a tremendous amount of damage. Families are advised against removing the pacemaker themselves as it involves cutting through the skin around the pacemaker to remove it and snipping the wires. If the pacemaker has been in for many years it could be difficult to remove as it will have become embedded in fibrous tissue in the chest.

Cardio defibrilators, which leave a similar scar to a pacemaker, must be deactivated before removal is attempted: a potentially fatal electric shock could otherwise occur. The family should be aware of the presence of a defibrilator.

Taking the body down a flight of stairs

If someone dies upstairs the body will need to be brought downstairs before placing in the coffin. You are advised to contract this out to a funeral director, as there is serious risk of back injury. However, if you insist on doing it yourselves it will take at least three people.

Borrow from a funeral director a stretcher which the body is strapped onto. Turn the body onto its side so any remaining stomach contents drain out through the mouth. If more than a tea cup full you may want to reconsider packing the throat with about five or more cotton wool balls, using a pair of tweezers. Then roll the body onto its back. Using the sheet or the mattress protector as a base lift the body onto the stretcher on the floor. Place a pillow under the head for protection and a thick towel over the face. Take the body down headfirst and use a gentle combination of sliding and lifting until you reach the bottom.

Taking the body home before the funeral

After Josefine Speyer's husband Nicholas Albery died suddenly, his body was kept at the hospital mortuary until two days before the funeral. Then it spent one day at the local funeral director's viewing room and one day back at home before being buried in private woodland by family and friends:

Nicholas died in a car accident of a broken neck. He had no visible injuries. Since we could not bring his body home, we brought the home to him. For three days we spent long periods of time with his body at the hospital mortuary, meditating, praying or just sitting with his body. Our closest friends and family came. The hospital responded generously to our request, allowing us more than the usual 20-minute time slot. A postmortem was performed on the fourth day after his death. The funeral, which I organised with the help of friends and family, took place nearly two weeks later.

Two days before the funeral we picked up his body in a van using a stretcher trolley from a local funeral director. Our local funeral director in London had a small air-conditioned viewing room. There, with help from four close friends, I prepared Nicholas' body for his coffin. We massaged his arms and legs with oils of frankincense, myrrh and lemon grass and dressed him in some of his favourite clothes. We lifted his body from the stretcher down into his bamboo coffin. John, the funeral director, assisted us with this as it proved quite tricky.

The coffin was lined with sweet-smelling hay freshly cut from our field as a kind of bedding, and a pillowcase filled with hay. It all fitted perfectly. In his hand we gave him a writing pen and in the breast pocket of his shirt the train ticket of his fatal journey. Nicholas was as handsome and young looking as he had been in his life. We lit a candle and left his 'Poem for the Day' book sitting on a little shelf beside him.

The next day we brought his body to the house and sat the coffin in the living room. We held a gathering, a kind of wake. We sat in silence for a long time. Then I spoke, standing by Nicholas' open coffin, touching him. I told the story of what had happened, from the day he had died to this moment, to give everyone a sense of how we had arrived at this point. It felt important that everyone knew what had happened and knew what was going to happen over the next two days. A friend remembered a dream Nicholas had told us some months earlier, which now seemed like a premonition of his death. We ended the ceremony around the coffin toasting Nicholas with sparkling wine and became quite merry. Together we watched Nicholas' memorial message video and had a huge buffet meal, which we ate squatting on the floor, sitting around a big tablecloth as there was no table big enough for us all. We recounted the past and one friend read a poem he had written for Nicholas. My brother sat next to me. It was a wonderful day in every way.

The next morning we set off for the country for the funeral. My son helped carry the coffin out into the van. It was the last time Nicholas' body left our house, to go on this last journey, and we were taking him there.

From Progressive Endings *(NDC, 2001; see Resources).*

Chapter 4

INEXPENSIVE, GREEN, FAMILY-ORGANISED FUNERALS

Almost all those who have tried it advocate looking after at least some aspects of the funeral of a friend or relative oneself, with the assistance of family and neighbours, rather than depending entirely on funeral directors. This chapter aims to help you find the courage to organise and design such a funeral by arming you with essential information and tales from some pioneers. The next chapter will give advice about getting the professionals in to help.

> **!** The more advance planning you can do, the better. It helps to be clear about what you want, and persistent about getting it. People (cemetery staff, health staff etc) may be helpful and sympathetic but also possibly shocked and uncertain about what they should do.

How to organise a DIY funeral

In brief, how to organise a funeral without a funeral director, in the most common of cases, tends to be as follows (many of these points will be amplified later):

• If the person died at home, you can normally keep the body there for a couple of days simply by turning off the heating in the room and by opening the windows. The nurse can lay out the body for you. (See the previous Chapter for more details on this.)

• If the person died in a hospital ward, get the sister there to sign a release form stating that you are doing your own undertaking (these release forms are not a legal requirement but many hospitals seem to use them). Phone the hospital mortuary to arrange a mutually convenient time to collect the body and ask how many assistants, if any, you will need to bring with you and what covering, if any, you will need for the body.

• Rent or borrow a transit van or a sufficiently large estate car. Turn up at the arranged time with a coffin, either one you have made or one you have bought. If the coffin and body are very heavy, you may be able to use sawn-off broomstick handles under the coffin to slide it in and out of the van.

• Before the funeral, you need in most cases to register the death with a registrar of births, deaths and marriages (under 'R' in the phonebook) and to pay for as many copies of the death certificate as you are likely to need for banks, etc. You need to decide if you want a natural burial ground, cemetery or crematorium. For a cremation you will also need three forms from the crematorium (which a good crematorium will no doubt help you to fill in; their form A needs countersigning by a householder who knows you, the applicant) and two doctors' certificates (for which you will have to pay about £101).

• Normally a coffin has six bearers matched in pairs for size, who carry the coffin on their shoulders (if possible, the bearers should practise together beforehand). But some burial grounds and crematoria may have a trolley you can use if you prefer. Or, you may be using a coffin with usable (ie non-decorative) handles. You may want to cover a cardboard coffin with a drape.

• You can have a service, celebration or ritual in whatever venue you prefer, ranging from your living room or a local hall, to the crematorium chapel or the graveside. You can ask a priest, minister, celebrant or officiant to preside over the service or perhaps a friend who is able to chair meetings in a sensitive way.

• At a crematorium it might be wise to choose the last slot of the day, in case your timing goes slightly out, or to book extra time – and to discuss with the staff well in advance the music you may want. If a natural burial ground is being used and it is far from your home, you might prefer to have a service locally, with just one or two members of the family going on with the coffin to the site.

DIY advantages

The suggested advantages for a DIY funeral are that:

• Participating in this way, according to psychotherapists, helps people to begin to come to terms with their loss.

• You have the option of trying for a 'greener' funeral if you so wish.

• It can be far less expensive – and potentially free, if the body is buried in a shroud on your own land, or from about £250 if cremation is used (whereas the average cost of a 'basic' funeral as detailed in Chapter 5 is currently £1,580 for a burial, or £1,218 for a cremation).

• You have more control over every aspect of the funeral, which can as a consequence be a much more personal and less 'assembly-line' affair.

Not having the body whisked away

No one [carrying out a DIY funeral] has had regrets about taking control but some do say how difficult it was, when the temptation was to let others take over. We hear how sharing responsibility with friends or relatives strengthened bonds, offering solid comfort – after one bond had been irrevocably broken.

In the case of burials in nature reserves, visits are made beforehand to select the positions of graves, to watch graves being dug, and to do the digging and filling themselves. Purposeful activities directly related to the death are then spread over a number of days. Emotions then move with these events and are less likely to become fixed or frozen. Having the body whisked away and a short, impersonal ceremony a few days later may be harmful for some.

An address to the Cremation Society given by John Bradfield who works for the A. B. Welfare and Wildlife Trust which offers support and legal advice on all types of funeral (☎ 01423 530900 or 868121).

The end of Chapter 3 explained how to keep a body at home until the funeral. Here we look at the importance of saying goodbye to the body for one last time, whether the death occurred at home or elsewhere. Incidentally, the Natural Death Centre proposes that the phrase 'visiting' the body replace 'viewing', as visiting includes the idea of touching the body. As Stephen Briggs has noted, 'the word "view" is coldly impersonal and conveys a sense of distance and slight distaste. It perpetuates the "keep at a distance and do not touch" inclination.'

From an academic perspective, one researcher, Therese Rando, has written, with reference to adult deaths as well as children's:

Visits to the body

Give the bereaved adequate private time to be with, touch, caress and hold the body, as time with the deceased may be very critical in helping them settle unfinished business and accept the reality of loss.

Those who did not view the body or had arranged for immediate disposal of the remains (excluding the normal Jewish custom of not viewing the body) reported the greatest hostility following the death, the greatest increase in consumption of alcohol, tranquillisers and sedatives, the greatest increase in tension and anxiety, the lowest positive recall of the deceased and greater problems in adjustment to the death, particularly among male respondents.

From Grief, Dying and Death *by Therese Rando (out of print) quoted in* Caring For Your Own Dead *by Lisa Carlson (see Resources).*

Even if the bereaved accept that a body is too damaged to be seen, there can be intermediate measures. The Child Bereavement Trust told the Guardian the story of the father of a very damaged stillborn baby. The father had a photograph taken of the baby's hand curling round his fingers – 'it was the most beautiful picture, and having something like that can make the difference to whether you can cope or not.'

Mary Wallace e-mailed the Centre to complain at the first edition of the Handbook's focus on the death of adults:

Death before birth

My babies died in the womb during pregnancy – one at around 20 weeks gestation (John), and another, less than a year later, at 14 weeks (Alex). Both were, medically speaking, miscarriages rather then stillbirths.

24 weeks gestation is the point at which the dead baby is referred to as stillborn rather than miscarried. ... Earlier than this, the baby born dead has no legal status as a human being and it is almost as if he or she never existed. This, and the fact that there are sometimes no identifiable remains, make the grieving process all the more difficult. The experience of miscarriage is often more distressing because others, including those in the medical profession, do not always regard it as particularly significant emotionally. It is as if there was no 'real' baby with no 'real' parents.

At one point whilst I was in hospital for example, a midwife asked me about 'the foetus' and I had to tell her that he was my baby and not a foetus. I felt like having a T-shirt printed saying 'I had a baby, not a miscarriage'! To me they were precious little beings – tiny, but fully formed and very beautiful.

In the case of Alex, who died in the womb at 14 weeks, the usual procedure would have been to have had an ERPC (Evacuation of the Retained Products of Conception) on a gynaecological ward. There would have been no identifiable body and disposal would have been in the hospital incinerator, possibly along with other hospital waste.

To me this was barbaric. I gave birth to my tiny babies naturally, held them, photographed them, and in Alex's case, took him home for a few days. My other children, both under seven years old at the time, saw and held their little brothers and were filled with wonderment and awe at their beauty and perfection. Before they were born I had been haunted by what they might look like and whether they would be deformed or damaged in some way. I need not have worried, but whatever they had looked like, they were mine and I would have loved them regardless.

I was also adamant that I didn't want other people touching them and we conducted the funerals ourselves, with the help of the hospital chaplain. Whilst we hold no religious beliefs, I needed a ceremony to say goodbye to them properly. The chaplain was a very a special man – kind and warm-hearted, with an ability to make an instant emotional connection with people. At no time did he attempt, even subtly, to find out what our religious beliefs were, and for this I am grateful.

My husband found solace in making the coffins. It was something he could do at a time when so much was beyond his control. He chose pine and made a simple little box just big enough for them. The boxes were pinned and glued and the lid was inset so that it sat flush. Two brass screws were put into either end of the lid to hold it firm. They were sanded and varnished, with a brass plaque showing the baby's name and dates – how strange, sad and profound to have death before a birth. Inside we lined the coffin with a quilted fabric. There we lay the babies, wrapped in a little shawl. We each chose a little gift to bury them with – a butterfly brooch, a carved wooden heart, little toys ...

They are buried next to each other in a rose garden especially for babies within one of the city cemeteries. The chaplain said some words and my husband and I also read some poetry. We threw flowers into the grave. We said our goodbyes and we have sad but lovely memories. ...

Since my babies died, I have become an Officiant of the Humanist Society of Scotland (eds: see Resources), and conduct non-religious funerals. I have officiated at ceremonies for babies and children and would be happy to offer advice to anyone who would like a non-religious ceremony of any kind.

Mary Wallace (☎ 01786 842239; e: mary@wallace.prestel.co.uk).

Laying out the body

As soon as the doctor has certified the cause of death, the body can be washed and dressed. The nurse can do this for you, but for how to do this yourself, see the end of the previous chapter.

Fear of being buried alive

A surprising number of people are frightened that they will be buried alive. Indeed this has occasionally happened, as the Funeral Service Journal reported:

> The Herald Tribune of May 1994 reported that Elenor Marks from New York, apparently dead and being taken in her coffin to the graveside, alarmed the men carrying it by a faint tapping from its interior. When the lid was removed, it was found that the supposed corpse was alive. She was then moved back to her residence and began recovering. She says that she had full knowledge all the time of what was passing, whilst arrangements were made for her burial, but was unable to give any sign of consciousness until the fear of being interred alive roused her to action.

One perhaps over-suspicious correspondent has complained to the Natural Death Centre about 'the unsavoury practice of removing people from nursing homes to undertakers' parlours before being certified or seen by a doctor, even though a qualified nurse may have expressed an opinion that the person was dead. The reason why this is unsatisfactory is that most undertakers either embalm, or refrigerate the person immediately they arrive on the premises. The consequences of a person not being actually dead are horrific.'

These are not wholly unrealistic fears in Western society today, according to a book by Rodney Davies (*The Lazarus Syndrome*, published by Robert Hale, 1999) – in 1996, two women in the UK were found alive after being pronounced dead and a study of 150,000 exhumed American war-dead from World War II in Europe it was revealed that no less than 6,000 (4 per cent) showed signs of having been buried alive.

Doctors, if very concerned to avoid, for instance, misdiagnosing a profound barbiturate- or morphine-induced coma as death, are advised to listen to the heart and lungs with a stethoscope for up to five minutes; to feel the carotid pulse at the side of the neck; to shine a light in the eyes (to see if the pupils stay dilated) and to check there is no blink reflex when the eye is touched. Other situations that can lead to mistakes include hypothermia, near-drowning, unconsciousness from electric shocks, alcohol intoxication and shock following blood loss. In any case, keeping the body at home for several days can reassure all concerned that the person is truly dead.

Which is greener, burial or cremation?

In the UK cremation was originally presented as the environmentally friendly option, with the anti-burial slogan of 'keeping the land for the living'. Nowadays cemeteries and churchyards help protect the land *from* the living, preventing land being used for development and often acting as a refuge for wildlife. Some of the few bits of green space left in Tokyo are graveyards.

In cremation, the coffins are all wastefully burnt, and the atmosphere and ground water is polluted by the glues used, from the plastics in artificial joints and other implants, and from the metals, hydrogen chloride (the cremator's pollution control systems do not catch these emissions), carbon dioxide, formaldehyde and furans emitted in the burning process. Eleven per cent of UK atmospheric dioxin resulting from combustion comes from crematoria (according to the National Atmospheric Emissions Inventory).

A report from Warren Springs Laboratory in Stevenage found that even one of the crematoria updated to bring it into line with the new standards emitted far more dioxins than permitted; dioxins can cause cancer and other illnesses even at low concentrations. Crematoria also account for up to 15 per cent of UK mercury emissions to air (DEFRA, March 2002; the mercury comes from tooth fillings). A report from the Environment Agency's Local Authority Unit has rather worryingly concluded that mercury emissions from crematoria will increase by two thirds by 2020 (FSJ, July 2003).

One reader has suggested 'greening' the cremation process by using solar energy but until that happens, the conclusion must be that burial is a greener option than cremation, particularly if the burial is in a natural burial ground, with a tree or wild flowers planted instead of having a headstone, as discussed later in this chapter. If cremation is chosen, coffins entering cremators should contain no substances that will pollute when burnt – for instance, no plastics, PVC, fibreglass, styrofoam, rubber or metals such as zinc.

Taking the notion of 'green' disposal of the dead to one extreme, a letter writer to the Independent quoted with approval an advertisement in James Joyce's 'Ulysses': 'Well preserved fat corpse, gentleman, epicure, invaluable for fruit garden. A bargain £3-13.6.' Andrew Kerr has suggested further research into how body composting could work:

Composting bodies

I suggest compost funerals. Animal wastes (and the human body belongs to the animal kingdom) are an integral part of the process by which the vegetable kingdom is sustained. If animal remains are mixed with vegetable wastes to the proportion of one in four, in a controlled system, turned and dampened correctly, the result will be a perfect product to be fed to any kind of plant. Most dangerous pathogens are dealt with in the process.

The corpse could be taken to the Compostorium and placed in a specially constructed autoclave or pressure cooker. The corpse would have already been disembowelled and that material placed into a methane digester; this would have averted the potential danger of pathogens. The gas so generated would contribute to the slow and steady heat required to render the remains to a condition ready to be ground up to a kind of slurry to be 'intimately mixed' with straw and other vegetable wastes.

The whole process would be completed in about 12 weeks: a decent time for mourning. The finished compost could then be incorporated into the family memorial garden.

This would be far better than burial which is too deep for aerobic processes, or wasteful incineration which is damaging to the environment.

From a letter from Andrew Kerr, Rectory Cottage,
Standlake, Nr. Witney, Oxon OX29 7SG
(☎ 01865 300125; f: 01865 301985; e: andrewpkerr@onetel.net.uk).

As a perhaps more immediately attainable alternative, Swedish biologist Susanne Wiigh-Mäsak, head of Promessa Organic AB (Färjeläget 7600, 474 96 Nösund, Sweden, ☎ 0046 30420809; e: info@promessa.se) recommends having your body freeze-dried in liquid nitrogen and then shattered to make a soil-enriching powder. Her proposals have already won approval from the Church of Sweden, and the Church of England would probably accept the procedure too, if done 'in a dignified manner', according to Geoffrey Rowell, the Bishop of Basingstoke and chair of a multi-faith committee on funerals.

A not dissimilar process, called alkaline hydrolysis, has been developed by Dr Gordon Kaye, a professor at the Albany Medical College in New York. In this process, high temperature, pressure and sodium or potassium hydroxide are used to break the remains down to a sterile liquid (that can be legally emptied into most sewer systems) and powdery bone residue. The process is now permitted in three US states, and technology is emerging that might make the process feasible for funeral homes to use.

In certain rural parts of the US, a far more natural form of 'recycling' of the body after burial, according to Stephen Levine, already takes place:

Fruit tree planted over body

Often, in the back country of Montana, a hole will be dug and the body, in a plain pine coffin or perhaps just wrapped in a tie-dyed cloth, will be lowered into the ground. Instead of a tombstone, a fruit tree is planted over the body. The roots are nourished by the return of that body into the earth from which it was sustained. And in the years to follow, eating the fruit from that tree will be like partaking in that loved one. It touches on the ritual of the Eucharist.

From Who Dies? *by Stephen Levine (see Resources).*

Incidentally, John Bradfield of the A. B. Welfare and Wildlife Trust has publicly expressed his fears about the significance of the UK government's recent ban on the burial of farm animals (which stemmed from advice given by the Environment Agency): 'It may only be a matter of time before it presses for a ban on human burials ... and if that happens, we will have to stop calling ourselves humans' (FSJ, July 2003).

Forms and procedures

The bureaucracy facing newly-bereaved relatives who are arranging a funeral is fairly minimal, although there will be many more forms to fill in for those looking after probate of the estate. The Which? Books *What To Do When Someone Dies* and *Wills and Probate* are useful; as is the free Department of Work and Pensions booklet 'What To Do After A Death' (see Resources). We can help the survivors before our own deaths by following the advice in Chapter 2: by leaving a will, telling people where to find it, and putting in the same place all our financial and other details, along with the information and documents that will be needed for the registration of death (again listed in that chapter); and by simplifying our affairs.

When the person is dying at home it is as well to ensure, if you can, that the doctor (not just the nurses) sees the patient at some time during the 14 days before the death occurs (28 days in Northern Ireland). This will normally avoid the death being referred to the coroner (see below). After the person has died, the doctor will (without charge) fill in a medical certificate as to the cause of death. (If cremation is wanted, the doctor charges for the relevant form – and will need to know about any operations in the past year – and the doctor gets another doctor to fill in a similar form, for a total charge of £101, known in the trade as 'ash cash'; the forms are issued by crematoria and also stocked by funeral directors.)

If the person dies in hospital, you can refuse permission for a postmortem (to learn more about the cause of death) if you wish. The coroner will have to issue a certificate as to the cause of death (and may insist on a postmortem) if there were unusual circumstances surrounding the death. The coroner can issue an interim certificate to allow the executors to begin work on sorting out the deceased's affairs, if an inquest will decide the cause of death at a later date.

Going to the Registry Office

As the next-of-kin or the person arranging the funeral, you take the medical certificate (if the doctor does not send it for you) to the Registrar of Births and Deaths. You are supposed to do this within five days (eight days in Scotland – the five days is extendable to 14 by agreement) or within three months in the case of a stillborn child (21 days in Scotland).

Find out which registrar covers the area where the death occurred by looking up under 'R' in the phone book, 'Registration of Births, Deaths and Marriages', and checking by phone which is the nearest office and asking whether or not you can have an appointment. (You can register the death anywhere that suits you but this can add a few days of delay for receiving the death certificate which may be needed to deal with legal matters.) In Scotland the registrar will want to know the time of death as well as the date and place of death.

Make certain the registrar has correctly recorded all the details in the registry as it is complicated getting them altered once it has all been signed.

You can get away with taking with you just the date of birth of the deceased, where the deceased was born and the maiden name of the deceased (and sending on later, if you can find it, the person's NHS number or medical card, so that NHS payments to the GP cease). But ideally take with you not only the full list of items listed in Chapter 2 but also information about the deceased's banks, friendly societies, life insurance and so on, and then the registrar should be able to estimate how many copies of the death certificate you will need to be able to claim these assets. Sometimes, however, banks and other institutions will simply take a copy of the certificate and give you back the original. It is easier and cheaper to obtain at the time (or within a month) as many copies as you may need and an extra one in case, for £7 each (£8 Scotland), rather than later when it can cost £11-50 (£13 Scotland).

The basic white certificate that you will also be given is free and contains a social security form for claiming benefit arrears and bereavement benefit.

For burial, either a doctor will have issued a free medical cause of death certificate (a white form) or the coroner will have issued a free pink form. One or the other is given to the registrar, who issues a free green form – which must be obtained before the burial goes ahead (in England and Wales). (However, this paragraph does not apply if there is to be an inquest. In such cases, the coroner will issue a free burial order, which again must be obtained before the burial goes ahead.)

Whether you receive the green form burial certificate from a registrar or the free burial order from a coroner, both have tear-off slips which need to be received by the registrar within 96 hours of the burial having taken place.

Cemeteries may want the certificate or order 24 hours before the burial. For burials in private land, give the certificate or order to the landowner or land manager. (The registrar can issue the free burial certificate for the burial to go ahead, before the death has been registered.)

For a cremation, the forms permitting it may be required by a crematorium at least 24 hours in advance of cremation.

Incidentally, the person who paid for the cremation has the right to collect the ashes at any time, even years later. However, if the crematorium gives a fortnight's notice and the ashes are not collected within that time, the ashes can be buried or scattered by the crematorium.

Sudden death

The following is based on notes sent to the Natural Death Centre by PC Rick Jones of the Coroner's Office in Essex.

GPs may issue a death certificate even if they have not seen their patient in the 14 days prior to death, provided that the person died from a disease for which the doctor was previously treating them. This would be acceptable for burial. However, the registrar at the crematorium would generally want a coroner's involvement in such cases. The patient's doctor contacts H. M. Coroner who may then agree to issue a Coroner's 'A' Certificate, a certificate for when there is no postmortem.

Where the person died unexpectedly but 'naturally', the coroner would issue a 'B' Certificate to the Registrar of Births and Deaths, giving the cause of death as found at postmortem. For cremation, the coroner would also issue an 'E' Certificate free of charge (instead of two medical certificates costing about £91).

For so-called 'unnatural' deaths (suicide, road and industrial accidents or deaths from industrial or notifiable diseases), an inquest has to be held. Once this is officially opened (although it may actually take place at a later date), the coroner issues a cremation form 'E' or a Burial Order.

The bodies of those who died abroad of 'unnatural' causes, when repatriated to this country, have to be referred to the coroner.

Anyone seeking to take a body out of England and Wales (even for sea burial) must obtain a coroner's Out of England Certificate.

Repatriation

There are moves afoot to make the process of repatriation simpler, specifically with regard to standardising consular formalities within the EU. Basically, however, repatriation is an area where a family will unfortunately be obliged to use a funeral director as the airline and their handling agents will require a 'certificate of sanitisation' to accompany the body. This must be prepared by the firm which hermetically sealed the zinc container in which the body must be placed for external flights. Embalming would normally be carried out prior to the production of this certificate but is not a specifically-named requirement.

Phoenix International of London (☎ 0800 783 4044) act as co-ordinators to the funeral trade with regard to repatriations. Managing director Steve Thomas says that the average cost of preparing the body for repatriation in a zinc-lined coffin, with suitable certification, and delivery from London to Heathrow is about £950. To this must, of course, be added the air freight charge and the costs of the arrangements at the destination.

For internal flights, London to Belfast, say, a certificate of sanitisation is still needed, but the zinc-lined coffin is not a requirement.

Moving the body

Jane Spottiswoode had problems moving her husband Nigel's body after he died:

> There was no way that Nigel in his coffin and with the coffin in a horizontal position, could be carried out of the room and around all the corners and down the stairs to where the Volvo was waiting. Since then I have learned that the way it is done by the professionals is in a body bag, which is much easier to handle, and then transferred to a coffin either in the pick-up vehicle or at the undertakers.
>
> From Undertaken with Love *by Jane Spottiswoode*.

For how to obtain a body bag see the next chapter but note that a strong sheet or curtain works even better.

You may need a van to transport your coffin. For instance, with a 76ins coffin the few estate cars it will fit into are the old Volvo 940, the old Vauxhall Carlton and the Ford Scorpio. The A. B. Welfare and Wildlife Trust tends to use a Renault 5 with the passenger seat removed.

If you do not have access to a suitable estate car or van for transport, and cannot find a friend with one, it may be possible to persuade your local funeral director to help (see Chapter 7) or to use a firm that hires out a chauffeur-driven hearse and bearers. See the section on Transport in the next chapter – this is liable to cost from about £85. Alternatively a transit van can be hired through the Yellow Pages for a few hours from about £40.

One correspondent to the Natural Death Centre found that fixing handles on the two ends of the coffin, helped to get it through the living room and front door, for a burial on their own land.

Sheila Page suggests that an ordinary stretcher can perhaps be borrowed from the local Red Cross or St Johns Ambulance to help move a body to the mortuary. Such a stretcher is long, however, and is likely to need a van. Another alternative is to borrow one from a funeral director or to buy the hessian carrier with eight handles which is detailed in the next chapter.

Carrying the coffin

Coffins are normally carried feet first.

Professional pallbearers tend not to use handles, which are decorative. The coffin is lifted from below and carried on the shoulders. However, handles are useful for burial, to thread the lowering webbing or straps through, so as to prevent the coffin from slipping.

When carrying a cardboard coffin with no handles, the A. B. Welfare and Wildlife Trust uses lowering straps, by placing them over and under for a secure hold, or a large curtain or blanket folded up all four sides.

Sheila Page advises that wooden lathes can also be used to carry a coffin, although only with great care and on the flat (unless you have people before and after to prevent the coffin slipping). She writes (from the experience of organising her husband Jan's funeral):

> We bought three four-foot long pieces of planed 2ins by 1in wood, sanded down about 6ins at the ends. Slipped under the coffin, these provided a very satisfactory way for six of us to carry the coffin...

> The gravediggers had put 2ins by 2ins wooden bars across the grave with the lowering straps laid neatly along these. We lowered the coffin on to these, our own wooden lathes fitting between, and, being only 1in deep, they were slipped out easily by a nominated friend. Then at a word from our previously appointed chief bearer, we picked up the coffin a few inches, using the straps, and the friend removed the wooden bars. At another word from the chief bearer, we gently lowered the coffin on to the bed of cut grass laid in it by the grave diggers. We placed the ends of the straps by the edge of the grave.

A family-organised cremation in Wales

Wales has a reputation as a difficult part of the world in which to organise a funeral without using funeral directors. But Jill Harcourt-Ray managed it:

In memory of my mother Marjorie

My mother died on February 25th 1998 at 3pm in Prince Phillip Hospital, Llanelli, South Wales.

After leaving the hospital, as I was driving home, I called into the local undertakers and of course they were nice, they gave me a quote for a basic funeral, but the voice inside told me to go home and contact the Natural Death Centre. I told the undertaker that I would think about it. He was very surprised. I don't think anyone had ever said such a thing to him before.

The following day, I phoned the Natural Death Centre and I was very pleased that I did. I was given the telephone number of Narberth Crematorium here in West Wales. I contacted the superintendent, the Rev Elwyn John, a wonderful man who has a copy of the *Dead Good Funerals* book in his office. I made an appointment to see him later the same day. He was very encouraging. He also took me to see behind the scenes at the crematorium to look at the ovens. It really was an education.

The hospital mortuary agreed to keep my mother's body until the Monday following her death, without charge. We used the Compakta Eco-Coffin. The man at Compakta told us to stuff old pillow cases with newspaper to put around my mother to keep her in place.

My daughter has one of the people-mover type vehicles, so, with the seats taken out, it was ideal to transport my mother. The mortician at the hospital was helpful. He assisted us in arranging Marjorie in the coffin and helped to put the coffin in the transport. He remarked how lovely it was to see a family involved in their loved one's funeral preparation.

Rev Elwyn John met us after a 45-mile journey to his crematorium. He and his assistant wheeled the coffin from the transport into the chapel of rest to await the funeral the following day, Tuesday, March 3rd 1998.

We had the last slot of the day, just in case anything did not go according to plan. However, all was well and we had a humanist ceremony and celebration of my mother's life. We draped a gold brocade cloth over the coffin and had a large photograph of my mother on top, with her favourite iris flowers.

We are a very small family but we found doing my mother's funeral ourselves very, very rewarding. It helped so much with the process of grief.

We did not have any opposition to our plans, but we did meet with surprise. When I registered my mother's death, I was handed a green form to give the undertaker. I then said that I was doing the funeral myself and the registrar looked aghast and said 'What are you going to do with your mother's body?' So we explained – and she was lost for words.

Jill Harcourt-Ray, Ty Bryn, Mountain Road, Betws, Ammanford,
Carmarthenshire SA18 2PL, Wales (☎ 01269 593017).

Burial on private land

Organising a burial on private land is much simpler than most people think, although it can be hard work physically, as the following account demonstrates.

A grave that took four days to dig

My friend Marcelle died as she lived, with great fortitude. Her husband John and their three children – Pierre, John-David and Marie, all young adults – along with John-David's girlfriend Stephie, had been on duty in a 24-hour rota caring for Marcelle during her last days, and in the event they proved quite capable of organising everything for the funeral too. John-David and Pierre helped the local furniture maker to make a beautiful coffin out of one-inch pine, with a wooden cross pattern on top and wooden handles wide enough for webbing to slip through, all covered with a light matt varnish. Pierre went down to the piece of land the family owns in the Cotswolds, and there a handful of friends spent no less than four days hacking with pickaxes through stony ground to dig a grave – a grave so deep, John remarked, that there would be room for him too in due course.

John-David collected the death certificate (with six copies for banks and institutions), and we noted the green form's tear-off slip which you have to return with details of where the burial took place and the date. The Gloucestershire County Council planning department confirmed that there was no need for permission from them, and that they had no concerns about a private land burial so long as no archaeological ruins were to be disturbed.

My friend drove his Toyota van with me and the boys on board, to the hospital mortuary to pick up Marcelle's body. We had a funeral director's release form which the hospital nurse had given John-David, and which we had filled in with our own names as the funeral directors. The hospital porter had never dealt directly with a family before, so for this special occasion he decided to leave Marcelle's body wrapped like a mummy taped up in their mortuary sheet. He helped us to put the body into the biodegradable body bag which Green Undertakings had sent us and to lift this unexpectedly heavy weight into the coffin.

Now I was glad that we had six strong bearers. We'd had a rehearsal in church with the empty coffin the evening before, when it had all seemed easy. But now we carefully repositioned the bearers so that they were all paired off in size and were all taking some of the weight.

A local woman had typeset the service sheets without charge, and Instant Print had also kindly printed them for free. And so the requiem mass began. 300 people crowded into the church. We followed the bishop in, with the coffin, and we left it in the centre of the chancel, on a low dais. Everyone had been invited to bring one flower only, which they all came up to place in front of the coffin.

Pierre read a bible extract. John, who is an assistant priest, made a moving address about his wife and his family, urging neighbours not to stop dropping by. The bishop outlined some of Marcelle's good works, forgetting to mention that it was largely thanks to her efforts that the beautiful church we were in had been saved from being turned into a block of flats.

The coffin stayed in the side chapel overnight, and the next day, in the afternoon, a small convoy of cars (which would have displeased car-hating Marcelle) drove to the Cotswolds.

We hauled the coffin up the steep hill, using webbing to lift it. Green Undertakings had run out of proper funeral webbing, but John-David had found furniture webbing in John Lewis department store which worked just as well.

John was both the priest conducting the service and husband for this final gathering, with 50 of us crowded round. He read some prayers and he recalled a touching poem by Vikram Seth:

> All you who sleep tonight
> Far from the ones you love,
> No hands to left or right,
> And emptiness above –
>
> Know that you're not alone.
> The whole world shares your tears,
> Some for two nights or one,
> And some for all their years.

Betsy played some Schubert on her flute, people wept and shared their memories of Marcelle and we sang Blake's Jerusalem from memory ('And did those feet ...'). We followed on from John's words 'ashes to ashes, dust to dust ...' with the African custom of everybody helping to fill the grave. We were throwing in very stony soil, which crashed down so hard I feared the coffin would split open.

It was, it is, all very sad. But I think the funeral helped.

From an article in 'Before and After' by Nicholas Albery.

In the UK, from the mid-17th century, the early Quakers were often buried in their gardens – indeed William Penn, the founder of Pennsylvania, is buried in the garden of the Friends Meeting House in Jordans, Buckinghamshire. But nowadays, how do people in the UK go about arranging a funeral on their own land? One of the Natural Death Centre's contacts arranged this after the sudden death of her husband from a heart attack by asking her lawyer to set aside a part of the large back garden for the grave, with its own access, so that this part would not be sold with the rest of the house and grounds. Some council officials still do not know how limited the laws are surrounding private burial – see Ian Alcock's struggles, overleaf – so if you approach them for their blessing, go armed with the information in this chapter.

Planning permission for private burial?

Ian Alcock in Aberdeenshire wanted himself and his wife to be buried in their wild flower pasture on their own hill in a special conservation area (SSSI). He was told to approach the Nature Conservancy Council for Scotland for initial permission and then had to pay £77 for a planning application for 'change of use of hill land to private burial ground' and £60 for a small ad in the local newspaper under 'developments which may cause concern in the neighbourhood'. There was no obligation to seek the approval of neighbours, and the environmental health officer confirmed that the burial was not likely to cause pollution.

Ian Alcock subsequently successfully appealed against the need for planning permission. The Scottish Office, in the person of the Deputy Chief Reporter R. M. Hickman (Ref. P/PPA/GD/342, Nov. 25th 1992), ruled that 'a limited number of unmarked and unfenced graves would not constitute a material change of use and I conclude that the planning consent issued to you by the district council is superfluous'. The decision letter also noted that the square area in the middle of grazing land, identified by Ian Alcock for the burial ground, was about 50 metres by 50 metres, and that Ian and his wife wished to be buried there, and to be able to 'afford this opportunity to another close member of the family, family retainer, or perhaps a close friend. ... As there would be no change in the surface land use, nor any upstanding physical features resulting from the intended burials, I am satisfied that a limited number of private graves would not result in a material change of use. If the ground were to be fenced off to become a cemetery, I would agree with the district council that a material change of use would have occurred. ... I have also considered whether the burials would constitute "engineering ... or other operations in, on, over or under the land" ... However, I am satisfied that the digging of a very limited number of graves by hand ... would not amount to a significant engineering or other operation. If there were a large number of burials, perhaps involving an access track or mechanical excavation, the situation would perhaps be different but that would be a matter of fact and degree to be considered on its merits.'

More cautiously, a spokesman for the Department of the Environment wrote to the Natural Death Centre on May 15th 1994: 'May I confirm that planning permission is not required for the burial of one or two persons in back gardens, it would only be required if there was an intention to bury a larger number of people.'

On one occasion, a case was won on appeal, a Lawful Development Certificate (variously termed either an LDC or a Certificate of Lawfulness or a Certificate of Lawful Use) having been refused. The A. B. Welfare and Wildlife Trust reports that, in May 1996, a man in East Sussex won his appeal to the Department of the Environment against the local authority, who had turned down his application for a Lawful Development Certificate to have two burials in his half-acre garden.

Applying to a local authority for a Lawful Development Certificate is a way of determining whether something is legal in planning law, without having to apply for planning permission. John Bradfield of the A. B. Welfare and Wildlife

Trust, who has been the Natural Death Centre's main source of information on the laws surrounding funerals, and who is now the UK's acknowledged expert on private land burial law, describes the following two cases in 'Green Burial' (now out of print):

• No planning consent was required for a private burial ground in the Harrogate area to be used for 'non-commercial' burials. There would be no fences or gravestones, and the site was within an organic smallholding that would continue to be grazed as before.

• No planning consent was required for 'private non-commercial burial of the householder, those resident with her at the time of their deaths and her relatives only' – for burial in a 300 square metre garden also near Harrogate.

This, then, is the Natural Death Centre's conclusion: **planning permission is not required for non-commercial sites, for a limited number of burials for family, friends and those living in the house**.

In Eire, by contrast, it is claimed that permission is required from the Health Department. One correspondent writes, however, that people have been taking the law into their own hands: 'In Eire, the way an inexpensive, green and DIY funeral is done is that you bury the remains on your own or the deceased person's property.' If the police later take action, with a prosecution and the courts, they will not exhume the corpse. Depending on how long it has been since the burial, a small fine could be imposed, but this would be unlikely.

Legal requirements concerning funerals

The Natural Death Centre published 'Green Burial – The DIY guide to law and practice' which is now out of print. John Bradfield, its author, who founded the A. B. Welfare and Wildlife Trust, put an immense amount of research into the two editions of 'Green Burial' and generously donated all the proceeds from sales to the Natural Death Centre. He demolished many legal myths that have surfaced in funeral guides, and has persuaded officials at the highest levels to alter their advice.

What follows is the Centre's understanding of some of the A. B. Welfare and Wildlife Trust's key findings, but readers are advised to refer urgent or complex enquiries to the Trust itself (☎ 01423 5309000):

• Some people organising funerals without using funeral directors have had trouble getting the hospital to give them the body. Unless the coroner is making an investigation into the cause of the death, it is a common law offence for a hospital to **refuse to release a body** to the executors. As one trial judge put it in 1882: 'executors have a right to the custody and possession of [the] body.'

If you are having problems getting the body released to you, contact the Natural Death Centre and they will willingly send a stiffly-worded fax to any hospital proving obstructive, citing chapter and verse as to their offence and its possible consequences.

• Although cemeteries and crematoria may have their own particular rules or guidelines, there is **no law requiring a coffin**. It is, however, an offence for a dead body to be exposed naked in a public place if this causes shock or disgust or is intended to do so.

• A body can be **transported across county boundaries** without permission and no fee is payable. Consent, given free of charge, must be obtained to move a body out of England/Wales (treated as one area), Northern Ireland or Scotland – which includes from one to the other.

• 'Subject to any restrictive covenants affecting the use of the land (see below), a place of burial may be established by any person without statutory authority, in private land, provided no statutory or other 'nuisance' such as smell or pollution is caused ...' (Halsbury's Laws of England, 1975:504, Butterworths). 'The statute law on burial is archaic ... and does not apply ... to **private burial grounds**' (Hickman, R. M. Deputy Chief Reporter in the Alcock case above).

• There may be very rare instances where a property's **restrictive covenants** prevent the creation of graves, but application can be made for such covenants to be lifted on the grounds that they have ceased to serve their original purpose.

• It is **a myth** that in England and Wales there must be **no neighbours within 100 yards of a burial** – this is a misreading of the 1855 Burials Acts (Ch. 128, S.9 and now repealed; and Ch. 68, S.7 – the latter does apply the 100 yards requirement but only to public burial grounds in Scotland).

• An 1847 Act may apply to some old cities or towns, requiring 30 inches of soil between the coffin top and the ordinary surface of the ground. Council cemeteries are governed by a 1977 Order requirement that there be 2 or 3 feet from the coffin top to the surface. But for any other burial grounds there is no national law specifying a **minimum depth**.

• There is no requirement to inform the council's **environmental health officers** of plans for burial on private land, nor do such burials require their advance permission. These officers have no powers to order exhumations. However, they do have legal powers to prevent any 'deposit' which might be 'prejudicial to health or a nuisance'.

The health risks from burial are very remote. Bradfield quotes a professor of forensic pathology and a consultant to the Home Office as concluding that 'the risks [from the] exhumation of ... recent burials are no greater than those of gardening. Antibiotic [precautions are] not required'.

• The **Environment Agency** is entitled to carry out works to prevent pollution of 'any controlled waters', but there is no legal obligation to consult it in advance of a burial.

• In England, Wales and Scotland, a **burial authorisation** must be obtained before the burial takes place.

• In England and Wales, the tear-off slip on the **burial authorisation** must be completed by the landowner or land manager, giving the date and place of burial, and must be received by the Registrar of Births and Deaths **within 96 hours** of any burial. This slip will be on a form issued before the burial either by the same Registrar (a 'green form' or Burial Certificate, also known as a Disposal Certificate) or by a coroner, if an inquest will be or has been held (a white form called a Burial Order).

• There must be a **land burial register** for all graves in England. Unless some other law applies, it is necessary to comply with the 1864 Registration of Burials Act, Ch.97, even for an isolated grave in a garden. It requires that Christian laws be followed, even by non-Christians, on the layout and storage of registers. It is difficult to make proper sense of this law and only if noncompliance is 'wilful' can a prosecution take place. Private burial grounds would be expected by any court to do their utmost to comply.

This durable burials register must record, in columns, the 'Entry No., Christian name and surname in block capitals, Address, Date of Birth, Age, Date of Burial, Plan Ref. No., Officiating Minister', with each entry separated by a printed line. The register must be kept in a specially protected steel cupboard.

• **Consecration** by the Church of England alters the legal status of the land, whereas consecration by other religions may 'bless' a piece of land but has no legal implications. Even the Church of England is moving away from consecrating its own property.

• There is a common law right for Christians to have a **Christian burial**, otherwise it is not legally necessary to have a Christian or other religious service or any officiant presiding over a funeral; or to be buried in a formal cemetery or consecrated land.

• 'No **Church of England minister**' writes John Bradfield, 'can be criticised for holding a religious service in an unconsecrated burial place. This includes a garden or house.'

• There are no laws which can force you to **move** a body in private land from one grave to another.

• No law mentions the **scattering of ashes** on ordinary land or in rivers. It is technically illegal to put anything on someone else's land or in rivers without consent but the A. B. Welfare and Wildlife Trust has never heard of anyone ever being prosecuted for doing so, presumably as it is too trivial for the courts to waste time on the matter.

• **Exhumations** in England and Wales, unless only from one legally consecrated place to another, may require some form of consent from central government (free licences can be issued by the Home Office, ☎ 0870 0001585).

• Exhumation from or to legally consecrated land requires a Church of England document called a '**faculty**'.

• In theory, a **funeral pyre** that causes no 'nuisance' (ie pollution or smell) seems to be legal, as long as no construction is made which could be defined as a crematorium. Bradfield has received several enquiries about the legality of funeral pyres and has warned that officials might press for a case to be taken to court, to test whether DIY cremations remain lawful. Some claim to have gone ahead with such plans, whilst mindful of the risks. There is less chance of a prosecution, to test the law, if the public cannot see the activity and have no idea what is happening. Bradfield was told that the police turned up to one event and left thinking it was some type of festival. Had a prosecution been sought at a later date, the fact that the police saw no requirement to intervene, would have helped prove that no 'nuisance' was caused.

Stephen White, a trustee of the Cremation Society and law lecturer who has published academic articles on cremation and funeral pyres, seems to take the same view as John Bradfield. They both stress the need to consult with someone who is insured for giving legal advice, before deciding whether to go ahead.

• Under the Anatomy Act 1984, S.4(9), a hospital, nursing home or other institution has the right to send a body for **anatomical use**, without consent, if no friend or relative takes possession of the body.

The fear that the bodies of paupers would be used for dissection purposes has haunted the poor ever since the 1832 Anatomy Act (as described by Ruth Richardson in her book 'Death, Dissection and the Destitute' published by Pelican, 1989). It may well be true that hospitals nowadays do not take advantage of this legal power, but it is ethically unacceptable that they should have the potential right to do so.

Burial recommendations (not requirements)

The above summarises the laws. The following are merely the Natural Death Centre's recommendations for good practice:

• **Farmland can be used for private land burial**. DEFRA has told the Centre that set-aside land can be used, 'provided there was no return to the farmer in cash or kind ... and the land remains croppable and in good agricultural condition.' Farmers could run natural burial grounds in association with wildlife charities, as in the case of Oakfield near Manningtree (see Chapter 6).

• **A large garden can be used for burial**. The Natural Death Centre helped one couple in their nineties choose a spot for burial on the edge of their ten-acre garden where their beloved boxer dogs were buried, with a way to reach the graves from the public footpath, in case the remainder of the property were later to be sold by the family. The couple also ordered cardboard coffins which they stored in their garage. They felt prepared for their deaths, but their plans were cruelly disrupted when increasing disabilities forced them to move to a residential home, and to sell their home to cover the costs.

The Natural Death Centre advises careful thought before creating a grave in a small urban garden. It is easier to bury a body than it is to exhume it; a garden burial can cause dissension amongst relatives; and neighbours, for whatever reason, may feel offended.

• **You do not need a Lawful Development Certificate**. If you nevertheless wish to have one to set your mind at rest, you may want to ask the council to keep the decision-making stage confidential – the outcome, however, must be recorded on a public register. The cost of applying for a Certificate is approximately half the cost of applying for planning permission (the full cost is payable if one or more burials have taken place). If the Certificate is refused or specifies unsatisfactory conditions, a free appeal can be made to the Department of the Environment, although their findings will then definitely be made public.

• In general, the Environment Agency is responsible for the protection and regulation of groundwater and surface water. They have advised the following wording: 'Although there is no formal requirement for authorising private land burials, it is a good idea to contact the Environment Agency by phoning 0845 9333111 (Eds: which number should automatically direct you to the nearest area or regional office; if you get no satisfaction you could try phoning Dr Rob Ward of their National Groundwater and Contaminated Land Centre on 0121 711 5800 who is knowledgeable on the issue at the national level). The Environment Agency is unlikely to have any objections provided that the grave is **not within ten metres of any standing or running water**, or **50 metres of a well, borehole or spring that supplies water for human consumption**. For graveyards or sites of multiple burials a more restrictive view may be taken. The Environment Agency will deal with enquiries sympathetically and will only advise against burial where there is potential for significant pollution to the environment.'

• A suitable grave should have **no water at the bottom** when first dug.

• It would be wise to **avoid burial in very sandy soil**, as it is unsuitable for shallow graves and digging a deep grave can be dangerous.

• The burial needs to be deep enough to prevent **foraging animals** from trying to dig up the body.

• Check with HM Land Registry that no-one else is on public record as the **owner of the land** which you wish to use. This may not seem necessary, but failure to do so in one case resulted in exhumations.

• It would be extremely sensible to store a detailed plan of where the body is buried (or a copy of any exhumation licence) with the **deeds of your property**. One council's Environmental Services Division arranged for an informal notice to be attached to the Land Charges Register so as to inform prospective purchasers of the private graves on the land. The following letter to the Natural Death Centre highlights the potential risks of omitting to take such precautions:

A cautionary tale

In 1996, I and my family were greatly helped by you to enable us to bury my husband on our own property in West Wales. The prompt service we received then was invaluable, and I have been intending to write to you since – but never got round to it. In the event, perhaps this was as well, as mine is a cautionary tale!

At the time we owned property which included a one-acre sloping field alongside our house, farm buildings and garden. We had been replanting much of this with young trees and so felt it appropriate to bury my husband among them when he died of cancer. We had a body bag from you, local people helped and the grave was dug by the chapel gravedigger. My husband knew and approved of our plans and despite the trauma at the time, everyone felt that the event was entirely appropriate – the ultimate recycling. I planted a special tree on the spot, and others in the general area, and when I sold the property last year there was no evidence to indicate a burial had ever taken place. Thus I did not inform either the estate agent or the new owners.

However, within weeks, a neighbour who had been frustrated at not knowing exactly what we had done, told the new owners a fairytale – you know, shallow grave, in the garden, no one told, etc – and in spite of all our reassurances, and after months of discussion, they obtained permission from the Home Office to exhume and cremate his body. We, of course, had no rights anyway, although the Home Office was very sympathetic, and obviously considered the attitude of the new owners totally ridiculous. But they could not actually find grounds to refuse, as the new owners felt so strongly and were prepared to pay for it all.

Fortunately I do have religious beliefs and never considered that it was my husband buried in the field, only his mortal remains appropriately disposed of. Nevertheless it was very distressing to have all the sadness of his illness, etc dragged up again, so unnecessarily. It was made worse by the new owners going to the local press with an extraordinary tale of 'body buried in garden sought with JCB' (apparently they had actually had someone with a JCB digging around wherever they thought there was some disturbed earth. They were, of course, looking for a coffin!). Fortunately the press did print an explanation from me, and of course it meant everyone knew what had happened and they were shocked and horrified at such crass insensitivity.

But it is a point which people planning unorthodox burials should consider. I had felt that since the use of the field was in no way compromised, there was no need to tell anyone what we had done. They could never have found out for themselves. The burial was some distance from the house. It is more understandable that problems will arise where burials have taken place in suburban gardens and shrines to the loved-one erected.

Barbara Vessey (e: barbaravessey@lineone.net).

Making the coffin

If expense is the main consideration, it is worth noting that making a coffin yourself will probably work out as if not more expensive just for materials as the cheapest coffin available from a funeral supplier (see the next chapter). Be careful by the way to make the coffin at least an inch or so longer than the person was tall – a body is longer lying down.

The Huelin DIY coffins

The Huelins, a couple in Oxford, gained a great deal of satisfaction from making their own coffins and found themselves quite a centre of media attention as a result. Barbara Huelin outlines the story:

My husband (now in his 80s) has built our coffins. We spent a most enlightening few months organising and preparing for our deaths; the idea has caught on amongst our friends in Oxford.

The coffins are made in blockboard at a cost of about £50 each (not including our time). They are painted green and have nautical-looking rope handles (from the boat chandlers). The coffins are stored in the workroom. We have bought a double-decker site in the local council cemetery for £150 to which we intend that family and friends shall physically bear us. We are leaving the commemorative gravestone for our survivors to add if they wish, so that they have something they can do.

There were a number of interested enquiries from members of the public so her husband David sent the Natural Death Centre the following detailed description and drawings of the design that he used:

Materials: The most convenient, though possibly not the cheapest, material is three quarter inch (18mm) blockboard; it is lighter and stronger than chipboard, and is much easier to work. It is normally sold in sheets measuring 8ft x 4ft (2.44m x 1.22m); each sheet costs about £30 (1992). The half inch (12mm) version is cheaper but seems rather flimsy for a coffin, and the one inch (25mm) appears unnecessarily heavy, and costs more.

Three sheets of 8ft x 4ft blockboard are enough for two coffins, with a little fiddling. It is possible, though more difficult, to make one coffin with a sheet and a half, though it is not always possible to buy half-sheets. The following suggestions are for making two coffins with three sheets of board.

Other materials (for two coffins):
- 36ft (11m) wood strip 35mm x 10mm (rim round lid)
- 42ft (12.8m) batten 25mm x 25mm; this is not needed if the joining is by dovetailing – see below
- 400 (2 boxes) steel wood-screws, gauge 8 x one and a quarter inch
- 100 panel pins three quarter inch
- 250ml (quarter litre) wood-working glue, eg Evo-Stik Wood Adhesive
- 1 litre paint (optional)
- Handles: special subject dealt with separately below.

Tools: A hand-held electric circular saw is invaluable for cutting the basic shapes in the blockboard, which by hand would be arduous work. If dovetailing is intended a coping saw is useful; beyond that, a tenon-saw, chisel, angle-gauge, and sanding equipment for finishing off.

Method: Take the measurements of the future occupant of each coffin, not forgetting the hip width; allow extra space for the possibility of putting on weight before the coffin is needed.

With these measurements the main components for the two coffins can be drawn out on the blockboard: floor and lid, sides and ends (see the illustrations). Since the basic measurements are internal, allowance must be made for the thickness of the wood when drawing the basic shapes.

It is advisable to defer cutting out the lids until the main boxes are built (see below).

Joining: Attaching the sides and ends to the floor of the coffin and to each other, can be done in several ways; the simplest would seem to be one of the following:

1. With internal battens or corner-blocks, using the 25mm x 25mm batten listed above. With plenty of glue and screws this can be quite satisfactory;

the batten joining the sides and ends to the floor of the box can be fixed below the floor for extra strength. As the four corners are not right angles, the internal block or batten will have to be shaped to the actual angle.

2. With dovetailing (so called, though it is not true dovetailing); that is by cutting alternating tongues and recesses all along the edges to be joined, so that they fit together. Each tongue and recess can be 3 or 4 inches long; once the whole thing fits snugly together, the joins can be glued and screwed with a one and a quarter inch screw through every tongue. The recesses need to be a whisker over three quarters of an inch (19mm) deep to match the thickness of the board.

Coffin A (woman)

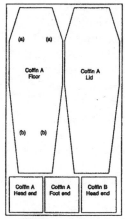

Blockboard sheet 1

Coffin B (Man)

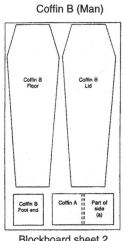

Blockboard sheet 2

Coffins A & B

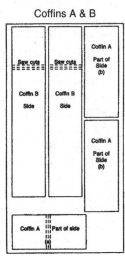

Blockboard sheet 3

This system involves more work and precision than the batten method, but the result is neat and very strong.

Shaped sides: To achieve the bends in the sides of the coffins, the inner surface of the board should have five or six saw-cuts made across it, to a depth of about three quarters of its thickness; it will then bend to the shape of the floor. The saw-cuts can be filled with glue to add to their solidity, but this is not essential. If the batten method is used, the batten itself can be treated in the same way.

In this particular layout for three sheets of board it has been necessary to divide the sides of coffin 'A' into two sections; they can be joined together by dovetailing at the appropriate angle. With four boards this dividing would not be necessary.

Lid: The precise shaping of the lid of each coffin can be left until the main body of the box is complete; this can be placed inverted over the piece of board reserved for the lid, and its outline drawn straight onto the wood. The lid should have a rim or lip all round its edge, made from the 35mm x 10mm strip listed above; this can be fixed with glue and panel pins.

Once it fits nicely, the lid can be drilled for screws, about 8 inches apart, using gauge 8, length one and a quarter inch screws and pilot holes can be drilled in the main box. The thoughtful coffin builder will provide a bag of screws for the purpose, and possibly a screwdriver too.

Headrest: A dead person's head falls back unbecomingly unless it is supported. The coffins should therefore have a small platform across the head end, slightly sloping, some two to three inches from the floor of the box.

Packing: Though not strictly part of the construction, there is the question of packing or lining. A very economical, attractive, and adequately absorbent packing is wood-shavings. If shavings of nice-smelling woods, such as cedar or pitch pine, can be obtained, so much the better. One dustbin-liner-full is probably enough.

Paint: Blockboard is not a very interesting colour; a litre of matt emulsion paint will make the two coffins look much more interesting; they can also be embellished with paintings of flowers or boats or castles, to taste.

Handles: The importance of handles depends on how the coffins are to be carried: if at shoulder height by skilled men, then no handles are required at all (professional bearers never use them). If the intention is that a coffin should be carried by family and friends, with their hands, then the handles are necessary and should be functional.

Metal or tough plastic handles, such as are used on swing and sliding doors, are inexpensive but great care is needed in fixing them. It may be advisable to use one and a half inch screws going through the comparatively soft blockboard into a hardwood block inside. Note that if cremation is chosen, then no large metal parts such as handles should be employed.

Another method is with nylon rope of half inch diameter. Half inch holes, some five inches apart, in three pairs, are to be drilled in the sides of the coffin; the rope (which must be nylon) is cut into lengths of 12 or 13 inches (30 to 33cm) and the ends are threaded into the holes from the outside, so that at least one inch projects on the inside of the box. Next a metal washer with exactly a half inch hole is fitted over the projecting end of rope, which is then melted with a hot-air gun so that it flattens down and spreads over the metal washer; when it cools and hardens it is very firm.

This method is easier than it may seem; it is extremely strong, and the rope loops on the outside of the coffin look attractive and appropriately modest.

Materials: 4 metres (2m each coffin) half-inch nylon rope obtainable at boat chandlers' shops. 24 half-inch washers.

Tool: Hot-air gun.

Barbara & David Huelin, 69 Kingston Road, Oxford OX2 6RJ.

A simple burial box

Ernest Morgan in his excellent book about funerals in the United States, 'Dealing Creatively with Death – A manual of death education and simple burial', describes the making of a simple burial box, which has top and sides of quarter-inch plywood, and the bottom and ends of three-quarter-inch plywood. Two reinforcing battens, three-quarters of an inch thick, run the length of the box on the inside, attached to the side pieces at the top edge, so the top of the box rests on them – as in this illustration. Ernest Morgan writes:

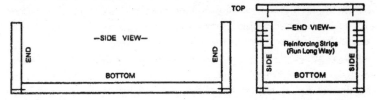

Using nails or screws (Eds: the latter, say gauge 8, length one and quarter inch, would give extra strength, particularly for the ends. Wood glue, such as Evo-Stik Wood Adhesive, would also give additional strength):

• Attach the reinforcing battens to the side pieces, flush with the edge and the end, making sure to have the good side of the plywood facing outwards.

• Attach the side pieces to the bottom.

• Attach the ends, again with the good sides out, to the bottom and to the side strips.

Four chest handles, two screwed to each end, could be useful for ease of carrying when going through doors (Eds: or rope handles could be used, as in the Huelin coffins, above). The handles could be stored in the box and screwed on when needed. Likewise, the cover could be tacked lightly in place until the box is needed and then when the time comes fixed firmly down.

A birch or pine coffin

For those who would like something finer, and who have the skills, a coffin made of birch or pine planks dovetailed together could look good, with the name carved into the wood and patterns around the edges as desired, and a final polish with beeswax or linseed oil.

DIY *willow coffin courses*

Hilary Burns at Windrush Willow, Higher Barn, Sidmouth Road, Aylesbeare, Exeter EX5 2JJ (☎ 01395 233669; **e**: windrushw@aol.com) offers courses suitable for beginners, intermediate and advanced weavers interested in producing traditional willow coffins. Alternatively, you could surprise your local basket-weaving class, as Ann Allen did:

> A mother of two joined a basket-weaving class – to make her own coffin. While the rest of the class set to work on vases and garden ornaments, Ann Allen asked the tutor to measure her up for a willow casket. 'If people think the fact that I made my own coffin out of wicker is a little odd then so be it,' the 50-year-old from Newent, near Gloucester, said. She added she wanted a biodegradable coffin to fit her environmentally-conscious philosophy. She found working on the coffin 'very therapeutic'.
>
> *From an item in the* Leeds Metro, *July 29th 2003.*

Coffins for cremation – avoiding pollution

If the coffin is destined for cremation rather than burial, there are various requirements for avoiding air pollution. The best approach is to check with your intended crematorium as to whether first, they would accept a home-made coffin (see Chapter 8); second, what the maximum size of the coffin may be – one US crematorium has said that home-made coffins tend to be made larger than they need be (Lisa Carlson in *Caring for your own Dead* writes that 'two feet wide and 18 inches deep is sufficient for most bodies'); third, whether the particular construction you are planning needs modifying in any way; fourth, whether any lining or handles you are planning for the coffin or clothing for the body are unacceptable (for instance, PVC linings and rubber-soled shoes are discouraged); and fifth, whether any medical implants in the body will be problematic. A pacemaker would need to be removed, for instance, in case it explodes during cremation (a doctor, a mortician at your local hospital or a funeral director can do this, although, writes Lisa Carlson, 'anyone can do it. A pacemaker is about the size of a small coin, embedded just under the skin, usually near the neck or lower on the rib cage. It is attached to wires which should be snipped').

Instructions for funeral directors have been issued by the cremation authorities, many of which would apply to those running a funeral themselves. P. J. Wilson, the secretary of the Federation of British Cremation Authorities, writes to the Natural Death Centre that 'Crematoria invariably require that bodies are conveyed to the building in a reasonable manner. A rigid coffin able to withstand any handling or transportation problems, adequately secured and identified and suitably lined to prevent leakage of fluids or other material will be required.'

Instructions from the Federation of British Cremation Authorities

- *Bearers:* Sufficient bearers should convey the coffin reverently from the hearse to the catafalque.
  - *Coffin construction:* The coffin must be made of a suitable material

which, when placed in a cremator and subjected to the accepted cremation processes, is easily combustible and which does not emit smoke, give off toxic gas or leave any retardant smears or drips after final combustion. No metal furniture or fittings whatever shall be used on a coffin for cremation. No metal of any kind shall be used in the manufacture of such a coffin except as necessary for its safe construction and then only metal of a high ferrous content [Eds: eg use ferrous screws]. Cross pieces must not be attached to the bottom of the coffin. If it is desired to strengthen the bottom of the coffin, wooden strips may be placed lengthwise for this purpose. The coffin must not be painted or varnished but may be covered with a suitable cloth [Eds: water-based paints *may* be allowed; for instance, Firwood Paints' Firaqua 482 (☎ 01204 525231; w: www.firwood.co.uk), a water-based acrylic gloss, has been fully crematoria tested, dries fast, is low odour, comes in a range of colours or as a clear finish for natural wood and can be applied by brush or as a spray]. Products containing any chloride or fluorides are prohibited, eg polyvinyl chloride (PVC), melamine. The use of polystyrene must be restricted to the coffin nameplate only, in which case it must not exceed 90 grams in weight.

No coffin shall be accepted unless it bears adequate particulars of the identity of the deceased person therein [Eds: normally this would include the name, age and date of death of the person].

• *Lining of the coffin:* The use of sawdust or cotton-wool must be avoided. If circumstances require, suitable sealing material may be used, but no metal, rubber or polyvinyl chloride (PVC) will be permitted and on no account must pitch or a similar substance be used. [Eds: no lead-lined coffins would be permitted.]

• *Size of the coffin:* Where the external dimensions of a coffin are likely to exceed length 81 inches (206 cm), width 28 inches (71 cm) and depth 22 inches (56 cm) the proper officer of the crematorium must be given advance notice.

• *Cremation of infants:* In cases when bereaved parents desire the cremation of the body of an infant, they should be warned that there are occasions when no tangible remains are left after the cremation process has been completed. This is due to the cartilagineous nature of the bone structure.

If the warning is not given the parents may have been denied the choice of earth burial and thereby been subjected to understandable distress.

• *Cremated remains:* An urn or casket for cremated remains should be of sufficient internal dimension to provide a minimum of 200 cubic inches (3,280 cubic cm) and securely labelled. The container should be strong enough to resist breakage in transit. The lid must fit tightly and the fastening should be strong enough to prevent the lid being forced open by distortion of the container through maltreatment in transit.

Adapted from a text sent by the Federation of British Cremation Authorities.

Deidre Martin sent the Natural Death Centre an encouraging description of the funeral of her mother, Dorothy, which they organised themselves and for which they made the coffin. The description, adapted extracts from which appear below, ties together many of the elements previously discussed in this chapter.

In memory of Dorothy Miller – a simple funeral

My mother had always said she wished to be buried 'simply' and we had already told the hospital matron that we would like to make the arrangements ourselves. She was extremely sympathetic and very helpful. She made an appointment for my husband and me to see the hospital registration officer that afternoon and told us the hospital would be able to keep my mother's body until we had made adequate arrangements. She also advised us to speak to the crematorium and to ask them for advice.

At 12.30 pm that day we visited Brighton's Woodvale Crematorium. The staff were marvellous. We asked if we could make the coffin and deal with all the funeral arrangements ourselves. 'Certainly.' They provided us with a leaflet and told us how to make the arrangements, but my main worry was what to do with Grandma. They said she can be kept as long as convenient in the borough mortuary for up to three weeks at no charge – after that a small sum would be necessary. I feel this is always a problem with death – everyone seems to want to dispose of the person too soon! The fact that we had time to think, and time to make arrangements was the first step. The staff said they would help with carrying Grandma into the chapel. We went to look at the chapel to see how high the platform was for the body to be placed on. They told us to telephone and come at any time if we wanted more help or information. At 3 pm that afternoon we were with the hospital registrar. She was delighted someone wished to arrange their own funeral – the ward sister had arranged for my mother to be taken to the hospital mortuary, and the registrar spoke to the mortician on our behalf. He was happy to keep my mother until the day of the funeral – no problem – no charge. He gave us the dimensions of the coffin. Width and length: 5ft 9ins by 18ins wide. All we had to do was to let him know the time for collection and they would help us lift her in and to seal the lid. So my mother's last resting place was the hospital mortuary until March 3rd.

This gave us time to make the coffin and sort ourselves out. I telephoned the Natural Death Centre for some information, which came very promptly, and for which I am grateful. The British Humanist Association sent me a booklet 'Funerals without God' [eds: see Resources]. It was very reassuring getting information from various sources, showing us that we could do this ourselves, and that our mother's passing had not been taken away from us and dealt with by strangers.

The coffin was made in our garage in a day. My husband enlisted the help of George Haines, a friend in his seventies, who said he always wanted to make his own coffin, so was delighted to have the chance to practise. Much tea and merriment went into the work, and chipboard and timber arrived from the local yard. Most of the neighbours and friends came to have a look and to try it out.

Really it was the fun bits that started to emerge, such as finding music that my mother liked. On a checkup trip to the crematorium to speak to them about the tapes and how to set them up, they told me they had loads of tapes available. They set all the taping up for us, again giving us every assistance. They also suggested that the funeral should be the last one of the day, to be able to give us assistance and extra time in case we had any hiccups.

The registrar was fascinated; she advised me to take several copies of the death certificate as any further copies would cost more later. That was wise advice as my brothers and the solicitor and crematorium all wanted copies. We dealt with all the paperwork which had come from the mortuary, hospital, etc, and that is usually handled by the funeral directors – it was simple. We needed burial certificates, doctors' certificates and one or two other certificates mentioned in the interment leaflet from Woodvale, and again we were assisted by everybody.

I tried to involve the family as much as possible. My eldest daughter made a lovely cake for the funeral tea, and also put together a wonderful photographic display, with photos of my mother's life, and the paintings she did in her later years. My brother's estate wagon was measured for the coffin – it would fit in OK. As a precautionary measure, we also hired an estate car for £42 in case of emergencies. Fortunately it was not required. The rest of the family prepared readings from my mother's favourite books and we prepared a programme containing readings, remembrances and music. We timed this for approximately 30 minutes. We requested no flowers, but did in fact have a lovely display of everlasting flowers made by my sister-in-law, in a basket, which was placed on the coffin with an Indian rug from my brother, and this looked really great.

So at 4 pm on March 3rd we were ready to conduct the service. What went wrong? Not a lot – one late-arriving relative wanted to view her grandmother and we did not think to let the mortician know in advance of collecting the body. The body was not prepared and obviously did not look its best for the occasion and there was an upsetting reaction. My husband, the friend who made the coffin, George, my brother from Kent, and his two children (a son and daughter) and another grandson from Wales, all went to fetch the body. Lesson number one – double check who knows who is coming, when and where. At the crematorium it was difficult getting the coffin out of the car – nobody realised quite how heavy it would be. One granddaughter wished to help carry the coffin, which was great, but this needed a rehearsal. The crematorium staff helped and it was OK. We made a mess-up of getting everyone into the chapel, and in the end they went in after the coffin was placed on the rostrum. The staff worked the tape recorder and I compered the show. My husband videoed the event and Mother would have been very, very pleased, because basically it went off OK. And it did – it dealt with a lot of emotions, and people were able to work on their own grief, mainly, I felt, because they had helped to get the show on the road.

We collected the ashes the next day from the crematorium, free of charge. We later gave the mortician a bottle of wine and the crematorium staff a Christmas box, saw to the nurses and staff at the hospital for their Christmas fare and hoped we had not forgotten anyone.

A hundred days after her death we held a Celebration for her death and life at the Chithurst Monastery, where a Dhana was given to the monks, and family and friends came once again to join with us in the memorial.

All this activity has helped me to deal with my grief and my feelings of guilt and resentment at having to look after quite a difficult lady. I feel I was also able to deal with my father's death: he died in 1961 at the age of 54 and the funeral was too quickly dealt with, with little time to realise how we all felt at that time. So I was able to lay to rest some unresolved grief over his loss.

Many people have spoken to us regarding making their own coffins and are surprised at how little we spent. For the record the absolutely necessary expenses were:

Fee for the crematorium £105 (£184 in 2003), fees for the doctors £57 (£91 in 2003), death certificates £8; purchase of chipboard and timber £30. Total: £200 (equivalent to about £313 in 2000).

In fact we spent a further £42 on the reserve car, for a grand total of £242. Several people asked, did we do this because we couldn't afford it? The answer to this is, No. I felt doing this ourselves was very rewarding, it helped to deal with our grief and the resentments that we had, and which had built up through the years as a result of some of the difficulties of looking after my mother during her lifetime. The main thought seemed to be that it was just as she would have wanted and this came over very strongly from all who helped and were present.

Dorothy Miller's coffin

Deidre's husband adds this note and the illustration below about the coffin:

We made the coffin from half inch chipboard and 2ins by 1in finished battens. First we cut the base and used this as a template for the lid. Although the hospital mortician gave us the width of 18ins we erred on the generous side, at 20ins, to make sure the shoulders would go in all right. On reflection, it would have been ample to make the sides and top with quarter inch chipboard or even hardboard if one really wanted to economise on expense and weight. Below the bottom (and flush with the edges) we fixed battens. We then cut the side pieces 12ins high and fixed these on to the battens so that the battens were concealed. Then we fixed battens on the inside of the side pieces a half inch from the top to accommodate a flush-fitting lid. We found it necessary to strengthen the joining to the lid-battens at the junction of the angle at the widest part of the coffin. We pre-drilled the lid so that it was simple to screw down after putting the old lady in at the mortuary.

We used ferrous screws throughout because after the cremation they were removed from the ashes with a magnet. In the foot end we fixed a small rope handle to use in pulling the coffin out of the car. It was not necessary to fit any other handles.

The mortician said that the coffin was one of the best he had seen.

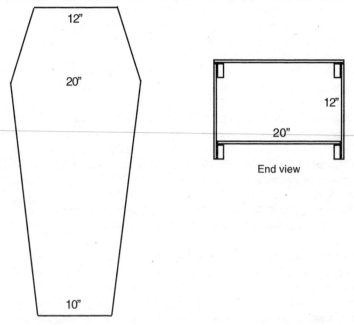

End view

Burial at sea

In theory, burial at sea seems an attractive proposition: the body becomes food for the fish, and it is just a matter of getting a free licence (for England and Wales) from the Department for Environment, Food and Rural Affairs (DEFRA) and then finding a person with a suitable boat to take the coffin out. In practice, sea burial is mildly discouraged by the authorities (with only about 20 such burials a year) and there are quite complex guidelines. On several occasions, bodies buried off the coast have been washed up on shore. There are concerns about commercial fishing trawling the bodies back up – these are busy shipping lanes and foreign trawlers do not always know the areas to avoid. There are now only three places around the coast where sea burials are allowed: one near Newhaven; the Needles Spoil Ground, to the West of the Isle of Wight; and an area nine miles from the mouth of the Tyne. For the free licence contact either the marine licensing person at DEFRA (Matthew Hampshire ☎ 020 238 5869; **e:** m.hampshire@gsi. maff.gov.uk) or your local fisheries District Inspector:

• *Newhaven, East Sussex*: Angus Radford (☎ 01424 424109; **f:** 01424 444642 ; **e:** a.radford@fish.defra.gsi.gov.uk). One of the vessels used for this site is the MVS launch East Sussex 1 from the Sovereign Harbour Marina,

Eastbourne. Local funeral directors in Seaford have used this ground and also Kenyon & Co in London.

• *Poole, Dorset:* Alex Mackenzie (☎ 01202 677539; **f:** 01202 678598; **e:** a.mackenzie@fish.defra.gsi.gov.uk). His site is the Needles Spoil Ground, shown on Admiralty Chart No 2045, 'Outer Approaches to the Solent'. The vessel normally used for the Needles Spoil Ground is the Island Rose (Sean Crain, Hurst Castle Ferries, Lymington, ☎ 01590 642500). Funeral directors who have organised sea burials there include: J. Bevis & Son in Southampton (Andrew George, ☎ 023 9277 2120); Britannia Shipping Co., Britannia House, Newton Poppleford, Sidmouth, Devon EX10 0EF (☎ 01395 568652); Davies Funeral Services of Milford-on-Sea (☎ G. R. Davies, 01590 644664); Bennett in Essex (Jane Bennett, ☎ 01277 210104); the Co-op in Weymouth (Allan Quatermain, ☎ 01305 772789 – 'our sea burials start from £1,500'); and A. H. Roger (☎ 023 8061 2435).

• *North Shields, Tyne and Wear:* Ian Campbell (☎ 0191 257 4520; **f:** 0191 257 1595; **e:** i.s.campbell@sfi.defra.gov.uk). The site off the mouth of the Tyne has only been open since 1999.

A sea burial organised by a funeral director may cost up to £4,000.

A private yacht can be used if it has accurate positioning equipment and if its skipper has a yacht master's certificate.

You should tell the registrar when registering the death that you plan a sea burial and you can then obtain from the registrar a 'Coroners Out of England Form' (Form 104) – and the local coroner's address to which this should be sent.

The Poole Fisheries Officer, Mr Bushell, has dealt with families making their own arrangements, without using funeral directors, and seems helpful. (For a full account of the formidable organisation involved in a DIY sea burial, look on the web at: www.globalideasbank.org/ndw/NDW-25.HTML). Guidelines vary slightly between the two regions, but, by talking to Mr Bushell and Mr Radford, and reading the various documents, the following consensus emerges – the aim of these conditions being to ensure that the coffin and body stay down on the sea-bed, that marine life has ready access to the body and that the body is readily identifiable should it be washed up:

• The coffin should not be made of any persistent synthetic material, nor of a species of timber, such as oak, which would endure in the marine environment. It may not include any lead, zinc or copper. (They recommend a solid softwood such as pine – no veneered board, chipboard or solid hardwood – with the coffin as strong as possible, reinforced on the bottom corners, and large enough to fit extra weights. Even the screws must not be zinc.)

• The wooden coffin should be weighted with approximately 200kg (4cwt) of iron, steel or concrete clamped to the base of the coffin with brackets of 10mm steel bar.

• Holes of at least three-quarter-inch diameter are to be drilled to allow rapid ingress of water and escape of air, so that the coffin may reach the sea-bed quickly and stay there. (They recommend two dozen holes in both the side and lid.)

- The body should also be weighted. (They recommend that the body should have chain wrapped round it, with the chains weighing about 20 kilos, or about 10 per cent more than the body.)
- The coffin should effectively retain the body on the sea-bed without unduly preserving it.
- The body may not be embalmed. (The body may be dressed, although DEFRA specifies a cotton sheet or paper substitute – or a biodegradable body bag may be used, but not a canvas shroud. Biodegradable absorbent padding can be used to contain any leakage of fluids.)
- A certificate of freedom from fever and infection should be obtained from the GP or hospital doctor, and this certificate, together with a copy of the death certificate and the form releasing the body for removal out of England, should be submitted to the district fisheries office.
- The body should have a plastic (or other durable) tag around the neck with the telephone number and identity of the licensee.

DEFRA reserves the right to inspect the coffin prior to the burial, although this rarely happens in practice. Normally, the local DEFRA office must be informed on the day prior to the date of burial and immediately after. An at-least-verbal amendment to the licence is needed if adverse weather or other circumstances delay the burial beyond the week of the licence.

Non assembly-line funerals

There are many ways that people have found to prevent funerals from becoming assembly-line affairs, including those events for which funeral directors are used. Below are some examples.

- **Reminders:** Have something on top of the coffin during the service, as a reminder of the person who has died - such as a favourite hat or scarf.
- **Fires, candles, lanterns**: John Fox of Welfare State International (see Resources) suggests a funeral or memorial service outdoors, the space framed with poles, bunting and music, tables decorated with cloth, flowers and papercuts, and the use of fires, candles and lanterns. 'The Dead Good Funerals Book' which he co-wrote, demonstrates the flair and genius of his group of 'Engineers of the Imagination' in designing innovative rituals (the book's first edition is unreliable on the legal side).

- **One flower each**: You could ask friends not to buy flowers but to bring one flower each, preferably from their garden, and to place it on the coffin. Here is Allegra Taylor's description of how everyone brought one daffodil each to the funeral of Claire, an eight-year-old girl who died of leukaemia:

A grave lined with moss and leaves like a bird's nest

The funeral, organised magnificently by Margot's husband, was a triumph of life over death. Many children from Claire's old school came, as well as some she'd known in hospital. Their drawings for Claire were stuck up all round the church: drawings of butterflies, flowers and big yellow suns. A few children stood up and read poems. Everyone was given a candle to hold – the place was ablaze with the illuminated faces of children – and a yellow daffodil to throw in the grave.

The minister – a friend of the family – held the little coffin in his arms as he spoke of Claire's courage and of the lightness and joy she'd brought into the world during her short life. The grave was lined with moss and leaves like a nest for a baby bird. We stood with our arms around each other as we threw in an avalanche of daffodils and sang 'The Lord of the Dance' together: 'Dance, dance, wherever you may be ... ' It was the most beautiful funeral I had ever been to and an inspiring example of how it can be. We have begun to reclaim birth and death from the medical profession after generations of abdication – begun to reinstate choice and personal responsibility. Let's do the same with funerals.

From Acquainted with the Night *by Allegra Taylor*.

• **A motorcycle funeral**: On June 13th 2003, Helen Armstrong's partner was knocked off his motorbike. He died of multiple injuries six days later. She decided to use the services of Motorcycle Funerals, under the guidance of Paul Sinclair, who rides the bike with sidecar hearse and can conduct the ceremony. The funeral took place at the natural burial ground at Great Bradley Cottage, Tiverton, Devon (see Chapter 6 for details):

The site is one of the most beautiful, peaceful, natural places on earth and I knew as soon as I saw it, and when I talked to the lovely Cath Hunt, that I could do the kind of crossing for Tigger that I wanted. The Rev Sinclair agreed that he and three of Tigger's friends would place Tigger in his coffin and then we would ride in a big bikers' procession from Reading to Devon.

The ceremony was very simple in concept. The chairs were arranged around the coffin. Many people spoke, many message were delivered. We had a massive group hug. The Rev Sinclair closed the ceremony, then we rode him to the burial site. Cath had thought of everything – she kept the lane clear so we didn't meet a tractor and she had mown around the site so the bikes could be parked in a ceremonious concourse. Tigger's mates lowered the coffin, and I spoke the words of blessing, crossing and love. The Rev Sinclair spoke the familiar burial words and people made their own farewells in their own way. His friends filled in the grave and decorated it, making a warrior figure of flowers and stones.

Many of us camped that night, my tent pitched directly against his grave so I could lie one last time beside him. We drummed and sang through the night and lit candles all around the grave. In the early morning we sat quietly around drinking tea and watching the birds and the butterflies settling on the wild flowers on the grave. It was beautiful, comforting, sad.

I have visited the grave three times since his burial and each time am comforted by the beauty and simplicity of the place. I should like to be buried there myself when my time comes.

Helen Armstrong, 61 Old Exeter St, Chudleigh, Devon TQ13 0JX
(☎ 01363 776465; m: 07811 783264).

• **Home funerals**: You could get the minister, officiant or celebrant to conduct the funeral or memorial service in your home or out in the garden. Amongst ministers, Unitarians are particularly willing to conduct a funeral service in your home or elsewhere and will officiate at very personalised or even humanist (that is, atheist or agnostic) funerals (see Resources). Anglican priests, too, are increasingly willing to conduct 'life-centred' funerals.

The Rosslyn Hill Unitarian Chapel in Hampstead (☎ 020 7433 3267) is committed to allowing people to hire the chapel for non-religious funerals, without strict time limits. An organist can be provided. Unitarian ministers will fit in with the wishes of the deceased and their families and may exclude what many see as a formal religious language. The Chapel does not quote a set of charges but prefers to talk of 'grateful donations'.

• **Secular funerals**: For a fee similar to that paid to a priest for a funeral, you can get a trained officiant or celebrant (see Resources) to act as master or mistress of ceremonies for a non-religious funeral. The officiant will normally ask you beforehand about the life of the person that died, so that their speech will be personalised. Or you or a friend or relative can conduct the service yourselves, perhaps referring to the very helpful pamphlet entitled 'Funerals Without God', by Jane Wynne Willson on how to run such services, with its sample texts and poetry (see Resources). The pamphlet explains how a humanist service, for example, tends to divide into distinct parts:

> First there is about eight minutes' worth of entry music, which is played until people have settled down in their seats – if an organist is not being used, this music should be recorded on side A only of a tape marked clearly 'Entry Music' and should be presented to the crematorium preferably the day before. The service proper opens with thoughts on life and death; then a tribute to the dead person (perhaps by a relative); followed by the committal (where everyone stands, the officiant turns towards the coffin, 'commits the body to its natural end' and a button is pressed to close the curtains). Up to about 40 seconds of slow and solemn music is sometimes used for the committal, with the person operating the machine cued to switch it on the moment specific words are said (a second tape should be clearly marked 'Committal Music' with the tape in position to deliver music the moment the Play button is pressed); and the service ends with closing words, after which the officiant walks over to the main mourners and leads them out of the exit door; a tape (marked 'Exit Music') can be played for about five minutes from the moment the officiant steps down from the lectern. Be sure to ask the crematorium to play the music loudly, if this is what you want.

• **No service**: A few of those organising a burial themselves on their own land prefer no service at all. As one correspondent wrote to the Natural Death Centre: 'With us the process went on long enough to comprise a kind of rite of its own. Most of the time we were silent. When we had finished we stood for a while more, still in silence, then I played a piece of music and we left.'

• **A made-to-measure CD:** Do it yourself, or use one of the online services, such as fond-farewells.co.uk: visit their website, select three songs for a funeral you are organising for someone else (or preparing for your own!) and have them delivered on a CD. Price from £14.95 (PO Box 216, Leeds LS15 9WX, ☎ 0113 216 7196; **w**: www.fond-farewells.co.uk).

• **A New Orleans band:** The Eureka New Orleans Jazz Band (☎ 0121 449 0119) plays traditional jazz and dirges at funerals. From a solo saxophone player to the full eight-piece (two trumpets, clarinet, trombone, sousaphone, banjo, snare drum and bass drum) leading the cortege from the gates of the cemetery or burial ground with happy or sad music. They can play a fanfare or requests inside or outside the chapel, or elsewhere. Prices range from £250 (four-piece) to £500 (eight-piece) for one hour's performance within 30 miles of Birmingham; £350 to £700 for the London area.

• **Longer services:** It may be possible to book two or even three sessions at the crematorium, if the standard time is not enough, and if there are many people who wish to speak; and to book the last service of the day, in case your timing is not as exact as the professionals. Chapter 8 details how much, if anything, each crematorium charges for extra time.

• **Other cultures, other times:** In the UK, two world wars made funerary pomp on the home front seem out of place and accentuated our Puritan heritage of simple funerals. Indeed in 1644 the Puritans directed that the dead were to be interred 'without any ceremony'. In 1648, when the body of King Charles I was brought to the Royal Chapel at Windsor, the governor of the castle refused to let Bishop Juxon read the funeral service from the Book of Common Prayer:

The funeral of King Charles I

The Bishop of London stood weeping by, to tender that his service might not be accepted. Then was Charles I deposited in silence and sorrow in the vacant place in the vault about three of the afternoon; and the Lords that night, though late, returned to London.

From The English Way of Death *by Julian Litten*.

There is a beauty of its own in the simplicity expected at a Quaker funeral today, where the disposal of the body is supposed to be done with no unnecessary expense and with no flowers. But the diversity of funeral practices in other cultures and religions around the world and the beauty or intricacy of some of their rituals can widen our vision of the potential of funerals to 'enchant' the participants, raising their consciousness above the mundane. The Ecuadorians, for instance, are buried with their eyes open so that they can see their way to heaven; the Yanonami Indians of the Amazon believe that it is barbaric that Westerners do not drink the ashes of their relatives; rural Greeks tend the graves daily for five years before the corpse is disinterred and placed in a communal ossuary, with clean bones being seen as a reflection of a good life; and for traditional Hindus even the grandchildren are closely involved:

The Hindu rites of death

Hindus should arrange for the dying person to be brought home to die. The dying person should concentrate upon the mantram given at initiation, or if the person is no longer conscious, a family member should chant the mantram softly in his or her right ear.

After death, the relatives place a simple cloth on the person. Each of the relatives comes and applies sesame oil to the deceased's head. The body is bathed with the water from nine kumbhas, and is placed in the coffin. Each of the grandchildren takes a small lighted stick and stands around the body and sings.

> *From* Death and Dying – A Hindu Point of View, *£1.50 from Himalayan Academy Publishers, Rakesh Mathur, 6 Carolyn House, 95 Larkhall Rise, London SW4 6HR.*

A pagan death

Both the Pagan Federation and LifeRites in the UK offer support to pagans (see Resources).

Pagans aim to design rituals that bring them very close to nature and the seasons. Here is an eloquent description of a pagan death and memorial ceremony organised by Tony Kelly and his friends, for his wife Betty who died from cancer:

> Betty was now lying in a green-covered bed in the sunshine at the window, the window open and the air full of warmth and birdsong, willow and birch branches in front of her and a great leafy birch bough at the foot of the bed and the littler branches by the open window. It looked like a woodland glade and she was pleased. Among all the greenery were two bunches of daffodils in big jars, and jars of dandelions and celandines and yellow polyanthus on the windowsill. And I put a few little branches of silver birch on the bed where she could take hold of them and handle them and feel them in the way she always liked to do ...
>
> I was sitting at Betty's side, speaking to her softly as she dreamed, saying, 'The Goddess loves you,' and other things that I knew would make her happy, and I was holding her hands. Betty stopped breathing ...
>
> We stripped all the alien words and the glitter off the coffin; the wood was beautiful. We laid Betty naked inside it and dressed her with daffodils, tastefully, beautifully, in her hair and about her body, some of them fresh and a few to speak her fading ...
>
> The cremation was without ceremony and we brought her ashes home and kept them with us in the box I made, its lid scalloped like the waves of the sea, till the Hag Moon of Samhain called us to a distant shore ...

The ceremony for the scattering of the ashes took place seven months later, at a remote spot by the sea:

> The Sea-lady came over the grass to where I was standing and she raised the lid of the box, and the ashes, speckled black and grey, lay open to the wide

open sky. As I held the box to my breast and she took the lid into her own two hands I spoke the message that for seven moons my heart had borne:

> I am come, beloved Mabh
> To do a thing for Betty
> And to do the thing for thee
> For love of Betty
> And for love of thee

Each spoke their own devotion and to each the priestess responded with the same words that had been Betty's own spontaneous response when their phone calls had been conveyed to her, and they sang a six-verse song they had composed for the occasion:

> ... Green Lady Earth,
> Deep Lady Sea ...
> Carry the ash ...
> Her life has flown;
> Thou dost abide ...

We joined our hands in a ring, all nine of us, and a kiss from the Green Lady passed from lip to hand all around the ring. 'With thee for always, Mabh,' I spoke as the love of the Goddess moved me. At last we loosened our hands.

Celebration Box

Yvonne Malik (see Resources) is a designer by trade and has in the past decorated coffins. She has designed a Celebration Box, which could be filled before death, as a kind of miniature art gallery, and placed at the back of the church or crematorium or memorial service, or be filled by the congregation with photographs, letters, poems, keepsakes and small items. The following is an extract from Yvonne Malik's leaflet:

> When a relative or close friend dies, we often find it impossible to find words to express our feelings. We remember special times, events and places which we shared together, or recall good deeds and kindnesses. These keys to our special memories have an intrinsic value only between ourselves and the one who has died.
>
> Using the Celebration Box is an opportunity to express and focus on a new way of saying 'goodbye'. Each box becomes unique and special, giving us the satisfaction of having taken part in filling it, as well as the ultimate feeling of something shared. This is a new way of including family and friends in a nonverbal act of celebration and comfort – a celebration of the life and shared experiences with the deceased and a later comfort for the bereaved, as well as something to be treasured by the next generation.
>
> Suggested items which have a private or intimate meaning and could be placed in the box include:
>
> Photographs; postcards which reminds us of a special day together; letters, poems, thank-you notes; birthday cards; tickets from a concert

which we shared, souvenir from a holiday; button from their favourite jacket, pair of earrings, pipe; copy of a team certificate, club badge, medal; special scarf or cap.

The events and times which we shared require no explanation from us and the tokens placed within the box are private statements. It is something which can be carried out by ourselves, alongside the traditional services of the funeral director.

The Celebration Box can be filled at home prior to the funeral or placed in an accessible situation at the back of the church or chapel and brought home after the final ceremony.

Each Celebration Box is hand decorated and therefore differs from any other. It also has the advantage of being portable, to suit today's more transient lifestyle.

A simpler approach, described by Tony Walter in the Funeral Director (April 1996) – or one which could work in tandem with the Celebration Box – is to place cards in the church pews inviting mourners to leave a sentence or two about the person who has died – for the later comfort of the family.

Public memorial

Remembering the dead begins immediately after death, and continues after the funeral. One suggestion for improving grieving is to set up 'open houses' for bereaved people who can't face going home. Nowadays, many people hold impromptu wakes after the funeral. The wake or after-funeral gathering is common in most cultures, like the wedding feast. However, it is the tone or style of the wake that is all-important. A feast that is too formal might accentuate the loneliness of the bereaved person once the guests have gone home. On the other hand, an informal gathering of mourners who want to share their feelings may begin a sharing process that will come to be of benefit to the bereaved. Laughter and jokes as well as tears are likely to erupt because remembering the dead person is also recalling the richness of life and relationships through stories and anecdotes.

Holding a memorial service at some time, perhaps months after the death and immediate obsequies, may be a way of bringing out the essential cheerfulness and spirit of life with which most of us would like to be remembered. We want to be celebrated as well as mourned. Here is such a celebration, designed by Margaret Chisman for her husband Stan. There is some human instinct that makes us want to be present at such a celebration of people who were our friends. It is rather like giving wedding gifts. We want to give the gifts, be part of the celebration. Why should we deprive ourselves of being part of such a ceremony, the feasting of a life?

A table of objects to commemorate the person

The celebration and commemoration of Stan was held at our home in the double rooms on the ground floor. About 40 friends and relations were present. It was a beautiful day, the garden was full of flowers and their scent drifted in through the open french doors. After welcoming everyone I took the cloth cover off the table and explained that on it were articles that Stan loved or that exemplified his life.

The first thing that everyone noticed about him was his outstanding physical vigour. By contrast many people seemed only half alive. He was fully and gloriously alive in every fibre of his being. He loved rambling – I held up his walking boots – and whenever he decided to go on a walk he began to get excited and I would know to get his boots out. He loved skiing – I showed his goggles – and sadly had a holiday fixed for January by which time he was too ill. There were several photos amongst those displayed of him enjoying this sport. When living in Ipswich he played in the Post Office Table Tennis Team, and they won the cup one year and each player received a small trophy, here displayed. He also played five-a-side football and his old football boots were still in the cupboard upstairs. He took up sailboarding within the last two years and there were several photos of him displayed. These were taken on our holiday in the South of France. I regret I have no photos of him hang-gliding (whoever heard of a man of 62 taking up hang-gliding?), but George, who also introduced him to this sport describes the last occasion; Stan had become airborne to a height of 50ft and was looking decidedly unhappy but absolutely determined to go through with it.

John White, who could not be present today said that for him he would always remember Stan for playing the glorious voice of Paul Robeson singing 'I thought I saw Joe Hill last night.' We played this record, and as I heard that vibrant voice singing the words of optimism in the face of death I felt once more overcome with grief and loss and wondered whether, despite all my supportive and loving relations and friends, all my active outside interests, my comfortable and satisfying home, I would manage to achieve serenity and full acceptance of his death.

The next part was pure joy. Nearly everyone had an anecdote or memory to share. Some of them were new to me, and I felt as if Stan came alive again for a few minutes.

Alan Mayne commented in the Visitors Book: 'I knew that Stan was a man of many parts but I didn't know how many.'

I asked everyone to end as Stan would have wished – to hug and kiss their neighbours.

By Margaret Chisman.

Incidentally, Ernest Morgan warns that those who speak up at memorial services should not allow themselves to be cut short by whoever is conducting the service. 'I have known family members who carried regrets for years that they had been cut-off from speaking because the service was running too long.'

Memorials by Artists

• Memorials by Artists helps people to commission individual memorials from the finest designers and lettercutters in Britain. These range from simple tablets to headstones, boulders, arches, sundials, birdbaths, urns, etc. Depending on the individual's needs, the service provides help with the formulation of ideas, finding the most suitable artist, making the introduction, arranging permissions with churchyard or cemetery authorities and administering the project throughout. Prices start from £900. An illustrated booklet is available from Memorials by Artists for £7.50 incl. p&p; also a free illustrated leaflet (see Resources).

Memorials by Artists was founded in 1988 by Harriet Frazer to help others through the kind of difficulties she experienced over the memorial to her stepdaughter, who died in 1985. There is also an associated charity, The Memorial Arts Charity, to promote memorial arts and crafts.

Elizabeth Lawlor, who used Memorials by Artists for her husband's headstone, commends them to the Natural Death Centre:

> The headstone is up. I wanted a wave on top for symbolic reasons – waves of consciousness, waves being re-absorbed into the ocean, etc – and for my husband's naval and sea-loving connection. The help I received from Memorials by Artists was wonderful.

• Eleanor Glover (76b Richmond Street, Totterdown, Bristol BS3 4TJ, ☎ 0117 971 9755; e: eleanor.glover@freeuk.com) produces painted sculptures and wooden reliefs (from £5 to £150, or £80 per day); 'no job is too small'.

• Small Remembrances is a range of wooden sculptures from Scottish woodcarver Alan Lees (Wood Artist, 38 Patna Road, Kirkmichael, Ayrshire KA19 7PJ (☎ 01655 750386; e: info@woodarts.co.uk; w: www.woodarts.co.uk). They are designed to be used in the interim between a funeral and the installation of a permanent memorial and may then be moved to the relatives' garden, say, as a second lasting memorial. Prices range from £200 to around £1,000. He is happy to undertake commissions for any kind of memorial.

• The Stile Company (☎ 01295 780372; f: 01295 780972; e: info@the-stile.co.uk; w: www.the-stile.co.uk) offer advice, planning and installation for celebratory and commemorative features – including stiles, sculptures, benches, signs, fences, gates and trees – in countryside or garden.

• If you simply need to find a quality person to design the headstone, a free register of artists is kept by the Council for the Care of Churches (☎ 020 7898 1866).

• A memorial of course need not be a gravestone: you may want to pay for a glass window in church; or to pay for a park bench; or to have a sponsored walk or children sponsored to learn poetry for a recital in aid of the person's favourite charity. If asking for donations to charity, suggest that these be paid by cheque, to help prevent donations going astray.

Alternative ashes disposal

• An astronomer's ashes were sent to the moon by NASA. An expensive American service to put ashes in orbit is available from Celestis Inc (☎ 001 713 522 7282; e: celestis@best.com; w: www.celestis.com).

• More feasible for the average deceased is for their ashes to be launched into the night sky in giant fireworks. None of the UK fireworks manufacturers seem particularly keen to be mentioned, although several have provided this service in the past (one charged £600 for a giant firework with all the ashes on board). You could try approaching them diplomatically (or try approaching firework display firms to ask them to refashion one of their bought-in rockets). Manufacturers include Pains Fireworks (☎ 01794 884040), Theatrical Pyrotechnics Ltd (☎ 01843 823545), Spectrum (☎ 01522 514016) and Kimbolton Fireworks (☎ 01480 860988).

• A firm called Air Navigation and Trading (☎ 01253 345396), based at Blackpool airport, will scatter your ashes over land or sea. They charge £82.25 an hour.

• The American company LifeGem Memorials (w: www.lifegem.com) says it will make a person's ashes into a diamond for a minimum cost of about £3,688. The process takes 16 weeks, and the firm say that any unused ashes will be returned to the family. The company is soon to open up a UK branch.

Memorial tree planting

If you want to plant a tree in a public place in memory of the person, you could ask your local park if this might be possible. Alternatively, the following organisations offer memorial tree planting:

• Woodland Creation, Little Bakes, Tredethick, Lostwithiel, Cornwall PL22 OLE (☎ 01208 873618) is an unregistered organisation set up by Tim and Nicky Reed where for £25 you can dedicate a tree in new broadleaved woodland in Cornwall. All trees can be located on site and dedications are recorded in a book with a mapped reference number. A certificate is sent out to the sponsor.

• Trees for London (registered charity), Prince Consort Lodge, Kennington Park, Kennington Park Place, London SE11 4AS (☎ 020 7587 1320; f: 020 7407 3830; e: treesforlondon@aol.com) say you can sponsor them to plant a young tree from £15 per annum to a grove of five trees for £72 per annum. You may nominate either a species or a site. Alternatively, you can choose to dedicate a single semi-mature memorial tree (12ft to 15ft) with a botanical (black) plaque, recording the Latin and English tree name and a message, for £175.

• The World Land Trust (UK-based conservation charity), Blyth House, Bridge Street, Halesworth, Suffolk IP19 8AB (☎ 01986 874422; w: www.worldland trust.org) will commemorate any donation of £150 (enough to save 1,500 rainforest trees in Ecuador) by planting a new tree in their 48-acre reserve at Kites Hill, Gloucestershire, and entering the benefactor's name, or that of the person they are commemorating, in their register of support, which is available for viewing at Kites Hill.

• The National Memorial Arboretum, Croxall Road, Alrewas, Staffordshire, DE13 7AR (☎ 01283 792333) offers dedicatory tree planting for £50 with a label or, for an extra £125, a named plaque. You may propose the type of tree, but the final selection is up to them. There is also a place for the scattering of ashes. The project RoadPeace has an area of woodland which forms part of the National Memorial Arboretum and offers the same dedicatory facilities there (see the Resources chapter).

• Ashes may also be scattered (not buried) in Woodland Trust woods, provided that no 'formal ceremony' is carried out in the wood and that the ground is not disturbed in any way. The Trust will also dedicate existing trees which have been planted within the last five years in 20 of its woods (details of the wood, along with a certificate, sticker and card will be sent to the purchaser's address): £10 for one tree; or £25 for three trees plus £5 per additional tree (☎ 0800 026 9650; w: www.woodlandtrust.org.uk).

Alternative Urns

John Fox of Welfare State International suggests redecorating the normal small wooden caskets used for ashes: remove the paint with varnish stripper, undercoat with filler and two coats of white wood primer; then paint imagery or words – he uses fluorescent enamel varnish (Brodie and Middleton); and re-varnish, allowing 24 hours for the drying. He adds this story:

> I commissioned a pottery urn from a friend who specialised in throwing decorative slipware. It was for the ceremony to scatter my father's ashes in the Humber Estuary, where he had earned his living as a sea captain.
>
> We ended up with a dome-shaped circular lidded pot about a foot high and a foot diameter at the base. A little like a tiny bee hive.
>
> The lid had to be surprisingly wide too – about six inches, for the ashes to scatter easily downwind.
>
> In white slip on the dark brown of the pot's surface, we inscribed: 'The last voyage of Captain Fox, MBE. May his spirit be at peace with the sea.'
>
> At the ceremony myself, my wife and our two children then ten and eight played 'Eternal Father' on brass instruments. (My father was a Christian.)
>
> It was memorable and healing for us all.

Welfare State International (artistic director John Fox – see the Resources chapter) offers a consultancy service for those wanting a very special memorial service.

If you might want to buy an artist-designed, pottery, bamboo or willow urn, or one shaped like a large acorn, or to inspired by such designs to create your own, see the next chapter.

For more on memorials and 'Living Memorials', see Chapter 10.

Probate

In Chapter 2 on Preparing for Dying, under the heading 'Simplifying Your Affairs Before Death', it was outlined how someone could leave their estate so that neither probate, inheritance tax nor Inland Revenue account was required. Probate otherwise involves the executors of the will applying to the probate registry for a grant of probate which confirms their power to process the will (if the person died without a will, or if the executors have died or are unwilling to act, the relatives apply for similar powers, known as letters of administration). Solicitors can do the whole thing for you, but in one typical recent instance they charged a rate of £90 per hour, plus 1per cent of all the cash, stocks and shares in the estate and 0.5 per cent of the property. To this total they then added 25per cent. Banks tend to charge even more for doing probate work.

Shop around for the cheapest appropriate solicitor you can find – for instance, avoid central London and choose a solicitor who specialises in probate work (they are likely to take less time) – perhaps within such a firm you could get a reduction by asking if a trainee solicitor could handle it for you. You could probably reduce the bill further by doing some of the work yourself, such as gathering in the estate's money from the bank and building society. (Incidentally, if the will names a professional executor and you are determined to do it all yourself, the professional may be willing to surrender the executorship to you for a nominal fee.) The Will Consultancy (☎ 01443 485147), as mentioned under wills in Chapter 2, also specialise in probate work nationwide and will tend to quote a fixed price.

But assuming the estate is relatively straightforward (with no business partnership, self-owned business, agricultural land, insurance syndicate or family trusts) it can be done by anyone businesslike, with patience enough to wade through all the fiddly details and to write the many formal letters. Again, as when preparing one's will, the most useful book is the Which? *Wills and Probate* book (see Resources), and there is also a new probate and inheritance tax helpline (☎ 0845 302 0900). The following is merely a sketch of what is involved:

You will need forms for a personal application for a 'grant of representation' from your local Probate Personal Application Department – if you were not given this address in a booklet at the time you registered the death, you can find it out from the Probate Registry (see Resources). The main local offices are also detailed in booklet PA4 (from probate offices, the Citizens Advice Bureau or w: www.courtservice.gov.uk) which outlines how to do things without a solicitor. Once you have filled in and returned these forms (PA1, the probate application form; and the account of the estate – IHT205, IHT44), you will be given an appointment to go to your local office in person to swear that the information is true. Before the grant is made you will need to pay the probate fee (a flat fee of £130). If the estate is demonstrably less than £5,000, there may be no need to apply for a grant of probate; in any event, where the estate is less than £5,000, no fee is payable. You will also need to have paid any inheritance tax owing (although inheritance tax on land or buildings can be paid over a ten-year period at a rate of interest that is in line with the average bank base lending rate). There may be a form of inheritance tax self-certification coming in soon, in which case tax issues are likely to be dealt with even before the grant application is made.

If the deceased's funds were in a bank the money should now, under a new agreement, be able to be transferred directly to the Inland Revenue from the bank or building society accounts before probate is granted. The IR will then issue a receipt which you can use to apply for a grant of probate. You will need a reference number and forms D21 and D20 for each bank or society. However, be aware that banks' and societies' participation in this scheme is voluntary; although most will allow payments before probate, some will not (eg Abbey National). Even when they do, you may, unfortunately, find that the branch staff are not yet up to speed with the new procedures.

The executors will also need to deal with the Land Registry to transfer any property (form 56 from Oyez, see Resources) and with the Income Tax people – their forms Cap 30 (to show that any inheritance tax has been paid), form 59 (an income tax return for the year in which the person died) and form R185E (income tax deduction certificates).

Valuing stocks and shares with the exactitude required for probate purposes (your bank may be willing, without charge, to find out the shares' value at the date of death), filling in the probate schedule of them and handling their transfer or sale are small bureaucratic nightmares. To repeat Chapter 2: any dying person who has accumulated the odd lot of shares would save their executors a great deal of trouble by selling them before death.

Executors will also need to deal with the deceased's mortgage company, house insurance company, district valuer (it is usually acceptable to get sales particulars for similar houses locally and to base your valuation on these), bank, building society, life insurance company, pension company, Benefits Agency and local post office (for forwarding of mail) – plus in some cases advertising in the newspapers for any unknown creditors.

Anyone appointed as an executor who, understandably, cannot face the work involved, can fill in a renunciation form or a form appointing an attorney to do it (forms available from Oyez, see Resources); or you can hand over to a professional part of the way through, but you will have to pay if there are insufficient assets in the estate.

Chapter 5

COFFINS &
PROFESSIONAL SERVICES

Chapter 4 described how people could organise a funeral themselves. This chapter is for those who want help from the trade. It is for those who may be trying to buy funeral goods – such as a cardboard or a regular coffin; a painted coffin or a recycled coffin; a bamboo or willow coffin or a coffin as bookcase; an urn; a body bag or lowering webbing. It describes the goods on offer from mail order suppliers and coffin manufacturers. It will also enlighten you if you are seeking just one service rather than a complete package – such as cold storage facilities, or a hearse or horse-drawn carriage you can rent, or the hiring of extra bearers. This chapter serves as an introduction to the detailed listings in the next three chapters and summarises the findings of the Natural Death Centre's nationwide survey of the funeral trade. It describes not only the Natural Death Handbook Award 2004 Winners, but which local authorities supply a cheaper municipal funeral service; how to get a free funeral; how best to choose a funeral director; why embalming may not be necessary; the snags that go with prepaid funerals (and a natural burial alternative for Londoners, including collection of the body); and the high standards being laid down by the best funeral directors, crematoria and cemeteries.

Natural Death Handbook Awards 2004

On Sunday April 18th 2004, as part of the National Day of the Dead ceremonies organised by the Natural Death Centre, the following five National Awards (and the 36 other Regional Awards detailed in Chapters 6, 7 & 8) will be publicly presented.

National Awards

• The Natural Death Handbook Award 2004 for the **Best Natural Burial Ground** in the UK goes to Rosie Bullough and colleagues at the South Downs Natural Burial Site, East Meon, Hampshire (☎ 01730 823005), who provide an exceptionally friendly and helpful service – a complete funeral at the site, including the grave, the digging, backfilling and top-soiling by hand, tree planting and staking, 4x4 transportation for elderly or infirm mourners, A3 page in memorial book, and staff attendance at funeral, costs £602.50. The Natural Death Centre has had an unprecedented amount of purely positive feedback about this site from the members of the public who have used it since it opened in 2000. (See the South section of Chapter 6 for their details and extracts of the glowing reports.) Highly commended in this category is Great Bradley Cottage, near Tiverton (see the South West section of Chapter 6).

• The Natural Death Handbook Award 2004 for the **Best Cemetery** in the UK goes, along with the crematorium award, to Carlisle. The Bereavement Manager in charge of both places is June Carswell (☎ 01228 625310) and the services she and her colleagues provide consistently win awards. They have a 'recycled funeral' for those who require a simple, inexpensive burial with no memorial, and maintain both conservation areas and conventionally attractive cemetery grounds. The Carlisle Cemetery makes available not only cardboard and regular coffins, but its own woollen shroud. (See the North West region in Chapter 8 for details.)

• The Natural Death Handbook Award 2004 for the **Best Crematorium** in the UK goes to the Carlisle Crematorium run by June Carswell and colleagues in Carlisle's Bereavement Services (☎ 01228 625310). They offer a reduced fee for those choosing a fuel-saving 'Environmental Cremation', which involves a cardboard coffin and cremation the same day or by the following morning, thus saving on pre-heating of the cremator. They publish excellent guidance for those arranging funerals without funeral directors and can help the public by providing cold storage for the body. They accept a wide variety of body containers from home-made to wicker coffins. They can provide cold storage for the body before the funeral and extra bearers to help the family. (See the North West region in Chapter 8 for details.)

• The Natural Death Handbook Award 2004 for the **Best Funeral Director** in the UK goes to Dr John Mallatratt and his firm Peace Funerals of Sheffield (☎ 0114 253 0505). They see it as their role to offer flexible options and to empower the bereaved. Their service is widely available and they have their own range of willow basket-work coffins and run two woodland burial grounds. The Natural Death Centre receives many unsolicited plaudits for this firm from the general public. (See the North East region in Chapter 7 for details.)

• The Natural Death Handbook Award 2004 for the **Best Coffin Manufacturer** in the UK goes to William Wainman and his firm SAWD Ltd (☎ 01795 472262). With the introduction of the Bamboo Eco Coffin they have pioneered the use of bamboo in coffin manufacturing. All bamboo, strong, light, and less expensive than the wicker models, they are attractive, and shipped 'Russian doll' style, one inside the other, to save on transport costs. The Natural Death Centre receives favourable comments regarding these coffins from both the public and the funeral trade. (See below in this chapter for their details.) Highly commended in this category is The Somerset Willow Company (☎ 01278 424003, and see below in this chapter for their details).

In making these awards, the editorial team have relied on their own surveys and investigations, and on feedback to the Natural Death Centre from the general public, so as to decide which services were the most helpful, the most innovative and the best value.

Good funeral directors

In our view, the ideal funeral director is a *facilitator*, one who helps the family to do as much of the funeral arranging themselves as they can bear, as exemplified in the following excerpts from an account by an American funeral director about what he learnt from the funeral of his father:

A funeral director helping with his father's funeral

I was sitting on the hospital bed holding my father's hand when he died. I hated the scene but I wouldn't have been anywhere else. Such helplessness and desperation I have never felt at any other time. When he died, we wept.

Two men came with a cot – men I had never seen before. They didn't know me or my profession. My emotion didn't leave room for explanations, so I simply asked them to stand aside. It was my dad and I would do it. Hesitatingly they obliged, while I took the cover from the cot, positioned the cot and gathered Dad's limp body into my arms. It was my job. I was his son. It was our love.

I felt a sense of desertion as I watched those two strangers disappear down the hall with Dad. Dad didn't know them.

One of my best friends, a funeral director from the next town, came to get Dad and did all the embalming work. I did the rest – the death certificate, the notification of newspapers, cemetery, minister, church, family, friends, neighbours, all the scores of details which accompany the task of being a funeral director.

My family did lots of other things: we tucked Dad in (it's rough but it's real) and closed the casket; we took him to church ourselves. My brother, sister and I carried Dad to his grave, we lowered him into his grave with straps and our own muscle power. We closed the vault and shovelled the dirt ourselves. We closed out his life ourselves.

Later, weeks later, I asked myself: how many sons, daughters, parents and spouses had I delayed the grief work for because I had performed all of the tasks for them, because I, as a functionary, had usurped their role as care-giving family members? How many times had I made decisions for a family without their opinion, because I had assumed 'they couldn't take it?' They have a right to be heard. The focus must be on their needs, reactions and prior experience. Immediately, my role in funeral service shifted to being that of a facilitator and it has remained there.

By Roy & Jane Nichols from Death – The Final Stage of Growth
edited by Elisabeth Kübler-Ross.

Buying a coffin

The last chapter dealt with making a coffin. This one, inter alia, tells you how to buy one ready-made – not always an easy purchase, as Jane Spottiswoode discovered. Many funeral directors refuse to sell just a coffin, or do so at grossly inflated prices.

Biodegradable coffins

Cardboard coffins

When the Natural Death Centre was launched in 1991, it called for cardboard coffins to be made available in the UK. Nowadays there is a wide variety of models to choose from. The first edition of *The Natural Death Handbook* in 1993 could identify only a handful of crematoria and cemeteries that would accept cardboard coffins. But by 1994, Jon Luby of The Federation of British Cremation Authorities was writing that 'my advice would be to accept such a coffin if requested'. Now almost every crematorium accepts them; and most funeral directors are willing to obtain a cardboard coffin on behalf of a client, although they will tend to charge a high price.

Cardboard coffins are regularly used for burials in natural burial grounds. Some people prefer to use them in conjunction with a body bag, or a liquid-proof liner or some other more environmentally-friendly padding or protection for the body such as hay, sawdust, cotton wool, torn-up sheets or old pillows or newspapers (if for cremation, consult the management as to whether the materials you plan to use are acceptable). Some like to paint the coffin (using water-based paints: again, ask the crematorium) or to put a drape over the cardboard coffin during the funeral service to hide its unorthodox appearance. It is as well to be aware that if the soil is clay or very stony, the cardboard lid may get smashed open as the grave is filled. Measures that could be taken to avoid this include: placing planks or a mattress-type filling on top of the coffin; dropping a layer of hay or bracken on top of the coffin; wrapping the coffin in some covering such as a rug; filling the grave very gently to begin with, using specially gathered loose soil; or filling the grave only when those who would be most upset have left.

If using an estate car, don't forget to check that your cardboard coffin will fit (see Chapter 4 for the relevant makes).

The cardboard coffins available, with the cheapest first, are as follows:

• CC Supplies (Office 6, 10 Buckhurst Road, Bexhill-on-Sea, East Sussex TN40 1QF (☎ 01424 733833; f: 01424 730180) sells the **Woodland Coffin** for £54.69 incl. VAT & delivery. Its dimensions are 72ins by 22ins by 15ins. It comes flatpack, in a white oyster (off-white) colour, and assembles into a normal coffin shape. It has a removable lid, but the flaps that hold it together are visible on the outside, so it is perhaps marginally less aesthetically pleasing than some of the other models listed below.

• Larger is the **Brighton Casket**, also marketed by CC Supplies (see previous entry). Its dimensions are 74ins by 22ins by 15ins. It looks a bit like a giant brown cardboard shoe box with a printed woodgrain-effect on the lid and uses part-plastic bolts to hold it together. It has a 'moisture-protected white liner' inside which gives 'enough protection for a cremation or a burial'. It is available flatpack, with instructions for assembly, at a price of £57.69 incl. VAT & delivery. The advantage of both the Brighton Casket and the Woodland Coffin (see above) is that they have removable lids, so they are more suitable for viewing the body than the Compakta (see below).

• **Celtic Caskets** (Unit 111, Fauld Industrial Estate, Fauld Lane, Tutbury, Burton upon Trent, Staffordshire DE13 9HS, ☎ 01283 521104 or 07949 122484 anytime) do a strong white cardboard coffin with a rigid chipboard base and a (removeable) cremfilm liner for £77 incl. delivery (or for £75. 'if a person orders directly by telephone without any postal correspondence,' says Alan Goldingay, MD). The coffin will arrive flatpack (76ins by 22ins by 2ins), assembly time approx. 3 mins.

It costs £10 extra for another colour – blue, green or maroon. Floral or 'cross' stencilling to the lid (£10). Lowering webbing set for burial, disposable into the grave (£10). Gift handle set, cosmetic only (£10).

• **P. A. Ginns** (Compakta Ltd, Environ, Parkfield, Western Park, Hinckley Road, Leicester LE3 6HX; ☎ /f: 01162 333566; **w**: www.eco-coffin.co.uk) sell an elegant white cardboard coffin, the **Compakta**, for £111.63 incl. delivery. It is lightweight, relatively strong and slightly tapered, needs no bolts or clips, and may be painted. A longer (77ins) woodgrain-effect version costs £123.38 incl. delivery. One snag with the Compakta is that it is tricky to remove the lid for those wanting access to the body. Also, we have received complaints that it is too lightweight and that the handles, which are made of cloth, are not strong enough. Internally, it is 72ins long by 18ins wide and 13.5ins deep. They also sell the **Environ** casket for £129 incl. delivery. Collections can be arranged from L. T. & R. Vowles Ltd, Longdon Heath, Upton upon Severn, Worcester WR8 0RL (☎ 01684 592212), or depots in Coventry or Leicester by telephoning the main number above. In urgent cases, the A. B. Welfare and Wildlife Trust (☎ 01423 530900/ 868121) may be able to arrange the delivery, adding on no more than £5 to whatever they have to pay the supplier. Alternatively, members of the public can find out their nearest stockist by phoning Compakta.

• **Greenfield Coffins** (Unit 6/7 Lakes Road, Braintree, Essex CM7 3SS, ☎ 01376 327074, **f**: 01376 342975; **e**: sales@greenfieldcoffins.com; **w**: www. greenfieldcoffins.com) sell brown, white, plain green, green or grey marble-effect and woodgrain effect cardboard coffins which hold up to 23 stone in weight, from 6ft 1in (185 cm; standard) to 6ft 7ins (200 cm; special). Prices start at £79.31 for a flatpacked plain brown coffin incl. three-day delivery; up to £275.54 for a ready-assembled printed coffin with decorative handles incl. next day delivery. Both types can be fitted with a range of handles.

• **Engrefco**, Alterchrome House, Murray Road, Orpington, Kent BR5 3QY (☎ 0800 018877) sell a new design of large, coffin-shaped cardboard coffin for £79.95 incl. next day delivery. This arrives as a partially assembled flatpack and takes about ten minutes to assemble. It includes a waterproof liner and carrying handles.

• The most expensive cardboard coffin, is the **Peace Box Ecology** coffin. It looks least like a cardboard coffin, with a wood-effect finish, and comes with an elasticated cotton lining, a liquid-proof insert, and a pillow. It is said to be the only one-piece cardboard coffin, 'is easily transported and can be slotted together in under five minutes'. It weighs 12 kilos and, it is claimed, can carry 200 kilos (although one reader complained to the Natural Death Centre that the coffin's bottom came loose). In the UK, it is distributed flatpack by P. B. UK, Triangle House, 62 Victoria Road, Cirencester, Gloucestershire GL7 1ES (☎ 01285 653298; **f**: 01285 653224; **e**: ecocoffinpbuk@hotmail.com) for £135.63 incl. delivery. A pack of ten works out at £93.94 each incl. delivery. (A purpose-made carrying-belt and metal clips – used when the lid sections of the coffin are folded down for viewing purposes – cost an extra £70.44 incl. delivery and can be reused for each funeral.)

• Some local authority cemeteries and crematoria sell cardboard coffins to members of the public not using their other services. Their prices are reasonable but they will usually require you to collect. They include:

Brighton, ☎ 01273 604020 (the Greenfield, sold ready-assembled only, for £78, 'to be collected from the mortuary with a suitable vehicle'); Cardiff, ☎ 029 2062 3294 (the Compakta for £95, flatpack, no liner); and Carlisle, ☎ 01228 625310 (the Compakta for £75).

• A number of private natural burial grounds also sell cardboard coffins. They include: Greenhaven near Rugby, (☎ 01788 860604) £70 to £95; Birdsong Burial Ground, Alford, Lincs. (☎ 01507 466644); South Yorkshire Woodland Burials,(☎ 01704 821900) £89. See Chapter 6 for details of other sites selling cardboard and other coffins.

The many funeral directors around the country who sell cardboard coffins will probably add considerably more mark-up than any of the above sources. Funeral directors tend to be ferociously opposed to local authorities selling coffins, sometimes getting together to threaten a boycott of those crematoria and cemeteries who do so. In 1996, the Natural Death Centre reported two such cases to the Office of Fair Trading.

Bamboo and willow coffins

❍❍❍ The SAWD Partnership, Highsted Farm, Highsted Valley, Sittingbourne, Kent ME9 0AG (☎ 01795 472262; **f**: 01795 422633; **e**: wainman@ sawd.demon.co.uk; **w**: www.bamboocoffins.cjb.net) sell handmade biodegradable Bamboo Eco Coffins which are non-toxic during cremation and come with a waterproof cotton liner and a bamboo headrest. They cost from £195 incl. next day delivery, depending on size (from 1.65m to 2m) and design (standard or lattice). (Eds: One FD has said: 'This coffin is great: the weave is dense, the base is very strong, the handles can be used to carry (unless the body is very heavy). William Wainman and Chris Garland are extremely helpful.') All callers who mention the Natural Death Centre will be offered a 10 per cent discount on their order. This firm are the winners of the Natural Death Handbook Award 2004 for Best Coffin Manufacturer.

• The Somerset Willow Company, Wireworks Estate, Bristol Road, Bridgwater, Somerset TA6 4AP (☎ 01278 424003; **f**: 01278 446415; **e**: enquiries@ somersetwillow.co.uk; **w**: www.somersetwillow.co.uk) supply a range of native-grown willow caskets costing from £345 to £381 for an adult curved end or coffin-shaped casket in natural buff or weatherbeaten gold (plus approximately £20 for delivery). Cotton liners are £34 each, and they can also make caskets to your own size or specifications on request.

• Tony Carter (The Basket Workshop, 121 Hargham Road, Attleborough, Norfolk NR17 2HQ, ☎ 01953 457893; f: 01953 457705; m: 0771 4101567) makes a 'woven willow chrysalis'. It is semi-elliptical in shape and is produced within a week to order, in sizes from giant to newborn baby, and costs £380 for an adult size, plus delivery. The chrysalis can be kept at home and used for storage. If tightly filled, it can serve as a bench. One bought years in advance 'should be kept completely dry in a large plastic bag' to prevent woodworm. Willow is of varied tints, ranging from white and buff, to green, red and brown, depending on the length of time it is left to steam before being woven.

• Peace Funerals (☎ 0114 253 0505 or see under Sheffield in the North West region in Chapter 7 for full contact details) now sell their own design of wicker coffin, the Mawdesley Willow, for £399 for the largest adult sizes, down to £75 for smaller sizes up to 24ins (delivery locally free). The Mawdesley is more coffin-shaped than the other willow coffins, without pointed ends, which makes it externally slightly shorter than the other designs, but it takes the same size internally. 'They are made in the village where my wife Mary was born in Lancashire. They have a two-part hinged lid, which closes together with a willow stick, attached to toggles on the side of the coffin. We can be very flexible with design and will try and accommodate all requests' (John Mallatratt). NB: to make this coffin truly biodegradable, ask for it with a cotton liner *only*, otherwise it will arrive with a cotton liner stapled to a non-biodegradable plastic liner which may not be acceptable for some natural burial grounds.

• Nigel Price (Linden Spinney, Chagford, Devon TQ13 8JF, ☎/f: 01647 432451; e: nigel@willowcoffins.co.uk; w: www.willowcoffins.co.uk) makes a woven willow coffin from willow harvested in the Sedgemoor area of Somerset. Available in brown or buff. Various sizes from 2ft to 6ft, from £100 to £385 *not* incl. delivery.

• Natural Fencing (Pastures Farm, Yardley Road, Olney, Buckinghamshire MK46 5EL, ☎ 01234 714240; f: 01234 714384; e: mail@naturalfencing.com; w: www.naturalfencing.com). This firm's premises are next to the Olney Green Burial Site. They can supply traditional and oval shaped 'bespoke and standard size' willow coffins from 5ft 11ins by 20ins to 6ft 8ins by 26ins, for £450 not incl. delivery; calico liners optional.

• Heaven on Earth in Bristol (☎ 0117 926 4999 or see full contact details above) sell a willow coffin with a hinged lid for £499.

Earthsleepers and ecopods

• Designer Andrew Vaccari sells an **earthsleeper** – a 'strong and rigid' biodegradable papiermache coffin, with wood studs and an organic lining – flatpack for £350 incl. UK mainland delivery. Vaccari Design, 52 Greenway, Crediton, Devon EX17 3LT (☎ 01363 83659; w: vaccari.co.uk). It comes in five colours: natural (grey), green, blue, black and red, and Vaccari says it takes 'under five minutes to put together'.

• The **ecopod** is a contoured pod-shaped coffin made from KEF, an entirely recycled and biodegradable material strengthened with cellulose fibres. It carries up to 116 kilos and weighs 14 kilos and thus 'easy to transport'. It is available in blue, red, dark green or cream, and decorated with a Celtic cross, flying doves, or an Aztec sun, all incl. a calico mattress. The ecopod costs £515.50 incl. delivery from ARKA, 39-41 Surrey Street, Brighton, East Sussex BN1 8PE (☎ 01273 684151; **e**: info@eco-funerals.com; **w**: www.ecofunerals. com).

Untreated wood coffins

• £129 for a simple, traditional (curved end) or casket-shaped (oblong) coffin made from untreated solid FSC-certified pine and non-toxic biodegradable glue. Rope handles are included and the price includes delivery. This is a strong coffin, but some families have described it as 'very heavy'. From Eco-coffins.com, Channel Business Centre, Castle Hill Avenue, Folkestone, Kent CT20 2RD (☎ 01303 850856; **e**: info@eco-coffins.com; **w**: www.eco-coffins.com).

Wood and chipboard coffins

As detailed below, regular coffins can be obtained from some local funeral directors, direct from a couple of manufacturers, from carpenters or from nationwide funeral suppliers. Wooden coffins can also be collected from several local authorities, such as Carlisle (see the North West region in Chapter 8).

Coffins from funeral directors

If you want to buy a coffin that is not a biodegradable or cardboard make, your cheapest option may be to approach one of the recommended funeral directors in your local region, as listed in Chapter 7. For instance, UK funeral directors who are prepared to sell their cheapest fully-fitted coffin (fitted with handles and lining) for £90 or under are as follows:

• £65 in Bolton: from Fulton Funeral Directors (☎ 01204 694999). Free local delivery.

• £75 in Faringdon: from G. & L, Evans (☎ 01367 242762). Local delivery £10.

• £80 in Hatfield: from J. J. Burgess & Sons (☎ 01707 262122). Local delivery £35.

• £90 in Birmingham: from Jonathan Walker Ltd (☎ 0121 693 0204). Delivery locally free.

Also, not fully-fitted, but good value:

• £60 in London: from Roger Gillman of J. E. Gillman & Sons (☎ 020 86721557), a chipboard-based lightly veneered coffin, 'without handles or fancy lining, just cremfilm, using wood from managed sustained-yield forests.' Delivery free within five miles of their premises in Tooting, London SW17.

In 2003, the Natural Death Centre circulated a questionnaire to all UK funeral directors. Of the 104 (excluding branches of the same firm) who deigned to reply – mostly the small independent firms – all except five were prepared to sell just a coffin, without other services, at prices ranging from £65 to £375 for the cheapest fully-fitted coffin. The resultant average price for a coffin was £149.60. This is a big improvement since the Centre's 1993 survey, which found a mere 45 funeral directors (53 per cent of all respondents) willing to sell just coffins.

Funeral directors who will supply a coffin to anywhere in the UK are listed under Funeral Suppliers below.

Coffins direct from manufacturers

The following are the cheapest wooden coffins available from those coffin manufacturers who are prepared to deliver directly to a member of the public. Most funeral suppliers remain unwilling to sell directly to the public, often because they are frightened that their main customers, the funeral directors, will object. Of the following brave few who will do so, surprisingly, their prices to the public tend to be higher than those charged by the funeral directors above. The firms with the cheapest coffins are listed first.

• £88.12 for a chipboard oak veneer coffin, fully-fitted with lining, handles and nameplate. Next day delivery £26 nationally. From E. C. Hodge (MF) Ltd, factory at New Drove, Off Weasenham Lane, Wisbech, Cambridgeshire PE13 2RZ (☎ 01945 587477; f: 01945 466063); or Norton Road, Stevenage, Hertfordshire SG1 2BB (☎ 01438 357341). They can also supply a solid oak coffin for £188, and pet caskets with name plates. 'We have over 100 coffins in stock for next day delivery' (Ted Hodge).

• £120 for an 'oak foil' standard coffin, fitted and lined, for cremation. Overnight delivery locally £20; nationally £50. From Vic Fearn & Co Ltd, Crabtree Mill, Hempshill Lane, Bulwell, Nottingham ND6 8PF (☎ 01159 771571; f: 01159 771571); and at Newbarn Farm, Calbourne, Isle of Wight PO30 4JA (☎/f: 01983 531734). 'All our coffins are of superior quality. We sell all funeral items. We refuse no one. Everything we sell is environmentally friendly' (D. G. Crampton).

• £160 for a fully-fitted coffin suitable for burial or cremation – wood veneer on chipboard with a taffeta lining, plastic handles and nameplate. Delivery locally free (not delivered nationally). From Henry Smith (Wandsworth) Ltd, 192-194 Garratt Lane, Wandsworth, London SW18 4ED (☎ 020 8874 7622/3). Their solid oak Wandle coffin with solid brass fittings costs £780. 'We are a small family firm and we pride ourselves on our ability to manufacture to any specification very quickly' (John C. Smith, director).

• £354 for an oak finish coffin with lining, handles and nameplate. Delivery £25 within M25, £85 nationally. From F. A. Albin & Sons Ltd, 52 Culling Road, Rotherhithe, London SE16 2TN (☎ 020 7237 3637; f: 020 7252 3205). Their top price coffins include the Winchester solid bronze casket for £4,208. 'We are now 220 years old. We sell everything to the trade and to the public. Owned by the family, we accept no pressure [from funeral directors]' (B. Albin).

Coffins from carpenters

Another way of obtaining a coffin, but not normally as cheaply, is simply to ask a local carpenter or to pick one at random from your local Yellow Pages.

The following carpenters have been in touch with the Natural Death Centre, indicating a willingness to provide a coffin:

• From £200 for a coffin made to order from the 'very flexible' Traditional Funeral Company, 212 Warwick Road, Park Hill, Birmingham B11 2NB (☎ 0121 773 9296). Call for more information.

• Artistic coffins made to order from several hundred to several thousand pounds, or less expensive self-assembly (flatpack) pine coffins for about £200, from Bryan Frisby, Sally Clarke and Neil Trinder, Burrowlee House, Broughton Road, Sheffield S6 2AS (☎ 0114 2852459 or 2853875).

Specialist coffins

Coffins for babies and children

• Compakta (☎ 01162 333566 or see above for more contact details) sell tiny white-finished cardboard 8ins containers for foetal remains for £1.74 each (about £2.50 with postage).

• Children's caskets and baby cribs can be obtained from Wells Caskets, Unit 1B, Little Dale Workshops, Colliers Green, Kent TN17 2LS (☎ 01580 212040). They range in price from £10.50 to £137.55, plus £13.50 for next day delivery.

• The SAWD Partnership (☎ 01795 472262, or see above for more contact details) make smaller bamboo coffins for babies and children cost from £40.

• The Somerset Willow Company (☎ 01278 424003, or see above for more contact details) have a baby's crib casket for £66 or a child's casket from £205 to £293 (not incl. delivery).

Coffins as furniture

• Heaven on Earth (☎ 0117 926 4999 or see full contact details above) sells coffins that can be used as bookcases from £395, made as furniture with mitred joints; and shelves to go inside, with removable brass brackets, for £8 each.

• Lisette de Roche (164 Westbourne Grove, London W11 2RW, ☎ 020 7221 8742) can provide coffins for initial uses as various pieces of furniture; as a wardrobe, bookcase or even a cocktail cabinet, for example, at prices from £500.

• The Scottish Vernacular Furniture Company (The Star Cottage Workshops, Dunglass Common, Cockburnspath, Berwickshire TD13 5YL, ☎ 01368 830583) design and manufacture coffins to be used beforehand as bookcases, linen presses, wardrobes and long-case clocks. Prices start from £390, incl. handles and a biodegradable lining. Delivery costs £35.

Reusable coffins

It is now possible to rent a decorous outer wooden coffin for the funeral service, with only the cardboard inner coffin cremated (normally a thin piece of pine or plywood is placed under the deceased to keep the cardboard rigid). A variety of 'outer coffins' are available, at Carlisle Crematorium, for example, they have available for cremations the reusable Carlisle Coffin with an inner Compakta cardboard coffin – only the inner coffin, which slides out, is cremated.

• Celtic Caskets in Staffordshire (☎ 07949 122484) offers free use of a reusable hardwood 'Cocoon' outer coffin for cremations using their funeral directing service. Four other UK funeral directors also offer this facility.

• Coffin Covers Ltd (470 Great Horton Road, Bradford, West Yorkshire BD7 3HR, ☎ 01274 571021) offers a reusable 'external protective and decorative shell' with a cardboard coffin inside. The cost of the cardboard inner coffin (which could be used separately) is £50 plus packaging, VAT and delivery. The funeral director would usually include the cost of the hire of the Coffin Cover in their fees; those not wishing to use a funeral director should contact the company for details of hire charges and arrangements within their area.

Painted coffins

• Ros Clarke (18 The Avenue, Belper, Derbyshire DE56 1WB ☎ 01773 820870) will handpaint a cardboard coffin to a client's design for £50 to £100. She needs at least five days.

• Heaven on Earth (☎ 0117 926 4999) will attractively stencil a cardboard coffin for £75, plus £55 for the coffin. Or, from £275 they sell a medium density Fibreboard coffin painted with water-based paints and decorated.

• Amy Douglas will paint a beautiful mural on a cardboard coffin from £150 per day, depending on the design (☎ 01273 623527).

• Susan Kinnear (37 Rainbow Street, London SE5 7TB, ☎ 020 7703 5830) handpaints coffins from £200 – she can supply the coffin.

• Creative Cardboard Coffins in Kent (☎ 01233 860153) will paint abstract/ floral designs in a 'contemporary Impressionist' style on a cardboard coffin from £200 plus the price of the coffin.

• Carol Aston (The Lodge, Roveries Hall, Bishops Castle, Shropshire SY9 5HQ, ☎ 01588 638444 or mobile 0781 502 8742) is a decorative artist who handpaints coffins using water-based paints and varnishes suitable for crema- tion (check with the crematorium), or for green or traditional burial. She is happy to assist with a design or work to a client's own preferences. She specialises in faux marble and verdigris, but takes commissions for religious and secular symbols, football and racing colours, Celtic knotwork, poetry, calligraphy and animal prints. Her prices start from £195 for cardboard coffins to £375 for regular coffins (incl. coffin and handles, plus £30-£100 for the lining). Delivery about £50 for London. Three working days minimum are required, more for extensive artwork.

• Lisette de Roche (164 Westbourne Grove, London W11 2RW, ☎ 020 7221 8742) accepts independent commissions from members of the public. She can paint a coffin within ten days. You can, if you wish, provide her with a cardboard or regular coffin to paint. Alternatively, her prices (including a coffin) start from £250 for a children's coffin, or from £450 for an adult's coffin. Personal commissions cost from £650.

• Vic Fearn coffin manufacturers (☎ Nottingham 01159 771571; or Isle of Wight 01983 531734 or see 'Wood and chipboard coffins' above for their full contact details) do an artist-designed coffin made from recycled pallets for about £500, and artist-painted coffins using water-based paints suitable for cremation from £350 to £800 depending on the choice of design. Some of their coffins are designed by Lisette de Roche (see above).

Shrouds, body bags and burial stretchers

Shrouds

• Carlisle Cemetery Office (☎ 01228 625310 or see the North West region in Chapter 6 for full contact details) sell their own design of woollen burial shroud complete with board and ropes for £132 (delivery extra).

• Heaven on Earth (☎ 0117 926 4999 or see full contact details above) have shrouds or robes in cotton, Indian wool or silk from £5 to £15 or more (delivery locally free).

• Su Colman (PO Box 234, Keighley BD21 5XH, ☎ 0845 458 1001; f: 0845 458 1003; e: su.c@sammaajiva.com) hand weaves fabrics from natural fibres suitable for garments or burial cloths for green funerals. Prices from £25 per square metre.

Body bags

The simplest way to obtain a body bag might be to approach an undertaker local to you listed in Chapter 7. Alternatively, a body bag can be bought from the following (make sure you get a body bag that is long enough for the body)

• Heavy duty body bags 7ft 5ins long (ex-Gulf War), semi-opaque and zipped along three sides, are available for £7 (delivery extra) from RBT (☎ 020 8684 1667, ask for Bob or Steve).

• Thorley Smith (Britannia Mill, Clayton Street, Wigan WN3 4DG, ☎ 01942 243331; f: 01942 821592; e: sales@thorleysmith.com; w: www.thorleysmith .com) sell zipped body bags for £8.51, or unzipped biodegradable ones for £9.89 to £8.83. They also sell clear film bags for £8.46. All prices are subject to delivery charges with a minimum charge of £6.26.

• Celtic Caskets (☎ 07949 122484, or see in 'Cardboard coffins for more contact details) sell a body bag for £12 (including delivery).

• Heaven on Earth (☎ 0117 926 4999 or see full contact details above) sell a cremation body bag for £12 (including delivery); or a heavier biodegradable body bag for burials for £15 (delivery extra).

• Gillman Funeral Service (☎ 020 8672 1557 or see under Greater London in Chapter 7 for full contact details) sell heavy gauge white plastic bags, 7ft 3ins x 34ins with full length zip for £18 and biodegradable body bags for £22.

• Peace Funerals (☎ 0114 2530505 or 08457 697822 or see under Sheffield in the North West region in Chapter 7 for full contact details) sell a biodegradable body bag with board from £20.

Burial stretchers

• A biodegradable hessian burial stretcher which can be carried by four or eight people, and incorporates a fluid-proof inner liner and a 'modesty cover' which rolls out from one end, is available for £49.95 incl. next day delivery, from Engrefco, Alterchrome House, Murray Road, Orpington, Kent, BR5 3QY (☎ 0800 0188877).

• Heaven on Earth in Bristol (☎ 0117 926 4999 or see full contact details above) say they have wicker makers who could make a wicker stretcher for £150 or less.

Other coffin equipment

Coffin handles

• Thorley Smith (☎ 01942 243331 or see full contact details above) supply handles ranging in price from £2.67 for a plastic set to £10.97 for a metal set and upwards. Delivery is extra.

• Heaven on Earth (☎ 0117 926 4999 or see full contact details above) sell hemp rope handles at £8 each (delivery locally free).

• Celtic Caskets (☎ 07949 122484 or see full contact details above) sell biodegradable cotton webbing handles from £5 for the set, or £10 for 'integrated cotton handles cum lowering webbing'. A set of six cremation-friendly handles, a name plate, six wreath holders and a crucifix costs £20, in brass or chrome effect (delivery extra).

Linings for coffins

A coffin could be lined with something naturally absorbent such as hay, torn up newspaper, an old sheet or clothing, or use a biodegradable body bag.

• Thorley Smith (☎ 01942 243331 or see full contact details above) supply patented plastic coffin liners, which can be used as cremfilm, from about £2 each, including a pillow, delivery extra.

• Heaven on Earth (☎ 0117 926 4999 or see full contact details above) supply coffin linings from £35 (or cremfilm for £1.50 a metre, about £4 per coffin) plus delivery.

• SAWD Partnership (☎ 01795 472262; w: www.bamboocoffins.cjb.net) who supply the Bamboo Eco-coffin (see above) sell what seems to be the cheapest non-plastic liner available at the moment. From them, a 'totally waterproof' and 'completely biodegradable' (tests indicate within nine months of burial), 100 per cent cotton liner costs £19.50 incl. VAT and p&p.

Coffin drapes

Heaven on Earth (☎ 0117 926 4999 or see full contact details above) have batik throws, to cover a coffin, costing from £118 (delivery locally free).

Lowering webbing

Heaven on Earth (☎ 0117 926 4999) sell lowering webbing from £15. Furniture webbing from a shop such as John Lewis (☎ 020 7629 7711) seems to work well too – 95p per metre.

Urns

• Heaven on Earth in Bristol (☎ 0117 926 4999 or see full contact details above) sell urns for ashes, plain or lacquered, from £5 upwards.

• Gemma Nesbitt (Wytherston, Powerstock, Bridport, Dorset DT6 3TQ, ☎ 01308 485 211; f: 01308 485 273) who designed the willow coffin (see above), also designs little clay pots for ashes, in the shape of beehives or mud-huts. These can be commissioned in white or in various colours from Tatina Mallinson (67 Camberwell Grove, London SE5 8JE, ☎ 020 7703 8080; f: 020 7703 6550; e: wjwm@btinternet.com), a potter and sculptor, who makes little pots from £8 or big ones for about £30.

• E. C. Hodge (MF) Ltd (☎ Wisbech 01945 587477 or Stevenage 01438 357341, or see full contact details in 'Coffins from manufacturers' above) supply a solid oak casket for ashes from £12.

• ARKA (☎ 01273 684151, or see full contact details above), makers of the ecopod, have an Acorn Urn made of the same material for £25 incl. delivery.

• Tim Hurn, a potter in Dorset (Home Farm House, Bettiscombe, Bridport, Dorset DT6 5NU, ☎ 01308 868171) makes funerary jars to commission – clay wood-fired stoneware jars for remains – from £25 upwards.

• SAWD Partnership (☎ 01795 472262, or see full contact details above) have bamboo urns for ashes which cost £30.

• Carol Aston (☎ 01588 672199 or see full contact details above) sells ashes caskets handpainted to her own or the client's design, from £45 (pet ashes caskets from £35). Delivery extra.

• Rupert Blamire (Ground Floor Unit, Bannerman Buildings, Bannerman Road, Bristol BS5 0RR, ☎ 01179 39 3914) has designed a striking neoclassical three-foot-high lidded ceramic urn, made of red terracotta clay from Staffordshire. They can be used for housing the ashes or simply as garden ornaments. The 3ft urn costs £150, a 4ft model is available for £325. Blamire will deliver the urn for about £50 locally.

Transport

If you are arranging a funeral yourselves and providing your own transport, see 'Body, transport' in the Index for advice and make sure that the coffin will fit your vehicle (see the advice in Chapter 4 about particular makes of estate car). If you need to pay for transport, a helpful local funeral director may well be as cheap as a local hire firm. Those who replied to our questionnaire were no doubt the more enlightened members of the profession; almost all of these would supply just transport for the body or coffin without other services – only three refused. The prices varied greatly, ranging from £35 for an estate car to £214 for a hearse and two bearers; one offered a mileage charge of 50p per mile. All the firms and their prices (if given) are detailed in Chapter 7.

Renting a hearse and bearers

Alternatively, you could try a car hire firm that rents out chauffeur-driven hearses, cars and limousines, such as Green's Carriage Masters (☎ 020 8692 9200; e: info@greens.co.uk) who charge from £85 for a choice of hearses including a Daimler, minimum 2 hrs, then £22 per hour, within the M25; or O'Brien Car Hire (☎ 020 8311 9591) who charge £85 for a Daimler hearse for two and a quarter hours (£15 per hour thereafter). Their 'full uniform' chauffeurs can also act as bearers for £10, and extra bearers are available at £25 each. A Daimler limousine is available for £65 for two hours (£15 per hour thereafter). You could find out the phone numbers of other such firms from the main journal in which they tend to advertise, the Funeral Service Journal (☎ 0113 2841177; e: info@fsj.co.uk). You can hire an 11-seater stretch limousine for the mourners from Rodeo Drive Limousines (☎ 020 8438 9577) for £195 for three hours.

Wheel biers

Those readers who are so 'green' that they cannot accept the idea of motor vehicles of any kind being used to transport the body, could try asking a local church or cemetery if they can lend or rent, with a suitable deposit, a wheel bier. For instance, Maldon Cemetery (see under East Anglia in Chapter 8) does have such a wheel bier.

Motorcycle funeral

Motorcycle Funerals, 89 Belvoir Road, Coalville, Leicestershire LE67 3PH (☎ 01530 834616, m: 07799 712682; e: info@motorcyclefunerals.com; w: www.motorcyclefunerals.com). The coffin is transported in a roofed motorcycle sidecar hearse. Prior to the funeral, friends and family can join in a commemorative ride out to the deceased's favourite café or run. Costs £220 within the East Midlands area; further afield £220 plus £1 per mile from Coalville, Leics, to the end of the funeral. For London add 20 per cent, for Manchester 10 per cent. Paul is an ordained church minister with 15 years experience of funerals and helping the bereaved. His wife, Marian, is a trained counsellor. 'We are are respectful of all traditions, requests, customs and open to unusual requests' (Paul Sinclair, 'the Revving Rev').

Motorbike Funerals of Essex Lodge, 26 East Street, Pritlewell, Essex SS2 6LH (☎ 01702 618315) offer Harley-Davidson bike-drawn hearses for hire, with driver, from £575.

Horse-drawn funeral

More feasible, more expensive and more dashing is to arrange for a horse-drawn hearse (which can be hired by the family direct, the use of a funeral director is not obligatory). A number of firms offer such vehicles, complete with black horses: Gibson Carriage Masters (from £500 in the London area and they also have branches in Huntingdon, Nottingham, Bolton and Blackburn, ☎ 01487 830045); Claytons Carriage Masters (from £500, based in Gayton, Northampton, ☎ 01327 830181); Classic Carriages (from £450, based in London,

Kingston and Runcorn, ☎ 0800 1975125); Foxdell Carriages (from £450 locally to £650 for the London area, based near Bromsgrove, Worcestershire, ☎ 01527 873865); Mews Carriages (from £550 for the London area, based in Hitchin, Hertfordshire, ☎ 01438 871622); Peter Taylor (from £650, a funeral director with various branches in East Anglia, ☎ 01603 760787); Chalfont Carriage Company (from £550, based in Chalfont St Giles, Bucks, ☎ 01494 872 304).

Mole Valley Green Burial Ground (☎ 01769 574512) in South Molton, North Devon (see the South West region in Chapter 6) offers the use of a horse and cart for funerals, free within their site and for £5 to £10 an hour elsewhere.

Trains and canal boats

Peace Funerals (☎ 0114 2530505) can help you to arrange a burial in a woodland burial ground at Alfreton in Derbyshire, with arrival there by steam train from the Midland Railway Centre at Ripley in Derbyshire.

The Calder and Hebble Navigation Society took one of their departed members, who lived in Calderdale, on the canal boat 'The Savile' to the crematorium, and were rumoured to be planning to make this a public service, with room on board for a dozen mourners and the coffin. Their phone number is ex-directory, however.

The woodland burial ground in Retford, Nottinghamshire (Ron Clark, Bassetlaw District Council, ☎ 01909 533487, or see the East Midlands region in Chapter 6) has boats passing the site along the Chesterfield canal. It could probably be arranged for a coffin to be delivered by boat.

Cold storage

Sixty-nine per cent of our progressive respondents were prepared to supply cold storage facilities to families who were not using the funeral director's other services. This could be reassuring for those, for instance, who have to wait for relatives arriving from abroad for the funeral. Some of the other funeral directors did not have cold storage facilities, using embalming instead. The price asked for cold storage ranged from no charge at all (in ten instances) to £60 per day, with an average price of £17.25 per day. All the firms and their prices are detailed in Chapter 7.

Embalming

Embalming, which is normally quite unnecessary, involves draining blood from the body, and replacing it with formaldehyde (plus a pinkish dye such as safranine) pumped in under pressure, which has a hardening and disinfecting effect. 'The cheeks become fuller and firmer, and the eyeballs and surrounding skin become harder,' writes Robert Wilkins in 'The Fireside Book of Death'. He describes how the mouth is prevented from hanging open, sometimes by a needle passed from the lower lip up through the nostril, and how the abdomen is suctioned clean. Unlike Egyptian embalmers, modern embalming aims only for a short-term preserving effect. The funeral trade argues that embalming helps prevent the body smelling and removes some of the trauma from the face. As one of our contacts put it: 'I would certainly look better after death pumped full of pink dye, with the lines on my face smoothed away.' Embalming will probably not appeal to those who dislike make-up for the living face; or to those who want the body to be handled only by close family; or to those who want to allow the body to look very evidently dead.

'Do you embalm the deceased as a matter of course or on request?' we asked the funeral directors in our questionnaire. Several firms replied 'Yes, we do embalm as a matter of course', some adding the proviso 'unless asked not to' – so it is important to make your wishes clear in this regard. The majority claimed only to embalm on request, but often again with provisos such as: 'unless the body is to be exported or conveyed long distance' or 'unless the family wishes to view the body'. One firm wrote: 'We embalm when we consider it necessary for hygienic reasons and for viewing purposes. If there is a risk of infection, we will insist on it for our own staff's sake.' At which point, the client may need to insist on a change of funeral directors. Indeed, embalming is not allowed for sea burial or for burial in most natural burial grounds.

Using a funeral director

It is hard to find an independent funeral director nowadays – many of the big firms hide behind the name of the small firm they have taken over, and often it takes some persistence to find this out. Many independent firms are members of SAIF, the Society of Allied and Independent Funeral Directors, so look out for their emblem. With other firms, the firm's parent company is likely to be Dignity (UK) Ltd, which used to be American-owned and called SCI, and which has acquired more than 500 funeral businesses around the UK and 21 crematoria, or the Co-op, which handled approximately 87,000 funerals last year, or the Alderwoods Group, formerly the Loewen Group, another of North American origin.

But a bigger problem in choosing a funeral director is that, in the first shock of a relative dying, 97 per cent of people, according to an Office of Fair Trading investigation, sign up with the very first funeral director they contact. Arranging a funeral is not like buying any other consumer service, and people need to be aware that this could lay them open to exploitation, even if most funeral directors are in fact well-meaning and dedicated people. Do not accept, for instance, a funeral director who just happens to be at the hospital, who may have a private 'arrangement' with staff. Ask the staff for a full list of local firms if they have one. Our advice is that you get a friend who is not so emotionally involved to phone around for you and to report back to you when a funeral director has been located who meets your criteria. Do not be wary of looking outside your area – any extra mileage charge is likely to be a small element of the final bill.

It is perhaps worth re-emphasising at this point that, although the Natural Death Centre is campaigning for improvements in the funeral trade, and advocates that families organise funerals themselves wherever possible, it acknowledges that funerals in the UK are as cheap or cheaper than most countries in Europe; they are cheap compared with what the average family is prepared to spend on a wedding; and they are carried out in the main by sensitive professionals doing a difficult and stressful job which most people would not have the courage to do.

All members of funeral associations are supposed to offer a basic funeral (eg the National Association of Funeral Directors now calls theirs 'The Simple Funeral Service'), but this needs asking for by name. In response to our questionnaire, a basic funeral costs from £400 to £1,250, with an average of £753 – an increase of 28.8 per cent on the £585 figure for 2000. This seems a remarkable jump compared to an increase of only 9 per cent in the average coffin price over the same period. To this £753, which represents the funeral director's charges, need to be added the so-called 'disbursements' paid out on behalf of the client by the funeral director: the cremation fee (averaging £284), doctors' fees (£101) and minister's fee (normally £90), an average extra total for disbursements of £465 (assuming it is a cremation). Thus the average complete cost for a basic funeral is currently £1,218 with cremation or £1,590 with a burial. However, it should be noted that there are wide regional variations, especially where the cost of a burial plot is concerned.

The best value basic funeral for those in the London area, for instance, seems to be that offered by J. F. Shackleton & Sons (see the Greater London region in Chapter 7), costing £550. Their cheapest fully-fitted coffin costs only £100.

For those wanting no involvement in the funeral at all, not even to know which crematorium was used, Rowland Brothers (see the Greater London region in Chapter 7) offer what they call a 'disposal service' for £400 (disbursements extra). Ken Gregory & Sons Ltd have a 'direct cremation' for £395 (disbursements extra); and J. E. Gillman & Sons Ltd, also in London, offer a similar funeral, more tactfully entitled a 'Direct Transfer Service', for £385 (disbursements extra).

If you are genuinely hard-up, many funeral directors are kind-hearted enough to make allowances and will not turn you away. One of our contacts offered a funeral director £400 cash on the spot (the most he could afford) for a £795 funeral and was accepted. The highly commendable and distinctive Islamic funeral service offered by Haji Taslim (see the London region in the Good Funeral Guide), based at the East London Mosque – 95 per cent of their clients are from the Muslim community – offers free burial to the indigent, besides being prepared to give cheap or free help of various kinds to those planning their own funeral.

If you need to complain about a funeral director, you can report the matter to their trade association, if they have one – normally either the National Association of Funeral Directors, the Funeral Standards Council or the Society of Allied and Independent Funeral Directors (see the Resources chapter for their addresses). In practice, you may get more satisfaction by going to your local county court (under 'C' in the phone book) or even to the local media. Or it may be a matter that could be reported to the Trading Standards Officer at your local council. The Natural Death Centre would be interested in receiving any brief written accounts that could help warn others – and in receiving positive feedback about funeral professionals whom you have found to be unusually helpful.

Less expensive funerals for council residents

A very simple but useful scheme has been started by the local authorities in Crewe ('The Local Funeral', ☎ 01270 212643; w: www.crewe.nantwich. gov.uk/worksservices) and in Nottingham ('The Nottingham Funeral', ☎ 0115 915 2340). It deserves copying by other councils nationwide. The councils in these cities provide the public with information on the cheapest funeral offered by a funeral director in their area plus a list of the other funeral directors. Nottingham pioneered this in 1996 and as a result, the cheapest funeral price has dropped from £1,000 to £799 – a price that includes a following car and disbursements. The winning funeral director is obliged to take out a certain number of advertisements about the scheme (which is guaranteed for two years, in the second year going up merely by the rate of inflation) and the council also advertises it.

Other councils have made similar agreements with local funeral directors for a special relatively inexpensive funeral package for local residents, but without perhaps the same exclusive focus on price. It may be worthwhile phoning your local council's cemeteries department (eg for Brent, this would mean looking under 'B' for Brent and then under 'Cemeteries' within the list of Brent's services) and asking if your council has made such an agreement (note that the requirement is normally that the deceased should have lived in the borough, not the person organising the funeral, but check this). Often, however, the prices are not that good. In London, one funeral director provided a service for certain boroughs and the cost was greater than that for the firm's basic funeral, whether for residents or non-residents, although including only a hearse and not the following limousine. **Bury** Metropolitan Borough Council has an arrangement with Hamers Funeral Directors (☎ 0161 797 7133) offering a funeral for £350 (disbursements extra – burial costs an extra £720). In **Cardiff**, the local authority funeral service provider is Rumney Funeral Services (☎ 029 207 97516), who charge £385 (disbursements extra). An inexpensive service is offered by the **St Helens** council which has an agreement with the local Co-op (☎ 01744 23675) whereby cremation costs £663 and burial costs £674, both prices including disbursements. In **Stockport**, the 'Civic Funeral Service' is provided for the council by the United North West Co-operative Society (☎ 0161 432 0818). They charge £841 for a cremation (including disbursements); and £1,526 for burial in a new grave (again including disbursements). In **Wigan**, the borough council uses the services of local funeral directors, Edwards Funeral Directors (☎ 01942 821 215) and L. Heyes Funeral Service (☎ 01942 261936) to offer cremation for £846 (including disbursements) and burial for £809 (including disbursements). The **Hounslow** Council also has a similar arrangement for a 'Hounslow Community Funeral Service' with local funeral directors: The CRS Co-op (☎ 020 8570 4741) and Frederick Paine (☎ 020 8994 0056) – the price being £650 (disbursements extra).

Free funerals

Approximately 8 per cent of the 623,000 deaths per annum in the UK result in claims to the government's Social Fund for help with funeral expenses. Up to £700 for the funeral is available from the government (with extra money for 'disbursements' – such as a grave, burial costs, the cremation fee, doctors' certificates and removing a pacemaker; for transporting a body more than 50 miles; and to pay for a return journey for a responsible person who is either arranging or attending the funeral). Claims must be made before or within three months of the funeral and can sometimes be paid out before the funeral takes place, if the invoice is submitted in time. Phone your local Benefits Agency office (under 'Benefits Agency' or 'Social Security' in the phone book) and ask for form SF200. Details and leaflets (but not the claim form) can be obtained from the Benefits Agency Public Enquiry Office (☎ 0845 604 0210; **w**: www.dss.gov.uk).

The deceased must have been ordinarily resident in the UK at the time of death, although the funeral can in specified circumstances take place anywhere within the European Economic Area. Recent research by a Friendly Society showed that a third of the population thinks the state will automatically help with the cost of funerals, even if benefits are not being received. It is not so. The person organising the funeral must be on Income Support, income-based Jobseeker's Allowance, Family Credit, Housing Benefit, Council Tax Benefit or Disability Working Allowance, although the person's money over £500 (£1,000 if 60 or over) will be used towards the costs. Any money in the estate of the deceased will go towards the costs, as will contributions from relatives, clients or charities. The cheque is usually made out to the funeral directors, not the claimant, but is sent to the claimant to give to them. If the person arranging the funeral is a war widow, or widower, help may be available from the War Pensions Agency, Norcross, Blackpool FY5 3WP (☎ 0800 169 22 77).

Since 1997 a greater attempt has also been made to find a non-estranged partner or relative who could afford to pay for the funeral. As the government puts it, in complex double negatives: 'Where there is no surviving partner, and where a parent, son or daughter of the deceased exists, and neither they nor their partner are in receipt of a qualifying benefit, it will be considered unreasonable for the person in receipt of the income-related benefit to take responsibility for the funeral expenses.'

A claim from an otherwise eligible single parent for the funeral of a child will fail if the absent parent lives abroad or has savings.

The Benefits Agency (see leaflet NP45, 'A Guide to Bereavement Benefits') may make a lump-sum Bereavement Payment of £2,000 to a husband or wife if their deceased partner paid enough National Insurance contributions (or their death was caused by their job), and was not getting retirement pension, or if the widow or widower is under state pension age.

The local authority is obliged (under the Public Health – Control of Disease – Act 1984 Part III Disposal of Dead Bodies Section 46) to arrange for the disposal of the body where 'no suitable arrangements have been made'. A. C. T. Connolly (of 26 Broadfields Avenue, Winchmore Hill, London N21 1AD) decided to test this Act by refusing to arrange for the disposal of a relative's body (which was in the mortuary at the local hospital). He resisted 'wrongful' pressure from the registrar of deaths to take various forms before he would register the death. Finally, a helpful official in the council's Social Services department agreed to arrange the funeral and to register the death in the name of the council, with the Connolly family reimbursing the council for the £315 cost. The family were notified in advance of the time for the service and the committal at the crematorium. Mr Connolly concludes: 'It is a legally imposed duty on local authorities to carry out this public health function *no matter what the financial position of the bereaved might be*. Yet very few people indeed know of this local authority option.'

In one instance, a local authority took control of a house and its contents in order to recover the cost of a funeral it had provided. The nearest relative was prevented from going into the house to find suitable clothes with which to dress the body. The case was referred by a law centre to John Bradfield, author of 'Green Burial', who is insisting that the local authority be taken to court to prove that relatives cannot be treated in this insensitive way.

Similarly, the ombudsman has issued a report criticising a local authority which tried to define the bodies of old people from private nursing homes as 'industrial waste' (with reference to the 1984 Act mentioned above).

Bereavement benefits

The Benefits Agency (see leaflet NP45, 'A Guide to Bereavement Benefits') may make a lump-sum Bereavement Payment of £2,000 to a husband or wife if their deceased partner paid enough National Insurance contributions (or their death was caused by their job), and was not getting retirement pension, or if the widow or widower is under state pension age. From April 2003, eligible relatives have up to 12 months to claim.

The same leaflet gives details of the Bereavement Allowance, which you may be able to get if you were aged 45 or over when your husband or wife died. The amount depends on your age and the relevant National Insurance contributions and is payable for a maximum of 52 weeks. To claim this, you need form BB1 and you should make the claim as soon as possible but within three months of the death to qualify for the full 52 weeks of the allowance.

Organ and body donation

Ernest Morgan quotes a poetic statement by Robert Test in favour of organ donation:

Give my sight to the man who has never seen a sunrise

The day will come when my body will lie upon a white sheet tucked neatly under the four corners of a mattress located in a hospital busily occupied with the living and the dying. At a certain moment, a doctor will determine that my brain has ceased to function and that, to all intents and purposes, my life has stopped.

When that happens, do not attempt to install artificial life into my body by the use of a machine and don't call this my deathbed. Let it be called the Bed of Life, and let my body be taken from it to help others lead fuller lives.

Give my sight to the man who has never seen a sunrise, a baby's face or love in the eyes of a woman. Give my heart to the person whose own heart has caused nothing but endless days of pain. Give my blood to the teenager who was pulled from the wreckage of his car, so that he may live to see his grandchildren play. Give my kidneys to a person who depends upon a machine to exist from week to week. Take my bones, every muscle, every fibre and nerve in my body and find a way to make a crippled child walk. Explore every corner of my brain. Take my cells, if necessary, and let them grow so that, someday, a speechless boy will shout at the crack of a bat or a deaf girl will hear the sound of rain against her window.

Burn what is left of me and scatter the ashes to the winds to help the flowers grow.

If you must bury something, let it be my faults, my weaknesses and all my prejudice against my fellow man. Give my sins to the devil. Give my soul to God.

If, by chance, you wish to remember me, do it with a kind deed or word to someone who needs you. If you do all I have asked, I will live forever.

Dealing Creatively with Death *by Ernest Morgan.*

If you feel the same way as Ernest Morgan and Robert Test, you need to persuade your next of kin (who will have charge of your body after death), to tell your doctor and your hospital ward and you need to get a donor card from your local library, health centre, doctor or chemist. Or contact the Department of Health Organ Donor Literature Line (☎ 0845 6060400) and ask to be sent a form and a donor card. You can choose to donate any part of the body or only the kidneys, heart, liver, corneas, lungs or pancreas. Animal Aid (The Old Chapel, Bradford Street, Tonbridge, Kent TN9 1AW, ☎ 01732 364 546) issues a Humane Research Donor Card which requests that the body be used for medical and scientific research. Organ donor cards are also available from the British Heart Foundation, Distribution Department, 14 Fitzhardinge St, London W1H 4DH (☎ 020 7935 0185). You can also tick the donor box on forms when getting a passport or a driving licence.

The cornea of the eyes is the only part of the body that can wait up to 12 hours for removal; the rest have to be removed immediately after 'brain-stem' death, with machines keeping the body's blood circulating after death. Normally the body is made available for the funeral within less than 12 hours, once the relatives have agreed. Relatives are still asked for their approval, even if a name is on the register.

It is not possible to guarantee a free disposal of your body by leaving it for dissection by medical students. Only a percentage of bodies are accepted. Medical schools generally accept only bodies that are within easy range of the school, unautopsied after death, relatively whole and non-cancerous – although more and more schools are taking cancerous bodies. To offer to donate your body, contact the professor of anatomy at your local medical hospital or HM Inspector of Anatomy, Department of Health, Wellington House, 133-155 Waterloo Road, London SE1 8UG (☎ 020 7972 4342 – on call 24 hours); or for those in the London area, contact the London Anatomy Office (☎ 020 8846 1216).

People who want to donate their bodies for purposes of medical research only (and not for dissection by medical students) can write to the Tissue Acquisition Unit, Peterborough District Hospital, Thorpe Road, Peterborough PE3 6DA (☎ 01733 874000, ext 5892) for an information pack and consent forms. The hospital makes use of the bodies for drug discovery research. Bodies are returned to the family for a funeral.

Incidentally, whoever is lawfully in possession of the body can donate it to a medical school, even if the person who died made no provision for this, as long as he or she did not object – either in writing or verbally in the presence of two witnesses; and as long as no relative or spouse objects.

Transplants can be authorised as long as there is no reason to believe that the next of kin would object.

Prepaid funerals

It has been estimated that the prepaid funeral market could become as big a business in the UK as it is in the United States, where about three quarters of all funerals are paid for before death. The advantages claimed include: people planning in advance tend to choose simple funerals; it allows for leisurely comparison shopping; in some of the plans you are protected against inflationary price rises; relatives do not suddenly face a big bill at a time of stress; it provides peace of mind for those who are elderly and without relatives; and it would reduce your capital and thus perhaps entitle you to social security benefits you might not otherwise have received.

In our view, the advantages of some of the schemes could be outweighed by the potential disadvantages: prepaid funerals militate against family participation – what if your family decide that they want to make your coffin or to look after your funeral arrangements? Many of the schemes tend to favour the big chains with their assembly-line funerals and to drive the smaller firms to the wall. They encourage TV advertising and other heavy marketing ploys. One firm in the UK went bankrupt. And there has been at least one horror story in the US where the money was simply pocketed, and the prepaid cremation bodies were stacked in the basement of the mortuary, with others buried in mass graves.

A first step is to consider questions such as: what happens if you do not need a funeral in the UK after all, for instance if you die abroad or if your ship sinks at sea? What happens if you die before completing payments? What happens if you need that capital sum in an emergency? Would you not have done better to put the money into a form of investment that you could recover? What happens if the trust or foundation backing your prepaid scheme goes bust or proves fraudulent? What if whoever attends your dying is not aware of your prepaid arrangement? If you want such an arrangement, would it not be more interesting to discuss your funeral wishes with your most trusted next of kin or partner and to pay money into an account or investment controlled jointly with them? Or, probably a less financially attractive option, to put regular premiums into a funeral insurance scheme (or to top up your life insurance) which would pay a lump sum to your relatives on your death, leaving your relatives with more freedom of action? **Axa Life** (☎ 0800 27 21 27), for instance, offers a funeral insurance scheme (Guardian Over 50 Plan) whereby a 70-year-old male, whatever his state of health, pays £20 a month for life, and, if death occurs during the first two years, the premiums plus 50 per cent are paid back; thereafter it pays out £2,325 on death.

Nevertheless, if your circumstances are such that one of the more high profile prepaid plans seems desirable, try to find a scheme which, as well as satisfactorily answering the above questions, is mainly for small independent firms; places at least 90 per cent of the prepaid funds in trust; will not add extras when the time comes; allows a wide range of choice if you move to another part of the country; allows for no-questions-asked cancellation with refund of money *and* interest (less any small administration fees); and returns any unspent money and interest after the funeral. There is no scheme currently available in the UK with all of the above (although the last two points are required by law in some US states).

• The **greenest best buy** for those needing to arrange the funeral in advance might be to set aside sufficient funds in a joint savings account to cover the full costs of one of the less expensive Natural Burial grounds (described in detail in Chapter 6) which have established arrangements for providing a coffin and for collecting the body. These include: Hinton Park in Dorset (☎ 01425 278910), Greenhaven near Rugby (☎ 01788 860604) and Oakfield in Essex (☎ 01255 503456). But be very cautious about handing over money in advance. It is one thing to buy burial rights, and quite another to hand over money years in advance for digging graves and body collection. It might also be worth approaching the charitable A. B. Welfare and Wildlife Trust in North Yorkshire (☎ 01423 530900 or 868121) to see if a special prearrangement can be made for one of their sites. Hinton Park, for instance, charge £1,195 in advance for a coffin and a plot, including the digging and filling of the grave, the planting of a tree, the provision of a small memorial plaque and the collection of the body locally. Collection from London costs an extra £190. Thus for a London family looking for a site within range of the city, some feasible sites are Hinton Park, Greenhaven or Oakfield. The total funeral charges, including collecting the body from London, would be about £1,448.75 for Oakfield; £1,385 for Hinton Park. Greenhaven would prefer to sell just the plot in advance for £300, and recommend that a sum for funeral expenses be deposited in a joint account at a bank or building society. Any of these figures will compare favourably with the plans described below.

• Possibly the least objectionable of the mass market plans is **Golden Charter** (☎ 0800 833800), since it is specifically designed for the small, independent funeral directors and their association SAIF (some of whom are also members of the larger National Association of Funeral Directors). It claims to have over 2,100 participating funeral directors. Golden Charter's cheapest Standard Way plan costs £1,325, which allows £525 towards the costs of disbursements. If disbursements cost more than this at the time of the plan's purchase, the extra sum can be paid then to ensure full future cover. The Woodland Trust is paid to plant a tree for each plan bought.

• Over 120 local funeral directors offer their own prepayment plans, backed by **Funeral Planning Trust** (for referrals to a local firm, ☎ 01508 532 632).

• The next best is probably the **Perfect Assurance Funeral Trust** run by the National Association of Funeral Directors (for details of your local participants, ☎ 0121 709 0019), which allows you to choose any firm, small or large, that offers the scheme and to tailor-make a plan to your requirements. The firm then pays the money into the presumed safety of the Perfect Assurance trust fund.

• The market leader and the first to advertise on TV has been Chosen Heritage, now **Dignity and Chosen Heritage Plan** (☎ 0800 344 6489), whose cheapest Basic Plan funeral costs £1,475 (no specific amount relates to disbursements). If the person dies abroad or ends up not needing their funeral, relatives are refunded. All the plan money goes into a trust fund. It has a 'personal choice' option for those wanting a nonstandard package. The snag is that a large number of its 600 funeral directors are part of the Dignity group, pre-empting choice of a funeral director, except in those areas where they were not represented,

• The Co-op's CRS and CWS divisions (☎ 0800 289120) offers a **Co-operative Funeral Bond** Funeral Plan, the price of which will be determined by a quote from your local Co-op funeral director. On asking for the cheapest basic funeral in the Kentish Town area of London, we were quoted £1,285, for their 'Bronze' plan, including disbursements, for a cremation. Once the full cost is paid, and the plan taken out, there will be no more to pay at the time of the funeral provided that the disbursement element has not risen by more than 40 per cent since the start. Cancellation is 'at the discretion of the society and any repayment is subject to an administration fee'.

Since January 2002, the 'provider' in funeral plan contracts must have authority from the Financial Services Authority. However, most, if not all, providers have opted for the exclusion available in that they have adequate trust fund or insurance measures in place. The Funeral Planning Authority maintains a list of companies who have been accepted as registered providers. The firms mentioned above are all registered with the FPA and consumers should look out for the 'FPA, Funeral Planning Authority Registered' logo. The FPA will provide a list of companies (☎ 01306 740878) and also offers an online search facility (**w**: www.funeralplanningauthority.com/php/providers.php).

Charter for the Bereaved

In recent years, adverse criticism about modern funeral practices has been increasing. The Institute of Burial and Cremation Administration (IBCA) recognised this, and in 1966 produced the Charter for the Bereaved specifically to improve funerals. It recognises the need for natural burial grounds and the right of a family not to use a funeral director, and has already been officially adopted by 83 cemeteries or crematoria with a further 30 'close to signing'.

Crematoria

In our view, the majority of crematoria are to be shunned. Who wants rushed funeral services in buildings which have been described as looking like waiting rooms in airports? Several people of late have suggested a different approach. Rather than, say, a service in church followed by just some of the family going on to a committal at the crematorium, with consequent confusion and disruption for any party or gathering afterwards, both the service and something similar to a committal can be held in the church (or other preferred location), with the coffin borne out towards the end of the service. Then just one member of the family goes with the coffin to the crematorium (or just the vicar goes if a committal service at the crematorium is wanted). Crematoria will prefer this too, suggests funeral director Philip Tomlins in the Funeral Director journal, as they then do not have the difficulty of finding a time that fits with the church service.

Perhaps the ideal crematorium would be a building that was designed to allow the mourners to gather round a high-tech version of a funeral pyre. Tony Walter in *Funerals and How to Improve Them* has suggested a number of slightly less radical design improvements: a coffin visible and central, near floor level throughout the service, which can be touched, kissed, circled round or filed past; a building in which the coffin can be moved by the mourners, possibly by being lowered under the floor; and a building as beautiful and significant as a church, so that the local community will want it for births and marriages too, and which is close to the elements – surrounded by forest and wildlife, rather than manicured lawns and regimented rows of rose bushes.

Of the 132 respondents to our survey of 243 crematoria nationwide, all seem to allow a small group of mourners (by arrangement) to witness the coffin entering the cremator. Eighteen per cent had flexible seating, which might help those wanting a more participatory 'half-moon' seating arrangement, rather than the 'audience facing the front' style – although changing the seating would no doubt mean paying for extra time.

One off-putting aspect of crematoria is the sense of being led along a factory conveyor belt: In – 30 minutes – Out – Next. However 44 excellent crematoria, as highlighted in Chapter 8, break the 30-minute norm and allow 45-minute services; three superb crematoria, the one in Aberystwyth (see Wales, Chapter 8), one in Banbury (see East Midlands, Chapter 8) and the other in Cinderford (see West Midlands, Chapter 8) allow 60 minutes; and most of the other crematoria allow the purchase of extra time at a reduced price.

Contrary to myth, crematoria do burn all the coffins (unless you use one of the newly available reusable coffin outers with a cardboard inner, see earlier in this chapter), and the ashes you get back will definitely be the right ones.

Most crematoria are run by local authorities and have reasonable fees, although these fees are being sharply increased (by as much as 15 per cent in some areas) to finance the cost of new facilities that meet stringent EC anti-pollution requirements. These will cost the average crematorium at least half a million pounds; as a result, some of the local authority operations are beginning to sell out to the larger private firms. For instance, Dignity (UK) Ltd, already owns 21 (8.7 per cent) of the 243 crematoria in the UK, despite the undesirability of a firm that sells funerals in an area also controlling its crematoria.

At present, the cheapest crematorium that met our other criteria for inclusion was Woodvale (Brighton and Hove) Crematorium (£185 for 45 minutes at certain times of day – see the South region in Chapter 8). The most expensive was West Bromwich crematorium (£325 for 20 minutes – see the West Midlands region in Chapter 8). The average price for a cremation was £284, as against £225 in 2000 (an increase of 26 per cent).

Our questionnaire was circulated to all 242 crematoria in the country. Our main interest lay in finding out how helpful they were to people organising a funeral without using a funeral director. Of the 114 who replied, every single one was prepared to deal directly with a family, with no funeral director involvement – whereas in 1993, 8 per cent said that they would deal only with funeral directors. Virtually all said that they would accept a home-made coffin, if it met all the anti-pollution requirements and if everything were done 'in a dignified manner without disturbance to other mourners or to staff' – this is a significant improvement on the figure of 19 per cent in 1993. Cardboard coffins are also now accepted by virtually all UK crematoria – as against a mere 15 per cent in 1993. The majority of the crematoria will accept basket coffins; 53 per cent would accept body bags (if supported on a piece of wood and covered with a drape); 50 per cent would accept a body in a shroud (if the shroud were kept rigid with a piece of wood).

Cemeteries

We wrote to over 800 cemeteries, and of the 230 respondents (some administering several cemeteries) deemed worthy for inclusion in our Good Funeral Guide (Chapter 8) all will accept burial by the family without involving funeral directors. Nearly all will accept a suitable home-made wooden coffin or one of the manufactured cardboard coffins. Seventy-four per cent will accept bamboo or wicker coffins. Fifty-six per cent will accept body bags, if supported on a plank and covered with a drape. Sixty-one per cent will accept shrouds.

Just as house prices vary by region, so too do the rights to a burial plot. The Natural Death Centre's survey found that, including the cost of digging the grave, the prices ranged from £142 at Lon Newydd Cemetery in Anglesey (see Wales in Chapter 8) to £2,500 at Brookwood Cemetery, Woking (see the South region in Chapter 8). The average price for the cheapest individual plot in a cemetery was £656 (incl. digging) as against £524 in 2000 (a 25 per cent increase). Some also charge non-residents either extra, double, treble, or even quadruple the normal price. The most expensive in 2000, Highgate Cemetery in London, will no longer quote a price for publication.

Luton Church Cemetery (see the East Midlands region in Chapter 8) is an example of a cemetery with a pleasantly liberal and enlightened approach to memorials, with virtually any design accepted.

Remember to request, if buying burial rights, that ownership is put in the name of the surviving partner, to ensure the eventual right to be buried together.

Chapter 6

NATURAL BURIAL GROUNDS

All the sites listed in this chapter are natural burial grounds – where burial usually takes place in a biodegradable coffin or shroud, and a tree, shrub or wild flowers are planted as a memorial instead of having a headstone. This is not a Good Funeral Guide to natural burial grounds, since all such sites, open or planned, are listed, even those not belonging to the Association of Natural Burial Grounds (ANBG). Therefore, before buying a plot at any of the sites listed, especially those that are *not* members of the ANBG, make sure to ask for how long the burial rights will last and what will happen to the grave when these run out or when the site is full (where necessary, ask for written proof of claims).

See Chapter 9 for the ANBG Code of Practice and for advice on how to set up a natural burial ground.

Please also write to the Natural Death Centre with your experience of using these sites, covering the following points if at all possible: name of site; a description of the landscape and ecology of the site; what you liked or didn't like about the site and service; the total price you paid and what this included; the name and address of the funeral director used, if any; if you would recommend the site to others and why; your contact details and if you would mind your story (if it is a story) published with or without your name and contact details, etc. If you feel up to writing a longer, perhaps more personal report of your experiences, this would be particularly helpful to others. Our listings are otherwise primarily based on information given to us by the sites themselves – the name of the informant is given (in brackets) wherever possible.

For updates to these listings, please see the Centre's website (www.naturaldeath.org.uk/updates.html) or send six first class stamps to the Centre saying you have the book and asking for the update sheets.

Abbreviations in this chapter are as follows:

[**] = Full Association of Natural Burial Grounds member
[*] = Provisional Association member (not yet open or still being assessed)
(**Name of place**) = Not yet open at the time of going to press
✪✪✪ = Winner of a Natural Death Handbook Award 2004
NAMM = National Association of Memorial Masons

Listings are by region, and then by town or nearest town to the site within the region, except in the Greater London region, which has been further subdivided into areas (see the map overleaf for a visual representation of where the sites are located).

Natural Burial Grounds in the UK and Eire

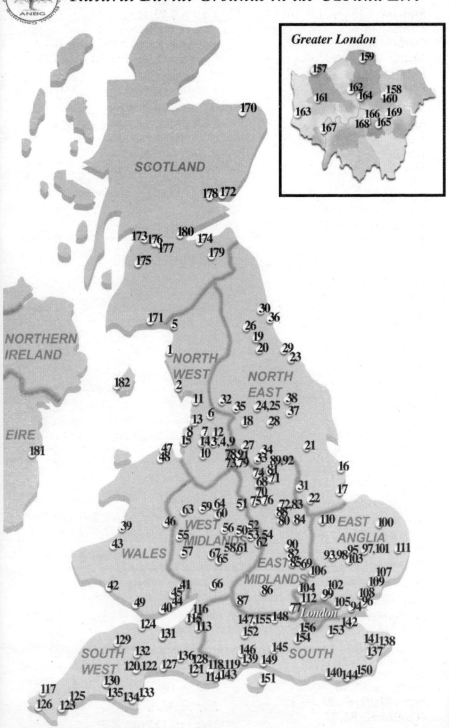

Greater London

The North West
Map ref: 1-15 (pp. 158-161)
Cheshire: **10**
Cumbria: **1, 2, 5**
Greater Manchester: **3, 4, 9**
Lancashire: **6, 7, 11, 12, 13, 14**
Merseyside: **8, 15**

The North East
Map ref: 16-38 (pp. 161-168)
Cleveland: **23**
Durham: **19, 20**
Lincolnshire: **16, 17, 22, 31**
Middlesbrough: **29**
Northumberland: **26, 30**
Yorkshire: **18, 21, 24, 25, 27, 28, 32, 33, 34, 35, 37, 38**
Tyneside: **36**

Wales
Map Ref: 39-49 (pp. 168-170)
Cardiff: **40**
Cardiganshire: **39**
Carmarthenshire: **42, 43**
Denbighshire: **47, 48**
Monmouthshire: **41**
Newport: **44**
Powys: **46**
Swansea: **49**
Torfaen: **45**

West Midlands
Map ref: 50-67 (pp. 171-175)
Birmingham: **50**
Coventry: **53, 54**
Dudley: **56**
Gloucestershire: **66**
Hereford & Worcs: **57, 61, 65, 67**
Shropshire: **55, 59, 63**
Staffordshire: **51, 60, 64**
Warwickshire: **52, 58, 62**

East Midlands
Map ref: 68-92 (pp. 175-181)
Bedfordshire: **69**
Buckinghamshire: **77, 85**
Derbyshire: **68, 70, 73, 74, 75, 76, 78, 79, 91**
Leicestershire: **80, 84, 88**
Northants: **82, 90**
Notts: **71, 72, 81, 83, 89, 92**
Oxfordshire: **86, 87**

East Anglia
Map ref: 93-112 (pp. 181-186)
Cambs: **93, 95, 98, 110**
Essex: **94, 96, 102, 105, 108, 109**
Herts: **99, 104, 106, 112**
Norfolk: **100**
Suffolk: **97, 101, 103, 107, 111**

The South West
Map ref: 113-136 (pp. 186-193)
Bath: **113**
Bristol: **115, 116**
Cornwall: **117, 123, 125, 126**
Devon: **120, 122, 127, 129, 130, 132, 133, 134, 135**
Dorset: **114, 118, 119, 121, 128**
Somerset: **124, 131, 136**

The South
Map ref: 137-156 (pp. 193-198)
Berkshire: **147, 148, 155**
East Sussex: **140, 144, 150**
Hants: **139, 143, 145, 146, 149, 152**
Isle of Wight: **151**
Kent: **137, 138, 141, 142, 153**
Surrey: **154, 156**

Greater London
Map ref: 157-169 (pp. 199-201)
Brent: **157**
Camden: **162**
Ealing: **161**
Enfield: **159**
Hillingdon: **163**
Islington: **164**
Lewisham: **165**
Newham: **158, 160**
Richmond: **167**
Southwark: **166, 168**
Woolwich: **169**

Scotland
Map ref: 170-180 (pp. 201-203)
Aberdeenshire: **170**
Central: **180**
Dumfries & Galloway: **171**
Lothian (Edinburgh): **174**
Tayside: **172, 178**
Scottish Borders: **179**
Strathclyde (incl. Glasgow): **173, 175, 176, 177**

Eire & Northern Ireland
Map ref: 181 (pp. 203)
Dublin: **181**

Isle of Man
Map ref: 182 (pp. 203)

The North West

Comprising Cumbria, Lancashire, Manchester, Sefton, Wirral, Liverpool, Knowsley, St Helens, Wigan, Bolton, Bury, Rochdale, Salford, Trafford, Manchester, Oldham, Tameside, Stockport & Cheshire.

1. **Allerdale, Cumbria**: Meadow burials offered in the Victorian cemeteries: Cockermouth (1856), Maryport (1856) and Harrington Road (1879); run by Allerdale Borough Council, Allerdale House, Workington, Cumbria CA14 3YJ (☎ 01900 326411; **e**: bereavement.services@allerdale.gov.uk). A meadow grave (75 years) costs £325; or £487.50 for non-residents. They accept all types of biodegradable coffin and shrouds. 'Cockermouth is wooded, with multiple specimen trees, a chapel, red squirrels, partridge, kestrels, bats and a stream running through it' (Robert Deacon, Bereavement Services Officer).

2. **Barrow-in-Furness**: Woodland burial ground in Barrow Cemetery, Devonshire Road, Barrow-in-Furness, Cumbria LA14 5PD (☎ 01229 894928); run by Barrow-in-Furness Borough Council. This half-acre site opened in 1998. There is space for 400 graves; eight burials have taken place so far. A grave costs £511 incl. digging and a woodland tree; £621 for non-residents. No memorials permitted. Ashes may be interred for £73.50. A memorial tree on its own costs £67.04. They will accept biodegradable coffins, body bags or shrouds. Families are not allowed to dig or fill the grave. 'The site is adjacent to the existing cemetery woodland' (Chris Pollard).

3. **Blackley**: Woodland burial ground in Blackley Cemetery, Victoria Avenue, Blackley, North Manchester M9 8JP (☎ 0161 740 5359); run by Manchester City Council. Space for 100 graves. A grave costs £890 incl. digging and a woodland tree. They accept biodegradable coffins, and body bags or shrouds. For details contact Paul Burton, Bereavement Services Manager, Longley Lane Depot, Sharston, Manchester M22 4RQ (☎ 0161 718 4811; **f**: 0161 718 4809).

4. **Bury, Greater Manchester**: Woodland burial site within Radcliffe Cemetery, Cemetery Road; run by Bury Metropolitan Borough Council. Contact Mrs Maria Swillo, Bury Cemetery, St Peters Road, Bury BL9 9RL (☎ 0161 762 9506). A grave costs £1,010 incl. digging; £1,410 for non-residents; tree or seedling to be supplied by the family or friends. They will accept biodegradable coffins and shrouds. Family and friends can help with a token amount of filling the grave. 'The site is on the perimeter of the cemetery by a housing estate, with fields on the other side' (Margaret Hall).

5. **[**] Carlisle**: Woodland Burial Site, Carlisle Cemetery Office, Carlisle City Council, Richardson Street, Carlisle, Cumbria CA2 6AL (☎ 01228 625310; **e**: bereavement@carlisle.gov.uk). A single grave costs £456, a double grave £606 (incl. digging and a tree; £94 extra for non-residents). This, the UK's first woodland burial ground, is a peaceful site looking out towards the river, with horses in an adjoining field. A local artist has made an oak seat. 252 burials and 51 ashes interments have taken place so far ; an average of 38 per year. They accept biodegradable coffins or shrouds, and sell Compakta cardboard coffins for £75, Ecology (Peace Box) cardboard coffins for £150, a standard fully-fitted chipboard coffin for £148, the Alverstone wooden coffin with rope handles from

£320, and their own Carlisle woollen burial shroud (complete with board and ropes) for £145. Mourners may help to fill, but not dig, the grave. A sheepfold has been built of recycled stone and bronze plaques can be placed inside. The site is accessed through the traditional burial ground. 'No chemicals are used. It is proposed as a site for a red squirrel reserve in the future' (June Carswell).

6. Clitheroe: Woodland burial ground as part of Clitheroe Cemetery, Waddington Road, Clitheroe, Lancashire; run by Ribble Valley Borough Council, Council Offices, Church Walk, Clitheroe BB7 2RA (☎ 01200 425111). 100 burials have taken place so far. A grave costs £240.75 plus £155.25 for the digging (incl. a tree or bulbs); double for non-residents. They will accept biodegradable coffins 'if to the required specification'. Mourners can help in a token way with filling the grave. Trees are planted, about one for every five graves, once a row of graves is completed. Individual memorial trees can also be planted around the perimeter of the site at extra cost. Ashes may be interred in an ashes glade for £58.25. The site is on the perimeter of the existing cemetery, adjacent to private woodland, in a rural setting overlooking the River Ribble. Over half of the council employees in a survey said that they would prefer this site for themselves. 'The site is managed to ensure maximum tree growth and to create conditions for wild flowers and nature to flourish' (Judith Paliga).

7. Entwistle, Lancashire: The West Pennine Remembrance Park, Entwistle Hall Lane, Entwistle, Turton, Lancashire BL7 0NG (☎/f: 01204 856848; **e**: info@remembranceparks.com; **w**: www.remembranceparks.com). A grave (100 years) costs from £650 to £1,200, plus approx. £150 for the digging (plots are set in circles around the park and the cost depends on the location, size and depth of the grave). Ashes may be buried from £250. Trees cost from £60 (family may plant, if they like). A children's woodland burial glade and a herbal garden are also being created. Families may help with the initial start and end filling in of the grave, and in the planting and maintenance of the park. There is a large car park and a mobility vehicle for the less able. Also a reception and family gathering room with a kitchen and disabled toilet, and a pavilion in the park for quiet meditation. A memorial hall is planned for the future. Entwistle railway station provides easy access by rail (on the Manchester to Blackburn line). A local inn offers food and accommodation for funeral parties. Musical and poetry events and talks throughout the year. Open to visitors 10am-4pm. A bereavement counsellor is available by appointment. 'Situated in an area renowned for its natural beauty and moorland views. Entwistle is a small hamlet at the end of a country road. Wild deer and other animals visit and there are bluebells and wild flowers. It is a mature landscape setting with maintained paths and burial areas plus wild areas' (Donald Boddy).

8. Liverpool: Woodland burial site in mature woodland at Allerton Cemetery, Woolton Road, Liverpool L19 5NF; run by Liverpool City Council. Contact Dale Willis, Cemeteries Manager (☎ 0151 233 3004; **w**: www.liverpool.gov.uk). Approx. 20 burials have taken place so far. A new grave costs £1,000 incl. digging and a woodland marker. They accept biodegradable coffins. Currently ashes can be interred in woodland at Springwood Crematorium, Woolton. The council has also earmarked local woodlands for use as woodland burial grounds in the future when the city's cemeteries reach capacity.

9. Nr. Manchester: The Woodland Cemetery, City Road, Ellenbrook, Worsley, Manchester M28 1BD (☎ 0161 790 1300; e: woodland.cemetery@virgin.net). A privately-run concern, this 12-acre site looks across open fields and is surrounded by trees. A grave costs £892 incl. digging (plus from £220 for a flat bedstone). Mourners may fill the grave and can help with a token amount of digging. They will accept home-made, cardboard, or wicker coffins, body bags or shrouds, and sell coffins to the public 'when available; prices on request'. There is a children and babies garden and a garden for the interment of ashes; name plaques and other facilities also available. Advance purchase of burial plots is possible. (Eds: reports suggest that weedkiller is regularly used at this site and it is 'mown constantly', but would perhaps suit those 'not too concerned about green issues'; 'The site staff are friendly, informative and efficient'.)

10. ✪✪✪ [**] Mobberley: Friends of Nature Burial Ground, Graveyard Farm, Newton Hall Lane, Mobberley, Cheshire WA16 7LJ; run by Mrs M. Arnison (☎ 0161 432 2131). Opened 1998. £400 for a single grave, £600 for a double, £700 for a treble, and £800 for a quadruple (plus £250 for the digging per burial). Ashes interred for £75. Coffins supplied from £120. All aspects of planning a funeral are available, from help with DIY funerals to full funeral arrangements. 'Graveyard Farm takes its name from a Quaker burial ground on the site which dates from the early 1600s. Located half a mile from the nearest road, the site is in an idyllic setting and is prolific in wildlife, flora and fauna, leading to the creation of a peaceful haven. Support from the Cheshire Wildlife Trust has ensured that environmental and ecological aspects of the site are being developed. An ecological study has been carried out and flora mapped. A wildflower area is being created and copses of trees planted each autumn' (Margaret Arnison). (Eds: users report, 'Ideal setting with fields all around'; 'Beautiful and tranquil. Thank you for the considerable help and assistance you provided'.)

11. Morecambe: Woodland burial ground at the rear of the Torrisholme Cemetery, Westgate Road, Morecambe, Lancashire. Contact Cemeteries Service, Lancaster City Council, Town Hall, Morecambe, Lancashire LA4 5AF (☎ 01524 582635). A grave costs £546 (incl. digging and a tree). Unfortunately, funeral directors must be used 'although DIY arrangements may be possible at a later date'. Families are also not allowed to assist with digging or filling the grave. 'An additional woodland burial site is open in the top corner of Hale Carr Lane Cemetery in Heysham' (Julie Clarkson).

12. [*] Nr. Oldham: Nature reserve burial ground, with space for 150 graves, as part of Saddleworth Cemetery, Uppermill; run by Saddleworth Parish Council, Civic Hall, Lee Street, Uppermill, Nr. Oldham OL3 6AE (☎ 01457 876665; e: enquiries@parishcouncil.saddleworth.org.uk). A grave costs £242 (incl. digging) plus from £12.20 for a tree or shrub; double for non-residents. They accept cardboard coffins and shrouds. Mourners may help fill the grave and do a token amount of digging. The woodland burial areas are in long grass (only cut directly near the grave) around a wild copse area, an integral part of the main cemetery which has been open since 1988 and which won a design competition. 'We want to make this a place that people come to see' (Dave Holland). (Eds: while early reports suggested that this was an attractive and well-run site – 'It really provides a green alternative with understanding and care'; 'The view from the site is stunning and I would highly recommend it' – a more recent user said it is 'starting to go downhill' and 'is no longer strictly speaking a nature reserve'. More feedback, positive or negative, welcome.)

13. **Preston**: Preston Cemetery, New Hall Lane, Preston, Lancashire PR1 4SY; run by Preston City Council (Manager Pam Duncanson, ☎ 01772 794585; **e:** p.duncanson@preston.gov.uk; **w:** www.preston.gov.uk). Eight burials have taken place with more graves pre-purchased. A grave costs £252.15 incl. a tree (plus £258.45 for the digging and burial; £516.90 for non-residents). The site is in the old cemetery lodge garden and is bordered by well-established trees and shrubs. They accept strong cardboard or home-made coffins. A choice of native species tree is planted for each grave. Mourners may help fill the grave.

14. **(Wigan)**: Cemeteries Section, Wigan Metropolitan Borough Council, Trencherfield Mill, Wallgate, Wigan WN3 4EF (☎ 01942 828855). 'The borough has plans to establish one, and possibly two, nature reserve burial areas in the future. Since there is no possibility of expansion at any of our existing sites, the facility will be established in a completely fresh, as yet unknown, location, probably selected from countryside land already owned by the borough. We are unable to say how soon this service will become available' (A. Bassett).

15. **The Wirral**: The Woodland Garden at Frankby Cemetery, Frankby Road; run by the Metropolitan Borough of Wirral. Contact the Cemeteries Manager, Landican Cemetery Office, Arrowe Park Road, Birkenhead, Wirral, Merseyside L49 5LW (☎ 0151 6772361). 70 burials have taken place so far. A grave costs £539 (incl. digging) for a Wirral resident (non-residents £809). Mourners may help fill the grave. Trees planted are native (eg pine, beech and hawthorn). Plots are mainly single graves but adjacent plots may be reserved for partners. Advance purchase of Right of Burial is no longer available. Any type of coffin may be used, but biodegradable ones are preferred. 'Part of an existing cemetery, with enough land available to extend it for many years to come' (Lisa Parkes).

The North East

Comprising Northumberland, Newcastle-Upon-Tyne, North Tyneside, Gateshead, South Tyneside, Sunderland, Durham, Hartlepool, Stockton-On-Tees, Middlesbrough, Redcar, North Yorkshire, York, East Riding of Yorkshire, Kingston-Upon-Hull, Bradford, Leeds, Calderdale, Kirklees, Wakefield, Barnsley, Sheffield, Rotherham, Doncaster, North Lincolnshire, North East Lincolnshire & Lincolnshire.

16. **[*] Alford, Lincolnshire**: Birdsong Burial Ground between Willoughby and Sloothby, eight miles from Skegness. Opened 2001. Contact Gay James, Willoughby Farms Ltd, The Estate Office, Well, Alford, Lincolnshire LN13 OET (☎ 01507 466644; **f:** 01507 463812; **e:** willfarm@otago.co.uk; **w:**

www.greenburialsite.co.uk). A five-acre site, with room for 1,300 graves. A single grave costs £400 incl. digging. Families may help dig and fill the grave. They sell the Compakta cardboard coffin for £80 (white) or £94 (woodgrain effect); the Bamboo Eco-coffin for £150; and the Mawdesley willow coffin for £543. They accept any fully biodegradable coffins, shrouds or body bags. Ashes may be interred in a 1 sq m plot for £150, or scattered for £50. A broadleaf tree may be planted for £50. 'We also have plans for a build-your-own coffin in the office if anyone is interested. The site is an old meadow surrounded by a tall hawthorn hedge with hedgerow trees. It is a quiet rural location, in slightly undulating open countryside. Access to the meadow is easy and is suitable for people with mobility problems. Birdsong may be visited at any time. People of all faiths are welcome' (Kitty Hamilton).

17. (**Boston, Lincs**): A green burial site planned by Boston Borough Council (☎ Martin Potts on 01205 364612) who run Boston Cemetery in Horncastle Road. No details as yet. Biodegradable coffins are currently accepted at the cemetery.

18. **Bradford**: A four-acre woodland burial area opened in 1997 within Thornton Cemetery; run by Bradford City Council (☎ 01274 571313). A grave costs £948 (incl. digging and a tree; £1,422 for non-residents). No memorials allowed. Ashes may be interred for £82. They accept biodegradable coffins, body bags or shrouds, and families are allowed to help fill, but not dig, the grave. 16 burials have taken place so far; approx. two per year. 'The site is on a hillside with some trees' (David Congreve).

19. [*] **Nr. Consett, Co. Durham**: A 4.5-acre green burial site within a 530-acre farm, opened April 2002. Seven Penny Meadows Green Field Burial Ground, Longclose Bank, north side of Medomsley Village, Consett; contact Alan & Marilyn Willey, Broomfield Farm, Chopwell, Newcastle upon Tyne NE17 7AS (☎ 01207 561229; **m**: 07831 707996). A single grave costs £475 (incl. a numbered plaque), a double £800; plus £150 for the digging, bulbs, wildflowers and maintenance of the grave. Seven burials have taken place so far. They accept all types of biodegradable coffins and shrouds. Families may help to dig and fill the grave. Ashes may be interred for £500 (up to two caskets and two numbered plaques). Trees are not planted on the graves, but may be dedicated elsewhere. 'Seven Penny Meadows will be allowed to mature into a wildflower meadow with scattered spinneys of native trees' (Alan Willey).

20. (**County Durham**): The County Durham Green Burials Partnership is actively researching green burial for the county and has produced an information leaflet 'Funerals and the Environment in County Durham'. Contact Christine Smith, Local Agenda 21, County Hall, Durham DH1 5TY (☎ 0191 386 4411; **w**: www.durham.gov.uk).

21. **Doncaster**: Woodland and meadowland burial areas at Rosehill Cemetery, Ascot Avenue, Cantley; run by Doncaster Metropolitan Borough Council. Contact Mrs Carr, Cemeteries Officer, Cantley Lane, Doncaster DN4 6NE (☎ 01302 535191; **f**: 01302 371948; **w**: www.doncaster.gov.uk; **e**: cems@doncaster. gov.uk). A grave (50 years) in the wooded area or the meadowland area – where the aim is to create grassland using local seed from Owston Hay Meadow, a site of special interest – costs £715 (incl. digging and a native tree typical for the area; £908 for 75 years). A surface level or submerged marker is included in the meadowland area and wildflowers can be planted on the grave. They accept all types of coffins and shrouds. Ashes may be scattered or buried.

22. Grantham: A two-acre green burial site as an extension to Grantham Cemetery; run by South Kesteven District Council (contact Mrs Steptoe, Grantham Cemetery, Harrowby Road, Grantham, Lincolnshire NG31 9DT; ☎ 01476 563083). Opened in 2000. Six burials have taken place so far. A grave costs £845 (incl. digging, a choice of tree and a small plaque). Oak, ash, field maple, silver birch, birch, mountain ash, hawthorn, holly, or hazel trees are offered. Only biodegradable coffins allowed. Families may help with a token amount of filling the grave, but may not dig for health and safety reasons.

23. Guisborough: A woodland burial ground in the corner of Guisborough Cemetery, Church Lane, Guisborough; run by Redcar and Cleveland Borough Council, Cemeteries Office, Central Depot, Limerick Road, Dormanstown, Redcar TS10 5JU (☎ 01642 444991; **f**: 01642 444992). Opened June 2002 with space for 39 side-by-side graves; there have been nine burials so far. A double grave costs £605.50 (incl. one interment and a tree; plus £307 for the second interment). 'For the first five years the authority will replace free of charge any tree which may die. As the woodland develops it may be necesessary to thin out some of the trees to maintain the character of the woodland' (Iain Dixon).

24. Harrogate: A. B. Welfare & Wildlife Trust (charity no. 1037444), 7 Knox Road, Harrogate, North Yorkshire HG1 3EF (☎ 01423 530900/868121; **w**: www.abtrust.info). This combined social work and wildlife charity was launched in 1994. It plans to create new nature reserves through temporary burial projects. Until suitable land becomes available burials are being arranged in existing nature reserves, without damaging the wildlife interest. It is hoped that the major landowning wildlife charities will soon offer what this Trust has pioneered. The Trust arranges burials or interment of ashes in pastures and wood-pasture. One nature reserve for burials (for benefactors only or for those able to raise substantial sums for the Trust's work) is on eight acres of the Brimham Rocks 400-acre Site of Special Scientific Interest, in the Nidderdale Area of Outstanding Natural Beauty, with permission for up to 25 burials. The land is named Kate's Fell after Kathleen Davies, one of the first occupational therapists and a modern-day pioneer of the therapeutic value of pets in hospitals. It is a mix of semi-natural woodland with pasture, including bilberry and heather on a warm, west-facing slope looking into the valley of Nidderdale. There are 250 large boulders scattered throughout and each has legal protection. The second site, and the Trust's main burial project, is Gertrude's Pasture (donations only, but possibly a charge in the future) a 3.5-acre site 'teeming with great crested newts, wild flowers, butterflies, grasshoppers, noctule bats with a wingspan of 355mm, and other wildlife. It is grazed by Hebridean black sheep'. The adjacent river gorge has spectacular walks and views, with more than 100 acres of woodland. Volunteers have health and social services backgrounds and many years of experience in managing nature reserves. One of the Trust's advisers is John

Bradfield, probably the UK's leading authority on laws surrounding funerals; he is certainly the source to whom the Natural Death Centre refers people with complex questions. The Trust can help arrange funerals paid for by the Benefits Agency, or if necessary, a grave can be made available free of charge; other charges are at the Trust's discretion. The land has long-term security being owned by a registered wildlife charity. The Trust accepts biodegradable coffins, shrouds, or stretchers made of natural materials, but not body bags – 'our experience is that body bags smack of a waste disposal operation'. The Trust can supply cardboard coffins for cost price plus £5. As for collection of the body or other services, 'all aspects of help can be provided free of charge, depending on circumstances and distance. Donations welcome'. Family and friends can dig and fill the grave. 'Most graves are difficult to see after a few weeks but some are mounded for wild flowers; and others have turfed cairns for great crested newts. Our priority is to meet the needs of those seeking help, whilst creating or helping to protect a wildlife area. We are experienced as conservationists' (John Bradfield). (Eds: this project is probably more for the serious green burial enthusiast; each grave can be located, but there is little if any obvious marking of most of the graves. One user reports: 'The public service philosophy of the Trust actively encourages independence. Its work is done for its own sake, to build strong personal relationships and strong communities. For me, dealing with death in a place which is bursting with life, made all the difference.')

25. Harrogate: For Harrogate residents only. A half-acre green burial site at Stonefall Cemetery, Wetherby Road, Harrogate, North Yorkshire HG3 1DE (☎ 01423 883523; f: 01423 884151); run by Harrogate Borough Council. A grave costs £965 incl. digging and burial, no tree. Families can help fill, but not dig, the grave. They will accept biodegradable coffins or shrouds. No trees are planted on the graves but each grave has a marker placed flat at ground level. The area is landscaped, and is planted with bulbs and flowers and cut twice a year. 'The site opened in 1995, five burials have taken place so far and there is space for 150-200 graves' (Philip Andrew, Bereavement Services Manager). (Eds: one visitor comments, 'Very small, but very pleasant, and would be better called a wildflower meadow area. Secluded and surrounded by mature trees and hedgerow. The flowers and seating make a lovely quiet and peaceful area.')

26. [**] Hexham: Woodland burial site run by Hexham Town Council; contact John R. Thirlwell, Cemetery Superintendent, Council Office, St Andrew's Cemetery, West Road, Hexham, Northumberland NE46 3RR (☎ 01434 609575; m: 077100 53732). Opened 1995. A grave costs £295 (incl. digging, a biodegradable coffin, a numbered flat stone marker, and a broadleaved tree planted within the woodland area; triple for non-residents). Family may provide their own tree (subject to approval of type) and casket, but there will be no reduction in the fee. Burial of infants and ashes within separate areas (fees are appropriately reduced). Families may organise the entire funeral themselves and help fill the grave. 'Sited in the countryside and in a secluded setting on the boundary of St Andrew's Cemetery, next to the golf course. Beautiful views westwards and northwards over the South and North Tyne valleys' (Derick Tiffin, Clerk).

27. **(Holmfirth)**: A woodland burial ground planned for four acres of land at Upper Ubberthong near Holmfirth owned by T. W. Birks & Son Ltd, funeral directors of Holmfirth. Contact Neil Birks for further details (☎ 01484 683322).

28. **Leeds**: Woodland burial site within Lawnswood Cemetery, Otley Road, Adel, Leeds LS16 6AH (☎ 0113 2673188); run by Leeds City Council. A grave costs £942 incl. digging and a tree; double for non-residents. Opened in 1997; two further woodland burial sites in the Leeds area are planned. They will accept biodegradable coffins. Mourners may fill the grave if they wish. 'The site is a flat area within the cemetery near some mature trees' (Phil Stephenson). (Eds: one visitor reported, 'We were very disappointed with this site. It is a patch of ground behind their offices next to a litter-filled ditch. They have simply replaced headstones with very closely spaced trees and there is no sense of creating a wood environment. In a few years they will have to vigorously thin out the trees. It is also very expensive for what you get. I would not recommend it.')

29. **Middlesbrough**: Woodland burial area in Acklam Cemetery, Acklam Road; run by Middlesbrough Borough Council. Contact Mr Gitsham, Bereavement Services Manager, Cemeteries and Crematorium Office, Teesside Crematorium, Acklam Road, Middlesbrough TS5 7HE (☎ 01642 817725, **f**: 01642 852424). Single or double grave (100 years) costs £610, plus £287 for each interment. An oak tree or similar, included in the price, is planted on each grave. 80 burials have taken place so far. Families can help fill, but not dig, the grave. All types of coffins are permitted, but biodegradable ones are preferred. They will consider body bags and shrouds. The woodland burial section lies between two lawn sections in the cemetery extension and can itself be extended. Similar plots are available at Linthorpe Cemetery.

30. ✪✪✪ [**] **Nr. Morpeth, Northumberland**: Northumbrian Woodland Burials, Bockenfield, Felton (☎ 01670 787067; **e**: steve.clarehugh@virgin.net; **w**: www.northumbrianwoodlandburials.co.uk). A six-acre site, with space for 3,000 graves initially, based at a former WWII airfield which has been planted out into a broadleaf forest. Burials began in 2001, with 20 so far. A single grave costs £500, a double £1,000 (plus £75 for the digging). Friends and relatives may help dig and fill the grave subject to health and safety guidelines. The use of cardboard coffins is strongly encouraged. A flat A4 remembrance plaque on the grave or a small bronze plaque on the stone sheepfold wall are allowed instead of headstones. There is also a half-acre area for babies and children. 'Bockenfield Wood is made up mostly of oak and ash trees with a sprinkling of pines for future red squirrel feedings. A large pond has been constructed at the side of the nearby Blackbrook stream which flows to the south. Curlews, oyster-catchers and skylarks nest on the site. The area benefits from some of the original roads constructed by the RAF in 1943 and has five circular aircraft parking blisters which are to be used as picnic areas' (Steve Clarehugh). (Eds: users report, 'Lovely – natural and peaceful'; 'Something we could easily envisage as an attractive woodland area within a few years. Steve and his family were welcoming, helpful, supportive and friendly. It's as though we all have an equal share in Bockenfield'; 'Rural and very environmentally friendly, so much that upland birds have nested on it'; 'Steve Clarehugh was extremely helpful'.)

31. **Norton Disney, Lincolnshire**: For locals only, 'Ecoburial' is offered in the 2.5-acre Hill Holt Wood, south of the A46. Contact Nigel Lowthrop, Hill Holt Wood, Norton Disney LN6 9JP (☎ 01636 892836; **e**: info@hillholtwood.tk). Only for residents of the parishes or Friends of Hill Holt Wood (who pay £10 per year per family to join; applications from the address above). Five burials have taken place so far. Plots by agreement and donation to the charitable business. Ashes can be scattered and a memorial tree planted for £150. Trees from local stock, mainly oak, are planted to form an avenue down the wood's main drive. 'Over 3km of paths cross the wood with plenty of seating to enjoy the wildlife and surrounding farmland. Hill Holt Wood is a not-for-profit, community-controlled membership organisation limited by guarantee' (Nigel Lowthrop).

32. **[**] Rathmell, Settle, North Yorkshire**: Brocklands Woodland Burial, a 1.5-acre site in the North Ribble Valley, near Skipton; run by Julia & Chris Weston, Cappleside House, Rathmell, Settle, North Yorkshire BD24 0LJ (☎ 01729 840102; **f**: 01729 840103; **e**: info@brocklands.co.uk; **w**: www.brocklands. co.uk). The first burial took place August 2000. A single grave costs £290; a side-by-side double £560 (plus £260 for the digging and a tree). They sell various coffins: cardboard (£95, or £105 woodgrain effect); solid pine (£180); bamboo (£180); and wicker (from £450); all coffins sold with a separate waterproof biodegradable liner. Trees planted are native and typical for the area; planting takes place November-March. Families may help with the digging and filling of the grave. A bronze number is embedded in each grave. Ashes can be interred for £100 incl. a tree. 'Secluded site with fine views up Ribble Valley, surrounded by pasture and small woods. Woodchip paths from the car park lead to the main areas. There is already a notable increase in bird and animal life, and we are now concentrating on wildflowers and butterflies. The site has been set up as a Trust so that it will remain a woodland burial site' (Julia Weston). (Eds: users comment, 'I liked the informality and personal touch. I would most positively recommend it'; 'Has a magnificent view and will develop into a wonderful area'; 'Peaceful pastureland with a fine view of the Dales'; 'Perfect'; 'You couldn't hope for a better setting. It beats looking at a collection of gravestones'.)

33. **Sheffield**: Wisewood Woodland Burial Ground, Loxley Road; run by Sheffield City Council. Contact Kay Rogers, Bereavement Services, City Road Cemetery, Sheffield S2 1GD (☎ 0114 239 6068; **w**: www.sheffield.gov.uk). This small site is within Wisewood Cemetery, in Sheffield's beautiful Loxley Valley, with a backdrop of trees. 57 burials have taken place so far. The cost of a grave is £743 (incl. digging, a tree and a small York stone memorial; same for non-residents). Adjacent plots may be pre-purchased. Trees can be alder, silver birch, rowan, whitebeam or ash. Families may help with a token amount of digging and may fill the grave. Leaflets are provided for families organising DIY funerals. Five types of cardboard coffin are on sale from £55-£114, and traditional coffins from £70. They accept other types of biodegradable coffins and shrouds and will sell a natural fibre shroud for £60. Ashes may be scattered (for £54) or buried (£106). A biodegradable urn can be supplied free of charge or they sell a range of ashes caskets and urns. They also offer mortuary and washing services (£20 for the first day, £10 per day after this).

34. [**] **Nr. Sheffield**: South Yorkshire Woodland Burial Ground, Turnshaw Road, Ulley, Nr. Rotherham; run by Peace Funerals, Gleadless Mount, Sheffield S12 2LN (☎ 0114 2530505 / freephone 0800 093 0505; **f**: 0114 2530503; **e**: peacefuner@aol.com; **w**: www.peacefunerals.co.uk). This 2.88-acre site opened October 1995; 150 burials have taken place so far (approx. 25 a year). It is surrounded by fields and is located down a lane by a small country village. A stream runs along the boundary with the next field. A hawthorn hedge has been planted. Their tree management policy is guided by a permaculturist and Friends of the Earth chairman. A grave (50 years) costs £550 (incl. digging and any native British tree). They accept biodegradable coffins, body bags or shrouds. They sell cardboard coffins (from £89) and their own design of wicker coffin, the Mawdesley Willow (from £409). Family and friends may dig or fill the grave if they wish. An A4-size York stone plaque, laid horizontally, costs £105. Ashes may be interred for £145 incl. a tree. They will collect the body from hospital for £55. There is a group for relatives and friends which discusses the management of the site and acts as a support group. 'A horse and dray can be hired and a restored thatched barn is available nearby for religious or secular ceremonies' (Mary Mallatratt). See also their 'railway funeral' site near Alfreton, Derbyshire, below. (Eds: users have commented, 'The site is beautiful and we were very satisfied with Peace Funerals' level of service - Excellent'; 'It was perfect'.)

35. [**] **Skipton, North Yorkshire**: Tarn Moor Memorial Woodland, White House Farm, Stirton, Skipton, North Yorkshire, BD23 3LH (☎/**f**: 01756 701688, **m**: 07968 205 880; **e**: enquiries@tarnmoor.co.uk; **w**: www.tarnmoor.co.uk). This ten-acre site opened in 2002. 22 burials have taken place so far, with 60 plots reserved. A single grave costs £500, a double £900; a plot for ashes £100 (plus digging costs which vary depending on season). Ashes may also be scattered for £25. Prices are 25 per cent lower for Skipton parishioners; 50 per cent higher for those who live outside of Craven. For pre-booking, 50 per cent of the plot price must be paid; this is non-refundable. Pets may also be buried (call for prices). 'Elevated site offers panoramic views over the adjoining countryside. Part of the Tarn Moor Estate, a charity with a limited portfolio of land and property, income from which is used to benefit the people of Skipton. We encourage environmental and conservation issues but are flexible' (Wendy Pratt, Manager). (Eds: users say, 'Beautiful, open, peaceful and timeless'; 'Very sympathetic management. Everything was superbly organised, nothing could have been improved upon'.)

36. (**Whitley Bay**): Plans for a meadow burial ground at Whitley Bay Cememtery; to be run by North Tyneside Council (contact Jim Finlay ☎ 0191 200 5861).

37. **York**. The York Cemetery Trust, The Warden, The Gatehouse, Cemetery Road, York YO10 5AJ (☎ 01904 610578). Prices from £700 (incl. digging). Not a woodland burial ground, since there are traditional headstones too, but 'nature is taking over. This is a Victorian park landscape gone wild and there is an ecological management plan in place to encourage wildlife' (Vanessa Temple). All types of biodegradable coffins and body bags accepted, and the warden can help supply these. There is a remembrance garden where an ashes plot for four sets of ashes costs £150, plus £140 for each interment or scattering. There is also a fine classical chapel in working order.

38. [**] North Yorkshire: The Mowthorpe Independent Garden of Rest c/o Robert Goodwill, Southwood Farm, Terrington, York YO6 4QB, (☎ 01653 648459; **f:** 01653 648225; **e:** robert@robertgoodwill.co.uk). A 2.5-acre site with lovely views, adjacent to a wood and an existing cemetery, in an Area of Outstanding Natural Beauty, set on the ridge of the Howardian Hills overlooking the Vale of York. A grave (in perpetuity) costs £475 (incl. digging). There have been 65 burials so far. 1,500 trees have been planted. Mourners may fill the grave if they wish. Memorials less than 1m high allowed. Undertaken With Love, the funeral directors, charge about £1,080 to carry out a funeral here. 'Mowthorpe is part of the 250-acre Southwood Farm at Terrington where the Goodwill family has lived since 1850. The families of all the people buried in Mowthorpe hold shares in the company and can attend the AGM.' (Eds: one reader has commented, 'As well as being a stupendously beautiful setting next to established woodland with outstanding views, it also has the reassurance that all people who buy a plot hold B shares in the company. £150 of the fee is invested for future maintenance after all the plots are full and you have some say in the ongoing maintenance of the site. The owners are flexible and sympathetic.')

Wales

Comprising Flintshire, Wrexham, Denbighshire, Aberconwy & Colwyn, Anglesey, Caernarfonshire & Merionethshire, Powys, Cardiganshire, Pembrokeshire, Carmarthenshire, Swansea, Neath & Port Talbot, Bridgend, Rhondda Cynon Taff, Vale of Glamorgan, Merthyr Tydfil, Caerphilly, Cardiff, Blaenau Gwent, Torfaen, Newport, Monmouthshire.

39. Aberystwyth: Aberystwyth Woodland Cemetery, Clarach Road, Aberystwyth, Cardiganshire SY23 3DG (☎ 01970 626942). A one acre site within Aberystwyth Cemetery, run by Crematoria Management Ltd. On a wooded hillside above the Cynfelyn valley. The garden of remembrance is a rare orchid site, and the sea is visible from part of the grounds. A single grave costs £500 incl. digging (same for non-residents). Families can help dig and/or fill the grave. They will accept any biodegradable coffin. Memorial benches and bronzed plaques on simple stakes are acceptable. Trees may be planted in the vicinity of, but not on, the grave. 'We would encourage people to visit the site as we believe the qualities will speak for themselves' (Sandra Gornal).

40. Cardiff: Woodland Burial Glade, Thornhill Cemetery, Thornhill Road, Llanishen, Cardiff, Wales CF14 9UA; run by Cardiff County Council (☎ 029 2062 3294; **f:** 029 2069 2904; **e:** ThornhillReception@Cardiff.gov.uk; **w:** www.cardiff.gov.uk). The Glade is on the perimeter of the cemetery, overlooked by Wenallt mountain, and looking down on Cardiff Bay. The site has mature oaks. A single grave costs £473.50 incl. digging; £689.50 for non-residents. An optional marker costs £58. The adjoining grave may be pre-purchased. No trees are planted in the current woodland section, or on the grave after burial, as the section is set within an existing wooded area. Biodegradable coffins are available, ring for costs. Either of the crematorium chapels may be hired for any burial service (religious symbols can be removed or covered by request) for £59. 'It is an excellent site, simply the best' (Roger Swan, Senior Registrar).

41. **(Gwent)**: Gwent Wildlife Trust (16 White Swan Court, Monmouth NP25 3NY, ☎ 01600 715501, e: gwentwildlife@cix.co.uk; w: www.wildlifetrust. org.uk/gwent) is looking into the possibility of establishing a green burial site in Gwent, to be run either as a charity or in conjunction with a local landowner.

42. **[*] (Llanelli, SW Wales)**: Proposed woodland burial ground of six acres (with potential expansion to ten acres) at Bryn Coch Farm, Upper Tumble, Llanelli SA14 6DL; to be run by Tim Pullen, Pant Y Bryn, Heol Ddu, Ammanford SA18 2UG (☎ 01269 822375). To open early 2004 (if the planning application is successful). A grave will cost £350 for a single or £600 for a double (2m x 2m). Ashes may be scattered for £25, or interred for £150. All types of biodegradable coffin or shroud may be used. Horse-drawn transportation from the car park to the graveside is planned. Graves will be marked with a tree or flowers, a bird or bat box, or a brass plaque on an oak stake or bench. Mourners may fill the grave if they wish, have the ground consecrated in any religion or none, and spend as much time at the graveside as they wish to say their farewells. 'We encourage DIY funerals and are happy to give advice. A place of peace and tranquility surrounded by hedges and just ten minutes from the M4. It is accessed through a 60-acre community woodland and hosts a wealth of wildlife from butterflies to red kites. Wildlife will be encouraged with carefully planned planting of native species trees and flowers around natural glades' (Tim Pullen).

43. **(Nr. Newcastle Emlyn)**: A 4.5-acre proposed burial site owned by Bede David in the middle of protected woodland nominated as a Site of Special Scientific Interest at Coed y Tyddyn, Tyddyn Du Farm, Cwm Coy, Nr. Newcastle Emlyn, Wales. Negotiations with local planners are still under way but due to Bede David's extended residence abroad, a new application will not be for some time. All enquiries to Bede David , Box 3019, 3911 Sisimiut, Greenland.

44. **Newport**: St Woolos Cemetery, Bassaleg Road, Newport NP9 3NA (Nigel Woodward ☎ 016332 263864), run by Newport Council, has a small woodland area. A grave costs £497 incl. digging.

45. **(Pontypool, Torfaen)**: The local authority is actively seeking a site for a new cemetery to include a small woodland burial area. Contact Mr A. P. Crewe, Cemeteries Manager, Panteg Cemetery Office, The Highway, New Inn, Pontypool, Torfaen, Wales NP4 8HW (☎/f: 01495 766339).

46. **[*] Powys, Mid-Wales**: Green Lane Burial Field; owned and operated by Eira and Ifor Humphreys, Upper Bryntalch Farm, Abermule, Montogomery, Powys SY15 6LA (☎01686 630331; e: iforbh@farmersweekly.net; w: www.greenlaneburialfield.co.uk). Opened December 2003. Grid ref. SO 179964. 11-acre field, of which 7.5 acres are being regenerated as native woodland. 3.5 acres are being managed to become a wildflower hay meadow, of which 3/4 of an acre is available for burials. A grave costs £350 plus £150 for the digging.

Burial of ashes costs £150, scattering £30. Only bulbs or wildflowers are allowed on the grave. A memorial tree with plaque, planted in the memorial area, costs an extra £150. A bench or sculpture may be sited by arrangement, or an existing tree may be 'adopted'. Families may dig and fill the grave, and may carry out the funeral themselves. Other facilities are available, such as marquee hire on site. Burials can take place at any time during daylight hours; 'we are a family business and are very flexible, please ask! We are working closely with Montgomeryshire Wildlife Trust and will donate £20 to the Trust for every right of burial that is sold. The field has excellent access, a good car park with a picnic area, several walks, and is wheelchair friendly. The area has a wealth of history; the burial field is considered to be an essential setting to the adjacent Cefnbryntalch Hall, once the home of composer Peter Warlock, and is overlooked by an ancient motte and bailey. The burial field is located on a small plateau with magnificent views over the Severn valley to the north and the Kerry Hills to the south. This is already a beautiful place and we want to make it even better!' (Ifor Humphreys).

47. ❁❁❁ Prestatyn, Denbighshire: Woodland burial at Coed Bell Cemetery, Llanasa Road, Prestatyn, Denbighshire, North Wales; contact Mrs S. K. Jones, Cemeteries Officer, Denbighshire County Council, Caledfryn, Smithfield Road, Denbigh, Denbighshire, Wales LL16 3RJ (☎ 01824 706938; e: sylvia.k.jones@ denbighshire.gov.uk). Opened 2001. A grave costs £470 incl. digging, assistance with lowering if required, a rowan or similar type of tree and wild flower seeds; double for non-residents. A neighbouring plot can be reserved for £100 (which will later be deducted from the cost of burial). Ashes may be interred for £130. Unfortunately, families cannot help dig or fill the grave. Biodegradable coffins only. 'The woodland burial site is on a hill above the existing cemetery, below a natural woodland, overlooking the Dee Estuary/Irish Sea' (Sylvia Jones).

48. St Asaph: Woodland burial at Y Llwyn Cemetery, Mount Road, St Asaph (Llanelwy), Denbighshire, North Wales (see previous entry for contact details and prices). 'The woodland burial ground is a field hedged on three sides, at the bottom of an existing graveyard that is rustic and peaceful' (Sylvia Jones). (Eds: reports confirm this description: 'A very pleasant traditional, ancient, wild and overgrown cemetery with plenty of character and atmosphere.')

49. Swansea: Woodland burial offered at Oystermouth Cemetery, Mumbles; run by the City and County of Swansea, Cemeteries and Crematorium Division, Room 304 Environmental Health, The Guildhall, Swansea SA1 4PE (☎ Andy Parsons, on-site supervisor, 07980 721559; or e: Noel.Evans@swansea.gov.uk). A grave costs £450 incl. digging. Ashes may be scattered for £30 (no charge if cremation took place at Swansea Crematorium). In all cases, they ask for a one-off payment of £35 as a contribution to the woodland area (appropriate planting, etc) instead of memorials. Biodegradable coffins or shrouds only. 'Each burial will be recorded on Cemetery plans but no headstones or fencing allowed, keeping the environment as wild and natural as possible, protecting trees, shrubs and wildlife' (Noel Evans, Registrar).

West Midlands

Comprising Shropshire, Staffordshire, Wolverhampton, Walsall, Dudley, Sandwell, Birmingham, Solihull, Coventry, Warwickshire, Hereford & Worcester, Gloucestershire.

50. Birmingham: Woodland burial sites for Quinton and Handsworth Cemeteries and as part of plans for a new cemetery which opened in 2002 in Sutton Coldfield; run by Birmingham City Council. Contact Mr Powell, Yardley Cemetery, Yardley Road, Birmingham B25 8NA (☎ 0121 708 2183).

51. Burton-upon-Trent: Woodland burial, Stapenhill Cemetery, 38 Stapenhill Road, Burton-upon-Trent DE15 9AE (☎ 01283 508572); run by East Staffordshire Borough Council. Stapenhill is a large traditional cemetery and the woodland burial area is at the far end on sloping ground. There have been 33 burials so far, with a further 34 plots pre-sold. A grave costs £566 (incl. digging, a tree and bulbs; double for non-residents). They will accept biodegradable coffins and body bags or shrouds. Family and friends may help fill the grave. A grave space must be bought if ashes are to be buried. 'The woodland burial area is situated on a hillside overlooking the cemetery, above the flood plain of the River Trent. It has been planted with bulbs, wild flowers and a variety of native trees – including ash, oak, cherry, hazel and birch' (Nick French).

52. (Coleshill, Warwickshire): For 2005/6, a woodland burial area planned for Woodlands Cemetery; run by Solihull Metropolitan Borough Council, Birmingham Rd, Coleshill (☎ 01675 464835, **f**: 01675 464351; **e**: ghull@solihull.gov.uk).

53. Coventry (1): Lentons Lane Cemetery and Nature Reserve, Lentons Lane, Walsgrave, Coventry; run by the City of Coventry Bereavement Services, The Lodge, Cannon Hill Road, Canley, Coventry CV4 7DF (☎ 024 7629 4411). Cardboard coffins can be supplied to people using this site. There is no time limit at the graveside. A grave costs from £715 (incl. digging and a biodegradable coffin; no tree as the woodland is already planted); same prices for non-residents). No memorials allowed. There is provision for ashes to be interred within the site. Free advice for families arranging a funeral without undertakers. Families can help dig and fill the grave. 30 burials have taken place so far, about six a year, and there is room for development of this two-acre site. 'The site is part of a larger traditional cemetery on the outskirts of the city, away from residential areas. The area is planted with local trees and there is a wild flower meadow and a pond with frogs and newts' (Mrs S. Turner).

54. Coventry (2): Woodland burial at St Paul's Cemetery, Holbrook Lane, Coventry; run by the City of Coventry Bereavement Services, The Lodge, Cannon Hill Road, Canley, Coventry CV4 7DF (☎ 024 7629 4411). For details see previous entry.

55. ✪✪✪ [**] Craven Arms: Westhope Church Meadow Green Burial Ground, Westhope Craft College, Craven Arms, Shropshire SY7 9JL (☎ 01584 861293). Landowner: Anne Dyer. The college is run by the Westhope Charity. The site is in an ancient orchard, about 1.5 acres, set in a quiet valley five miles from Craven Arms. Westhope itself is a small widely-scattered community. A single grave costs £250, a double £300; plus £150 for each digging (the soil is shaley and difficult to dig by hand). Spring bulbs may be planted on the graves. An apple tree costs £60, a wild cherry tree £50 (incl. aftercare). An oak bench with plaque costs £250; an engraved stone, price on application. Ashes may be buried for £50, or scattered in an area beneath some walnut trees. All types of biodegradable coffins, body bags and shrouds accepted ('we have a small stock of coffins, wicker stretchers, etc'). Families may help dig and fill the grave and organise a funeral without undertakers; the site can offer help in the form of bearers and general advice. A Victorian chapel, rebuilt on the site of a Norman building, is available for ceremonies (£30 for the organist) and for holding bodies before funerals if wished (£25 for up to a week). Minibus hire costs £10 (or £40 incl. a driver). The undertakers Hoskins & Son (☎ 01584 872048) can help with arrangements for inexpensive funerals at this site. There is a pet cemetery attached. 'The orchard is being replanted with memorial apple trees whose species are under threat and there are wild cherry trees along the hedgerows. We have been open since 1996 and about 15 burials take place each year. There are rare breed sheep, and the farm is organic. When I die, the Westhope Charity takes over' (Anne Dyer). (Eds: one user says, 'I wholeheartedly recommend it. In fact, many of my friends said they wished they had known about it'.)

56. Dudley: A woodland burial ground at Gornal Wood Cemetery, Chase Road, Gornal Wood, Dudley DY3 2RL (☎ 01384 813970; **f**: 01384 813971; **e**: bereavementsvcs.due@dudley.gov.uk); run by Dudley Metropolitan Borough Council. This small site for up to 34 graves – approximately 300 sq m – is adjacent to the Seasonal Gardens of Remembrance. Since 1999, six burials have taken place. A grave costs £548 (incl. digging, native bulbs and a tree: hawthorn, birch, hazel or mountain ash; double for non-residents). They accept homemade, cardboard or wicker coffins. Mourners may help fill the grave. Free advice for DIY funerals. No memorials or flower containers allowed. A minimum two-line inscription in the Book of Remembrance costs £38. 'There are buildings and grassed areas to one side, a cremated remains area at the front, and woodland and seasonal gardens of remembrance to the rear' (Ian Bailey).

57. [**] Nr. Leominster, Herefordshire: Humber Woodland of Remembrance, situated four miles from Leominster; run by Mrs Diane Thomas of Risbury Court, Risbury, Leominster, Herefordshire HR6 0NG (☎ 01568 760443, **f**: 01568 760384; **e**: rgmdthomas@lineone.net). A grave costs £545 incl. digging (plus cost of tree or shrub which varies depending on type chosen). Families may dig the grave themselves, subject to health and safety guidelines. A small stone marker may also be purchased for £90, or a bronze plaque on a tree stake for £110. Scattering of ashes £50; burial of ashes £105 (there is a separate area for this on a hillside where people may 'adopt' a tree). Biodegradable coffins or shrouds are preferred. 'Families may use their preferred funeral director or we can put them in touch with a local 'green' funeral director, or they may organise the funeral themselves – we could assist in the purchase of a coffin. The site is bordered to the west by a Roman road and to the east by a winding stream. The beautiful little parish church, St Mary's, only 200m away, is available for funeral services. Mature trees grow alongside the stream and 1,600 young trees have been planted' (Diane Thomas).

58. Mappleborough Green, Warwickshire: Wildlife Churchyard, Mappleborough Green, Warwickshire; contact Rev. Richard Deimel, The Vicarage, 3 Manor Mews, Studley B80 7PR (☎ 01527 852830). A five-acre meadow with trees situated 15 miles south of Birmingham, with views out onto undulating farmland, and adjoining a Victorian church and churchyard. They accept most kinds of biodegradable body container. A grave costs £200; or £550 for non-residents. Families can either do their own digging and filling of the grave or pay a local digger £100. Families can also provide a tree, although there is a tree planting plan, rather than an individual tree, for each grave.

59. Newport, Shropshire: A two-acre woodland burial ground as an extension to Newport General Cemetery on Audley Avenue; contact the Town Clerk, Newport (Shropshire) Town Council, The Guildhall, High Street, Newport, Shropshire TF10 7TX (☎ 01952 814338; **f:** 01952 825353; **e:** townclerk@ newportsaloptowncouncil.co.uk). Since the site opened in 1998 there have been 15 burials and 27 plots reserved. A single grave costs £270 (incl. digging; £390 for non-residents). A tree costs from £20 to £30 depending on the species, and can be bought separately for someone whose funeral was elsewhere. Ashes can be interred for £177 (£295 for non-residents). Any biodegradable body container is acceptable, including cardboard, but not home-made ones or shrouds. Family and friends can help fill the grave. Free advice will be offered to DIY families. The existing cemetery, which the site abuts, was opened in 1859, and is complete with mature trees and a full complement of wildlife. There is a chapel, which can be used for services, religious or secular.

60. (Penkridge, South Staffs): Woodland burial area proposed for Penkridge Cemetery, Pinfold Lane, Penkridge; run by Penkridge Parish Council. Contact Lesley Griffiths, Deputy Parish Administrator, Haling Dene Centre, Cannock Road, Penkridge, Stafford ST19 5DT (☎ 01785 714157; **f:** 01785 715682).

61. [*] Redditch, Worcestershire: Westall Park Woodland Burial, Holberrow Green B96 6JY (☎ 01386 792806, **f:** 01386 793253; **e:** tolley.d@ westallpark.fsnet.co.uk). A grave ('without limit as to time') costs £645 (incl. digging; same for non-residents). Mourners may help fill the grave and help is offered for DIY funerals. Trees are planted randomly once the burial area is full. A wooden name plaque on a stake costs an extra £35 (plus engraving). A dedicated Norwegian maple tree on the drive costs £100. Ashes may be interred from £162 or scattered on the hillside for £25. Plots can also be paid for in advance. Standard, home-made and biodegradable coffins or shrouds accepted. 'We are out in the country, six miles due south of Redditch, well away from public roads and within sight of the Brecon Hills. The main six-acre field is reached by a private drive and is bowl-shaped with beautiful views. A second five-acre field will eventually be brought into use. There are some very old oak trees, 100 landscaping trees, and woodpeckers, owls and foxes. I am often congratulated on the site and I am proud of the choice we offer to families. We opened in 1997' (Dave Tolley, MD). (Eds: users say, 'We would 110 per cent recommend Westall Park, in fact we have reserved our own plots there'; 'Very rural, part of a farm, very peaceful'.)

62. [**] **Rugby, Warwickshire**: Greenhaven Woodland Burial Ground at New Clarks Farm; run by Christine Atkin and Nicholas Hargreaves of Yelvertoft Road, Lilbourne, Rugby, Warwickshire CV23 OSZ (☎ 01788 860604; **e**: nichargreaves@hotmail.com; **w**: www.greenhavenwoodland.com). A 14-acre field on the outskirts of Rugby. There were 23 burials in the first year (1994); now approx. 75 per year. A grave costs £300 (incl. planting of a small tree). Family and friends may dig the grave or pay £75 to have it dug for them. Home-made, cardboard, bamboo or wicker coffins, and body bags or shrouds are accepted. They sell the following coffins: cardboard £70-£95; pine £200; basket £200. They will collect the body at a cost of 90p per mile (eg about £90 for London collections) with a minimum fee of £50. From £30, staff will attend at graveside, church, etc. The priest or vicar charges £39 for a graveside service. A church service would cost an extra £128.50 (plus £30 for heating, if required). The village hall may be hired for £35. All-inclusive burial from £500. Wooden plaques are allowed as memorials. 'The site is situated in an elevated position with good views. It is typical Northamptonshire countryside, at present with not many trees, but lots of old hedges dotted with ash trees and a pond. All our trees are grown from native seeds. Wild flower seeds and bulbs are also planted. Clients' pre-payments are safeguarded as they have a legal deed to their plots and other monies are kept in a separate clients' account. It is a family-run site, very relaxed, with very reasonable prices and centrally placed' (Christine Atkin).

63. **(Shrewsbury, Shropshire)**: A natural burial area is planned for sometime in the longterm future (no date specified) at the new Emstrey Cemetery which opened in 2002. For further information please contact Mr M. D. Wraith, Shrewsbury & Atcham Borough Council, Bereavement Services, Oakley Manor, Belle Vue Road, Shrewsbury SY3 7NW (☎ 01743 281385, **f**: 01743 281377).

64. **Stafford**: A 1.5-acre woodland burial ground as part of Stone Cemetery (off the A34); run by Stafford Borough Council, Stafford Burial Grounds, Tixall Road, Stafford ST18 0XZ (☎ 01785 242594; **f**: 01785 228521). The section opened in 1995. A double grave costs £525 (incl. the first interment and an ash, lime or beech tree; same for non-residents). £75 for interment of ashes in a previously purchased grave. They allow all types of biodegradable coffins and shrouds and will give assistance for DIY funerals. Families are permitted to fill graves. There are plans for a memorial wall. The site is a 'naturalised area with marsh, open fields as a boundary to two sides. Mature trees and shrubs in the old section of the cemetery. 15 burials have taken place so far, with another eight plots pre-purchased; there is space for 300 burials in total' (Anthony Evans).

65. **(Strensham, Worcestershire)**: A new site planned by Green Woodland Burial Services who already manage two natural burial sites. They have planning permission and it is hoped that the site will be operating shortly. Further information incl. a price list can be obtained from Green Woodland Burial Services, see Manningtree, Essex, below for contact details. 'This site is in a rural location yet has easy access from the M5 motorway' (Peter Kincaid).

66. Stroud: For locals only. Brimscombe woodland burial area, a difficult-to-reach part of a regular cemetery, with no seat to rest on at the top: 'I have never carried a coffin as far under such difficult conditions,' reports one undertaker. It is also rather expensive at £1,386 a grave (incl. digging, and a rowan, wild cherry, field maple or birch tree planted November-March). Burial of ashes costs £1,139. They allow biodegradable coffins (not chipboard ones) and shrouds. They cannot supply coffins, but can help DIY families in other ways. The site is on a hillside adjacent to open country, with views across the valley. Only for those who lived or were born in the area (but if non-residents can show a 'tenable link with the area, individual cases, and costs, will be considered at the discretion of the council'). A plot can be reserved in advance for £541. Contact George Damsell, Housing & Environmental Services, Stroud District Council, Ebley Mill, Westward Road, Stroud GL5 4UB (☎ 01453 754425; **f**: 01453 754409).

67. Worcester: A wild flower meadow green burial ground at Astwood Cemetery, Tintern Avenue, Worcester WR3 8HA; run by the City of Worcester Council (☎ 01905 22633). A grave costs £520 (incl. digging, a memorial inscription and tree planting 'in accordance with the development plan'). They will accept home-made, cardboard or wicker coffins. An inscribed stepping stone in the grass pathway costs £180; a two-line inscription in the nearby crematorium's Book of Remembrance is free. Bird and bat boxes have been put up. Family and friends can fill the grave if they wish and can help in a token way with the digging. 'The site is a wildlife area surrounded by hedges in an old part of the cemetery, with lots of very large established trees nearby. We are currently adopting the Charter for the Bereaved' (Marion Boulter).

East Midlands

Comprising Derbyshire, Nottinghamshire, Leicestershire, Northamptonshire, Bedfordshire, Oxfordshire, Buckinghamshire.

68. ✪✪✪ [**] Nr. Alfreton: Golden Valley Woodland Burial Ground, Nr. Newlands Road, Riddings, Nr. Alfreton, Derbyshire; run by Peace Funerals, Gleadless Mount, Sheffield S12 2LN (☎ 0114 2530505 or freephone 0800 093 0505; **f**: 0114 2530503; **e**: peacefuner@aol.com; **w**: www.peacefunerals.co.uk). Opened September 1996; 50 burials have taken place so far. A grave costs £335 (incl. a British native tree; digging £195 extra, unless families do their own digging); same for non-residents. York stone memorial plaque with room for 50 characters costs £105. All types of coffin and shrouds accepted. Ashes may be interred for £145 (incl. a tree). Transportation of the coffin and the funeral party can be by steam train to the track-side cemetery (from the Midland Railway Centre at Ripley in Derbyshire); the funeral would then cost about £1,500. Full catering options are available on the train. A preserved tin tabernacle near the site may be used for religious or secular funeral ceremonies. The one-acre burial ground can only be reached by train or through the Golden Valley Country Park. 'A lovely secluded setting, away from any road or housing, with woodland on two sides. Families can choose their own tree type and plot. A Friends group meets for mutual support and to advise on policy' (John Mallatratt). Other arrangements as for the South Yorkshire Woodland Burial Ground (see above). Prepaid plan: Golden Leaves. Funds are put in a Trust.

69. **Bedford**: One-acre woodland burial site at Norse Road Cemetery, 104 Norse Road, Bedford MK41 0RL (☎ 01234 353701/359986; **e**: crem@bedford.gov.uk); run by Bedford Borough Council. A grave (75 years) costs £330 incl. a small granite marker or plaque; £214 for a second interment in an existing grave. An approved native tree, shrub or rose bush may be planted at the head of the grave. Recycled cardboard coffins are sold at the Cemetery Office. 'Embalming is not allowed. 600 burials are planned for the area. No chemicals are used in maintaining the area. There is a large wild bird population' (Michael Day).

70. **Belper, Derbyshire**: Woodland burial is offered at Belper Cemetery, Matlock Road, Broadholme, Belper. Contact Borough Development Dept, Amber Valley Borough Council, PO Box 18, Town Hall, Ripley, Derbyshire DE5 3SZ (☎ 01773 841418; **f**: 01773 841539; **e**: enquiry@ambervalley.gov.uk; **w**: www.amber valley.gov.uk). A grave costs £473 incl. digging; £710 for non-residents. Biodegradable coffins, shrouds or other appropriate containers (wood should be from managed forests) preferred. Ashes may be buried or scattered. No memorials allowed within the woodland area. 'A Helping You leaflet is available on request' (Paul Martin, Cemetery Officer).

71. (**Blidworth, Notts**): Green burial at Undermill Woodland Cemetery; run by Steve Taylor, 14 Dale Lane, Blidworth, Nr. Mansfield, Nottinghamshire, NG21 OTG (☎ 01623 798842). Reapplying for planning permission.

72. (**Bulwell, Nr. Nottingham**): For 2005/6, a three to four-acre woodland burial site planned for High Wood, Bulwell, five miles north of Nottingham City centre; to be run by Nottingham City Council. Contact Alec Thomson, Bereavement Services Manager, Lawrence House, Talbot Street, Nottingham NG1 5NT (☎ 0115 915 6106; **e**: alec.thomson@nottinghamcity.gov.uk). To complement an area of existing ancient woodland within a 30-acre site.

73. **Buxton, (Glossop, Hope, Thornsett)**: Four small green burial areas have been created by the High Peak Borough Council within their cemeteries. Contact Terry Redfern, HPBC, 22 Market Street, Buxton, SK17 6LY (☎ 01298 74570; **e**: terryr@highpeak.gov.uk). A grave costs £374.50 (incl. digging and a 'contribution towards the planting of trees and bulbs on the grave and continuing maintenance'). Ashes may be interred for £217. No memorials allowed. Families may arrange a DIY funeral, but no assistance will be given. All types of biodegradable coffins and shrouds accepted. 50 burials have taken place so far.

74. (**Nr. Chesterfield, Derbyshire**): A natural burial park is being developed by Green Celebrations, a not-for-profit social firm, at: Williamthorpe Hills, Holmewood & Heath, Nr. Chesterfield, Derbyshire. The site is situated on three acres of land near to M1 junction 29. Adjacent to a nature trail which links former coalfield sites in the area, the site overlooks Williamthorpe Ponds with an adjoining nature reserve and open countryside. It is already wooded but further planting and landscaping work is being completed. It is planned to open the site formally in 2004. For information contact Tim Dowdell (☎ 01629 823421).

75. Derby: Woodland Grave section at Nottingham Road Cemetery; run by Derby City Council, Nottingham Road Cemetery Office, Nottingham Road, Derby DE21 6FN (☎ 01332 672761; e: cemetery@derby.gov.uk). A grave costs £400, incl. digging and a contribution towards planting and landscaping. Ashes may be scattered for £100 or buried for £130. All fees double for non-residents. No embalmed bodies allowed. All types of biodegradable coffin or shroud are acceptable, provided that the body is covered and labelled and the coffin has not been treated with varnishes or preservatives. 'The woodland area will be disturbed as little as possible at the time of each interment, as we wish to encourage wildflowers and wildlife to become established in the area. No pesticides will be used. We will provide benches in the area for everyone to use. At the time of each interment a brass plaque will be placed on one of the benches unless the applicant does not require this' (Bereavement Services).

76. Erewash, Derbyshire: Two natural burial sites: one at Park Cemetery, Ilkeston, and one at Longmoor Cemetery, Breaston; run by Erewash Borough Council, Customer Services, Town Hall, Derby Road, Long Eaton NG10 1HU (☎ 0115 9072319; e: enquiries@erewash.gov.uk; w: www.erewash.gov.uk). A grave costs £284-76 (incl. digging, a sapling and planting); double for non-residents. Ashes may be scattered or buried. 'Embalming is not allowed, indeed the Council no longer use any chemicals in these areas' (Caroline Price).

77. [**] Gerrards Cross, Buckinghamshire: Parkside Woodland Burial Ground, Parkside Cemetery, Windsor Road, Gerrards Cross, Bucks SL9 8SS (☎ 01753 662426); run by South Bucks District Council. Open since 1996. 40 burials so far, with a further 30 plots pre-sold. A grave costs £241 (£321 for non-residents). A child's grave (half-size) costs £107 (£187 for non-residents). Digging has to be arranged with a private contractor such as Mr Heyburn on 07967 651586 (he charges around £300). There is also an interment fee of £53. So, for a non-resident, a burial would cost about £674. Ashes can be interred from £53. For £55 a tree or bush will be planted and taken care of for ten years; 'trees are often supplied by the grave owner, we don't object to non-native types'. All sorts of wild flowers, perennials, small shrubs, bulbs etc are allowed, providing they are kept within the confines of the 10ft x 5ft grave area. They accept home-made, cardboard or wicker coffins, body bags or shrouds. Mourners may fill the grave if they wish. Limited assistance is offered to DIY families. A small wooden or slate plaque at the bottom of the tree would be possible, if arranged by the family. 'The two-acre site is an extension of the existing lawn cemetery, with a field with ponies beyond and woodland behind the field. Until the woodland matures, the area will be treated as a wild flower hay meadow. We allow areas of long grass to encourage invertebrates and we are not too tough on brambles and nettles. Many of the wild flowers have naturalised themselves. Our prices are reasonable for this area. Graves can be prepurchased. The M4 and M40 are readily accessible' (Ian Richens, Superintendent). (Eds: this site, and Mr Richens, seem to be popular with North Londoners who cannot afford London grave prices.)

78. Glossop: Green burial ground created by the High Peak Borough Council within their cemetery in Glossop, Derbyshire. See Buxton above for details.

79. Hope: Green burial ground created by the High Peak Borough Council at their cemetery in Hope, Derbyshire. See Buxton above for details. (Eds: users comment, 'Natural setting, at a distance from the main cemetery. Grassland, with thinly-planted trees and thicker trees in the background, on a slight slope. Approached from a country lane'; 'Reserve your plot to avoid disappointment'.)

80. [**] Nr. Leicester: Scraptoft Natural Burial Ground, five miles from the centre of Leicester and one mile from Scraptoft towards Keyham; run by the Natural Burial Company, Parkfield Western Park, Hinckley Road, Leicester LE3 6HX (☎ 0116 2220247, f: 0116 2552343; e: info@naturalburial.co.uk; w: www.naturalburial.co.uk). Eight burials have taken place since the site opened in 2002, with many more pre-bookings. For prices, see Prestwold entry below. 'Scraptoft burial ground is situated on a gentle slope in a quiet valley in one of the most attractive and historic areas of Leicestershire. Woodland with open wildflower glades to be created as the burial ground develops' (Nicola Duffield).

81. Mansfield, Nottinghamshire: Woodland burial ground as an extension to Mansfield Woodhouse Cemetery; run by Mansfield District Council. Contact Mrs Sally Curtis, Assistant Registrar of Cemeteries, Mansfield and District Crematorium, Derby Road, Mansfield, Notts NG18 5BJ (☎ 01623 621811). 11 burials have taken place so far with 20 plots pre-sold. An adult grave (75 years) costs £196; a child's from £80 to £119. Plus £196 for the digging. Biodegradable caskets encouraged, but not obligatory. There is space for 206 double graves arranged in clusters to permit the development of a woodland copse. Following guidance from the Woodland Trust, oak, ash, birch and rowan trees are planted in appropriate blocks. For maximum encouragement of wildlife, wild flowers and trees, no memorials are allowed on the site, but there is a memorial wall and a Book of Remembrance available.

82. Northampton: Green burial area, Kingsthorpe Cemetery, Harborough Road North, Kingsthorpe, Northampton; run by Northampton Borough Council, Community Services, Cemetery Office, Cliftonville House, Bedford Road, Northampton NN4 7NR (☎ 01604 838903; e: cemeteries@northampton.gov.uk). Green burial offered in this large cemetery since 1996. A grave (99 years) costs £517.50 (incl. digging); double for non-residents. Home-made, cardboard, wicker and bamboo coffins and shrouds accepted. Will assist with DIY if asked. 100-year-old chapel, with seating for approx. 60 people, available. 'Welcoming to everyone who visits. Helpful ground staff. Mature shrubs and trees' (Irene Thompson, Cemetery Officer).

83. Nr. Nottingham: Tithe Green Burial Ground, The Estate Office, Grange Farm, Oxton, Nottinghamshire NG25 ORG (Ian Johnson, ☎ 01623 882210). This 40-acre site, five miles north of Nottingham, near Calverton and the A614, is in peaceful countryside, adjacent to a forest, with a stream, the Dover Beck, running alongside. Memorial trees are planted to form large clumps of trees, and wild flower seed is scattered. A grave costs £280, plus £120 for the digging, if required. Families may arrange the digging and filling themselves if they wish. A native British species tree – ash, oak, lime, wild cherry, rowan or birch – costs £70. Biodegradable coffins are available. A prepaid grave plot costs £250. There have been 120 burials so far. 'The concept is appropriate as the burial ground is within the boundary of the historic Sherwood Forest' (Ian Johnson). (Eds: users have described this site as: 'Meadowland bordered on one side by mature woodland'; 'Very peaceful. Having been present at the burial, my parents have now expressed a wish to be buried there. However, I was disappointed that some of the trees that had been planted didn't look very well cared for'.)

84. **Oakham, Rutland**: Ketton Park Green Burial, run by Roger Mills, Hawthorn Cottage, Ketton Road, Empingham, Oakham, Rutland LE15 8QD (☎ 01780 460000; **m**: 07801 090777; **e**: mail@greenburial.co.uk; **w**: www.greenburial.co.uk). This 35-acre site opened in 2000. A grave costs £400 (incl. digging, for a 99-year lease). A broadleaf tree costs £50. A granite plaque 12ins by 12ins, set at ground level, costs £75. Ashes may be interred for £150, or scattered for £50. Prices are the same for non-residents. The site will become a wildflower meadow with trees. It is situated in the bottom of the River Chater valley; typical rolling Leicestershire countryside, protected from the A6121 by a band of trees. Ten per cent of the income from sale of plots is paid into a trust fund to maintain the site in the long-term. (Eds: the first member of the public to use Ketton Park said, 'I went back three weeks after the funeral and have never seen a more breathtaking sight: thousands of flowers of every type and hue covered the entire field.' Other users say, 'We particularly liked the tranquility and peacefulness, the copses, the horses in the adjoining field'.)

85. **Olney, Buckinghamshire**: Olney Green Burial Ground, Yardley Road, Olney, Bucks MK46 5EH (☎ 01234 241808; **f**: 01234 240363; **e**: information@ thegreenburialcompany.plc.uk; **w**: www.thegreenburialcompany.com). This 9.5-acre site opened May 2000. 200 burials have taken place so far, and a similar number of rights to burial purchased. Plots cost from £375 in the 'high' density' meadow area, to £895 (for a large 4m x 4m grave and a native tree) in the 'low density' area. Prices incl. digging; same for non-residents. Ashes may be interred for £275 or scattered for £245. A simple complete funeral costs from £995 (incl. a meadow plot). DIY is welcomed with help available as required. Families can help dig and fill the grave, subject to supervision. A full range of coffins and biodegradable containers can be supplied. 'Located on peaceful but not isolated undulating pastureland on the outskirts and overlooking the small country town of Olney (famous for its annual pancake race). The site, much acclaimed by visitors for its attractiveness and atmosphere, is in various stages of gradual change to natural oak woodland and has two distinct areas for burial, ashes burial or scattering or just memorial tree planting. There are few signs that the area is used for burials with every effort made to encourage wildlife and natural change whilst meeting the client's expectations of a caring environment and a safe, cared for resting place for their loved ones' (Warwick Clark, MD).

86. **Oxford**: Hugh Dawson, Cemetery Manager, Wolvercote Cemetery, Banbury Road, Oxford OX2 8EE (☎ 01865 513962). Woodland burial plots are located at three cemeteries in Oxford: Wolvercote (a corner of the cemetery on the boundary with the recreation ground and sports ground); Headington Cemetery (Dunston Road); and Botley Cemetery (North Hinksey Lane). A grave costs

£450 (incl. digging; double for non-residents). A tree costs £63 extra and bulbs £34. They accept biodegradable coffins, but no body bags or shrouds. Trees are planted October-May and relatives can help – choosing between a whitebeam, silver birch, hazel, field maple or wild service tree. Individual trees are guaranteed for 20 years; if a tree is lost during that period it will be replaced free of charge. Beyond that period, some coppicing and thinning will be required. In addition, a maximum of 100 wild flowers may be planted from a selection of bluebells, snowdrops, wood anemones or wood violets.

87. (Oxfordshire): A three-acre woodland burial site in Oxfordshire (with room for 3,000 to 3,500 graves) expected to be open by 2005. Contact Liz Rothschild of Colleymore Farm, Coleshill, Highworth, Swindon, Wiltshire SN6 7PU (☎ 01367 240508). No prices yet. 'Surrounded by organic farmland near Watchfield Village off the A420 in sight of the Offington white horse and downs. The River Cole flows nearby and there is an ancient Roman spring. I can also offer support with creating ceremonies to mark the burial as I have been working with people in this field for over ten years' (Liz Rothschild).

88. [**] **Prestwold, Nr. Loughborough**: Prestwold Natural Burial Ground. A 1.5-hectare site, set in a 4-hectare nature reserve at Burton Bandalls (1.5 miles east of Loughborough); run by the Natural Burial Company, Parkfield Western Park, Hinckley Road, Leicester LE3 6HX (☎ 0116 2220247, f: 0116 2552343; e: info@naturalburial.co.uk; w: www.naturalburial.co.uk). Opened March 2000. A grave in the meadow area costs £395. A grave in the Memorial Tree area, where families can choose a specific plot and a native tree, costs from £545 for a silver birch, up to £845 for an oak tree. £495 for a grave with a shared tree only (incl. plaque and marker). Plus £150 for the hand-digging of the grave. Families may help fill the grave, but not dig. No visible grave markers allowed apart from the tree and plaque. Graves are marked with a microchip. Biodegradable coffins are preferred. Local-grown oak plaques can be fixed on posts around the burial areas for £35. Ashes may be buried in a small wood or in grave plots (eg a full grave with a tree for six ashes interments). Memorial bird and bat boxes can be placed in trees. Memorial seats, benches and trees for those buried or cremated elsewhere are also available. They have a list of friendly local undertakers, and offer advice and help for DIY. 'This site is one mile from the main road in a quiet setting with views of open countryside and Charnwood Forest. From Loughborough, take A60 to Nottingham, after 3/4 mile take B676 to Prestwold, after about 3/4 mile the site is on the right, well-indicated with road signs. Entrance via private road and large car park. Landscaped gently with over 10,000 tons of fine subsoil laid to provide a suitable medium for wildflowers' (Paul Ginns).

89. **Retford, Nottinghamshire**: Woodland burial area at The Cemetery, North Road, Retford, Nottinghamshire; run by Bassetlaw District Council, Carlton Forest House, Hundred Acre Lane, Carlton, Worksop S81 OTS (☎ 01909 533487). The site opened in 1999 with room for 700 burials. A grave costs £750 (incl. digging, a tree and a name plaque; £1,125 for non-residents). Trees are birch, holly, hawthorn, hazel, yew or mountain ash. They will accept biodegradable coffins, and body bags or shrouds. This one-acre woodland burial ground is in an old cemetery with established trees. Boats pass up and down the Chesterfield canal, and it could probably be arranged for a coffin to be delivered by boat. The grave area is deep enough for single graves without disturbing any remains that may still be there (the last burial was at least 100 years ago). Mourners cannot help with the digging for safety reasons. 'The Cemetery has a country park character' (Ron Clark).

90. Rothwell: Green burial ground opened as an extension to Rothwell Cemetery, Loddington Road, Rothwell, Northants. Contact Burials and Cremations Manager, Kettering Borough Council, East Lodge, Kettering Crematorium, Rothwell Road, Kettering NN16 8XE (☎ 01536 525722). Ten burials have taken place so far and six plots reserved. A grave costs £295 incl.digging, and to register an interest in a plot for the future costs £50 double for non-residents). They will accept biodegradable coffins and cardboard coffins can be supplied at cost. The staff are available to assist DIY families. The area is being developed as a meadowland site and no memorials or additional trees are permitted.

91. Thornsett, Nr. New Mills, Derbyshire: Green burial ground created by the High Peak Borough Council within their cemetery in Thornsett, Nr. New Mills. See Buxton above for details. (Eds: one visitor called this site 'nice enough'.)

92. Worksop, Nottinghamshire: A two-acre woodland burial ground opened in January 1999, attached to Hannah Park Cemetery, Netherton Road, Worksop, Nottinghamshire. 16 burials have taken place so far and there is room for about 1,400 graves. Enquiries to Bassetlaw District Council, Carlton Forest House, Hundred Acre Lane, Carlton, Worksop S81 OTS (☎ 01909 533487). A grave costs £750 (incl. digging, a tree – birch, holly, hawthorn, hazel, yew or mountain ash – and a name plaque; £1,125 for non-residents). They accept biodegradable coffins, body bags or shrouds (and can advise on where to obtain these). Families cannot help with the digging for safety reasons. 'The entrance is through a natural copse of woodland, opening up into an eight-acre cemetery with panoramic views of the town. The site will help to extend the ancient Hannah Park Wood.' (Ron Clark). (Eds: one visitor says, 'A south-facing slope with woods visible all around. Some noise from the nearby bypass travels up, somewhat detracting from an otherwise idyllic site.')

East Anglia

Comprising Norfolk, Suffolk, Essex, Cambridgeshire & Hertfordshire.

93. ✪✪✪ [**] Barton, Cambridgeshire: The Church of England has chosen for its first green cemetery a consecrated 38-acre site on a quiet hill just west of Cambridge between Barton and Comberton (The Arbory Trust, Bishop Woodford House, Barton Road, Ely CB7 4DX, ☎ 01284 749974; **e**: info@arborytrust.org; **w**: www.arborytrust.org). The site opened June 2001. There is room for up to 2000 graves. 60 burials have taken place so far; 168 graves have been pre-purchased. A grave costs £500 (plus £120 for the digging, paid direct to the gravedigger). Ashes may be interred for £250 (plus £60 for the digging). Graves are located in glades and the site has already been planted with beech tree saplings. All types of biodegradable coffin or shroud are accepted and it is preferred that bodies are not embalmed. Families may help with the digging and filling of the grave. There is a memorial tree scheme and memorial seats available. 'The site is set in the Cambridgeshire countryside on a slight hill which rises up facing south. The Arbory Trust is a charitable Christian Foundation (charity no. 1079635) which welcomes all regardless of race or religion. Everybody who works for the Arbory Trust has been given training in bereavement counselling. We hope to have many more woodlands in the future' (Anita Gregory). (Eds: one early user of this site wrote in to say, 'The vicar said how refreshing it was and how right it felt. I am satisfied that this site will exist for many centuries to come'.)

94. Benfleet, Essex: Woodland Burial Ground, Woodside Cemetery, Manor Road, Thundersley, Essex SS7 4PH; run by Castle Point Borough Council, Cemeteries Office, Leisure Services Directorate, Council Offices, Kiln Road, Benfleet, Essex SS7 1TF (☎ 01268 882200; **e**: gsnook@castlepoint.gov.uk). There is room for 328 graves; eight plots have been used so far. A grave costs from £190 (same for non-residents) plus £23 for a tree. Ashes may be interred for £25 (£50 for non-residents). They will accept cardboard, wicker and bamboo coffins. 'The site stands by the main car park facing a green valley backed by trees and hedges. All graves are dug for one person only; adjacent spaces can be reserved at the time of the first interment' (Gerald Snook, Cemeteries Officer).

95. Brinkley, Cambs: Brinkley Woodland Cemetery, Balsham Lane, off Six Mile Bottom Road, Brinkley; run by Countryside Burials Ltd, The Old Courts, 147 All Saints Road, Newmarket, Suffolk CB8 8HH (☎ 01638 600693; **f**: 01638 560869; **e**: bwc@countryside-burials.co.uk). Phase 1 of this 33-acre rural woodland burial site opened July 2000. An adult grave costs from £550; or £450 for a child and £360 for an infant (all prices incl. digging; same for non-residents). Families can help fill, not dig, the grave. A tree: ash, oak, lime, beech, larch, wild cherry, silver birch or hazel, may be purchased (£150 incl. planting and a five-year replacement guarantee). Home-made, cardboard, wicker, bamboo or pine (from managed forests) coffins, and body bags or shrouds of natural fibres accepted. Ashes interred from £275. Although not encouraged, a ground-level granite tablet (14ins x9ins) as a memorial costs from £200 incl. inscription and installation. 'Open rolling countryside interspersed with woodlands. Trees will be planted to build up the woodland, leaving an area as meadow to be cut only in the autumn to encourage wild flowers, birds, insects and other wildlife' (Bernard Edge).

96. Burnham-on-Crouch: Woodland burial offered at Burnham-on-Crouch Cemetery, Southminster Road; run by Maldon District Council. 'Trees are gradually being planted. A pergola for climbing plants and memorial plaques is planned' (Richard Yelland). Prices and contact details as for Maldon below.

97. Bury St Edmunds: A small green burial area is included within Borough Cemetery, King's Road, Bury St Edmunds. Contact Maggie Moss, Cemetery Registrar, St Edmundsbury Borough Council, Angel Hill, Bury St Edmunds IP33 1XB (☎ 01284 763 233). A grave costs £430 incl. digging and memorial trees planted from £100. They will accept biodegradable coffins.

98. (Cambridge): Green burial area of about an acre included in plans for a new cemetery near the City Crematorium, Huntingdon Road, Cambridge CB3 0JJ (Cemeteries Manager, David Giles, ☎ 01954 780681); run by Cambridge City Council. Set to open late 2003. No prices have been fixed as yet (a plot in the traditional part of the cemetery costs £760; £1,660 for non-residents). No provision planned for family assistance in digging and backfilling graves.

99. (Cheshunt, Herts): One-acre woodland burial area with room for 400 graves planned for 2005 at Cheshunt Cemetery, Bury Green, Cheshunt EN7 5AG; run by Broxbourne Borough Council (Jim Duncan, The Cemetery Office, Bishops College, Churchgate, Cheshunt EN8 9XF, ☎ 01992 785507; e: leisure@broxbourne.gov.uk). Current cost of a woodland grave in the conventional section is £560 (quadruple for non-residents; £50 extra for a tree). Families can help with the digging. A brass plaque memorial on a wooden stake costs £60. They will supply biodegradable coffins for trade prices plus 12.5 per cent.

100. [**] Colney, South Norfolk: Colney Woodland Burial Park, Watton Road, Colney, Norwich NR4 7TY (☎ 01603 811556, f: 01603 811770; e: enquiries@woodlandburialparks.co.uk; w: www.woodlandburialparks.co.uk). Graves cost £1,500, £2,000, £2,500 and £3,000 (incl. digging); same prices for non-residents. Most graves are sited around an already mature tree, but families may also purchase a tree to plant near their plot if required. Ashes may be scattered for £100, or interred for £500 or £750. English oak memorials are also available. An elegant Woodland Hall for funeral services may also be used by those not buying a plot at Colney. A Gathering Hall provides a warm and welcoming meeting point. Refreshments can be offered, ample WC facilities are available and the needs of the disabled are fully supported. A woodland shelter is available for families to use when visiting the park. There is an area dedicated solely to animals; and another area providing for burials of pets with owners. The park is manged by an independent trust, ensuring longterm management and maintenance for the site and its occupants. (Eds: users say, 'Wonderful'; 'Extremely satisfied. Handled in a gentle and considerate way. Picturesque ambience'; 'Informal friendliness, willingness to offer instant help and advice, obvious expert wildlife knowledge'; 'A mature woodland, well-maintained, with friendly, helpful staff'; 'All your staff are the best anyone could wish for'.)

101. (Culford, Nr. Bury St Edmunds, Suffolk): A new site planned by Green Woodland Burial Services; see Manningtree below for contact details.

102. Harlow, Essex: A woodland burial ground in Parndon Wood, Parndon Wood Road, Great Parndon, Harlow CM19 4SF (☎ 01279 423800/446199; e: chris.brown@harlow.gov.uk); run by Harlow District Council. Opened 2001. Eight burials have taken place so far. A grave costs £560 (incl. digging). Trees are not planted by the graves, but families may contribute to the Living Memorial Fund which subsidises the planting of trees on site to create an area of natural woodland. Indigenous wild flowers are sown on each grave.

103. Haverhill Suffolk: A small green burial area is included within Haverhill Cemetery. Contact Maggie Moss, Cemetery Registrar, St Edmundsbury Borough Council, Angel Hill, Bury St Edmunds IP33 1XB (☎ 01284 763 233). A grave costs £430 incl. digging and memorial trees planted from £100. They will accept biodegradable coffins.

104. **Hemel Hempstead**: Woodland burial ground; run by Linda Gizzie, Cemetery Manager, Dacorum Borough Council, Woodwells Cemetery, Buncefield Lane, Hemel Hempstead, Herts HP2 7HY (☎ 01442 252856). Opened in 1999. A grave costs £506 (incl. digging; double for non-residents) plus extra at cost for any one of nine native British species trees. Families can fill the grave if they wish and can help with a token amount of digging. The woodland area is a one-acre patch near the main cemetery, bounded by a fence and trees, on flat ground. It is part of what used to be a farm until bought by the council. It is near the M1 and near a caravan storage area.

105. **[**] Herongate, Essex**: A 14-acre green burial ground to the south of Billericay Road, Herongate, Brentwood; owned by the Woodland and Wildlife Conservation Co. Ltd (a new green burial company set up 'to preserve the green spaces around London'). Contact Ray Ward or Jackie Sawtell, Birch Hall Farm, Coppice Row, Theydon Bois, Essex CM16 7DR (☎ 01992 814909, f: 01992 814910; e: enquiries@woodlandandwildlife.co.uk; w: www.woodlandand wildlife.co.uk). Burials began in May 2003. A grave costs £750 (incl. the digging, use of the Hall of Remembrance, if available, and an electronic locator tag). Familes may help with the digging and filling, at their own risk. Ashes may be scattered for £150, or buried from £400. £25 from every plot payment is paid to the Trust Company to create a fund for longterm maintenance. In the dormant season young trees are planted across the burial area; individual trees with name plaques may also be purchased for an additional £250. An oak (£85) or granite (£300) grave marker may also be purchased. The ashes of a small family pet may be buried in the owner's plot. 'An open meadow site, looking down a natural valley with existing woods on two sides, carpeted in bluebells in the spring. A pond is being restored and planted as a quiet area of contemplation. No grave will ever be re-used or disturbed' (Ray Ward). (Eds: early users have commented, 'It has great potential and is in an ideal location. The staff were very helpful'; 'It will be very beautiful when the trees are planted. The staff were very caring. Excellent facilities. One couldn't wish for a more peaceful burial'.)

106. **(North Hertfordshire)**: Woodland and flower meadow burial areas planned for two new cemeteries to be run by North Hertfordshire District Council, Leisure & Community Devlopment, Gernon Road, Letchworth SG6 3JF. Contact Mr Andrew Mills (☎ 01462 474272) for more information.

107. **(Nr. Ipswich, Suffolk)**: The owners of part of Walk Farm Woods in Martlesham have a new planning application for a green burial site with Suffolk Coastal District Council. Plans include a proposal to build nine shelters, one large building and a car park at the site. For information, contact the owners' agent: Tim Worthington-Chapman, The Burrell Partnership (☎ 01603 760588).

108. **Maldon, Essex**: Woodland Glades, Maldon Cemetery, London Road, Maldon; contact Maldon District Council Offices, Princes Road, Maldon, Essex CM9 5DL (☎ 01621 875747; e: richard.yelland@maldon.gov.uk). Opened 1996. A grave costs £305 (£650 for non-residents). Plus, at the time of burial, an admin fee of £204 (£408 for non-residents) and the digging fee (approx. £170). There is no fee for the supply and care of trees, shrubs and bulbs where applicable. They accept biodegradable coffins and shrouds. Mourners cannot help dig or fill the grave. Ashes may be scattered or interred and a plaque placed either on a plinth by a tree or on the memorial wall. The woodland area borders farmland within the walled boundary of an existing mature cemetery. 'On a Day of Dedication in Winter the bereaved are invited to plant trees, shrubs and bulbs' (Richard Yelland, Cemeteries Officer).

109. [**] **Manningtree, Essex**: Oakfield Wood Green Burial Ground, Wrabness Hall, Wrabness, Manningtree, Essex CO11 2TQ (☎ John Acton 01255 880182). General enquiries and enquiries about the other sites they operate to the site agent: Peter Kincaid, Green Woodland Burial Services, 256 High Street, Dovercourt, Harwich CO12 3PA (☎ 0800 37 47 59/ 01255 503456, f: 01255 554833; e: gburials@talk21.com; w: www.greenburials.co.uk). Farmer John Acton manages this seven-acre burial ground overlooking the River Stour, but has given ownership of the land to Essex Wildlife Trust. A grave (perpetuity) costs £598.75 (incl. digging, a tree, a wooden plaque, a tree guard, and entry into Register of Burials with an Ordnance Survey grid reference). The £1448.75 funeral price includes a biodegradable coffin, the burial and collection of the body from anywhere within a 100-mile radius of the site (including London). Interment of ashes costs £548.75. They will accept biodegradable coffins, body bags or shrouds. Mourners may assist in digging and filling. A native broadleaf tree is planted at every plot in the dormant planting season. The ground is in set-aside farmland. The perimeter is planted with about 22,000 hardwood native hedging plants. Any monies paid in advance go into a Trustee account. 'Our prices are competitive, and it's a special scenic location that will be preserved by a charitable Wildlife Trust' (Peter Kincaid).

110. **Peterborough, Cambs**: Green burial area in Fletton Cemetery, Peterborough; run by Peterborough City Council Community Services, Peterborough Crematorium, Mowbray Road, North Bretton, Peterborough PE6 7JE (☎ 01733 262639, f: 01733 265698; e: kate.day@peterborough.gov.uk). Space for 400 graves. A grave costs £710 incl. digging and a bronze plaque on the memorial wall (less for children; £1,710 for non-residents). They accept biodegradable or softwood coffins from managed forests, or shrouds. Relatives may help fill the grave. 'After five years of burials we have started the first phase of soft landscaping – planting trees and shrubs on the graves where burials have already taken place. Visitors often comment on the fedge, a living fence of woven willow, when they visit the section for the first time. This is now well-established, making an attractive boundary between traditional burial areas and the green section on this mature cemetery site' (Kate Day).

111. **Saxmundham**: Greenwood Burial Ground run by the undertaker Tony Brown, The Funeral Service, New Cut, Saxmundham, Suffolk IP17 1DJ (☎ 01728 603108; f: 01728 604346). There have been 65 burials and intinterments of ashes so far. A grave costs from £1,235 (incl. digging, a coffin and transport within Suffolk, but no tree as the site is already planted; plus extra for mileage outside Suffolk, a chapel or graveside service, reception etc). A pre-booked plot costs £350 plus £135 for the digging. Charles Barnett of the Green Party was the first person to put his name down for burial at this 20-acre site which comprises about a quarter of Racewalk Covert, a private nature reserve in the parish of Farnham, East Suffolk. Already planted with deciduous native trees in rows. Burial plots are about ten feet square, so a single grave 'will occupy a central position between four trees in about 100sq feet of land. All wreaths removed after 14 days, after which a small flat wooden plaque is allowed, but the only decoration is to be wild flowers. No marble, metal pots or jam jars are permitted so that the graves integrate with the trees in a natural fashion. There is even a separate area for your pets' (T. Brown). (Eds: Tony Brown has an excellent reputation as a funeral director, but unfortunately this site had to be turned down for Association membership as families are not permitted to organise the funeral themselves, but must use Brown's services and coffins.)

112. [**] **Three Rivers, Hertfordshire**: A woodland burial site at Woodcock Hill, Harefield Road, Rickmansworth; run by Three Rivers District Council, Rickmansworth, Hertfordshire WD3 1RL (☎ 01923 776611/727031; **e**: Lindsey.Trodd@threerivers.gov.uk). A grave costs £402 (incl. digging and a one-off contribution towards the annual planting of native trees and bulbs); double for non-residents. Plot only £190. Only biodegradable coffins, shrouds and body bags allowed. No memorials. 'We want a natural woodland to develop over the years, where future generations can walk, or sit and contemplate. Some areas will be left to form natural meadowland. The only grave markers will be small numbered tablets' (Lindsey Trodd, Environmental Support Officer).

The South West

Comprising South Gloucestershire, Bristol, Bath & North East Somerset, North West Somerset, Somerset, Dorset, Devon, Cornwall.

113. **Bath**: Woodland burial section in Haycombe Cemetery, Whiteway Road, Bath BA2 2RQ (☎ 01225 423682; **f**: 01225 316339; **e**: Cemeteries_Crematorium @bathnes.gov.uk; **w**: www.bathnes.gov.uk/directservices/cemcrem). Site with rural views. A grave costs £1,100 incl. digging, a tree and a small metal plaque; £1,540 for non-residents. Ashes can be interred at a separate site for £550. Free advice and help with paperwork is offered to those not using undertakers. Families may help dig and fill the grave. All types of coffins or shrouds accepted. 'There is a list of trees suited to the soil here, but any reasonable request will be considered' (Rosemary Tiley, Bereavement Manager).

114. **Bournemouth**: Woodland Burials at Bournemouth North Cemetery; run by Bournemouth Borough Council (Cemeteries Manager, North Cemetery Office, Strouden Avenue, Bournemouth, Dorset BH8 9HX, ☎ 01202 526238; **e**: crematorium@bournemouth.gov.uk). A grave costs £583 incl. digging, a small plaque and a tree (12 types, incl. maple, silver birch, cedar and weeping willow); double for non-residents. Biodegradable coffins preferred. Mourners may help fill the grave. 'The woodland burial area forms part of the attractive

North Cemetery. The Cemetery contains many mature trees of a variety of species, and the woodland burial area enhances the range and appearance of the site, as well as offering a further choice to families' (Julie Dunk).

115. **Bristol**: Woodland Burial Site, South Bristol Cemetery, Bridgewater Road, Bedminster Down, Bristol BS13 7AS (☎ 0117 903 8330; **e**: simon_westbrook @bristol-city.gov.uk); run by Bristol City Council. A secluded woodland burial site of several acres overlooking Bristol, the Avon Gorge and the Suspension Bridge. The site opened in 1996; 70 burials have taken place so far, about ten per year. A grave for burial or cremated remains costs £850 incl. digging and a choice of seven native trees; same price for non-residents. Mourners may help fill the grave. They accept biodegradable coffins, body bags or shrouds. 'Wild flower seeds have been introduced and the grass is cut one or two times a year' (Simon Westbrook). (Eds: one visitor said that this site is set in the grounds of a stark 1960s crematorium, with mown lawns and Tarmac. However, the woodland burial area is 'impressive', with trees planted on the graves, and the staff are enthusiastic about the scheme. Further reports welcome.)

116. [**] **Nr. Bristol**: Bristol Memorial Woodlands, Earthcott Green, Alveston, Bristol BS35 3TA (☎ 01454 414999, **f**: 01454 419081; **w**: www.woodland cemeteries.com). A 25-acre burial ground in the valley. A grave (incl. digging, a tree, a small engraved flagstone and the use of the converted Georgian barns which provide a chapel and function rooms) costs from £850. Ashes may be buried (for a fee) or scattered free of charge. 'The site is approached by a driveway leading down from the Old Gloucester road to a car park. Access to the burial field is either on foot or by car if needed. The Memorial Woodland Trust is responsible for the choice of tree to ensure that the woodland develops as a coherent whole. Arrangements can be made for family pets to be buried. A proportion of the cost of each plot goes to the Memorial Woodland Trust which will ensure the longterm maintenance of the woodland' (Christopher Baker).

117. **Camborne, Cornwall**: Woodland burial at Killivose Cemetery, Camborne; run by Kerrier District Council, Direct Services, 2a Forth Kegyn, Dudnance Lane, Pool, Redruth TR15 3QU (☎ 01209 614050, **f**: 01209 717465; **e**: direct.services@kerrier.gov.uk; **w**: www.kerrier.gov.uk). A grave costs £667 (incl. digging) plus £78 to supply, plant and maintain a tree (oak, ash, alder, hazel, hawthorn or wild cherry). Only biodegradable coffins and adornments allowed. Wooden coffins must be made from timber felled in managed tree forests. 'Woodland burial will be chosen by those who love birds and wildlife and who wish to create a woodland for future generations, providing environmental benefits for the people of Kerrier for many years to come'(Kerrier DC).

118. (**Canford Magna, Dorset**): A woodland burial area planned for 2004/5; to be run by Poole Borough Council, jointly with Bournemouth Borough Council (see entry above). Contact Mr Steve Carter, Manager, Poole Crematorium, Gravel Hill, Poole, Dorset BH17 9BQ (☎ 01202 261347). The council has planning permission for a new 28-acre cemetery near Magna Road in Canford Magna, and the periphery will be set aside for woodland burial, with 'dense tree planting'. No more details as yet as funding is still being finalised.

119. [**] **Colehill, Nr. Wimborne, Dorset**: The Poole & Wimborne Woodland Burial Ground, Greenhill Road, Colehill, Wimborne, Dorset BH23 7EJ (☎ 01202 888887; **e**: info@woodlandburial.com; **w**: www.woodlandburial.com); owned by Woodland Burial Grounds Ltd, who also manage the award-winning Hinton Park Woodland Burial Ground at Christchurch. A 24-acre site in the Dorset countryside, which opened in 2002. A single grave (99 years) costs £395 (incl. digging and a tree). An additional £550 covers collection of the body within a 20-mile radius, provision of a place of rest before the burial, and complete arrangements for the burial. Ashes can be interred for £195 if Woodland Burial Grounds Ltd have arranged the cremation; otherwise ask for prices. A name plaque costs £65. They sell polished oak veneer, cardboard and wicker coffins from £200. Collection of the deceased can be at any time and from any area in the UK. Eg collection from London would cost approx. £190. The hearse used is a green-coloured Mercedes estate. A fleet of Mercedes vehicles, including a limousine, is also available for transportation of relatives and friends on the day of the burial. Outdoor religious services or a short committal service can be held in the meadow next to the plot for no charge if a church has not been attended beforehand. A service at any denomination of church can be arranged for £275. A range of catering is available for after the service. 'Colehill is a large area of fields with mature oak trees. The fields are on different levels and produce wonderful views of the surrounding countryside' (Keith Gillison).

120. [*] **Cheriton Bishop, Exeter, Devon**: Woodland burial site situated on a small family farm; run by M. D. & J. Chatfield, Crossways Farm, Cheriton Bishop, Exeter, Devon EX6 6JD (☎ 01647 24382; **e**: xways0@farmerweekly. net). A grave costs £400 incl. digging and a local native tree (chosen by the site managers, to get the balance correct) planted at the next planting season; £600 for non-residents of Devon. £50 for ash scattering on the grassy area, which will only to be cut twice yearly to encourage wild flowers. No embalming, and all coffins must be fully biodegradable. Funerals with or without funeral directors allowed. Family can help fill graves but not with the digging for safety reasons. 'The low-input farm is run under the Countryside Stewardship scheme and thus works with local flora and fauna. There are exceptional views across to Dartmoor and it is in an area of great landscape value – therefore no headstones etc. will be allowed, only a small tag to hang on the tree. Our aim is to provide what people want whether informal or otherwise' (Martin Chatfield).

121. **Dorchester**: Green burial at Poundbury Cemetery, run by Dorchester Council. Enquiries to Sue Cheeseman, Dorchester Joint Burial Committee, 19 North Square, Dorchester, Dorset DT1 1JF (☎ 01305 266861; **f**: 01305 266085; **e**: s.cheeseman@dorchester-tc.gov.uk). The cemetery, opened 2001, is located to the west of Dorchester between the historic town and the Poundbury development, and can be accessed from Poundbury Road. A grave costs £537 incl. digging and a microchip for identification. Ashes may be interred for £180. Only biodegradable coffins and shrouds, or coffins made from timber from managed forests allowed. Brass memorials embedded in flagstones available. 'The Cemetery has been designed with help from the Dorset Wildlife Trust. The green burial area will be sown with wildflower seeds each spring, and is intended to be a wild, natural habitat, so no individual graves will be identifiable by the planting of a tree or any other sort of memorial' (Sue Cheeseman).

122. **Exeter, Devon**: A one-acre woodland burial site on a steeply-sloped part within the boundary of Exwick Cemetery, Exwick Road, Exeter EX4 2BT; run by Exeter City Council. Contact the Cemeteries Registrar, Civic Centre, Paris Street, Exeter EX1 1RQ (☎ 01392 665704; f: 01392 665935; e: john.ocallaghan@ exeter.gov.uk; w: www.exeter.gov.uk). A dozen burials have taken place and there is room for about 50 more. Other areas have been identified for future use on the same slope. A grave costs £689 (incl. digging and an English native tree; double for non-residents). £76 for the interment of ashes. Biodegradable coffins are preferred, but chipboard or natural wood coffins of timber from managed forests would also be accepted. 'At the appropriate time of year we will plant an approved tree just off the grave, or maybe wild flowers, as we consider appropriate for the management of the site' (John O'Callaghan).

123. **(Falmouth, Cornwall)**: The organisation Last Rights (45 Grenville Road, Falmouth TR11 2NP, ☎ 01392 01326 317587; e: lorely@reallifetools.org.uk), supports last human rights and rites, and is working locally to promote green burial. 'The land could be provided from a variety of sources from local councils to landowners with half an acre or more to spare' (Lorely Lloyd).

124. **Old Cleeve, Somerset**: Priory Woodland Burial Ground opened in 1996 next to the residence of the owner, Mrs Almuth Groos, Cleeve Priory, Watchet, Somerset TA23 OJS (☎ 01984 631098). Two acres of woodland, not over-looked from the road, with a view of the Quantocks and Brendon Hills. 85 burials have taken place so far. A grave costs £200; a site for an urn £50. Gravedigging can be done by the family, or costs from £120 to £150 depending on the weather. A tree can be planted by or on the grave, and a plaque fixed to the supporting pole. Flat-lying stones are also allowed as memorials. Family and friends or funeral directors may arrange the funeral. Any type of biodegradable coffin, body bag or shroud is accepted. A specially-designed trolley is available to bring the coffin to the grave. (Eds: one user has commented, 'Will in time return to a lovely copse for birds and wild animals. I highly recommend it.')

125. **Par, Cornwall**: Pontsmill Human Green Burial and Pet Cemetery, c/o Patrick Squires, Terraine, Pontsmill Lane, Par PL24 2RR (☎ 01726 813975). A two-acre site with room for about 300 graves adjoins a pet cemetery on a gentle slope looking out onto woodland in this Designated Area of Outstanding Natural Beauty in the Luxulyan Valley. It costs £580 for the grave (incl. an oak tree and a plaque if wanted) plus £120 for the digging. Ashes can be interred for £40. A memorial tree can be planted for someone whose funeral was elsewhere for £40. They can also supply coffins (a softwood oak, ash veneer costs £130). Mourners may help fill or dig the grave. They will supply grass mats for around the grave, tools etc. Owners can have their pets buried with them. Any kind of body container is acceptable. Rules are kept to a minimum. Bearers are available, as are car parking and toilet facilities. '28 burials have taken place so far and 29 plots have been paid for in advance. This area of wooded valley and green fields is regularly visited by the royal family. Mines in the hillside were used by the Phoenicians. There is no through road' (Patrick Squires). (Eds: one funeral director says, 'Pontsmill is in a beautiful setting. Through a country lane you come to a truncated drive, then walk through the pet area, all on sloping ground, higher up to the human cemetery.' Another user writes, 'We liked the location. The ground was a gently sloping green field joining two areas of woodland and overlooking the woodland of Luxulyan valley'.)

126. [**] **Penzance, Cornwall**: Penwith Woodland Burial Place; run by John & Penny Lally, Rose Farm, Chyenhal, Buryas Bridge, Penzance TR19 6AN (☎ 01736 731310; **f**: 01736 731808; **e**: john@rosefarmcornwall.co.uk; **w**: www.pets andpeopletogetherforever.co.uk). 14 burials have taken place, and 60 plots have been reserved. A grave costs £400 incl. a native tree, planted at a suitable time of year, plus about £120 for the digging. An adjoining plot for pets costs £200. Ashes may be buried for £100, or scattered for £25. They allow biodegradable coffins, wooden coffins 'made from managed-forest and ecologically-sound timber', and shrouds. DIY funerals welcome. People and pets can be buried together. A horsedrawn hearse is available, and a chapel of rest is planned. 'On a gentle hillside where there are already over 150 trees with a tranquil view of distant Cornish hills and church towers of West Penwith' (Penny Lally).

127. **Seaton, Devon**: Green Burial Ground, Colyford Road, Seaton; run by Douglas Jackson & colleagues, c/o The Registrar, Chief Exec Dept, East Devon District Council, Knowle, Sidmouth, Devon EX10 8HZ (☎01395 516551). This site for 160 graves in meadowland is part of Seaton Cemetery, in an Area of Outstanding Natural Beauty on a hillside with panoramic views out over the valley. They accept biodegradable coffins. A grave costs only £67 (incl. a tree; double for non-residents), but the digging must be done and paid for either privately (Mr Simmons ☎ 01297 489530; £105) or through a funeral director. Mourners may help with a token amount of digging or filling of the grave. 'Any family-organised funeral must be done properly. A tree or shrub will be planted in accordance with a site plan' (Douglas Jackson). (Eds: one user writes, 'Ideal, natural, rural setting. An area surrounded on three sides by hedges, looking over fields and trees to the Axe Valley. Will produce a copse of trees and shrubs'.)

128. [**] **Shillingstone, Dorset**: Ham Down Woodland Burial Ground at Bere Marsh Farm, Shillingstone, Dorset DT11 0QY; run by Mrs A. Hughes OBE, Box Bush House, Broadoak, Sturminster Newton, Dorset DT10 2HD (☎ 01258 471370; **w**: www.hamdown-greenburial.co.uk). This two-acre site overlooking the River Stour and Hambledon Hill has room for approximately 350 burials per acre. Individual plots may be consecrated. A grave costs £475 incl. a tree (field maple, silver birch, oak, whitebeam, rowan and small-leaved lime), plus the cost of the digging. Families may help fill the grave. Wild flowers may also be planted on the graves. An approved wooden plaque with the name of the deceased and their lifespan can be ordered. A small wooden cross supplied by the relatives of the deceased is allowed as a memorial. 'Nightingales nest next to the site, and rare butterflies breed in the oaks adjoining the site. A seat will be provided for mourners and there is a small spinney within the site where ashes can be scattered for £50. We supply a list of county undertakers. A sum is set aside from each burial fee for the longterm maintenance of the woodland' (A. W. Hughes). (Eds: one user reported, 'We liked the location – wonderful views of the the Dorset landscape – and the informality – a family business, not overtly commercial. It will be a wonderful place in years to come'.

129. **South Molton**:Mole Valley Green Burial Ground, Wood House Farm, Queens Nympton, South Molton (just south of George's Nympton), North Devon EX36 4JH (☎/f: 01769 574512). Five acres in a 12-acre field adjoining existing woodland, with views over the river valley. A grave costs £450 plus the cost of the digging (£150). A number of tree species growing on the farm are available free of charge. Other species may be planted, however families are expected to supply these themselves. Full undertaking service available – cost depends on services required – and various coffins and shrouds can be supplied at the retail price. Families can help fill, but not dig, the grave. Ashes can be interred for £50. Relatives of a deceased buried on the site can reserve adjoining plots free of charge. A horse and cart is to be bought for those who wish to use it. The meadow is planted with local trees and shrubs. 'The site is on an organic farm in rural Devon and is easily accessible via a private lane. There is an unconfirmed ancient woodland, hedgebanks, badgers, deer, birds, hares and foxes. It is hoped that a wildlife trust will be brought on board to ensure the site's development as a nature reserve. We have a good working relationship with a number of funeral directors. However, those not wishing their involvement are invited to discuss alternative arrangements' (Brian and Jeanne Nicholas). (Eds: one reader, who liked this site, commented in 2001: 'The scenery is wonderful'.)

130. **Tavistock, Devon**: Green burial facility offered on two acres of consecrated land at Tavistock Cemetery, 119 Plymouth Road, Tavistock PL19 8BY; run by Teignbridge District Council (contact the Cemetery Superintendent, ☎ 01822 612799). A grave costs £298 for parishioners incl. digging; £780 for non-parishioners. Ashes can be interred for £55; £165 for non-parishioners. Only biodegradable coffins and adornments are allowed. Grass, wild flower seeds or a small native shrub may be planted on the grave. Ten burials have taken place so far. DIY funerals allowed, but families cannot help dig or fill the grave. Pre-purchase of a burial plot is possible. 'The site is secluded, surrounded by mature oaks, limes and copper beeches. We hope to contribute to a new sanctuary for wild plants, birds and other wildlife, thus bringing enjoyment to the community and to future generations' (Brian Brown).

131. **(Taunton & Wellington)**: Taunton & Deane Borough Council are actively seeking land suitable for use as a woodland burial ground. For further details contact Mr P. D. Rayson, Taunton Deane Crematorium, Wellington New Road, Taunton, Somerset TA1 5NE (☎ 01823 284811).

132. ❂❂❂ [**] **Tiverton, Devon**: Great Bradley Cottage Natural Burial Ground, Templeton, Tiverton, Devon EX16 8BJ (☎ 01884 256098); run by Mrs Catherine Hunt. This one-acre green burial ground set in a five-acre wildflower hay meadow opened in August 2001. 14 Burials have taken place so far. A single grave costs £450 (incl. digging). Ashes can be interred for £95 or scattered for

£25. Families and friends can choose to arrange and carry out either part of or the entire funeral themselves, with help from Mrs Hunt, or use the services of a conventional funeral director. ('Two DIY burials were very successful, with over 60 people attending each burial.') Any kind of biodegradable coffin, body bag or shroud is acceptable; a small selection is available, please ask. Following health and safety guidelines, familes may help fill but not dig the grave; tools are provided. As this is a natural meadow no memorials are permitted. The grave is sown with grass and a scattering of seeds saved from the meadow each year; bulbs and spring flowers may be added by the family if they wish. A native tree may be planted in remembrance in the area. The ground is level, with easy access, and there is a small stoned parking area. 'My plan is to form a small orchard with benches where people can sit in private with their thoughts. It is a very peaceful site set in the beautiful mid-Devon countryside, enclosed by natural hedges and has panoramic views across unspoilt farmland to the hills beyond. The hedgerows are a bit wild and untamed, but this is how I would like it to remain as the wildlife appreciate it that way' (Catherine Hunt). (Eds: users have commented: 'If you want a natural burial in a beautiful unspoilt area with a very friendly owner, it's ideal'; 'We particularly liked Catherine's helpful and caring nature'; 'A lovely field with outstanding views over Dartmoor. Beautifully done. It's the most gorgeous place to be buried, next to heaven'; 'A local pub was able to provide excellent and reasonably priced hot food in a separate area for 50-plus people'; 'Mrs Hunt was efficient, helpful and respectful of our wishes. Excellent'; 'Cath Hunt was wonderful. The site is one of the most beautiful, peaceful, natural places on earth'.)

133. **(Torquay)**: Woodland burial is to be offered in the future by Torbay Council, but there are no details as yet. Contact Jana Britton, Torquay Cemetery, Hele Road, Torquay, Devon TQ2 7QG (☎ 01803 327768) for more details.

134. **Nr. Totnes, Devon**: Six acres of recently-planted woodland adjacent to the mature Bidwell Wood and farmland; run by Andrew Lithgow, Bidwell, Cummings Pond Lane, Rattery, Devon TQ10 9LU (**m**: 07973 459065; **e**: andrew@bidwell woodland.co.uk; **w**: www.bidwellwoodland.co.uk). Burials are spaced between existing trees, allowing about ten sq metres per burial. Ten burials have taken place so far (approx. ten per year). A grave costs £500 (plus digging as required; the trees are already planted). Only biodegradable coffins or shrouds are allowed. Mr Lithgow says that the trees in the burial area will not be harvested for 150 years, but beyond this he cannot offer longterm security for the graves, and has not applied for planning permission for change of use. 'This is high quality timber-producing woodland subject to Forestry Commission rules on maintenance, felling and replanting, and burials take place where the trees are wider spaced. While access is normally unrestricted there may be short periods of forestry activity where restriction must apply for safety reasons. This is not a reserve – no memorials, no special trees – just a nice place to remember saying some goodbyes. There are presently some disputes with the local planning authority over whether such activity constitutes development. The website will contain up-to-date information and pictures' (Andrew Lithgow). (Eds: at the time of writing the District Council have issued a Planning Contravention Notice relating to a suspected breach of planning control. We would recommend enquiry on this point at the outset.)

135. [*] **Yealmpton, Devon**: Lower Heddon Field, Ashcombe Farm, Yealmpton, Plymouth; run by Linda Durman of Wrescombe Court, Yealmpton, Plymouth, Devon PL8 2NL (**m**: 07739 806898, messages replied to within 12 hours; **e**: linda.durman@virgin.net). Opened May 2003. A grave costs £400 excl. the digging. Burial of ashes costs £100 and scattering of ashes £25. 'We charge £50 per tree for us to buy, plant, label, maintain and replace if necessary. We hold two tree-planting events each winter if people wish to come and plant their own tree. Until 2003 it was a productive arable field. Set on a hill overlooking Yealmpton and Brixton villages, and within an Area of Outstanding Natural Beauty, it has the lovliest views, with Dartmoor in the background. The field is nearly ten acres and will be managed as a wildflower meadow, then gradually planted with locally sourced trees of native species to create a woodland that will last hundreds of years' (Linda Durman).

136. (**Yeovil, Somerset**): Woodland burial ground planned for land near Yeovil, possibly near the Ham Hill beauty spot; to be run by South Somerset Council. Contact George Smith (☎ 01963 435 006) for further details.

The South

Comprising Wiltshire, Berkshire, Surrey, Kent, Hampshire, East & West Sussex.

137. **Ashford**: The Woodland Garden Cemetery, Bybrook Cemetery, Cemetery Lane, Ashford, Kent (on the A28); run by Christine Smith, Cemeteries Officer, Ashford Borough Council, Civic Centre, Tannery Lane, Ashford, Kent TN23 1PL (☎ 01233 637311 ext 472, **f**: 01233 665413). A single grave costs £360, a double £670 incl. digging and a tree (double for non-residents). Biodegradable coffins can be supplied. Cremated remains can be interred for £300 incl. a biodegradable casket and a tree; further interments £75 (incl. the casket). A child's grave (up to 16 years old) costs nothing, except for the cost of a coffin and a tree. The cemeteries office is happy to advise DIY families. A grave can be reserved in advance for £110 plus £55 to select a particular grave space. 'The Woodland Garden Cemetery was started in 1995 to the southern side of Bybrook Cemetery. As with any natural woodland, it will take time to establish and is managed for the benefit of its trees, shrubs and wildlife. A path is maintained for visitors. The area includes two flowering cherry orchards, a wildflower meadow and carefully-placed seating. One tree can be planted on each grave and relatives can choose from a variety of native species such as oak, birch and hornbeam. Wooden marker posts and a memorial tag on each tree enables graves to be located easily. If desired, relatives can plant the tree themselves after the ground has settled. For those who want an additional memorial, a bench can be dedicated with a plaque for £400' (Christine Smith). (Eds: one user said of this site in 1999, 'I cannot speak of it too highly. It is young, and the trees are still small, but in a few years it will be very beautiful and the screening of broad leaved saplings will have hidden the main cemetery from view.')

138. **(Aylesham, Kent)**: An area has been cleared for future woodland burial in Aylesham Cemetery, Barham Downs, Aylesham. Contact Darren Solley, Client Officer Horticulture, Dover District Council, White Cliffs Business Park, Dover, Kent CT16 3PG (☎ 01304 872436).

139. **Beaulieu**: Beaulieu Woodland Burial Ground, Grindingstone, Beaulieu, Hampshire; run by Mrs Linda Coote, New Forest District Council, Client Services Division, The Town Hall, Avenue Road, Lymington SO41 9ZG, (☎ 023 8028 5952). A grave costs £497 (incl. digging and a tree or shrub; £994 for non-residents). They will accept biodegradable coffins. It is a section within an existing cemetery in a rural area. (Eds: One funeral director describes this site as 'an idyllic country churchyard, one mile from the village, with mature trees in the traditional part and the woodland burial ground in the right hand corner, with, as yet, only very small trees. About 25 burials have taken place. Numbered plates only, without names, are placed on the graves; but it is beautiful.')

140. **[**] Brighton**: Brighton & Hove Woodland Burial Ground at Bear Road Cemetery; run by Brighton & Hove City Council, The Woodvale Lodge, Lewes Road, Brighton, East Sussex BN2 3QB (☎ 01273 604020; **f**: 01273 292320; **e**: woodvale@brighton-hove.gov.uk; **w**: www.brighton-hove.gov.uk). A grave (50 years) costs £476 (incl. use of a nearby chapel, the digging, a choice of eight varieties of native species tree, and a small metal grave marker); double for non-residents. This local authority woodland burial site is within a large meadow overlooking the City of Brighton and the sea in one direction, and Sussex downland in the other. More than 600 graves have either been reserved or used for burial, and there is room for a further 900 graves. Services are tailored to meet individual requirements. Free consultation, an interview and a guide is offered to families organising funerals without funeral directors. Refrigerated storage facilities available. The Woodvale Cemetery chapel may be used. They sell the Greenfield cardboard coffin for £78, and accept all biodegradable coffins. If they wish, mourners can assist in filling the grave and planting the tree. A Book of Remembrance is available at Woodvale's Hall of Memory. The meadow is cut only twice a year to encourage wildlife. No chemicals are used in maintaining the area. 'The site and scheme have won three awards since it became operative in 1994' (Stephen Horlock, Bereavement Services Manager).

141. **Canterbury**: Green Burial offered within the centre of Section H in Canterbury City Cemetery, Westgate Court Avenue; run by Mrs Leita Honey, Cemeteries Registrar, Architecture & Engineering, Canterbury City Council, Military Road, Canterbury, Kent CT1 1YW (☎ 01227 862490; **f**: 01227 862020; **e**: leita.honey@canterbury.gov.uk). A grave (50 years) costs from £872 incl. digging (ask for the grave to be hand-dug to avoid petrochemicals being used) and the use of a bier (from £1,104 for non-residents). Embalming is discouraged. Home-made, cardboard and bamboo coffins are allowed, but not body bags or shrouds. They usually have at least one Brighton (£88) or Woodland (£64) cardboard coffin in stock. Families cannot help dig or fill the grave. No memorials are permitted and no trees are planted on the graves as this 'creates difficulties for providing new graves', but graves are sprinkled with grasses, a wild flower mix and bulbs for the spring. For £155 you can dedicate an existing tree anywhere at Canterbury, Whistable or Herne Bay Cemeteries (where ashes may also be scattered by appointment for £109). A Book of Remembrance and an advice leaflet are also available. The chapel may be hired for £57 per 30 minutes. 'You are advised to visit the site before making your final decision. The area was consecrated when the Cemetery first opened in 1877. Existing young trees and wild flowers will create a sunlit glade attracting wildlife and assisting the selfseeding of flowers. The area will be cut twice a year' (Leita Honey). (Eds: one visitor remarked, 'This is merely lip service to the green burial movement. There is no discernable difference between this area and any other area in the cemetery.' Further reports welcomed.)

142. **Chatham**: A small natural burial ground at Chatham Cemetery, Maidstone Road, Chatham, Kent; run by Medway Council (01634 861639; **e**: paul. edwards@medway.gov.uk). Recently opened within an existing cemetery, six burials have taken place so far and two plots have been reserved. A grave (99 years) costs £380 incl. digging and a native species tree. Only biodegradable coffins are permitted. Ashes can be interred for £160 incl. a small tree. Assistance would be given to DIY families.

143. **[**] Christchurch**: The Hinton Park Woodland Burial Ground, The Burial Centre, Wyndham Road, Walkford, Nr. Christchurch, Dorset BH23 7EJ (01425 278910 ; **f**: 01425 278920; **e**: info@woodlandburial.com; **w**: www.wood landburial.com). This 14-acre site on the Dorset/Hampshire border opened in 1995. A peaceful meadow containing over 1,000 burials, each with a tree, surrounded by mature oak and pine trees, with red deer in an adjoining meadow. Hinton House, an old English manor, is visible overlooking the lake. Horses, squirrels, wild deer and pheasants wander around the grounds and there are many species of birds. A single grave (99 years) costs £395 (incl. digging and a tree). An additional £550 covers the collection of the body within a 20-mile radius, provision of a place of rest before the burial and complete arrangements for the burial. Collection of the deceased can be at any time of the day or night and from any area in the UK. Collection from London would cost approximately £190. (The all-in price, incl. collection of the body from London, comes to about £1,385.) Ashes can be interred in a separate area for £195 if Hinton Park have arranged the cremation; otherwise, call for prices. A name plaque costs £65. They sell polished oak veneer, cardboard and wicker coffins from £200. A church service of any denomination can be arranged for £275 (excl. the minister's, organist's and choir fees); or a service can be held in the meadow during fine weather. Graves can be subsequently visited any time during daylight hours. A purpose-built building with lounge and refreshments serves the catering needs of mourners and services can also be held there. B&B can be arranged locally. 'We can collect the body from home, hospital or nursing home and can look after the deceased until the burial (we have a mortuary unit). We can make arrangements for newspaper advertisements and flowers. Many are simple family burials; doing their own lowering, reading their own thoughts and poems, occasionally prayers and often music. We have had one person saying goodbye alone to her husband, and on another occasion, 300 people saying farewell to a popular nurse from a local hospital' (Mike Hedger, Proprietor). (Eds: one user reports, 'Well signposted from the A35. We particularly liked the sensitive way in which we were allowed to do everything in our own way and time – no sense at all of being rushed. No longer as cheap as it used to be – now quite upmarket. But still, we thought the service and friendliness was great!')

144. **Eastbourne**: Woodland burial at Langney Cemetery; run by Eastbourne Borough Council. Enquires to the Manager & Registrar, Eastbourne Crematorium, Hide Hollow, Langney, Eastbourne, East Sussex BN23 8AE (☎ 01323 761093/766536; **f**: 01323 760637; **e**: cemeteries@eastbourne.gov.uk). A single grave (75 years) costs £275, a side-by-side double £400 (plus £490 for each interment). Advice is offered for families arranging a funeral without a funeral director. 'The area has already been planted with native trees, wild grasses and flowers and there is space for about 400 graves. Only interments in shrouds, cardboard or wicker coffins will be permitted' (Mrs Gill Bewick A.Inst BCA). (Eds: one user has helpfully described the site in detail, 'It is a small grassy enclave with some young bushes and saplings fenced in around it – not exactly woodland, more like a park, as it is only recently established, and there are houses overlooking it on two sides. However, it feels open and airy. There is a back road into the site which is convenient for access from the main road and parking, and avoids one having to drive in via the horrid crematorium'.)

145. **✪✪✪ [**] East Hampshire**: South Downs Natural Burial Site, Sustainability Centre, Droxford Road, East Meon GU32 1HR (☎ 01730 823005; **m**: 07719 702195). There have been 156 burials so far. A single grave costs £602-50 (incl. digging, backfilling and top-soiling by hand, tree planting and staking, 4x4 transportation for elderly or infirm mourners, A3 page in memorial book, individual attention throughout and staff attendance at funeral, music sytem, admin, etc). Single plots may be purchased in advance for £390. Double plots and a few large family plots are available – from £495 to £1,655. DIY funerals welcome. Families can do everything with help and guidance from Rosie and staff. Basic collection service £110 within 30-mile radius (beyond add 45 pence per mile). Families can choose a plot within the site. No chipboard or rainforest timber coffins allowed. Coffins are transported from the reception building to the graveside on a replica Victorian hand bier. Grave goods acceptable if made from natural materials: horseshoes, bottles of whiskey, etc. There is a large room available for services and there are restaurant facilities on site (£60 plus VAT). There is no time limit. It is a one-acre site within 55 acres of mature woodland, owned by the EarthWorks Trust, on a south-facing slope of the South Downs. 'Local funeral directors, clergy and humanist officiators are very happy with the service we provide and recommend this option' (Rosie Bullough). (Eds: one FD has said: 'This site is beautiful. The property is large and the burial area is a nine-minute walk down into a valley. And they hand dig the grave!' Other users write: 'Mature woodland, well away from any roads'; 'The arrangements made for our mother's burial were calming and beautiful. Thanks a million; I have no praise high enough for Rosie and her colleagues, truly astounding'; 'Rosie was incredibly supportive and kind. If you are searching for a perfect end to a life I would recommend this site'; 'Visit it if you can: there are no words to describe how beautiful, peaceful and comforting it is'; 'Nothing but praise for the staff. I would recommend this burial ground to anybody'; 'Exceptional'.)

146. **Eling**: Eling Woodland Burial Ground, Eling Hill, Totton, Southampton; run by Mrs Linda Coote, New Forest District Council, Client Services Division, The Town Hall, Avenue Road, Lymington, Hampshire SO41 9ZG (☎ 023 8028 5952). A grave costs £497 (incl. digging and a tree or shrub; £994 for non-residents). They will accept biodegradable coffins. 'A section within an existing cemetery, in a rural area' (Linda Coote). (Eds: One visitor has described this site as 'really bleak and windswept. Only one burial has taken place.' Other reports from the public, positive or negative, welcomed.)

147. **[**] Enborne, Nr. Newbury**: Acorn Ridge Natural Burials, Red Hill, Enborne; run by Mrs S. Lynes, Yew Tree Farm, Ball Hill, Newbury, Berks RG20 0NG (☎ 01635 255441; **f**: 01635 254018). This 20-acre site is set on a hillside overlooking the South Downs leading down to the River Enbourne. Native trees, shrubs and bulbs are planted. Any eco-friendly casket or covering accepted, but burial of embalmed bodies is not permitted. A grave (50 years) costs £800 incl. digging (plus £75 for a tree); same prices for non-residents. £275 for the interment of ashes. £100 to plant a memorial tree for someone whose funeral was elsewhere. Families may help dig and fill the grave. 'The exceptional views and the peace and quiet make this a perfect site for reflection' (Sadie Lynes).

148. **[*] (Goring Heath, Nr. Reading)**: Martin Wise of 5 Coombe End, Goring Heath RG8 7TD (☎ 01189 843071) plans to establish a natural burial ground on two hectares of set-aside land in the parish of Goring Heath, NW of Reading.

149. **(Gosport, Hants)**: Proposed woodland burial ground still looking for support in the Gosport area. Contact: Ian Jeffery, 11 Harcourt Road, Gosport PO12 3NR (☎ 023 92523358; **e**: ian@gosport.info; **w**: www.gosport.info).

150. **Hastings**: Woodland Burial, Hastings Borough Cemetery, The Ridge, Hastings, East Sussex TN34 2AE (☎ 01424 781302; **e**: gford@hastings.gov.uk); run by Hastings Borough Council. A grave costs £270 incl. digging (double for non-residents); plus £53 to use the chapel. Ashes may be buried in the Woodland Walk area for £52. Biodegradable coffins accepted. Mourners may fill the grave. Graves are seeded with wild flowers and have a tree planted on them (silver or downy birch, rowan, crab apple, guelder rose or fastigiate hawthorn planted in rotation). 'The site is a peaceful spot on the edge of an existing copse in a quiet corner of an 80-acre cemetery, well shielded by banks and trees' (George Ford).

151. **Isle of Wight**: Springwood Woodland Burials, run by William Hall, Independent Funeral Directors, Winford Road, Newchurch, Sandown, Isle of Wight PO36 0JX (☎ /**f**: 01983 868688). 700 interments have taken place so far (incl. ashes). A single grave costs £650 incl. digging and an oak, mountain ash or beech tree; a double costs £810. They accept biodegradable coffins, body bags or shrouds. They sell the Brighton cardboard coffin for £190. Mourners may help dig or fill the grave. The five-acre cemetery is in a peaceful setting. Paths lead to a small memorial garden where bronze plaques may be placed. Extensive tree

and bulb planting has taken place and there is also a pond with a small marsh area. Bird, bat and kestrel boxes have been erected and a slow worm pit constructed.
152. St Mary Bourne, Hampshire: Breach Farm Woodland Burial Ground, Bank Top, St Mary Bourne, Andover, Hampshire SP11 6BG (☎ 01264 738278, **f**: 01264 738118; **e**: info@breach-farm.co.uk; **w**: www.breach-farm.co.uk). A one-acre woodland burial site, set within a ten-acre nature reserve. A grave (99 years) costs £450 (incl. a native tree, plus about £150 for the digging; same for non-residents). Trees will be replaced free 'as the wild deer have a liking for them!' Scattering of ashes is free. Pets allowed. 'A peaceful resting place, bordered by mature woodland, on a hillside overlooking the beautiful Bourne Valley in Hampshire. All forms of faith are welcome. Friendly local churches and hostelries, also an excellent village hall available for hire' (Lisa Hirst).
153. Sevenoaks, Kent: A woodland burial ground as part of a small cemetery in Otford parish; run by Mrs Barbara Darby, Clerk, Otford Parish Council, School House, 21 High Street, Otford, Sevenoaks, Kent TN14 5PG (☎ 01959 524808). Part of the old deer park of Otford Palace, adjacent to new woodland. Established trees include a 600-year-old oak. A grave costs £535 (incl. a native British species tree, normally planted a year after the burial; £700 for non-residents). Graves must be dug by the Parish Council's contractor, for about an extra £150. Coffins may be cardboard, wicker or wood. A small memorial stone may be placed adjacent to the tree. There is no chapel.
154. [**] Shamley Green, Nr. Guildford, Surrey: A second 18-acre site run by Green Woodland Burial Services along the same lines as Oakfield Wood Green Burial Site (see Manningtree in East Anglia) on land between Shamley Green and Cranleigh, near the Gaston Gate Garage is now open. A grave costs £495 (incl. a broadleaf tree, a wooden plaque with name and lifespan, and 'sinking fund contribution to Surrey Wildlife Trust for maintenance in perpetuity'). Digging costs £165. The all-in price for a funeral is £1,610 and includes collection within a 100-mile radius, including London, a biodegradable coffin, the grave and the burial. Ashes can be interred for £395 (incl. tree and plaque). Contact: Green Woodland Burial Services, 256 High Street, Dovercourt, Harwich, Essex CO12 3PA (☎ 0800 374759 / 01255 503456; **e**: gburials@talk21. com; **w**: www.greenburials.co.uk). 'The site is overseen with a detailed management plan by the Surrey Wildlife Trust' (Peter Kincaid). (Eds: one user reports: 'We want to record how friendly and obliging the gravedigger, Gavin Brown, was. We recommend the site to others. It is of course only a field, but we soon adjusted to being pioneers for this site – the first in Surrey.')
155. (Shaw-cum-Donnington, Newbury): Parish Councillors are considering 'finding some land to use for environmentally-friendly interment' (John Brunskill, Clerk to the Council, ☎ 01635 248366).
156. Woking: Woodland burial at Brookwood Cemetery, Woking, Surrey GU24 0BL (☎ 01483 472222; **e**: enquiries@brookwoodcemetery.com); run by Brookwood Park Ltd. A grave costs £1,500 for adults, £500 for children; plus £400 for the digging. For people living in a 17-mile radius, woodland burials are available at an all-inclusive price of £1,600. Pre-paid plots available.

Greater London region

Including old Middlesex. See also South region.

157. Brent: One-acre woodland burial area within 30-acre Carpenders Park Cemetery, Oxhey Lane, Carpenders Park, Watford; run by Brent Council Cemetery Service, Cemetery Office, Clifford Road, Alperton, Middlesex HA0 1AF (☎ 020 8902 2385; f: 020 8795 0273; e: langford@brent.gov.uk; w: www.brent.gov.uk). The section opened in 1998; 20 woodland burials have taken place so far. A single grave (50 years) costs £1,075 (incl. digging, an indigenous tree – hawthorn, oak, rowan, field maple, beech, holly, yew, silver birch, ash, hazel, sloe, sycamore, cherry or hornbeam – and a plaque); £1,577 for non-residents. Ashes may be interred for £572; £698 for non-residents. Families may help fill the grave, but not dig. Advice can be offered for DIY funerals. Only biodegradable coffins are allowed: cardboard coffins can be supplied from £53; wooden coffins must be made from managed forest timber. A wooden plaque can be placed on the grave until the tree is planted. No horticultural chemicals are used in the woodland section. The only possible drawback is that there are no direct buses and the nearest train station is a 30-minute walk through woodland that is unlit at night. Thus the site is best reached by car. 'The cemetery has 14 acres of mature woodland, where no burials take place, two lakes and the Hartsbourne stream rolling through. Already the cemetery is a haven for wildlife: ducks and moorhens nest on small islands in the lakes and kingfishers, jays and herons can be seen quite regularly' (Bob Langford, Director).

158. ✪✪✪ City of London Cemetery's woodland burial ground, Aldersbrook Road, London E12 5DQ (☎ 020 8530 2151; w: www.cityoflondon.gov.uk/cemetery). A two acre site where 30 burials have taken place so far. New graves with exclusive right of burial (50 years) cost £1,258 (incl. digging; £774 for a second interment). Interment in a grave without exclusive burial rights (owned by the corporation, who may carry out a second interment at a later date) costs £508 (incl. digging). All graves are double graves. Ashes may be interred for £125. They accept biodegradable coffins. Families may help fill the grave if they wish. The site already has established trees, so they may not always plant new ones. Absolutely no memorials are permitted on the woodland site, although families may sponsor a bench or other memorial elsewhere in the cemetery. 'The site is within the existing, world-renowned City of London Cemetery, a 200-acre site with well-kept grounds and excellent security. We are happy to advise DIY families' (Ian Hussain, Director).

159. (Enfield): This site is experiencing difficulties due to poor ground conditions. A woodland burial area is planned as an extension to Lavender Hill Cemetery at Strayfield Road; run by the London Borough of Enfield. Families will be permitted to help fill, but not dig, the grave. For more information contact the Cemetery Registrar, London Borough of Enfield, PO Box 58, Civic Centre, Silver Street, Enfield EN1 3XJ (☎ 020 8379 3767).

160. Forest Gate: Woodland burial areas offered within Manor Park Cemetery, Sebert Road, Forest Gate, London E7 0NP (☎ 020 8534 1486); run by the

Manor Park Cemetery Company. A grave costs £800 (incl. digging, a tree and a small brass plaque). There are several possible areas within the cemetery to choose from. Any native British species tree can be planted. The place already contains mature trees, and has a traditional chapel with spire. There is housing adjoining the site but it is relatively quiet. Biodegradable coffins or shrouds are acceptable. Families can help to fill or dig the grave.

161. (**Greenford**): Green burial is to be offered, in the long term, in Greenford Park Cemetery, Windmill Lane, Greenford UB6. Contact Elaine Robinson, Cemetery Manager, London Borough of Ealing, Perceval House, 14-16 Uxbridge Road, London W5 2HL (☎ 020 8825 6030; **e**: cemeteries@ealing.gov.uk).

162. **Highgate**: Highgate Cemetery, Swains Lane, London N6 6PJ (☎ 020 8340 1834) may be able to arrange woodland burial on individual request. They accept home-made and cardboard coffins. 'As a privately-run charity, Highgate is able to offer a much more flexible service than most' (Richard Quirk).

163. [**] **Hillingdon**: West Drayton woodland burial ground is a wild flower meadow with trees, with West Drayton Cemetery to one side and public open space to the other; run by the London Borough of Hillingdon. A grave costs £713 for residents (incl. digging); £38 extra for non-residents. Families can help fill, but not dig, the grave. Contact David Bryant, Cemetery Office, Civic Centre (4W/08), Uxbridge, Middlesex UB8 1UW (☎ 01895 250416) for more details.

164. (**Islington**): A woodland burial area is being discussed as part of a feasibility study for Trent Park Cemetery, Cockfosters Road, Cockfosters, also Islington Cemetery Grounds; run by The London Borough of Islington. Contact Mr D. Pryor, Islington Crematorium, High Road, East Finchley, London N2 9AG (☎ 020 8883 1230) for more information.

165. (**Lewisham**): Woodland burial area planned by the London Borough of Lewisham (Shirley Bishop ☎ 020 8697 2555) for its cemetery at Grove Park SE12. A traditional grave costs £796 incl. digging; quadruple for non-residents.

166. **Linden Grove**: Woodland burial at Nunhead Cemetery, Linden Grove, London SE15; run by Southwark Council. A half-acre woodland burial area opened in 1998 in association with the Friends of Nunhead Cemetery, extends the existing cemetery. A single grave costs £1,068 (incl. digging and a tree; £3,246 for non-residents). Ashes can be interred for £115 (£335 for non-residents). Mourners may help fill the grave and assistance will be offered with DIY funerals at no extra cost. All types of biodegradable coffin or shroud are accepted 'if suitably covered'. 'Strictly no headstones, plastic or wire fences or any other type of memorial permitted, just a tree or shrub (with many varieties to choose from including mountain ash, ash, yew, chestnut, poplar) or seasonal bulbs (bluebell, daffodil, tulip, crocus). The area is very natural and peaceful and the staff are very helpful. The site will be maintained as a meadow when it is full' (T. M. Connor). 54 burials have taken place so far. All correspondence should be to Terry Connor, Superintendent, Camberwell New Cemetery, Brenchley Gardens, London SE23 3RD (☎ 020 7639 3121; **f**: 020 7732 3557).

167. **Richmond**: The Natural Burial Area, East Sheen Cemetery, Sheen Road, Richmond, Surrey TW10 5BJ (☎ 020 8876 4511; **f**: 020 8878 8118; **w**:

www.richmond.gov.uk/cemeteries/cems.html); run by the London Borough of Richmond Upon Thames. There have been 20 burials so far. Single-depth unmarked graves cost £1,100 (incl. digging; £3,360 for non-residents). Biodegradable coffins are to be used in this small area of the cemetery. The cemetery staff can advise on where to buy a cardboard coffin and are happy to assist DIY families. Ashes can be interred (up to eight interments in one grave plot). Metal caskets are not permitted. 'The natural burial area is a haven for wildlife and native flowers, at the edge of the cemetery between existing older-style traditional graves and the tree-lined boundary to East Sheen Common. No form of individual memorial, flowers or any other item may be placed here. Trees, shrubs, bulbs etc will be selected and planted by the cemetery staff. Hedges and bird boxes encourage wildlife' (Natasha Mahon-Smith).

168. **Southwark**: A three-quarter-acre woodland burial area at Camberwell Old Cemetery, Forest Hill Road, Dulwich SE22, run by Southwark Council. Since 2003, one burial has taken place. (For all other details, see Linden Grove above.)

169. **(Woolwich)**: 'Tentative' plans for a woodland burial area in the future at New Woolwich Cemetery; run by Greenwich Council. No further details. Plans are in the hands of Chris Barr, Cemeteries Supervisor (☎ 020 8856 0100).

Scotland

170. ✪✪✪ [**] **Aberdeenshire**: A 35-acre woodland and nature preserve, Clovery Woods of Rest, Brackenrig, Fyvie, Turriff, Aberdeenshire AB53 8QR (☎ 01651891654, **f**: 01651891166, **m**: 07789171574; **w**: www.greenburials-scotland.co.uk). In 2002, Alexander and Fiona Rankin opened this, the first site in the north/north-east of Scotland. A grave costs £600 (incl. digging and planting of grass and wildflowers). Graves are machine-dug, but families may help with the filling subject to health and saftey rules. Biodegradable coffins and shrouds only (pine, wicker, cardboard, etc, without metal handles or nameplates; no hardwoods). Ashes may be scattered (and a tree dedicated), but not interred. They will soon be offering a rest room attached to a Hall of Celebration. Up to 2,000 words about the deceased plus ten photographs may be recorded onto a CD-ROM for approx. £50. Five per cent of the burial fee is paid into the Clovery Woods of Rest Trust fund for ongoing maintenance of the site. 'The site is laid out with a shelter belt of 2.5 acres of trees. Half the site is set aside for the scattering of ashes and tree dedication, with a nature walkway. The woodland will develop as people are interred. Trees, shrubs and wild flowers offered will be native to this locality as our winters can be quite harsh' (Alexander Rankin).

171. **(Dumfries & Galloway)**: For the natural death and green burial group Another Way (Registered Charity SCO29726) please contact: Jean Pilborough, Secretary, Another Way, 16 Midtown, Dalry, Castle Douglas, Dumfries DG7 3UT (☎ 01644 430324; **e**: jeanniep@bushinternet.com).

172. **Dundee**: A woodland burial ground adjacent to Birkhill Cemetery. The site is landscaped and planted with trees and wild flowers, two interments have taken place so far. A grave costs £719 incl. digging. No memorials allowed with the exception of plaques on a memorial wall. They accept biodegradable coffins.

Contact Gary Robertson, Dundee City Council Leisure & Parks, Floor 13, Tayside House, Dundee, Scotland DD1 3RA (☎ 01382 433388).

173. **East Dunbartonshire**: One-acre meadowland burial area for residents only at Langfaulds Cemetery, Baljaffray Road, Bearsden; run by East Dunbartonshire Council (Mr Copeland, Parks & Amenity Development Officer, Connect Services, Broomhill Industrial Estate, Kilsyth Road, Kirkintilloch G66 1TF, ☎ 0141 574 5549). A block of four lairs costs £798; a single £409.50. Digging costs £336 for a coffin, £157.50 for ashes. 'Each lair is used only once in this section. They are sold in blocks of four so that family members can be close together' (Alan Copeland). (Eds: a local resident says, 'the site is secluded, and in time they intend to plant trees and bushes to make it more so'.)

174. **Edinburgh**: Woodland burial section, Costorphine Hill Cemetery, Edinburgh EH12; run by the City of Edinburgh Council. Contact the Bereavement Services Manager, Mortonhall Crematorium, Howden Hall Road, Liberton, Edinburgh, Scotland EH16 6TX, ☎ 0131 664 4314). Opened 1995. A grave costs £875 incl. digging, burial and a tree; same for non-residents. They accept biodegradable coffins, shrouds or body bags. Mourners may help fill the grave. Memorials are allowed on a pathway. Current graves on the edge of the site are easily accessible, but visits to the central area are discouraged in order to let the wild flowers grow. 'There is room for 500 graves; 37 burials have taken place so far. Silver birch trees (supplied by the Scottish Wildlife Trust), bluebells and wild flowers are planted. It is a quiet woodland site' (G. P. Bell). (Eds: visitors have said, 'We liked what we saw very much. The cemetery is small and very quiet, with plenty of trees; not unkempt, but not over-tidy either. It's in a residential area with a school on one side and houses on the other. The woodland burial area is an area of grass about the size of two tennis courts. Off to one side is a section planted with flowers designed to attract butterflies'; 'The site is being managed for the development of trees and the benefit of wildlife and the environment generally; and will become a very special woodland in years to come'.)

175. **[**] Fenwick, Ayrshire**: A woodland burial ground at Craufurdland Woods, Midland Farm, Fenwick, Ayrshire KA3 6BY; run as a limited company made up of family members of Mr J. P. Houison-Craufurd. Opened July 2002. Correspondence to: Craufurdland Castle, Kilmarnock, East Ayrshire KA3 6BS (☎ 01560 600 767; e: woods@craufurdland.co.uk; w: www.craufurdland.co.uk). A 10ft x 6 ft grave costs £600 (incl. digging and a tree). Ashes may be interred for £100 in a smaller plot. No embalming allowed. Biodegradable coffins only, with no metal handles. They can supply cardboard, pine or bamboo coffins. A wooden plaque may be placed on the grave. Families are allowed to fill, but not dig, the grave. Leaflets about arranging a funeral without a funeral director are available. Trees are planted in the autumn together with woodland bulbs between the graves. A pet cemetery is planned for nearby. 'A three-acre site which can be extended as required. It is in the middle of a farm, a long narrow field with mature trees in the hedgerows only overlooked by three farms in the distance. Although close to a village it is quiet and peaceful. The farm is part of the Craufurdland Estate, owned by the Craufurds since 1245' (Peter Houison-Craufurd).

176. Largs, Nr. Glasgow: A new cemetery in Largs on the west coast of Scotland, just south of Glasgow, which opened July 2003, will include an area for woodland burial. DIY funerals will be permitted. Contact David MacColl, Cemeteries Services Manager, North Ayrshire Council, Cemeteries Office, 43 Ardrossan Road, Saltcoats, Ayrshire, Scotland (☎ 01294 605436, **f**: 01294 324144; **e**: CemeteriesOffice@north-ayrshire.gov.uk).

177. (North Lanarkshire): A mixed woodland and traditional lairs cemetery for a 3.5-acre site in Coatbridge; run by North Lanarkshire Council. For further information about the site, which may allow woodland burial style graves with trees, contact John Russell, Cemeteries Manager, Dept of Community Services, Old Edinburgh Road, Bellshill, Scotland ML4 3JF (☎ 01698 506304, **f**: 01698 506249; **e**: groundsmaintenance@northlan.gov.uk; **w**: www.northlan.gov.uk).

178. (Perth & Kinross): The Perth & Kinross District Council are actively seeking a site specifically for use as a natural burial ground. For more information contact Richard Smith (☎ 01738 475000).

179. (Scottish Borders): 'We are working to set up a charity to: maintain and create one or more woodland nature reserves; encourage greater understanding of death as an holistic part of the life cycle; develop a centre where people can conduct their own ceremonies marking life events; enable the personal involvement in and direction of funerals by family and friends of the deceased; use local resources (as far as possible) and provide employment locally; use sustainable and environmentally sound practices; and enhance and maintain the ecology and biodiversity of the area. We welcome contact with other interested individuals and organisations – those who have relevant skills and knowledge as well as those who would like to support or find out more about the idea' (Heather Johnston, South Cottage, Watherston, Stow, Selkirkshire TD1 2ST; ☎ 01578 730507; **e**: naturalwayburial@southcottage.co.uk).

180. (Stirling): Stirling Council is taking a 'positive' approach to green burial by consulting the community and raising local awareness. So far they say they have had no 'negative feedback' from the public to their proposals, which include woodland burial, memorial gardens and the end to the advance selling of family lairs. For more information contact Jim McBrier, Cemeteries Services, Viewforth, Stirling FK8 2ET (☎ 01786 442559).

Eire and Northern Ireland

181. (Dublin): The Sustainable Ireland Cooperative, 15-19 Essex Street West, Dublin 8, Ireland (Erik van Lennep-Hyland ☎ 00 353 16746396; **e**: erik@sustainable.ie; **w**: www.sustainable.ie) have a small but growing interest group formed around the concept of ecological burials.

Isle of Man

182. (Isle of Man): Pat Kneen of Lhie Ny Greiney, Surby Mooar, Port Erin, Isle of Man IM9 6TD (☎ 01624 834104) hopes to open a natural burial ground on the Island. There is a group of people interested, but no further progress so far.

Italy

• **Milan**: The Capsula Mundi Project (**e**: Capsula@capsulamundi.com; **w**: www.capsulamundi.com) is the first ever project to promote ecological burial in Italy: 'to try to transform the tradition of urban wall cemeteries and to offer the alternative of memorial woodland burial sites. If you can help make this happen or give advice from personal experience, please get in touch' (Anna Citelli).

United States of America

• **Florida**: Glendale Memorial Nature Preserve (297 Railroad Avenue, De Funiak Springs, Florida 32433, USA; ☎ 001 850 8592141; **e**: john@glendale naturepreserve.org). 'We charge $1,000 for opening and closing the grave. The rules are: no embalming; caskets must be biodegradable (shroud or sheet is OK); flat markers or stones native to the area are allowed. Controlled burning is rapidly returning the ecosystem to pre-white man conditions, mainly wild flower production that is awesome' (John Wilkerson).

• **South Carolina**: Memorial Ecosystems (113 Retreat Street, Westminster, SC 29693, USA, ☎ 001 864 647 7798; **f**: 001 864 647 7796; **e**: information@memorial ecosystems.com; **w**: www.memorialecosystems.com) runs the 32-acre Ramsey Creek Preserve at the edge of the Blue Ridge Mountains in Oconee County, Western South Carolina, which opened in 1998. It costs $1,950 for the plot (or $2,300 incl. digging, a biodegradable casket and marker). They also have plans for a site on a 500-acre ranch near San Diego, California: 'complete with panthers, coyotes, golden eagles and a host of other bird life' (Billy Campbell).

Canada

• **British Columbia**: The Memorial Society of British Columbia is looking for land to establish a Green Burial Park in the near future, most likely on Vancouver Island: 'This will be a community-run, non-denominational, not-for-profit venture' (contact Ellen Le Fevre, Executive Director, Memorial Society of British Colombia, 212-1847 West Broadway, Vancouver, BC V6J 1Y6, ☎ 001 604 733 7705; **f**: 604 733 7730; **e**: memsocnw@telus.net; **w**: www.greenburials.ca).

New Zealand

• **Living Legacies** (PO Box 140, Motueka, NZ, ☎ 03 526 8100; **e**: lynda@living legacies.co.nz). An environmental funeral consultancy with an 'innovative, sustainable and celebratory approach to life, death and funerals' is trying to establish woodland burial grounds in New Zealand. 'I have made submissions to two councils about establishing Natural Burial Parks in the South Island. They both received the idea with interest. I will be changing New Zealand law to allow for the burial of bodies in places other than existing cemeteries, so that folk can set up such Parks or Living Legacies right around the country. Watch this space' (Lynda Hannah, whose book *Living Legacies: A family funeral handbook for an evergreen world* is available for NZ$35 incl. p&p).

Chapter 7

GOOD FUNERAL DIRECTORS

Unless otherwise stated, you can assume that all the funeral directors in this nationwide guide provide an à la carte service and will, for instance, sell you just an inexpensive fully-fitted coffin without your having to use any of their other services. Abbreviations in bold are as follows:

FD = Funeral director

✪✪✪ = Winner of a Natural Death Handbook Award 2004

☎ = Telephone number

f: = Fax number

e: = E-mail address

w: = Web address

Abbreviations for professional associations are as follows:

BIFD = British Institute of Funeral Directors
BIE = British Institute of Embalmers
CFSA = Co-operative Funeral Services Association
IAFD = Irish Association of Funeral Directors
FSC = Funeral Services Council
MBIE = Member of the British Institute of Embalmers
NAFD = National Association of Funeral Directors
NAMM = National Association of Memorial Masons
NAPFP = National Association for Pre-Paid Funeral Plans
SAIF = Society of Allied and Independent Funeral Directors
SIFH = Selected Independent Funeral Homes

Listings are by region or country, and then by town within the region, except in the Greater London region, where services are listed alphabetically. Contents:

Please write to the Natural Death Centre (see Resources for contact details) with your experience of using the services of these or other funeral directors, whether positive or negative. Please include as much detail as possible and say if you wish to nominate them for a future Award. Our listings are otherwise based on information given to us by the services themselves; the name of the informant is given wherever possible.

The North West

Comprising Cumbria, Lancashire, Manchester, Sefton, Wirral, Liverpool, Knowsley, St Helens, Wigan, Bolton, Bury, Rochdale, Salford, Trafford, Manchester, Oldham, Tameside, Stockport and Cheshire.

• **FD Blackburn**: Iqbal Funeral & Memorial Services, Cashmere Cottages, 53/55 Furthergate, Blackburn, Lancashire BB1 3HQ (☎ 01254 695303); also at Hollins House, 419-421 Hollins Road, Oldham OL8 3TL (☎ 0161 628 6289). Cheapest fully-fitted coffin only: £350 (delivery locally £50). Cold storage only: No. Body transport only: No. Advice for DIY: No. Basic funeral: £760 (disbursements extra). 'We are a Muslim funeral service who serve all of the communities and religions for funerals and memorials' (Rashid Iqbal). Prepaid plan: Perfect Choice. Member of NAFD & BIFD.

• **FD Bolton**: Fulton Funeral Directors, 81 Mason Street, Horwich, Lancashire BL6 5QP (☎ 01204 694999). Cheapest fully-fitted coffin only: £65 (delivery locally free). Cold storage only: Yes, £30 per day. Body transport only: Yes. Advice for DIY: Yes, '£100 flat fee for all help and guidance required'. Basic funeral: £705 – or 'about £450 for cremation with cardboard coffin' (disbursements extra). 'The decor and furnishings are just as you would find in a normal, comfortable domestic house; we have gone to great lengths to get away from what most funeral "homes" aspire to. Where the deceased is female, my wife takes on the embalming and preparation. We have been trading independently since 1998. We are prepared to carry out separate parts of the funeral arrangements as individual items' (John & Samantha Fulton). Prepaid plan: Perfect Assurance. Member of NAFD & BIE.

• **Bury**: Bury Metropolitan Borough Council has an arrangement with Hamers, 7 Rochdale Road, Bury (☎ 0161 797 7133) whereby residents can obtain a funeral for £350 (disbursements extra; eg burial costs an extra £720).

• **FD Carlisle**: Beattie & Co, 41-43 Warwick Road, Carlisle, Cumbria CA1 1EE (☎ 01228 527413). Cheapest coffin only: £122 (Compakta cardboard) delivery locally free). Cold storage: Not available. Body transport only: Yes, price on request. Advice for DIY: Yes. Basic funeral: £725 (disbursements extra). 'We are a small but very experienced family firm who offer a personal and caring service 24 hours a day, seven days a week. We respect and care for all our clients and treat them as people not numbers' (Adam Thomson). Prepaid plans: Golden Charter, Help the Aged. Member of no association.

• **Crewe**: The Council has a scheme called the Local Funeral where you can phone 01270 212643 (or see: www.crewe.nantwich.gov.uk/worksservices) to find out the funeral director in Crewe who provides a service which the council has agreed and which is inclusive of all unavoidable disbursements. This therefore includes interment or cremation but not the cost of rights of burial in a new grave. The current funeral director is Co-op Funeral Services in Crewe (☎ 01270 584329) and the price is £750 incl. a following car and disbursements.

• **FD Crewe**: South Cheshire Funeral Services, 6 Brierley Street, Crewe, Cheshire CW1 2AY (☎ 01270 582628; f: 01270 586350). Cheapest fully-fitted coffin only: £135 (delivery locally £35). Cold storage only: No. Body transport only: Yes, £1.25 per mile, minimum £40. Advice for DIY: Yes, £45 ph. Basic funeral: £590 (disbursements extra). Do not have a printed price list available, but say they are 'prepared to give price breakdowns over the phone. The same funeral director who interviews the client at home also prepares the coffin and the deceased, digs the grave if required and directs the funeral. We have a service that assists clients to claim benefits, also a probate service' (C. L. Harthern). Prepaid plan: FPS. Member of BIE.

• **FD Manchester**: R. Pepperdine & Sons Ltd, Alexandra House, 5 Manchester Road, Chorlton-cum-Hardy, Manchester M21 9JG (☎ 0161 881 5363; **f**: 0161 862 9443; **w**: www.pepperdine.co.uk). Cheapest fully-fitted coffin only: £155 (delivery locally £40). Cold storage only: Yes, £35 per day. Body transport only: Yes, hearse and driver £195. Advice for DIY: Yes, £60 ph. Basic funeral: £795 using a cardboard coffin (disbursements extra). 'Independent family firm. Our service is excellent value for money and flexible. What a family wants, a family gets' (Frank Barrett). Prepaid plans: Golden Charter & Perfect Assurance. Member of NAFD & SAIF.

• **✪✪✪ FD Manchester**: S. Wellens and Sons Ltd, 121 Long Street, Middleton, Manchester M24 6DL (☎ 0161 643 2677; **f**: 0161 653 7085; **e**: info@wellens-funerals.co.uk; **w**: www.wellens-funerals.co.uk). Also branches at: 347 Hollinwood Avenue, New Moston, Manchester M40 OJX (☎ 0161 681 4377); and 313 Washbrook, Chadderton, Oldham OL9 8JL (☎ 0161 624 4132). Cheapest fully-fitted coffin only: £110 (free local delivery). Cold storage only: Yes, £15 per day. Body transport only: Yes, from £30. Advice for DIY: Yes, £35 ph (all figures plus VAT). Basic funeral: £680 (disbursements extra). 'Proudly an independent family firm, established 1870 by present owners' great-grandfather. We can order cardboard coffins. We provide a local bereavement support service' (Norman Wellens). Prepaid plan: Golden Charter. Member of NAFD, SAIF & BIE.

• **Rochdale**: Rochdale Council provides a municipal funeral service for local residents through a local funeral director: Clifford Oldham Funeral Service, 203 Drake Street, Rochdale OL11 1EF (☎ 01706 646186). Cremation costs £820. Burial £805 for the re-opening of an existing family grave or £1,060 for a new grave. All prices include disbursements (but not flowers, notices etc). 'The charge for using the cemetery chapel is an extra £40' (Mr Tudor, Manager).

• **St Helens**: The St Helens Council has an agreement with the Co-op (☎ 01744 23675) to provide a municipal funeral for local residents, whereby cremation costs £807 and burial costs £846, both prices include disbursements.

• **Stockport**: A 'Civic Funeral Service' is provided by the local authority for residents, run by the United North West Co-operative Society (☎ 0161 432 0818). They charge £841 for a cremation incl. disbursements and £1,526 for a burial in a new grave, again incl. disbursements.

• **FD Stockport**: George Ball & Son, 39 Derby Range, Heaton Moor, Stockport SK4 4AB (☎ 0161 432 2131; **w**: www.georgeball.co.uk). Cheapest fully-fitted coffin only, £225. Cold storage: Yes, £50 per day. Body transport only: Yes,

£120 for vehicle incl. 20 miles. Advice for DIY: Yes £80 ph. Basic funeral £748 (excl. disbursements). 'As owners of Friends of Nature Woodland Burial Ground [eds: see Chapter 6] we are experts in all forms of alternative funerals. Every funeral that is arranged by us is individually designed according to the requirements of the family and any requests of the deceased' (Margaret Arnison). Member of NAFD.

• **Wigan**: Wigan Council offers a low cost but dignified funeral service to local residents. Two funeral directors provide this service: Edwards Funerals Directors (see the entry below) and L. Heyes Funeral Service of Leigh (☎ 01942 261936). Cremation costs £846 and burial costs £809 incl. disbursements.

• **FD Wigan**: Edwards Funeral Directors Ltd, Holmwood, Dicconson Terrace, Wigan WN1 2AA (☎ 01942 821215). Cheapest fully-fitted coffin only: £130 (delivery £1.20 per mile). Cold storage only: Yes, £20 per day. Body transport only: Yes. Advice for DIY: Yes, £30 ph. Basic funeral: £846 (incl. fees for doctors, minister and cremation). 'Our family has been associated with quality funeral service in the town for nearly 120 years' (R. B. Edwards). Prepaid plans: Golden Charter & Help the Aged. Member of SAIF.

The North East

Comprising Northumberland, Newcastle-Upon-Tyne, North Tyneside, Gateshead, South Tyneside, Sunderland, Durham, Hartlepool, Stockton-On-Tees, Middlesbrough, Redcar, North Yorkshire, York, East Riding of Yorkshire, Kingston-Upon-Hull, Bradford, Leeds, Calderdale, Kirklees, Wakefield, Barnsley, Sheffield, Rotherham, Doncaster, North Lincolnshire, North East Lincolnshire and Lincolnshire.

• **FD Bradford:** Joseph A. Hey & Son Ltd, 470 Great Horton Road, Bradford, West Yorkshire BD7 3HR (☎ 01274 571021; **f**: 01274 521258; **w**: www.funeral assist.co.uk) branches at: Low Moor, Bradford (Tordoff & Hey ☎ 01274 578220); Tong, Bradford (F. & A. Bottomley ☎ 01274 681944); Undercliffe, Bradford (Holmes & Hey ☎ 01274 626210); Thornton, Bradford (Brook Chapel of Rest ☎ 01274 834602); Leeds (Welborn & Hey ☎ 0113 2751413 and W. H. Newton & Co ☎ 0113 2705703). Cheapest fully-fitted coffin only: £220; cardboard 'Coffin Cover' £50. Delivery locally free; nationally, p&p only. Cold storage only: Subject to space availability, yes (no charge). Body transport only: Yes, £55 plus £1.50 per mile over 10 miles (one way). Advice for DIY: Yes, no charge. Basic funeral: £590 excl. disbursements. Direct service funeral (no service or mourners) £350 excl. disbursements. 'Our company provides a service over and above the normal. Our website offers help, guidance and prices online. We also publish every obituary notice free of charge on the internet. Those who log on have an option to send a message of sympathy by e-mail to the immediate family' (R. J. Morphet). Prepaid plans: Perfect Assurance, Golden Leaves. Member of NAFD, BIE & NAMM. (Eds: a recent client said 'Everything was superbly organised'.)

• **FD Dewsbury**: George Brooke Ltd Funeral Directors, 27 Bradford Road, Dewsbury, West Yorkshire WF13 2DU (☎ 01924 454476; **e**: office@george brooke.com). Cheapest fully-fitted coffin only: £295 (delivery locally £35). Cold storage only: Yes, £12.50 per day. Body transport only: Yes, minimum charge £60 for local area, then 75p per mile. Advice for DIY: Yes, 'no charge, we automatically help'. 'We are a truly small family business caring for our community, advising on all aspects of funeral services and we try to fulfil a family's requests. We have cardboard coffins in stock' (Helen Wilson). Prepaid plan: Golden Charter. Member of NAFD, BIFD.

• **FD Grimsby**: Kettle Ltd Funeral Directors, 135 Granville St, Grimsby, North East Lincs DN32 9PB (☎ 01472 355395; **f**: 01472 267383; **e**: kettle@kettle funerals.co.uk; **w**: www.kettlefunerals.co.uk); also 110 Kidgate, Louth LN11 9BX (☎ 01507 600710; **f**: 01507 354912). Cheapest fully-fitted coffin only: £210 (delivery locally free, nationally 50p per mile). Cold storage only: Yes, £15 per day. Body transport only: Yes, hearse £95. Advice for DIY: Yes, £10 ph. Basic funeral: £760 (disbursements extra). 'We even supplied handles, plate and linings to a client who had made a coffin for his mother's funeral' (Michael Chevins). Prepaid plan: Golden Charter. Member of NAFD, BIFD & SAIF.

• **FD Harrogate**: W. Bowers Services to the Bereaved, Birstwith Road, Hampsthwaite, Harrogate HG3 2EU (☎ 01423 770258; **f**: 01423 772474; **e**: rbowers186@aol.com; **w**: www.w-bowers.co.uk) and at 3 Sykes Grove, Harrogate HG1 52DB (☎ 01423 505543). Cheapest fully-fitted coffin only: £125 (delivery £35 within 10 miles). Cold storage only: Yes, £10 per day. Body transport only: Yes. Advice for DIY: Yes, £25 ph. Basic funeral: £1,350 (incl. disbursements). Prepaid plan: Golden Charter. Member of no association, although a member of the Small Business Federation. 'We seek to meet individual requirements with sensitivity, care and support. Our attitude is customer first at all times, nothing is too much trouble' (Roger Bowers). (Eds: one family emailed the Centre to say of this firm, 'We are getting excellent service'.)

• **FD Hebburn**: Mr Peter Kerrigan, Tynedale Funeral Services, Victoria House, Prince Consort Road, Hebburn, Tyne and Wear NE31 1BE (☎ 0191 4281018). See South Shields below for details.

• **FD Holmfirth**: T. W. Birks & Son Ltd, Holme Valley Funeral Home, Woodhead Road, Holmfirth HD7 1PR (☎ 01484 683322). Cheapest fully-fitted coffin only: £150 (delivery locally £25; nationally £1 per mile). Cold storage only: Yes, £20 per day. Body transport only: Yes, £1 per mile, minimum £25. Advice for DIY: Yes, no charge. Basic funeral: £800 (disbursements extra). 'We are a family firm that pride ourselves in giving a service to the community we live and work in. We also own land that we plan to use as a green burial site subject to planning permission' (Neil Birks). Prepaid plan: Golden Charter. Member of NAFD, BIFD, SAIF & BIE.

• **FD Huddersfield**: D. J. Screen & Sons, 222 Bradford Road, Huddersfield HD1 6LJ (☎ 01484 452220). Cheapest fully-fitted coffin only: £98 (delivery locally free, nationally 50p per mile). Cold storage only: Yes, £5 per day. Body transport only: Yes, 50p per mile. Advice for DIY: Yes, no charge. Basic funeral: £600 (disbursements extra). 'As a small local family business, we try to assist. Barter if required, we are not stuck to fixed prices' (Denis Screen). Prepaid plan: Golden Charter. Dip FD.

• **FD Lincoln**: Lincoln Co-operative Funeral Services, 12 Portland Street, Lincoln LN5 7JX (☎ 01522 534971). They also have offices in: Gainsborough (☎ 01427 612131); Holbeach (Clubley's ☎ 01406 422333); Horncastle (M. England ☎ 01507 523385) [eds: this branch has been particularly commended to us for its helpful approach]; Newark (G. E. Rose ☎ 01636 703808); Sleaford (☎ 01529 306311); and Spalding (Clubley's ☎ 01775 723199). Cheapest fully-fitted coffin only: £205 incl. a gown (delivery locally £30). Cold storage only: Yes, £15 per day. Body transport only: Yes, £1.30 per mile, minimum charge £40. Advice for DIY: Yes, £40 ph. Basic funeral: £620 (disbursements extra). 'We are a small independent co-op society offering a personal service. Trained counsellors offer free bereavement support service to all clients; own floristry and memorial masonry service' (David Dernley). Prepaid plan: Co-operative Funeral Bond. Members of the local society automatically get up to £387 off the funeral price. Member of FSC.

• **FD Newcastle-upon-Tyne**: Phillips Acorn Funeral Service, Acorn House, 309 Salters Road, Gosforth, Newcastle-on-Tyne NE3 4HN (☎ 0191 2840777). Cheapest fully-fitted coffin only: £195 (delivery locally free). Cold storage only: 'We do not have cold storage but charge £25 per day to hold a body in our chapel of rest.' Body transport only: Yes, estate car £50, hearse £75 plus 50p per mile over 10 miles. Advice for DIY: Yes, £20 ph. Basic funeral: £625 (disbursements extra); but a 'simple green service would cost from approximately £525, then add fee for burial in the Hexham woodland burial ground'. 'We will advise fully on all options. Funerals should be made more personal and distinctive. Green/eco-friendly options and issues discussed and made available whenever required' (Philip Harrison). Prepaid plans: Help the Aged, Golden Charter.

• **FD Newcastle-upon-Tyne**: Go as you Please Funeral Directors Ltd, 84-84a Park Road, Wallsend, Newcastle-on-Tyne NE28 6QY (☎ 0191 2369797; **e:** goasyoupleasefunerals@yahoo.co.uk). Cheapest fully-fitted coffin only: £195 (delivery locally £20, nationally £40). Cold storage only: Yes, £10 per day. Body transport only: Yes, minimum charge £65. Advice for DIY: Yes, no charge. Basic funeral: £1,150 (incl. disbursements). Woodland burial: £1,350 incl. plot at Seven Penny Meadows Green Field Burial Ground and all disbursements. 'We believe that a funeral should be a personal and special occassion where you dictate what happens' (Jonathan Purdy). Prepaid plan: Golden Leaves. Member of no association.

• **FD Sheffield**: B. & C. Funeral Service, 51 Suffolk Road, Sheffield S2 4BX (☎ 0114 2760211); also at 473 Herries Road, Sheffield S5 8AH (☎ 0114 2852984); Bevan Way, Chapeltown S35 1RP (☎ 0114 2467971); Market Street, Eckington S21 4EN (☎ 01246 433093); 8 Bridge Street, Killamarsh S31 8AH (☎ 0114 2474095); 512 Manchester Road, Stocksbridge S36 2DU (☎ 0114 2888612); and Market Square, Woodhouse S13 7JX (☎ 0114 2697750). Parent company: Sheffield Co-operative Society. Cheapest fully-fitted coffin only: £140 (delivery locally £50, nationally 50p per mile). Cold storage only: Yes, £10 per day.

Body transport only: Yes, £70 plus 50p per mile over 15 miles. Advice for DIY: Yes, £30 ph. Basic funeral: £420 (disbursements extra). 'We work within a 15 mile radius of the city centre at no extra charge. We would try to accommodate any request' (M. R. Bratton). Prepaid plan: Funeral insurance with vouchers. Member of FSC.

• **FD Sheffield**: T. W. Birks & Son Ltd, 100 Manchester Road, Deepcar, Sheffield S36 2RE (☎ 01142 885555). For details see their entry under Holmfirth, above.

• ✪✪✪ **FD Sheffield**: Peace Funerals, Gleadless Mount, off Ridgeway Road, Sheffield S12 2LN (☎ 0114 253 0505 or freephone 0800 093 0505; **e**: peacefuner@aol.com; **w**: www.peacefunerals.co.uk). Cheapest fully-fitted coffin only: £149; cardboard £89 (delivery locally free). Cold storage only: Yes, £12 per day. Body transport only: Yes, £55. Advice for DIY: Yes, £30 ph. Basic funeral: £600 (disbursements extra). 'We have our own design of willow basket-work coffins and plain and painted cardboard coffins. We are concerned with empowering the bereaved and providing any funeral choice whatsoever as long as it is legal. We run two woodland burial grounds (see Chapter 6) and have provided woodland burial at over 20 different sites across the UK. We arrange many secular funerals (which we help families to design and implement) and we originated the Railway Funerals concept' (John Mallatratt). Prepaid plan: Golden Leaves. Member of no association. (Eds: we have received more positive feedback from the public about this firm than any other in the UK. Recently received letters say, 'Wonderfully sympathetic, courteous and efficient service ... Peace Funerals would be my choice for any future funerals'; 'Wonderful, helpful, kind and patient'; 'What could have been an awful experience turned out really to be a celebration of his life'; 'Absolutely excellent, they were able to provide exactly what we wanted'.)

• **FD South Shields**: Mr Peter Kerrigan, Tynedale Funeral Services, Tynedale House, Stanhope Road, South Shields, Tyne and Wear NE33 4TB (☎ 0191 4550904). Cheapest fully-fitted coffin only: £190 (delivery locally £10, nationally negotiable). Cold storage only: Yes, £10 per day. Body transport only: Yes, £40 one-off payment. Advice for DIY: Yes, £15 ph. Basic funeral: £590 (disbursements extra). 'Full horse-drawn hearse from £500' (Peter Kerrigan). Prepaid plan: Golden Charter. Member of FSC & BIFD.

Wales

Comprising Flintshire, Wrexham, Denbighshire, Aberconwy and Colwyn, Anglesey, Caernarfonshire and Merionethshire, Powys, Cardiganshire, Pembrokeshire, Carmarthenshire, Swansea, Neath and Port Talbot, Bridgend, Rhondda Cynon Taff, Vale of Glamorgan, Merthyr Tydfil, Caerphilly, Cardiff, Blaenau Gwent, Torfaen, Newport, Monmouthshire.

• ✪✪✪ **FD Anglesey**: W. O. Williams, Tan Graig, Rose & Thistle, Llanedwen, Anglesey, North Wales LL61 6PX (☎ 01248 430312). Cheapest fully-fitted coffin only: £125 plus VAT (includes gown; delivery locally £20). Cold storage only: Yes, £16 the first night, £8 per day thereafter. Body transport only: Yes (£50). Advice for DIY: Yes, £40. Offers what it terms a 'DIY Funeral' for £245 (disbursements extra) where 'all the forms and certificates are collected and delivered by the client, there is no embalming included and the client provides own bearers (or pays extra). This includes the provision of a hearse for the funeral (20 miles) but not the cost of a coffin which is supplied from a selection. Reductions made for unrequired services' (W. O. Williams). Prepaid plan: Golden Charter.

• **FD Barry**: W. Spickett and Son, 181 Court Road, Cadoxton, Barry, Vale of Glamorgan (☎ 01446 407962). Basic funeral: £850 excl. disbursements. Cheapest fully-fitted coffin only: £320, delivery locally free. Cold storage only: £15 per day. Body transport only: £195 for local removal and delivery to cemetery/crematorium. Advice for DIY: Yes, two visits free. 'We have cardboard, bamboo and wicker coffins available, also horse drawn vehicles and access to a local woodland burial site (Cardiff). We will tailor our services to the needs of the bereaved; if budget is limited we will attempt to provide requested services within the budget' (John Marsh). Prepaid plan: Golden Leaves. Member of NAFD.

• **FD Cardiff**: A local authority funeral service for Cardiff residents is provided by the firm Rumney Funeral Services of Cardiff (☎ 029 20797 516), who charge £385 excl. disbursements. Add to this the crematorium fee of £270.50 and the doctors' fees of £91. Burial costs £582.50.

• **FD Cardiff**: J. Pidgeon and Son, 539 Cowbridge Road East, Victoria Park, Cardiff CF5 1BD (☎ 029 2022 6604; **w**: www.pidgeonsofcardiff.co.uk). Basic funeral: £700, excl. disbursements. Add to this the crematorium fee of £270 (non-residents £436) or the cemetery fee of £622.50 (non-residents £983.50); the officiant fee of £51 (plus) and the doctor's fee of £91. They will cut costs to meet small budgets. They will not supply coffin only but will give wholesaler details. Cold storage only: £8 per day. Advice for DIY: Yes. 'We have cardboard coffins available, but think our recovered wood chipping Cotswold coffin is more environmentally friendly. We also have bamboo and wicker coffins available' (John Pidgeon). Prepaid plan: Golden Leaves. Member of NAFD.

• **FD Cardiff:** Green Willow Funerals Ltd, 33 St Isan Road, Cardiff, Wales CF4 4LU (☎ 029 2046 2100). See Newport for details.

• **FD Newport:** Green Willow Funerals Ltd, Pillmawr Road, Newport, Wales NP20 6WN (☎ 01633 855350; **e**: enquiries@greenwillowfunerals.co.uk; **w**: www.greenwillowfunerals.co.uk). Cheapest fully-fitted coffin only: £150; or £110 for a cardboard coffin (delivery free within 20 miles). Cold storage only: Not available. Body transport only: Yes. Advice for DIY: Yes, no charge. Basic funeral: £625 (excl. disbursements). Also offer a 'Direct Sevice', where there is no attendance of mourners and where the funeral is carried out at a time convenient to the funeral directors: £399 (excl. disbursements). 'The company specialises in tailoring the arrangements for a funeral service to meet the total needs of the family. We can give a full estimate by phone or by post' (John Bettles). Prepaid plan: Golden Charter. Member of no association.

West Midlands

Comprising Shropshire, Staffordshire, Wolverhampton, Walsall, Dudley, Sandwell, Birmingham, Solihull, Coventry, Warwickshire, Hereford & Worcester, Gloucestershire.

• **FD Birmingham**: Samuel James & Sons, 313 Foxhollies Road, Acocks Green, Birmingham B27 7PS (☎ 0121 7082766). Cheapest fully-fitted coffin only: £125 (delivery locally free). Cold storage only: Yes, £4.99 per day. Body transport only: Yes. Advice for DIY: Yes, no charge. Basic funeral: £750 (excl. disbursements). 'As a small and new company we try to give the best personal service possible' (Tony James). Prepaid plan: Golden Leaves. Member of no association.

• **FD Birmingham**: Jonathan Walker Funeral Directors Ltd, 288 Church Road, Sheldon, Birmingham B26 3YH (☎ 0121 6930204). Cheapest fully-fitted coffin only: £90 (incl. crematorium handles and plate, delivery locally free). Cold storage only: Yes, £10 per day. Body transport only: Yes. Advice for DIY: Yes, no charge. Basic funeral: £600 within 50-mile radius of Birmingham (disbursements extra); beyond 50 miles, slight additional charge. 'We provide a range of services specifically geared to what the family wants rather than pre-packaged funerals' (Jon Walker). No prepaid plan. Member of NAFD.

• **FD Burton upon Trent**: Family Care Funeral Services, Unit 111, Fauld Ind Estate, Fauld Lane, Tutbury, Burton upon Trent, Staffordshire DE13 9HS (☎ 01283 521104 or 07949 122484 anytime). Cheapest fully-fitted coffin only: 'eco-coffin' £35 (delivery locally £5; nationally £20); 'also the Celtic (cardboard) Casket at £55, bamboo coffins from £155, stretchers, etc.' Cold storage only: Yes, £5 per day. Body transport only: Yes, £15 plus 80p per mile. Advice for DIY: Yes. Basic funeral: £550 (excl. disbursements). 'We are proprietors of the Cocoon system and therefore provide this service to the public from a unique position' (Holly Ryalls). Prepaid plan: 'Own plan, Final Security, in conjunction with Nat West. Client retains control of account and interest.' Member of no association.

• **FD Cirencester**: Cowley & Son Ltd, Triangle House, 62 Victoria Road, Cirencester, Gloucestershire GL7 1ES (☎ 01285 653298; **f**: 01285 653224; **e**: cowleyandson@hotmail.com; **w**: www.iofab.com). Cheapest fully-fitted coffin only: £120 (delivery locally £15; nationally £45 plus VAT). Cold storage only: Yes, £10 per day. Body transport only: Yes, 75p per mile (£50 minimum). Advice for DIY: Yes, £50 all-in. Basic funeral: £595 (disbursements extra). 'We will do anything the client requires. We are also the main importers of the Peacebox Ecology coffins into the UK' (Robert Orford). Prepaid plan: Golden Charter. Member of SAIF & NAFD.

• **FD Coventry**: Henry Ison & Sons (Coventry) Ltd, 76-78 Binley Road, Stoke, Coventry CV3 1FQ (☎ 024 7645 8665; **e**: info@henryison.co.uk; **w**: www.henryison.co.uk); also at 49 Allersley Old Road, Chapel Fields, Coventry CU5 8BU (☎ 024 7671 3643). Cheapest fully-fitted coffin only: £135 (delivery locally free). Cold storage only: Yes, £25 per day. Body transport only: Yes,

£115 for a hearse. Advice for DIY: Yes, £65 ph. Basic funeral: £850 (disbursements extra). 'A Christian firm offering the highest standards' (Bryan Powell). Prepaid plan: Golden Charter. Member of SAIF & NAFD.

• **FD Dursley**: L. W. Clutterbuck, 24-26 High Street, Cam, Dursley, Gloucestershire GL11 5LE (☎ 01453 542754; **w**: www.lwclutterbuck.co.uk). Cheapest fully-fitted coffin only: £240. Cold storage only: Yes, £7 per day. Body transport only: Yes (no fixed price). Advice for DIY: Yes, £17.50 ph. Basic funeral: 'Funerals are not sold as packages; we start with nought and build up.' 'Now in our third generation of being a family-run firm, offering a personal and caring service catering for any and all individual needs. We will provide cardboard, willow or bamboo coffins for cremation or woodland burial' (Jeremy Clutterbuck). Prepaid plan: Golden Charter. Member of no association.

• ✪✪✪ **FD Nailsworth**: Fred Stevens Funeral Directors, Newmarket Road, Nailsworth, Gloucestershire GL6 ODQ (☎ 01453 832188). Cheapest fully-fitted coffin only: £170 (delivery locally £20). Cold storage only: Yes, £15 per day. Body transport only: Yes (private ambulance £73 incl. first 40 miles; hearse and driver only £214 incl. first 40 miles). Advice for DIY: Yes, no charge. Basic funeral: £890 (disbursements extra). Direct transfer service with no funeral service or mourners £465 (disbursements extra). 'We try to empower clients through clear advice and exploration of suitable options relevant to each circumstance. We try to be more imaginative in our approach, encouraging clients to do what is right for them rather than necessarily follow the perceived "way that things are done" unquestioningly' (J. J. Baker). Prepaid plan: Perfect Assurance. Member of NAFD.

• **FD Solihull**: Simply Funerals, 65 Rowood Drive, Solihull, West Midlands B92 9NG (☎ 0121 711 1173). Cheapest fully-fitted coffin only: £135 (delivery locally free). Cold storage only: Yes, £25 per day. Body transport only: Yes, £115 for a hearse. Advice for DIY: Yes, £65 ph. 'We are a privately owned company who specialise in simple funerals. Being low cost doesn't mean low standards – our staff are fully trained and we use the latest Daimler hearses and limousines complete with uniformed chauffeur/bearers. We do insist on payment in full before the funeral takes place' (B. Powell). Prepaid plan: Golden Charter. Member of no association.

• **FD Stroud**: Lansdown Funeral Service Ltd, 64 Slad Road, Stroud, Gloucestershire GL5 1QU (☎ 01453 762276). All other details as for Fred Stevens Ltd (see Nailsworth above) which owns it. Member of NAFD & SAIF.

• **FD Tamworth**: Co-operative Funeral Service, The Mews, Upper Gungate, Tamworth, Staffordshire B79 7NZ (☎ 01827 62094; **e**: tamworthfuneral@lineone.net; **w**: www.tamworth.coop). Run by the Tamworth Co-operative Society Ltd which also has offices at: 68 Station Street, Atherstone (☎ 01827 712105); 14 Queen Street, Cheadle (☎ 01538 755260); 34 High Street, Uttoxeter (☎ 01889 565561); and 107 Granville Street, Woodville (☎ 01283 217237). Cheapest fully-fitted coffin only: £150 (delivery locally free). Cold storage only: Yes, £5 per day. Body transport only: Yes, £100. Advice for DIY: Yes, no charge. Basic funeral: £935 (disbursements extra). 'We are a small independent co-op society offering a personal service' (Amanda Woodward). Prepaid plan: Tamworth Co-op Funeral Bond. Member of FSC.

East Midlands

Comprising Derbyshire, Nottinghamshire, Leicestershire, Northamptonshire, Bedfordshire, Oxfordshire, Buckinghamshire.

• **FD Amersham**: H. C. Grimstead Ltd, 10 Hill Avenue, Amersham, Buckinghamshire HP6 5BG (☎ 01494 434393). See Grimstead in the London region, below, for details.

• **FD Beaconsfield**: Arnold Funeral Service, 32 Gregories Road, Beaconsfield, Bucks HP9 1HQ (☎ 01494 685000; f: 01494 680101). See High Wycombe, below, for details.

• **FD Beaconsfield**: H. C. Grimstead Ltd, Tilbury House, Shepherds Lane, Beaconsfield, Buckinghamshire HP9 2DU (☎ 01494 672668). See Grimstead in the London region, below, for details.

• **FD Biggleswade**: Woodman & Son, a branch of Lodge Bros, at 3 Market Square, Biggleswade, Bedfordshire SG18 8AP (☎ 01767 315700; **w**: www.lodgebros.co.uk). See Lodge Bros in the London region for details.

• **FD Chalfont St. Peter**: H. C. Grimstead Ltd, Churchfield Lodge, Churchfield Road, Chalfont St Peter, Buckinghamshire SL9 9EW (☎ 01753 891200). See Grimstead in the London region, below, for details.

• **FD Derby**: G. Wathall & Son Ltd, 101-111 Macklin Street, Derby DE1 1LG (☎ 01332 345268). Cheapest fully-fitted coffin only: £235. Cold storage only: Yes, £15 per day. Body transport only: Yes. Advice for DIY: Yes. Basic funeral: £910 (disbursements extra). 'We offer all aspects of service relating to green funerals and aim to provide each family with a service to suit their own needs and requirements' (Helen Wathall). Prepaid plan: Golden Charter. Member of SAIF.

• ✪✪✪ **FD Faringdon**: G. & L. Evans, 8 Marlborough Street, Faringdon, Oxfordshire SN7 7JP (☎ 01367 242762; **e**: geoff@deadman.ghound.net). Cheapest fully-fitted coffin only: £75 (delivery locally £10). Cold storage only: Yes, £10 per day. Body transport only: Yes, £85 locally. Advice for DIY: Yes, £10 ph. Basic funeral: £685 (disbursements extra). 'We are a family firm who believe in service. We will do as much or as little as our clients require' (Geoff Evans). Prepaid plan: Golden Charter. Member of SAIF.

• **FD Gerrards Cross**: Arnold Funeral Service, 38 Oak End Way, Gerrards Cross, Buckinghamshire SL9 8BR (☎ 01753 891892; f: 01753 884941). See High Wycombe, below, for details.

• **FD High Wycombe**: Arnold Funeral Service, 891 London Road, Loudwater, High Wycombe, Buckinghamshire HP10 9TB (☎ 01494 472572 f: 01494 538968). Cheapest fully fitted coffin only: £165 (delivery locally £20). Cold storage only: Yes, £10 per day. Body transport only: Yes, removal from place of death direct to cemetery or crematorium inclusive of 20 miles, £150. Advice for DIY: Yes, no charge. Basic funeral: £760 excl. disbursements. 'We offer traditional, green, alternative and environmentally-friendly funerals and pride

ourselves in providing a wide range of products and services. This enables us to cater for all our clients' needs at reasonable cost' (Peter Kenyon). Prepaid plans: 'We offer all'. Member of NAFD.
• **FD Luton**: Neville Funeral Service Ltd, Neville House, Marsh Road, Leagrove, Luton LU3 2RZ (☎ 01582 490005; **e**: peteraspinall@nevillefuneralservice.com; **w**: www.nevillefuneralservice.com). Cheapest fully-fitted coffin only: £185 (delivery locally free). Cold storage only: Yes, price on application. Body transport only: Yes. Advice for DIY: Yes, no charge. Basic funeral: £625 (disbursements extra). 'We are a family business in a local tradition and offer our clients the opportunity to plan the sort of funeral they want' (Peter Aspinall). Prepaid plan: Chiltern Plan. Member of NAFD & BIE.
• **FD Mansfield**: Ken Gregory & Sons Ltd, 365 Nottingham Road, Mansfield, Notts NG18 4SG (☎ 01623 466620; **f**: 01623 466621; **e**: admin@ kgsfunerals.co.uk). Also at: Sutton-in-Ashfield (☎ 01623 466600) and Kirkby-in-Ashfield (☎ 01623 466610). Cheapest fully-fitted coffin only: £120; cardboard £105 (delivery locally £15). Cold storage only: Yes, £5 per day. Body transport only: Yes. Advice for DIY: Yes, £120 flat fee. Basic funeral: £650 (disbursements extra). A Direct Cremation is also available for £395 (cardboard coffin, no mourners, no funeral ceremony, closed vehicle, undisclosed date and time at local crematorium, with ashes left in the crematorium grounds). 'Family-owned and managed with dedicated and caring staff, we are able to offer total freedom of choice to ensure our clients arrange a unique funeral' (Peter Gregory). Prepaid plan: Golden Charter. Member of NAFD & SAIF.
• **FD Marlow**: Arnold Funeral Service, The Old Forge, Wethered Road, Marlow, Bucks SL7 3AH (☎ 01628 898866; **f**: 01628 898867). See High Wycombe, above, for details.
• **FD Milton Keynes**: The Funeral Company Ltd, 19 Stratford Road, Wolverton, Milton Keynes MK12 5LJ (☎ 01908 225222; **f**: 01908 220588). Cheapest fully-fitted coffin only: £195 (delivery locally free). Cold storage only: Yes, no charge. Body transport only: Yes, 50p per mile, minimum charge £50. Advice for DIY: Yes, no charge. Basic funeral: £795 (incl. disbursements). 'We specialise in green funerals as we are linked to a green burial ground. We offer all aspects of a green funeral nationwide. We are a young modern company and fully flexible in our approach' (Allen Scott). Prepaid plan: Golden Leaves. Member of no association.
• **Nottingham**: The council runs an excellent free scheme called the Nottingham Funeral where you phone 0115 915 2340 to find out the funeral director in Nottingham who provides a service which the council has agreed and which is inclusive of all unavoidable disbursements. This therefore includes interment or cremation but not the cost of rights of burial in a new grave. W. Bamford & Son Ltd (571 Mansfield Road, Sherwood, Nottingham NG5 2JN, ☎ 0115 962 6403) currently provide this service for £799.
• **FD Nottingham**: A. W. Lymn, The Family Funeral Service, Robin Hood House, Robin Hood Street, Nottingham NG3 1GF (☎ 0115 950 5875). Their 14 other offices are: Arnold (☎ 0115 967 6777); Aspley (☎ 0115 919 0011);

Beeston (☎ 0115 922 0433); Bingham (☎ 01949 837211); Bulwell (☎ 0115 979 4944); Carlton (☎ 0115 961 6180); Clifton (☎ 0115 945 6232); Derby (☎ 01332 348800); Hucknall (☎ 0115 968 0737); Long Eaton (☎ 0115 946 3093); Mansfield (☎ 01623 623765); Radcliffe (☎ 0115 933 2257); Ruddington (☎ 01115 921 1075); and West Bridgford (☎ 0115 969 6006). Cheapest fully-fitted coffin only: £150; cardboard £129 (delivery locally £20). Cold storage only: Yes, £5 per day. Body transport only: Yes, £99 locally. Advice for DIY: Yes, £157 flat fee. Basic funeral: £880 (disbursements extra). A 'Budget Cremation' is also available for £700. 'Family owned and managed. We encourage distinctive funerals arranged with the lifestyle, character and individuality of the deceased in mind. We are specialists in woodland burials. Fully itemised pricing allows the client to select a number of different options' (Jacqui Etches). Prepaid plans: Perfect Assurance & Golden Charter. Member of NAFD.

• **FD Rushden**: A. Abbott & Sons (Rushden) Ltd, Bedford Road, Rushden, Northamptonshire NN10 OLZ (☎ 01933 312142 or 410365; **f**: 01933 410500; **e**: abbot_funerals@yahoo.co.uk; **w**: www.abbotfunerals.co.uk). Cheapest fully-fitted coffin only: £375 (delivery locally free; nationally by mileage). Cold storage only: Yes, £25 per day. Body transport only: Yes. Advice for DIY: Yes, no charge. Basic funeral: £1,250 (disbursements extra). 'Family-owned and operated. Full bespoke service. Full green services' (M. Abbott). Prepaid plans: Golden Charter & Perfect Choice. Member of NAFD & SAIF.

• **FD Southwell**: David J. Hall, 62 King Street, Southwell, Nottinghamshire NG25 0EN (☎ 01636 812481). Cheapest fully-fitted coffin only: £150 (delivery at cost). Cold storage only: Yes, 'goodwill'. Body transport only: Yes, locally £75. Advice for DIY: Yes, no charge. Basic funeral: £755 (disbursements extra). 'We are a small village funeral directors and we are also joiners. We can provide cardboard, willow or bamboo coffins' (Simon Hall). Prepaid plan: Golden Charter. Member of SAIF.

• **FD Uppingham**: E. M. Dorman, 10 Main Street, Bisbrooke, Uppingham, Rutland LE15 9EP (☎ 01572 823976). Cheapest fully-fitted coffin only: £85 (delivery locally 'at a negotiable price'). Cold storage only: Yes, £11 per day. Body transport only: Yes. Advice for DIY: Yes, £12 ph. Basic funeral: £480 (disbursements extra). 'As a small family-owned funeral director, all arrangements are carried out by myself. It is a family concern that has served the community for over 150 years' (E. M. Dorman). Prepaid plan: Golden Charter. Member of SAIF.

• **FD Winslow**: Heritage & Sons, 63 High Street, Winslow, Buckinghamshire MK18 3DG (☎ 01296 713341). Cheapest fully-fitted coffin only: £210 (delivery locally £27; nationally by carrier depending on distance, with a £48 hessian wrapping). Cold storage only: Yes, £20 per day. Body transport only: Yes, £1.20 per mile. Advice for DIY: Yes, £35 to cover home visit. Basic funeral: £628 (disbursements extra). 'Quality funerals at reasonable prices, plus our own flexible funeral plan' (David J. Lloyd). Prepaid plan: Heritage & Sons. Member of NAFD.

East Anglia

Comprising Norfolk, Suffolk, Essex, Cambridgeshire and Hertfordshire.

• **FD Cambridge**: F. W. Cook Funeral Service, 49 Church Street, Willingham, Cambridge CB4 5HS (☎ 01954 260325; **f**: 01954 204073). Basic funeral: £675 (disbursements extra). 'The Cook family have been funeral directors for over 40 years. We strive to offer a personal service and in 99 per cent of cases families will have the funeral personally handled by a member of the owning family' (Andrew Cook). Prepaid plan: Golden Charter. Member of NAFD. (Eds: although not providing services for DIY such as selling just a coffin, this firm is included on the basis of testimonials received by us. One correspondent writes that they 'went far beyond the call of duty to provide a service that I can only describe as second to none'.)

• **FD Clacton-on-Sea**: R. Gwinnell & Sons, 351 Holland Road, Clacton-On-Sea, Essex CO15 6PD (☎ 01255 815600). See Manningtree, below, for details.

• **FD Colchester**: R. Gwinnell & Sons, 112 Ipswich Road, Colchester, Essex CO4 4AA (☎ 01206 868585). See Manningtree, below, for details.

• **FD Colchester**: Hunnaball Funeral Services, York House, 41 Mersea Road, Colchester, Essex CO2 7QS (☎ 01206 760049; **e**: hunnaball-funeral@talk21.com; **w**: www.hunnaball.co.uk). Branches in Braintree, Ipswich, Manningtree, Sudbury and West Mersea. Cheapest fully-fitted coffin only: from £115; cardboard coffin £135. Cold storage only: Yes, £60 per day. Advice for DIY: Yes, £40-£50 ph. Basic funeral: £600 (disbursements extra). 'Independent family business. Non-religious officiants available. Oakfield Wood, Wrabness, is the nearest woodland burial ground' (Trevor Hunnaball). Prepaid plan: Perfect Assurance, Chosen Heritage. Member of NAFD.

• **FD Dovercourt**: R. Gwinnell & Sons, 193 Main Road, Dovercourt, Essex CO12 3PH (☎ 01255 241900). See Manningtree, below, for details.

• **FD Finchingfield**: G. W. Hardy & Son, Finchingfield, Essex (☎ 01371 810324). See R. Gwinnell & Sons, Manningtree, below, for details.

• **FD Great Yarmouth**: Arthur Jary & Sons Ltd, 213/4 Northgate Street, Great Yarmouth, Norfolk NR30 1DH (☎ 01493 844363; **w**: www.arthurjary.co.uk). Also at: 43 High Street, Gorleston, Great Yarmouth NR31 6RR (☎ 01493 662389); 15 Yarmouth Road, Caister, Great Yarmouth, Norfolk NR30 5DL (☎ 01493 722472); Calthorpe Green, Old Road, Acle, Norfolk NR13 3QL (☎ 01493 752122); 1 Golden Court, Bridge Road, Oulton Broad, Lowestoft, Suffolk NR32 3LU (☎ 01502 538820) Cheapest fully-fitted coffin only: from £265 (delivery locally free). Cold storage only: Yes, £50 per day or part-day. Advice for DIY: Yes, approx. £25 ph. Basic funeral: £710 (disbursements extra). 'We are a family-owned company. Our staff go out of their way to be friendly and helpful, and nothing is too much trouble. We pay great attention to detail' (Mrs S. Thompson). Prepaid plan: 'Our own, through Funeral Planning Services.' Member of SAIF.

• **FD Hadleigh**: R. Gwinnell & Sons, 77 High Street, Hadleigh, Suffolk IP7 5DY (☎ 01473 824440). See Manningtree, below, for details.

- **FD Halstead**: Colne Valley Funeral Services, 47 High Street, Halstead, Essex (☎ 01787 477500). See R. Gwinnell & Sons, Manningtree, below, for details.
- **FD Hatfield**: J. J. Burgess & Sons, Alfred House, 20 The Common, Hatfield, Hertfordshire AL10 0ND (☎ 01707 262122/ 262171). Also at James House, 5 Cole Green Lane, Welwyn Garden City, Herts AL7 3PP (☎ 01707 391808); and at Jacob House, 23 Station Road, Knebworth, Herts SG3 6AP (☎ 01438 815656). Cheapest fully-fitted coffin: £80 (delivery locally £35). Cold storage only: Yes, £10 per day. Body transport only: Yes, £35 locally by estate car. Advice for DIY: Yes, £20 ph. Basic funeral: £650 (disbursements extra). 'We do however prefer to discuss the various options. We have carried out woodland burials with the family involved at the point of burial, using both wicker and cardboard coffins. Any denomination catered for. Our business is now being run by its fifth generation' (Justin J. Burgess). Prepaid plan: Golden Charter & Help the Aged. Member of SAIF, BIFD.
- **FD Ipswich**: Farthing, Singleton & Hastings Funeral Service, 650 Woodbridge Road, Ipswich, Suffolk IP4 4PW (☎ 01473 272711; **e**: fsh650@hotmail.com). Cheapest fully-fitted coffin only: £150 (delivery locally £25). Cold storage only: Yes, £25 per day. Body transport only: Yes, locally, minimum charge £70. Advice for DIY: Yes, 'modest negotiable fee'. Basic funeral: £640 (disbursements extra); direct cremation service £455 (excl. disbursements). They also offer a range of cardboard, willow and bamboo coffins. 'We are a small family firm with experienced and sympathetic staff who are keen to ensure clients receive excellent service tailored to their specific requirements. We pay great attention to detail and will go to any lengths to ensure a well-organised funeral' (Luke Farthing). Prepaid plan: NAFD Perfect Assurance. Member of NAFD & SIFH.
- **FD Ipswich**: Ipswich Funeral Service, Dove House, 291 Norwich Road, Ipswich IP1 4BP (Melanie Hunnaball ☎ 01473 748808). See Hunnaball Funeral Services in Colchester, above, for full details.
- **✪✪✪ FD Manningtree**: R. Gwinnell & Sons, 24 High Street, Manningtree, Essex CO11 1AD (☎ 01206 391506). Cheapest fully-fitted coffin only: £135 (delivery dependent on mileage). Cold storage only: Yes, £15 per day. Advice for DIY: Yes, basic advice free. Basic funeral: £700 (disbursements extra). 'We are a family firm happy to perform any task that is ethically and legally correct' (Roy Gwinnell). Pre-paid plan: Golden Charter. Member of SAIF and NAFD.
- **FD Manningtree**: Paskell Funeral Service, 15 High Street, Manningtree, Essex CO11 2RS (☎ 01206 396709). Contact Saul Hunnaball. See Hunnaball Funeral Services in Colchester, above, for details. Oakfield Wood, Wrabness, near Manningtree, is the local woodland burial ground
- **FD Norwich**: Peter Taylor Funeral Services, 85 Unthank Road, Norwich, Norfolk NR2 2PE (☎ 01603 760787, **f**: 01603 620298; **e**: taylors@ angliafunerals.co.uk; **w**: www.angliafunerals.co.uk). Branches include: Holt (☎ 01263 711992); Halesworth (☎ 01986 872204); Bungay (☎ 01986 892178); Long Stratton (☎ 01508 531806); Dereham (☎ 01362 699484); Watton (☎ 01953 881229); Diss (☎ 01379 642321); Harleston (☎ 01379 853094);

Horstead (☎ 01603 737729); Wroxham (☎ 01603 783797); Aylsham (☎ 01263 733176); Wymondham (☎ 01953 603138); Thetford (☎ 01842 766221); Attleborough (☎ 01953 452798); and North Walsham (☎ 01962 402603). Cheapest fully-fitted coffin only: £120 (delivery locally £20; nationally 45p per mile over 20 miles). Cold storage only: Yes, £20 per day. Body transport only: Yes, £60 minimum charge up to 20 miles, 45p per mile thereafter. Advice for DIY: Yes, £50 ph. Basic funeral: £795 (disbursements extra). 'We also offer a range of ecology funerals, incl. a cardboard coffin and a craftsman-made woven willow chrysalis. We have a strong association with, and support, the woodland burial ground at Colney. We are open-minded. We are here to help provide a funeral in accordance with the customers wishes, not ours' (Anne Beckett-Allen). Prepaid plans: Anglia Funeral Plan with Funeral Planning Services. Member of NAFD & The Alderwoods Partnership Ltd.

• **FD Royston**: Cecil Newling, a branch of Lodge Bros, at Newling House, Market Hill, Royston, Herts SG8 9LL (☎ 01763 243048; **w**: www. lodgebros.co.uk). See Lodge Bros in the London region, below, for details.

• **FD St Neots**: T. L. Cobbold, a branch of Lodge Bros, at 11 & 13 New Street, St Neots, Huntingdon, Cambridgeshire PE19 1AE (☎ 01480 472398). See Lodge Bros in the London region, below, for details.

• **FD Saxmundham**: Tony Brown's Funeral Service, New Cut, Saxmundham, Suffolk IP17 1DJ (☎ 01728 603108; **f**: 01728 604346). Would not supply coffin only. Cold storage only: Yes, £10 per day. Body transport only: Yes ('the charge would depend on distance, with a minimum fee of £60 to cover the cost of the limousine hire'). Advice for DIY: Yes, no charge. Basic funeral: £750 (disbursements extra). Prepaid plan: No: 'privately if required, but I do not believe in it.' Would give price breakdowns over the phone, but does not have a price list for members of the public to take away. Also run a green burial site in Farnham near Saxmundham (see Chapter 6). 'I conduct a personal family business and I object to all unnecessary red tape. I give a very good Christian service and treat everybody the same unless they want something elaborate. We probably know 95 per cent of the people we deal with' (Tony Brown). (Eds: Libby Purves, writing in Country Living magazine, referred to Brown's 'cheerful sensitivity that makes bereavement more bearable'.)

• **FD Sible Hedingham**: Harvey Darke Funeral Services, Swan Street, Sible Hedingham, Essex (☎ 01787 461138). See R. Gwinnell & Sons, Manningtree, above, for details.

• **FD Thorpe-le-Soken**: R. Gwinnell & Sons, High Street, Thorpe-le-Soken, Essex CO16 OEA (☎ 01255 861818). See Manningtree, above, for details.

• **FD West Mersea**: J. K. May Funeral Service, Blackwater House, Barfield Road, West Mersea, Essex CO5 8JG (☎ 01206 382235). Contact John May. See Hunnaball Funeral Services in Colchester, above, for details.

The South West

Comprising South Gloucestershire, Bristol, Bath and North East Somerset, North West Somerset, Somerset, Dorset, Devon, Cornwall.

• **FD Ashburton:** F. Christophers & Son, Bridge House, 9 Kingsbridge Lane, Ashburton, Devon (☎ 01364 654065). Cheapest fully-fitted coffin only: £270 (delivery locally £1 per mile). Cold storage only: Yes, £10 per day. Body transport only: Yes. Advice for DIY: Yes, £30 ph. Basic funeral: £990 (incl. disbursements up to £250 only). 'Oldest family firm in Devon, established 1846, covering area of Southern Dartmoor' (Frederic Christophers). Member of SAIF.

• ✪✪✪ **FD Bideford**:A. D. Williams, The Pill, Kingsley Road, Bideford, North Devon EX39 2PF (☎ 01237 472108). Cheapest fully-fitted coffin only: £120 (delivery locally £10). Cold storage only, £5 per day. Body transport only: Yes. Advice for DIY: Yes, no charge. Basic funeral: £450 (disbursements extra). 'Happy to help people achieve a green burial option' (Alan David Williams). Prepaid plan: Golden Charter. Member of SAIF.

• **FD Bristol:** Heaven on Earth, 18 Upper Maudlin Street, Bristol BS2 8DJ (☎ 0117 926 4999; **e**: heaven.earth@virgin.net; **w**: www.heavenonearth bristol.co.uk). Cheapest fully-fitted coffin only: £199 (delivery locally free). Range of coffins: cardboard £160 or £299; bamboo from £299; reclaimed pine £399; willow from £550; biodegradable body bags £38. Cold storage only: Yes, £10 per day. Body transport only: Yes. Advice for DIY: Yes, donation to charity suggested. Basic funeral: £600 (disbursements extra; 'family involvement can reduce the price'). 'We positively encourage DIY. We can recommend pagan, secular, religious or Buddhist celebrants' (Paula Rainey Crofts & Simon Dorgan). No pre-paid plan. Member of no association.

• **FD Crewkerne:** Stoodley & Son, The Park, The George Shopping Centre, Crewkerne, Somerset TA18 7LU (☎ 01460 73229). Cheapest fully-fitted coffin only: £275 (delivery locally free). Cold storage only: Yes, £15 per day. Body transport only: Yes. Advice for DIY: Yes, £10 ph. Basic funeral: £995 (disbursements extra). 'We provide cardboard coffins, bamboo coffins and urns and have undertaken many green funerals. Will always try to meet family's "green" needs' (Tracey Warren). Pre-paid plan: Golden Charter. Member of NAFD & BIFD.

• **FD Dawlish:** B. G. Wills & Son, 22 Brunswick Place, Dawlish, Devon EX7 9PD (☎ 01626 862426; **e**: geoffwills@btinternet.com; **w**: www.bgwillsfuneral directors.co.uk). Cheapest fully-fitted coffin only: £175 (delivery locally £20). Cold storage only: Yes, £10 per day. Body transport only: Yes, £50 within 12 miles during working hours. Advice for DIY: Yes, £20 ph. Basic funeral: £640 (disbursements extra). Cardboard, bamboo and willow coffins and ashes caskets available. 'We feel we are here to help families in any way we can either with just advice or supplying odd items or vehicle hire' (G. Wills). Prepaid plan: Golden Charter. Member of NAFD & SAIF.

• **FD Ilfracombe**: A. D Williams, 31 Portland Street, Ilfracombe, North Devon EX34 9NL (☎ 01271 866332). See Bideford above for details.

• **FD Launceston:** Cornish & Devon Green Burials, Trekenner Mill, Treburley, Launceston, Cornwall PL15 9PN (☎ 01579 370039). Cheapest fully-fitted coffin only: 'would put family in direct touch with the manufacturers'. Cold storage only: Yes, £10 per day. Body transport only: Yes, pick-up with hearse and two people, £150. Advice for DIY: Yes, no charge over the phone or at our place of business. Basic funeral: £400 (disbursements extra). 'We offer as green a funeral service as possible. Our coffin range includes cardboard and bamboo as well as coffins produced by local craftsmen using willow and wind-felled green oak. We do not embalm. Our strength is in helping families facing unexpected bereavement. We are helping and advising a number of people who wish to set up woodland burial sites in Devon and Cornwall' (Rupert Callender and Claire Phillips). No prepaid plan. Member of no association.

• **FD Weymouth:** Stockting Funeral Service, 22 Crescent Street, Weymouth, Dorset DT4 7BX (☎ 01305 785915; **f:** 01305 760626; **w:** www.grassby-funerals.co.uk; **e:** info@stocktingfunerals.co.uk). Parent company: Grassby & Sons Ltd. Cheapest fully-fitted coffin only: £195 (delivery locally £20; won't deliver nationally). Cold storage only: Yes, £30 per day. Body transport only: Yes. Advice for DIY: Yes, £17 ph. Basic funeral: £680 (disbursements extra). 'We would be prepared to supply a cardboard coffin if requested' (David Grassby). Member of NAFD.

• **FD Winscombe:** C. V. Gower & Son Funeral Directors, The Square, Winscombe, North Somerset BS25 1BS (☎ 01934 842945; **f:** 01934 843130; **e:** johngower@supanet.com). Cheapest fully-fitted coffin only: £150 (delivery locally £10; nationally 50p per mile). Cold storage only: Yes, £5 per day. Body transport only: Yes, basic charge plus 50p per mile. Advice for DIY: Yes, no charge. Basic funeral: £550 (disbursements extra). Prepaid plan: Golden Charter. Member of SAIF, NAFD, FSC. (John Gower)

The South

Comprising Wiltshire, Berkshire, Surrey, Kent, Hampshire, East & West Sussex

• **FD Banstead**: A branch of W. A. Truelove & Son Ltd at 121 High Street, Banstead, Surrey SM7 2NS (☎ 01737 212 160). For details see Sutton, below.

• **FD Battle**: Arthur C. Towner Ltd, 19 Market Square, Battle, East Sussex TN33 OXB (☎ 01424 775515). See St Leonards, below, for details.

• **FD Bexhill-on-Sea**: Arthur C. Towner Ltd, 19-20 Station Road, Bexhill-on-Sea, East Sussex TN40 1RE (☎ 01424 733700). See St Leonards, below, for details.

• **FD Brighton:** Arka Original Funerals, 39-41 Surrey Street, Brighton, East Sussex BN1 (☎ 01273 684151; **e:** info@eco-funerals.com; **w:** www.eco-funerals.com). Cheapest fully-fitted coffin only: £150 (delivery locally £8; nationally £30). Cold storage only: Yes, £20 per day. Body transport only: Yes, £50 minimum charge (15 mile radius) then £1 per mile. Advice for DIY: Yes, no charge. Basic funeral: £900 (disbursements extra). 'Brighton's first alternative death centre. We promote personalised green funerals and assist people to make informed choices in the areas of death, bereavement and funeral planning' (Cara Mair). No prepaid plan at present. Member of SAIF.

• **FD Burgess Hill**: C. & T. Radmall Funeral Services, 223 London Road, Burgess Hill, West Sussex RH15 9QU (☎ 01444 871212). Cheapest fully-fitted coffin only: £190 (free delivery within five miles). Cold storage only: Yes (air conditioned room, no fridge), £10 per day. Body transport only: Yes £55 for collection from hospital, plus £130 to crematorium in a hearse or £65 in a car/ private ambulance. Advice for DIY: Yes: no charge for general guidance; £35 ph for in-depth assistance. Basic funeral: £995 (incl. disbursements, coffin in place at crematorium, no hearse or bearers). 'We can supply cardboard, bamboo or willow coffins. We are an independent family-owned and family-run firm and are happy to offer whatever level of service or assistance a family requires' (Matthew Keysell). Prepaid plan: Golden Charter. Member of SAIF.

• **FD Byfleet**: G. Boutell & Son, a branch of Lodge Bros, at 50 High Road, Byfleet, Surrey KT14 7QL (☎ 01932 345037; **w**: www.lodgebros.co.uk). See Lodge Bros in the London region, below, for details.

• **FD Calne**: E. Wootten & Son, a branch of Lodge Bros, at 1 North Street, Calne, Wiltshire SN11 OHQ (☎ 01249 812258; **w**: www.lodgebros.co.uk). See Lodge Bros in the London region, below, for details.

• **FD Canterbury**: Terry Davis Funerals, 5 Builders Square, Court Hill, Littlebourne, Canterbury, Kent CT3 1XU (☎ 01227 720924). Cheapest fully-fitted coffin only: £220 (delivery locally free). Cold storage only: Yes, £15 per day. Body transport only: Yes (£70 within 20-mile radius). Advice for DIY: Yes, £40 ph. Basic funeral: £910 (disbursements extra). Green funeral option with cardboard coffin, removal from place of death, professional services prior to the funeral, transport to the funeral and provision of funeral director: £660 (disbursements extra). 'We encourage every bereaved family to make each funeral as unique a celebration of the life of their loved one as possible. It may be appropriate in some cases to arrange the celebration around a particular interest that the deceased had during their life' (Terry Davis). No prepaid plan. Member of no association. (Eds: one client reported back to the NDC, 'Terry Davis was helpful, discreet, self-effacing, interested and concerned'.)

• **FD Carshalton**: A branch of J. E. Gillman & Sons at 16 Green Wrythe Lane, Carshalton, Surrey SM5 2DW (☎ 020 8669 0483). See their entry in the London region, below, for details.

• **FD Caterham**: A branch of W. A. Truelove & Son Ltd at Leslie House, 187 Croydon Road, Caterham, Surrey CR3 6PH (☎ 01883 345 345). For details see Sutton, below.

• **FD Cheam**: A branch of W. A. Truelove & Son Ltd at 31 High Street, Cheam, Surrey SM3 8RE (☎ 020 8642 3300). For details see Sutton, below.

• **FD Chertsey**: Lodge Bros, 7 Windsor Street, Chertsey, Surrey KT16 8AY (☎ 01932 565980; **w**: www.lodgebros.co.uk). See Lodge Bros in the London region, below, for details.

• **FD Couldson**: A branch of W. A. Truelove & Son at 55 Chipstead Valley Road, Coulsdon, Surrey CR3 2RB (☎ 020 8660 2620). For details see Sutton below.

• **FD Epsom**: A branch of W. A. Truelove & Son Ltd at 14-18 Church Road, Epsom, Surrey KT17 4AB (☎ 01372 723 337). For details see Sutton, below.

• **FD Guildford**: J. Monk & Sons, a branch of Lodge Bros, at 3 Artillery Terrace, Guildford, Surrey GU1 4NL (☎ 01483 562780; **w**: www.lodgebros.co.uk). See Lodge Bros in the London region, below, for details.

• **FD Haywards Heath**: P. & S. Gallagher Funeral Directors, Fraser House, Triangle Road, Haywards Heath, West Sussex RH16 4HW (☎ 01444 451166; **e**: patgallagher@aol.com). Cheapest fully-fitted coffin only: £130 (delivery locally £25; nationally at cost). Cold storage: Yes. Body transport only: Yes. Advice for DIY: Yes, £35 ph. Basic funeral: £715 (disbursements extra). 'A family-run business with complete facilities. We are only too pleased to be able to assist members of the general public in any way that we can, not only on costs but also with advice and support when needed' (Patrick Gallagher). Prepaid plan: Golden Charter & own plan. Member of SAIF, BIE & BIFD.

• **FD Henfield**: C & T Radmall Funeral Services, 2 Stanhope House, High Street, Henfield, West Sussex BN5 9JJ (☎ 01273 494577). See Burgess Hill above for details.

• **FD Horsham**: C & T Radmall Funeral Services, 3/4 Shelley House, Bishopric, Horsham, West Sussex RH12 1QF (☎ 01403 257444). See Burgess Hill above for details.

• **FD Lewes**: Richard Green Funeral Service, 28 Western Road, Lewes, East Sussex (☎ 01273 488121). See Uckfield below for details.

• **✪✪✪ FD Lindfield**: Masters & Son (Lindfield) Ltd, Lewes Road, Lindfield, West Sussex RH16 2LB (☎ 01444 482107; **e**: masters@mistral.co.uk). Cheapest fully-fitted coffin only: £95 plus VAT (delivery locally £15). Cold storage: Yes, £5 per day. Body transport only: Yes, £1.25 per mile, minimum charge £25. Advice for DIY: Yes, no charge. Basic funeral: £725 (disbursements extra). 'As a small family-run business we believe it is our role to provide the support and services which our clients need, however great or small that need is. Two weeks ago we delivered a pine coffin to someone who wanted to make the arrangements for his wife's funeral himself; I booked a gravedigger and gave him some advice, and that is where our involvement ended. We can supply cardboard, wicker, bamboo, solid pine coffins and ecopods. We advise on woodland burial, supply bamboo ashes caskets and are very supportive of green issues' (Susan Masters). Prepaid plans: Golden Charter, Help the Aged. Member of NAFD & SAIF.

• **FD Melksham**: D. J. Bewley Funeral Directors, 15 Bank Street, Melksham, Wiltshire SN12 6LE (☎ 01225 702521). Also at Corsham (☎ 01249 716008) and Trowbridge (☎ 01225 353521). Cheapest fully-fitted coffin only: £203 (free delivery locally). Cold storage: Yes, £30 per day. Body transport only: Yes. Advice for DIY: Yes, £50 ph. Basic funeral: £988 (disbursements extra). 'We provide eco-friendly coffins and advise on green funerals and private land burial in the area' (Patrik Bewley). No prepaid plan. Member of NAFD & SAIF.

• **FD Mitcham**: A branch of J. E. Gillman & Sons at 205 London Road, Mitcham, Surrey (☎ 020 8685 0349). See their entry in the London region, below, for details.

• **FD Mitcham**: Donald Drewett & Sons, a branch of W. A. Truelove & Son Ltd, at 49-51 Upper Green East, Mitcham, Surrey CR4 2PF (☎ 020 8648 2905). For details see Sutton, below.

• **FD Newbury**: Camp Hopson Funerals, 90 West Street, Newbury, Berkshire RG14 1HS (☎ 01635 522210; **f**: 01635 569471; **e**: petercox@camp hopsonfunerals.fsnet.co.uk). Cheapest fully-fitted coffin only: £195 (delivery locally £20). Cold storage only: Yes, £12.50 per day. Body transport only: Yes. Advice for DIY: Yes, £50 for the first hour; £30 ph thereafter. Basic funeral: £700 (excl. disbursements). 'We are the largest private, family-run funeral directors in the area and have the resources, staff and equipment to cope with whatever is required. We are currently developing an "Enviro funeral". We're here to help!' (Peter Cox). Prepaid plan: Golden Charter. Member of NAFD &d SAIF.

• **FD Newbury**: R. C. Smallbone Ltd, Starwood House, 37 Pound Street, Newbury, Berkshire RG14 6AE (☎ 01635 40536). Cheapest fully-fitted coffin only: £130 (delivery locally £10; delivery nationally 'variable'). Cold storage only: Yes, £15 per day. Body transport only: Yes. Advice for DIY: Yes, £25 ph. Basic funeral: £850 (excl. disbursements). 'Small independent family-owned company that strives to carry out every request of the bereaved' (Michael Smallbone). Prepaid plan: Golden Charter. Member of SAIF.

• **FD Portsmouth**: Co-operative Funeral Directors, 157 Fratton Road, Portsmouth PO1 5EJ (☎ 023 9286 3031; **e**: stevepearce@southerncoops.co.uk). Other Southern Co-op Funeral Directors with the same terms of business at: Andover, Hampshire (☎ 01264 334798); Ascot, Berkshire (Lines Bannister & Co Ltd ☎ 01344 620266); Basingstoke, Hampshire (A. Monger Funeral Directors ☎ 01256 851124); Bognor Regis, West Sussex (☎ 01243 865119); Camberley, Berkshire (Camberley & District Funeral Directors ☎ 01276 33241); Chichester, West Sussex (☎ 01243 782209); Fareham, Hampshire (☎ 01329 280249); Farnborough, Hampshire (☎ 01252 542236); Fleet, Hampshire (☎ 01252 623098); Gosport, Hampshire (☎ 023 9258 1032); Havant, Hampshire (☎ 023 9248 4499); Portsmouth, Hampshire (G. Andrew & Sons Funeral Directors ☎ 023 9266 2534); Portsmouth (Dashwood & Denyer Ltd ☎ 023 9282 3853); Waterlooville, Hampshire (☎ 023 9226 6105); Waterlooville, Hampshire (Edwards Funeral Directors ☎ 023 9226 2194); Wokingham, Berkshire (J. B. Hall Funeral Directors ☎ 0118 979 3623). Cheapest fully-fitted coffin only: £100 (delivery locally £25). Cold storage only: Yes, £15 per day. Body transport only: Yes, £85 minimum charge. Advice for DIY: Yes, £20 ph. Basic funeral: £960 excl. disbursements but incl. a hearse and limousine). Bamboo, willow and cardboard coffins available. Green options are offered on funeral plan. Motorcycle and horse drawn packages. 'We will help any client in their time of need as much or as little as they request. We offer a complete service; whatever part of that service the client wishes is down to them' (Steve Pearce). Prepaid plan: Co-operative Funeral Bond. Member of FSC.

• **FD Ryde**: Langdon Browning Funeral Services, South View House, Edward Street, Ryde, Isle of Wight PO33 2SH (☎ 01983 565599; **f**: 01983 812394).

Cheapest fully-fitted coffin only: £200 (delivery locally £20). Cold storage only: Yes, £25 per day. Body transport only: Yes, minimum charge £50. Advice for DIY: Yes, £20. Basic funeral: £650 (disbursements extra). 'We offer a bespoke funeral and monumental masonry service which enables bereaved families to tailor the arrangements to their specific requirements. We are able to offer cardboard, willow or bamboo coffins and also have access to a local woodland site in Newchurch, Isle of Wight' (Simon Browning). Prepaid plan: Perfect Choice. Member of NAFD.

• **FD St Leonards**: Arthur C. Towner Ltd, 2-4 Norman Road, St Leonards-on-Sea, East Sussex TN37 6NH (☎ 01424 436386; **w**: www.towners.co.uk). For branches in Battle and Bexhill, see above. Cheapest fully-fitted coffin only: £148 (delivery locally £20). Cold storage only: Yes, flat fee of £38. Body transport only: Yes – first 10 miles free, then £1 per mile; with a minimum charge for a van of £51, for a hearse £98. Advice for DIY: Yes, £50 ph. Basic funeral: £618 (disbursements extra). 'Bamboo, chipboard or cardboard coffins available. Woodland burial site available locally. We are a small family firm offering a service to the highest ethical standards and committed to providing our clients with the funeral they want, not the funeral that is easiest for us to provide' (Edward Towner). Prepaid plan: Golden Charter. Member of SAIF.

• **FD Salisbury**: Richard T. Adlem Funeral Director Ltd, Park Cottage, Brushy Bush Lane, Sixpenny Handley, Salisbury, Wiltshire SP5 5NJ (☎ 01725 552496). Cheapest fully-fitted coffin only: £100; phone for delivery costs. Cold storage only: Yes, no charge as long as no other funeral director is involved. Body transport only: Yes, 70p per mile. Advice for DIY: Yes, no charge. Basic funeral: £800 (excl. disbursements). 'Families who have used us are willing to discuss the high level of service they have received from us. We do not have to satisfy shareholders or directors so we charge the lowest prices we can afford' (Richard Adlem). Prepaid plan: Golden Charter. Member of no association.

• **FD Southsea**: Mayfields Funeral Directors, 90 Elm Grove, Southsea, Hampshire PO5 1LN (☎ 02392 875575; **f**: 02392 751172; **e**: dcolbourne@line one.net). Cheapest fully-fitted coffin only: £105 (delivery locally free). Cold storage only: Yes, £10 per day. Body transport only: Yes, £1 per mile, minimum £30. Advice for DIY: Yes, £15 ph. Basic funeral: £725 (excl. disbursements). Prepaid plans: Golden Charter & Golden Leaves. Member of no association. 'We are an independent family funeral directors and every funeral is tailor-made for each family. We will meet any request for green aspect' (David Colbourne).

• **FD Sutton**: W. A. Truelove & Son Ltd, 118 Carshalton Road, Sutton, Surrey SM1 4RL (☎ 020 8642 8211; **e**: funerals@wa-truelove-and-son.ltd.uk; **w**: www.wa-truelove-and-son.ltd.uk). Also at 20 Mulgrave Road, Sutton SM2 6LE (☎ 020 8642 0089) and 278 High Street, Sutton SM1 1PG (☎ 020 8642 0327). For branches in other areas, see Truelove (London region, for the Wallington branch), Caterham, Cheam, Coulsdon, Banstead, Epsom and Mitcham. Cheapest fully-fitted coffin only: £225, plus VAT (delivery locally £40). Cold storage only: Yes, £15 per day, subject to availability. Body transport only: No. Advice for DIY: Yes, £75 ph. Basic funeral: £765 (advance payment price, disbursements extra). 'Family owned and run. Seven of our staff are diploma holders, two having won the Harold Rivett Award for excellence. A range of services, simple or elaborate' (Simon Truelove). Prepaid plan: Truelove Funeral Plans Ltd. Member of NAFD & SIFH.

• **FD Swindon**: Hillier Funeral Service, 170 Victoria Road, Swindon, Wiltshire SN1 3DF (☎ 01793 522797, **f**: 01793 422591). Also at Hillier Chapel of Rest, Broadway, Whitworth Road, Swindon SN25 3BL (☎ 01793 522145). Cheapest fully-fitted coffin only: £130 (delivery locally £15). Cold storage only: Yes, £3 per day. Body transport only: Yes (£75 for a hearse and driver). Advice for DIY: Yes, free. Basic funeral: £630 (disbursements extra). 'We provide comprehensive information to our clients and we also provide Hillier Bereavement Care (free of charge) to any family that requires help, for as long as is necessary' (Lesley Petherick). Prepaid plan: Golden Charter & own plan. Member of NAFD & SAIF.

• **FD Swindon**: A. E. Smith & Son, a branch of Lodge Bros, at Queens Drive, Swindon, Wiltshire SN3 1AW (☎ 01793 522023; **w**: www.lodgebros.co.uk). Also at 16 Commercial Road, Swindon SN1 5NF (☎ 01793 521125). See Lodge Bros in the London region, below, for details.

• **FD Tonbridge**: Abbey Funeral Services Ltd, 173 High Street, Tonbridge, Kent TN9 1BX (☎ 01732 360328; **f**: 01732 352376; **e**: info.abbey@talk21.com; **w**: www.abbey-funerals.co.uk). Cheapest fully-fitted coffin only: £156 (delivery locally £50 during office hours). Cold storage only: Yes, £50 per day. Body transport only: Yes, £100 during office hours. Advice for DIY: Yes, £50 ph ('forms to be provided by family'). Basic funeral: £968 (for deaths attended between 9am and 5pm, Monday-Friday, and bills settled within seven days of the funeral; disbursements extra). 'Small, independent, family-owned and managed business' (Jo Prescott). Prepaid plan: Golden Charter. Member of SAIF.

• **FD Uckfield**: Richard Green Funeral Service, 125 High Street, Uckfield, East Sussex TN22 1RN (☎ 01825 760601). Cheapest fully-fitted coffin only: cardboard £95; chipboard £130 (free delivery within ten miles). Cold storage only: Yes, £2 per day. Body transport only: Yes, from £60. Advice for DIY: Yes, £18.75 ph. Basic funeral: £510 (disbursements extra). 'We will try to help as we have in the past with any request that a family may have. These requests have included cardboard, painted or home-made coffins. We always tell families that the funeral should be as they want it' (Richard Green). Prepaid plan: Perfect Assurance, Golden Charter & Help the Aged. Member of NAFD & SAIF.

• **FD West Byfleet**: Lodge Bros, 33 Old Woking Road, West Byfleet, Surrey KT14 6LG (☎ 01932 355897; **w**: www.lodgebros.co.uk). See Lodge Bros in the London region, below, for details.

• **FD Weybridge**: Lodge Bros, 36-38 High Street, Weybridge, Surrey KT13 8AB (☎ 01932 854758; **w**: www.lodgebros.co.uk). See Lodge Bros in the London region, below, for details.

• **FD Wokingham**: R. Aubrey Miles & Sons, 128 Ashridge Road, Wokingham, Berkshire RG40 1PH (☎ 0118 979 7004). Cheapest fully-fitted coffin only: £100, delivery locally free. Cold storage only: Yes, £12 per day. Body transport only: Yes, minimum charge £90 removal; £105 hearse. Advice for DIY: Yes, no charge. Basic funeral: £1,100 (incl. disbursements). 'Willow, cardboard and pine coffins are all available with green transport and burial options. We are very much a family firm. Highly qualified as funeral directors, our motto is people before profit' (Adam Miles). Prepaid plan: Perfect Choice. Member of NAFD.

• **FD Worthing**: TMC Funeral Services (Monumental Company), 92-94 Broadwater Street West, Broadwater Green, Worthing, West Sussex BN14 9DE (☎ 01903 235353; e: pennykeen@monumental.co.uk; w: www.monumental.co.uk); also at Bognor Regis (☎ 01243 820431). Cheapest fully-fitted coffin only: £295 (free local delivery). Cold storage only: Yes, £20 per day. Body transport only: Yes, £95 minimum charge. Advice for DIY: Yes, either free, or £25 'arrangement fee'. Basic funeral: £925 (disbursements extra). 'Family-owned and managed' (Penny Keen). Prepaid plans: Help the Aged & Golden Charter. Member of SAIF.

Greater London region

Incl. old Middlesex. See also South region.

• **FD: F. A. Albin & Sons** Funeral Directors, Arthur Stanley House, 52 Culling Road, London SE16 2TN (☎ 020 7237 3637). Also at 164 Deptford High Street, London SE8 3DP (☎ 020 8694 1384) and 65 Mottingham Road, London SE9 4QZ (☎ 020 8857 0330). Cheapest fully-fitted coffin only: £354 (delivery locally £25; outside M25 £85). Basic funeral: £1,123 incl. disbursements. Also offers a 'Disposal Funeral Package' with no viewing, no service and no one in attendance for £600 (excl. disbursements). 'Owned by the family, we are now 220 years old' (B. Albin). (Eds: this firm will recommend embalming in certain circumstances; be sure to make it clear to them at the time if this is not your wish.)

• **FD: H. J. Bent & Co** Funeral Directors, 343 Ladbroke Grove, London W10 6HA (☎ 020 8969 1170). Also at 1c Westminster Court, London NW8 8JN (☎ 020 7723 1186); and 86 Old Oak Common Lane, London W3 7DA (☎ 020 8743 3338). Cheapest fully-fitted coffin only: £120. Cold storage only: Yes. Body transport only: Yes, if practical. Advice for DIY: Yes, £20 ph. Basic funeral: £895 (disbursements extra). 'We were the first company to be ISO 9004 registered for Funeral Services' (Terry Foreman). Prepaid plans: Own & Chosen Heritage. Member of no association except Federation of Small Businesses.

• **FD: Chelsea Funeral Directors**, 260(b) Fulham Road, Chelsea, London SW10 9EL (☎ 020 7352 0008; e: funerals@chelseafunerals.co.uk; w: www.chelseafunerals.co.uk). Also at 91 Rochester Row, Westminster, London SW1P 1LJ (☎ 020 7834 3281) and 235 Munster Road, Fulham, London SW6 6BT (☎ 020 7385 0866). Cheapest fully-fitted coffin only: £125 (delivery locally £10). Cold storage only: Yes, £10 per day. Body transport only: Yes, £80 minimum charge for first 20 miles plus £1 per mile thereafter. Advice for DIY: Yes, no charge. Basic funeral: £675 (disbursements extra). 'Full range of coffins available, also burials in designated woodland burial grounds. We are sensitive to all personal funeral requests and are willing to help people organise the kind of funeral they wish to have, however simple or complex the arrangement may be' (Neil Cocking). Prepaid plans: Golden Charter, Help the Aged. Member of NAFD. (Eds: a recent correspondent said, 'This firm provided a very helpful and considerate service for which I am most grateful'.)

• **FD**: **T. Cribb & Sons** Funeral Directors, Victoria House, 10 Woolwich Manor Way, Beckton, London E6 4PA (☎ 020 7476 1855; **w**: www.tcribb.co.uk). Branches at: 154-155 Barking Road, Canning Town, London E14 4HB; and 112 Rathbone Street, Canning Town, London E16 1JQ. Cheapest fully-fitted coffin only: £183 (delivery locally £15). Cold storage only: Yes, £10 per day. Body transport only: Yes. Advice for DIY: Yes, no charge. Basic funeral: £764 (disbursements extra). 'Our horse-drawn service is still available at £775; we have a probate service. Our phone lines and office are always open to give families advice and help – regardless of the fact that we may or may not be carrying out the full funeral arrangements' (John Harris). Prepaid plan: Golden Charter. Member of SAIF.

• **FD**: **William Dunphy** Funeral Directors, 294 Brockley Road, London SE4 2RA (☎ 020 8691 7943); also at 135 Evelina Road, London SE15 3HB (☎ 020 7 358 1330); Cheapest fully-fitted coffin only: £180, delivery locally £20. Cold storage only: Yes, £10 per day. Body transport only: Yes, £60 minimum, plus £1 per mile outside local area. Advice for DIY: Yes. Basic funeral: £910 (disbursements extra). Offer woodland burials, coffins with FSC accreditation, cardboard, wicker and pine; non-embalmed viewing, burial at sea, etc. 'We ensure that each funeral is tailored to meet the wishes of those arranging it. We offer the lowest priced options first and are happy to give advice on costs over the phone' (N. Dunphy). Member of no association.

• **✪✪✪ FD**: **J. E. Gillman & Sons Ltd**, 971 Garratt Lane, Tooting, London SW17 0LW (☎ 020 8672 1557; **e**: info@funeral.org.uk; **w**: www.funeral.org.uk). Branches: Balham High Road, London SW12 (☎ 020 8673 8719); Battersea, London SW11 (☎ 020 7228 0360); Carshalton, Surrey (☎ 020 8669 0483); Mitcham, Surrey (☎ 020 8685 0349); Norbury, London SW16 (☎ 020 8679 7422); Tooting, London SW17 (☎ 020 8672 6515) and West Norwood, London SE27 (Wilson Funeral Service ☎ 020 8670 4126). A lightly veneered chipboard coffin, 'without handles or fancy lining, just cremfilm, using wood from managed sustained-yield forests', is available in a range of sizes for £60 incl. delivery within 5 miles. Cold storage only: Yes, £15 per day. Body transport only: Yes, £75 ph 'base-to-base'. Advice for DIY: Yes, 'free advice from experienced and flexible staff'. Direct Transfer Service: 'Where there is no service, religious or secular, and no mourners', £385 (disbursements extra). Basic funeral: £860 (disbursements extra). 'Independent family firm, very qualified staff. We always try to be helpful, understanding and maintain a flexible attitude. We have a record of serving people who require any funeral that is out of the ordinary' (Roger Gillman). Prepaid plan: Golden Charter. Member of NAFD & SAIF. (Eds: the Natural Death Centre receives much positive feedback from the public about this firm. One recently received letter says, 'Excellent. They listened and did just as I asked. I paid only for what they provided. Please continue giving them your maximum star rating.')

• **FD**: **Green Endings**, 141 Fortess Road, London NW5 2HR (☎ 020 7424 0345; **e**: info@greenendings.co.uk; **w**: www.greenendings.co.uk). Cheapest wooden coffin: £150; cardboard coffins: 'rectangular shape with waterproof lining' £155; shaped £195 (all plus £10 local delivery or £1 per mile outside central London). Cold storage only: No. Body transport only: Yes. Advice for DIY: Yes, £20 ph. Basic funeral (cremation): £1,300 (incl. use of reusable wooden coffin containing inner cardboard coffin, transport within 10 miles of Camden, and all disbursements). 'My aim is to offer choice and to create the kind of funeral which would reflect the life of the person who has died. I encourage participation' (Roslyn Cassidy). Prepaid plan: Funeral Planning Services Ltd, custodian trustee HSBC Trust Company (UK) Ltd.

• **FD**: **H.C. Grimstead Ltd**, 58 Swan Road, West Drayton, Middlesex UB7 7JZ (☎ 01895 431000). Branches at Eastcote (☎ 020 8866 0688), Harefield (☎ 01895 822297) and Ruislip (☎ 01895 623000); and at Amersham, Beaconsfield and Chalfont St. Peter (see the East Midlands region above for details). Cheapest fully-fitted coffin only: £245, delivery locally free; cardboard coffin £180. Cold storage only: Yes, £25 per day. Body transport only: Yes, £60 plus £1 per mile. Advice for DIY: Yes, free of charge if local. Basic funeral: £725 excl. disbursements. 'A cardboard coffin can be used for many of our range of funerals. At a time when many funeral directors are reluctant to assist DIY families, I feel it better to give them professional advice' (Colin Thompson). Member of The Alderwoods Partnership Ltd. Prepaid plan: Advance Funeral Planning. Member of NAFD.

• **FD**: **Haji Taslim Muslim Funerals**, East London Mosque, 45 Fieldgate Street, London E1 1JU (☎ 020 7247 2625/ 9583). Cheapest fully-fitted coffin only: approx. £100. Cold storage only: Yes, no charge. Body transport only: Yes, £60 for two hours with a driver within a 25-mile radius. Prices can be reduced for those in financial difficulty. 'Although 95 per cent of the firm's business is Islamic, it is not exclusively so' (Mr Taslim).

• **FD**: **Holmes & Daughters**, 3 Church Road, Ashford, Middlesex (☎ 01784 421015; **f**: 01784 880626). Branches at: 461 Upper Richmond Road West, East Sheen SW14 7PU (☎ 020 8392 1012); 4 Cavendish Terrace, High Street, Feltham TW13 4HE (☎ 020 8893 1860) and 161 High Street, Teddington TW11 8HH (☎ 020 8977 9532). Cheapest fully-fitted coffin only: £305 (delivery locally free). Body transport only: Yes, from £180. Advice for DIY: Yes, no charge. Basic funeral: £995 (disbursements extra). 'Small independent business. Vintage 1934 hearse no extra cost. Female conductors on request. Many staff are family or longstanding family friends' (David Holmes). This firm publishes a full breakdown of its pricing. Prepaid plan: Holmes Plan. Member of SAIF.

• **Hounslow**: The Council has an arrangement with local funeral directors to supply a 'Hounslow Community Funeral Service' to residents at a cost of £650 (disbursements extra). The firms taking part are: The CRS Co-op (☎ 020 8570

4741), and Frederick Paine (☎ 020 8994 0056). In addition the council has a Community Funerals Officer to advise on bereavement, benefits and related issues (Christine Clark ☎ 020 8583 5009).
• **FD**: **Indian Funeral Service**, Chani House, Alexander Place, Lower Park Road, New Southgate, London N11 1QD (☎ 020 8361 6151; **e**: chandu@aol.com; **w**: www.indian-funeral.co.uk). Cheapest fully-fitted coffin only: £230 (delivery locally £50). Cold storage only: Yes. Body transport only: Yes, £90 for first 20 miles, £1 per mile thereafter. Advice for DIY: Yes, no charge. Basic funeral: £1,100 (disbursements extra). 'The only Asian family-owned funeral directors in London. We provide a quick and helpful way of completing a funeral in all circumstances for the Hindu and Sikh communities' (Chandu Tailor). Prepaid plan: Golden Charter. Member of SAIF.
• **Lewisham**: A municipal funeral service for local residents, by arrangement with the local authority, is provided by the CWS Co-op (☎ 020 7698 3244) at a cost of £1,030 (disbursements extra).
• **FD**: **Lodge Bros (Funerals) Ltd**, Ludlow House, Ludlow Road, Feltham TW13 7JF (☎ 020 8818 7710; **e**: info@lodgebros.co.uk; **w**: www.lodge bros.co.uk). Branches include: Ashford (☎ 01784 252226); Bedfont (☎ 020 8890 7902); Brentford (☎ 020 8560 7499). Feltham (☎ 020 8890 2231); Hampton Hill (☎ 020 8941 4022); Hanworth (☎ 020 8894 9731); Hillingdon (☎ 01895 234011); Hounslow (☎ 020 8570 0118); Northolt (☎ 020 8845 0660); Shepperton (☎ 01932 220081); Paddington (☎ 020 7286 8718); Shepherds Bush (☎ 020 8723 6862); Sunbury-on-Thames (☎ 01932 785402); Uxbridge (☎ 01895 233018); West Ealing (☎ 020 8567 0227); Yiewsley (☎ 01895 446686). Cheapest fully-fitted coffin only: £140. Body transport only: Yes, £125 minimum charge for up to two hours and 20 miles in normal working hours. Advice for DIY: Yes, 'free for those who purchase goods or services from us'. Basic funeral: £894 (disbursements extra). 'Our family business has been established for over 200 years. Full range of services at all branches. Our duty director receives all out-of-normal-hours phone calls to ensure that we give a continuous and helpful personal service at all times' (John Lodge). Prepaid plan: Family Funerals Trust Ltd. Member of NAFD, BIFD, NAPFP & NAMM. (Eds: this firm is to be commended for its particularly clear itemised price lists which include the comment: 'Any items listed can be purchased separately by clients wishing to make their own arrangements'.)
• **FD**: **Mears & Cotterill**, 169 Merton Road, Wandsworth, London SW18 5EF (☎ 020 8874 7698). Cheapest fully-fitted coffin only: £115 (delivery locally £30). Body transport only: Yes. Advice for DIY: Yes, £50 set fee. Basic funeral: £590 (disbursements extra). 'We are family owned. We supply coffins, hearse, embalming and advice as required, without insisting that we complete the whole of a funeral' (John William Mears). Prepaid plans: Golden Charter & Golden Leaves. Member of FSC.
• **FD**: **W. G. Miller**, 93-95 Essex Road, Islington, London N1 2SJ (☎ 020 7226 3886). Cheapest fully-fitted coffin only: £265 (delivery locally £30). Body transport only: Yes. Advice for DIY: Yes. Basic funeral: £995 (disbursements

extra). Cold storage only: Yes, £20 per day. 'Small family company which still cares for the family's wishes' (Peter Henry). Prepaid plan: none, but would advise. Member of NAFD & SAIF.

• **FD**: **Oakleigh Funerals Ltd**, 423 Oakleigh Road North, Whetstone, London N20 0RU (☎ 020 8368 6688, **f**: 020 8361 2299). Cheapest fully-fitted coffin only: £250 (delivery free within 10 miles). Body transport only: Yes, £35 plus £1 per mile. Advice for DIY: Yes, £40 ph. Basic funeral: £880 (disbursements extra). Cold storage only: Yes, £25 per day. 'As a new company we offer funerals at a lower cost than many competitors. Families will usually speak to the same person after calling. We treat people the way we would expect to be treated ourselves and do not cut corners. All funerals are conducted to the highest standard' (Ian Argent). Prepaid plan: Golden Leaves. Member of SAIF.

• **FD**: **Rowland Brothers**, 301 Whitehorse Road, West Croydon CR0 2HR and at 44 High Street, Purley, Surrey CR8 2HA (☎ 020 8684 1667; **e**: info@rowlandbrothersinternational.co.uk). Body transport only: Yes, £120 within 10 miles, £1 per mile thereafter. Advice for DIY: No. Basic funeral: £820 (disbursements extra). 'We also have a disposal service which costs £400 for those who want no involvement at all' (Steve Rowland). Prepaid plan: Golden Leaves. Member of NAFD.

• **FD**: **J. F. Shackleton & Sons**, 102 Percy Road, Shepherds Bush, London W12 9QB (☎ 020 8740 1481; **w**: www.shackletonfunerals.co.uk). Cheapest fully-fitted coffin only: £100, local delivery £20. Body transport only: Yes, £2 per mile, no minimum. Advice for DIY: Yes. no charge. Basic funeral: £550 (disbursements extra). 'We specialise in catering for the lower waged and can offer a rent-an-outer-coffin with a cardboard inner' (James Shackleton). Prepaid plan: Company's own. Member of no association.

• **FD**: **W. A. Truelove & Son Ltd**, a branch at 109 Stafford Road, Wallington, Greater London SM6 9AP (☎ 020 8647 1032). See their entry under Sutton, South region, above, for details.

• **FD**: **Willow Independent Funeral Service**, 21 Wellington Street, Woolwich, London SE18 6PQ (☎ 020 8854 6222). They have a branch at 347 Bexley Road, Northumberland Heath, Kent. Cheapest fully-fitted coffin only: £285. Cold storage only: Yes, no charge. Body transport only: Yes, minimum charge within M25 £100, plus £1 per mile thereafter. Advice for DIY: Yes, no charge. Basic funeral: £660 (disbursements extra). 'We are independent and give value for money' (Mr Hopper). Prepaid plans: Golden Charter, Golden Leaves & Help the Aged. Member of SAIF.

Scotland

• **FD**: **Cumbernauld,** Cumbernauld Funeral Services Ltd, 45 Main Street, Cumbernauld Village, Cumbernauld G67 2RT (☎ 01236 733744). Cheapest fully-fitted coffin only: £310. Cold storage only: Yes, no charge. Body transport only: Yes, £110 hearse, £90 estate car. Advice for DIY: Yes, no charge. Basic funeral: £960 (disbursements extra). 'My firm is family-owned

and run. I would help any family regardless of their financial circumstances' (William Paterson). Prepaid plan: Golden Leaves. Member of no association.
• **FD**: **Dunfermline,** Dunfermline Funeral Services, Dickson House, Dickson Street, Dunfermline, Fife KY12 7SL (☎ 01383 622882). Cheapest fully-fitted coffin only: £150, delivery locally free. Cold storage only: Yes, £55 per day. Body transport only: Yes, £75 minimum charge. Advice for DIY: Yes, £25 ph. Basic funeral: £700 (disbursements extra). 'Low cost dignified funerals with personal service. We will carry out any request for green funerals' (Andrew Donald). Prepaid plan: Golden Leaves. Member of no association.
• **FD**: **East Kilbride**, Heritage Funeral Services Ltd, 10 Montgomery Street, The Village, East Kilbride G74 4JS (☎ 01355 271717, **f**: 01355 330500). Cheapest fully-fitted coffin only: £140 (delivery locally £10). Cold storage only: Yes, £10 per day. Body transport only: Yes, estate car and hearse available. Advice for DIY: Yes, no charge. Basic funeral £855 (disbursements extra). 'We realise the importance of the client making decisions and will always put their needs both emotional and financial before the profitability of the company. Being a family business, we are not governed by targets or budgets and can provide a higher level of personal service than some of the larger companies' (Keida Mackenzie). Prepaid plan: Golden Charter. Member of SAIF, BIFD, BIE & FSC.
• **FD**: **Edinburgh,** Barclay's Funeral Services, 4 Taylor Gardens, Edinburgh EH6 6TG (☎ 0131 553 6818; **e**: david.deery@dignityuk.co.uk; **w**: www.dignityuk.co.uk). Parent company Dignity (UK). Cheapest fully-fitted coffin only: £300. Cold storage only: Yes, no charge. Body transport only: Yes, £150 hearse, £125 limousine. Advice for DIY: Yes, no charge. Basic funeral: £950 (disbursements extra). 'We go above and beyond the call of duty' (David Deery). Prepaid plan: Dignity. Member of FSC.
• ✪✪✪ **FD**: **Greenock,** P. B. Wright & Sons, Grey Place House, 131 West Blackhall Street, Greenock PA15 1YD (☎ 01475 724248; **f**: 01475 720400; **e**: info@pbwright.com; **w**: www.pbwright.com). Cheapest fully-fitted coffin only: £130, delivery locally £70. Cold storage only: No. Body transport only: No. Advice for DIY: Yes, £70 ph. Basic funeral: £900 (disbursements extra). 'We are a sixth-generation family firm with total concern for the families we serve. We have a very open attitude and will discuss anything with families including green funerals and woodland burials' (Nigel Wright). Prepaid plan: Golden Charter. Member of NAFD, BIFD, BIE & FSC.

Eire

• **FD County Leitrim**: Luke Early, Main Street, Mohill, County Leitrim, Eire (☎ 07196 31081 / 0872 470795; **e**: earlyfunerals@eircom.net). Cheapest fully-fitted coffin only: £390 (delivery locally £60; anywhere in Eire for £140). Cold storage only: No. Advice for DIY: Yes, £20 ph. Basic funeral: £590 (disbursements extra). 'Our firm is family-owned and run so we have personal contact with the bereaved family' (Luke Early). Prepaid plan: Golden Charter. Member of IAFD.

Chapter 8

GOOD CREMATORIA
& CEMETERIES

Unless otherwise stated, you can assume that all the cemeteries and crematoria listed are prepared to deal with families not using funeral directors. Abbreviations in bold are as follows:

Cem = Cemetery
Crem = Crematorium
✪✪✪ = Winner of a Natural Death Handbook Award 2004
☏ = Telephone number
f: = Fax number
e: = E-mail address
w: = Web address
☾ = Length of service
NAMM = National Association of Memorial Masons
CFTB = Has adopted the Charter for the Beareaved (see Chapter 5 for details)

Those crematoria listed as willing to take home-made coffins do so on condition that such coffins meet the anti-pollution requirements of the Federation of British Cremation Authorities (FBCA), as set out in Chapter 4. Shrouds, if listed as acceptable by either crematoria or cemeteries, are normally required to be made rigid with a plank; likewise body bags, which would also normally need to be covered with a drape of some kind. These institutions do not want to cause offence to staff or to other members of the public.

Listings are by region, and then by town within the region, except in the Greater London region, which has been further subdivided into areas. Contents:

Please write to the Natural Death Centre (see Resources for contact details) with your experience of using your local crematorium or cemetery, whether positive or negative, and including as much detail as possible; please add if you are nominating them for a future award. Our listings are otherwise based on information given to us by the services themselves – the name of the informant is given wherever possible.

The North West

Comprising Cumbria, Lancashire, Manchester, Sefton, Wirral, Liverpool, Knowsley, St Helens, Wigan, Bolton, Bury, Rochdale, Salford, Trafford, Manchester, Oldham, Tameside, Stockport and Cheshire.

• **Cem Accrington (1)**: Accrington (Huncoat) Cemetery, Burnley Road, Accrington, Hyndburn, Lancashire BB5 6HA (☎ 01254 232933). Plot (100 years) incl. digging and burial £636. ⊙ 30 mins (extra time £62). They accept home-made (after prior consultation), cardboard and bamboo coffins. Free advice available for DIY funerals. Chapel: As for Crematorium below. Grounds: Well-tended; seating areas. Memorials: Standard headstone style and type, within size restrictions. There are separate plots for different religious denominations and an infant memorial area for foetal remains, stillborn children and small infants. 'Staff are caring and dedicated' (Janice Tolson). CFTB.

• **Cem Accrington (2)**: Dill Hall (Church of Clayton-le-Moors) Cemetery, Dill Hall Lane, Church, Nr. Accrington, Hyndburn, Lancashire. Contact and other details as for previous entry, except for: Grounds: 'A small cemetery with plots for Church of England and Roman Catholics. A memorial wall has been built for the burial and memorial of cremated remains' (Janice Tolson). CFTB.

• **Crem Accrington**: Accrington Crematorium, The Cemetery Office, Burnley Road, Accrington, Hyndburn, Lancashire BB5 6HA (☎ 01254 232933). Price: £237. ⊙ 20 mins within a 40-min period (extra time £90). They accept home-made (after prior consultation, must comply with regulations), cardboard and bamboo coffins. Free advice available for DIY funerals. Chapel: 'Church-like; traditional nonconformist, cruciform design, seating 80.' Grounds: 'Burial plots on all sides of the chapel. We are always willing to assist and be flexible to requests. Good disabled access' (Janice Tolson). CFTB.

• **Cem Alderley Edge**: Alderley Edge Cemetery, Chelford Road, Alderley Edge SK9 7TQ; run by Macclesfield Borough Council, from Macclesfield Cemetery, Prestbury Road, Macclesfield SK10 3BU (☎ 01625 422330/422408; **f**: 01625 616350; **w**: www.macclesfield.gov.uk). Plot (100 years) incl. digging and burial £813 (£1,562 for non-residents). They accept cardboard, wicker and bamboo coffins. ⊙ 30 mins (extra time £138). No chapel. Grounds: 'Quiet rural setting, with a view of the town and the Edge' (B. Richardson).

• **Cem Alston**: Alston Cemetery, Adjacent to the Firs, Alston, Cumbria (☎ 01768 86215) & Newthead Cemetery, Newthead, Alston, Cumbria. (☎ 01768 86215); both run by Eden District Council. Details as for Penrith Cemetery below except for: No chapel. Grounds: 'Quiet, attractive location overlooking open countryside. Mature trees in older sections' (Mrs Christine Millington).

• **Cem Appleby**: Appleby Cemetery, Cross Croft, Appleby in Westmoreland, Cumbria. (☎ 01768 86215); run by Eden District Counci. Contact and other details as for Penrith Cemetery below except for: No chapel. Grounds: Peaceful location adjacent to fields. 'High standard of maintenance' (Mrs Millington).

• **Cem Askam-in-Furness**: Ireleth Cemetery, Broughton Road, Askam-in-Furness, Cumbria. Contact and all other details as for Barrow-in-Furness

Cemetery entry below except for: No Chapel. Grounds: 'A small cemetery next to the local churchyard with superb views of the Duddun estuary' (C. R. Pollard).
• **Cem Atherton**: Atherton Cemetery, Leigh Road, Atherton, Lancashire M46 0LX. Contact and all other details as for Leigh Cemetery below.
• **Cem Nr. Atherton**: Howebridge Cemetery, Lovers Lane, Near Atherton, Lancashire M46 0PZ. Contact and all other details as for Leigh Cemetery below.
• **Cem Barrow-in-Furness**: Barrow-in-Furness Cemetery, Devonshire Road, Barrow-in-Furness, Cumbria (☎ 01229 894928). Plot (99 years) incl. digging and burial £511 plus maintenance £191. They accept home-made, cardboard, wicker and bamboo coffins and body bags and shrouds. ① 45 mins (extra time can be booked without charge). Chapel: 1960s crematorium chapel. Grounds: 'On a hillside overlooking the town, with views across the Irish Sea.' Memorials: Natural stone; size restrictions. 'Several areas are left uncut to encourage wild flowers' (C. R. Pollard). For details of the natural burial ground, see Chapter 6.
• **Crem Barrow-in-Furness**: Thorncliffe Crematorium, Cemetery Office, Devonshire Road, Barrow-in-Furness, Cumbria LA14 5PD (☎ 01229 894928). Price: £273. ① 45 mins (extra time can be booked without charge). They accept home-made and cardboard coffins. Chapel: Modern, non-denominational with flexible seating. Grounds: Surrounded by a cemetery and glade of remembrance. 'Because we are a smaller crematorium, the staff offer a more personal, friendly service' (C. R. Pollard).
• **Cem Burnley**: Burnley Cemetery, 93 Rossendale Road, Burnley BB11 5DD (☎ 01282 664600/664615). Plot (40 years) incl. digging and burial: standard £1,026; lawn £1,137 (double for non-residents, except 'former residents who purchased the exclusive Right of Burial when residing within the Borough'). They accept home-made or cardboard coffins. ① Not strictly limited. Chapel: 'Victorian, sombre.' Grounds: 'Woodland to rear. Part of cemetery in tranquil setting.' Memorials: 'Restrictions vary in different sections of the cemetery; no new sidestones, etc allowed; inscriptions not to cause offence. There are separate plots for different religious denominations, an infant memorial area, and caring and dedicated staff. Currently adopting CFTB' (Cemeteries Manager).
• ❂❂❂ **Cem Carlisle**: Carlisle Cemetery, Richardson Street, Carlisle CA2 6AL (☎ 01228 625310; **e**: junec@carlisle-city.gov.uk; **w**: www.carlisle.gov.uk); run by City of Carlisle. Plot (50 years) incl. digging and burial £306. They accept home-made, biodegradable coffins, body bags and shrouds. ① 40 mins. Chapel: 'Attractive, Gothic design. Warm, with seating for 100.' Grounds: 'Parkland in wooded setting with conservation zones. There are waterfalls on a natural beck, a squirrel feeder, a lichen reserve, nesting herons, etc.' Memorials: Traditional graves are not subject to restrictions, lawn memorials must be within size limits. 'Our range of graves and coffins enable us to meet all religious and personal needs without difficulty. We have added a further choice, the 'recycled funeral' for those who require a simple, inexpensive burial with no memorial. We maintain both conservation areas and conventionally attractive cemetery grounds. We have arranged many funerals with families and know that funerals arranged without a funeral director are at least as good, and often better, than those that

take the conventional path' (June Carswell, Bereavement Services Manager). CFTB. For details of their woodland burial ground, see Chapter 6.

• **✪✪✪ Crem Carlisle**: Carlisle Crematorium, Bereavement Services, Cemetery Office, Richardson Street, Carlisle CA2 6AL (☎ 01228 625310; **e**: junec@carlisle-city.gov.uk). Price: £305. ✪ 40 mins (extra time can be booked without charge). They accept home-made and biodegradable coffins, body bags and shrouds. (For their full range of coffins, see their woodland burial site entry in Chapter 6.) For cremation, a reusable coffin is available, with an inner Compakta cardboard coffin, for £102. They can provide cold storage for the body at a charge of £7.65 for up to 24 hrs; £15.30 for up to 48 hrs; or £22.95 for over 48 hrs. Extra bearers to help the family can be supplied at £8 per person. Chapel: Non-denominational with flexible seating. Grounds: 'Four different zones: the Peace Garden is bedded out and highly-maintained providing the principal view from the Hall of Remembrance; the monthly gardens are planted to a seasonal pattern; the woods are for those who prefer a return to nature and may oppose high maintenance regimes; the memorial wall offers the only cremation memorial option. The service offers both traditional and environmental options (the latter also prove far less expensive). Our attitude is one of complete openness, giving the bereaved complete access to the information they need in order to obtain a meaningful funeral. There is no commercial pressure or bias towards so-called conventional funerals' (June Carswell). CFTB.

• **Cem Cheadle**: Mill Lane Cemetery, Manchester Road, Cheadle; run by Norwest Co-operative Ltd (contact details as for Stockport Crematorium below). Plot (75 years) incl. digging and burial £980 (£870 extra for non-residents). They accept home-made, cardboard, wicker and bamboo coffins. ✪ 45 mins (extra time can be booked). No chapel. Grounds: 'A lawn cemetery, newly laid out with roads and drives designed for modern corteges; mostly native species trees.' Memorials: Only flat desk-shaped, made of granite or slate. 'The modern layout has made this cemetery very popular. It has a high standard of maintenance' (Cemetery Manager)

• **Cem Chester**: Blacon Cemetery, Blacon Avenue, Chester Cheshire CH1 5BB (☎ 01244 372428; **e**: crematorium@chestercc.gov.uk; **f**: 01244 382189, **w**: www.chestercc.gov.uk); run by Chester City Council, Plot (99 years) incl. digging and burial £695 (double for non-residents). ✪ 30 mins (extra time £80). They accept home-made, wicker and bamboo coffins (cardboard coffins currently being considered). Advice available for DIY funerals. Chapel: Crematorium chapel available if required, see entry below. Grounds: 'Incorporates Commonwealth war graves. On the bus route.' Memorials: Lawn sections: a maximum of 3ins high and a minimum of 2" thick; natural materials only. 'Competitive prices and a flexible approach. Cremated remains plots and a separate baby cemetery which contains a memorial garden with a water feature' (Christine Wedge). Considering establishing a natural ground.

• **Crem Chester**: Chester Crematorium (contact details as for previous entry). Price £280 (£380 for non-residents). ✪ 30 mins (extra time £80). They accept cardboard, wicker and bamboo coffins. Advice available for DIY funerals. Up to six mourners may view the coffin entering the cremator. Chapel: 'Built 1965. Non-denominational, with pew type hardwood seating. Disabled access, hearing loop and toilets. Interior floral display area. The organ incorporates the old organ pipes of Liverpool Cathedral.' Grounds: Gardens with waterfalls, ponds and rockery. Seating for quiet reflection, memorial garden and a book of remembrance. 'Committed staff, flexible service to public. Excellent facilities for the disabled. Private interview facilities. Constant awareness of changing trends and requirements. Mourners' CDs and tapes accepted. Competitive prices' (Christine Wedge).

• **Cem Clitheroe:** Clitheroe Cemetery, Waddington Road, Clitheroe, Lancashire (☎ 01200 414478; **e**: Judith.Paliga@ribblevalley.gov.uk; **f**: 01200 414488, **w**: www.ribblevalley.gov.uk); run by Ribble Valley Borough Council, Church Walk, Clitheroe, BB7 2RA. Plot (100 years) incl. digging and burial £396 (double for non-residents). ⊙ No limit at the graveside. They accept cardboard, wicker and bamboo coffins. No chapel. Grounds: 'Beautiful rural location.' Memorials: Hard stone only. Size restriction in the lawn cemetery. 'We maintain a high standard of customer care' (Judith Paliga). For details of the natural burial area on the cemetery's perimeter, see Chapter 6.

• **Cem Cockermouth:** Cockermouth Cemetery, Cockermouth, Cumbria (☎ 01900 326411; **e**: bereavement.services@allerdale.gov.uk; **w**: www.allerdale. gov.uk); run by Allerdale Borough Council, Allerdale House, New Bridge Street, Workington, Cumbria CA14 3YJ. The council also runs cemeteries at Brigham, Dearham, Silloth, Flimby, Maryport, Salterbeck and Harrington Road for which the following details all apply unless stated otherwise: Plot (75 years) incl. digging and burial £445 (plus 50 per cent for non-residents). Meadow plot at Cockermouth, Maryport and Harrington Road only: £325 (plus 50 per cent for non-residents). ⊙ No limit at the graveside. They accept all coffins, body bags and shrouds. Chapel: 1856 with spire (Cockermouth only). Grounds: 'All cemeteries have well-maintained lawns and most have traditional areas. Cockermouth is wooded with specimen trees, a stream running through and extensive wildlife.' Memorials: Height restrictions in the lawn cemetery. 'We have a dedicated team committed to providing the best possible advice who will happily assist DIY families' (Robert Deacon). Meadow burial areas at Cockermouth, Maryport and Harrington Road, see Chapter 6 for details.

• **Cems Crewe**: Crewe Cemetery, Badger Avenue, Crewe; run by Crewe & Nantwich Borough Council, Cemetery Office, Market Close, Crewe, Cheshire CW1 2NA (vehicular access Badger Avenue only; ☎ 01270 212643; **e**: mary.slinn@crewe-nantwich.gov.uk; **w**: www.crewe-nantwich.gov.uk). Plot (50 years) incl. digging and burial £564.50 (£200.50 extra for non-residents). They accept cardboard, wicker and bamboo coffins, and shrouds. Grounds: Rural surroundings, within easy access of all local transport; wildlife area. They accept bodies directly from a family for a DIY funeral. They also run: Coppenhall Cemetery, Ford Lane ('the oldest cemetery under our control, contains a church within its grounds); and Weston Cemetery, Cemetery Road, Weston ('Small village cemetery in pleasant surroundings'). CTFB.

• **Crem Crewe**: Crewe Crematorium, Badger Avenue (contact details as for previous entry); run by Crewe & Nantwich Borough Council. Price £295.50. ◷ 40 mins full service, 20 mins committal (extra time £48). They accept home-made, cardboard, wicker and bamboo coffins, body bags and shrouds. They will accept a body directly from a family for a DIY funeral. Chapel: Non-denominational, with flexible seating, for a maximum of 88 people. Grounds: 'Good, with flower beds' (Mary Slinn). CFTB.

• **Cem Dalton-in-Furness**: Dalton-in-Furness Cemetery, Cemetery Hill, Newton Road, Dalton-in-Furness, Cumbria (☎ 01229 894928). No chapel. Grounds: 'Edge of town with views to the neighbouring countryside. It is an old cemetery with graves dating back to 1800' (C. R. Pollard). Other details as for Barrow-in-Furness Cemetery above.

• **Crem Distington**: Distington Hall Crematorium, Distington, Workington, Cumbria CA14 4QY (☎ 01946 830561; **f**: 01946 830023; **e**: sbenn@copeland bc.gov.uk). Price: £279 (£300 for non-residents). ◷ 30 mins. They accept cardboard, wicker and bamboo coffins. Chapel: Modern, non-denominational. Grounds: Woodland. 'Reasonably priced and well-maintained' (S. J. Benn).

• **Cem Fleetwood**: Fleetwood Cemetery, Beach Road, Fleetwood, Lancashire; run by Wyre Borough Council, Cemetery Office, Wyre Civic Centre, Breck Road, Poulton-le-Fylde, Lancashire FY6 7PU (☎ 01253 887662; **e**: aallen@wyrebc.gov.uk; **w**: www.wyrebc.gov.uk/bereavementservice.htm). Plot (50 years) incl. digging and burial £532 (double for non-residents). They accept home-made, cardboard, wicker and bamboo coffins, body bags and shrouds. ◷ Unlimited. No chapel. Grounds: 'Well kept and tidy.' Memorials: Lawn types; however, the Council will 'view and consider' other choices. 'The constant concern is to try to honour and meet our customer's needs at all times, at a realistic price, with a realistic attitude' (Anita Allen).

• **Cem Garragill:** Garragill Cemetery, Garragill, Cumbria. (☎ 01768 86215); run by Eden District Counci. Contact and all other details as for Penrith Cemetery below except for: No chapel. Grounds: Quiet rural location overlooking open countryside. 'Maintained to a high standard' (Mrs Millington).

• **Cem Great Harwood**: Great Harwood Cemetery, Blackburn Road, Great Harwood, Nr. Blackburn, Lancashire. Contact and all other details as for Accrington Cemetery above. 'Set in a quiet side of town. The cemetery is well-maintained with a caring foreman' (Mrs Janice Tolson). CFTB.

• **Cem Hindley**: Hindley Cemetery, Castle Hill Road, Hindley, Nr. Wigan, Lancashire WN2 4BU. Contact and other details as for Leigh Cemetery below.

• **Cem Knowsley**: Knowsley Cemetery, Fox's Bank Lane, Whiston, Knowsley (☎ 0151 443 5231); run by Knowsley Metropolitan Borough Council, Cemeteries Section, Council Offices, Prescot, Knowsley L34 3LH. Plot (99 years) incl. digging and burial £575 (50 per cent extra for non-residents). No maintenance charge. ◷ 45 mins. No chapel. Grounds: Open countryside. Memorials: 3ft 3ins high, 2ft 8ins wide. (John Profitt.)

• **Cem Knutsford**: Knutsford Cemetery, Tabley Hill Lane, Tabley, Knutsford WA16 OEW; run by Macclesfield Borough Council, from Macclesfield Cemetery, Prestbury Road, Macclesfield, SK10 3BU (☎ 01625 422330/422408; **f:** 01625 616350; **w:** www.macclesfield.gov.uk). Plot (100 years) incl. digging and burial £813 (£1,562 for non-residents). They accept cardboard, wicker and bamboo coffins. ⓧ 30 mins (extra time £138). Chapel: 'Victorian octagonal building atop Tabley Hill, compact, airy and light, with space heating.' Grounds: 'The cemetery stands out on top of the hill, overlooking the town.' Memorials: 'Lawn-type memorials only, with size restrictions' (B. Richardson).

• **Cem Leigh**: Leigh Cemetery, Manchester Road, Leigh, Lancashire WN7 2NP (☎ 01942 828507); run by Wigan Leisure & Cultural Trust, 1-3 Worsley Terrace, Standishgate, Wigan WN1 1XW (☎ 01942 828993/4; **f:** 01942 828877; **e:** T.Bassett@wiganmbc.gov.uk). See below for their cemeteries in the Wigan area. Plot (99.9 years) incl. digging and burial £565 (50 per cent extra for non-residents). ⓧ 30 mins (extra time can be booked without charge). They accept home-made and biodegradable coffins. No chapel. Memorials: Lawn style and marker stones only, within size restrictions. No kerbs.

• **Cem Lytham St Annes**: Park Cemetery, Regent Avenue, Lytham St Annes, Lancashire FY8 4AB (☎ 01253 735429). Plot (100 years) incl. digging and burial £658 (£1,316 non-residents). They accept home-made, cardboard, wicker and bamboo coffins. Free advice and assistance with paperwork available for DIY funerals. ⓧ 30 mins (extra time can be booked without charge). Chapel & Grounds: As crematorium below. Memorials: 'Within size restrictions; no kerbing' (Mr A. Royston).

• **Crem Lytham St Annes**: Lytham Park Crematorium, Park Cemetery, Regent Avenue, Lytham St Annes, Lancashire FY8 4AB (☎ 01253 735429). Price: £250. ⓧ 30 mins minimum (extra time can be booked without charge). They accept home-made coffins made from natural wood; cardboard coffins and body bags if FBCA-approved. Chapel: Standard 1950s. Grounds: 'In rural area, large pond in centre, lots of wildlife. Saturday services are available' (Mr A. Royston).

• **Cem Macclesfield**: Prestbury Road, Macclesfield SK10 3BU (☎ 01625 422330 or 422408; **f:** 01625 616350; **w:** www.macclesfield.gov.uk); run by Macclesfield Borough Council. Plot (100 years) incl. digging and burial £813 (double for non-residents). They accept home-made and biodegradable coffins, and shrouds. ⓧ 30 mins (extra time £138). Chapel: See Crem below. Grounds: 'Near town centre, adjacent to a park and arboretum. Mature trees and a rhododendron shrubbery.' Memorials: Lawn-type only, within size restrictions. 'Beautiful surroundings with well-trained, happy staff offering a sympathetic service' (D. Gosling).

• **Crem Macclesfield**: Macclesfield Crematorium, Cemetery Lodge, Prestbury Road, Macclesfield SK10 3BU (☎ 01625 422330/422408; **f:** 01625 616350; **w:** www.macclesfield.gov.uk); run by Macclesfield Borough Council. Price: £299.50. ⓧ 30 mins (extra time £138). They accept cardboard and other coffins. Free advice and paperwork help given to DIY families. Chapel: 'Victorian, non-denominational, made from local stone. Movable seating for up to 70 people; centrally heated.' Grounds: 'Overlooking a pool and stream in an established arboretum valley' (D. Gosling).

• **Cem Manchester**: Southern Cemetery, Barlow Moor Road, Chorlton, Manchester M21 7GL (☎ 0161 881 2208); also Blackley Cemetery, Victoria Avenue, Blackley M9 8JP (same details except for Chapel & Grounds). Plot (50 years) incl. digging and burial £890 (£1,365 for non-residents). They accept home-made, cardboard, wicker and bamboo coffins after prior consultation, and shrouds in the Muslim section. ☼ 20 mins in chapel. Chapel: Victorian Gothic. Grounds: 168-acre site with listed buildings and a 'great variety' of trees and shrubs. Memorials: 56-page rule booklet (eg wooden crosses, 'except those supplied by the city council', sea shells, rockery and other stones prohibited). Those bringing the coffin to the cemetery in other than a funeral director's hearse must transfer it at the entrance gate to a wheeled bier. Not unreasonably, it also wants to be notified if the coffin size will exceed 6ft 4ins by 22ins width, 15ins depth, allowing for any protruding handles ('it is difficult and may be dangerous to alter the width of the grave once it has been excavated'.) 'We will give advice on coffins or anything relating to the cemetery. We pride ourselves on being experienced in all manner of problems associated with burial – and how to solve them! We follow the principles of the CFTB closely and hope to adopt it in the near future' (Paul Burton). See Chapter 6 for planned woodland burial area.

• **Crem Manchester:** Blackley Crematorium, Victoria Avenue, Blackley Manchester M9 8JP (☎ 0161 881 2208). Price: £260. ☼ 20 mins in chapel. They accept home-made, cardboard, wicker and bamboo coffins – and DIY funerals – after prior consultation. 'We will give advice on coffins or anything relating to the crematorium' (Paul Burton).

• **Crem Manchester:** Barlow Moor Road Crematorium, Chorlton, Manchester M21 7GZ (☎ 0161 881 5269); run by Manchester Crematorium Ltd. Price: £240 for 30 mins in the mornings (£15 extra with music); or £297 for 40 mins in the afternoons (£18 extra with music). Extra time £115 per half hour. They accept home-made or biodegradable coffins. Chapels: 'One Romanesque chapel is from the late 19th century and seats 108; the other is modern and seats 60.' Grounds: 'In the suburbs of Manchester with a 168-acre cemetery next door. Families are treated as individually as possible' (Andrew Paul Helsby).

• **Crem Manchester**: Howe Bridge Crematorium, Lovers Lane, Atherton, Manchester M46 OPZ (☎ 01942 870811); run by Crematoria Management Ltd. Price: £265. ☼ 30 mins. They accept home-made, cardboard, wicker and bamboo coffins, body bags and shrouds. Advice available for DIY funerals. Chapel: 'Modern, natural materials.' Grounds: 'Open countryside' (P. J. Wilson).

• **Cem Nantwich:** Nantwich Cemetery, Whitehouse Lane, Nantwich. Contact and all other details as for Crewe Cemetery above, except for: No chapel. Grounds: 'Small well-maintained cemetery in rural surroundings near to town.'

• **Cem Padiham**: Padiham Public Cemetery, St John's Road, Padiham, Lancashire (☎ 01282 425011/664602); run by Burnley Borough Council. Contact and all other details as for Burnley Cemetery above, except for: Grounds: 'No adjacent dwellings.' No lawn section.

• **Cem Penrith:** Penrith Cemetery, Beacon Edge, Penrith, Cumbria CA11 7RZ (☎ 01768 86215); run by Eden District Counci, Mansion House, Penrith,

Cumbria CA11 7YG. Plot (50 years) incl. digging and burial £469 (double for non-residents). ⓧ Unlimited. They accept home-made, cardboard, wicker and bamboo coffins, body bags and shrouds. Chapel: Twin Grade II listed buildings; only one of which is in use. Grounds: Hillside location overlooking Penrith and Lake District Fells. Mature trees in older sections attract birds and red squirrels. Memorials: Height restricted to 1.2m. They will accept bodies directly from a family for a DIY funeral. 'Beautiful location, high standard of maintenance. All staff are helpful and considerate' (Mrs Millington)

• **Cem Poulton-le-Fylde:** Carleton Cemetery, Stocks Lane, Carleton, Poulton-le-Fylde FY6 7QS: (☎ 01253 882541); run by Blackpool Borough Council. Plot (75 years) incl. digging and burial £629 (double for non-residents). ⓧ 30 mins (extra time £102.50). They accept cardboard coffins (made rigid with plank), wicker and bamboo coffins. Chapel: Use of crematorium chapel (church-like with forward facing pews). Memorials: Lawn type arranged back to back, maximum height 4ft; crosses 5ft 6ins. 'We will accept bodies directly from a family for a DIY funeral' (Suzanne Moden).

• **Cem Poulton-le-Fylde**: Poulton New Cemetery, Garstang Road East, Poulton-le-Fylde, Lancashire (☎ 01253 887662; e: aallen@wyrebc.gov.uk; w: www.wyre bc.gov.uk/bereavementservice.htm); run by Wyre Borough Council (see also Fleetwood above). Plot (50 years) incl. digging and burial £532 (double for non-residents). They accept home-made, cardboard, wicker and bamboo coffins, body bags and shrouds. ⓧ Unlimited. Chapel: 'Quaint.' Grounds: 'Well-kept, surrounded by trees.' Memorials: Lawn types; the Council will 'view and consider' other choices. 'Free advice available for DIY funerals' (Anita Allen).

• **Crem Poulton-le-Fylde:** Carleton Crematorium, Stocks Lane, Carleton, Poulton-le-Fylde FY6 7QS (☎ 01253 398426, e: crematorium@black pool.gov.uk); run by Blackpool Borough Council. Minimum charge for crema-tion is £275. ⓧ 30 mins (extra time £102.50). They will accept cardboard coffins (made rigid with a plank), wicker and bamboo coffins. Two mourners can view the coffin entering the cremator at a time. 'The crematorium has church-like pews, facing forward. It is situated within Carleton Cemetery' (Suzanne Moden.)

• **Cem Preesall**: Preesall Cemetery, Cemetery Lane, Preesall, Lancashire (contact details as for Poulton New Cemetery above). Plot (50 years) incl. digging and burial £532 (double for non-residents). They accept home-made, cardboard, wicker and bamboo coffins and body bags and shrouds. No chapel.

• **Cem Preston**: Preston Cemetery, The Cemetery Office, New Hall Lane, Preston, Lancashire PR1 4SY (☎ 01772 794585, e: m.birch@preston.gov.uk; w: www.preston.gov.uk); run by Preston City Council. Lawn plot (75 years) incl. digging and burial £644.10 (double digging fee for non-residents). They accept home-made, cardboard, wicker and bamboo coffins, and shrouds. ⓧ Unlimited. No chapel. Grounds: '75-acre site divided into two cemeteries, the old and the new. The old cemetery is Grade II listed and contains many Victorian memorials.' Memorials: Must be NAMM-fitted; maximum height 6ft. Free advice and leaflet for DIY funerals. 'We offer a specially dedicated area for the burial of infants, and also cater for the needs of ethnic groups' (Mr Martin Birch

MIBCA Dip). CFTB. See Chapter 6 for details of the woodland burial section.
• **Crem Preston**: Preston Crematorium, Longridge Road, Preston, Lancashire; run by Preston City Council (contact details as for previous entry). Price: £263.35. ☉ 30 mins (extra time £100, they are considering extending the standard time to 40 mins). Up to four mourners may view the coffin entering the cremator. They accept home-made, cardboard, wicker and bamboo coffins, and body bags. Chapel: Seats up to 100 people on fixed pews. Religious symbols can be removed. Grounds: Long driveway from main road leads to a quiet area where the crematorium is bordered by woodland and fields. Free leaflet and advice available for DIY funerals. CFTB. 'The crematorium is classic 1960s architecture' (Mr Martin Birch MIBCA Dip).
• **Crem Southport**: Southport Crematorium, Southport Road, Scarisbrick, Southport PR8 5JQ (☎ 01704 533443); run by Sefton Metropolitan Borough Council. Price: £230 (£290 for non-residents). ☉ 30 mins (extra time £230). They accept home-made or cardboard coffins. Chapel: 'Modern, airy, interdenominational, well-maintained.' Grounds: 'Natural woodland, augmented by ericaceous planting, pheasants, woodpeckers and jays. Our greatest asset has to be our surroundings. Our peat soil provides a magnificent display of rhododendrons and azaleas in May and June. The red squirrel feeding programme has ensured the survival of a healthy colony; they are a delight and comfort to the bereaved' (John Proffit).
• **Cem Stockport**: Highfield Cemetery, Highfield Avenue, Bredbury, Stockport; run by Norwest Co-operative Ltd. Contact details as for Stockport Crematorium below. Plot (75 years) incl. digging and burial £870 (double for non-residents). They accept home-made, cardboard, wicker and bamboo coffins. ☉ 45 mins (extra time can be booked). No chapel. Grounds: 'Wide open, rural aspect, no houses visible nearby.' Memorials: Height restriction of 3ft, stone or ceramics only. 'The cemetery is adjacent to Goyt Valley and has fine views, with woods nearby' (Cemetery Manager).
• **Crem Stockport**: Stockport Crematorium, 31a Buxton Road, Heaviley, Stockport SK2 6LS (☎ 0161 480 5221; **f**: 0161 480 6992, **e**: cemeteriescrematorium@stockport.gov.uk); run by United Co-operative Ltd. Price: £278. ☉ 30 mins (extra time £65 per half hour). They accept home-made, cardboard, wicker and bamboo coffins. Up to eight mourners may view the coffin entering the cremator. Chapel: 'Built 1934: dark brick, simple Byzantine style with church-like pews, disabled access and loop system. Organist provided.' Grounds: Formal gardens of remembrance. Advice available for DIY funerals at no set fee. 'Regular praise for helpfulness of staff at the crematorium. Flexible in assisting bereaved eg weekend services and late times during the week. Provision for bereaved to bring their own tapes, music etc' (N. Buckley). CFTB.
• **Cem Tyldesley**: Tyldesley Cemetery, Hough Lane, Tyldesley, Lancashire M29 8WN (contact and all other details as for Leigh Cemetery above).
• **Cem Whitehaven**: Whitehaven Cemetery, Low Road, Whitehaven, Cumbria (☎ 01946 692329); also administering Hensingham, Netherwasdale, Millom, and St John's Beckermet Cemeteries. Plot (50 years) incl. digging and burial

£461 (£112.75 extra for non-residents). They accept home-made or cardboard coffins. No chapel. Grounds: 'Natural woodland setting.' Memorials: Within size restrictions. 'Reasonably priced and well-maintained' (Mr S. J. Benn).
• **Cem Widnes**: Widnes Cemetery, Birchfield Road, Widnes WA8 9EE (☎ 0151 471 7332); run by Halton Borough Council. Plot (99 years) £316 incl. digging and burial (double for non-residents). They accept home-made, cardboard, wicker and bamboo coffins, body bags and shrouds. ☾ 30 mins (extra time can be paid for). Chapel: 'Grade II listed sandstone chapel, with ramped entrance and loop system, seats 70 with standing room in entrance alcove.' Grounds: 'Well maintained.' Memorials: 'Back-to-back lawn type fitted to NAMM standard.' 'For those not using a funeral director, staff will assist in any way possible; no charge made' (Michelle Carter). CFTB.
• **Crem Widnes**: Widnes Crematorium, Birchfield Road, Widnes WA8 9EE; run by Halton Borough Council (contact details as for previous entry). Price: £266. ☾ 30 mins (extra time £44). They accept home-made, cardboard, wicker and bamboo coffins, body bags and shrouds. The service is held in the chapel, as described above. Six to eight mourners may view the coffin entering the cremator if they wish. There is a new four seasons garden of remembrance in the grounds. 'Lowest cremation charge in the area; no extra charge for non-residents; 24-hour booking system for the booking of services. Helpful staff' (Michelle Carter).
• **Cems Wigan**: Gidlow Cemetery, Wigan Road, Standish WN1 2RF; Ince-in-Makerfield Cemetery, Warrington Road, Lower Ince WN3 4NH; and Westwood Cemetery, Westwood Lane, Lower Ince WN3 4NX (contact and other details as for Leigh Cemetery above). Wigan Cemetery, Cemetery Road, Lower Ince WN3 4NL (contact details as for Wigan Crematorium below; other details as for Leigh Cemetery above).
• **Crem Wigan**: Wigan Crematorium, Cemetery Road, Lower Ince, Wigan WN3 4NL (☎ 01942 866455); run by Wigan Leisure & Cultural Trust. Price: £220. ☾ 30 mins (extra time can be booked without charge). They accept home-made, cardboard, wicker and bamboo coffins, and body bags. They accept a body directly from a family for a DIY funeral. Advice and help with the paperwork costs £20. Chapel: 'Church-like, converted from a nonconformist cemetery chapel.' Grounds: 'In the middle of Wigan Cemetery surrounded by burial plots and Gardens of Remembrance. The crematorium is church-like with stained-glass windows. It may not be a modern purpose-built crematorium, but is well received for its service and feeling' (Tony Bassett).
• **Cem Wilmslow**: Wilmslow Cemetery, Manchester Road, Wilmslow SK9 2LE; run by Macclesfield Borough Council, from Macclesfield Cemetery, Prestbury Road, Macclesfield, SK10 3BU (☎ 01625 422330/422408; **f**: 01625 616350; **w**: www.macclesfield.gov.uk); run by Macclesfield Borough Council. Plot (100 years) incl. digging and burial £813 (double for non-residents). They accept home-made, cardboard, wicker and bamboo coffins, and shrouds. ☾ 30 mins (extra time £138). Chapel: Victorian with space heating. Memorials: 'Lawn-type only, with size restrictions' (B. Richardson).

The North East

Comprising Northumberland, Newcastle-Upon-Tyne, North Tyneside, Gateshead, South Tyneside, Sunderland, Durham, Hartlepool, Stockton-On-Tees, Middlesbrough, Redcar, North Yorkshire, York, East Riding of Yorkshire, Kingston-Upon-Hull, Bradford, Leeds, Calderdale, Kirklees, Wakefield, Barnsley, Sheffield, Rotherham, Doncaster, North Lincolnshire, North East Lincolnshire and Lincolnshire.

• **Cem Barnsley**: Barnsley Cemetery, Cemetery Road, Barnsley; run by Barnsley Metropolitan Borough Council (Paul Beardsley, Bereavement Services Manager, Barnsley Crematorium, Doncaster Road, Barnsley S71 5EH, ☎ 01226 206053), which also runs the following cemeteries: Ardsley, Hunningley Lane; Bolton, Furlong Road; Brierly, Church Street; Carlton, Royston Lane; Cudworth, Church View; Darfield, Saltesbrook Road; Dodworth, Green Road; Elsecar, Church Street; Great Houghton, Park Lane; Grimethorpe, Cemetery Road; Hemingfield/Jump, Cemetery Road; Hoyland, Kirk Balk; Monk Bretton, Cross Street; Penistone, Thurlstone Road; Royston, New Street; Silkstone, Cone Lane; Thurgoland, Halifax Road; Thurnscoe, Southfield Lane; and Wombwell, Cemetery Road. Plot (99 years) incl. digging and burial from £856. They accept cardboard coffins. ⏱ 30 mins. Advice available for DIY funerals. No chapel. Memorials: 'Restrictions as to size and wording' (Margaret Parry).

• **Crem Barnsley**: Barnsley Crematorium, Doncaster Road, Ardsley, Barnsley S71 5EH (☎ 01226 206053). Price: £316. ⏱ 30 mins (extra time £91). They accept all FBCA-approved coffins. Chapel: Built in 1963. Grounds: 'Peaceful and quiet garden. A service that meets the changing demands' (Margaret Parry).

• **Cem Barrow-on-Humber**: Barrow-on-Humber Cemetery, North Lincs. Contact and all other details as for Woodlands Memorial Cemetery, under Scunthorpe below, except for: Grounds: 'A tranquil cemetery with farmland on two sides and screened on one side by a belt of mixed trees.' Memorials: Headstones, without kerbing, within size restrictions.

• **Cem Barton-upon-Humber**: Barton-upon-Humber Cemetery, Barrow Road, Barton-upon-Humber, North Lincolnshire. Contact and all other details as for Woodlands Memorial Cemetery, under Scunthorpe below, except for: Grounds: 'With farmland on two sides and a fine view across to the Humber Bridge and estuary.' Memorials: Headstones, without kerbing, within size restrictions.

• ✪✪✪ **Cem Boston**: Boston Cemetery, Horncastle Road, Boston, Lincs (vehicular access Marian Road only; ☎ 01205 364612; **e**: martin.potts@ boston.gov.uk; **w**: www.boston.gov.uk); run by Borough of Boston, Bereavement Services Offices, Boston Crematorium, Marian Road, Boston PE21 9HA. Plot (100 years) £580 incl. digging and burial (non-residents £850); 'please note that only people who have purchased a plot are allowed to erect memorials.' They accept home-made, cardboard, wicker and bamboo coffins, body bags and shrouds. ⏱ 30 mins (£105 for extra 30 mins). Chapel: 'Comfortable 1960s crematorium chapel, with live organ and central heating.' Grounds: 'Wooded setting with beautiful spring flower display.' Memorials: 'Size restrictions, but we have kerb and lawn sections. No plastic, wire, metal or wooden fences or wooden carvings allowed.' Free advice and leaflets available for DIY funerals. 'We are not too restrictive and try to help rather than hinder, whilst balancing this with common sense. The cemetery is a green haven not far from the town centre. Friendly approachable staff' (Martin Potts). For planned woodland burial ground, see Chapter 6. CFTB.

• **Crem Boston**: Boston Crematorium, Marian Road, Boston, Lincolnshire PE21 9HA (☎ 01205 364612); run by Borough of Boston, contact details as for previous entry. Price: £275. ⏱ 30 mins. They accept home-made, cardboard, wicker and bamboo coffins, body bags and shrouds; other containers must be rigid and smooth-bottomed. Two or three mourners may view the coffin entering the cremator. Chapel: Removable Christian symbols. Grounds: Extensive lawns with many trees and formal rosebeds. 'Our attitude is friendly, and the ambience inviting' (Martin Potts).

• **Cem Bradford**: Scholemoor Cemetery, Necropolis Road, Bradford BD7 2PS (☎ 01274 571313). Plot (100 years, exclusive rights) £864 incl. digging and burial. They accept home-made, cardboard, wicker and bamboo coffins, body bags and shrouds. ⏱ No limit. Chapel: As crematorium below. Grounds: Maintained to a high standard. 'Our highly trained staff are committed to delivering a sensitive service to meet the needs of the user' (David Congreve). Woodland burial area within Thornton Cemetery; see Chapter 6 for details.

• **Crem Bradford**: Scholemoor Crematorium, Scholemoor Cemetery, Necropolis Road, Bradford BD7 2PS (☎ 01274 571313). Price: £277. ⏱ 30 mins (extra time can be booked without charge). They accept home-made, cardboard, wicker and bamboo coffins, body bags and shrouds. Chapel: Non-denominational, converted Victorian. Grounds: Well-maintained. 'Caring, helpful staff' (David Congreve).

• **Cem Brigg**: Brigg Cemetery, Wrawby Road, Brigg, North Lincs. Contact and all other details as for Woodlands Memorial Cemetery, under Scunthorpe below, except for: Grounds: 'On the edge of a pleasant market town, includes an older section with traditional memorials.' Memorials: Headstones, without kerbing, within size restrictions.

• **Cem Doncaster**: Rose Hill Cemetery, Ascot Avenue, Cantley, Doncaster (☎ 01302 535191; **e**: cems@doncaster.gov.uk; **w**: www.doncaster.gov.uk); run by Doncaster Municipal Borough Council. Plot (50 or 75 years) incl. digging and burial £660. Maintenance: £475 pa. They accept home-made, cardboard, wicker and bamboo coffins, and shrouds. ⏱ 30 mins (£17 per extra 20 mins). Chapel: 'Adequate size with a very private church-like feel.' Grounds: 'Well kept; woodland, meadowland and children's section. Curved paths and extensive tree planting.' Memorials: Lawn type and traditional kerb sets. Will give assistance with DIY funerals. 'This cemetery offers a wide choice of both regular burial plots and a varied choice of memorials. We cater for CofE, RC, Jewish, Muslim and Greek Orthodox' (Amanda Carr).

• **Crem Doncaster**: Rose Hill Crematorium, Cantley Lane, Cantley, Doncaster (contact details as for previous entry). Price: £288. ⏱ 30 mins (£129 for an extra

20 mins). They accept home-made, cardboard, wicker and bamboo coffins, and shrouds. Two mourners may view the coffin entering the cremator. Grounds: Tranquil setting surrounded by mature woodland and well-kept ornamental gardens. Free advice and leaflet available for DIY funerals. 'We have an Environmental Plan which aims to encourage and conserve wildlife. We are open Saturday mornings (admin only), to help those who cannot visit the office during the week' (Amanda Carr).

• **Crem Durham**: Central Durham Crematorium, South Road, Durham, County Durham DH1 3TQ (☎ 0191 3848677). Price: £249 (£309 non-residents). ⏱ 30 mins (extra time £40 per half hour). They accept home-made or cardboard coffins. Chapel: Modern, non-denominational. Grounds: 'Open parkland with distant views. Our service is dignified and fitting to the needs of individual families. We are happy to arrange any music (within reason) and have recently hosted jazz bands, trumpet solos, etc at services' (Mr Alan S. M. Jose).

• ✪✪✪ **Crem Great Grimsby**: Great Grimsby Crematorium, Weelsby Avenue, Great Grimsby, North East Lincs DN32 0BA (☎ 01472 324869; w: www.ne lincs.gov.uk); run by North East Lincolnshire Council Environmental Services. Price: £327 for residents or those who left the area within the last five years (£399 non-residents). Children up to and incl. 12 years: Free. ⏱ 40-min intervals with 30 mins chapel time (extra time on request). They accept home-made, cardboard, wicker and bamboo coffins, body bags and shrouds (made rigid with a plank). Mourners may witness the coffin entering the cremator by prior arrangement only. Chapel: 'Early 1950s, spacious with a high ceiling and balcony. Good acoustics. Comfortable, flexible seating for 144 people, with 23 additional seats in the balcony. A wheelchair is available.' Grounds: 'Nine acres, with lawns surrounded by mature trees, shrubs, bulbs and seasonal bedding. Wildlife is encouraged with bird-boxes and feeders.' Free advice available for DIY funerals. 'An experienced, dedicated team with a flexible, approachable attitude. We will do our utmost to meet specific requests and will explain why if for some reason we have to say no' (Allison Fisher). Working towards the CFTB.

• **Crem Harrogate**: Harrogate Crematorium, Stonefall Cemetery, Wetherby Road, Harrogate, North Yorkshire HG3 1DE (☎ 01423 883523). Price: £332. ⏱ 20 mins within a 40-minute period. They accept home-made and cardboard coffins; others if FBCA-approved. Chapel: Church-like. Grounds: Well-maintained, traditional. 'We recognise that bereaved people have differing needs and we accommodate these wherever possible' (Philip Andrew). For woodland burial area, see Chapter 6. In the process of adopting the CFTB.

• **Cem Hexham**: St Andrews Cemetery, West Road, Hexham, Northumberland NE46 3RR (☎ 01434 609575); run by Hexham Town Council. Plot (99 years) incl. digging and burial £220 (double for non-residents). They accept cardboard coffins. ⏱ 'As required.' Chapel: 'Victorian, built 1865, non-denominational.' Grounds: 'Set in the picturesque River Tyne valley.' Memorials: '30-years rights renewable.' They will accept a body directly from a family for a DIY funeral. For details of their woodland burial area, see Chapter 6. CFTB.

• **Cems Houghton-le-Spring**: Easington Lane Cemetery, Murton Lane, Easington

Lane, Houghton-le-Spring, Tyne & Wear; Hetton Cemetery, Houghton Road, Hetton-le-Hole; and Houghton Cemetery, Durham Road; all run by City of Sunderland. Contact and other details as for Bishopwearmouth Cemetery under Sunderland, below, except for: No chapel. Grounds: Small rural cemeteries.

• **Crem Hull**: Chanterlands Crematorium, Chanterlands Avenue, Hull HU5 4EF (☎ 01482 614976; **e**: nicci.hewitt@hullcc.gov.uk); run by Hull City Council. Price: £300.◕ 45 mins. They accept hand-made, wicker and bamboo coffins, and sell cardboard coffins. Chapel: 'Two modern multi-faith chapels, one with 36 seats, the other with 120 (plus an upper balcony seating 23). Each chapel has organ, CD, tape and record playing facilities.' Grounds: '23 acres with memorial areas and rose trees, shrubberies and lawn areas' (Nicci Hewitt).

• **Cems Keighley**: Utley Cemetery, Skipton Road, Keighley, Bradford BD20 6EJ (☎ 01535 603162; **f**: 01535 690933, **w**: www.bradford.gov.uk); run by Bradford Metropolitan District Council, which also runs the following cemeteries: Ilkley, Haworth, Morton, Oakworth, Silsden, Stanbury, and Steeton ('small village type, all now lawned, some with fine view of moorland'). Plot (100 years) incl. digging and burial £389 (for 4ft 6ins deep). ◕ No limit. No chapel. Grounds: 'Victorian, now lawned; an attractive park-type layout.' They accept home-made and biodegradable coffins, body bags and shrouds. Free advice and assistance with the paperwork for DIY funerals. 'We hope to offer the public a funeral that meets all their requirements regarding form of service, coffins, etc, and we are very flexible in this respect' (John Elsbury). CFTB.

• **Crem Keighley**: Oakworth Crematorium, Wide Lane, Oakworth, Keighley, Bradford BD22 0RJ; run by Bradford Metropolitan District Council (contact details as for previous entry). Price: £271. ◕ 45 mins (extra time can be booked without charge). They accept home-made, cardboard, wicker and bamboo coffins, body bags and possibly shrouds. Up to two mourners may view the coffin entering the cremator. Chapel-like crematorium building with flexible seating. Organ if required. Disabled access with a loop system for the deaf. Grounds: Set in acres of countryside. 'Ours is a small and friendly crematorium. We charge the lowest fees in West Yorkshire, and allow the public to have whatever type of service they request. We were, I believe, the first crematorium to allow a service to be filmed over the internet so relatives abroad could watch the service' (John Elsbury).

• **Cem Leeds**: Lawnswood Cemetery, Otley Road, Adel, Leeds LS16 6AH (☎ 0113 2673188). Plot for two people (50 years) incl. digging and burial £819 (£1,638 for non-residents). They accept home-made or cardboard coffins. ◕ 40 mins. Chapel: Dark stone, late 19th century, with seating for 80 people. Grounds: 'Historic 40-acre cemetery with beautiful old memorials' (Phil Stephenson).

• **Crem Leeds**: Leeds City Council Cemeteries and Crematoria Section, Otley Road, Adel, Leeds LS16 6AH (☎ 0113 2673188). Price: £315. ◕ 40 mins (extra time £124). They accept home-made and cardboard coffins. Chapel: Church-like, with seating for 80 people. Grounds: 'A mix of formal and woodland areas' (Phil Stephenson).

• **Cems Middlesbrough**: Acklam Cemetery, Acklam Road, Acklam, Middlesbrough TS5 7HE; run by Middlesbrough Council (☎ 01642 817725; e: peter_git sham@middlesbrough.gov.uk). Plot (100 years) £724 incl. digging and burial (25 per cent extra for those living outside the former Cleveland County boundary). ⏲ Up to 60 mins. They accept home-made, cardboard, wicker and bamboo coffins and 'will consider' body bags and shrouds. Grounds: 'Adjacent to Teesside Crematorium. Open space with views of Cleveland Hills, and an environmental centre.' Chapel: 'Use of the two crematorium chapels: both seat over 80; one built 1961, with central altar; the other built 1985.' Memorials: 'Natural quarried stone, wood or other suitable material subject to approval' (P. Gitsham). The Council also runs Linthorpe Cemetery, Burlam Road, Middlesbrough TS5 5AP (52 acres; Middlesbrough's largest remaining woodland; no new graves; woodland burial area); North Ormesby & St Joseph's Cemeteries, Ormesby Road, Middlesbrough TS3 7AP; and Thorntree & Thorntree RC Cemeteries, Cargo Fleet Lane, Thorntree, Middlesbrough TS3 8AL (with 1930s style chapel seating 30-40). For details of the woodland burial areas, see Chapter 6.

• **Crem Middlesbrough**: Teesside Crematorium, Acklam Road, Acklam, Middlesbrough TS5 7HE (☎ 01642 817725); run by Middlesbrough Council. Price: £287. ⏲ 30 mins (extra time £67). They accept home-made, cardboard, wicker and bamboo coffins and 'may consider' body bags and shrouds. Chapels: 'One was built in 1961, with a very high ceiling, seating 80; the other is more modern, light and airy, seating about 100.' Grounds: 'Shrubberies and lawn with views of Cleveland Hills' (P. Gitsham). CFTB.

• **Crem Newcastle-upon-Tyne**: West Road Crematorium, West Road, Newcastle-upon-Tyne (☎ 0191 2744 737); run by Newcastle City Council. Price: £312.50. ⏲ 30 mins (extra time £65). They accept home-made, cardboard, wicker and bamboo coffins, body bags and shrouds. Chapel: 'Very simple and traditional.' Grounds: Well-kept gardens. 'All family requests by way of music, etc are accommodated whenever possible' (Tracey Harrison). CFTB.

• **Cem Newton Aycliffe**: West Cemetery, School Aycliffe Lane; run by Great Aycliffe Town Council, Council Offices, School Aycliffe Lane, Newton Aycliffe, County Durham DH5 6QF (☎ 01325 300700; e: info@great_aycliffe.gov.uk). Price (99 years) incl. digging and burial £164 (£109 for public grave, no purchase). ⏲ No limit. No chapel. Grounds: 'Very quiet, secluded location with views over adjacent land.' They accept home-made, cardboard, wicker and bamboo coffins. Memorials: Upright stones for grave plots must be fixed in underground concrete shoe; flat or angled stones for ashes area. They will accept a body directly from a family for a DIY funeral. 'Modern well-kept cemetery with garden of remembrance and floral beds. Lawned in appearance with separate denominational plots' (Andrew Bailey).

• **Crem North Shields**: Tynemouth Crematorium, Walton Avenue, North Shields, North Tyneside (☎ 0191 2005861); run by North Tyneside Council. Price: £273. ⏲ 30 mins (30 mins extra time £45). They accept home-made and cardboard coffins; all other types 'would be considered by the registrar'. Chapel: 'Church-like, with removable crosses and seating for 60 people.' Grounds: 'Heavily wooded, older part of mature cemetery – one part is a conservation area' (Mr Jim Finlay). CFTB.

• **Cem Scawby**: Scawby Cemetery, Scawby, North Lincolnshire. Contact and all other details as for Woodlands Memorial Cemetery below, except for: Grounds: 'Tranquil, natural setting in open farmland.' Memorials: Headstones, without kerbing, within size restrictions.

• **Cem Scunthorpe (1)**: Brumby Cemetery, Cemetery Road, Scunthorpe, North Lincolnshire. Contact and all other details as for Woodlands Memorial Park Cemetery, below, except for: Grounds: 'An old cemetery with a mix of traditional kerbs and headstones, plus a lawn section set amongst birch trees.' Memorials: Stone headstones, without kerbing, within size restrictions.

• **Cem Scunthorpe (2)**: Crosby Cemetery, Ferry Road, Scunthorpe, North Lincolnshire. Contact and all other details as for Woodlands Memorial Park Cemetery, below, except for: Grounds: 'An old cemetery with traditional memorials.' Memorials: Headstones, without kerbing, within size restrictions.

• **Cem Scunthorpe (3)**: Woodlands Memorial Park Cemetery, Brumby Wood Lane, Scunthorpe, North Lincolnshire DN17 1SP (☎ 01724 280289; **e:** jack. startin@northlincs.gov.uk). Administers Barrow-upon-Humber, Barton-upon-Humber, Brigg, Brumby, Crosby, Scawby and Winterton branch cemeteries. Plot (50 years): £520 (lawn grave) £650 (traditional) £350 (ashes); plus digging and burial £385 (ashes £51). They accept home-made and cardboard coffins. ☼ 20 mins (extra time £54). Chapel & Grounds: See next entry. Memorials: No headstones in Sections A & B, only bronze plaques set at an angle, off the ground, in a garden border. Headstones and kerbing permitted in other sections. 'Every effort is made to accommodate the family's wishes' (Jack Startin). CFTB.

• **Crem Scunthorpe**: Woodlands Crematorium, Woodlands Memorial Park, Brumby Wood Lane, Scunthorpe (contact details as for previous entry). Price: £313. ☼ 20 mins within a 30-minute period (extra time £54). They accept home-made, cardboard, wicker and bamboo coffins, body bags and shrouds. Chapel: 'Light and airy, the upper portion in glass, with a non-denominational stained-glass window.' Grounds: Shrubberies, specimen trees and avenues creating long vistas across lawns. 'We strive to provide an excellent service to all our customers and to help them have the funeral of their choice. We have an open door policy, and the public may visit without prior booking for a guided tour' (Jack Startin). CFTB.

• **Crem Sheffield**: Greneside Crematorium, Sikes Hill Lane, Sheffield S35 (☎ 0114 2453999); run by Sheffield Co-op Society. Price: £305. ☼ 45 mins (extra time £150). They accept cardboard, wicker and bamboo coffins. Two mourners may view the coffin entering the cremator. Crematorium building: 'Modern, light decor with flexible seating.' Grounds: 'Set on hillside overlooking Sheffield. Free advice available for DIY funerals' (M. R. Bratton). CFTB.

• **Cem Shipley**: Nab Wood Cemetery, Bingley Road, Shipley, Bradford BD18 4EW (☎ 01274 571313; **f:** 01274 521176). Plot (100 years) incl. digging and burial £864. They accept home-made, cardboard, wicker and bamboo coffins, body bags and shrouds. Advice available for DIY funerals. ☼ Open. Chapel & Grounds: As crematorium below. 'Highly-trained staff are committed to delivering a sensitive service to meet the needs of the user' (David Congreve). CFTB.

• **Crem Shipley**: Nab Wood Crematorium, Bingley Road, Shipley, Bradford BD18 4BG (☎ 01274 584109; **f**: 01274 521176). Price: £271. ☉ 30 mins (extra time can be booked without charge). They accept home-made, cardboard, wicker and bamboo coffins, body bags and shrouds. Advice available for DIY funerals. Chapel: Non-denominational, converted Victorian. Grounds: Well-maintained. 'Caring, helpful staff' (David Congreve). CFTB.

• **Cems Sunderland**: Bishopwearmouth Cemetery, Chester Road, Sunderland SR4 5SU (☎ 0191 553 1687; **e**: john.blyth@sunderland.gov.uk); run by City of Sunderland. Plot (99 years) incl. digging and burial £598 (double for non-residents). They accept cardboard coffins. ☉ 30 mins. Chapel: '1850s, small and quite pleasant.' Memorials: Lawn and kerbed, provided that the kerb is limited to 5ft in length. Offer a useful guide for DIY families. 'A very large cemetery of 88 acres, dating from 1856' (John Blyth). The City also runs the following cemeteries along the same lines: Castletown, Hylton Castle Road, Castletown (no chapel; 'small, pleasant, well-tended cemetery'); Mere Knolls, Torver Crescent, Fulwell ('Victorian chapel, in reasonable condition; next to the resort of Seaburn; mature trees along a stream at the northern boundary; a meadow area is under consideration'); Ryhope, Burdon Lane, Ryhope ('no chapel; small established cemetery situated in a conservation area'); Southwick, Wembley Road, Witherwack ('very basic, seldom used'); and Sunderland, Ryhope Road, Grangetown ('Victorian chapel, quite basic'). CFTB.

• **Crem Sunderland**: Sunderland Crematorium, Chester Road, Sunderland (contact details as for previous entry). Price: £260.50. ☉ 30 mins. They accept home-made or cardboard coffins. Chapels: 1950s design with a fixed catafalque. Grounds: Well-tended, with a small garden of remembrance, adjoining a large cemetery. 'We offer a high quality and flexible service' (John Blyth). CFTB.

• **Cem Washington**: Washington Cemetery, Glebe Crescent, Washington Village, Tyne & Wear (☎ 0191 553 1687); run by City of Sunderland. Contact and other details as for Bishopwearmouth Cemetery above, except for: Grounds: 'Small established cemetery situated in a conservation area' (John Blyth).

• **Cem West Rainton**: West Rainton Cemetery, County Durham (☎ 0191 3720616); run by West Rainton Parish Council. Plot (99 years) incl. digging and burial: £70 for a single; £100 for a double; plus gravedigger's and rector's fees (double fees for non-residents). ☉ Approx. 45 mins. They accept home-made coffins. No chapel. Memorials: Height and width restrictions.

• **Crem Whitley Bay**: Whitley Bay Crematorium, Blyth Road, Whitley Bay (☎ 0191 200 5861); run by North Tyneside Council. Price: £273. ☉ 30 mins (extra time £45). They accept home-made and cardboard coffins; other types of container 'at the registrar's discretion'. Chapel: 'Converted church with attractive domed ceiling, seating for about 60. Removable cross.' Grounds: 'Mature, off an attractive drive lined with memorial seats' (Jim Finlay). CFTB.

• **Cem Winterton**: Winterton Cemetery, Cemetery Road, Winterton, North Lincolnshire. Contact and all other details as for Scunthorpe: Woodlands Memorial Cemetery above, except for: Grounds: 'Tranquil cemetery alongside

farmland. A garden of remembrance for the scattering of cremated remains.'
Memorials: Headstones, without kerbing, within size restrictions.
• **Cem York**: York Cemetery, The Gatehouse, Cemetery Road, York YO1 5AJ
(☎ 01904 610578 day); run by York Cemetery Trust (charity no. 1075408). Plot
(99 years) incl. digging and burial £700. Maintenance: £25 pa lawned areas; £35
pa non-lawned areas grass cutting scheme. ◒ Unlimited. They accept home-
made, cardboard, wicker and bamboo coffins, body bags and shrouds. DIY
funerals allowed. Chapel: Late neo-classical Grade II* listed building; furniture
can be arranged to suit requirements; £55 for service; £85 service plus reception.
Grounds: 'Open and staffed seven days a week until 5pm. Mature 24-acre site
of historical and ecological interest. Grounds combine formal, wild, wooded and
managed areas to encourage wildlife. Surrounded by quiet residential areas and
allotments.' Memorials: Natural stone only, fixed by a trustee-approved stone-
mason. Memorials in the Victorian section must reflect the style and architecture
of the Victorian stones. No multiple part memorials allowed. 'Grounds include
Grade II* listed Victorian layout with a privately-owned florist on site. Educational and informal recreational use encouraged with a summer programme of
guided walks organised by the friends of York Cemetery' (Vanessa Temple).
• **Crem York**: City of York Crematorium, Bishopthorpe Road, York YO23 2QD
(☎ 01904 706096; **f**: 01904 701369); run by City of York Council. Price: £410.
◒ 30 mins (20 mins in chapel; extra time £65). They accept home-made,
cardboard, wicker and bamboo coffins, and shrouds. Chapels: 'Main chapel,
built in 1962, seats 120; a second, smaller chapel seats from 15-20.' Grounds:
'Parkland and trees with a small garden of remembrance' (Mr Milsted).

Wales

*Comprising Flintshire, Wrexham, Denbighshire, Aberconwy and Colwyn, An-
glesey, Caernarfonshire and Merionethshire, Powys, Cardiganshire,
Pembrokeshire, Carmarthenshire, Swansea, Neath and Port Talbot, Bridgend,
Rhondda Cynon Taff, Vale of Glamorgan, Merthyr Tydfil, Caerphilly, Cardiff,
Blaenau Gwent, Torfaen, Newport, Monmouthshire.*

• ✪✪✪ **Crem Aberdare**: Llwydcoed Crematorium, Aberdare, Mid Glamorgan,
Wales CF44 0DJ (☎ 01685 874115; **e**: enquiries@crematorium.org.uk; **w**:
www.crematorium.org.uk); run by Llwycoed Crematorium Joint Committee.
Price: £202 (up to and including 16-years, free of charge). ◒ 25 mins within a
40-minute period (extra time £60). They accept home-made, cardboard, wicker
and bamboo coffins, body bags and shrouds. Six to eight mourners may view the
coffin entering the cremator. Chapels: 'Capel Mair seats 120, Capel Tydfil 50.
Traditional pew seating but we are able to supply 16 chairs for other seating
arrangements.' Grounds: 'Landscaped with trees, shrubs and ornamental pools,
and the gardens provide a haven for quiet contemplation in tranquil surroundings.' They stock the Compakta, Ecology Peace Box and Woodgrain eco-
coffins, and provide a leaflet for DIY funerals (which they have carefully
researched eg: 'Enquiries have been made at local hospitals and we are informed
that the body will be dressed in a shroud and placed in the coffin by mortuary

staff. A copy of the Authority for Removal of a Body from the mortuary of local hospitals is attached'). 'We believe we offer a reasonably priced service. We try to meet all environmental needs and to offer a personalised service. On request, we can tape or video record services' (Clive G. Lewis). CFTB.

• **Crem Aberystwyth**: Aberystwyth Crematorium, Clarach Road, Aberystwyth, Cardiganshire, Wales SY23 3DG (☎ 01970 626 942); run by Crematoria Management Ltd. Price: £298. ◑ 60 mins (extra time can be booked without charge). They accept home-made, cardboard, wicker and bamboo coffins, body bags and shrouds. Advice available for DIY funerals. Chapel: 'Modern, with a large window overlooking Cynfelyn Valley. Comfortable furnishings.' Grounds: 'A wooded hillside above the beautiful and peaceful Cynfelyn Valley. The garden of remembrance is a rare orchid site, and the sea is visible from parts of the grounds' (P. J. Wilson). For their natural burial site, see Chapter 6.

• **❀❀❀ Cem Anglesey**: Lon Newydd Cemetery, Lon Newydd, Llangefni, Anglesey, Wales LL77 7TW (☎ 01248 723 332); run by Llangefni Town Council. Plot incl. digging and burial £142 (double for non-residents). No maintenance costs. ◑ Unlimited. Check for coffins. Will accept DIY funerals with prior consultation. Chapel: 'Small, Victorian, nonconformist, well-constructed of local stone.' Grounds: 'Opened in 1867, the cemetery occupies a central position in town. The number buried stands at 2,630.' Memorials: Headstone limited to 3ft in height, 2ft 6ins in width. 'The neat cemetery is a matter of pride to the workers, council and local inhabitants. Our prices are quite low compared to other nearby cemeteries' (M. T. Jones). Closely follows CFTB.

• **Crem Bridgend**: Coychurch Crematorium, Coychurch, Bridgend, Wales CF35 6AB (☎ 01656 656605); run by Coychurch Crematorium Joint Management Committee (for the following county councils: Bridgend, Vale of Glamorgan & Rhondda Cynon Taff). Price: £241.30. ◑ 30 mins (extra 30 mins £48.80). They accept home-made, cardboard, wicker and bamboo coffins. Chapel: 'The main Christian chapel has a wooden ceiling and solid wooden pews and a catafalque of black slate; the second inter-denominational stone chapel is sheeted both internally and externally with cedar wood, roofed in copper, and has a floor of patterned brick. The crematorium is built of natural stone taken from old demolished buildings in the area. Both chapels have outstanding pipe organs and full sound systems for CDs and tapes.' Grounds: 'The crematorium is set on a rolling hillside on the dividing line between open countryside and ancient woodland. 29 acres, of which 15 are woodland, within which the car parks are screened. A beautiful natural lake adjoins the main chapel entrance canopy. The tranquil setting, coupled with a highly-trained and motivated team, provides a truly sympathetic environment' (Joanna Hamilton).

• **Crem Cardiff**: City & County of Cardiff Crematorium, Thornhill Road, Llanishen, Cardiff, Wales CF14 9UA (☎ 029 206 23294; **f**: 029 206 92904); run by Cardiff County Council, Bereavement Services Division, Thornhill Road, LLanishen, Cardiff CF14 9UA. Price: £270.50 (non-residents £436). ◑ 45 mins (extra 45 mins £59, request when booking). They accept home-made, cardboard, wicker and bamboo coffins, body bags and shrouds. Four to six mourners may view the coffin entering the cremator. Chapels: 'Wenallt Chapel opened in 1953, seats 160; Briwnant chapel opened in 2001, seats 50. Either of the chapels may be hired for any burial service for £59.' Grounds: 'Views of surrounding countryside and hills. Staff will help families organise DIY cremations' (Roger Swan). See Chapter 6 for details of their woodland burial ground. CFTB.

• **Cem Mold**: Mold Public Cemetery, Alexandra Road, Mold, Flintshire, Wales CH7 1HJ (☎ 01352 753820). Plot incl. digging and burial £350. No time limit for the service. No chapel. Grounds: 'This is the town cemetery with flower borders and trees, surrounded by a football field and playing ground.' Memorials: 'To be made of stone with reverent wording.' 'Friendly management. Family mourners often lower the coffin. The cemetery won a best-kept cemetery award in 1993' (Arfon Williams-Cooke).

• **Crem Narberth**: Parc Gwyn Crematorium, Narberth, Pembrokeshire, Wales SA67 8UD (☎ 01834 860622; e: parcgwyn@hotmail.com). Price: £207.50 incl. organist's fee. ◷ 20 mins (extra time £207.50). They accept home-made, cardboard and wicker coffins, and shrouds. They will accept a body directly from a family for a DIY funeral. Chapel: 1960s, removable cross. Grounds: 'Beautifully laid out with trees, borders, etc in 7.5 acres of gently rolling countryside.' 'A friendly service in accordance with the wishes of the bereaved' (Revd Elwyn J. John). CFTB.

• **Cem Newport**: St Woolos Cemetery, Bassaleg Road, Newport NP9 3NA, South Wales (☎ 01633 263864); also Christchurch Cemetery, Christchurch Road, Newport; and Caerleon Cemetery, Coldbath Road, Caerleon (for which the same details apply). Plot (99 years) incl. digging and burial £497. ◷ 1 hour for services, plus 1 hour is left between services. No chapel in use. Grounds: 'Three old listed buildings in St Woolos and one in Christchurch.' Memorials: 'Headstones limited to 2ft 8ins in height, 3ft in width and 8ins in thickness' (N. S. Woodward). For the woodland burial section, see Chapter 6.

• **Cem Penarth**: Penarth Cemetery, Castle Avenue, Penarth, Wales CF64 3QY (☎ 02920 700721; e: townclerk@penarthtowncouncil.fsnet.co.uk). Plot (75 years) incl. digging and burial £215.15 (double for non-residents). No chapel. Grounds: 'Traditional, edge-of-town location but accessible; elevated position giving views over the town.' Memorials: Newer sections are lawn-type; older sections are traditional. 'Well-maintained. Being the local cemetery in a small town, there is a need to be responsive to local views' (Edward J. Vick).

• **Crem Port Talbot**: Margam Crematorium, Longlands Lane, Margam, Port Talbot, Neath & Port Talbot, Wales SA13 2PP (☎ 01639 883570). Price: £225 (same for non-residents). ◷ 30 mins (extra time £21). They accept cardboard coffins. Chapel: Main non-denominational chapel seats 150. The family chapel seats 12. Grounds: 'Both lawn and natural woodland areas within 17 acres, with oak and elm trees, rhododendrons and other shrubs' (D. Hywel Selway).

• **Cem Powys**: Guilsfield Cemetery, Cemetery Lane, Guilsfield, Powys, Wales (☎ 01938 551249/ 551120; e: nicolam@powys.gov.uk). Plot (100 years) incl. digging and burial £389 (double for non-residents). ◷ No allotted time, but two hours between funerals. Home-made, cardboard and wicker coffins accepted.

No chapel. Grounds: Rural. 'Caring service. Attitude and practice is designed to help the bereaved as much as possible' (Nicola Morris).

• **Cem Wrexham**: Wrexham Cemetery, Ruabon Road, Wrexham, Wales LL13 7RE (☎ 01978 263159); run by Wrexham County Borough. Plot (99 years) incl. digging and burial £502 (double for non-residents). No maintenance costs. They accept home-made, cardboard, wicker and bamboo coffins. Advice available for DIY. Chapel: Victorian Gothic with spire. Grounds: 'Preserved Victorian layout, initially described as a garden cemetery. The buildings, chapel and monuments are Grade II listed.' Memorials: Maximum 3ft 6ins height on lawn sections, any design, any colour. 'Computerised records for family history research. Original landscape preserved. Few prescriptive regulations' (Alan McMahon).

• **Crem Wrexham**: Wrexham Crematorium, Pentrebychan, Wrexham, Wales LL14 4EP (☎ 01978 840068); run by Wrexham County Borough. Price: £265 (£307 for non-residents). ◔ 30 mins (extra time £76). They accept home-made, wicker and bamboo coffins, and cardboard coffins made rigid. Advice available for DIY. Chapels: 'Modern, from 1960s. Glazed side wall with view of a water feature.' Grounds: 'Riverside walk, ponds, wildlife habitats, woodland. Traversed by Offa's Dyke. We aim to preserve and enhance the natural beauty of the setting' (Alan McMahon). CFTB.

West Midlands

Comprising Shropshire, Staffordshire, Wolverhampton, Walsall, Dudley, Sandwell, Birmingham, Solihull, Coventry, Warwickshire, Hereford and Worcester, Gloucestershire.

• ✪✪✪ **Cem Burton upon Trent**: Stapenhill Cemetery, 38, Stapenhill Road, Burton upon Trent, Staffordshire DE15 9AE (☎ 01283 508572, **e**: cemetery@east staffsbc.gov.uk); run by East Staffordshire Borough Council. Plot (50 years) incl. digging and burial £566 (double for non-residents). They accept home-made, cardboard, wicker and bamboo coffins, body bags and shrouds. ◔ 45 mins (extra time can be booked without charge). Chapel: 'Victorian, traditional feel softened by carpeting; well-maintained, with seating for about 60 people.' Grounds: 'Attractively landscaped Victorian cemetery rich in wildlife, overlooking flood plain of River Trent.' Memorials: Size restrictions (1,350 mm in height, 914 mm in width and 460 mm front to back); must be erected by a registered memorial mason. Free advice available for DIY funerals. 'Well-maintained grounds. Helpful and knowledgable staff' (Nick French). For details of their woodland burial area, see Chapter 6. CFTB.

• **Crem Burton upon Trent**: Bretby Crematorium, Geary Lane, Bretby, nr Burton upon Trent, Staffordshire DE15 OQE (☎ 01283 221505, **e**: bretby.crematorium@eaststaffbc.gov.uk); run by East Staffordshire Borough Council. Price: £293. ◔ 45 mins (extra time £117). They accept home-made, cardboard, wicker and bamboo coffins, body bags and shrouds. Chapels: 'Two chapels, seating 80 and 18 respectively, in a natural and uplifting style using

Columbian pine and Welsh slate.' Grounds: 'Set in natural woodland in the countryside between Burton upon Trent and Swadlingcote.' Free leaflets and advice available for DIY funerals. 'Civic Trust Award-winning architecture and landscaping. Natural woodland: no plaques, memorial vases or rose bushes, etc. We welcome family-managed funerals' (Nick French). CFTB.

• **Crem Cinderford**: Forest of Dean Crematorium, Yew Tree Blake, Speech House Road, Cinderford, Gloucestershire GL14 3HU (☎ 01594 826624); run by Crematoria Management Ltd. Price: £310. ⏱ 60 mins (no charge for extra time). They accept home-made or cardboard coffins. Chapel: 'Simple yet dignified, comfortable, views of the forest.' Grounds: 'Forest location – very attractive' (P. J. Wilson).

• **Cem Coleshill:** Woodlands Cemetery, Birmingham Road, Coleshill, Warwickshire (☎ 01675 464835; **f**: 01675 464351; **e**: ghull@solihull.gov.uk); run by Solihull Metropolitan Borough Council. Plot (75 years) incl. digging and burial £1,070 (£3,140 for non-residents). They accept home-made, wicker and cardboard coffins. Families may help fill, but not dig, the grave. 'Set in a rural location, this site is well-maintained within mature landscaped grounds' (Gordon Hull). Woodland burial area planned for 2005/6.

• **Crem Coleshill**: Woodlands Crematorium, Birmingham Road, Coleshill (contact details as for previous entry). Price: £330. ⏱ 30 mins (extra time may be booked). They accept home-made and cardboard coffins. Chapel: 'Modern, church-like, but intimate in size with fixed pews.' Grounds: 'Well-maintained, landscaped gardens of remembrance and wooded areas' (Gordon Hull).

• **Cems Coventry**: Canley Cemetery, Cemeteries & Crematorium Office, Cannon Hill Road, Canley, Coventry CV4 7DF (☎ 02476 294411; **f**: 02476 693863). Plot (75 years) incl. digging and burial £857. ⏱ No limit at graveside. They accept home-made and cardboard coffins and 'will consider' wicker and bamboo coffins; selection of coffins for sale. Information pack available for DIY funerals. Chapels: As Crematorium below. 'A modern lawn-type layout with Garden of Rest and pond' (Mrs S. Turner). Also the following cemeteries: Lentons Lane, Walsgrave ('opened in 1994, with a wild flower meadow and woodland burial area'); St Paul's, Holbrooks Lane ('set in the industrial North of the city, with lawn, traditional and natural burial sections'); and Walsgrave, Woodway Lane ('small, on outskirts of the city, with lawn and kerb sections and a section for Muslim burials'). CFTB.

• **Crem Coventry**: Canley Crematorium, Cannon Hill Road, Canley, Coventry CV4 7DF (☎ 02476 294411). Price: £315. ⏱ 45 mins (extra time £70). They accept home-made, wicker and cardboard coffins. Chapel: 'Recently modernised to provide second chapel.' Grounds: 'Eight acres of gardens of remembrance, with rose gardens, pond, seasonal lawns and English woodland. A flexible interpretation of rules is always applied' (G. D. Marshall). CFTB.

• **Cem Dudley**: Gornal Wood Cemetery, Chase Road, Gornal Wood, Dudley DY3 2RL (☎ 01384 813970; **e**: bereavementsvcs.due@dudley.gov.uk; **w**: www.dudley.gov.uk); run by Dudley Metropolitan Borough, which also administers cemeteries at Stourbridge, Halesowen, Cradley, Lye & Wollescote,

Brierley Hill and Dudley. Plot (75 years) incl. digging and burial £852 (double for non-residents). They accept home-made and cardboard coffins. ◐ 30 mins if in the chapel (which can be booked for £45). Chapel: 'Modern, light and airy.' Grounds: Landscaped. Memorials: Health & safety restrictions. 'Helpful staff' (Liz Mansell). There is also a natural burial area, see Chapter 6 for details.

• **Crem Dudley**: Gornal Wood Crematorium, Chase Road, Gornal Wood, Dudley DY3 2RL; run by Dudley Metropolitan Borough (contact details as previous entry). Price: £300. ◐ 20 mins at half-hourly intervals (extra time £49). They accept home-made, cardboard, wicker and bamboo coffins, and will consider body bags and shrouds. Four mourners may view the coffin entering the cremator. Chapel: Modern, light and airy. Grounds: 'Pleasant and spacious landscaped settings, seasonal gardens of remembrance.' Free advice and leaflets available for DIY funerals. 'Tranquil setting amongst memorial rows to a less formal garden of remembrance.providing a haven for wildlife. The staff are helpful and dedicated' (Liz Mansell). They will shortly adopt the CFTB.

• **Cem Hereford**: Hereford Cemetery, Westfaling Street, Hereford (☎ 01432 383200; e: jgibbon@herefordshire.gov.uk); run by Herefordshire Council, Client Services, Kemble House, Broad Street, Hereford HR4 9AR. Plot (50 years) £582; double for non-residents. Maintenance: £55 pa. ◐ Unlimited. They accept home-made, cardboard, wicker and bamboo coffins. Chapel: Traditional. Grounds: Quiet, peaceful, well-landscaped. Memorials: Dependent on the section eg headstones not to exceed 105cm in height and 76cm in width in the lawn area. DIY families must provide their own bearers. 'The cemetery is well-planted and maintained and is a haven for wild birds. It is a very peaceful setting and a good place for quiet contemplation' (David Ravenscroft). They are working towards achieving the CFTB.

• **Crem Hereford**: Hereford Crematorium, Westfaling Street, Hereford (contact details as for previous entry). Price: £289. ◐ 40 mins (extra time £221). They accept home-made, cardboard, wicker and bamboo coffins. Up to four mourners may view the coffin entering the cremator. Chapel: '1950s church-like building with a comforting atmosphere; seating for 60 people.' Grounds: 'Mature, well-landscaped, well maintained and provide a tranquil setting for contemplation.' Free advice available for a DIY funeral. 'Offers a wide range of services to the public. Car parking is rarely a problem. 11 services per day; weekend or Bank Holiday services can be arranged' (David Ravenscroft).

• **Cem Kington:** Kington Cemetery, Eardisley Road, Kington. Contact and all other details as for Hereford Cemetery above.

• ✪✪✪ **Crem Leamington Spa**: Mid-Warwickshire Crematorium, Oakley Wood, Bishops Tachbrook, Leamington Spa, Warwickshire CV33 9QP (☎ 01926 651 418); run by Warwick District Council. Price: £233.50 (£263.50 for non-residents). ◐ 30 mins (extra time £46 per 30 mins). They accept home-made, cardboard, wicker and bamboo coffins, body bags and shrouds. Chapels: 'Modern: the North Chapel seats 50 people; the South Chapel seats 80 and has an organ. Music systems and collection in both chapels.' Grounds: Informal woodland. 'Our crematorium must be one of the most flexible and helpful crematoria in the UK. The atmosphere is extremely peaceful and the woodland is home to many forms of wildlife. We have opened a woodland memorial garden. There is no commercialism' (Andrea Barnett). CFTB.

• **Cem Leominster:** Leominster Cemetery, Old Hereford Road, Leominster. Contact and all other details as for Hereford Cemetery above.

• **Cem Madeley**: Madeley Cemetery, Manor Road, Madeley, Nr. Crewe, Cheshire. Contact and all other details as for Newcastle-under-Lyme Cemetery below except for: No office or chapel.

• **Cems Newcastle-under-Lyme**: Newcastle-under-Lyme Cemetery, Lymewood Grove, Newcastle-under-Lyme, Staffordshire ST5 2EH (☎ 01782 616379; **f**: 01782 630498); run by Newcastle-under-Lyme Borough Council. Plot (50 years) incl. digging and burial £751; £353 for ashes grave. ① 30 mins (extra time available). They accept home-made, cardboard, wicker and bamboo coffins. Chapel: 'Grade II listed Victorian; small and cosy.' Grounds: 'Peaceful, well-maintained Victorian cemetery, close to town centre with easy access by car and public transport. Our offices offer a comfortable reception room where people can sit and discuss matters in private.' Memorials: Within stipulated dimensions and NAMM fitted. They will accept a body directly from a family for a DIY funeral. 'We aim to offer a caring, efficient and dignified service' (Jeanette Hollins). The Council also runs the following Cemeteries: Chesterton, Loomer Road (plots for ashes only; no office or chapel); Knutton, Cotswold Avenue; and Silverdale, Cemetery Road (no office or chapel). In the process of adopting the CTFB.

• **Crem Newcastle-under-Lyme**: Bradwell Crematorium, Chatterley Close, Bradwell, Newcastle-under-Lyme, Staffordshire ST5 8LE (☎ 01782 635498). Price: £294. ① 30 mins (extra time can be booked without charge). They accept home-made, cardboard, wicker and bamboo coffins, and will consider body bags and shrouds. Advice available for DIY funerals. Chapel: 'Multi-denominational, timber-clad, seating about 100.' Grounds: '13 acres of themed gardens with a multitude of memorial trees and shrubs and a new cremated remains section' (Steve Wells). CFTB.

• **Cem Newport (Shropshire)**: Newport General Cemetery, Audley Avenue, Newport, Shropshire (☎ 01952 814338; **e**: townclerk@newportsalop towncouncil.co.uk); run by Newport Town Council. Plot (50 years) incl. digging and burial £370 (£220 extra for non-residents). They accept cardboard, bamboo or wicker coffins, body bags and shrouds. ① No restriction. Chapel: 'Built in 1859 in Gothic style, recently restored. Seats 50.' Memorials: No restrictions in the new children's burial area; otherwise size and height restrictions (see information sheet). 'There is a reserved area for Jewish burials and a separate area for other faiths' (Miss Dee Halliday). For details of their woodland burial extension, see Chapter 6.

• **Cem Redditch**: Abbey Cemetery, Bordesley Lane, Redditch, Worcestershire B97 6RR (☎ 01527 62174; **e**: stuart.connelly@redditchbc.gov.uk); run by Redditch Borough Council. Plot (75 years) incl. digging and burial £790 (treble for non-residents). Ashes may be buried for £85. They accept home-made, cardboard, wicker and bamboo coffins, body bags and shrouds. ⏱ 30 mins (extra time £50). Free advice and a leaflet available for DIY families. Chapel: As Crem below. 'A new cemetery is being planned, with a proposed woodland burial area' (Stuart Connelly). CFTB.

• **Crem Redditch**: Redditch Crematorium, Bordesley Lane, Redditch, Worcestershire B97 6RR (contact details as for previous entry). Price: £213 (early services); £285 (others). ⏱ 30 mins (extra time £52). They accept home-made, cardboard, wicker and bamboo coffins, body bags and shrouds. Up to six mourners may view the coffin entering the cremator. Chapel: 'Modern with large plate glass window overlooking the attractive scenery of the Worcestershire countryside.' Grounds: 'Scenic elevated views, natural aesthetic, quiet surroundings and unspoilt lawned scattering areas.' Free advice and a leaflet available for DIY funerals. 'The staff are excellent and show an awareness and understanding of the needs of the bereaved. They continually look for ways to improve the service. The surroundings have exceptional beauty adjacent to the historical site of Bordesley Abbey. Magnificent location on top of a hill overlooking the Arrow Valley Park' (Stuart Connelly). CFTB.

• **Crem Shrewsbury**: Emstrey Crematorium, London Road, Shrewsbury, Shropshire SY2 6PS (☎ 01743 359883; f: 01743 245477); run by Shrewsbury & Atcham Borough Council. Price: £260. ⏱ 40 mins (extra time can be booked). They accept home-made, cardboard, wicker and bamboo coffins, body bags and shrouds. They have a leaflet for DIY funerals. Chapel: Modern, church-like. Grounds: 'A quiet restful atmosphere with private formal gardens set in open countryside. The Chapel of Remembrance contains a screen where personalised memorials including photographs and drawings can be viewed' (M. D. Wraith).

• **Cem Solihull**: Robin Hood Cemetery, Streetsbrook Road, Shirley, Solihull (☎ 0121 744 1121; f: 0121 733 8674; e: ghull@solihull.gov.uk); run by Solihull Metropolitan Borough Council. Plot (75 years) incl. digging and burial £1,070 (£3,140 for non-residents). They accept home-made, cardboard, wicker and bamboo coffins. Chapel: 'Church-like and intimate.' Memorials: Maximum 5ft high. Grounds: 'Mature urban woodland site. Visitors may sit or walk through the well-maintained, landscaped gardens of remembrance and woodland areas' (Gordon Hull). The Council also runs Widney Manor Cemetery, Widney Manor Road, Bentley Heath, Solihull, along the same lines (no chapel; set in a rural location with maturing grounds').

• **Crem Solihull**: Solihull Crematorium, Streetsbrook Road, Shirley, Solihull (☎ 0121 744 1121; f: 0121 733 8674; e: ghull@solihull.gov. uk); run by Solihull Metropolitan Borough Council. Price: £330. ⏱ 30 mins (extra time can be booked). They accept home-made and cardboard coffins. Chapel: 'Church-like and intimate with fixed pews.' Grounds: Woodland approach; well-maintained. 'All services are quality assured. The buildings are attractive' (Gordon Hull).

• **Cem Stafford**: Tixall Road Cemetery, Tixall Road, Stafford ST18 0XZ (☎ 01785 242594; f: 01785 228521, e: stafford_crem@yahoo.co.uk); run by Stafford Borough Council, Civic Offices, Riverside, Stafford. The Council runs two other cemeteries – Eccleshall, Eccleshall Road, Stafford; and Stone,

Stafford Road, Stone – to which the following details also apply, unless otherwise stated. Plot (50 years) incl. digging and burial £555 (double for non-residents). ⏱ 30 mins (extra time £40). They accept home-made, cardboard, wicker and bamboo coffins, body bags and shrouds. Chapel (only at Tixall Road): 'Mid-1960s, warm and subtle.' Grounds: 'From lawn cemeteries to mature old type. Eccleshall Road backs onto Doxey Marches, a recognised wildlife sanctuary.' Memorials: No restrictions at Eccleshall Road; lawn type at Tixall Road & Stone. Free leaflets and two bearers available for DIY funerals; prior notice needed. 'Helpful, experienced staff. Excellent grounds and maintenance' (Anthony Evans). There is a small natural burial area within Stone Cemetery, see Chapter 6 for details. CFTB.

• **Crem Stafford**: Stafford Crematorium, Tixall Road, Stafford ST18 0XZ; run by Stafford Borough Council (contact details as for previous entry). Price: £295. ⏱ 30 mins (extra time £40). They accept home-made, cardboard, wicker and bamboo coffins, body bags and shrouds 'at the registrar's discretion'. Up to ten mourners may view the coffin entering the cremator. Chapel: 'Seating for 96 people. Warm and comfortable with a loop system and music facilities.' Grounds: 'A parkland effect with slight undulations, in a countryside area with mature trees.' They will accept a body directly from a family for a DIY funeral. Leaflets and advice are available for a small donation. 'Competitive prices, professional staff. High standard of grounds' (Anthony Evans). CFTB.

• **Cem Stoke-on-Trent**: Attwood Street Cemetery, Attwood Rise, Kidsgrove, Stoke-on-Trent, Staffs; run by Newcastle-under-Lyme Borough Council. Contact and all other details as for Newcastle-under-Lyme Cemetery above, except for: Plots for ashes only; no office or chapel.

• **Cem Stoke-on-Trent**: Carmountside Cemetery, Leek Road, Milton, Stoke-on-Trent, Staffordshire ST2 7AB (☎ 01782 235050; **f**: 01782 234698; **e**: sandraramsay@stoke.gov.uk); run by Stoke-on-Trent City Council. Plot (50 years) incl. digging and burial £915 (treble for non-residents). Maintenance: £35. ⏱ 30 mins burial service (no extra time allowed). They accept home-made, cardboard, wicker and bamboo coffins; and can supply cardboard coffins. Information pack for DIY funerals available. Chapel. Memorials: Size restrictions. 'We have twice won the Cemetery of the Year competition' (Sandra Ramsay, Admin Officer). They have plans for a natural burial area. CFTB

• **Crem Stoke-on-Trent**: Carmountside Crematorium, Leek Road, Milton, Stoke-on-Trent, Staffordshire ST2 7AB. Contact and all other details as for previous entry, except for: Price: £300. ⏱ 30 mins for full service; 15 mins for committal only (15 mins extra time £75). Up to 12 mourners may view the coffin entering the cremator. Chapel: 1930s, seats 175. Grounds: Gardens including woodland, garden of remembrance and baby and children's garden.

• **Crem Stourbridge**: Stourbridge Crematorium, South Road, Stourbridge DY8 3RQ (☎ 01384 813985); run by Dudley Metropolitan Borough. Price: £300. ⏱ 20 mins at half-hourly intervals (extra time £49). They accept biodegradable coffins. Chapel: 'A converted cemetery chapel with a church-like atmosphere.' Grounds: 'A pleasant, mature, traditional cemetery landscape' (Liz Mansell).

• **Cem Telford**: Castle Green Cemetery, Beeches Road, Ironbridge, Telford; run by Leisure & Community Services, Telford & Wrekin Council, Darby House, Telford TF3 4LA (☎ 01952 202754; **e**: lcc@wrekin.gov.uk). The Council runs two other Cemeteries – Wellington, Linden Avenue; and Wombridge – to which the following details also apply, unless otherwise stated. Plot (75 years) incl. digging and burial £149 (single, unpurchased; purchase price £225); double for non-residents. They accept home-made, cardboard, wicker and bamboo coffins, body bags and shrouds. No chapel. Memorials: Maximum 3ft 6ins height. 'Flexible, accommodating service' (Phil Pritchard). CFTB.

• **Cems Walsall**: Contact details for all the following cemeteries as for Streetly Crematorium below: Streetly Cemetery, Little Hardwick Road, Aldridge, Walsall WS9 0SG; and Willenhall Lawn Cemetery, Bentley Lane, Short Heath, Willenhall. Plot (100 years) incl. digging and burial £1,253; cremated remains £656 (both fees triple for non-residents). ⏱ 30 mins (extra time £52). They accept home-made, cardboard, wicker and bamboo coffins. Chapel: 'Modern, non denominational, small and intimate.' Grounds: 'Landscaped, secure areas, close to amenities and transport links.' Memorials: Regulation sizes; made of natural stone only. 'A friendly, flexible and helpful service to all. We are willing to answer any questions and guide family members through the process of a DIY funeral free of charge' (Steve Billings). The same details apply for the following Cemeteries which do not have chapels: Bentley, Wolverhampton Road West; Bloxwich, Field Road, Bloxwich; James Bridge, Cemetery Road, Darlaston; North Walsall, Saddleworth Road, Bloxwich; and Ryecroft, Coalpool Lane.

• **Crem Walsall**: Streetly Crematorium, Little Hardwick Road, Aldridge, Walsall WS9 0SG (☎ 0121 353 7228; **e**: billingss@walsall.gov.uk; **f**: 0121 353 6557); run by Walsall MBC, Bereavement Services Division. Price: £286 (same for non-residents). ⏱ 30 mins (extra time £102). They accept home-made, cardboard, wicker and bamboo coffins, and body bags. Two family members may view the coffin entering the cremator. Advice available for DIY funerals. Chapels: Modern, non-denominational. Live music available. Grounds: Semi-rural area close to local population, set in landscaped grounds.

• **Crem West Bromwich**: West Bromwich Crematorium, Newton Road B71 3SX (☎ 0121 569 6700); run by Sandwell Metropolitan Borough Council. Price: £325. ⏱ 20 mins (extra time £125). They accept cardboard coffins. Chapel: Modern; seats 160. Grounds: 'Landscaped gardens' (Mr K. Howard).

• **Cem Wigmore:** Wigmore Cemetery, Wigmore, Herefordshire. Contact and all other details as for Hereford Cemetery above.

• **Crem Wolverhampton**: Bushbury Crematorium, Underhill Lane, Bushbury, Wolverhampton (☎ 01902 556070); run by Wolverhampton City Council. Price: £310. ⏱ 30 mins (extra time £70). They accept cardboard, wicker and bamboo coffins. Modern chapels: in West Chapel (seats 80) coffin lowers; East Chapel (seats 50) curtain draws across. One chapel can be non-denominational.' Grounds: 47-acre site with flower borders and a wooded area for cremated remains. 'We are happy to accept different-style services and coffins, and have a variety of memorial options available' (Adam Clelland). Adopting CFTB.

• **Crem Worcester**: Worcester Crematorium, Tintern Avenue, Astwood Road, Worcester WR3 8HA (☎ 01905 22633); run by City of Worcester Council. Price: £270. ⏱ 30 mins (£60 for extra time; 'a double service is available if we are not busy'). They accept home-made, cardboard, wicker and bamboo coffins, body bags and shrouds, 'as long as they have extra support for carrying'. Free advice and leaflet for DIY funerals. Chapel: '1960s building with a conventional layout, with seating for 100 people.' Grounds: 'Attractive lawns and borders with a stream running though. The garden of remembrance is adjacent to the old cemetery with its many fine old trees. We will deal with any requests that do not adversely affect other users' (David Seaman). Adopting CFTB.

East Midlands

Comprising Derbyshire, Nottinghamshire, Leicestershire, Northamptonshire, Bedfordshire, Oxfordshire, Buckinghamshire.

• **Crem Amersham**: Chilterns Crematorium, Whielden Lane, Amersham, Buckinghamshire HP7 0ND (☎ 01494 724263; **f**: 01494 433065). Price: £241. ⏱ 30 mins. They accept home-made and cardboard coffins, and will consider other body containers after inspection. They publish a useful five-page guide for DIY families. Chapel: Non-denominational, 1960s brick with copper roof. Grounds: Woodland setting in open countryside on the edge of the Chiltern Hills. 'Flexible attitude; willing to consider every reasonable request on its merits' (Charles Howlett).

• **Cem Banbury**: Scutham Road Cemetery, Scutham Road, Banbury OX16 (☎ 01295 263436, **w**: www.banbury.gov.uk); run by Banbury Town Council. Plot (99 years) incl. digging and burial £140 (double for non-residents). Maintenance: £30. They accept home-made, cardboard, wicker and bamboo coffins. ⏱ 1 hour (no extra time available). No chapel. Grounds: 'Old established cemetery, built in 1858 with many memorials of architectural interest.' Memorials: Headstones not exceeding 91.5 cm high, 75 cm wide and 10 cm thick. They will accept a body directly from a family for a DIY funeral. Special assistance is available; prices on application. 'Attractively landscaped with many mature and specimen trees. Caring and sympathetic staff' (Tony Webster). Natural burial ground planned for 2008. Considering adopting CFTB.

• **Crem Banbury**: Banbury Crematorium, Hardwick Hill, Scutham Road, Banbury OX16 (☎ 01295 226500); run by London Cremation Company plc. Price: £325. ⏱ Bookings on the hour Mon-Fri; weekends by appointment (£425 for a double slot). They accept cardboard, wicker and bamboo coffins. Six to eight mourners may view the coffin entering the cremator. Chapel: Modern and light. Grounds: Modern, mainly lawned cemetery, well maintained, clean and tidy. Free advice available for DIY funerals. 'Beautiful gardens set in Oxfordshire countryside' (J. T. Cox).

• **Cem Bedford**: Kempston Cemetery, Green End Road, Kempston, Bedford MK42 8BG (☎ 01234 851823); run by Kempston Burials Joint Committee. Plot (30 years) incl. digging and burial £250 (50 per cent extra for non-residents).

They accept home-made, cardboard, wicker and bamboo coffins. They will accept a body directly from a family for a DIY funeral. ⊕ Unlimited. No chapel. Grounds: Rural, quiet and well-maintained. Memorials: Not exceeding 900 mm in height, 100 mm in thickness and 600 mm in width. 'Kempston Cemetery excels in its rural position with positive divisions, eg Victorian-Natural, Victorian-Monuments, New-Spacious' (Lynda Smith). Considering adopting CFTB.

• **Cem Bedford**: Norse Road Cemetery, 104 Norse Road, Bedford (☎ 01234 353701). Plot (75 years) incl. digging and burial £277. They accept home-made, cardboard, wicker and bamboo coffins, body bags and shrouds. ⊕ 45 mins (extra time £30). Chapel: Modern, secular. Grounds: Modern, heavily wooded. Memorials: Lawn-type, back to back. 'Well-kept' (Michael Day). There is also a one-acre woodland burial area, see Chapter 6 for details. CFTB.

• **Crem Bedford**: Bedford Crematorium, Cemetery Complex, 104 Norse Road, Bedford (☎ 01234 353701; e: mday@bedford.gov.uk). Price: £275 (£300 non-residents). ⊕ 45 mins (extra time £100 per slot). They accept home-made, cardboard, wicker and bamboo coffins, body bags and shrouds. Advice available for DIY funerals. Chapel: 'Modern, with wall-hangings and oak seating.' Grounds: Designed for ease of access. 'Each funeral an individual experience' (Mr Michael Day). CFTB.

• **Cem Belper**: Belper Cemetery, Matlock Road, Belper, Derbyshire (☎ 01773 841418; e: enquiry@ambervalley.gov.uk; w: www.ambervalley.gov.uk); run by Amber Valley Borough Council, Environment & Leisure Department, PO Box 18, Town Hall, Ripley, Derbyshire DE5 3TU. The Council also runs five other Cemeteries – Alfreton, Rodgers Lane; Crosshill, Heanor Road, Codnor; Heanor, Ilkeston Road, Marlpool; Leabrooks, Albert Street; and Ripley, Cemetery Lane – for which the following details apply, unless otherwise stated. Plot (99 years) incl. digging and burial £337 (£405.50 for non-residents). They accept home-made and cardboard coffins and are prepared to assist DIY families. ⊕ Approx. 40 mins. Chapel: At Leabrooks Cemetery and Heanor Cemetery only. Memorials: 'Max height 1m; no metal' (Gale Stapleford). For the woodland burial area within Belper Cemetery, see Chapter 6. CFTB.

• **Crem Bramcote**: Bramcote Crematorium, Coventry Lane, Bramcote, Beeston, Nottingham NG9 3GJ (☎ 0115 9221837; f: 0115 9430067); run by Bramcote Crematorium Joint Committee. Price: £300. ⊕ 45 mins. They accept home-made, cardboard and wicker coffins; also the Cocoon System (see Chapter 5) 'as long as there is a signed statement'. Chapel: 'Modern, with large window giving view of small enclosed garden; seating for 125 people. A further chapel with seating for 40 is planned.' Grounds: Parkland with lots of trees, seats and walks, as well as immaculate gardens. 'We aim to make each service very personal, and keep costs low to help families' (Mrs Richards). CFTB.

• **Cem: Buxton:** Buxton Cemetery, Ashbourne Road, Buxton (no post please; ☎ 0845 1294876; e: terryr@highpeak.gov.uk); run by High Peak Borough Council, 22 Market Street, Buxton, Derbyshire SK17 6LD (☎ 0845 129 4868; f: 01298 27640; e: buxton@highpeak.gov.uk; w: www.highpeak.gov.uk). Plot (80 years) incl. digging and burial £660-50; or £374.50 for the woodland areas.

They accept home-made (within reason), cardboard, wicker and bamboo coffins, and shrouds; other containers only after prior inspection. ◷ 45 mins (extra time on request). There is a chapel. Grounds: 'Quiet, well-wooded, well-kept. Views across to nearby hills. Easily accessible, including disabled access.' Memorials: None allowed in woodland areas; in other areas there are size restrictions and new memorials must be in keeping with those currently in the cemetery (lawn-type mostly, some monolith tablets, crosses etc). They will accept a body directly from a family for a DIY funeral: 72 hours notice is required at all times, and the family must supply the coffin or shroud. 'Helpful staff. Family-organised burials of ashes already take place regularly. There is a garden of remembrance for bronze plaque memorials' (Terry Redfern). For details of their woodland burial area, see Chapter 6. They are considering adopting the CFTB.

• **Cem Derby**: Nottingham Road Cemetery, Nottingham Road, Derby DE21 6FN (☎/**f**: 01332 672761; **e**: cemetery@derby.gov.uk); run by Derby City Council. Plot (100 years) incl. digging and burial £230 (double for non-residents). ◷ Unlimited. They accept home-made coffins, body bags and shrouds ('any biodegradable container as long as the body is covered and labelled'). Leaflets and advice are available for DIY funerals; however, no assistance can be offered with bearing the coffin. Chapel. Victorian. Grounds: Established mature trees. Woodland area and green open spaces. Memorials: Lawn and traditional sections: 137cm high, 90cm wide and 10cm deep; cremated remains section: granite 45.7cm by 35.5cm. 'Helpful and attentive staff. Local for Derby City with good road and rail links' (Susan Cannan). CFTB.

• **Crem Derby**: Markeaton Crematorium, Markeaton Lane, Derby DE22 4NH (☎ 01332 341012; **e**: crematorium@derby.gov.uk); run by Derby City Council. Price: £260. ◷ 30 mins (extra time £55). They accept home-made, cardboard, wicker and bamboo coffins, body bags and shrouds. Up to four mourners may view the coffin entering the cremator. Leaflets and advice available for DIY funerals. Chapel: 'Modern, 1956, church-like but non-denominational with no religious symbolism. Flexible seating, can face any direction.' Grounds: 'Open park-like setting, mature trees and secluded corners. Attractive foliage and flower beds. Helpful and attentive staff' (Susan Cannan). CFTB.

• **Cem Didcot**: Didcot Cemetery, Kynaston Road, Didcot (☎ 01235 812637, **e**: council@didcot.gov.uk); run by Didcot Local Council. Plot (40 years) £105 (50 per cent extra for non-residents). Plus digging and burial. Ashes: £42 for a plot only. It is advisable to check with the cemetery as to which body containers they accept. ◷ Unlimited. No chapel. Memorials: Size restrictions. 'The cemetery is maintained to a high standard. We keep our prices as low as possible. We provide help and support to families. We arrange interment of ashes without a funeral director by preparing the grave before and after interment' (Julia Underwood).

• **Cem Gerrards Cross**: Parkside Cemetery, Windsor Road, Gerrards Cross, Bucks SL9 8SS (☎ 01753 662426); run by South Bucks Local Council. Plot (50years) incl. digging and burial £554 (£160 extra for non-residents). They accept home made, cardboard, wicker and bamboo coffins, body bags and shrouds. They will accept a body directly from a family for a DIY funeral, but the family must supply all the bearers. ⓘ Unlimited. Chapel: 'Very small chapel for book of remembrance. 1960s brick-built, copper roof, light and airy. Holds about 12 people'. Memorials: 2ft sq stone tablets in some areas. Small staked plaques in woodland area. 'Attractive surroundings and easy to get to. Flower beds well-maintained. We provide assistance in choosing plots; and will help the family on the day of the burial. Grass kept under control to allow easy access to graves' (Ian Richards). See Chapter 6 for details of the woodland burial area.

• **Cem Glossop:** Glossop Cemetery, Cemetery Road, Glossop, Derbyshire; run by High Peak Borough Council. Contact and other details as for Buxton Cemetery above, except for: Grounds: 'Open since the 1850s. Well-wooded, hill-top cemetery with views of Kinder Scout & Peak District National Park. Rural; quiet location surrounded by farmland. There is a garden of remembrance for bronze plaque memorials. We are currently restoring and enhancing the Cemetery' (Terry Redfern). See Chapter 6 for the woodland burial area.

• **Cem Hope Valley:** Hope Cemetery, Green Drive, Edale Road, Hope, Hope Valley Derbyshire; run by High Peak Borough Council. Contact and all other details as for Buxton Cemetery above, except for: Grounds: 'Peaceful rural location in the Peak District National Park. Mature woodland and fields around. The Cemetery has been open since the1930s; it is small, secluded, and away from main roads. There is a natural spring water supply' (Terry Redfern).

• **❁❁❁ Crem Kettering**: Kettering Crematorium, East Lodge, Rothwell Road, Kettering, Northamptonshire NN16 8XE (☎ 01536 525722; **f**: 01536 524209); run by Kettering Borough Council. Price: £275 (£300 with organist). ⓘ 45 mins (extra time £50). They accept home-made, cardboard, wicker and bamboo coffins, body bags and shrouds. Free advice available for DIY funerals. Chapels: 'One modern, non-denominational, the other church-like; one seats 105, the other 50.' Grounds: Pleasant gardens with mature woodland areas. 'Funerals are viewed as the family's, not ours' (Sue Williams). There is a natural burial ground, see Chapter 6 for details. Working towards adopting the CFTB.

• **Crem Leamington Spa:** Mid-Warwickshire Crematorium, Oakley Wood, Bishops Tachbrook, Leamington Spa CV33 9QP (☎ 01926 651418); run by Warwick District Council. Price: £233.50 (£263.50 for non-residents) ⓘ 30 mins (extra slot £46). They accept home-made, cardboard, wicker and bamboo coffins, body bags and shrouds. Chapels: 'Modern. The North Chapel seats 50 people and the South seats 80 and has an organ. Music collection and system in both.' Grounds: Informal woodland. 'Our crematorium must be one of the most flexible and helpful in the UK. The atmosphere is extremely peaceful and the woodland is home to many forms of wildlife. We have opened a woodland memorial garden. There is no commercialism' (Andrea Barnett). CFTB.

• **Cems Leicester**: Gilroes Cemetery, Groby Road, Leicester LE3 9QG (☎ 0116 2995522/ 2527382; **f**: 0116 222 8706; **e**: doohj001@ leicester.gov.uk); run by Leicester City Council, from the Cemeteries Office, New Walk Centre, Welford Place, Leicester LE1 6ZG. They also run Saffron Hill Cemetery, Stonesby Avenue; Welford Road Cemetery, Welford Road; and Belgrave Cemetery, Red

Hill Way. Plot (99 years) incl. digging and burial £650 (double for non-residents). ⏲ 45 mins (extra time £50). They accept home-made, cardboard, wicker and bamboo coffins; check for body bags and shrouds. Chapel: 'Traditional, Gothic-cum-Tudor, seating 85 people, with large assembly hall attached. Music facilities.' Grounds: 'As well as the architecture, the assembly hall is a distinguishing feature of particular interest to Hindu, Sikh and Jain families.' Memorials: No kerbsets. Nothing above 4ft 6ins high. 'We will give as much assistance to families not using a funeral director as they require' (Lisa Handy).

• **Crem Leicester**: Gilroes Crematorium (see previous entry for contact details, chapel & grounds). Price: £275. ⏲ 45 mins (extra time £50). They accept home-made, cardboard, wicker and bamboo coffins.

• **Cems Leighton Buzzard**: Vandyke Road Cemetery, Vandyke Road, Leighton Buzzard (☎ 01525 219320; **e**: barry.wardle@leighton-linslade.org.uk); run by Leighton-Linslade Town Council, The White House, Hockliffe Street, Leighton Buzzard, Bedfordshire LU7 1HD. They also run Old Linslade Cemetery (no chapel; rural setting) .Plot (75 years) incl. digging and burial £300 (triple for non-residents). Maintenance: £52 pa. ⏲ 30 mins. They accept home-made, cardboard, wicker and bamboo coffins, body bags and shrouds. Free advice available for DIY funerals. Chapel: '1880s, late Victorian Gothic, quite small, being restored, services held infrequently. Grounds: Urban setting, peaceful, very well-maintained and has a history in the local area. Memorials: Maximum 2ft 9ins high and 6ins wide. 'The site is appreciated and respected by the the community. It is constantly being upgraded so that it remains a credit to both the community and the Town Council' (Barry Wardle).

• **✪✪✪ Cem Luton**: Luton Church Cemetery, 26 Crawley Green Road, Luton, Bedfordshire (☎ 1582 722874; **f**: 01582 451496; **e**: admin@stmaryssluton.org); run by Luton Church Cemetery Trustees. Plot £150 (single); £175 (double); prices for the digging vary. Maintenance: £55 pa. 'We positively encourage home-made, cardboard, wicker and bamboo coffins, body bags and shrouds.' ⏲ No time limit, given four days' notice. Chapel: Not in use at the moment. Grounds: 'A varied site with chalk grassland, copses and a wild flower meadow. Within it can be found 180 different species of plants, three species of orchid and 12 endangered plants. Grass cut frequently.' Memorials: Restrictions in certain sections. 'Understanding and helpful staff' (Richard Field).

• **Crem Luton**: Luton Crematorium, The Vale, Butterfield Green Road, Stopsley, Luton, Bedforshire LU2 8DD (☎ 01582 723700/ 730761); run by Luton Borough Council. Price: £245 (£256 non-residents). ⏲ 45 mins between services (extra time can only be booked by paying for a double slot). They accept home-made, cardboard, wicker and bamboo coffins; body bags and shrouds require prior consultation. Free advice and leaflet available for DIY funerals. Chapel: 'Modern and functional, with seating for 120 people.' Grounds: Pleasant semi-rural setting. 'Helpful staff' (N. Schonewald). CFTB.

• **Crem Mansfield**: Mansfield & District Crematorium, Derby Road, Mansfield, Nottinghamshire NG18 5BJ (☎ 01623 621811; **e**: sallycurtis@btconnect.com; **w**: www.mansfield.gov.uk); run by Mansfield District Council. Price: £210 (£35 extra for non-residents). ⓒ 20 mins, with services at 45-minute intervals (extra time £42). They accept cardboard, wicker and bamboo coffins. Advice available for DIY funerals. Chapels: 'Two chapels, one traditional and church-like, seating 80; the other modern, light wood and glass.' Grounds: 'Surrounded by woodland, pleasant gardens. No chemicals used unless absolutely necessary. Easily accessible by motorway, train, etc. We are forward thinking and open to suggestions' (Sally A. Curtis). CFTB.

• **Cem New Mills:** Thornsett Cemetery, High Hill Road, New Mills, High Peak, Derbyshire; run by High Peak Borough Council. Contact and other details as for Buxton Cemetery above, except for: Grounds: 'Semi-rural location in river valley, secluded woodland burial area, next to Sett Valley Trail footpath. Well-kept small cemetery. Good car parking close to graves. Open since the 1980s.'

• **Cem Northampton**: Kingsthorpe Cemetery, Harborough Road North, Kingsthorpe, Northampton (☎ 01604 838903; **e**: cemeteries@northampton gov.uk); run by Northampton Borough Council, Community Services, Cemetery Office, Cliftonville House, Bedford Road, Northampton, NN4 7NR. Administers other cemeteries locally at Dallington, Duston and Hardingstone. Plot (99 years) incl. digging and burial £517.50 (double for non-residents). Maintenance free. They accept home-made, cardboard, bamboo and wicker coffins, body bags and shrouds in the green burial area. ⓒ Normally 25 mins; extra time available at no charge. Chapel: 100-years old with seating for approx. 60. Grounds: Large cemetery opened 1900 with mature trees and a mix of traditional areas and lawns. Memorials: Kerbs permitted in traditional area, others restricted to 3ft high. 'The Cemetery is welcoming to everyone who visits. The ground staff are helpful' (Irene Thompson). CFTB.

• **Cem Oxford**: Wolvercote Cemetery, Banbury Road, Oxford OX2 8EE (☎ 01865 513962; **e**: wolvercote.cem@oxford.gov.uk); run by Oxford City Council. Administers branch cemeteries at Headington, Rosehill, and Botley (same details apply). Plot (75 years) incl. digging and burial £450 (double for non-residents). Maintenance: £63 pa. They accept home-made, cardboard, wicker and bamboo coffins. ⓒ 30 mins (extra time £40). Chapel: 'Victorian, with fully-equipped organ.' Grounds: 'Late Victorian; wide variety of trees.' Memorials: No kerbs. 'Service to the public is paramount. We received the IBCA & MAB Cemetery of the Year Award 1999 & 2001' (H. P. Dawson). For their woodland burial areas, see Chapter 6. CFTB.

• **Cem Retford**: The Cemetery, North Road, Retford, Nottinghamshire; run by Bassetlaw District Council, Environment & Health Services, West House, Hundred Acre Lane, Carlton Forest, Worksop, Nottinghamshire S81 0TS (☎ 01909 533487). Plot (99 years) incl. digging and burial £698 (50 per cent extra for non-residents). They accept home-made, cardboard, wicker and bamboo coffins, body bags and shrouds in the Woodland area (see Chapter 6). ⓒ As required. No chapel. Grounds: 'Like a country park, with about 1,000 trees and the Chesterfield Canal running through.' Memorials: 'Maximum 3ft high on lawn sections. Kerb memorials allowed in some sections' (Hazel Davison).

• **Cem Wigston**: Wigston Cemetery, Welford Road, Wigston, Leicestershire (☎

0116 2880942 or 0116 2720572); run by Oadby & Wigston Borugh Council, The Depot, Wigston Road, Oadby LE2 5JE. Plot (100 years) incl. digging and burial £475. Accept all coffins, body bags and shrouds. Advice available for DIY funerals. Chapel: Victorian. Grounds: 'Neatly laid out.' Memorials: 'None above 2ft 6ins high; no kerbs' (N. R. Coy). CFTB.

• **Cem Worksop**: Hannah Park Cemetery, Netherton Road, Worksop; run by Bassetlaw District Council. Contact and all other details as for Retford Cemetery above, except for: Chapel: 'Made in 1900 from large, Yorkshire stone bricks.' Grounds: 'Adjoining woodland, with a panoramic view of the town.' Woodland burial area, see Chapter 6 for details.

East Anglia

Comprising Norfolk, Suffolk, Essex, Cambridgeshire and Hertfordshire.

• **Crem Basildon**: Basildon and District Crematorium, Church Road, Bowers Gifford, Basildon, Essex SS13 2HG (☎ 01268 584411; **f**: 01268 584422); run by Crematoria Management Ltd. Price: £295. ◷ 30 mins. They accept home-made and cardboard coffins. Chapel: 'Modern. Natural wood used. Facilities for organ or tape music.' Grounds: 'Open countryside' (L. G. Yarham).

• **Cem Benfleet**: Woodside Cemetery, Manor Road, Benfleet, Essex (☎ 01268 882472); run by Castle Point Borough Council, Leisure Services Department, Council Offices, Kiln Road, Benfleet, Essex SS7 1TF (☎ 01268 882200; **e**: gsnook@castlepoint.gov.uk). Plot (50 years) incl. digging and burial £190 (double for non-residents). Maintenance: Free. ◷ 1 hour (no charge for extra time). Chapel: Modern. Memorials: Height and width restrictions. They will accept a body directly from a family not using a funeral director. 'In a green valley' (G. F. Snook). There is a natural burial area.

• **Cem Benfleet:** South Benfleet Cemetery, Jotmans Lane, South Benfleet, Essex. All details as for previous entry.

• **Cem Braintree**: Braintree Cemetery, London Road, Braintree; run by Community Services, Braintree District Council, Causeway House, Bocking End, Braintree, Essex CM7 9HB (☎ 01376 551414 x 2324). The Council runs three other Cemeteries – Bocking, Church Lane, Bocking; Halstead, Colchester Road, Halstead; and Witham, Manor Road, Witham – to which the following details also apply, unless otherwise stated. Plot (100 years) incl. digging and burial £602 (double for non-residents). Maintenance: £64.62 for twice-yearly planting of full grave. ◷ Approx. 60 mins. They accept home-made, wicker and bamboo coffins. Families may carry and lower the coffin, but the grave must be excavated by the Council's contractors. Chapels at Braintree, Bocking & Witham. Memorials: 'Varying restrictions depending on the area. Families may reserve or select a grave space at no extra cost. Our regulations closely follow the principles of the CFTB, which we hope to adopt in the near future' (Michael Ashby).

• **Cem Burnham on Crouch:** Burnham on Crouch Cemetery, Southminster Road, Burnham on Crouch, Essex; run by Maldon District Council, Council Offices, Princes Road, Maldon, Essex CM9 5DL (☎ 01621 875747, **w**:

www.maldon.gov.uk). Plot (30 years, renewable every ten years) excl. digging and burial £509 (double for non-residents); plus digging fee approx. £170. ☼ Unlimited. They accept home-made, cardboard, wicker and bamboo coffins, body bags and shrouds. They will accept a body directly from a family for a DIY funeral with prior notice. No chapel. Grounds: Rural. Memorials: 'No memorials in the woodland area; there is a pergola which accommodates plaques; in the traditional area memorials are subject to Cemetery regulations' (Richard Yelland). There is a natural burial ground, see Chapter 6 for details. 'Closely follow' the principles of the CFTB.

• **Crem Bury St Edmunds**: West Suffolk Crematorium, Nr. Risby, Bury St Edmunds, Suffolk IP28 6RR (☎ 01284 755118); run by Crematoria Management Ltd. Price: £335. ☼ 45 mins between services, but they request that services take no longer than 25-30 mins. They accept home-made, cardboard, wicker and bamboo coffins. Up to four mourners may view the coffin entering the cremator. Chapel: 'Design based on old Suffolk hay barn. Carved oak woodwork throughout with fixed seating.' Grounds: 'Peaceful rural setting, non-formal layout. People seem to find the crematorium comforting and calm.' There is free advice available for DIY funerals. Families who are organising a DIY funeral are requested to provide the crematorium with their selection of music the day before the service. 'All the staff work hard to give a first class service, by working with funeral directors and ministers to ensure that the public get what they want for their funeral service' (Royna Brunskill). The crematorium has applied for planning permission to establish a cemetery and a natural ground; see Chapter 6 for details.

• **Cem Cambridge**: Cambridge City Cemetery, Newmarket Road, Cambridge (☎ 01954 780681). Plot (50 years) incl. digging and burial £760 (£1,660 for non-residents). They accept home-made, cardboard, bamboo or wicker coffins. ☼ 45 mins (extra time £160). Chapel: 'Traditional, church-like, or use of crematorium chapels' (see below). Memorials: Traditional section: not restricted, but must be agreed; lawn section: headstone/vase only. 'Well-established cemetery with identified areas for special religious groups, and a separate children's section' (David Giles). Their new Huntingdon Road Cemetery will incorporate a natural burial area, see Chapter 6 for details.

• **Crem Cambridge**: Cambridge City Crematorium, Huntingdon Road, Cambridge CB3 0JJ (☎ 01954 780681). Price: £360. ☼ 45 mins (extra time £160). They accept home-made, cardboard, wicker and bamboo coffins. Free advice available for DIY funerals. Chapel: Traditional East chapel (1938); modern, light and airy West chapel (1991). Grounds: 'The memorial woodland is particularly attractive during the spring' (David Giles).

• **Cem Cheshunt**: Cheshunt Cemetery, Bury Green Road, Cheshunt, Herts EN7 5AG; run by Broxbourne Borough Council, Cemetery Office, Bishops College, Churchgate, Cheshunt, Herts EN8 9XF (☎ 01992 785507; **e**: leisure@broxbourne.gov.uk; **w**: www.broxbourne.gov.uk). Plot (100 years) incl. digging and burial £560 (£2,240 for non-residents). Maintenance: £50. They accept home-made, cardboard, wicker and bamboo coffins, body bags and shrouds;

other containers 'upon discussion'. ⓘ Unlimited; over one hour by prior arrangement. Chapel: 'Large stone and brick with a spire and arched doors and windows; carpeted, white painted walls, central heating, padded seats and a music system.' Grounds: 'Half urban, half rural in feel. Quiet, many trees, extensive wildlife. Well-maintained.' Memorials: Lawn graves: maximum height 3ft; conventional graves: maximum height 4ft 6ins. Any natural stone; no restrictions on inscriptions (within public decency). Free advice and leaflets available for DIY funerals. 'We always try to meet the requirements of the bereaved and provide beautiful surroundings for their loved ones' (Jim Duncan). A woodland burial ground is planned for 2005 (see Chapter 6 for details). Meanwhile, individual woodland graves are possible. CFTB.

• **Cem Clacton-on-Sea**: Clacton Cemetery, Burrs Road, Clacton-on-Sea, Essex (☎ 01255 831108; **e**: wcrem@wcrem.freeserve.co.uk); run by Tendring District Council. Contact details as for Weeley Crematorium below. Plot (99 years) incl. digging and burial £794 (£447 extra for non-residents). They accept home-made, cardboard, wicker and bamboo coffins, body bags and shrouds. ⓘ 45 mins for the chapel and graveside (extra time £93). Chapel: Older style cross-shaped building. Grounds: 'Open aspect, Lawn type with back-to-back memorials.' Memorials: Not exceeding 3ft high, 2ft wide and 1ft in depth. 'Our service and help to the public and funeral directors is second to none' (Janet Beech).

• **Cem Colchester**: Colchester Cemetery, Mersea Road, Colchester, Essex CO2 8RU (☎ 01206 282950; **e**: penny.stynes@colchester.gov.uk; **w**: www.colchester.gov.uk); run by Colchester Borough Council. Plot (50 years) incl. digging and burial £645 (£136 extra for non-residents). Maintenance: Free in lawn area; £37 pa elsewhere. They accept home-made, cardboard, wicker and bamboo coffins, and shrouds. ⓘ 'As long as it takes.' Chapel: Victorian Gothic with music facilities and organ. Grounds: 'Victorian, with a variety of long-established trees.' Will give assistance with DIY funerals. Memorials: Within size and materials restrictions. 'Cemetery excels in its standards of service to the bereaved families and public' (Penny Stynes).

• **Crem Colchester**: Colchester Crematorium, Mersea Road, Colchester, Essex CO2 8RU (☎ 01206 282950); run by Colchester Borough Council. Price: £342. ⓘ 20 mins (an extra 20 mins can normally be booked for £155). They accept home-made, cardboard, wicker and bamboo coffins. Two members of the family may view the charging procedure if they wish. Chapel: Modern, non-denominational. Grounds: 'Formal gardens in attractive 1850s cemetery with fine, mature specimen trees' (P. Stynes).

• **Cem Ely**: Ely Cemetery, Beech Lane, Ely, Cambridgeshire (☎ 01353 669659); run by City of Ely Town Council, 72 Market Street, Ely. Plot (99 years) incl. digging and burial from £151-50 (double for non-residents). They would consider cardboard or unusual coffins; likewise, funerals by families not using funeral directors. ⓘ Unlimited. Chapel: Brick and stone (1856). Grounds: 'Rural setting. Relatives can put bulbs and plants on graves.' Memorials: Must not exceed 4ft in height and no new kerbstones.

• **Cem Epping**: Lower Bury Lane, Epping, Essex (☎ 01992 579444, **e**:

bwhittome@eppingtowncouncil.gov.uk); run by Epping Town Council, Council Offices, Epping Hall, St John's Road, Epping, Essex CM16 5JU. Price: (99 years) £235 (quadruple for non-residents); digging fee to be arranged with grave digger. ① Unlimited. They accept home-made, cardboard, wicker and bamboo coffins. The Council will assist families who arrange funerals not using a funeral director; £20 for assistance with the paperwork. Chapel: 'Basic, no electricity.' Grounds: 'Well-maintained.' Memorials: Old burial area: flat or full kerb not exceeding 2 m in height and 76 cm in width; headstones and vertical memorials: not exceeding 1.2 m in height, 15 cm in depth and 75 cm in width. Restrictions also apply in the extension and cremated remains section. 'Surroundings are extremely attractive' (G. Chorley).

• **Cem Harlow**: Parndon Wood Cemetery, Parndon Wood Road, Harlow, Essex CM19 4SF (☎ 01279 423800/ 446199; **e**: chris.brown@harlow.gov.uk); run by Harlow Council. Plot (50 years) incl. digging and burial £1,158. They accept home-made, cardboard, wicker and bamboo coffins, body bags and shrouds. ① 30 mins. Advice available for DIY funerals. Chapel: Non-denominational. Grounds: 'Tranquil woodland setting.' Memorials: Within size restrictions; no kerbing. 'A separate baby and children's area' (Mrs Chris Brown). For details of the natural burial area, see Chapter 6.

• **Crem Harlow**: Parndon Wood Crematorium, Parndon Wood Road, Harlow, Essex CM19 4SF; run by Harlow Council (contact details as for previous entry). Price: £265. ① 30 mins (extra time: variable charge). They accept home-made, cardboard, wicker and bamboo coffins, body bags and shrouds. Advice available for DIY funerals. Grounds: Woodland. They intend to adopt the CFTB.

• **Cem Harpenden**: Westfield Road Cemetery, Westfield Road, Harpenden, Herts; run by St Albans City & District Council. Contact and all other details as for Hatfield Road Cemetery below, except for: Plot (100 years) £396 (double for non-residents). No chapel. Memorials: Height restrictions of 3ft in lawn sections.

• **Cem Harwich**: Dovercourt Cemetery, Main Road, Dovercourt, Harwich, Essex (☎ 01255 831108; **e**: wcrem@wcrem.freeserve.co.uk); run by Tendring District Council. All other details as for Clacton Cemetery above, except for: Chapel: Small and intimate.

• **Cem Heybridge**: Heybridge Cemetery, Goldhanger Road, Heybridge, Maldon, Essex (☎ 01621 875747; **w**: www.maldon.gov.uk); run by Maldon District Council, Princes Road, Maldon CM9 5DL (☎ 01621 875836). All details as for Maldon Cemetery below, except: Chapel: Small, basic, Victorian, seats approx. 50. Rural site. No woodland burial area.

• **Cem Hoddesdon**: Hoddesdon Cemetery, Warr Road, Hoddesdon, Herts EN11 9AE; run by Broxbourne Borough Council, Cemetery Office, Bishops College, Churchgate, Cheshunt, Herts EN8 9XF (☎ 01992 785507; **e**: leisure@ broxbourne.gov.uk; **w**: www.broxbourne.gov.uk). All details as for Cheshunt Cemetery above, except: 'Since the site is nearly full, plots are only available for residents, unless it is for a very close relative of a resident, in which case the interment fee is quadrupled.' Memorials: 'Although there is no natural burial ground, trees or wild flowers can be planted instead of having a memorial.'

Chapel: 'Red brick walls with oak-beamed and panelled ceiling, centrally heated, music playback and PA' (Jim Duncan).

• **Cem Hunstanton**: Hunstanton Cemetery, Alexandra Road, Hunstanton, Norfolk; run by Borough Council of King's Lynn & West Norfolk. Contact details as for Mintlyn Crematorium below. For all other details see next entry, except: Grounds: no details available.

• **Cems King's Lynn**: Gayton Road Cemetery, Cemetery Drive, Gayton Road, King's Lynn, Norfolk (☎ 01553 630533, **e**: colin.houseman@west-norfolk.gov.uk; **w**: www.west-norfolk.gov.uk); run by Borough Council of King's Lynn & West Norfolk. Also Hardwick Road Cemetery, Hardwick Road (no grounds details available), for which the following details also apply. Plot (99 years) incl. digging and burial £707 (double for non-residents); £305 for ashes (double for non-residents). Optional extras: two bearers £11.80; organist £10.60. ⏲ Unlimited. They accept home-made, cardboard, wicker and bamboo coffins, and shrouds. Memorials: 'Only allowed on purchased plots; maximum 1 m wide, 61 cm deep.' Grounds: 'Small, well-maintained, beautiful trees and boundary laurel bushes. Listed cemetery office and chapel buildings (chapel not in use).' Free assistance, leaflet and advice for DIY funerals. 'Natural aspect in a built-up area. Well-ordered and quite easy to find your way about. Helpful staff on site and in office. High standard of maintenance' (Colin Houseman). CFTB.

• ✪✪✪ **Crem King's Lynn**: Mintlyn Crematorium, Lynn Road, Bawsey, King's Lynn, Norfolk PE32 1HB; run by Borough Council of Kings Lynn & West Norfolk (contact details as for previous entry). Price: £305. ⏲ 45 mins (extra time £70). They accept home-made, cardboard, wicker and bamboo coffins, and shrouds. Free advice and leaflet available for DIY funerals. Chapel: 'Modern, of unusual design. Natural brick and wood throughout including pews, with seating for 100 people. Lowering catafalque.' Grounds: 'Mature woodland site, extending to 15 acres, planted with memorial shrubs and conifers. Well-maintained gardens. Staff are friendly and helpful and complete their duties with unobtrusive dignity and decorum. The bereaved may tailor the funeral service to their own needs' (Colin Houseman). CFTB.

• **Cem Kirby Cross**: Kirby Cross Cemetery, Holland Road, Kirby Cross, Essex (☎ 01255 831108; **e**: wcrem@wcrem.freeserve.co.uk); run by Tendring District Council. Contact details as for Weeley Crematorium below. All other details as for Clacton Cemetery above except for: No chapel. Grounds: Open aspect. Memorials: Lawn type, back-to-back.

• **Cem Loughton**: Loughton Cemetery, Church Lane, Loughton, Essex (☎ 020 8508 5164); run by Loughton Town Council, 1 Buckingham Court, Rectory Lane, Loughton, Essex IG10 2QZ (☎ 020 8508 4200, **e**: loughton_tc@compuserve.com, **w**: www.loughton-tc.gov.uk). No new interments. Plot for ashes only (25 years) incl. digging and burial £301 (double for non-residents). Public grave £154. To re-open 4ft 6ins plot £217 (resident of neighbouring parish £434; those outside the borough £651). ⏲ Two hours between services. Advisable to check as to which body containers they accept. No Chapel. Memorials: 'Height, width and material restrictions; appropriate design and wording.' Free assistance and advice for DIY funerals. 'Natural aspect in a built up area and well-kept. Helpful staff' (Ms Fuller/ Mrs Gilbert).

• ✪✪✪ **Cem Maldon**: Maldon Cemetery, London Road, Maldon, Essex (☎ 01621 875747; **w**: www.maldon.gov.uk); run by Maldon District Council, Princes Road, Maldon, Essex CM9 5DL (☎ 01621 875836). Plot (30 years, then renewable every ten years) £305 (£710 for non-residents) excl. digging and burial fee. A family organising a funeral themselves would need to make a private arrangement with one of the gravediggers locally (the cemetery can provide a list) – the cost is likely to be about £150. Maintenance: No charge. They accept home-made, wicker, bamboo and cardboard coffins, shrouds and body bags. ⏱ No restriction. Chapel: 'Simple Victorian chapel, refurbished 1996, seats 40. Available without extra charge.' Grounds: Rural, semi-woodland. Memorials: Traditional cemetery area subject to memorial regulations. No memorials on plots for woodland burials. Memorial wall for plaques. 'Our Victorian hand-pull bier has been renovated and brought into service' (Richard Yelland). There is also a Primrose Garden for children's burials and a woodland burial ground, see Chapter 6 for details. CFTB.

• **Crem Norwich**: St Faith's Crematorium, 75 Manor Road, Horsham St Faith, Norwich NR10 3LF (☎ 01603 897727); run by Dignity (UK) Ltd. Price: £325. ⏱ 45 mins (extra time £162.50). They accept home-made, cardboard, wicker and bamboo coffins, body bags and shrouds. Advice available for DIY funerals. Chapel: '1930s, church-like, with seating for 100; it has a PA and hearing loop system and a catafalque with curtains.' Grounds: '26 acres. Our Gardens of Remembrance are of particular peace and beauty. Saturday and Sunday services; opening hours may be extended to accommodate client preferences. 'No reasonable request is refused' (Mr C. M. Ward).

• **Cem Peterborough**: Eastfield Cemetery, Eastfield Road, Peterborough, Cambridgeshire (☎ 01733 262639; **w**: www.peterborough.gov.uk); run by Peterborough Bereavement Services, which also administers Broadway, Fletton, Stanground and Woodston Cemeteries (no new burials at Broadway, Stanground or Woodston). Plot (50 years) incl. digging and burial £835 (£1,835 for non-residents). They accept home-made, cardboard, wicker and bamboo coffins, body bags and shrouds. Advice available for DIY funerals. Small chapel at Fletton Cemetery. Grounds: 'Eastfield Cemetery has some conservation areas, vaults and a Muslim and a children's section. Broadway Cemetery has a conservation area, mausoleum, vaults, a children's section and a superb range of wild flowers.' Memorials: Lawn and traditional types. 'We work to ensure that each service is as individual and meaningful as possible' (Kate Day). For their woodland burial area at Fletton Cemetery, see Chapter 6. CFTB.

• **Crem Peterborough**: Peterborough Crematorium, Mowbray Road, North Bretton, Peterborough PE6 7JE (☎ 01733 262639; **w**: www.peterborough. gov.uk); run by Peterborough Bereavement Services. Price: £280. ⏱ 30 mins (extra time £125). They accept home-made, cardboard, wicker and bamboo coffins (subject to prior consultation). Advice available for DIY funerals. Chapel: Modern, church-like; glass wall looking out to semi-woodland. 'If we are asked for something unusual we consider why not? rather than just plain no. One gentleman organised a DIY funeral and stayed to watch throughout the whole, three-hour cremation process. This had been his uncle's wish. This is an example of how we will go out of our way to help' (Kate Day). CFTB.

• **Cem Southend-on-Sea**: Sutton Road Cemetery, Sutton Road, Southend-on-Sea, Essex SS2 5PX (☎ 01702 603907); run by Southend Borough Council. Plot (50, 75 or 100 years) incl. digging and burial £850 (same for non-residents; no interment fee for children). Maintenance: Fees for contracts. They accept home-made and cardboard coffins. ◔ 30 mins (extra time £49). Chapel: Stone church (1902) with new seating for 30. Non-denominational chapel also available. Grounds: Over 40 acres, with traditional and lawn sections. Memorials: Lawn type only. 'Picturesque cemetery with knowledgeable staff' (G. Green).

• **Crem Southend-on-Sea**: Southend-on-Sea Crematorium, Sutton Road, Southend-on-Sea, Essex SS2 5PX (☎ 01702 603908); run by Southend Borough Council. Price: £273 (no fee for children up to age 16). ◔ 40 mins (extra time £84). They accept home-made or cardboard coffins. Chapels: 'Two chapels, one church-like, the other modern. Good acoustics, hearing loop system installed, easy access, wheelchairs available on request.' Grounds: 'Gardens back onto open fields. Woodland memorial garden, densely planted with native trees, underplanted with hollies, ferns and dog-roses. A small stream emanates from a rock pool, through gardens into a large pond. However, there is a busy road at the front and small industrial area to the south. Environmental awareness and support for conservation' (G. Green).

• **Cem St Albans**: Hatfield Road Cemetery, Hatfield Road, St.Albans, Herts AL1 4LU (☎ 01727 819362; **e**: stalbans@cemeteries.freeserve.co.uk); run by St.Albans City & District Council. Plot (100 years) £344 (double for non-residents). ◔ Unlimited. Maintenance: Grass cutting free; £28 to £72 for bedding plants and maintenance. They accept home-made, cardboard, wicker and bamboo coffins, body bags and shrouds. Chapel: 'Victorian, built 1884, recently renovated and redecorated. Seats approx. 40. Lovely stained-glass window.' Memorials: Height restrictions of 3ft on lawn sections and 5ft on traditional sections. It is advisable to enquire beforehand regarding DIY funerals. 'Committed staff and reasonable prices' (Mrs Barbara Thompson). CFTB.

• **Cem St Albans**: London Road Cemetery, London Road, St Albans, Herts; run by St Albans City & District Council. Contact and other details as for previous entry, except for: Plot (100 years) £417; maintenance: £28 for lawn section planting (fees double for non-residents). No chapel. Memorials: Height restriction of 3ft on lawn sections. A natural burial area is planned.

• **Crem Upminster**: South Essex Crematorium, Okendon Road, Corbets Tey, Upminster, Essex RM14 2UY (☎ 01708 222188); run by London Borough of Havering. Price: £312 (with recorded or organ music). ◔ 30 mins (extra time £61.50). They accept home-made, cardboard, wicker and bamboo coffins. They will accept a DIY funeral with prior consultation. Chapels: 'North Chapel seats 30; the South Chapel has flexible seating for up to 100.' Grounds: 'Glades, seats, rosebeds and a columbarium' (Sharon Herbert). CFTB.

• **Crem Weeley**: Weeley Crematorium, Colchester Road, Weeley, Essex CO16 9JP (☎ 01255 831108; **e**: wcrem@wcrem.freeserve.co.uk); run by Tendring District Council. Price: £335. ⏰ 45 mins for the service (£105 for extra 45 mins). They accept home-made, cardboard, wicker and bamboo coffins. Six to ten mourners may view the coffin entering the cremator. Chapel: 'Modern brick with a warm feel. Seating is fixed and L-shaped.' Grounds: 'Park-like grounds. Fish pond with waterfall and fountain.' Free advice and leaflet for DIY funerals available. 'We are a small family-like team. I hope that friendliness and a caring attitude are conveyed to our visitors' (Janet Beech).

• **Cems Wisbech**: Marshland Smeeth Cemetery, Smeeth Road, Marshland St James; Upwell Cemetery, St Peters Road, Upwell; and Walpole St Andrew Cemetery, Police Road, Walpole St Andrew; all run by Borough Council of King's Lynn & West Norfolk. Details as for Gayton Road Cemetery above, except for: Plot (99 years) incl. digging and burial £563 (double for non-residents).

The South West

Comprising South Gloucestershire, Bristol, Bath and North East Somerset, North West Somerset, Somerset, Dorset, Devon, Cornwall.

• **Crem Barnstaple**: North Devon Crematorium, Old Torrington Road, Barnstaple, Devon EX31 3NW (☎ 01271 345431; **f**: 01271 328116); run by Joint Committee, North Devon & Torridge District Council. Price: £260. ⏰ 30 mins (extra time £53 per half hour). Provided they conform to regulations, home-made, cardboard, wicker and bamboo coffins, body bags and shrouds accepted. Due to limited space, only three mourners may view the coffin entering the cremator. Chapel: 'Opened in 1966. Serene atmosphere. Manual closure of gates. Seating for up to 100.' Grounds: 'Seven acres of secluded grounds with woodland on two sides. Mostly roses for dedication with trees and shrubs. Staff on duty 365 days of year for advice and information. Personal service when choosing a memorial. Brochure sent to all applicants' (Mr Graham Bailey).

• **Cem Bath**: Haycombe Cemetery, Haycombe Cemetery, Whiteway Road, Bath BA2 2RQ (☎ 01225 423682; **e**: cemeteries_crematorium@bathnes.gov.uk); run by Bath & North East Somerset Council. Plot (75 years) incl. digging and burial £880 (£440 extra for non-residents). They accept home-made, cardboard, wicker and bamboo coffins, body bags and shrouds. ⏰ 30 mins. Chapel: 'Built in 1930s of Bath stone. Dignified but light and airy. Refurbished in 1993.' Grounds: 'Overlooks a rural valley.' Memorials: 'Restrictions vary in different sections of Cemetery; in some areas there are no restrictions' (Rosemary Tiley). See Chapter 6 for details of the woodland burial section.

• **Crem Bath**: Haycombe Crematorium, Whiteway Road, Bath BA2 2RQ; run by Bath & North East Somerset Council (contact details as for previous entry). Price: £320 (same for non-residents). ⏰ 30 mins (20-minute service; Mon-Thurs: extra 30 mins £115). Free use of chapel for 30 mins before committal. They accept home-made, cardboard and wicker coffins, body bags and shrouds.

Chapel: Modern, with a glass wall overlooking rural valley. Grounds: Open countryside with beautiful views. 'The staff have mostly been here for a long time and take great pride in providing a good service' (Rosemary Tiley).

• ✪✪✪ **Cem Bournemouth**: North Cemetery, Strouden Ave, Bournemouth, Dorset BH8 9HX (☎ 01202 526238; **e**: crematorium@bournemouth.gov.uk); run by Bournemouth Borough Council. Plot (50 years) incl. digging and burial £580 (double for non-residents). Maintenance: £44 pa. ⏱ 60 mins. They accept home-made, cardboard, wicker and bamboo coffins, body bags and shrouds. Advice available for DIY funerals after prior consultation. Chapels: 'One chapel is small and intimate; the other large, more formal, housed within an attractive stone building forming part of the crematorium complex.' Grounds: 'Many established trees, nicely landscaped.' Memorials: Currently only natural stone is allowed but this is being reviewed. 'Regulations are regularly reviewed to ensure that as many requests as possible are met' (Julie Dunk). The council also runs three other cemeteries, for which the above details apply, except where stated: East Cemetery, Gloucester Road, Boscombe (late Victorian chapel); Kinson Cemetery, South Kinson Drive (modern chapel); and Wimborne Road Cemetery, Wimborne Road (late Victorian chapel with fine stained-glass windows). CFTB.

• **Crem Bournemouth**: Bournemouth Crematorium, Strouden Avenue, Bournemouth, Dorset BH8 9HX (☎ 01202 526238; **e**: crematorium@bournemouth.gov.uk); run by Bournemouth Borough Council. Price: £270.50. ⏱ 30 mins (double time £270.50). They accept home-made, cardboard, wicker and bamboo coffins, body bags and shrouds. Two non-denominational chapels with modernised fittings and disabled access: North Chapel seats 30; South Chapel seats 80-90. Grounds: 'Glades, seats, rosebeds and a columbarium' (Julie Dunk). CFTB.

• **Cem Bristol (1)**: Canford Cemetery, Canford Lane, Westbury-on-Trym, Bristol BS9 3PQ (☎ 0117 9038280; **e**: simon_westbrook@bristol-city.gov.uk); run by Bristol City Council. Plot incl. digging and burial £940. ⏱ 30 mins (extra time can be booked for a fee). They accept home-made, cardboard, wicker and bamboo coffins, body bags and shrouds. Advice available for DIY funerals. Chapel: Traditional, seating 100. Memorials: 'We try to maintain a flexible approach' (Simon Westbrook).

• **Crem Bristol (1)**: Canford Crematorium, Canford Lane, Westbury-on-Trym, Bristol BS9 3PQ; run by Bristol City Council. Contact and all other details as for previous entry, except for: Price: £325.

• **Cem Bristol (2)**: South Bristol Cemetery, Bridgewater Road, Bedminster Down, Bristol BS13 7AS; run by Bristol City Council (☎ 0117 9038330). Other details as for Canford Cemetery above. There is a natural burial ground, see Chapter 6 for details.

• **Crem Bristol (2)**: South Bristol Crematorium, Bridgewater Road, Bedminster Down, Bristol (contact details as for previous entry). Price: £325. ⏱ 30 mins (extra time may be booked). Grounds: 'Open plan, with picturesque views.'

• **Crem Bristol (3)**: Westerleigh Crematorium, Westerleigh Road, Westerleigh,

Bristol BS37 8QP (☎ 01179 374619); run by Crematoria Management Ltd. Price: £325. ⏱ 30 mins (extra time). They accept home-made, cardboard, wicker and bamboo coffins, body bags and shrouds. Advice available for DIY funerals. Chapel: Modern. Grounds: 'Open countryside' (P. J. Wilson).

• **Cem Clevedon:** Old Church Road Cemetery, Clevedon, Somerset; run by North Somerset Council. Contact and all other details, except for chapel & grounds, as for Ebdon Road Cemetery, under Weston-super-Mare, below.

• **Cem Crediton**: Crediton Cemetery, Old Tiverton Road, Crediton, Devon. Contact and all other details as for Tiverton Cemetery below except for: 'Rebuilt 15th Century chapel; small, quiet and peaceful'.

• **Cem Exeter**: Exwick Cemetery, Exwick Road, Exeter, Devon EX4 2BT. Contact and all other details as for next entry, except for: Chapel: 'Seats 70; volcanic stone and brick. Light and airy inside.' Grounds: 'Some fine angels. Attractive hillside setting in the newer areas with views across the valley to the cathedral and the city centre. A special section for stillborn and pre-term babies. Facilities for Muslim and Jewish burials available' (John O'Callaghan). For details of the woodland burial area, see Chapter 6.

• **Cem Exeter**: Higher Cemetery, St Marks Avenue, Heavitree, Exeter, Devon EX1 2PX (☎ 01392 265707, **e**: john.ocallaghan@exeter.gov.co.uk; **w**: www.exeter.gov.uk). Plot (30 years) incl. digging and burial £664. They accept home-made, cardboard, wicker and bamboo coffins. Advice available for DIY funerals. ⏱ 60 mins. Chapel: Seats 50, fee £64 ph. 'Of distinctive red-hued Heavitree stone. Old but cosy.' Grounds: '1860s urban cemetery with a Commonwealth war graves section, an older section laid out as a quiet garden and a small area for wildlife. Featured in the local historical society's trail.' Memorials: 'Within size restrictions' (John O'Callaghan). CFTB.

• **Cem Exeter**: Topsham Cemetery, Elm Grove Road, Topsham, Exeter, Devon EX3 OEJ. Contact and all other details as for previous entry, except for: Chapel: 'Seats 60; light, airy and comforting atmosphere with lovely stained-glass window.' Grounds: 'A typical small-town cemetery. Old-established trees and nearby allotments make this a very tranquil spot' (John O'Callaghan). CFTB.

• **Cem North Weston:** Portishead Cemetery, Clevedon Road, North Weston, Somerset. Contact and all other details, except for Chapel & Grounds, as for Ebdon Road Cemetery under Weston-super-Mare below.

• **Cems Plymouth**: Efford Cemetery, Efford Road, Plymouth, Devon PL3 6NG (☎ 01752 306104, **e**: fearnehj@plymouth.gov.uk); run by Plymouth City Council, Civic Centre, Plymouth PL1 2EW. For Weston Mill Cemetery, Ferndale Road, Plymouth PL2 2EP (☎ 01752 304837), the following details also apply. Plot incl. digging and burial £598.50 (plus £345.50 for a 25-year lease; 50- & 100-year leases also available). ⏱ 30 mins (extra time £28.50). They accept home-made, cardboard, wicker and bamboo coffins; other containers upon request. They will accept a body directly from a family for a DIY funeral. Chapel: 'Non-denominational, opened 1934. In recent years the building has been modernised but its original character has been preserved. Seating for 40 people.' Grounds: 'Formal, with some wooded areas.' Memorials: Older part of Cemetery: headstones and kerbstones; newer part: headstones only. 'Well laid-out grounds backing onto woodland. Plenty of trees and rose beds. Dedicated team of staff, all highly trained' (Jean Fearnehough). They are working to adopt the CFTB.

• **Crem Plymouth**: Efford Crematorium, Efford Road, Plymouth, Devon PL3 6NG (☎ 01752 306104); run by Plymouth City Council (who also run Weston Mill Crematorium, Ferndale Road, Plymouth PL2 2EP, ☎ 01752 304837; contact details as for previous entry). Price: £270.50 (non-residents £309). ◑ 30 mins (extra time £28.50). They accept home-made, cardboard, wicker and bamboo coffins. Up to four mourners may view the coffin entering the cremator by prior arrangement. Chapel: Non-denominational, static seating facing the front. Grounds: Well laid-out with rose beds. Easy access from the Devon Expressway and Tamar Bridge. 'Realistic pricing. Dedicated team of environmentally-aware staff. Varied choice of memorials' (Jean Fearnehough).

• **Crem Poole**: Poole Crematorium, Gravel Hill, Poole, Dorset BH17 9BQ (☎ 01202 602582); run by Poole Borough Council. Price: £286. ◑ 20 mins in a 30-minute period (extra time £60). They accept home-made, cardboard, wicker and bamboo coffins 'at the discretion of the registrar'. Advice available for DIY funerals. Chapel: 'Established in 1986, it has disabled access. Seating for 80, with room for 50 standing. There is an organist and a recorded music selection.' Grounds: 'We have a woodland scattering area themed to the four seasons, available free to users of the crematorium. Our working practices comply to the principles of the CFTB which we hope to adopt shortly' (Karen Fry).

• **Cem Poundbury**: Poundbury Cemetery, Poundbury Road, Dorchester, Dorset (☎ 01305 266861; f: 01305 266085; e: s.cheeseman@dorchester-tc.gov.uk); run by Dorchester Joint Burial Committee. Plot incl. digging and burial £527; ashes £170 (non-residents double). ◑ No time limit. All coffins accepted (wood must be from a sustainable source). Advice available for DIY funerals. No chapel. Grounds: 'Well-maintained, secure and pleasant site.' Memorials: 'Lawn: small headstones; traditonal: no restrictions' (Sue Cheeseman). CFTB.

• **Cem Sturminster Newton**: Sturminster Newton Cemetery, The Bridge, Sturminster Newton, Dorset DT10 2BS (☎ 01258 471351, e: towncouncil.stur minsternewton@virgin.net); run by Sturminster Newton Town Council, 1 Old Market Cross House, Market Cross, Sturminster Newton DT10 1AN. Plot (100 years) £225 excl. digging; £112.50 for garden of remembrance (fees double for non-residents). Maintenance: £20 pa. ◑ Unlimited. Chapel: Victorian (used as a chapel of rest, not available for services). Grounds: 'Open countryside, wildlife, good access and parking.' Memorials: Size restrictions; no restrictions on wording. 'Competitive pricing and surroundings' (Michael J. Fagg).

• **Cem Tavistock**: Tavistock Cemetery, 119 Plymouth Road, Tavistock, Devon PL19 8BY (☎ 01822 612799); run by Teignbridge District Council. Plot (100 years) £185 (£480 for non-parishioners) plus digging fee £138 (£360 for non-parishioners). There is a chapel. Advice available for DIY funerals. Grounds: 'The entry to the Cemetery is through a large archway, with a view to the chapel along an avenue of trees. There are many mature trees and shrubs. There is a cremated remains burial plot.' Memorials: Lawn type. 'The Cemetery was established in 1881 on land donated by the Duke of Bedford and is listed. There is a book of remembrance' (Brian Brown). See Chapter 6 for details of their natural burial ground. CFTB.

• **Cem Thornbury**: Thornbury Cemetery, Kington Lane, Thornbury, South Gloucestershire (☎ 01454 412103; e: towncouncil@thornburytown.free serve.co.uk); run by Thornbury Town Council. Plot (50 years) incl. digging and burial £310. Maintenance: £32 to £42 pa. They accept home-made, cardboard, wicker and bamboo coffins, body bags and shrouds. ⏲ No limit. Chapel: 'Small and intimate.' Grounds: 'Very well-maintained in rural surroundings.' Memorials: 'Appropriate designs', subject to approval. No kerbing. 'One of the best kept cemeteries in the west of England' (Mrs Judith Payne). Working towards adopting the CFTB.

• **Cem Tiverton**: Tiverton Cemetery, Park Road, Tiverton, Devon (☎ 01884 234343; e: bereavement services@middevon.gov.uk); run by Mid Devon District Council, Bereavement Services, Ailsa House, Tidcombe Lane, Tiverton, Devon EX16 4DZ. Plot (30 years) £340 (double for non-residents). Maintenance: £61 to 69 pa. ⏲ 30 mins (extra time by prior arrangement). They accept home-made, cardboard, wicker and bamboo coffins, body bags and shrouds; will consider all requests. Advice available for DIY funerals. Chapel: 'Small but quiet and peaceful.' Grounds: 'Semi rural location with views over rolling Devon Hills.' Memorials: No restrictions. 'We are keen to see diversification in terms of ceremony and memorialisation and will work with the bereaved to achieve their needs' (Ian Quance). CTFB.

• **Cem Torquay**: Torquay Cemetery, Hele Road, Torquay, Devon TQ2 7QG (☎ 01803 327768; e: janabritton@torbay.gov.uk); run by Torbay Council. Plot (100 years) incl. digging and burial £885 (double for non-residents). They accept home-made and cardboard coffins. ⏲ As required. Chapel: Modern, church-like. Grounds: 'Mature trees, clear views.' Memorials: No kerbs, no metal. 'Staff endeavour to make funerals as personal as possible. A woodland burial area is currently under review' (Pam Swain). CFTB.

• **Crem Torquay**: Torquay Crematorium, Hele Road, Torquay, Devon (☎ 01803 327768/ 329977; e: janabritton@torbay.gov.uk); run by Torbay Council. Price: £340. ⏲ Services booked at half-hourly intervals (extra time can be booked without charge). They accept home-made, bamboo, wicker or cardboard coffins; possibly others by arrangement. Chapel: 'Modern non-denominational; simply but tastefully decorated and with movable seating.' Grounds: Crematorium buildings set in landscaped cemetery. 'We are very willing to help families who wish to arrange their funerals with or without a funeral director. We will provide as much information and advice as we can. We try to meet individual needs as far as possible and encourage environmental awareness' (Jana Britton).

• **Cem Weston-super-Mare**: Ebdon Road Cemetery, Ebdon Road, Worle, Weston-super-Mare, North Somerset BS22 9NY (☎ 01934 511717); run by North Somerset Council. Also Milton Road Cemetery, Milton Road, Weston-super-Mare, for which the following details, except for Chapel & Grounds, also apply. Double plot to purchase (80 years) £495 (double for non-residents). Interment fees £415 single depth, £440 double depth and £490 triple depth (double for non-residents). Subject to inspection, they accept home-made, cardboard, wicker and bamboo coffins. Advice available for DIY funerals. Ⓦ 20 mins in chapel, no time limit at graveside. Chapel: See crematorium chapel below. Grounds: 'Attractive, well-maintained grounds with farmland on two sides.' Memorials: 'Within size restrictions.' 'The staff will do their utmost to facilitate special requests. Our working practices comply to the principles of the CFTB, which we hope to adopt shortly' (Russell Gadsby).

• **Crem Weston-super-Mare**: Weston-super-Mare Crematorium, Ebdon Road, Worle, Weston-super-Mare, North Somerset BS22 9NY (☎ 01934 511717); run by North Somerset Council. Price: £325. ⓌMU 20 mins for the service, ten mins for entry and exit (extra time £162.50). Subject to inspection, they accept home-made, cardboard, wicker and bamboo coffins. Advice available for DIY funerals. Chapel: 'Seats 75. Has CD, tape and organ facilities, a wheelchair and hearing loop.' Grounds: 'Attractive, well-maintained, with farmland on two sides. The crematorium opened in 1966. The staff will do their utmost to facilitate special requests' (Russell Gadsby). Adopting CFTB.

• ✪✪✪ **Crem Weymouth**: Weymouth Crematorium, Quibo Lane, Weymouth, Dorset DT4 0RR (☎ 01305 786984; **e**: crem@weymouth.gov.uk; **f**: 01305 761782); run by Weymouth & Portland Borough Council. Price: £291.50. Ⓦ 45 mins (extra time £82). They accept home-made, cardboard, wicker and bamboo coffins, body bags and shrouds. Advice available for DIY funerals. Chapel: Church-like, seats 80. Grounds: Large, lawned gardens of remembrance with trees and rose beds. 'Being a relatively quiet crematorium, we can spend time on details and go out of our way to meet the family's wishes' (Ian Morton). CFTB.

• **Cem Yeovil**: Yeovil Cemetery, Preston Road, Yeovil, Somerset (☎ 01935 476718); run by Yeovil Cemetery & Crematorium Committee. Plot (75 years) incl. digging and burial £459 (double for non-residents). Maintenance: £29 pa for basic upkeep; £41 extra for twice-yearly planting. Ⓦ No limit. They accept home-made and cardboard coffins, body bags and shrouds. People organising a DIY funeral may carry and lower the coffin, but the grave must be excavated by the Committee's contractors. Chapel: 'In keeping with the cemetery, with seating for 50 people and a ramp for disabled access.' Grounds: 'Formal' (Joy Coombs). CFTB.

• **Crem Yeovil**: Yeovil Crematorium, Bunford Lane, Yeovil, Somerset (☎ 01935 476718); run by Yeovil Cemetery & Crematorium Committee. Price: £270. Ⓦ 20 mins in a 30-minute period (extra time £113). They accept home-made, cardboard, wicker and bamboo coffins, body bags and shrouds, with prior consultation. Advice available for DIY funerals. Chapel: Stained-glass window; seating 70; disabled access and a braille box for the blind. Grounds: 'Set in a ten-acre site' (Joy Coombs). CFTB.

The South

Comprising Wiltshire, Berkshire, Surrey, Kent, Hampshire, West Sussex, East Sussex.

• **Cem Arundel**: Arundel Cemetery, Ford Road, Arundel, West Sussex. Grounds: 'Attractive view.' No chapel. Memorials: 'No restrictions.' All other details as for Littlehampton Cemetery below.

• **Cem Basingstoke**: Worting Road Cemetery, Worting Road, Basingstoke, Hampshire RG21 8YZ (☎ 01256 321737; **f**: 01256 843255; **e**: g.bowles@basing stoke.gov.uk). Plot (75 years) incl. digging and burial £325 (double for non-residents). They accept home-made, cardboard, bamboo and wicker coffins, body bags and shrouds. ① At least an hour (and as long as time allows). Chapel: 'Old English. Organ and CD facilities. £30 for up to one-hour service.' Grounds 'We have a natural (heritage) area and also provide outside columbarium niches for cremated remains on a 75-year lease for £200 incl. closure tablet.' Memorials: Lawn sections: headstone up to 3ft high (up to 5ft for additional fee); also size restrictions on kerb sections. 'We have not adopted the CFTB but we do work and provide the burial services in the spirit of it. We are more than happy to help those families arranging a burial without a funeral director' (Garry Bowles).

• **Crem Basingstoke**: Basingstoke Crematorium, Manor Farm, Stockbridge Road, North Waltham, Basingstoke RG25 2BA (☎ 01256 398783); run by Dignity (UK) Ltd. Price: £300. ① 45 mins (extra 45 mins £150). They accept home-made, cardboard, wicker and bamboo coffins, and may consider body bags and shrouds. Chapel: Brand-new, with a PA system and room for 100 seated; 20 standing. Grounds: 'Also very new with a rose garden and an ornamental lake. We follow the spirit of the CFTB' (Maureen Waddell).

• **Cem Beckenham**: Beckenham Cemetery, Elmers End Road, Beckenham, Kent BR3 4TD (☎ 020 8658 8775; **f**: 020 8663 3242); run by Dignity (UK) Ltd. Plot (100 years) incl. digging and burial £560. ① 30 mins (no limit at graveside). They accept home-made, cardboard and wicker coffins. Chapel: 'A very old-fashioned Victorian chapel, with seating for 70 people or standing room for 100.' Grounds: 32 acres, of which five acres are for a garden of remembrance and the rest are for graves. 'Services are available on both Saturdays and Sundays. There are very few restrictions' (Mr Nashfold).

• **Crem Beckenham**: Beckenham Crematorium, Elmers End Road, Beckenham, Kent BR3 4TD (☎ 020 8658 8775); run by Dignity (UK) Ltd. Price: £345. ① 30 mins (no limit at graveside). They accept home-made and cardboard coffins, and will consider wicker coffins. Other details as for above entry.

• **Cems Bognor**: Bognor Cemetery, Town Cross Avenue; and Chalcraft Cemetery, Chalcraft Lane, Bognor Regis, West Sussex ('attractive views, peaceful setting; no chapel'). Contact details as for Littlehampton Cemetery below.

• **Crem Brighton**: Woodvale (Brighton & Hove) Crematorium, Lewes Road, Brighton, East Sussex BN2 3QB (☎ 01273 604020; **e**: woodvale@brighton-hove.gov.uk); run by Brighton & Hove City Council. Price: from £175. ① 45 mins (extra 45 mins allowed, without charge, if required). They accept home-made, cardboard, wicker and bamboo coffins. Chapels: 'One consecrated with traditional church-like fittings and stained-glass window; the other inter-denominational and suitable for non-religious services. Both Victorian flint buildings with movable seating (80 each).' Grounds: 'Set in a grade II listed site in pleasantly landscaped grounds. A waterfall, stream, rockery, gardens, benches and flowering trees provide a peaceful and tranquil atmosphere. Awarded Charter Mark 1994, 1997 & 2000. Services are tailored to meet individual requirements and assistance will be given to families organising funerals without funeral directors. A free self-help guide is also available. Full facilities for the disabled are provided' (Stephen Horlock). See Chapter 6 for details of their woodland burial ground.

• **Cem Canterbury**: Canterbury City Cemetery, Westgate Court Avenue, Canterbury, Kent; run by Cemeteries Registrar, Architecture & Engineering, Canterbury City Council, Military Road, Canterbury, Kent CT1 1YW (☎ 01227 862490, e: leita.honey@canterbury.gov.uk; w: www.canterbury.gov.uk). Plot (50 years) incl. digging and burial £399 for new single plot, £295 for re-opening (double for non-residents). Maintenance: £100. They accept home-made, cardboard, wicker, bamboo and wood coffins (any wood to be from ecologically-managed woodlands). ⏰ 30 mins in chapel (chapel fee £57) and time to complete a graveside service with assistance in lowering the coffin. Chapel: 'Victorian with comfortable interior.' Grounds: 'Tree arbours and colourful bedding.' Memorials: Headstones not to exceed 4ft in height. 'We have not adopted the CFTB but we work towards its aims and objectives' (Leita Honey). There is also a small natural burial area, see Chapter 6 for details.

• **Crem Chatham**: Medway Crematorium, Robin Hood Lane (Upper), Chatham, Kent ME5 9QU (☎ 01634 861639; e: paul.edwards@medway.gov.uk); run by Medway Council. Price: £267 (double for non-residents). ⏰ 40 mins between services. They accept home-made, cardboard and wicker coffins; body bags and shrouds may be accepted 'by arrangement'. Chapel: Church-like, with movable seating for 60-70 people. Grounds: Semi-formal rose gardens and woodland. 'We aim to meet all cultural, religious and personal preferences where possible' (Paul Edwards). For details of their natural burial ground, see Chapter 6.

• **Cem Crawley**: Snell Hatch Cemetery, The Dingle, West Green, Crawley, West Sussex (☎ 01293 438503; e: burials@crawley.gov.uk); run by Crawley Borough Council, Town Hall, The Boulevard, Crawley RH10 1UZ. Plot (50 years) incl. digging and burial £366 (double for non-residents). They accept home-made, cardboard and wicker coffins, and shrouds. ⏰ Unlimited. No chapel. Grounds: 'Large open area with some mature trees.' Memorials: All materials allowed. Height and width restrictions: 2ft 10ins high, 2ft wide. Free advice for DIY funerals. 'Helpful and caring' (Barbara Conley).

• **Crem Crawley**: Surrey and Sussex Crematorium, Balcombe Road, Crawley RH10 3NQ (☎ 01293 882345); run by Dignity (UK) Ltd. Price: £345. ⏰ 30 mins (extra time can be booked). They accept home-made and cardboard coffins. Chapels: 'Church-like, 1950s architecture. One seating 90, the other 50.' Grounds: 'Attractive woodland glades' (Dennis Lambe).

• **Cem Dorking**: Dorking Cemetery, Reigate Road, Dorking, Surrey (☎ 01306 879299; **e**: carole.broug@mole-valley.gov.uk); run by Mole Valley District Council. Plot (50 years) incl. digging and burial £625; burial of ashes £217 (fees treble for non-residents). They accept home-made, cardboard and wicker coffins, and will accept a body directly from a family for a DIY funeral. ◑ No limit. Chapel: 'Built in 1855 of local materials, a fine example of Victorian Gothic architecture.' Grounds: 'The Cemetery contains native and exotic trees, and is sited at the foot of Box Hill, the famous Surrey landmark in the beautiful Mole Valley.' Memorials: Headstones up to 3ft high (ashes: 2ft high). 'An area of peace and tranquillity little changed since 1855' (Carole Brough).

• ✪✪✪ **Cems Eastbourne**: Langney Cemetery, Hide Hollow, Langney, Eastbourne, East Sussex BN23 8AE and Ocklynge Cemetery, Willingdon Road, Eastbourne BN21 1TL (☎ 01323 766536; **f**: 01323 760637; **e**: gillbewick@ eastbourne.gov.uk / cemeteries@eastbourne.gov.uk); both run by Eastbourne Borough Council. Plot (75 years) incl. digging and burial £540 (double for non-residents). They accept home-made, cardboard, wicker and bamboo coffins, suitable shrouds, and eco-friendly containers. ◑ Unlimited. Chapel: 'Victorian (1883), red brick, intimate.' Grounds: Well-kept. Memorials: 'No glass, wood, or plastic, otherwise most stone allowed.' Free advice available for DIY funerals. 'We offer a wide choice of graves, memorials and types of service, catering for many individual needs' (Mrs Gill Bewick). For details of the woodland burial area, see Chapter 6. CFTB.

• **Crem Eastbourne**: Eastbourne Crematorium, Hide Hollow, Langney, Eastbourne, East Sussex BN23 8AE (☎ 01323 761093); run by Eastbourne Borough Council (other contact details as for previous entry). Price: £300. ◑ 30 mins (extra time £80). They accept home-made, cardboard, wicker and bamboo coffins, and shrouds. Up to six mourners can view the coffin entering the cremator, by appointment. Chapel: '1960s fascia, secular, modern.' Grounds: 'Beautiful gardens with views to the sea.' A leaflet is being prepared for DIY funerals. 'All advice is free, memorial choices are varied. All staff are trained and all needs are met where possible. The grounds are well-kept and the buildings are being renovated to accommodate the needs of our visitors' (Mrs Gill Bewick). CFTB.

• **Cem Guildford**: Stoke New Cemetery, Stoughton Road, Guildford; run by Guildford Borough Council (contact details as for next entry). Plot incl. digging and burial: lawn-type £840; traditional £1,040. ◑ Unlimited. Chapel: Seats approx. 35 people and has a power point so that people may play CDs, tapes etc. Advice available for DIY funerals.

• **Crem Guildford**: Guildford Crematorium, Broadwater, New Pond Road, Godalming, Surrey, GU7 3DB (☎ 01483 444711; **f**: 01483 532 637; **e**: crematorium@guildford.gov.uk; **w**: www.guildford.gov.uk); run by Guildford Borough Council. Price: £295. ◑ 30 mins (extra time £120). They accept home-made, cardboard, wicker and bamboo coffins. Chapel: Modern, non-denominational, with seating for 100 people. Grounds: 'Open-fronted, well-maintained' (Keith Hendry). They follow the spirit of the CFTB.

• **Cem Hastings**: Hastings Borough Cemetery, The Ridge, Hastings, East Sussex TN34 2AE (☎ 01424 781302). Plot (50 years) incl. digging and burial £476 (double for non-residents). They accept home-made, cardboard, wicker and bamboo coffins. ① 25 mins maximum. Use of 'church-like' chapel £53. Grounds: As Crem below. Memorials: Headstones only, within size restrictions. 'Unrivalled views' (George Ford). There is a natural burial area in a quiet corner of the site, see Chapter 6 for details.

• **Crem Hastings**: Hastings Crematorium, 234 The Ridge, Hastings, East Sussex TN34 2AE (☎ 01424 781302). Price: £259. ① 30 mins (extra 30 mins £53). They accept home-made and cardboard coffins. Chapel: 1850s. Grounds: Trees, lawns and flower beds; 80 acres. 'On a hillside overlooking Rye Bay to the East, and the Sussex countryside to the North and West' (George Ford).

• **Cem Herne Bay**: Herne Bay Cemetery, off Canterbury Road, Herne, Herne Bay; run by Canterbury City Council (contact details and prices as for Canterbury City Cemetery above).

• **Crem Isle of Wight**: Isle of Wight Crematorium, Station Lane, Whippingham, East Cowes, Isle of Wight PO32 6NJ (☎ 01983 882288; **f**: 01983 883010); run by Isle of Wight Council. Price: £351 (or £425 for a double slot). ① 45 mins. They accept biodegradable coffins with a 'solid bottom'. Chapel: 'Typical 1960s with room for 120 people.' Grounds: 'Rural, wooded, peaceful' (Malcolm Houghton). In the process of adopting the CFTB.

• **Cem Kingston**: Kingston Cemetery, Bonner Hill Road, Kingston upon Thames, Surrey, KT1 3EZ (☎ 0208 546 4462; **f**: 0208 546 4463; **e**: howard.greenoff@rbk.gov.uk); run by the Royal Borough of Kingston, Bereavement Services, Bonner Hill Road, Kingston upon Thames, Surrey KT1 3EZ. Plot (75 years) incl. digging and burial £780; £635 for a lawn grave; £225 for a child's grave (no charge for burial of a child up to 16 years). All fees double for non-residents. ① Chapel service is shared with the crematorium (see below) at 40-minute intervals (extra time available). They accept home-made, cardboard, wicker and bamboo coffins, body bags and shrouds. Chapel: See Crem below. Memorials: Regulations are flexible, allowing for mausolea, wooden memorials, crosses, local artistic craft, ceramic plaques and colloquial inscriptions; only limitations are 'nothing likely to cause offence'. Free advice and leaflet available for families organising a DIY funeral. 'Staff can assist in arranging a funeral and have examples of available coffins. A remembrance chapel houses the children's book of remembrance, and a flower chapel is available' (Howard Greenoff). CFTB.

• ✪✪✪ **Crem Kingston**: Kingston Crematorium, Bonner Hill Road, Kingston upon Thames, Surrey, KT1 3EZ; run by Royal Borough of Kingston (contact details as for previous entry). Price: £305; or 'environmental cremation' available for £190 before 10am. ① 40 mins (extra time available). Acceptable containers as above. Chapel: 'Non-denominational with central descending catafalque. Mix of traditional padded pews and movable seats. Seats 50 with standing room for ten. For large attendances there are 'stage' speakers fully integrated with the induction loop along with the organ and lectern microphone.

Services may be recorded and a professional organist is available at no additional charge.' Free advice and leaflet available for DIY funerals. 'An electronic Book of Remembrance is available offering the opportunity to view entries any day of the year when the original book is off display. We can create a family memorial of up to 99 pages including film' (Howard Greenoff). CFTB.

• **Cem Littlehampton**: Littlehampton Cemetery, Horsham Road, Littlehampton, West Sussex; run by Arun District Council, Bognor Town Hall, Clarence Road, Bognor Regis, West Sussex PO21 1LD (☎ 01243 863141). Plot (75 years) incl. digging and burial £264 (double for non-residents). ⏲ 45 mins. They accept home-made, cardboard, wicker and bamboo coffins, body bags and shrouds. Chapel: 'Plain.' Grounds: 'Daffodils and crocuses are an attraction.' Memorials: 'Restrictions only on lawn section' (Dawn Gathergood).

• **Cem Maidstone**: Sutton Road Cemetery, Sutton Road, Maidstone, Kent ME15 9AF (☎ 01622 738172; **e**: bereavementservices@maidstone.gov.uk). Plot (30 years) incl. digging and burial £597 (£897 for non-residents). Maintenance: planting grave with heather £113, four-year term. They accept home-made, cardboard, wicker and bamboo coffins, and shrouds; 'anything different would require prior consultation'. ⏲ 90 mins (extra time may be booked without charge). Chapel: 'Built in 1850, with typical gargoyles, stained-glass, spire, etc.' Grounds: '49 acres of parkland with mature trees and a variety of lawn and general sections.' Memorials: Size restrictions. Lawn section: headstone only; general section: headstone, kerbs and vase. 'Good location, experienced staff and reasonable prices. A tree memorial may be sponsored, without plaques, and not adjacent to the grave. A natural burial ground is planned for the near future' (Mrs Debra Herbert-Evers). CFTB.

• **Crem Maidstone**: Vintners Park Crematorium, Bearsted Road, Maidstone, Kent ME14 5LG (☎ 01622 738172). Price: £295. ⏲ 30 mins (extra time £76). They accept biodegradable coffins. Up to six mourners may view the coffin entering the cremator. Chapel: Modern, bright, accommodating 80. Grounds: Surrounded by a conservation area, with formal gardens and a woodside walk.

• **Crem Morden**: North East Surrey Crematorium, Lower Morden Lane, Morden, Surrey SM4 4NU (☎ 020 8337 4835; **f**: 020 8337 8745; **e**: nescb-crematorium@talk21.com; **w**: www.nes-crematorium.org.uk). Price: £280. ⏲ 30 mins (extra time £78). They accept biodegradable coffins. Up to six mourners may view the coffin entering the cremator. Chapel: 'Converted late Victorian church, seats 85 in pews.' Grounds: '400-yard, poplar-lined drive and 3.5 acres of gardens.' Free advice and help with paperwork for DIY funerals. 'We have our own trained staff (no contractors) who take pride in their work and helping relatives' (J. E. Skinner).

• **Crem Portchester**: Portchester Crematorium, Upper Cornaway Lane, Portchester, Hampshire PO16 8NE (☎ 01329 822533); run by Portchester Crematorium Joint Committee. Price: £270. ⏲ 30 mins (extra time negotiable). They accept home-made and wicker coffins. Chapels: 'One built in 1958 seats 80; and the other, built in the 1980s, seats 44. Both have organ music available at extra charge.' Grounds: 'Natural gardens' (J. Clark). CFTB.

• **Cem Reading**: Henley Road Cemetery, All Hallows Road, Caversham, Reading, Berkshire RG4 5LP (☎ 0118 947 2433/ 4102). Plot (75 years) incl. digging and burial £914 (£2,054 for non-residents). They accept home-made and cardboard coffins. ⏱ 30 mins (extra time £96 per half hour). Chapel: See Crem below. Grounds: 'No traffic noise, park and farmland to the rear, mansion on the hillside.' Memorials: 'Tablet and headstone size restrictions for new graves.' They provide seven pages of guidance notes for families arranging funerals without funeral directors. 'Graves are individually numbered, making finding graves very easy' (Mrs Ruth Winch).

• **Crem Reading**: Reading Crematorium, All Hallows Road, Caversham, Reading, Berkshire RG4 5LP (contact details as for previous entry). Price: £294. ⏱ 30 mins (extra time £96). They accept home-made, cardboard, wicker and bamboo coffins. Chapels: 'Large 1930s chapel with excellent organ, interior of dome visible, seats 108; small, modern, brick and pine chapel, seats 26.' Grounds: 'Set in centre of 50-acre cemetery, with five-acre gardens of remembrance secluded by tall hedges.' Guidance notes for DIY funerals. 'We aim to meet all cultural, religious and personal preferences where possible' (Mrs Winch).

• **Cem Sevenoaks**: Greatness Park Cemetery, 194 Seal Road, Sevenoaks (☎ 01732 457565; **e**: council@sevenoakstown.gov.uk; **w**: www.sevenoaks.gov.uk); run by Sevenoaks Town Council, Town Council Offices, Bradbourne Vale Road, Sevenoaks, Kent TN13 3QG. Plot (75 years) incl. digging and burial £520. Maintenance: Lawn plot £49.25 pa; kerb £73.50. ⏱ 35 mins (extra time £50). They accept home-made, cardboard, wicker and bamboo coffins. Chapel: 'Built 1911: Bath stone and soft red brick.' Grounds: 'Hill-top site with commanding views of the North Downs, contains fine mature trees, cedars etc.' Memorials: Lawn type, maximum 2ft 6ins by 2ft x 1ft. Must be installed to NAMM standards. 'Flexible caring service, willing to consider all reasonable requests. Attractive mature site, space still available with no re-use issues at present' (Nicholas Cave).

• **Cem Surbiton**: Surbiton Cemetery, Lower Marsh Lane, Kingston upon Thames, Surrey, KT1 3BN (☎ 020 8546 4463); run by Kingston Bereavement Services. Details as for Kingston Cemetery above, except for: ⏱ Unlimited.

• **Cem Sutton**: Sutton Cemetery, Alcorn Close, off Oldfields Road (A217), Sutton, Surrey SM3 9PX (☎ 020 8644 9437; **f**: 0208 644 1373; **e**: don@suttoncemetery.freeserve.co.uk; **w**: www.sutton.gov.uk); run by Sutton Borough Council. Plot (50 years) incl. digging and burial £693. Maintenance: £92 pa. ⏱ 60 mins between bookings (extra time free 'with sufficient notice'). They accept home-made, cardboard, wicker and bamboo coffins, body bags and shrouds. Leaflets and advice for DIY funerals. Chapel: 'Victorian Gothic, warm and intimate with seating for 50-60. Disabled access.' Grounds: 'Well-maintained, secure and pleasant.' Memorials: Approved natural stone only, within size restrictions. 'Experienced and caring staff with our priorities given to the bereaved and the funeral service. Grave site viewing and selection, by appointment, very welcome' (Mr Don Ward). CFTB.

• **Crem Trowbridge**: West Wiltshire Crematorium, Devizes Road, Semington, Trowbridge BA14 6HL (☎ 01380 871101); run by Crematoria Management Ltd. Price: £320. ⏰ 30 mins (extra time at no charge). They accept home-made, cardboard, wicker and bamboo coffins, body bags and shrouds. Chapel: 'Natural stone, comfortable.' Grounds: 'Open countryside' (P. J. Wilson).

• **Cem Whitstable**: Whitstable Cemetery, off Mill Strood Road, Herne, Whitstable; run by Canterbury City Council (contact details and prices as for Canterbury City Cemetery above).

• **Cem Woking**: Brookwood Cemetery, Cemetery Pales, Woking, Surrey GU24 0BL (☎ 01483 472222; **f**: 01483 2223); run by Brookwood Cemetery Ltd. Plot (50 years) incl. digging and burial from £2,500 (various prices). Maintenance: £150 pa (12 visits per year). ⏰ As long as needed. They accept home-made, cardboard, wicker and bamboo coffins, body bags and shrouds. Advice available for DIY funerals. Chapel: Seats up to 50. Grounds: 'Vast 420-acre cemetery with beautiful trees and Victorian monuments.' Memorials: Virtually any design of memorial is allowed up to 3ft. 'One of the oldest cemeteries. We always use virgin ground for new interments and all graves remain undisturbed forever' (R. H. Guney). For details of the woodland burial area, see Chapter 6.

• **Cem Wokingham**: Easthampstead Park Cemetery, Nine Mile Ride, Wokingham, Berkshire RG40 3DW (☎ 01344 420314; **e:** cem.crem@bracknell-forest.gov.uk); run by Bracknell Forest Borough Council. Plot (75 years) incl. digging and burial £880 (£1,265 for non-residents). ⏰ 30 mins (extra time £140). They accept home-made, cardboard, wicker and bamboo coffins, body bags and shrouds. Advice available for DIY funerals. Chapel: 'Modern with wood panelling, seating 98 people. Organ, CD and tape machine.' Grounds: 'Landscaped, 22 acres, with pergolas and hanging baskets separating the lawned and traditional sections.' Memorials: Maximum height 3ft. Charter Mark winners in 1996 and 1999. 'We provide a staff member at every burial to oversee the funeral. The cemetery is set in Berkshire countryside. It is of a lawned style, offering traditional memorials and flat tablets' (Gary Fewkes). CFTB.

• **Crem Wokingham**: Easthampstead Park Crematorium, Nine Mile Ride, Wokingham, Berkshire RG40 3DW; run by Bracknell Forest Borough Council (contact details as for previous entry). Price: £300. ⏰ 30 mins (extra time £120). They accept home-made, cardboard and wicker coffins, and 'will consider' body bags and shrouds. Advice available for DIY funerals. Chapel: 'Modern and well-lit, seating 98.' 'Extensive memorialisation available' (Gary Fewkes). CFTB.

• **Cem Worthing**: Findon Cemetery, Findon By-Pass, Findon, Worthing, West Sussex. Grounds: 'Attractive views and peaceful setting.' No chapel. Memorials: No restrictions. All other details as for Littlehampton Cemetery above.

• **Crem Worthing**: Worthing Crematorium, Horsham Road, Findon, West Sussex BN14 0RQ (☎ 01903 872678; **f**: 01903 872051; **e**: Crematorium@ worthing.gov.uk; **w**: www.worthing.gov.uk); run by Worthing Borough Council. Price: £336. ⏰ 40 mins (extra time £40). They accept home-made, cardboard, wicker and bamboo coffins, body bags and shrouds. Chapel: '1960s, Swedish-style, non-denominational.' Grounds: 'Wildlife sanctuary. We also have spring, summer and autumn scattering glades for ashes. The local coroner's department and the mortuary department at Worthing Hospital are particularly helpful to people organising a DIY funeral' (Ian Rudkin).

Greater London region

Including old Middlesex. See also South region.

• **Cem: Alperton** Cemetery, Clifford Road, Alperton HA0 1AF (☎ 020 8902 2385; **f**: 020 8795 0273; **e**: langford@brent.gov.uk; **w**: www.brent.co.uk); run by London Borough of Brent. Plot (50 years) incl. digging and burial £1,635 (£817 extra for non-residents). Maintenance: Nil, or £84 if grave to be planted with flowering plants twice yearly. They accept cardboard, home-made and wicker coffins, and shrouds. ⏲ As long as required. Chapel: Simple brick chapel with Welsh slate roof and stained-glass windows. Grounds: 'A very pretty ten-acre cemetery with a nature reserve, bordering a canal and a golf course.' Memorials: No restrictions. 'Fees are fair and in line with competing cemeteries. Very peaceful, with an abundance of wildlife' (Bob Langford). They have a natural burial ground at Carpenders Park, see Chapter 6 for details. CFTB.

• **Cem Barking:** Rippleside Cemetery, Ripple Road, Barking, Essex IG11 9PF (☎ 020 8270 4740; **e**: damien.parker@lbbd.gov.uk); run by London Borough of Barking & Dagenham. Plot (50 years, residents only) incl. digging and burial £1,210. Maintenance: £50 pa, optional. They accept cardboard, home-made and wicker coffins, and shrouds. ⏲ 1 hour (£60 per additional hour). Chapel: 'Gothic style, interesting stained-glass windows.' Grounds: 'Classic Victorian design.' Memorials: 'Strict policy in lawn and traditional areas.' Free leaflets and advice for DIY funerals. 'Our sites are well-maintained, our staff well-qualified' (Damien Parker). They have plans for a natural burial ground. CFTB.

• **Cem: Bedfont** Cemetery, Bedfont Road, Bedfont, Middlesex (contact and all other details as for Feltham Cemetery below).

• **Cem: Camberwell** New Cemetery, Brenchley Gardens, London SE23 3RD (☎ 020 7639 3121; **e**: terry.connor@southwark.gov.uk); run by London Borough of Southwark. Plot (50 years) incl. digging and burial £1,063 (£3,246 for non-residents). Public grave £393. They accept home-made, cardboard, bamboo and wicker coffins. ⏲ 20 mins (extra time £100). Chapel: 'Plain, well-kept and regularly redecorated. Designed by Aston Webb, who designed Buckingham Palace.' Grounds: 'Well-kept formal gardens.' Memorials: Headstone only, natural stone, within size restrictions. 'Our prices are in line with other authorities' (Terry Connor). They also run the woodland burial area at Nunhead Cemetery, Linden Grove, see Chapter 6 for details.

• **Crem Camberwell**: Honor Oak Crematorium, Brockley Way, London SE23 3RD; run by London Borough of Southwark (contact details as for previous entry). Price: £276. ⏲ 20 mins (extra time £276). They accept home-made, cardboard, bamboo and wicker coffins, and will accept a body directly from a family. Up to six mourners may view the coffin entering the cremator. Chapel: 'Set in beautiful gardens; built in 1793, in a Greek Temple design. Catafalque is lowered into floor. Front-facing seating.' Grounds: Formal gardens. 'Our prices are cheaper than surrounding cremetoria. The chapel and floral display area has a ramp for disabled access. The public toilets are disabled-friendly' (Terry Connor).

• **Cem: Charlton** Cemetery, Cemetery Lane, London SE7 8DZ; run by London Borough of Greenwich, Greenwich Direct Services, Sun Yard, Archery Road, Eltham, London SE9 1HA (☎ 020 8856 0100). Plot (50 years) incl. digging and burial £910 (extra for non-residents, prices on request). Maintenance £50 pa; planting: £90 pa. ⏲ 20 mins (extra time available). Chapel: 'Small Victorian, with original fixtures and fittings.' Grounds: Well-maintained. Memorials: 2ft 6ins wide by 4ft high; kerbs 6ft 6ins by 2ft 6ins. 'No new graves except in the children's section' (Chris Barr).

• **Cem: Chingford** Mount Cemetery, Old Church Road, Chingford, London E4 6ST (☎ 020 8524 5030; f: 020 8523 7944); run by London Borough of Waltham Forest. Plot (75 years) incl. digging and burial £1,343 (new graves for residents only; double fees for non-residents in existing graves). ⏲ 30 mins (extra time can be booked without charge). They accept wicker and wooden home-made coffins. No chapel. Grounds: 'Large, older cemetery (1884), with lots of trees.' Memorials: Lawn-type headstones only, within size restrictions. 'We will accommodate all the wishes of all families to the best of our abilities within the limits of cemetery regulations' (John Billson). CFTB.

• **Cems: Chiswick** New Cemetery, Staveley Road, and Chiswick Old Cemetery, Corney Road, Chiswick; contact details as for Feltham Cemetery below.

• **Cem: City of London** Cemetery, Aldersbrook Road, London E12 5DQ (contact details as for next entry). Plot (100 years) incl. digging and burial £1,372. Maintenance: from £43 to £87 to wash & weed. ⏲ 30 mins (£100 per extra 15 mins). Memorials: 'Nine options ranging from catacomb and vault, to lawn and woodland. Restrictions depend on grave type. Rules and regulations available on request' (Mrs X. Naylor). Other details as for City of London Crematorium (following entry). See also natural burial entry in Chapter 6.

• **Crem: City of London** Crematorium, Aldersbrook Road, London E12 5DQ (☎ 020 8530 2151; f: 020 8530 1563; e: cityoflondoncemetery@corpoflon don.gov.uk; w: www.cityoflondon.gov.uk/cemetery); run by Corporation of London. Price: £222 (under 16 years free). ⏲ 30 mins (£100 per extra 15 mins). They accept home-made, cardboard, bamboo and wicker coffins. Up to 12 mourners may view the coffin entering the cremator. Chapels: Traditional Gothic and two modern. Grounds: 'Landscaped, with comfortable waiting rooms, refreshments and public toilets. Ample parking and disabled access.' Free advice and a leaflet available for DIY funerals. Winners of Cemetery of the Year 2001 and Green Flag award 2001 and 2002. 'The staff are trained and professional. Modern cremators ensure compliance with environmental require-ments' (Mrs X. Naylor). CFTB.

• ✪✪✪ **Cem: Croydon** Cemetery, Mitcham Road, Croydon CR9 3AT (☎ 020 8684 3877; e: bereavement@croydon.gov.uk; f: 020 8689 7795, w: www.croy don.gov.uk); run by Croydon Council Cemeteries & Crematorium Office. Plot (50 years) incl. digging and burial £1,602 (£707 extra for non-residents).

Maintenance: £46 or £80 pa. ⊕ 90 mins graveside and 30 mins in the chapel (extra chapel time £100). They accept biodegradable coffins, body bags and shrouds. They allow DIY funerals. Chapel: Traditional with modern music options. Memorials: Full memorials welcomed; no restrictions. 'Centrally located and aiming to meet the needs of the whole community. Dedicated and responsible staff with an innovative approach to customer service' (Ken West). The Council also runs Queens Road Cemetery, which will open for reclaimed graves in 2004. CFTB.

• **Crem: Croydon** Crematorium, Mitcham Road, Croydon (contact details as for previous entry). Price: £220. ⊕ 30 mins (extra time £100). They accept biodegradable coffins, body bags and shrouds. Up to five mourners may view the coffin entering the cremator. Leaflet for DIY funerals currently being prepared. Chapels: 'Traditional with modern music options.' Grounds: 'Landscaped, with award-winning water gardens, a large water feature and garden of remembrance' (Ken West). CFTB.

• **Cem Dagenham**: Eastbrookend Cemetery, The Chase, Dagenham. Contact and all other details as for Rippleside Cemetery under Barking above, except for: Chapel: 'Well-maintained brick chapel with bell tower.' Grounds: 'Surrounded by Eastbrookend Country Park and Chase Nature Reserve. There is an apiary.'

• **Cem: East Finchley** Cemetery, East End Road, London N2 0RZ (☎ 020 8567 0913; e: hanwell@cemcrem.com); managed for the City of Westminster by Cemetery Management Ltd (based at Hanwell Cemetery, see below). Plot (75 years) incl. digging and burial £745 (£1,275 extra for non-residents). They accept home-made, wicker, bamboo and cardboard coffins. ⊕ 45 mins in chapel. Chapel: 'Victorian, totally refurbished inside in 1992.' Grounds: 'Monumental memorials, Victorian architecture, exclusive location.' Memorials: 'Size restrictions; inscriptions and fittings must be approved' (Thomas McDowell).

• **Cem: East London** Cemetery (Co Ltd), Grange Road, Plaistow, London E13 OHB (☎ 020 7476 5109; e: supt@elond-cemetery.demon.co.uk; w: www.elond-cemetery.demon.co.uk). Plot (50 years) incl. digging and burial £1,400 (same for non-residents). Basic maintenance: £42 pa. ⊕ 30 mins.(£75 per extra 30 mins). They accept home-made, cardboard, wicker and bamboo coffins, and shrouds made rigid with plank. Advice and assistance with paperwork available for DIY funerals. Chapels: 'One Victorian with high roofs; one traditional Anglican style with magnificent stained-glass windows.' Grounds: 'Tree-lined avenues, tranquil and dignified setting.' Memorials: 'Size restrictions. Memorial masons must be registered with the Cemetery before they are allowed to work on site. A list of approved masons is available on request' (Paul Mallatratt).

• **Crem: East London** Crematorium, Grange Road, Plaistow, London E13 OHB. Price: £275. ⊕ 30 mins (£75 per extra 30 mins). They accept home-made, cardboard, wicker and bamboo coffins. Up to six mourners may view the coffin entering the cremator. Chapels: 'Modern, non-denominational, very comfortable, flexible seating. Recently refurbished. Organ, taped music and CD facilities. Option to record funeral service if desired.' Contact and all other details as for previous entry.

• **Cem: East Sheen** Cemetery, Sheen Road, Richmond, Surrey TW10 5BJ (☎ 020 8876 4511; **f**: 020 8878 8118; **w**: www.richmond.gov.uk). Administers similar cemeteries in Hampton, Mortlake, Teddington & Twickenham. Plot (50 years) incl. digging and burial £1,100 (£3,360 for non-residents). They accept home-made, cardboard and wicker coffins (subject to approval). ⏰ As long as required. Chapel: Non-denominational, seats 80. Grounds: 'Rural, in an urban environment.' Memorials: Lawn-style or traditional kerbed; natural stone, within size restrictions. 'We can provide cardboard coffins (for £121 plus VAT) and assistance' (Natasha Bradshaw). For details of the natural burial area, see Chapter 6.

• **Cem**: **Edmonton** Cemetery, Church Street, Edmonton, London N9 9HP (☎ 020 8360 2157); managed for London Borough of Enfield. Plot (100 years) incl. digging and burial £898 (£1,708 for non-residents). ⏰ 30 mins (only if the chapel is used, extra time may be booked for £43). Chapel: 'Victorian-Porte cochere.' Grounds: 'Well-kept.' Memorials: Lawn type, back-to-back or single rows; traditional headstones and kerbs in older sections. 'The staff have a caring attitude. We have a very low number of complaints' (Mrs M. Vetere).

• **Cem: Eltham** Cemetery, Rochester Way, Eltham, London SE9 2RF; run by London Borough of Greenwich. Contact and all details as for Charlton Cemetery above except for: Chapel: 'Brick, Gothic.' Grounds: 'A flat site with trees and plants on the edge of the pathways and edges of the grounds. Well-maintained.' Grounds contain Eltham Crematorium (see next entry).

• **Crem: Eltham** Crematorium, Crown Woods Way, Eltham, London SE9 2AZ (☎ 020 8850 7046; **f**: 020 8859 6991; **w**: www.greenwich.gov.uk); run by Greenwich, Bexley & Dartford Crematorium Joint Committee. Price: £280. ⏰ 30 mins (extra time £100). They accept home-made, cardboard, wicker and bamboo coffins. Up to ten mourners may view the coffin entering the cremator. Chapels: 'Modern, non-denominational: one built 1956 with flexible seating; the other built 1970 with fixed seating. Both chapels have an organ, music system and loop system for the hard of hearing.' Grounds: Beautiful enclosed garden of remembrance; lawns, herbaceous and shrub borders, a pond and waterfall with a woodland area. 'The caring and professional staff make every effort to meet the needs of the bereaved. They will provide advice and assistance with the paperwork for DIY funerals' (Crematorium Manager). CFTB.

• **Crem: Enfield** Crematorium, Great Cambridge Road, Enfield, London EN1 4DS (☎ 020 8363 8324); run by London Borough of Haringey. Price: £295. ⏰ 20 mins (extra time £140). They accept home-made, cardboard, wicker and bamboo coffins; shrouds and body bags 'would be considered'. Advice available for DIY funerals. Chapels: 'Pre-war, red brick, both seating 100 people.' Grounds: Attractive rock and water gardens. 'We provide a comprehensive and caring service' (Nigel Morgan). Adopting CFTB.

• **Cem: Feltham** Cemetery, Ashford Road, Feltham; run by Community Initiatives Partnership, Feltham Air Parcs Leisure Centre, Uxbridge Road, Hanworth, Middlesex TW13 5EG (☎ 020 8894 2677; **e**: info@cip.org.uk). Plot (60 years) incl. digging and burial £473 (treble for non-residents). Maintenance:

£52. ⏲ 45 mins (extra time no charge). They accept hand-made, cardboard, wicker and bamboo coffins, and shrouds. No chapel. Memorials: 'Few restrictions in traditional areas; lawn areas fairly restrictive' (Alan Rice). Adopting CFTB.
• **Cem**: **Hampstead** Cemetery, Fortune Green Road, West Hampstead, London NW6 1DR (☎ 020 8883 1231; **e**: cemeteries@camden.gov.uk); run by London Borough of Camden. No new graves available. They accept home-made, cardboard, wicker and bamboo coffins. ⏲ Unlimited. No chapel. Grounds: '20-acre site opened in 1876. Pleasant, fairly well-maintained with lots of Celtic crosses.' Memorials: Lawn style on lawn sections, otherwise flexible. 'Mature surroundings, excellent architecture' (Richard Baldwin).
• **Cem**: **Hanwell** Cemetery, 38 Uxbridge Road, London W7 3PP (☎ 020 8567 0913; **e**: hanwell@cemcrem.com); managed for the City of Westminster by Cemetery Management Ltd. Plot (75 years) incl. digging and burial £745 (£1,275 extra for non-residents). They accept home-made, cardboard, wicker and bamboo coffins. ⏲ 45 mins in chapel. Chapel: 'Victorian Gothic style with hammer beam roof. Renovated in 1994.' Grounds: 'Kept to a high standard. Grand avenue of cedars lining the main drive. There are always staff available 365 days a year to help with queries and to provide a safe atmosphere for families' (Thomas McDowell).
• **Cem: Hatton** Cemetery, Faggs Road, Feltham (contact details as for Feltham Cemetery above).
• **Crem: Hendon** Crematorium, Holders Hill Road, London NW7 1NB (☎ 020 8346 0657); run by London Borough of Barnet. Price: £260. ⏲ 45 mins (extra time £49). They accept home-made, cardboard, wicker and bamboo coffins, body bags and shrouds. Two traditional chapels seating 100 or 75 people. Grounds: 'Country churchyard set in 40 acres of wooded cemetery grounds. Practical, sympathetic and sensible service to the bereaved' (Maurice Salmon).
• **Cem Highgate** Cemetery, Swains Lane, London N6 6PJ (☎ 020 8340 1834; **e**: highgatec@tiscali.co.uk; **w**: www.highgate/cemetery.org). Prices available on request. They accept home-made and cardboard coffins. No chapel. Grounds: 'One of the most famous cemeteries in the world, with many eminent Victorians buried in grand style in a beautiful woodland setting. The Cemetery is a Grade II* listed site.' Memorials: 'Any memorial installed must reflect some sympathy with Highgate's historic status. As a privately-run charity, Highgate is able to offer a much more flexible service than most. For instance, within the limits imposed by available space, we would arrange woodland burial on individual request' (Mr Richard Quirk).
• **Crem: Honor Oak** Crematorium, Brockley Way, London SE23 3RD (☎ 020 639 3121; **f**: 020 7732 4075); run by London Borough of Southwark. Price: £276 (organist £29 extra). ⏲ 30 mins. They accept home-made, cardboard, wicker and bamboo coffins, body bags and shrouds. Chapel: 'Listed building, in a Grecian style, built in 1939. Seats 100 people. Christian symbols can be covered if desired.' Grounds: 'Formal gardens, shrubbery, wooded area, garden of remembrance, sports field and cemetery. The coffin is lowered on a catafalque to

symbolise the lowering of a coffin in a grave' (Terry Connor). Adopting CFTB.
• **Cems: Hounslow** Cemetery, Hanworth Road, and New Brentford Cemetery, Sutton Road, Hounslow, Middlesex (contact and all other details as for Feltham Cemetery above).
• **Cem Isleworth**: Isleworth Cemetery, Park Road, Isleworth, Middlesex (contact and all other details as for Feltham Cemetery above).
• **Crem: Islington** Crematorium, High Road, East Finchley, London N2 9AG (☎ 020 8883 1230; **f**: 020 8883 2784); run by London Borough of Islington. Price: £245 (£25 extra with organ music). ◷ 30 mins (extra time £100). They accept biodegradable coffins. Advice available for DIY funerals. Chapel: 'A light and warm 1930s building, with movable seating for 85 people.' Grounds: Garden of remembrance. Memorials: Various forms of memorial are permissible. 'Families are left to do their own thing. The crematorium follow the guidelines of the CFTB for improvement of their services, although we have not officially adopted it' (Crematorium Manager).
• **Cem**: **Kensal Green** (All Souls) Cemetery, Harrow Road, London W10 4RA (☎ 020 8969 0152; **f**: 020 8960 9744); run by General Cemetery Company. Plot (perpetuity) incl. digging and burial from £1,700. Maintenance, if required, from £64 pa. ◷ Up to an hour (extra by prior arrangement). They accept home-made, cardboard, wicker and bamboo coffins, and shrouds; 'whatever container is used must be made to an acceptable standard and have a long lasting means of identification'. Chapel: 'Greek style (Doric) with a grandiose feel and Victorian ambience.' Memorials: 'Few restrictions, all applications subject to scrutiny by our cemetery superintendent.' Grounds: 'Historic ambience, wonderful architecture and beautiful trees, plants and bird and animal life. Helpful and considerate staff, reasonable rates and good working practices. For families organising funerals without funeral directors, we provide as full co-operation and advice as possible. There is no extra charge for this' (David Burkett).
• **✪✪✪ Crem Kensal Green:** West London Crematorium, Kensal Green Cemetery, Harrow Road, London W10 4RA; run by General Cemetery Company (contact details as for previous entry). Price: £195 at 9am, 9.30am and 10am; rest of the day £295. ◷ 30 mins (extra time £195 per 30 mins by prior arrangement). They accept home-made (if smooth underneath), cardboard, wicker and bamboo coffins; shrouds and body bags must be opaque and attached to a board. Chapels: 'The East Chapel is in art deco style with oak pews and solid marble catafalque; the West is modern and light with light oak fixtures and catafalque.' Grounds: 'Trees, bushes, shrubs and seasonal flower beds; attractive and colourful the whole year round. Also a rose garden and lawns.' The Superintendent is a licensed FD who would be happy to help anyone trying to arrange a funeral on their own. There is no charge for this service. 'The aim of our crematorium staff is to provide a dignified and caring service to mourners, and to seek always to provide a service which they will remember. We aim to excel in customer service in every way possible' (David Burkett).
• **Cem**: **Lavender Hill** Cemetery, Cedar Road, Enfield, London EN2 OTH (☎ 020 8363 0608); run by Borough of Enfield. No new graves available, but the

Strayfield Road extension still has spaces. Plot (100 years) incl. digging and burial £701 (£1,708 for non-residents). ⏱ 30 mins (only if the chapel is used, extra time £43). Chapel: Victorian, Gothic. Grounds: Green belt. Memorials: Lawn-type, back-to-back or single rows; traditional headstones and kerbs on older sections. 'The Cemetery is extremely well-kept and the staff caring' (Mrs M. Vetere). A woodland burial area is planned, see Chapter 6 for details.
• **Cems Lewisham:** Hither Green Cemetery, Verdant Lane, London SE6 1TP (☎ 020 8698 4955, **e**: shirley.bishop@lewisham.gov.uk); run by London Borough of Lewisham, which also administers Brockley Cemetery, Brockley Road, London SE4 (no new graves); Grove Park Cemetery, Marvels Lane, London SE12 9PU; and Ladywell Cemetery, Ladywell Road, London SE13 (no new graves). Plot (50 years) incl. digging and burial £1,225 (quadruple for non-residents). They accept home-made, cardboard, wicker and bamboo coffins and, at Grove Park only, shrouds (if transported in coffins). ⏱ 60 to 90 mins (extra time negotiable). Chapels: Hither Green (Victorian); Grove Park (1930s); Ladywell & Brockley (none at present). Grounds: 'All the Cemeteries have an abundance of wildlife and a tranquil atmosphere.' Memorials: Size restrictions. See Chapter 6 for further details of the planned natural burial ground.
• **Crem: Lewisham** Crematorium, Verdant Lane, Catford, London SE6 1TP (☎ 020 8698 4955). Price: £283. ⏱ 30 mins (extra time £100). They accept home-made, cardboard, wicker and bamboo coffins. Chapel: Non-denominational. Grounds: Landscaped gardens of remembrance featuring a pond which attracts a wide variety of wildlife. 'We will always try to accommodate specific requests' (Shirley Bishop).
• **Cem: Manor Park** Cemetery, Manor Park Cemetery Company Ltd, Sebert Road, Forest Gate, London E7 0NP (☎ 020 8534 1486; **f**: 020 8519 1348; **e**: supt @manorpark15.fsbusiness.co.uk). Plot (50 years) incl. digging and burial: £800. ⏱ 30 mins (extra time £130). They accept home-made, cardboard and wicker coffins. Chapels: 'Traditional Kentish ragstone church design with original steeple dated 1874. Two chapels with tapestry wall-hangings.' Memorials: No restrictions for traditional grave area; height restrictions in lawn and public areas. Grounds: 'Wide drive-through cemetery: large area for flowers, attractive rose gardens, florist on site and a night security patrol. We have credit facilities available for pre-purchase of grave space' (Norman Stephens). There is a natural burial area, see Chapter 6 for details.
• **Crem: Manor Park** Crematorium , Manor Park Cemetery Company Ltd., Sebert Road, Forest Gate, London E7 0NP (☎ 020 8534 1486; **f**: 020 8519 1348; **e**: supt@manorpark15.fsbusiness.co.uk); run by Manor Park Cemetery Co Ltd. Price: £195 till 10.30am; £295 thereafter. ⏱ 30 mins (extra time can be booked). They accept home-made, cardboard, bamboo and wicker coffins. Large area for flowers. Other details as for previous entry.
• **Cem**: **Mill Hill** Cemetery, Milespit Hill, Mill Hill, London NW7 2RR (☎ 020 8567 0913; **e**: hanwell@cemcrem.com); managed for the City of Westminster by Cemetery Management Ltd (based at Hanwell Cemetery, see entry above). Plot (75 years) incl. digging and burial £745 (£1,275 extra for non-residents).

They accept biodegradable coffins. ⏲ 45 mins in chapel. Chapel: Modern redbrick. Grounds: 'Peaceful setting.' Memorials: 'Up to 3ft or 3ft 6ins in height. Portland stone is banned' (Thomas McDowell).

• **Crem: Mortlake** Crematorium, Kew Meadow Path, Richmond TW9 4EN (☎ 020 8876 8056). Price: £215 (£380 for a double slot). ⏲ 30 mins. They accept home-made, cardboard and wicker coffins; body bags and shrouds 'with prior consultation' only. Chapels: 'Comfortable ambience, non-sombre atmosphere.' Grounds: 'Overlooking River Thames' (Bob Coates).

• **Cem: New Southgate** Cemetery, Brunswick Park Road, London N11 1JJ (☎ 020 8361 1713; **e**: nsg@cemcrem.com; **w**: www.newsouthgate.com); run by New Southgate Cemetery & Crematorium Ltd, with all profits ploughed back into the site. Plot (50 years) incl. digging and burial £2,400. Maintenance: 'Range of services from £5 (plus cost of bouquet of flowers) to £145.' They accept home-made, cardboard, wicker and bamboo coffins, body bags and shrouds. ⏲ 30 mins (extra time £90). Chapel: '£90 per service. Built in 1858, with a high steeple and (screenable) ornate oak altar. Mourners are encouraged to donate flowers for the walls so that other funerals can benefit.' Grounds: 'One of the best selections of conifers in London, together with native trees. The Cemetery is used by Reform Jews and the Cypriot community. There are new Roman Catholic and Greek Orthodox sections.' Memorials: 'All new memorials must be supplied by the Cemetery for safety reasons. The Cemetery will make contributions of up to £2,000 for memorial designs with particular artistic merit. Flowers cover the bottom, head and corners of all graves. Special facilities provided as and when required' (Richard Evans). CFTB.

• **Crem: New Southgate** Crematorium, Brunswick Park Road, London N11 1JJ. Contact and all other details as for previous entry, except for: Price: £310. ⏲ 20 mins (extra time £75). Advice available for DIY funerals. Up to six mourners may view the coffin entering the cremator: 'The crematory has been decorated in a style which offers warmth and comfort to the bereaved. The cremators can accommodate coffins up to 36ins wide. There is a remembrance service in November and a Christmas carol service' (Richard Evans). CFTB.

• **Cem: Plumstead** Cemetery, Cemetery Road, Wickham Lane, Abbeywood, London SE2 0NS; run by London Borough of Greenwich. Contact and all other details as for Charlton Cemetery above, except for: Chapel: 'Victorian, well-maintained, with polished wooden floors and stained glass.' Grounds: 'Sited on a hillside. From the arched gateway the main path ascends to the chapels' (Chris Barr).

• **Cem Putney Vale** Cemetery, Stag Lane, Putney, London SW15 3DZ (☎ 020 8788 2113; **f**: 020 8785 3448; **e**: candrews@wandsworth.gov.uk; **w**: www.wandsworth.gov.uk); run by London Borough of Wandsworth, which also runs Wandsworth Cemetery, Magdelen Road, Earlsfield SW18 (new graves available); and Battersea New Cemetery, Lower Morden Lane, Morden, Surrey ('dedicated Muslim area'). Plot (40 years) incl. digging and burial £2,200 (£1,200 extra for non-residents). Maintenance: £120 pa. ⏲ 45 mins (extra time available). They accept biodegradable coffins and shrouds. Chapel: One modern, one traditional. Grounds: 'Scheduled high maintenance horticultural standards with a choice of grave plot.' Maintenance: Must not exceed the allocated dimensions of the plot (6ft 6ins x 2ft 6ins) or 5ft in height. Free advice for DIY funerals. 'We pride ourselves on delivering a quality, sensitive, caring service to all sections of the community. The public are encouraged to ask questions. The cemeteries complement the care provided by the staff' (Clive Andrews).

• **Crem: Putney Vale** Crematorium, Stag Lane, Putney, London SW15 3DZ. Contact and all other details as for previous entry, except for: Price: £263 (non-residents £336). ◐ 45 mins (extra time £150). They accept home-made, cardboard, wicker and bamboo coffins. Up to eight mourners may view the coffin entering the cremator. Grounds: 'Borders Wimbledon Common with a large, well-maintained garden of remembrance and babies memorial garden. The service encourages an open door policy, showing people around and answering any questions. The chapel can accommodate all religious denominations and provides facilities for the disabled' (Clive Andrews).

• **Cem: St Pancras** Cemetery, High Road, East Finchley, London N2 9AG; run by London Borough of Camden (☎ 020 8883 1231). Plot (60 years) incl. digging and burial £1,185 (double for non-residents). ◐ 30 mins (extra time free, by arrangement). They accept home-made, cardboard, wicker and bamboo coffins. Chapel: 'Gothic character, single spire, cruciform shape, cosy.' Grounds: 180-acre site opened in 1854., mature treed landscape. Memorials: 'Lawn style in lawn sections, otherwise flexible' (Richard Baldwin).

• **Crem: South London** Crematorium, The Garden of Remembrance, Rowan Road, London SW16 5JG (☎ 020 8679 4164). Price: £325. ◐ 45 mins (£100 to book an extra 45 mins). They accept cardboard and home-made coffins, and 'will consider' wicker coffins. Chapels: 'Edwardian, church-like, with seating for 60, and room for 100 standing.' Grounds: Formal gardens with mausolea at the front of the building. 'Services are available on both Saturdays and Sundays. There are very few restrictions' (Lee Snashfold).

• **Crem: South West Middlesex** Crematorium, Hounslow Road, Hanworth, Feltham, Middlesex TW13 5JH (☎ 020 8894 9001). Price: £140. ◐ 30 mins (extra time £105). They accept home-made, cardboard wicker and bamboo coffins, and body bags. Up to ten mourners may view the coffin entering the cremator. Chapel: 'Three traditional chapels seating 25, 80 and 150 respectively.' Grounds: 'Both formal and informal.' Free advice and assistance with the paperwork for DIY funerals. 'Very striking architecture; the grounds give a feeling of tranquillity and peace' (Peter Alan Cronshaw). CFTB.

• **Cem Warlingham:** Greenlawns Memorial Park, Chelsham Road, Warlingham, Surrey CR6 9EQ; run by Croydon Council (contact details as for Croydon Cemetery above). Plot (50 years) incl. digging and burial £1,147 (non-residents £707 extra). ◐ 90 mins at graveside. They accept biodegradable coffins, body bags and shrouds. Leaflet for DIY funerals. No chapel. Grounds: 'Lawn cemetery established as a park. A section has been set aside for use by our Muslim community. Dedicated and responsible staff' (Ken West). CFTB. Applying for planning permission for a natural burial ground.

• **Cem Watford**: Carpenders Park Lawn Cemetery, Oxhey Lane, Nr. Watford; run by London Borough of Brent, Brent Cemetery & Mortuary Service, Clifford Road, Alperton HA0 1AF (☎ 020 8902 2385; **f**: 020 8795 0273; **e**: langford@ brent.gov.uk). Plot (50 years) incl. digging and burial £1,635 (£2,452 for non-residents). Interment of ashes: £344 (£516 for non-residents). Maintenance: £84 for twice yearly planting. ⊙ Unlimited. They accept biodegradable coffins and shrouds. No chapel. Grounds: 'Countryside with mature woodland, a lake and a pond.' Memorials: Bronze plaques only in lawn section. 'Very peaceful, with an abundance of wildlife. Our fees are fair' (Bob Langford). CFTB. There is also a one-acre woodland burial area, see Chapter 6 for details.

• **Cem Whitton**: Borough Cemetery, Powdermill Lane, Whitton, Middlesex; contact and all other details as for Feltham Cemetery above.

• **Cems Willesden:** Paddington (Old) Cemetery, Willesden Lane, London NW6 (14th century style chapel; wildlife area, children's play and quiet area, bee-hives); and Willesden New Cemetery, Franklyn Road NW10 (old, established cemetery); both run by London Borough of Brent. Contact and all other details as for Watford entry above, except for: Memorials: No restrictions. A tree with memorial plaque can be planted and maintained for 15 years for £250. CFTB.

• **Cem: Woolwich** Cemetery, Kings Highway, Plumstead, London SE18 2DS; run by London Borough of Greenwich. Contact and other details as for Charlton Cemetery above, except for: Chapel: 'Brick, Early English style; on the brow of the hill.' Grounds: 'The old cemetery is an excellent example of how a Victorian cemetery can be adapted successfully into something like a country park whilst preserving its main features; the newer cemetery is on flat ground with very little landscaping but does have a Muslim section' (Chris Barr). A natural burial ground is planned, see Chapter 6 for details.

Scotland

• **✪✪✪ Cem Baldernock:** Baldernock Cemetery, Craigmaddie Road, Baldernock, East Dunbartonshire (☎ 0141 942 0363); run by East Dunbartonshire Council, Parks & Amenities, Broomhill Depot, Kilsyth Road, Kirkintilloch. Plot (perpetual) £745.50 (non-residents cannot purchase a plot). ⊙ Unlimited. They accept cardboard, wicker and bamboo coffins, and body bags. Free advice available for DIY funerals. No chapel, 'but the church is used for Church of Scotland congregation'. Memorials: 'Mostly lawn-type, back-to-back. Rules available on request.' Grounds: 'Rural cemetery surrounding a listed church. Some of the memorials date from 1600s' (Alan Copeland).

• **Cem Bearsden:** Langfaulds Cemetery, Baljaffrey Road, Bearsden, East Dunbartonshire (☎ 0141 931 5792). Contact and all other details as for previous entry, except for: Environmentally-friendly lair £798 (four lairs in a block). Chapel: Modern, non-denominational with movable religious symbols. Grounds: Maturing (cemetery opened 1995), well-landscaped. An area is set aside for meadowland burials.

• **Cem Bishopbriggs:** Cadder Cemetery, Crosshill Road, Bishopbriggs, East Dunbartonshire (☎ 0141 772 1977). Contact and all other details as for

Baldernock Cemetery above, except for: No chapel. 'Situated in the greenbelt on the edge of town. Panoramic views of the Campsie Hills. A pleasing blend of traditional (opened 1895) and a modern extension (opened 2001).'
• **Crem Buckie**: Moray Crematorium, Broadley, Clochan, Buckie, Aberdeenshire AB56 5HQ (☎ 01542 850488); run by Christies (Fochabers) Ltd. Price: £380. ◐ 25 mins (£65 per extra 20 mins). They accept cardboard, wicker and bamboo coffins. Four to six mourners may view the coffin entering the cremator, but only from within the chapel and by prior arrangement. Chapel: '19th century Gothic style church with a warm atmosphere. Non-denominational services often held. Seating on cushioned fixed pews.' Grounds: 'Set in six acres of garden: fountains, waterfalls and a koi-stocked pond with a hand-crafted bridge.' Memorials: A wide choice available, details available on request. 'We pride ourselves on offering our mourners a service second to none. We encourage clients to come and see us prior to their service (by appointment) so that we can discuss the sequence of events and any special requirements they may have regarding music or facilities for disabled mourners' (Manager).
• **Cem Edinburgh**: Seafield Cemetery, Seafield Place, Edinburgh EH6 7QP (☎ 0131 554 1500). Plot £850. They accept cardboard and wicker coffins and ecopods. Chapel: 1930s listed art-deco building with original interior and pipe organ. Grounds: Peaceful setting with many mature and stunning trees. Free advice and leaflet available for DIY funerals.
• **✪✪✪ Crem Edinburgh (1)**: Seafield Crematorium, Seafield Road, Leith, Midlothian EH6 7LE (☎ 0131 554 3496). All other details as for previous entry, except for: Price £360 (no charge for children under 16). ◐ bookings on the hour, 40 mins service time (£150 per extra hour). Eight mourners at a time may view the coffin entering the cremator. 'The staff are keen to help the family in any way possible and to provide a very personalised funeral service' (Jane Darby).
• **Crem Edinburgh (2)**: Mortonhall Crematorium, 30 Howdenhall Road, Edinburgh EH16 6TX (☎ 0131 664 4314). Price: £369.77 for 40 mins (Pentland Chapel, seats 60); or £442-90 for 60 mins (Main Chapel, high ceilings, piped organ, seats 300). Both chapels designed by Sir Basil Spence. They accept cardboard coffins. Grounds: Mature woodland, lawns and mounds. 'Memorial plaques available from £400' (George Bell).
• **Cem Kirkintilloch:** Old Aisle Cemetery, Old Aisle Road, Kirkintilloch, East Dunbartonshire (☎ 0141 776 2330). Contact and all other details as for Baldernock Cemetery above, except for: No chapel. 'Well-maintained lawn cemetery with an old wooded churchyard area that is returned to native flora.'
• **Cem Lennoxtown:** Campsie Cemetery, Main Street Lennoxtown, East Dunbartonshire (☎ 01360 311127). Contact and all other details as for Baldernock Cemetery above, except for: No chapel. Grounds: 'Rural setting with panoramic views of the Campsie Hills. Well-maintained, well-wooded churchyard surrounded by three extensions.'
• **Crem Masonhill**: Masonhill Crematorium, Masonhill, By Ayr, South Ayrshire KA6 6EN (☎ 01292 266051; **f**: 01292 610096). Price: £273. ◐ 30 mins (extra slot £242). They accept home-made, cardboard, wicker and bamboo

coffins, and will consider shrouds. Chapel: 1960s, non-denominational, seating 154. Grounds: Open country, established trees. 'The service will adapt to meet the needs of the bereaved' (Manager). Natural burial ground proposed for 2004.

• **Crem Perth**: Perth Crematorium, Crieff Road, Perth PH1 2PE (☎ 01738 625068; **e**: dpmartin@pkc.gov.uk); run by Perth & Kinross Council. Price: £350. ◔ 45 mins between each service (extra time £100). They accept home-made, cardboard, wicker and bamboo coffins, body bags and shrouds. Chapel: 'Built in 1962: wooden beams, wooden floors; seats 156.' Non-removable cross. Grounds: 'Lovely, landscaped. This is the most unusual crematorium in Scotland. The gates in the chapel by the coffin close manually, so the family can ceremonially close the gates at the committal if they wish. There is a family waiting area adjacent to the entrance foyer of the crematorium. We are always looking for further improvements to give the best possible service' (Donald Martin).

• **Cems Ross & Cromarty**: For a full list of burial grounds in the following Service Points, please contact the Highland Council, Council Offices, High Street, Dingwall IV15 9QN (☎ 01349 868429, **e**: katrina.taylor@ highland.gov.uk): Fortrose (Black Isle), Tain (Easter Ross), Poolewe (West Coast), Muir of Ord (Black Isle), Alness (Easter Ross). Dingwall (Dingwall Area), Locharron (West Coast), Ullapool (West Coast), and Invergordon (Easter Ross). Plot (perpetual) £206. ◔ Unlimited. They accept home-made, cardboard, wicker and bamboo coffins. No chapels. They will accept a body directly from a family for a DIY funeral.

Northern Ireland

• **Crem Belfast**: City of Belfast Crematorium, 129 Ballygowan Road, Crossnacreevy, Belfast, Northern Ireland BT5 7TZ (☎ 028 9044 8342; **w**: www.belfastcrematorium.co.uk). Price: £140 (double for non-residents). ◔ 30 mins (extra time can be booked without charge). They accept home-made, cardboard, wicker and bamboo coffins, body bags and shrouds. Advice available for DIY funerals. Chapel: 'Modern, church-like, but without religious symbolism.' Grounds: Beautiful lawns and memorial trees. 'Nothing is too much trouble for our staff and every family, regardless of their circumstances or background, is treated with courtesy and respect. Families who wish to carry out their loved one's funeral arrangements themselves are given help and encouragement by all the staff. We have a new waiting room facility with coffee shop. We can also provide catering for funeral services at the crematorium' (Mrs Sharon McCloy). CFTB.

Chapter 9

HOW TO SET UP A NATURAL BURIAL GROUND

The most important part of our woodland burial ground is the people who use our facilities and the reason why. We must obviously be aware of business plans, health and safety, maintenance, planting, administration, but never forget the true reason for our facility: for people who live and people who die. We are responsible for helping families deal with a very emotional and intimate situation. No one can stop what may have happened, but we can certainly provide a facility that may help the family feel more comfortable and accept their loss.

Wendy Pratt, Tarn Moor Memorial Woodland, Skipton.

The Natural Death Centre, cemeteries manager Ken West MBE, and others have for over a decade publicly promoted the concept of natural burial grounds – where a tree or wild flowers are planted instead of having a headstone. Such a site provides an elegant solution to a number of problems:

• Cemeteries in many areas are filled to capacity – and when visits to graves cease, the cemeteries could be destroyed to make way for building development.

• It would not be desirable to continue for centuries into the future covering the countryside with row upon row of headstones. Furthermore, headstones can become dangerous and are very costly to maintain.

• Burial has become pricier than cremation, particularly in and around cities.

• Cremation causes pollution and adds to the greenhouse effect.

• Crematoria are generally bleak places in which to hold funerals.

• Natural burial grounds are less costly to develop than crematoria.

• The planet needs more trees.

• People are seeking less expensive funerals.

• Natural burials organised by family and friends, without necessarily using funeral directors, are more therapeutic for those who are grieving than a short impersonal service in a crematorium.

• Farmers need to diversify to bring in more sources of income – many have land for which they are paid very little under the set aside scheme.

• People prefer burials in beautiful rural settings.

• Natural burial grounds will provide a refuge for wildlife.

• The Green generation – Friends of the Earth supporters and the like – will not want to cause pollution with their deaths. They will be attracted by the concept of 'giving the body back to nature'. As Jonathon Porritt puts it: 'The combination of built-in fertiliser, plus unlimited tender loving care from the relatives, would pretty well guarantee a thriving woodland in next to no time.'

The Centre made these points in a number of media interviews from 1993 onwards. Farmers were not slow to respond to the challenge. The Centre also gave a talk to the Institute of Burial and Cremation Authorities, urging that every local authority should follow the example of Carlisle and set up a natural burial ground within its area. Again, progress has been rapid.

The first Church of England woodland burial ground opened in Cambridgeshire in 2001. In 2003, bishops from nine other dioceses met to discuss the setting up of similar sites across the country. It was hoped that other charitable and nonprofit bodies such as the National Trust, the Woodland Trust, and the Forestry Commission would follow suit, and also start making provision for natural burial. In this instance, however, progress has been more cautious, with the Woodland Trust, for example, deciding not to develop any such burial grounds within its land for the time being.

Incidentally, 'natural burial grounds' has become the accepted general term for these new sites; woodland is just one sort of habitat being created, and does not convey the diversity of meadows and pastures that are being used.

The rate at which new natural burial grounds are opening is impressive. By 1996 there were 17 such grounds known to the Natural Death Centre; by 1997 there were 52; by 2000 there were 90; and by July 2003 there were 182 (of these, 45 are at various stages in the planning process).

Of these 182 natural burial grounds (all of which are detailed in Chapter 6), 115 are run by local authorities, 57 are run as businesses by farmers, private individuals or companies, and ten are run as charitable or non-profit concerns.

The cost of a grave, including the digging and usually a tree, ranges from £172 at Seaton in Devon to £1,900 at Brookwood Cemetery in Surrey. The average cost is £612.68. The average cost for the local authority-run sites is £631.76 (with most charging considerably more for non-residents); for the sites run as businesses the average cost is £577.36.

The preferred form of funeral in 40 years?

A recent study suggests that, at the lowest estimate, 1,270 natural burials took place in the UK in 2002; approximately 0.2 per cent of the total number of burials and cremations that year. The study concluded:

> Government policy makers and those within the industry should be aware that green burial is currently in demand and the demand is rising. This research has shown that the green burial movement has grown three times as fast as the cremation industry from its inception. It means that within 40 years green burial could be the most popular form of funeral.
>
> *'Green burials: Is there a growing demand?', Masters dissertation; Kelly Green, 32 Annesdale, Ely, Cambs CB7 4BN (☎ 01353 612627).*

The Association of Natural Burial Grounds

In 1994, the Natural Death Centre set up an Association of Natural Burial Grounds in order: (a) to put forward a Code of Practice for its members to adhere to, so that potential clients approaching such a burial ground can be more confident that it reaches these standards; (b) to help members through planning and other hurdles; (c) to help reassure neighbours of potential sites that they have nothing to fear; (d) to refer members to legal, ecological and other advice; (e) to provide information for members on obtaining coffins and other funeral supplies; (f) to promote the concept of using land for Natural Burial Grounds; (g) to provide publicity leaflets, information and a referral service for the public concerning individual sites; (h) to help publicise and defend the movement in the media and with the government and local authorities.

Membership, whether full membership or provisional applicant membership, costs £50 per annum (with cheques payable to 'NDC') although members are also encouraged to pay one per cent of the ground's gross income to the Natural Death Centre, a project of the educational charity, the Nicholas Albery Foundation (registered charity number 1091396).

To be allowed to become a full member of the Association, a natural burial ground must be willing to allow the use of biodegradable coffins; it must allow families to organise a funeral without a funeral director if they so wish; it must safeguard funds paid in advance; it must guarantee long-term security for the graves and the wildlife; and it must manage its site ecologically.

The Association relies primarily on the probity of statements made by its members and on feedback from the public, as it does not yet have the resources for regular site inspections.

The Association of Natural Burial Grounds' Code of Practice

• Association members agree to take all reasonable steps for the conservation of local wildlife and archaeological sites and to manage their sites according to sound and consistent ecological principles. (Written evidence must be provided to the Association that the views of local or national bona fide wildlife and archaeological organisations have been sought and that plans have been modified as necessary to take account of any objections.)

• Association members must be in a position to guarantee the long-term security of both the graves and the wildlife, and have a satisfactory plan for when the site reaches its capacity. (Except for local authority sites, written evidence must be provided as to freehold ownership, any mortgages on the site, the legal title that clients receive, any planned transfer of the site to a wildlife charity or other relevant factors. Give full details of the long-term security offered to clients.)

• Association members other than local authority sites must satisfy the Association as to the quality, financial probity and non-indebtedness and relevant qualifications of their directors, trustees, managing body or similar. (Adequate references must also be provided.)

• Association members accept for burial bodies whether wrapped in a shroud or placed in a cardboard or wooden coffin or alternative container or wrapping, provided these are environmentally acceptable.

• Association members will not require that a funeral director be used. Those using the Natural Burial Ground will be informed that they may organise the funeral themselves, including conducting any service. They may do a token amount of digging or dig a single depth grave, subject to any equipment, training, safety or regulatory constraints; and they may help with filling in the grave.

• Association members will keep a permanent record of exactly where each grave is. A copy of the burial ground register entry will be made available to the client and the register will be open for public inspection.

• Association members will either sell coffins and shrouds to clients or provide information as to where these can be obtained.

• Association members, whose charges must be fair and reasonable, will provide fully itemised price lists for potential clients on request, and will also reveal these prices on the telephone on request.

• Association members will provide a copy of this Code of Practice to clients using their services, and will have copies available on request for others.

• Association members will provide each client using their services with a feedback form, either the site's own form or the Association's form, asking for the client's comments on the service provided and for any suggested improvements, with a request that a copy of the feedback form be sent direct to the Association. This feedback form is to include the address and phone number of the Association and to note that any complaints can be sent to the Association.

• Association members, if taking money for funerals in advance, agree to abide by the Financial Services and Markets Act 2000 Regulation of Funeral Plan Contracts.

• Association members accept that in the event of a complaint from a client that is not dealt with to the Association's satisfaction within three months of the complaint being made, the Natural Burial Ground's membership will cease without refund. A serious complaint may result in immediate suspension of membership whilst the complaint is investigated.

• Before membership is granted or renewed, the Association may require further evidence on the above or any other relevant matters.

• Provisional Association members must provide the information required to convert to full membership within a year of their site opening.

The Association of Natural Burial Grounds
c/o The Natural Death Centre (see Resources).

Advice for those setting up a natural burial ground

The main obstacle facing any individual or group wanting to set up a relatively large scale natural burial ground is likely to be obtaining planning permission. Several grounds have only won permission on appeal; the Mowthorpe Independent Garden of Rest, which is located in an Area of Outstanding Natural Beauty in North Yorkshire, was awarded £20,000 costs against the local authority in its successful appeal against refusal of planning permission. Local objections can be ferocious and irrational, fuelled by fear of death and the taboos surrounding the subject. Applicants who want to spare themselves a long-drawn out process and the hostility of their neighbours would do well to choose a site not overlooked by neighbours and where neighbours will not even see the funeral cars. Even to be invisible may not help them sufficiently however: the landscape officer in one application reported that even though the site could not be seen from the road, the mere knowledge that the site was there, would make driving past it a 'depressing experience' – what a contrast with Victorian days when to have picnics in cemeteries was a quite normal occurrence.

• Applicants might also be well advised, if they have a choice between forecasting for 700 burials a year or for 50 burials, to go for the smaller number initially; likewise, if there is a choice between applying for the whole property of 50 acres to become a burial ground, or for a mere seven-acre field within it, to apply for the smaller site. The burial ground will take many years to fill up and by then the momentum in favour of such developments will be that much greater than it is now. In the meantime, a small site may arouse fewer passions.

• Applicants should also choose a site where the council cannot claim that access from the road will be dangerous or the car-parking inadequate and they should seek the advice of council officers at an early stage.

• But even when the council officers support an application, the applicant should be wary if there is local opposition. Local petitions and letters against the applicant need to be matched by petitions and letters in favour.

• It could also be good tactics to arrange a five-minute meeting with each councillor on the relevant planning committee to show them your plans, to answer any doubts that they may have and to let them see that you are not the devil incarnate. Produce a detailed landscaping plan and illustrate how the site will look when the trees are mature. At one planning meeting a site was rejected, with one councillor remarking: 'The trees are small, it doesn't look like a wood', not seeming to realise that it is in the nature of trees to grow bigger.

• To find a natural burial site to buy, it might be worth approaching an agent dealing in woodland such as John Clegg & Co (☎ 01844 215800; please note that they do *not* sell individual plots for burial).

• John Bradfield of the A. B. Welfare and Wildlife Trust is wary of commercial burial projects, 'as some have unsound foundations and most commercial cemeteries started in the 19th century became bankrupt'. He will give free advice to credible wildlife charities thinking of starting natural burial projects. 'Initial enquiries should always be in writing,' he stresses, 'giving the charity registration number'.

Questions from local people

The following are some of the typically probing questions that a proposed natural burial ground aroused and that were sent in by local objectors to their planning department. The list will give those proposing to set up grounds food for thought.

• What are the management plans for the site, who will retain the long-term maintenance of the site, what assurances are there against the site falling into disrepair, who will look after the site when it reaches capacity?

• Will be the gates be opened or locked? Will there be any form of security?

• How many people will be employed at the site? How will the graves be dug?

• Where will the machinery and tools be stored?

• Are there any buildings, structures (eg storage buildings), shelters, benches, memorials, etc, proposed for the future?

• How are bodies transported from the car park to the graves and what are they carried in?

• Is it only for human remains or would animals and pets be buried on the site?

• What evidence do you have of only one burial per fortnight? How long will the site take to reach capacity?

• What boundary fencing is proposed? How will the grass be cut? Who will see to the removal of dead flowers and rubbish?

• What evidence is there of the demand or need for this site?

• What is the total number of graves that the site will hold?

• From where will the site be administered?

• Will the scattering of ashes occur on the site, if so exactly where?

• What evidence have you to demonstrate that there will be no contamination of any watercourses?

• What external lighting is proposed?

• What civil law exists over the establishment and use of the burial ground?

• What is the proposed tree planting density for the site? (The indicative plans do not allow the trees to reach full maturity.)

• The site does not benefit from public transport provision. Have any plans been made or provided to reduce the need for everyone visiting the site to use a private vehicle?

• What signage is proposed for the site?

Advice from existing sites

Additional tips have been sent in by existing natural burial grounds:

Several correspondents suggest that the first person to get on your side is the local vicar, then the chair of the parish council, before approaching bodies like the Environment Agency (EA). Linda Durman of Yealmpton Woodland Burial in Devon says 'it is a huge advantage if you have a letter of support from the Church of England when applying for planning approval'. Once you have an outline letter from the Environment Agency saying that they cannot see any immediate objection, you can then spend the money on a planning application.

One cemetery registrar adds that, at the earliest opportunity, groups should meet not only with council people and local clergy but also with the local authority cemetery and crematorium people – you need to explain that you are not in competition but are offering an alternative service. When choosing a site, groups should consider whether the area floods or has water problems. Have a colour plan drawn up and put on display, with permission, in local authority buildings and the town hall, hold meetings with the local press and public to smooth out problems before a planning application is submitted.

Another correspondent advises that the site must be acceptable to the EA. Apply for a change to mixed use if the site is presently farmland. She emphasises the points made above that 'local people need to know what is happening or they will imagine the worst – always!' and that access must be easy and acceptable to the highway authorities. Wendy Pratt of Tarn Moor Memorial Woodland in North Yorkshire adds, 'Before putting in any plans, we did all the ground work by meeting the highways department on site, to assess the proposed entrance. If the site lines are not acceptable, the whole thing could be a non-starter and complete waste of time. We also put together the environmental assessment ourselves and liaised with the hydrologist at the EA to ascertain a low risk status.' Linda Durman explains how the system works in practice:

The planning department (now sometimes called Development Control) will refer all applications for natural burial sites to the EA and the relevant highways authority. The EA will require a written Risk Assessment for the site, in respect of possible pollution of groundwater. You should obtain their booklet 'Assessing the Groundwater Pollution Potential of Cemetery Developments', March 2002 (from the Environment Agency, Rio House, Waterside Drive, Aztec West, Almondsbury, Bristol BS32 4UD (☎ 01454 624400 or 0845 933 3111; w: www.environment-agency.gov.uk). [Eds: this booklet reports that natural burial sites 'usually exhibit accelerated decay rates due to the relatively shallow depth of burial, the biodegradable nature of the coffins or shrouds and the lack of embalming fluids.' Notably: 'the infiltration rate may be lower on such sites due to evapotranspiration by trees and shrubs. Decay will principally be aerobic, producing carbon dioxide, water, nitrate and sulphate, which are generally less polluting that those from anaerobic decay.']

The Risk Assessment is a daunting prospect, but the key issues seem to be a) whether the proposed site is within a Special Protection Zone (SPZ) for groundwater collection, and b) the potential for waterlogging. The EA will supply you with a list of approved consultants with hydrogeological site investigating experience. Such experts could undertake the risk assessment for you. Or you could find your nearest one, be very nice to them, and get a look at their Groundwater Vulnerability Map for the area. It will probably be the first time anyone has asked them. (Copy of Yealmpton's Risk Assessment available for £5 incl. p&p; see under Yealmpton, Devon, in Chapter 6, for Linda Durman's contact details.)

The highways department will make sensible suggestions about visibility splays and car parking. This needs to be good because the public will be entering and leaving the site by car.

It will help your case if you enclose letters of support with your planning application from the local churches and other local groups, if possible. It is also prudent to invite a sympathetic funeral director to view the site and advise on practicality of use by a hearse. The planning officer dealing with your application will draft a report to the planning committee. This report forms part of the agenda and is available to the public prior to the meeting, on request. Visit the planning department before the meeting so that you can check what the planning officer has said about your application, and see any letters of objections or support that have been sent in. You will then know the information on which the members of the planning committee will base their discussion, apart from the information you have sent. Some planning committees now allow applicants a three-minute presentation to the committee immediately before their planning application is heard. This is an opportunity to put your side if there have been any objections.

If your planning authority has not approved an application for a natural burial ground before, it may be prudent to reduce the scope for objections by omitting seating, toilets and buildings from the initial application. Once the use of the site for burials has been approved in principle, you can apply later for additions to the site.

Some sites have needed to upgrade their public liability insurance because of the 'change of use'. The standard insurance fee seems to be in the region of £250-£350 per annum, but Linda Durman says this could perhaps be cheaper if the site was being run as part of a farm business. Regarding other costs, she adds:

We avoided a lot of costs by asking people to work for free on things, this being a community project (probably the equivalent of £10,000 in professional fees and other work and expenses that we would have had to pay to someone if we were an ordinary business). Still we incurred the following:

• About £100 for market research and writing the business plan

• £220 for the planning application plus £18 for mandatory OS maps

• Over £600 for legal fees

• £300 for a consultant to draw up the landscape design

• Over £5,000 for enabling works on the field: ploughing, harrowing, rolling, seeding, initial tree planting, fence posts, gate and signs

• Could have been £500 for the risk assessment required by the Environment Agency but I managed that myself in the end.

The steering group members eventually helped fund Yealmpton Woodland Burial's start-up costs, but the ICOF (Industrial Common Ownership Finance) group, which offers 'finance for co-operatives and the social economy', also would have been willing to lend them the capital, providing they became an incorporated association (or similar). Loans from £5,000-£50,000 are 'normally available'; there is no set lending term, and loans can be for up to ten years. Initial enquiries should be made to Martin Hockley at the ICOF head office (115 Hamstead Road, Handsworth, Birmingham B20 2BT, ☎ 0121 523 6886; **e**: icof@icof.co.uk).

Bernard Edge, director of Brinkley Wood Cemetery, suggests taking up the grants that may be available for early development tree planting and hedging.

For those wishing to plant trees either near to the graves or elsewhere on the site, Philip Pearce, an environmentalist who has visited a few sites with an eye to examples of good practice, notes:

> It really does seem important to choose trees (or provide a choice of trees) that are grown on from local stock or at least native to the area. This not only increases the chances of survival of the individual tree but also the prospects of creating a woodland that is an integral part of the local environment and landscape. Individual specimen trees of non-native origin may work in certain circumstances (perhaps where an arboretum is being created) but otherwise it should be discouraged. The chances of survival of the tree are increased if the trees are planted properly in the first place. Recent advice suggests that small plants establish the best, do not require stakes and ties but are not very visible. Half-standards, on the other hand, usually need stakes and ties. Here low staking is best which allows roots to develop well and a special tie used to prevent chafing. Also trees need to well spaced and planted at the appropriate time of year. And after-care is crucial. Trees can be stifled by competing vegetation or strangled by unattended ties. The best sites have a policy of guaranteeing the replanting of any tree that fails within the first few years.

Tarn Moor Memorial Woodland has taken a slightly different approach, as Wendy Pratt explains:

> We took into account that the wood would develop over many years and therefore planting of oaks at 9m intervals means they will not be disturbed, yet the interim nursery crop trees will be coppiced out over the years. Families understand that our principle is not 'a tree per person interred': it is not practically possible to produce a long term oak woodland without coppicing and possibly upsetting a family, when 'Grandma's tree' has gone. Each group of 12 interments therefore has a dedicated tree. Taking this principle one stage further, we encourage families to think of the woodland as a whole as 'The Memorial'. As we have started our planting, we encourage immediate interments to be by the existing oak trees.

Incidentally, the Natural Death Centre has had reports of at least one natural burial site using tanalised wood, also called pressure-treated or CCA-treated timber. Wood is treated in this manner for protection and durability, and so the chemicals used are, by their very nature, persistent, toxic products. Two of the chemicals used, chromium and arsenic, are poisonous enough to humans to mean that the treatment is only ever carried out under carefully controlled conditions, and, arsenic has been known to leach into soil and water. For more information, contact HDRA, the organic organisation (Ryton Organic Gardens, Coventry CV8 3LG, ☎ 024 7630 3517; **e**: enquiry@hdra.org.uk).

One alternative, which is naturally rot-resistant and may be used for stakes, posts or elsewhere outdoors without prior treatment, is chestnut wood. It lasts just as long, if not longer, than tanalised wood, and will not contaminate the environment or those who come into contact with it. In addition, chestnut is a native, natural and sustainable resource. J. E. Homewood & Son (20 Wey Hill, Haslemere, Surrey GU27 1BX, ☎ 01428 643819), will sell chestnut stakes for little more per stake than tanalised wood.

Philip Andrew, who manages the woodland area within Harrogate's Stonefall Cemetery, suggests that 'two [grass] cuts per year are essential to give some control, and yet to maintain a wild area'.

Tania Thornley, who unfortunately lost her appeal for a site in Devon, gives the tip that 'one should mix the topsoil and subsoil' in order to 'reduce the couch grass and other invasive weeds on the back-filled grave, while encouraging the wild flowers and herbs'. She also addresses the problem of double graves:

Individuals often wish to be buried next to their loved ones, and this can be a problem for a woodland burial site for two main reasons. Firstly, the excavation of a grave next to one that has been filled (up to 40 years previously) could disturb the tree roots of neighbouring trees; and secondly, as the area will by then be a wildlife woodland, access through the undergrowth could be difficult. On my site, double burials will not be permitted on top of each other, but double burials could be acceptable if a separate area were provided with a slightly different management regime – for instance, a native shrub (guilder rose, dog rose, spindle tree or honeysuckle) could be planted on the first interment and a long-life tree only on the second interment.

Tania wondered how her site would have been rated:

Will the woodland burial site be rated under agriculture (in which case no rates are payable) or business? There seem to be no set rules applying to woodland burial grounds, and the Regional Rates Valuation Officer will not come up with an answer until the site is up and running. Once a burial has taken place the grave area becomes woodland; and before this it is grazed or cut for hay. Because none of the land therefore lends itself to being a definite business (except the car park area) it has been implied that I will be rated on the land that looks like a business – ie areas with paths, etc.

A number of site owners have expressed concern that the current relatively hefty rating valuation of natural burial grounds may threaten the viability of sites in the future. On the other hand, some local valuation officers seem to be turning a blind eye to their local natural burial grounds. While this is clearly not fair to those that are being asked to pay rates, the sites that are currently being let off the hook, as it were, are understandably afraid of 'rocking the boat' by offering such evidence as might help other sites appeal against their own valuation.

Incidentally, it has been suggested by one chartered surveyor that if there is a chapel or 'designated place of worship' at the site, the land should then fall under the general heading of 'charities', whereby no rates will be payable (there may, however, still be an assessment). How far that chapel's influence can be said to extend is debatable. Please note that it has not been possible to confirm this advice with a valuation officer at the time of going to press.

As the valuation currently stands, 'where a hereditament consists wholly of a natural burial site, whether operated by a Local Authority, a Charity or commercially, it should be presumed that it is capable of profitable operation', and is consequently valued at £4,000 for a one-acre site. The Valuation Office Agency admitted that the valuation, implemented in 2000, was based upon 'pretty scrappy evidence', as there was little known about the running costs of natural burial sites. It was surprised to learn of the discrepancies between individual sites and suggested that the current system, in which all sites are valued separately but by reference to overall guidelines, was quite feasibly 'too unyielding and uniform'. In 2002, in order to enable a fairer evaluation to be made, the Association of Natural Burial Grounds asked its members to provide the relevant supporting information. The new valuations, yet to be confirmed, will take effect from April 2005.

John O'Callaghan of Exwick Cemetery says to think carefully about methods of shoring up the grave, particularly if the family wish to back-fill.

Billy Campbell at Memorial Ecosystems Ramsey Creek Preserve in South Carolina, the first natural burial ground in the States, writes that to begin with they were completely opposed to inorganic grave markers:

Are grave markers ever appropriate?

We decided that any grave markers should be made of stone from the same geological strata as the preserve. Stones have a very important ecological role in most temperate forests. Ants in particular benefit from an ample supply of stones. According to Holldobler and Wilson (1990), stones provide cover for establishing colonies, and (when flat and shallow) are important for colony thermoregulation, and overall colony success. Ants are now understood to be major players in forests, with impressive total biomass/acre. They are important distributors of certain wild flower seeds. In fact, Pudlo et al (1980) reported that ants might distribute 'as much as 70 per cent' of the flora of mesic forests of the temperate areas of the world.

Our preserve consulting biologist, Dr L. L. Gaddy, published a report based on his research in our area of the US that gives credence to Pudlo's conjecture (Gaddy, 1986). Ants do more than just spread seed and are involved in plant pollination and protection as well (Beattie, 1985). They are also important for some other invertebrates and host the larva of the lycaenid butterflies (blues and hairstreaks). I understand that in the UK, the big blues are pretty much extirpated, and I wonder what role the enclosure acts (and subsequent stone gathering) had on them. It is interesting that in certain ecological restoration efforts in the US, ant diversity has lagged, perhaps because we have not paid enough attention to restoring the forest and prairie floor structure.

In any event, we have come to the conclusion that, at least in the case of Ramsey Creek, returning stones to the forest floor is a good thing ecologically.

For those sites that do not want to allow any form of permanent grave marker, or for those that wish to guard against the 'occasional mistaken exhumation', ASSETtrac Ltd (The White House, Oakendene Industrial Estate, Bolney Road, Cowfold, West Sussex RH13 8AZ; ☎ 01403 860063; **e**: info@assettrac.co.uk) sells radio frequency microchip pegs, which can be read by a hand-held reader, for 'long-term unalterable' grave identification in natural burial sites.

And a final few words of advice from Anne Dyer of the burial ground at Craven Arms: 'Don't try to hard sell – the site should sell itself. Have a roof, lavatory and tea-making nearby.'

Charitable natural burial grounds

Linda Durman has this recommendation for those who are at the stage of considering whether to form a company or a charity:

> I recommend that you first contact Co-operatives UK (Holyoake House, Hanover Street, Manchester M60 0AS, ☎ 0161 246 2959; **w**: www.cooperatives-uk.coop) who have an excellent information sheet and form to select a structure.

The trailblazing green burial charity has been the A. B. Welfare and Wildlife Trust in Harrogate (see Chapter 6 for their full details). In 1993, John Bradfield, the Trust's founder, said: 'I believe that by being able to select burial in land in which nature has a prior claim, there will be a qualitative shift in emotional experience, away from the "warehousing of the dead" in cemeteries and churchyards.' In letters to the Centre, John Bradfield has added:

The A. B. Welfare and Wildlife Trust

I'm concerned that we should be able to take *full* control over dying and death. This means being able to avoid the use of funeral directors (et al) or to buy only those services required from them. It could mean digging the grave oneself having chosen the location, or digging it with a group of friends and relatives. Health and safety factors need to be fully taken account of, but are not barriers in themselves. Risks can be reduced by making shallow graves, which are also more environmentally benign.

There is no minimum depth for graves in national laws for private land, unless the Towns Improvement Clauses Act 1847 applies, in which case the minimum is 30 inches from the ground level to the top of the coffin, if a coffin is used. The minimum for public cemeteries is 24 inches and we know of a hospital burial ground, closed in 1969, where coffins were at ground level.

I'm also keen that coffins not be used unless environmentally benign, such as second-hand timbers from doors, floors and pallets. A ban will be placed on tropical hardwoods, even those from assumed sustainable sources. A coffin is wrongly said by some to be required for transporting the body, but a choice may be exercised simply to use a shroud, the person's own clothes, or some other alternative, such as basket from willow or sustainable osier beds, cardboard or carpet.

Burials are arranged by the Trust in existing nature reserves. As a combined social work and wildlife charity, it is a tangible example of a seamless voluntary service based on 'joined-up' thinking.

It is the only charity in the country able to give sound advice about dying, death and funerals. By now it should be having a major impact on the health and welfare services, cemeteries, crematoria and wildlife charities. If the government ever sets up an agency to go in search of pioneering work – work which could transform standards in the public services – this Trust should be at the top of the government's list for scrutiny. But in fact further progress is being hindered by a bureaucratic stranglehold imposed by the planners and by the failure of politicians to help.

For a donation of £5, the A. B. Welfare and Wildlife Trust will send any group trying to start a charitable natural burial ground a copy of its constitution – or no doubt a copy could be obtained from the Charity Commission library at 57 Haymarket, London SW1 (☎ 020 7210 4477). The Trust is also seeking donations of land and money to run further burial grounds under its own aegis. Fabian Hamilton MP, who was persuaded by his constituents to visit the Trust, wrote to the Deputy Prime Minister saying, 'The Trust is run by its users and is modern in every other sense. I was very impressed and very moved by this innovative and brilliant project. It is one of the most impressive developments in public service. It is a model for community care, social participation and inclusiveness and one of the most visionary public services I have ever seen, run by one of the most dedicated public servants I have ever met.'

John Bradfield noted in *Green Burial* that the Charity Commission agreed that the trustees of the Harrogate Trust for Wildlife Protection had power to allow a small numbers of burials within its nature reserves, without having to mention burials in its constitution. Such burials have since taken place.

A Lawful Development Certificate or 'LDC' (also known as a Certificate of Lawfulness), he adds, which costs about half the fee for applying for planning permission, could be sought to ascertain how many graves your local authority would permit without requiring planning permission.

If the graves are dug by hand, and there are none of the various identifying signs of a cemetery, such as roads, sale of burial rights, gravestones and large fencing, John Bradfield argues in *Green Burial* that there will have been no 'substantial' or 'material' change of use and therefore the local authority should not require planning permission to be sought. Natural burial sites should make it clear that they have no interest in setting up cemeteries.

John Bradfield prefers to rely, not on tree planting, but on allowing woods naturally to plant themselves, or using a good seed supply from near at hand, thus promoting local strains and genes, and conserving genetic diversity. Burials should be on parts of the site with the least ecological importance, rather than in areas of existing wildlife value such as old woods with woodland flowers, bogs, marshes or wild flower meadows or pasture. 'It is too easy to overlook important wild flower areas, so it is worth asking someone with a trained eye to study the area between early spring and late autumn.'

John Bradfield warns that if the burial ground is on old meadow land that has interesting wild flowers, trees should not be planted. It should, however, continue to be mown. He also warns that wild bluebells have been given extra legal protection and should not be dug up for replanting in burial grounds.

Burials should happen only exceptionally, Bradfield adds, in Sites of Special Scientific Interest – but even these may have areas with little ecological value such as old refuse tips or nettle beds, areas once churned up by heavy machinery, large areas of bracken, old bonfire sites, areas where topsoil may need to be stripped off, or agriculturally 'improved' grassland where the aim is to recover some degree of species diversity.

In one planning appeal by a burial ground, monitored by John Bradfield, the inspector pointed out that 'cemeteries are not "inappropriate" development in terms of the guidance on Green Belts (contained in Planning Policy Guidance note 2 (PPG2) or local planning policies)'.

The A. B. Welfare and Wildlife Trust has sent in a number of other tips for those seeking to set up charitable natural burial grounds:

Persuade a local and well-established wildlife charity to agree to one or more burials in existing nature reserves, so as to begin the process and start changing attitudes (see *Green Burial* 1994, p. 61) but to avoid complex charity law, do not sell access or burial rights.

Work with a local wildlife charity to extend an existing nature reserve, by purchasing adjacent land for burials. Ask that charity to agree, from the outset, to take over the project after a number of years (as the Essex Wildlife Trust will do at Wrabness) or when burials have ceased.

Even if an established wildlife charity is wary of involvement, it is still worth buying land which it is likely to accept as a gift at some distant date.

Don't accept unsuitable land just to get started, as the land can't be sold or exchanged for a better site – burials are permanent. Small life rafts of wildlife in seas of barley and sugar beet, will be of no interest to most wildlife charities. They would take over small sites if adjacent to existing nature reserves, so the total area is increased.

Don't start until the long-term security of both graves and wildlife can be guaranteed.

If you are aiming for more than a handful of burials in the long-term, decide whether or not to have a few burials first, before applying for planning permission.

You must get a Lawful Development Certificate or planning permission, if graves will be sold in advance of need, to make the arrangement watertight.

To avoid complex charity law, it can be easier for an individual or non-charitable group to own the land and agree to burials, if reasonable donations are made to a named charity, with ownership passing to that or some other charity at a later date (as with Kate's Fell, which is owned by Bradfield, but with all money going to the Trust).

So that there is no doubt when questions are asked, have a clear and long-term plan from the outset on (a) the protection of graves, (b) access to the land for visits to graves, and (c) the conservation of existing wildlife or how wildlife will be established and managed over time.

Perpetual rights and perpetual protection cannot be guaranteed by non-charitable landowners, unless covered by some aspect of law, such as the Cemeteries Clauses Act 1847. The maximum length of time in law which public cemeteries and the Church of England can guarantee is 100 years, but even these rights can be ended if the correct steps are taken.

The A. B. Welfare and Wildlife Trust will not accept embalmed bodies. It has also banned hearses for its Kate's Fell site, partly to keep the planners happy (no one will know a funeral is taking place if no hearses are around) and partly to encourage people to use their own vehicles.

A. B. Welfare and Wildlife Trust (see under Harrogate in Chapter 6).

A *natural burial network for the bereaved*

The following is adapted from letters from a district council cemetery officer.

A nationwide network of local groups could be formed to bring together those families and friends who have made use of a natural burial ground. Activities for group members could include:

• Establishing bark pathways within the site.
• Assisting with planting trees and bulbs on an annual day of dedication, with refreshments served afterwards.
• Providing assistance with the placing of memorial seats.
• Assisting with the after-care of tree plantings.
• Providing additional planting days for bulbs.
• Providing talks to people on a variety of topics.

Such a group offers the opportunity for the development of friendship between people who have been brought together through bereavement and through an interest in the natural burial concept.

Each group would have its own committee. It would have to pay for its own outings or out-of-pocket expenses, but the local authority would provide meeting rooms, materials and the printing of newsletters. In due course, there could be a network magazine.

Maldon Cemetery, which has a woodland burial area, offers days of dedication and keeps a database of relatives connected to the woodlands area to enable occasional 'working parties' to be organised. Peace Funerals, which runs the South Yorkshire and Golden Valley woodland burial grounds (see Chapter 6 for details), has set up Friends groups at both sites – these groups meet regularly for mutual support and to advise on policy.

Local authority natural burial grounds

As mentioned, the first natural burial ground was the woodland burial site set up by the City of Carlisle. Ken West, Cemetery Manager there at the time, wrote during the planning stages in 1993 (and revised 2003):

> The creation of a memorial woodland resource would benefit the environment and could be returned to the community after the expiry of grave rights. It could then form part of a country park or a green lung, for walking, pony trekking or similar. Part of the intangible benefits are a return to nature and the need to encourage insects, birds and mammals.
>
> For the layout of the graves, I prefer a double grave with burials side-by-side, at a depth of 4ft 3ins. There will be space for 440 graves per hectare [composed of 5 x 3 metre squares set out as a star. The central square is pre-planted with four trees, one to each side, to help people locate the grave. Against each of the four sides sits a three-metre square which accepts two burials side-by-side, head-end to the tree, to create a star pattern. The tree marks the head of each grave but allows the burial square to remain free of trees. Fitting these 'stars' together creates a staggered planting regime, but ensures that a mini-excavator can approach each grave foot-end without being impeded by a tree. After the burial an understorey plant could be placed on the grave and as groups of graves are filled, some more permanent trees could be planted. The central three-metre square only has trees and is never used for interments].
>
> The reduction in density is more than compensated for by the reduced excavation costs, drainage problems, backfilling, reinstatement of sunken graves, etc. Additionally, the cost of a traditional new graveyard had to include new roads, deep drainage, etc, which will not apply in the same degree with this scheme.
>
> People choosing the woodland concept before death will have gained a real psychological benefit – a piece of woodland and a real, living memorial instead of a dull, dead stone. Perhaps the test of any product is 'Would you use it yourself?' I can state clearly that I would and refer you to these lines from 'Drummer Hodge' by Thomas Hardy:
>
> > His homely Northern breast and brain
> > Grow to some Southern tree
> > And strange eyed constellations reign
> > His stars eternally.

> *Extracted from an article by Ken West, now Cemeteries and*
> *Crematorium Manager at Croydon Council (see Chapter 8).*

Dawn Eckhart, erstwhile community development officer at Seaton Cemetery in Devon, suggests that the quickest and simplest way for a local authority to begin a natural burial ground is as a pilot project within an existing cemetery. The cemetery will already have planning permission and so there are no negotiations needed with other agencies about health and safety or water pollution. The disadvantage of a small scheme, she says, is not being able to allow people to buy adjacent plots in advance; the site has no sign of the graves on the surface, so graves are being dug in sequence to avoid error.

Brendan Day, who now works for West Bromwich Crematorium, advises that a natural burial section is a good way of utilising cemetery ground where only a depth of 4ft 6ins can be obtained. Families do not expect two-depth graves in a natural burial ground, once they are aware of the need for the body to be as close to the surface as possible so as to encourage the bacterial action and decay. Thus a local authority may be able to make use of a site with a relatively high water table or with a rocky layer beneath it.

David Lobb, erstwhile officer of Maldon Cemetery, Essex, wrote in the Funeral Service Journal (1996) that their woodland burial glades were being created within an existing mature cemetery. Families choose a grave space within burial islands of between 20-40 graves which eventually link up together. Pathways constructed from bark with log edgings are developed as the need arises. The grounds are managed as wild flower meadow. For the wild flower planting, they use pre-grown plant plugs, 'these being of much more immediate impact and far easier to establish. Species include red campion, ragged robin, white campion, harebell and oxeye daisy'.

John Bradfield of the A. B. Welfare and Wildlife Trust cautions, however, against indiscriminate use of wild flower seed – 'no wild flowers should be grown without obtaining advice from a credible wildlife charity on the species and genetic origin.'

The 'Good Bulb Guide' (which can be downloaded for free from the website of Fauna & Flora International, Great Eastern House, Tenison Road, Cambridge CB1 2TT, ☎ 01223 571000; w: www.fauna-flora.org/around_the_world/ good_bulb_guide.pdf) details companies that have pledged never to sell wild-collected bulbs but buyers would still need to satisfy themselves as to their provenance. Some experts argue strongly for local provenance:

> Too often wild flower seed is imported from the Netherlands or raised by nurseries from European sources. Many of the wild hyacinth or English bluebell strands have become seriously introgressed by pollen from garden introductions, resulting in hybrid stock. Common sources of seed homogenise the flora and threaten our floral genetic inheritance. If cemetery planners could take account of these concerns by ensuring only indigenous plant material is encouraged in situ it could go some way to prevent the erosion of our native genetic resources.
>
> *From a letter to the Natural Death Centre from Alan Fairweather.*

Linda Durman says that you can check the species that are indigenous to your area by logging onto the Postcode Plants database (maintained by the Natural History Museum) at: www.nhm.ac.uk/science/projects/fff

The following adapted extracts are from a long feasibility study prepared by Ken West, one of the pioneers of natural burial. More recently Ken West has written a draft ecological classification scheme for natural burial sites; please contact the Centre for further information.

The Woodland Burial – A Return to Nature

• Most local authority cemeteries operate at a deficit. In Carlisle, for instance, all cemetery income simply covers the grave digging and associated administrative costs. There is no surplus whatsoever for subsequent grave maintenance. [Eds, 2003: Ken West points out that many cemeteries, including Croydon, where he now works, have started to charge realistic fees.] The woodland burial site, by contrast, will have insignificant maintenance costs and long term liabilities. Income from coffin sales and plaques on the Memorial Wall offers the possibility of woodland cemeteries actually making a profit.

• The format of the funeral has been changed by those favouring the woodland concept. The number of secular funerals is slightly above average. One funeral has already occurred with the family requesting that all staff attending, both from the cemetery and the funeral director, should wear jeans and tee-shirts. A further funeral is being planned along these lines for the future. I have not previously experienced this request in my 35 years in this work.

• Chipboard coffins are lined with a plastic sheet. Expert opinion suggests that although chipboard acts like a sponge and breaks down very quickly in damp or wet soil, the plastic wraps itself around the body and may cause mummification. This will be avoided if a biodegradable coffin [lined with a biodegradable liner] is used. [See Chapter 5 for details of such coffins and liners.]

• Woodland burial is perceived as being much more successful than it really is. Woodland burial represents only 1.5 per cent of the total funerals we complete, including cremation ... (although), for the period October 1995 to March 1996, 19 per cent of our grave sales were in the woodland, and by January 2000, 30 per cent of new grave sales were in the woodland.

• If a new woodland burial scheme reduces memorial or other sources of income, either to the funeral director or associated memorial outlet, it may be opposed. An advance reservation scheme for graves may defeat negative advice the bereaved may receive from funeral directors at the time of death.

• Graves are marked with a concrete block sunk level with the ground, engraved with a number from 1 upwards. Each 20th grave marker will be erected 24ins high to facilitate measurement to locate other grave markers in dense vegetation.

• The graves take up more space than in conventional cemeteries, as two coffins are put side by side. But the graves are shorter length and width per coffin than usual, because they are dug to a shallow depth and collapse will not become a problem.

• We initially planted many of the unused graves with an oak whip, mainly to give the site a 'woodland' appearance. Subsequently, we find that these trees are easily moved and replanted onto graves which have recently been used for burial. This is useful as it generally allows the partner or family to plant the tree on their grave during the summer months.

• Reports of some other woodland burial schemes have been disappointing. One had graves located around cemetery perimeters, creating a line of trees rather than woodland. Another was situated on a compost heap formed by the cemetery grass mowings accumulating over years. At another location, the staff had little idea about the concept.

The woodland should replicate the type of woodland which exists naturally in the area. One woodland scheme offers a choice of three tree species, one of which is Mountain Ash. Unfortunately, most people using the scheme are choosing this and creating a Mountain Ash wood. Such a wood is rarely found naturally, particularly in lowland, and these trees are often short lived.

Other schemes are using the typical garden centre type tree, the 'lollipop' tree, with a cleared stem up to (say) 4ft to 5ft and the branches radiating from a single apical point. These trees never attain the typical forest tree appearance and they often possess structural weaknesses. They may also be grown from European rather than native seed.

In Carlisle, we located some landowners who have been growing Oaks from acorns harvested from old trees growing on their land [eds: if supplied from a local source, the genetic base of the tress must be wide. Otherwise, if the acorns come from one tree, disease might arise locally and kill all the trees]. These young trees cost £1 each and are about 2ft to 2ft 6ins high and with a good fibrous root system. Any seed trees you use should be old enough to predate the period of potential introduction from abroad. About 100 years should suffice.

Oak offers many benefits – the number of insect species found on the oak is 284, which exceeds any other tree. Oak is not suited, however, to chalk soils or industrial spoils.

• Tree shelters (translucent polypropylene tubes) would look unattractive across burial areas. Spiral guards (loosely coiled plastic tubes which wrap around the stem) are used instead. They are only suitable on feathered whips with a stem diameter of at least 25mm.

• Weeds around the tree are controlled by mulching using black polythene mulching mats (600mm by 600mm square), minimum 500 gauge with ultra violet inhibitor. The mat is dug in around its edges and covered by leaf mould or wood chips.

• Evidence from existing crematoria memorial planting schemes shows that trees, which, on the woodland burial ground will be only 1.5 metres apart, can be thinned after five years, with few, if any people, concerned.

• The Forestry Commission 'Woodland Grant Scheme' gives money per hectare for Oak woodland, if a minimum 0.25 hectare is planted within a five year period. This figure can be reached by including shelter and other types of planting achieved for the opening of the burial area.

• 20 weeks after burial (depending on the time of year), the grave will be forked/rotovated and levelled approximately 75mm below the normal ground surface. Approximately 210 bluebell bulbs will be laid evenly over the grave surface, covered by 75mm of top soil [see note on sourcing wild bulbs above]. The Oak tree whip will be planted and the plastic mulch mat at its base will be covered with 65mm of leaf mould. The remaining soil surface will be levelled.

• Environment Agency objections to the setting up of a cemetery may be based on reports of watercourse pollution from cemeteries in the USA. This is apparently due to the high percentage of bodies treated with embalming fluid, and formaldehyde has been found in the water. If this objection arises, it might be sensible to prohibit the embalming of bodies accepted for burial for the woodland burial site.

• The types of people using the woodland graves include those who seek an alternative to cremation; those who like the no-memorial anonymity; single people who do not need to buy the conventional double grave space; the broadly green – gardeners and those who love birds, countryside, trees and wild flowers; those who like the low cost aspect; and those wanting secular or independent funerals.

• A dedication ceremony can formally open the burial area. This involves a religious ceremony jointly performed by representatives of all the churches.

• Although I coined the phrase 'return to nature', other fertile minds are already improving on this. I particularly like 'leave the world a better place', devised by a funeral director operating a woodland site in the Isle of Wight.

The full set of papers is available for £20 from Carlisle Cemetery Office, Richardson Street, Carlisle CA2 6AL (☎ 01228 625310).

The following article is by Andy Clayden – a landscape designer with a special interest in cemeteries, who is currently conducting a research study into the design and management of UK natural burial grounds.

Design of natural burial grounds

The creation of a 'natural burial' ground would on the face of it, appear to be a relatively straightforward task. An area of land to be set aside for burial, where there is little or no marking of the grave, except perhaps with a native tree or wildflowers, and where nature will ultimately become the collective memorial landscape. Although this basic concept would appear relatively straightforward to implement there are important issues which need to be considered when designing a natural burial ground.

There are practical issues; for example, how will the burial plots be arranged, allocated and registered? How will the proposed burial ground accommodate a large funeral party and enable access to the graveside? There are also issues relating to the aesthetic and experiential qualities of the burial ground. For example, what is 'natural'? Natural burial grounds are frequently created in agricultural settings where the landscape has been managed and 'improved' over a thousand years. This is a cultural landscape with its own unique qualities and identity. It may also be a habitat in which native species may now struggle to thrive and assert themselves. How will the new burial ground 'fit' with that cultural landscape and what management strategies need to be considered to give 'nature' a chance to thrive? Finally, there are also the needs and expectations of the bereaved. To what extent will they be able to mark and tend the grave and for how long? How will the burial ground support their needs as a safe and secure place to visit where they can comfortably spend time in peaceful contemplation and reflection? These are just some of the issues which will need to be addressed in developing a burial ground which balances the needs of people and nature whilst also being economically viable.

It is not possible in this short section to provide comprehensive guidance on the design of natural burial grounds, partly because of the constraints of space, but primarily because of the wide range of interpretations and different settings in which they occur. The following notes do however aim to raise key questions and to encourage those who are considering developing a natural burial ground to think long and hard and to plan carefully how their project will evolve. Much of the advice focuses on the creation of new woodland burial grounds because these are the most common, and because typically they represent the most significant change to an existing landscape.

A vision for the site – design aims

Before you can begin to design and lay out a new burial ground it is important to establish early on what it is you are trying to achieve and why. Many new natural burial grounds have been developed in recent years and some of these will prove to be more successful than others. In this context 'success' is not necessarily measured in terms of demand for burial plots. For example some natural burial grounds may see the preservation and improvement of an existing habitat as their principle objective. Success in this case may be in identifying early on a clear set of guiding principles, which minimise the impact of burial upon that habitat. For example this may place constraints on what is permissible in the preparation of the deceased for burial but also after burial with regard to the bereaved and their access to the grave. Without a clear sense of purpose or what might be described as a 'vision' for the burial ground there is a danger that it will evolve in a piecemeal fashion, reacting to different pressures rather than presenting a clearly resolved design and management strategy.

A clear and unambiguous 'vision' for the burial ground will therefore be important in guiding the development of the design and also in communicating to potential clients how the burial ground will function and evolve. This is particularly true for new woodland burial grounds which by their very nature necessitate a significant change to an existing habitat (typically open grassland) and which may take several decades to establish. In presenting a vision it will be important to convey in more than words how the landscape will develop over time. Plans are very useful for showing the layout of a design but they say very little about the experience of a place, especially to those people who are unfamiliar in reading them. Sketches or photomontages showing how the burial ground might look after set intervals of time and drawn from a users perspective have the potential to say much more about what the burial ground will be like as a place to visit and how it will change. This is particularly important for new woodland burial grounds, which will vary considerably between one another as a result of different species selection, planting and distribution. Different management strategies will also have a major impact on the evolving character of the woodland. Illustrations that convey this information will help those who may be considering natural burial in understanding, for example, the long-term implications of woodland management in relation to access to the grave. The accompanying illustration shows a sequence of views set at approximately five-year intervals for the same area of the burial ground. They illustrate how a plaque may initially mark the grave (fig 1) but will biodegrade over time (fig 2) and also how the memorial tree, which had been planted on the grave, might be removed as part of the woodland management strategy (fig 3). This illustration also helps to convey the changing relationship between the bereaved and their access to the grave as the woodland matures.

Fig 1

Fig 2

Fig 3

Site investigation: survey and analysis

Care needs to be taken in evaluating the land proposed for burial and understanding the landscape in which it sits. What is it that is special about this land and how might these qualities be retained or enhanced within the new design proposal? What opportunities are there to address any problems, which may exist on the site? In evaluating the site and developing design proposals it may be advisable and necessary to employ specialist consultants, for example, Landscape Architects and ecologists. Landscape Architects have specialist training in site evaluation and developing appropriate design solutions. The following notes identify key areas for consideration.

Site context: An appreciation of the context for the new burial ground will, for example, help in deciding what might be an appropriate woodland character and how this may also enhance existing woodland habitats. There may also be opportunities to connect the burial ground to nearby communities by linking with existing footpaths and bridleways. This approach may be helpful in developing public awareness and also the security of the site through increased surveillance.

Physical characteristics: Soil, climate and microclimate, drainage and topography. In the case of new woodland burial these will have an impact on the species selected and how well they will establish. It may also influence the potential recreational and therapeutic value of the burial ground. For example, are there sheltered, south facing areas that might be appropriate for seating? What is the quality and diversity of the existing flora and fauna? Wherever possible and appropriate mature vegetation should be retained as this represents a significant investment in time and will contributes to the sense of maturity of the burial ground.

Visual survey: This should be considered in two parts, a visual survey within the site and a visual survey looking into and out of the burial ground. There may be views within the site which are important to retain and enhance. For example, an existing mature tree or other prominent feature could prove to be invaluable in helping users to orientate themselves and locate graves within the site. This opportunity may be lost if it is not recognised at the design phase. Views from within the site which look out into the surrounding landscape or towards significant local landmarks should also be retained, whilst unsightly views may be hidden with new planting. It will also be important to consider what impact the burial ground will have when viewed from the surrounding landscape and how this will change over time.

Historic survey: Are there any interesting historic or cultural associations, which should be retained or worked with to help inform the character of the design? It is worth looking at historic maps to see how the land may have changed. Local studies libraries can also be a valuable source of information. A burial ground is a new 'cultural' mark on the landscape but it still has the potential to respect and embrace patterns of land use developed by previous generations. Historic interpretations may, for example, seek to reinstate traditional field boundaries or use local stone and building techniques to create new entrance gateways.

Developing a design proposal

Issues relating to design have already been touched upon with regard to the development of a vision and set of aims for the burial ground. The following notes focus on specific components of the design which will need to be considered in the development of an effective design solution. How these are interpreted will be guided by the vision for the burial ground.

Burial plots and memorials. There is a legal requirement for the burial ground manager to keep a register of the location of each grave. It is possible to do this in a completely unobtrusive way using, for example, a hand held digital reader which can identify an electronic chip buried in the ground or alternatively through modern surveying methods. Although these techniques are important in maintaining the burial register they may be of little help to those who are trying to locate the grave of a loved one in a landscape which may have changed significantly from the day of the burial.

How this issue is addressed may have significant implications for site management, the bereaved and the habitat value of the burial ground. Where space permits it may be appropriate to offer within the burial ground different approaches to natural burial. For example, one area could offer greater access to the grave and a more relaxed approach to how the grave might be marked. This could be in contrast to a different area where access would be restricted and no marking of the grave would be permitted. However, trying to enforce such restrictions can prove to be problematic as the needs of the bereaved may prove to be different to the desires of the deceased. Temporary markers, including ornaments, cut and artificial flowers and personal letters wrapped in plastic are a common feature of many natural burial grounds even where these are not permitted. This type of display may be offensive to those who support the ethos of the unmarked 'natural' burial site. Clear guidelines will help to minimise this problem. These will be important not only in informing the decisions of those who chose natural burial for themselves but perhaps more importantly in educating their families and friends in the choice that they have made.

Entrances. These need to be clearly located and appropriately signed. Depending on the context there is the potential to make entrance areas legible through a more formal treatment, which will be in contrast to the informal character of the natural burial ground. This may be achieved through changes in materials and planting. This does not have to compromise the environmental credentials of the burial ground. It might, for example, be achieved through a more formal arrangement of native species and by pruning. The management regime may be changed when the burial ground is full to allow a more informal character to evolve. Perhaps there is also the potential to include edible native plants such as blackberry, hazel and crab apple. In addition to their wildlife value they might provide a welcome distraction for young children visiting the burial ground with their families.

Boundaries. There is potential for conflict with ecological aspirations if this is not handled sensitively. Many natural burial grounds already have clearly defined perimeters, which are marked by existing hedgerows. Where these do not already exist it will important to create a boundary that makes the burial ground feel secure and protected but which is not intrusive. Fencing may be a temporary solution whilst perimeter planting becomes established.

Parking. Thought needs to be given as to how the burial ground would cope with a large funeral cortege and how the deceased would be transported to the grave. It may be that parking can spill over into an adjacent road. Will there be space for the hearse to access the site and, more importantly, exit without the need for the bereaved to move their cars?

Shelter. It may be desirable to provide toilet facilities and a place to get a drink. Any structure within a burial ground is potentially vulnerable to misuse although this will be partly dependent on the type of structure, the location of the site and the degree of surveillance. The catchment area for a natural burial ground may be much larger than that of a municipal cemetery and they are typically more isolated. People may be travelling a considerable distance and therefore shelter and facilities can be very important in enabling the bereaved to spend time at the burial ground, and to provide a point of contact for any concerns they might have. A building or similar structure may also be used as a focus for the purposes of remembrance and thereby reduce the desire to personalise the grave. An example of this approach is at the Carlisle woodland burial site where a stone sheepfold, which is appropriate to that landscape, provides a setting in which to fix a memorial plaque.

Pathways, places and seating. What is the potential recreational value of the burial ground? What opportunities are there to take a short walk, to find somewhere private and peaceful to sit? Good design will exploit the microclimate of the site, surrounding views and different character areas. The design may also link the burial ground with local walks. These qualities will be important to the bereaved but also to members of the wider community as the function of the site shifts from an active burial ground to a nature reserve and memorial landscape. Consideration should also be given to the safety and security of users, by for example creating pathways which allow for clear and open sight lines.

Woodland establishment, selection and distribution

The following notes specifically focus on new woodland burial.

Woodland establishment. What type of tree stock will be planted and when? Many of the new woodland burial grounds are typically established on improved agricultural land. This land is a competitive environment of nutrient rich soils in which grass and weeds will thrive and potentially out-compete new woodland planting. Bare-root stock (small inexpensive trees one to two years old) should be planted in preference to larger and more expensive container grown or containerised trees. The small bare-root trees should be planted in the dormant season (October to March) when their demand for water is low. Containerised stock should be avoided; even though it may initially look more impressive, it is unlikely to thrive unless it can be regularly watered and weeded. This level of management is unlikely, especially for sites which are isolated and have no onsite access to water.

Species selection and distribution. If the intention is to design and manage the site with a view to creating a specific type of woodland character and experience then there is a need to control species selection and distribution. It is not possible to design a woodland if you don't know what trees are going to be chosen and where they are going to be planted. If habitat diversity is important then woodland understorey species, for example, holly and hazel, should also be included. Where choice is permitted these species are unlikely to be selected.

By keeping the selection and planting of trees separate from the grave it is possible to have much greater control over the management and design of the woodland without upsetting the bereaved by removing or coppicing a memorial tree. The disadvantage, however, is that there is no longer the direct symbolic value attached to the planting of a tree on the grave. As already noted, it may be possible to adopt a mix of different strategies catering for different needs, within the same natural burial ground.

For more detailed information on woodland design, history and management, please refer to the following literature:

Ferris-Khan, R. (1995). *The Ecology of Woodland Creation*. John Wiley & Sons, Chichester.

Hodge, S. J. (1995). *Creating and managing Woodlands around Towns*. Forestry Commission Handbook 11. HMSO, London.

Rackham, O. (1986). *The History of the Countryside*. J. M. Dent & Sons Ltd, London.

Rodwell, J. & Patterson, G. (1994). *Creating New Native Woodlands*. Forestry Commission Bulletin 112. HMSO, London.

Andy Clayden, Lecturer, Department of Landscape, University of Sheffield (e: A.Clayden@sheffield.ac.uk).

If any site manager, or potential site manager, would like some advice or guidance on design, landscape architect Kelley Green (who has recently written a Masters dissertation on green burial, see the beginning of this chapter) advises contacting the Landscape Institute (6-8 Barnard Mews, London SW11 1QU, ☎ 020 7350 5200, **f:** 020 7350 5201; **e:** mail@l-i.org.uk; **w:** www.l-i.org.uk) for a list of qualified landscape architects who will give management advice along-side design guidance.

The following company has been in contact with the Association of Natural Burial Grounds to offer their services in this area:

> We are a small specialist landscape architecture practice with a background in nature conservation and planning issues relating to sensitive sites. We are particularly interested in working on woodland burial sites, memorial gardens and commemorative gardens. We are based in Wales and also in an artspace in central Bristol. We recently worked on an unusual woodland burial site with glades in Norfolk.
>
> *Les Baker, Reckless Orchard Landscape Consultants Ltd, The Old Ship, LLandogo, Monmouth, Monmouthshire NP25 4TD (☎ /f: 01594 530081; w: www.recklessorchard.com).*

A final thought on the reasons for setting up such sites from a managing director of a new green burial company set up 'to preserve the green spaces around London':

> We have had two burials with graveside services, both from terminally ill people who particularly wanted a green funeral. ...
>
> What struck me about these funerals was the informality and the absence of gloom that normally accompanies these events, without in any way reducing the love and respect for the deceased. It seems to me that this allows the mourners to cope with their loss and also permits even quite small children to be included in the final parting from their relative.
>
> *'First Thoughts of a Green Burialist', by Ray Ward of the Woodland & Wildlife Conservation Co (contact details under Herongate, Essex, Chapter 6).*

Chapter 10

GRIEF

'All changes involve loss, just as all losses require change.'
Robert A. Neimeyer, PhD

Grief is a natural healing reaction to loss. It is not unlike trying to heal a wound after an injury occurs. A minor wound may heal quickly – a major one is another matter; healing may take place over time, but the scars will always be there.

After losing someone or something that was a significant part of one's life, grieving is often a long process of assimilating the reality of that loss and adapting to it. This can consume a huge amount of energy. In time, this continues on in the background of all daily activity, but in the early days it usually predominates. From time to time, emotions may re-emerge with unexpected intensity, as if out of the blue, as present and fresh as if the death had occurred yesterday. It is unpredictable. Sometimes bereavement hits the person hard at a time when they themselves are vulnerable and without the strength to recover from this blow. It is not uncommon amongst elderly couples for instance, that after one partner dies, the other dies soon after. In terms of stress levels, bereavement ranks very high on the scale of what is considered a serious threat to physical and emotional or mental health. Multiple losses can complicate the grieving process and raise the level of stress.

There are many personal losses in life which can provoke a powerful experience of grief: a painful divorce, the loss of an important relationship, retirement, redundancy or being diagnosed with a life-threatening or life-limiting illness. It is helpful to realise that these situations can amount to a form of bereavement, and that due care and consideration should be given. If we do not adequately grieve these 'little deaths' they may return with a vengeance later, when a major loss happens.

People usually associate disturbing emotional states with grieving, but there can also be a strong physical aspect to grief. One mourner, just when he thought he was recovering from his wife's death, broke out in a violent rash. It took him a further 18 months to realise what had happened:

> I was much debilitated; the body had to excrete the accumulated stress of several years. Some mourners, I was to discover, are prey to nervous breakdowns, ulcers and much, much worse: chronic arthritic conditions, heart attacks, even cancer. This is probably what accounts for so many instances, in centuries gone by, of persons dying of grief or 'a broken heart'.

From an article by Libby Purves in The Times *(April 3rd 1992).*

Anticipatory grief

When someone is diagnosed with a life-threatening illness, the person and their loved ones may grieve a multitude of losses. Depending on the severity of the illness and its progression, there is the loss of the anticipated future, loss of health and physical ability, loss of status in relation to the changing role within the family and the social circle or at work, and, in many cases, loss of income. Shock and numbness is often what carries a person through the early days following a diagnosis (or at difficult turns during the illness). In some way this acts as a form of protection to allow the person to take in the painful reality of their situation bit by bit. One woman in her fifties, who was diagnosed with breast cancer, fainted on hearing the news. Although she knew the consultant was an oncologist, and that the hospital she was in was a cancer hospital, she felt totally unprepared:

> I don't know how I got home. For days after that, I just felt everything was unreal. It wasn't until after the operation that I was able to take in what happened. I cried a lot. My family knew of the cancer and some of our closest friends did too, but there were lots of people I did not want to know about it. I was furious when my husband ignored my wishes. I have been very angry with him on many occasions since then, I never used to be. Having this illness has made me more outspoken in many ways. A lot of old grievances I have harboured for years and years, they have come out. I feel sad at all the things I have not done in the past, holding myself back. I am angry and sad and ashamed that I did not think more of myself before.

Many people are profoundly changed by the experience of illness, particularly cancer. Anticipatory grief can break our heart and, in doing so, break the heart open, to giving and receiving love on a more profound level than previously experienced. If the experience of a terminal illness is managed well, it may ease some of the pain of dying, help towards achieving a good and peaceful death. It may also alleviate some of the pain of grief for the bereaved.

We grieve also for what we have not had, but have hoped for. As for instance in the case of a couple who married young but waited to start a family. They were in their thirties, happy, and expecting their first baby, when the wife suddenly died. The husband was devastated by the loss:

> I was beside myself. I felt terrible, as if I had undergone major surgery and needed months to recover. I spent days in bed, unable to do anything. The first few weeks I had a lot of support from people. But since then I am alone, trying to carry on with my job and my life. Sometimes it is just too much for me. When I feel like that, I wonder if I will ever be alright again. When my wife died, nobody mentioned the baby, I could not either. It was only a small foetus at the time, but now I have a sense of it as a real person. I feel I lost my wife, my child and our future. I still cannot imagine a future without them. They are on my mind everyday, although I don't talk about it. If people ask me how I am and I say I am having a hard day, they ask 'Why?' I feel weird reminding them that I am suffering from bereavement. And I am annoyed; it seems to me they have forgotten that my wife died. I haven't. It has been over a year now. To me that is no time at all.

A tentative 'map' of grieving

There have been many attempts to create a 'map' of grieving, in order to help professionals and the bereaved to maintain a sense of orientation, as they try to manage what sometimes may seem like an emotional roller coaster. But as everyone grieves in their own way, this 'map' can only provide a broad outline of what a person may experience as part of the grieving process. A classic example is William Worden's 'Four Tasks of Mourning', first written about in 1983 in his book *Grief Counselling and Grief Therapy* (see Resources):

Task 1: To accept the reality of the loss
Task 2: To experience the pain of grief
Task 3: To adjust to an environment in which the deceased is missing
Task 4: To withdraw emotional energy and reinvest it in another relationship.

The following variation accommodates a broader spectrum of grief responses:

1. Shock and a sense of disbelief, moving to accepting the reality of the death
2. Experiencing the pain of loss in a multitude of ways; or experiencing a sense of relief
3. Accepting the new reality
4. Experiencing continuing bonds with the person who died

It is important to recognise shock and disbelief as a part of grief. The suggestion is that mourners may go through and return to various emotional states at various times. For most people it is not a question of getting 'over' what has happened, but rather getting through it. Colin Murray Parkes (in *Bereavement: Studies of Grief in Adult Life*, 1996) speaks of pangs of grief, which are frequent to begin with and lessen over time. Some say grief does not end, it becomes part of us, part of our life story. Following a death, a person can feel their life has been shattered by the loss. If this experience can be integrated, it might lead to a new and different sense of self; perhaps even a transformation to a deeper, more meaningful connection with oneself and with the world. This can in turn lead to having a sense of wisdom and insight that may benefit oneself and others.

The post-war baby boomer generation, experiencing peace and affluence, had time to explore their emotions, and it is this generation that writes books advocating a more expressive way of grief. The evidence, though, is that this works better for some than for others, and in some situations better than others. Margaret Stroebe and Henk Schut, two psychologists from Utrecht in Holland, show that grieving involves two things: experiencing the emotional pain and learning new tasks and roles. Stroebe and Schut argue that both dimensions – emotion-focused and task-focused – are important, but that it is not usually possible to do both at the same time. So, mourners oscillate from one to the other. The oscillations may occur over a matter of hours, or months. In this 'dual process model', there are no stages, as grief and getting on with life swing back and forth. And unlike stage and phase models of grief, it cannot be used to police mourners' emotions with suggestions like 'you ought to have moved on by now'.

Various emotions evoked by grief

Although the following list was compiled with the bereaved adult or child in mind, much of it is also relevant in cases of anticipatory grief:

Shock: Feeling numb, fainting, feeling physically weak. Inability to think, denial, feeling emotionally switched off or removed, disbelief, forgetfulness, not wanting to think about what has happened, imagining the dead person has not really died. Being on 'automatic pilot'.

Relief: Feeling relieved of the burden of caring for the dying person. Relief that the person is 'gone' in cases where there was a lot of conflict. Relief at 'a chapter in one's life' having come to an end and feeling free to move on. Relief at being newly able to develop parts of oneself that were previously not given a chance. Relief at the negative aspects of the relationship having gone.

Guilt: Feeling responsible for what happened. 'Survivor guilt'. Guilt at not having done enough. Guilt at not having spent more time with the dying person before they died. Guilt for not having made peace with the dying person. Guilt at not having expressed one's love more in actions or in words. Guilt at not having appreciated the person more.

Anger: Resentment, feelings of frustration, outrage, blaming and finding fault, irritability, criticising and verbally or physically attacking others. Inner tension, outbursts of anger, exploding temperament, shouting, starting or getting into arguments or fights. Self-harming.

Searching, Pining, Longing: Wishing to be reunited with the person who died. Wishing the death had not occurred.

Depression: Feeling low in energy and spirit, feeling a lack of pleasure in usual routines, tiredness, feelings of heaviness, loss of appetite, overeating, lack of confidence, low self-esteem, feelings of hopelessness, despair, a lack of purpose, inability to concentrate, ruminating or negative thoughts. Anxiety, inability to sleep, disrupted sleep, sleeping during the day, feeling isolated and not understood by others at school, at work or within the family. Inability to perform household duties, inability to perform at work, refusal to go to school, drop in performance level at school, not taking care of one's appearance or personal hygiene, feeling suicidal, feelings of abandonment. Loss of or doubting spiritual or religious beliefs previously held.

Sadness: Feeling tearful, weeping, wanting to be hugged or held. Withdrawing or wanting to be alone. Feeling physical, mental or spiritual pain at the loss. Regret at what has been left unsaid or undone, or at what had been said and done which did not feel positive. Feeling lonely. Missing the person who died. Sadness at all the good things that were shared and now no longer can be shared.

Love and Gratitude: Experiencing a deep sense of love for the person who has died. Gratitude for all the good things that have been shared and received. Having a sense of the person who died in their totality. Feeling enriched through what was shared with the person and how one's own life was affected or transformed as a result of opportunities and other relationships that came into one's life through the person who died. A renewed or strengthened sense of spiritual or religious beliefs.

Fear and anxiety: Fear of the future. Separation anxiety. Fear of the dark. Phobias about hospitals or doctors. Fear of developing the same illness as the person who died; fear of dying in similar circumstances. Fear of travelling by car, plane or train in case of accident. Fear of dying. Fear of losing other important persons close to one. Nightmares, panic attacks. Psychosomatic symptoms due to anxiety and shock (eg tension, tummy ache in children, headache, migraine, irritable bowel syndrome, lowered immune system, frequent colds). Desire for routine that provides sense of security, continuity and safety. Fear of loss of control. Needing to assert and have a sense of control.

Shame: Feeling ashamed at how the person died (AIDS-related illness, suicide, murder, circumstances that violate the person's dignity). Shame at having suffered a loss; at feeling emotional or not in control; at feeling needy.

Coping strategies

These are strategies that facilitate the grieving process in a positive, life-enhancing way. These may include the following: taking a reasonable amount of time off work or other demanding engagements, to allow for regaining one's inner balance. Talking about the dead person with family and friends, recounting memories, writing or reading poetry, playing or listening to music. Going on country walks with family or friends (the combination of nature and exercise can have a very soothing effect). Spending extra time in bed resting or sleeping to restore one's energy. Taking exercise and eating well to restore one's strength. Accepting support from friends such as helping with chores around the house. Awareness that emotional states will pass, allowing emotional expression without overly holding on to them. Having a religious or spiritual belief that is sustaining. Having a sense of community and of being a valued member of that community; reaffirming the sense of community. Being able to ask for help or support where needed. Feeling that there is no shame attached to being and feeling weak. Adopting strategies which are nurturing and health promoting. Joining a support group. Having aromatherapy or massage treatment. Taking up painting and drawing or creative and diary writing. Retaining a positive outlook on life. Working towards a new identity that incorporates the loss of the person.

Avoidance strategies

These strategies are a protective or defensive measure, which may lead to a decline in health if they are not sufficiently varied with coping strategies. Avoidance strategies include: developing excessive behaviour of any kind such as drinking excessive amounts of alcohol, drug abuse, comfort eating, excessive exercise, watching more TV than usual, promiscuity, over-working, destructive or violent behaviour of any kind. Denial of grief in attempt to protect self or others (children, parents, spouse). Avoiding contact with other people, avoiding talking about the dead person, trying to forget the dead person, generally withdrawing emotionally or socially. Not telling close friends and work colleagues that the death occurred.

Continuing bonds

Tony Walter has argued (*Mortality*, 1996) that people need permission to retain the dead person, not to let them go. Some bereaved people begin to recall more and more memories of their lost spouse, a process described (in Jane Littlewood's delightful phrase) as 'falling in love backwards'. The essence of grieving, Walter believes, is for the community of people that knew the deceased, to discuss and elaborate an accurate and durable 'biography', a shared condensation of the person, to integrate the memory of the person into their lives, mainly through conversation, so as to move on with, as well as without, the deceased. In *Bereavement Care* (Spring 1991), he wrote:

> The Jews understand this. They bury the body within a day or so and then the close family 'sit shiva'. They sit in the living room at home for a week, while friends, relatives and neighbours come to visit, bringing food, talking about the departed. Talking endlessly. Laughing, crying, sharing memories. And then, after that week, the family slowly get back to ordinary life.

Is it because we do not share memories like this, he asks, that the demand for bereavement counselling has arisen? Talking about the dead can be difficult in a mobile, urban society. Fellow mourners may live in different towns, or even different countries. Or divorce, or the stigma of AIDS, may make it difficult for them to agree on 'the story'. Or extreme old age means there are few contemporaries left who knew the deceased. But without telling the story of the dead, not only can we not grieve, but society loses the sense of its own history. South Africa's Truth and Reconciliation Commission understood: telling the story of the disappeared not only helped individual families to mourn, but enabled an entire nation to rewrite its recent history.

Tony Walter suggests that the modern funeral that celebrates the life of the deceased is not about 'closure' (whatever that means) but about opening up the possibilities for creating a shareable story, so that the dead can become *our* ancestor and not just *my* private loss.

After death contact experiences

Some bereaved people experience that the person who has died makes contact with them. The person who has this experience can feel greatly comforted to see, hear or feel their loved one again – feeling that the one who has died is safe, that he or she is not lost, to them, but continues to exist in another dimension.

These experiences can happen at any time after a death, and come in many different forms – most commonly in dreams, but also on waking or going to sleep, or even whilst fully awake:

> I had my first after death contact experience ten days after my husband died. By that time I was only sleeping with pills and I felt hypersensitive. I was busy organising two major events, with help from others: the funeral and another celebration the next day, both for a large number of people. All my days were taken up with tasks relating to this. I could hardly eat. Constantly on the phone, I had energy only to be factual, none to repeat what I had said

and absolutely no time for chats. I was sitting on the stairs crying to a friend on the phone, one of the moments when I allowed myself to connect with the feelings I had. I felt my husband putting his arms over me, touching my elbows. I saw his left hand very clearly, resting on my left elbow and knew his other hand was on my right elbow. Simultaneously I was overcome by complete peace. A feeling of neither longing nor withdrawing. Just neutral peace. It was so comforting to see and feel his hand, and to feel his presence. I felt his gesture was saying that he was alright and I was alright.

When I told close friends and family about this, who did not have these experiences, their view was that there is nothing after death, no afterlife. Although I keep an open mind, to me these experiences speak of an existence after death, that consciousness lives and exists beyond the physical body.

Many people who have such experiences do not talk about them; perhaps for fear of being thought of as mentally unstable, or being told that their experience is unreal or simply due to their intense longing for the dead person. Although a self-described skeptic, Dr Louis LaGrand has researched After Death Contact Experiences (ADCEs). In his books *After Death Communication* and *Messages and Miracles* (see Resources), he gives many fascinating accounts of the phenomena, explains their various aspects, and offers insight into how many bereaved people have been able, through ADCEs, to finish unfinished business, cope with their loss, and let go of stress-producing regrets and emotions.

In 1975, Raymond Moody's classic book, *Life After Life*, discussed in great detail the phenomena of Near-Death Experiences (NDEs). It ignited tremendous interest and research into that particular phenomena. Perhaps ADCEs, which seem to be much more commonplace than NDEs, but cannot claim to be acknowledged and accepted by society in the same way, also need a champion.

The invisible community

Robert Lord, editor of the 'Invisible Community' newsletter, believes that humanity lives in two worlds, that of the incarnate and that of the disincarnate, and wherever these two worlds meet there exists an invisible community:

> Everyone knows someone who has died. Many feel that their connection with that person still continues in some form. Others even feel it continues to develop: increasingly one hears of examples of communications from the departed.

Such a community is made up of those who live and those who have died and those who are not yet born. The idea is that all the people we connect with in our lifetime remain connected with us, through love, and are part of our community. Dying means 'disincarnating' – the giving up of the physical body, and continuing to live on in another dimension. Everyone belongs to such a community, but only some people are aware of it. The Invisible Community organisation aims to foster such an awareness. The newsletter includes book reviews, poetry and inspirational stories (see Resources for more information).

Grief expression in men and women

Allowing for personality, cultural background and the nature of the relationship with the person who died, men and women have been shown to respond differently to bereavement. In very general terms, women are more likely to have a social network that can offer them support, while men may appear to be responding in a manner that is seen as not being emotionally affected. Women have permission to be emotional in certain ways that men do not have. Cross-cultural studies show that, generally, women are more expressive of their emotions and men more restrained (Haig, *The Anatomy of Grief*, 1990). Regardless of how expressive a culture is, women tend, within that cultural context, to be more expressive than men. The result of this may well be a reason, why for instance, following a child's death, less support is made available to fathers than to mothers from family, friends and professionals ('When a Child Dies', a video by the Acorn Children's Hospice Trust; see Resources).

It is not uncommon for men to cope with bereavement by throwing themselves into work more than ever before. If work is a place where one has a sense of power and control and where one's mind can be diverted away from grief for a time, it can also be used in an affirmative way. This is increasingly so for women as well. Because our society discourages 'soft' feelings in boys, in that boys traditionally, after a certain age, are not supposed to cry or show that they are frightened or feel helpless; men may feel they are expected to be emotionally in control of themselves, to be tough. Traditionally, men are more likely to show anger and resentment or become withdrawn rather than talk about what is going on for them, and women tend to become depressed.

Different styles of grieving in men and women can cause problems. Consider, for example, the situation of a family where a child has died after a long illness such as cancer. The parents' marriage may have been under tremendous strain throughout the time of the illness, and may be in danger of collapsing when the child dies if outside help is not provided. Because both partners are affected by grief, they may not be able to support each other or their remaining children sufficiently and some marriages break down as a result.

Society exerts a major influence on what we consider to be proper and acceptable in bereavement. Crying in public or in front of a stranger, for instance, most people wish to avoid, because it is associated with young children and is seen as shameful. As a result of this fear, of being seen as weak or not in control, we repress our tears and sometimes are unable to cry, even in private. Depression also, a normal and common part of grief, is rarely openly admitted. It is this shaming attitude that prevents us as a society to grieve as part of everyday life. A 'good cry' can bring tremendous relief and release, the tears flushing out stress hormones in the process. Perhaps by allowing ourselves to be heartbroken in this way, we could prevent more serious illnesses? If tears were more widely encouraged generally amongst all ages and both sexes, might it contribute to an increase in mental health?

Sudden death

When a person dies unexpectedly, there has been no time to prepare for it and no time to say goodbye. The shock of the finality of death is compounded by the shock that, at a stroke, life has been completely altered. The circumstances of the death also contribute to how the bereaved are able to manage the crisis. Statistically speaking, the number of sudden deaths are on the increase in comparison to the total number of deaths in our society. Causes of sudden death include: road traffic accidents, accidental death by drowning, burning, falling, poisoning, natural causes, sporting accidents, accidents at work, cot death, stillbirth and miscarriage, suicide, murder, street violence, natural or other disasters. In some cases there may not be a body that the family can identify or only body parts may be found. The anguish this causes can be extreme. Dorothy Becvar writes:

> The distinguishing features in the case of sudden or accidental death are the stresses and challenges to the coping ability of the bereaved (Rando, 1988). Survivors confront the pain of the loss at the same time that they must deal with the shock, disbelief, and extreme disruption which suddenly are manifest in all areas of their lives. It is in such a state that they must make decisions regarding essential issues such as organ donation, funeral preparations and burial arrangements. In addition, they must contact family and friends, who also are shocked, and are faced with the necessity of recounting the details of what happened over and over.

Becvar identifies the unique challenge for those bereaved by a sudden death:

> It involves the struggle to make sense of an event that both occurred 'out of the blue' and also may seem totally meaningless and incomprehensible. ... It is not surprising then, that in this case the grieving process may take longer or be more complicated than in other instances of bereavement. In addition, a host of emotional manifestations that may run the gamut from numbness to heartrending reactions and outbursts are not at all uncommon.
>
> *From* In the Presence of Grief *by D. Becvar (see Resources).*

The initial impact of sudden death on the bereaved may cause extreme shock: physical and mental numbness, disbelief and a sense of unreality, being unable to focus one's mind, helplessness, heightened sensory awareness or paranormal experiences, powerful emotional reactions (or a complete absence of these), an inability to eat or digest food due to a high level of adrenaline, an inability to relax or to sleep, fear of the dark, and fear of being alone.

Here one woman describes her own unique immediate reponse:

> It was nearly midnight when the police came to my door. At first I could not imagine why they were there. When I asked, 'Is it my son?' They said no. 'Is it my husband?' They said yes. I was completely calm. For years I had embraced the reality of death and the transciency of life as a daily practice. I used the reminder of death as a way to appreciate the present moment. When I heard that my husband had been killed in a car accident, I felt 'Yes,

this is now. What I had been dreading has happened.' I did not cry or feel emotional in any way. That night I went to bed at 3am, but I could not sleep. I did not feel sad or tearful as my friend expected me to be. Instead I felt the presence of my husband very strongly, which made me feel very happy.

Josefine, psychotherapist, 52.

Often there is anger at what happened – a searching for someone to blame for the tragic event; sometimes total acceptance. In some cases of suicide, a sense of inevitability, or terrible feelings of guilt. The police may be involved, the body may be kept by the coroner, the media may intrude in the family's private grief and there may be a courtcase following the death. This is added trauma for the bereaved and their grief may be prolonged or suspended in part, until all these matters are settled.

Some sudden deaths are peaceful, as in the case of an elderly person dying in their sleep. Although such deaths will not usually cause the same level of pain as an untimely or violent death, even here, as the story below exemplifies, it may not be helpful to make assumptions about another's grief response.

When a parent dies

The death of a parent is a turning point in the emotional, personal and social lives of most adults – an event which initiates a period of substantial change and redirection in the way we view ourselves, our relationships to others, and our place in the world.

From *Death of a Parent* by Debra Umberson (see Resources).

A son's response to his mother's death after years of illness

Several friends hoped I would be over it within a fortnight – not for my sake, for theirs. They were afraid they'd have to handle my grief. They were embarrassed at the thought of seeing me, a middle-aged man, going to pieces over the death of his mother. I went along with them. I acted as though I was getting on with my life. Without my mum. I wasn't. I treated my fear, pain, loss and confusion as symptoms of a secret illness. Almost two years down the line I still do, with certain people. When they ask how I am I smile as though everything's fine. Only I know that it's not.

When an actor, writer or politician refers to the death of his father the subject is regarded as profound and deserving of great respect and reverence. A tragic milestone in their lives. But few public figures – men especially – talk of the devastation of losing a mother. Perhaps they're afraid of being seen as weak, cissy or something more sinister if they show that they're distraught at the loss of the woman who gave them life.

My mother's wheelchair never impeded her visits to my house in London where, in the last years of her life, she spent roughly half the week. If I suggested dinner out or a trip to France she'd simply ask what time we'd be leaving. She would do her hair – masses of soft, silver-white curls – and we'd be off. She trusted me.

On the night I was born my mother was entirely alone at home – it was just the way things turned out. By the time my father arrived with the midwife it was all over. My mum said it was by far her best experience of childbirth – she had five children in all – because she could follow her instincts without anybody interfering.

55 years later, on one of her frequent visits to my house, she died in the night, having smiled faintly an hour or so before, and told me she was 'all right'. Again only she and I were in the house.

To some that seems touching and poetic. I find it weird, overwhelming. Yes, she was 85 and had had Parkinson's for over 25 years. But why do people think it reasonable that she died at that point? Couldn't it have been two, five, ten years later?

When I think about never seeing her again it's an effort not to panic. I might be more accepting of it if I could strike a deal with someone who, with some magical power, would arrange for her to tell me, face-to-face, that she's 'all right'. Perhaps then I'd stop wondering where she is, how she is.

Peter, journalist, 56.

A son's response to his father's sudden death

My father died two years ago in an accident. I was 25 years old. At first I didn't feel much about my father dying. I could look down at him lying in the coffin. Touch him. Maybe cry. But I was quite detached. After a few days I noticed feeling a bit emotionally unstable. I couldn't tolerate anyone but close friends, and I wanted to scream at people making idle conversation with me. The last thing I wanted was to tell anyone that my dad had died. I hated the awkward reactions, or the knowing consolations.

By the way I was feeling towards people close to me, I reasoned that this was the point; that the most valuable thing was having good friends and family. All this took place over a period of about a month. Then things seemed to settle down. I was mildly down for about the next two months, although I put it largely down to being out of work and aimless. I decided that to break out of it, action was what I needed. I moved to France for three months. That went well. Up until September 11th 2001. That sparked off my rollercoaster of emotions. I actually found the rapid flow of erratic emotions uplifting. It wasn't at all stressful. I worked out straight away that none of the emotional spells lasted. I felt like I was experiencing years of emotions all packed into hours. I was almost carefree.

It didn't last. I soon returned to normal, except that the confidence I'd always had in myself was absent. Two years on, and I'm mostly the old me I remember. I get periods when I'm down; at their worst I feel like my body's too heavy to move, and why should I even want to? I've learnt that the best thing to do is not to resist. The times I've resisted with energetic activity, I've just dragged it out into weeks. The times I surrender to the feeling of not getting out of bed are the times that pass in a couple of days.

Merlyn, student, 27.

Parental loss in childhood

> *The younger adult who is just beginning to create an independent life, faces the resurgence of grief as each succeeding milestone is achieved without the presence of the parent who has died. Significant events such as graduations, weddings, the birth of a child, career successes, holidays and birthdays thus become bittersweet experiences, with happiness tinged always by a longing for the missing parent.*
>
> From *In the Presence of Grief* by D. Becvar (see Resources).

In the past children's grief has often been ignored. Parents who are themselves overwhelmed by grief and who have no model of open communication in the face of death, may not be able to adequately support children who are bereaved. Children were often sent away to stay with relatives for a time and excluded from the funeral preparations and funeral. In many cases they were also not adequately told how the death occurred, and were not able to visit the body. Adults believed they were protecting the children, but it served only to increase their anxieties, causing insecurity and a lack of confidence.

The Irish traditionally teach children how to cope with and manage the reality of death by including them in the wake and funeral. The following apocryphal tale places the responsibility of talking about death onto the child:

When an eight-year-old Irish boy's grandfather died, his grandmother came to sit with him. She held his hand and said, 'Your grandfather is dead. Someone must go out to the back yard and tell the dogs what happened. Will you do this for me?' The young boy went out the back, called the family dogs, and proceeded to tell the two animals, in his own words and in his own way, that grandfather was dead.

Often parents are not aware of the child's grief and therefore do not attend to it. A hospital or hospice counsellor, chaplain or art therapist might be able to offer guidance and support. Some children feel more comfortable with peers in a similar situation where they can speak freely about what they are going through and offer support to each other. Support groups for children of different ages might be available at your local hospice (see Resources, or ask your GP or your palliative care nurse, if you have one).

A child's response to his father's death

My father died suddenly when I was five years old. My sister and I were whisked away to stay with an aunt and uncle. I have no recollection of being given any reason other than 'something's very wrong ... your father ...'.

We stayed with my aunt for two weeks and when mother came to pick us up I already knew, deep within myself that my father was dead. But when my mother uttered a well-rehearsed phrase, 'He's gone to live with Jesus', I simply asked 'How is Scruffy?' (our beautiful collie-dog). I remember staring dreamily out of the schoolroom window with the thought that I later approximated as, 'So, everything seems to be going to plan'. Tears came in abundance a year later when Scruffy passed away. People at school who didn't know, would ask what my father did and I would dryly supply the necessary information. I felt nothing, just floated above it all. 30 years later I was idly chatting to a woman counsellor friend when the subject of parents came up and bang, that was it, it hit me like a freight train: extreme grief, yes, but with it intense power, as if I suddenly arrived in my body for the first time ever. I felt as if I'd been plugged into the mains and I cried for most of the week, less so for the rest of the year, and still less, on and off, for the next ten years, including several occasions when, in a conducive setting, my psyche would rush back to the moment of his death. At school I noticed that, in response to the teachers' questions most of the boys expressed a cynicism far beyond their years; it seemed to me that they were answering what their fathers would have answered as if each had their own pet monkey sitting on their shoulder. They weren't aware of this. I was glad that when I spoke, the answer came from me.

Nigel, osteopath, 52.

When a child dies

Grief, for a time, can seem larger than life. Your anguish is your response to that, but do not relate solely to your pain; remember your child, however painful the memories at first; recall your lives together, however short or long they were, so that restoration may take place and, in time, you will realise that he or she is still with you in the deepest sense, bonded to you and living within your heart. You are parents of your child for eternity. Nothing can alter that. Nothing can take that away.

Jenny Kander in the Compassionate Friends paper (No. 16) on 'The Death of an Only Child'.

The Bereaved Parent by Harriet Sarnoff Schiff is a sensitive exploration of the complex emotions and realistic living circumstances surrounding the bereaved parent, offering both insight and comfort in great measure. Another book which deals explicitly with this area of loss is *On Children and Death* by Elisabeth Kübler-Ross. There are various subcultures of shared feelings created by men and women who have suffered the loss of a child, from whatever cause. Nowhere is this more fully expressed than in the extraordinary and moving series of pamphlets and newsletters issued by the Compassionate Friends (they even do a special newsletter called Sibbs for bereaved brothers and sisters).

The death of a child puts an enormous strain on all family relationships but particularly on that of the parents. The death of a child goes against the natural order of things, and can rock the very foundations of a family unit. For emotional support and advice for parents and siblings, most children's hospitals and hospices offer individual or group support (see Resources).

Supporting the bereaved

> 'After my husband's funeral', Ellen said, 'a member of my church called to ask how I was doing. When I began to cry, she said, "I'll be right over." She sat beside my recliner until I finally sobbed myself to sleep. When I awoke the next morning, she was sleeping on the couch. That was one of the kindest things anyone has ever done for me, and now I do that for other widows.'
>
> From *Life After Loss* by Raymond Moody (see Resources).

Other kind gestures might include sending flowers a month after the funeral to the family of the deceased to let them know they are still in one's thoughts; and requesting donations after the death not to charity, as often happens, but to the surviving partner, who may in some cases be reliant only on a state pension. Why, asks Maggie of Cambridge in a letter to the Natural Death Centre, should it be customary for there to be gifts for the wedding couple, but not for the funeral partner?

Sending a letter of condolence

When someone has died, those left behind are usually in a state of shock. Letters, flowers and cards sent to the bereaved can be a wonderful way of offering a touch of comfort and support. But knowing what to say when someone has died is not an easy task. This is especially true if you have never been bereaved yourself. Not everyone has the gift of finding the right words at the right time. A condolence card bought from a shop with a printed message can be a bit of a hit or miss affair. So much better to be personal if you can manage it. A letter saying, 'I am thinking of you and send you my love', and then recounting some memories of the person who died, or what the person meant to you, will act as a real acknowledgement and a reaching out to the person or persons left behind.

Virginia Ironside related in the Times how surprised she was to be consoled by letters after her father's death:

> I will never let another death go by without dropping the relatives a line. Letters that say things like: 'He will live on for ever in your heart' – trite lines I'd usually wrinkle a lip at – seem to have huge significance, laden with meaning. 'I am down the road if you want an ear,' came from an old schoolfriend I barely know. And a lovely line from my son's godfather: 'These sad deaths are like signposts which direct you into a new and unknown route. I can only wish you well.'

I didn't know what to say ...

It may be hard to know how to show your love and support and 'get it right' by the mourner. Getting things 'wrong' is a frustrating business, and both mourners and supporters alike can feel hurt and upset by the other's lack of understanding. Everyone grieves differently, and although it can be said that there are certain reactions which are very common, perhaps the mourner could help those close to him or her by letting them know what he or she finds helpful in the way of support or what they need at that particular moment.

People wish to make the grieving person feel better, but often do not know what to say or do. Making comments such as, 'Don't worry, you can have another baby' or 'You will find another partner' are usually the wrong thing to say. Also, expecting the grieving process to take place according to a prescribed formula or to be over within a certain period of time is generally not helpful. Because intense grief is something that makes one very much live in the moment, asking the person to look into the future may be a hurtful thing to do. Bereaved people often cannot bear to think far ahead, instead taking it a day at the time. As one woman said: 'Don't tell me what I should be feeling or what you expect me to be feeling. Ask me how I *am* feeling and let *me* tell *you*. And then I will feel that you care.'

> '*After the death of our infant son, my wife and I were visited by the couple who lived next door. Instead of having the florist deliver the flowers, they carried a beautiful bouquet in their arms and handed it to us. We were so comforted by their gesture, along with their silent presence, that I wondered if they too had survived the death of a child. Silence is difficult for those who have not needed it themselves.*'
>
> From *Life After Loss* by Raymond Moody (see Resources).

Inviting a grieving person to tell you how they are and then really listening to them is something not everybody can bear. However, being given permission to listen without having to say anything in response, literally, can be a relief and can actually make listening easier.

Some grief never really goes away, it just might lessen in intensity over time. Remembering and accepting that this is so can also help those who are close to someone who has lost a 'significant other' such as a child, a sibling, a young parent or a partner. Grief is the price we pay for love; a price worth paying: 'It is better to have loved and lost than never to have loved at all.'

A happily married woman whose husband died unexpectedly, has good advice for those who want to offer support to a bereaved friend:

I want to feel my family and friends care about me and that they too have not forgotten my husband. I really appreciate when they make a point in phoning me to see how I am, ask me out to dinner, to the cinema, or to a concert, or just come round to have a meal that we cook together. I love their company and their concern and I love their encouragement and interest in how I am getting on and being able to remember my husband together. I keep in touch with them also. Sometimes when I am low, I just want to be alone. Then everything is too much effort. I withdraw for a while.

In the early days, when I had a lot of sorting out to do in the house, one friend helped me and we took a car load of things to a charity shop and another lot to the dump. It is great being offered practical help and company. It makes it so much easier to manage things.

Memorials and living memorials

Keeping the memory of the person who died alive through life-celebrating funerals, an uplifting memorial service, a stone-setting ceremony in the cemetery a year after the death, or a tree-planting ceremony after a green burial has taken place, these are just some of the ways we can express our love, our loss, and share it with others in a life-affirming way.

For help and advice on planting a tree in a park or street, donating a park bench, or designing a celebratory feature (whether stile or sculpture, in the countryside or garden), see Chapter 4.

In some cases a living memorial may be achieved through setting up a charity or trust fund, as in the case of The Suzy Lamplugh Trust, named after the young estate agent who disappeared from her workplace in 1986, which has become Europe's leading authority on personal safety. RoadPeace, a national charity for road traffic victims, founded in 1992 by Brigitte Chaudry after her 26-year-old son was killed by a red-light offender, is now the national voice for victims of all types of road offences (see Resources).

Grief can be a powerful motivator to do something good for others, particularly when a person died young as a result of tragic circumstances. It can lead to a wish to transform society, to create a better future.

Where do the dead go?

The notion of where the dead go, of their presence becoming felt as an intrinsic part of nature, is expressed in a poem by Percy Bysshe Shelley written in 1821 in honour of his friend and fellow poet John Keats, who died earlier that year of tuberculosis aged 25:

> He is made one with Nature: there is heard
> His voice in all her music, from the moan
> Of thunder, to the song of night's sweet bird;
> He is a presence to be felt and known
> In darkness and in light, from herb and stone,
> Spreading itself where'er that Power may move
> Which has withdrawn his being to its own;
> Which wields the world with never-wearied love,
> Sustain it from beneath, and kindles it above.

From Adonais
An Elegy on the Death of John Keats

Chapter 11

THE POLITICS
OF DYING

The Natural Death Centre has drawn up the following Declaration of Rights of the Person Dying at Home. The attainment of many of these rights would require a fairly drastic redirection of NHS resources and a reanimation of Neighbourhood Care type schemes in both urban and rural areas. The statements that follow are thus perhaps more in the realm of desirable goals than enforceable rights and are limited by how much a family can cope with, since so much of the caring depends on the family at present. It could be made into a more personal declaration by crossing out bits that do not apply to you or by adding others.

A Declaration of the Rights of the Person Dying at Home

• I have the right to sufficient support from the NHS and the community to enable me to die at home, if I so wish.

• I have the right not to die alone; although with the right to be left alone, if desired.

• I have the right to expect the local minister or other community leader to ask the neighbourhood to support me and those caring for me.

• I have the right to have 'midwives for the dying' or their equivalent to attend to my physical, emotional and spiritual needs.

• I have the right to the same expertise of pain relief as I would obtain if occupying a hospital or hospice bed.

• I have the right not to be taken without my consent to hospital as my condition deteriorates, or, if a hospital operation is required to relieve pain, I have the right to be brought home again afterwards.

• I have the right to have any Advance Directive I have signed respected and, if not fully conscious myself, to have the wishes of my proxy respected.

• I have the right to reject heart stimulants, blood transfusions or other medical interventions to prolong my life.

• I have the right, to the extent that I so wish, to be told the truth about my condition and about the purposes of, alternatives to, and consequences of, any proposed treatments.

• I have the right to fast as death approaches, if I so desire, without being subjected to forced feeding in any form.

• I have the right to discuss my death and dying, my funeral or any other related matters openly with those caring for me.

• I have the right to as conscious and dignified a death as possible in the circumstances.

• I have the right, if I so express the wish and if the circumstances allow, for my body to remain undisturbed at home after death for a period, and for my funeral to be handled by my relatives and friends, if they so desire, without intervention by funeral directors.

All comments please to the Natural Death Centre (see Resources).

Policy changes needed

This book and indeed the above Declaration have implied the need for a number of changes in policies and practices relating to dying and death. These are summarised here:

Education

• Children need less exposure to violent death on television and in the media and yet they need to be more involved in the natural dying of their relatives and friends; to have the opportunities to visit the body if they wish and to participate in the funeral. Teachers in schools can help where appropriate by introducing relevant literature to do with bereavement (see Resources) or, for instance, by helping the children to make Memory Books or Memory Boxes that compile their thoughts and memories and photos of the dead or dying person.

• A number of people learn first aid, which they may not ever need to use. But everybody would benefit from learning the basics about preparing for dying and about looking after a dying person, if only to be better prepared for their own death. A short first-aid-style course in practical care for those who are dying should be popularised, and open to the public, not just to the nursing profession.

• Death needs to become less socially invisible. Towards this end, the Natural Death Centre promotes an annual National Day of the Dead, inspired by the Mexican Day of the Dead, both as an opportunity for rituals in remembrance of friends and relatives who have died, with a flavour of festival to it, and also as a chance for discussions and exhibitions related to death and dying. The UK Day of the Dead is on held on one Sunday in April each year.

The National Health Service and the community

• The natural death movement must be as insistent as the natural birth movement in pressing for changes in the NHS. First, there needs to be a feasibility study leading to a pilot project that would look at the relative costs for a particular region if the policy were to become one of enabling those who are terminally ill to die at home rather than in hospital or elsewhere; and the study would encourage and collect suggestions from carers about how services for those who are dying could be improved. Second, existing palliative care services and other nursing and hospice home-care services need to be adapted, or new organisations founded, for extending services to people dying of other causes besides cancer, motor neurone disease and AIDS. Third, there needs in the long term to be a new holistic profession of 'Midwives for the Dying', trained to look after the physical, emotional and spiritual needs of the dying and their carers; backed up by a nationwide network of volunteer befrienders for those who are dying, who will sit with them, carry out errands for the carers, provide transport, etc (eg see Resources for The Befriending Network scheme). Fourth, we need more take-up of the Canadian experimental brokerage scheme, whereby those with disabilities or who are terminally ill, together with their carers, identify their own financial and other needs, interviewing and selecting would-be helpers, with generous funding coming from the state. Carers taking time off work should receive an allowance equivalent to their net salary (they are currently eligible for a 'carer's assessment', though some feel this is purely paying lip service to the 1998 National Strategy for Carers, and not making a real difference to people's lives). Fifth, respite breaks for carers should be frequently and flexibly available, preferably through a vast extension of the Crossroads-type arrangements, whereby a replacement carer comes into the home and takes over all the tasks involved. Sixth, night nurses need to be routinely available for all those receiving home palliative care. (The Department of Health is aiming that all palliative care services have at least night *telephone* service by 2004; however this is not yet being seen reflected in current practice).

• There are many Neighbourhood Watch anti-crime schemes that have provided the foundations for neighbours to get to know each other. There need to be grants for pilot projects to extend these into Neighbourhood Care schemes where neighbours would gradually begin to care for each other in crisis, including helping those who are dying, their carers, and the bereaved. It would be natural in many areas for the local doctor or other respected figurehead to provide the impetus to get such schemes going. For example, Harriet Copperman writes in *Dying at Home* of an instance where the vicar 'organised a rota of people to sit with a patient who lived alone, in order that he could die at home'. Indeed, a great deal of neighbourhood care already takes place, often under the aegis of church groups, but formalised Neighbourhood Care schemes, receiving funding from Social Services and others, could encourage such activity in neighbourhoods where it is currently lacking.

Spirituality

• There needs to be an English Book of the Dead (there are already several American ones) that would translate Tibetan insights into the experience and psychology of dying into anglicised and even Christian rituals that could become part of a prearranged Dying Service for those wanting it – for instance an elaboration of the 'go towards the light' message whispered into the ear of the dying person, along with breathing and other meditations; and perhaps accompanied by music. People could be encouraged to design their own Dying Plans specifying the kind of material of this nature that they might like. (See the Centre's own Death Plan in Chapter 2, for example.)

• People seem to appreciate dying close to nature, as near outdoors as the elements will allow. Either the patient needs to be able to get a taste of the outdoors or nature needs to be brought into the house or even the hospital – not only flowers, but branches, trees and animals. (One of the burial grounds listed in Chapter 6, Donald Boddy's West Pennine Remembrance Park, is apparently considering providing a building on site for dying people to come and spend their last days, surrounded by nature.)

Hospital

• A hospital palliative care ward should have as much a 'home from home' atmosphere and design as possible – imagine, for instance, a country house hospital with open fires and meals around long tables, with patients' interests accommodated, whether for pets, music or complementary treatments.

• Dr Marie Louise Grennert's excellent palliative care work at the Malmö Clinic in Sweden deserves imitating. To encourage patients to talk freely, she has an informal discussion with each one at the outset and asks: 'What are your most pressing problems right now? What do you want from the care provided here? What is your outlook on the future? How do you feel about entering this palliative care ward?' Next-of-kin also talk with the doctor about anything that is on their mind, not just medical matters – and are invited back to the hospital two weeks after the death for a further talk. Two hours or so after the death, all the ward staff gather briefly to discuss the patient who has died, any problems that arose and any lessons that can be learnt.

• In the hospital setting, the partner needs acceptance as part of the caring team (that is, if both partner and patient would like this). Ideally, just as a parent can sometimes stay with a child in hospital, the partner should be able to share a bed with the dying person, as is possible at home, or to have another bed alongside. Justin Hawkins even goes so far as to suggest that hospitals should have double beds so that those who are terminally ill could have their partners lie down close to them; and children who were ill could have their parents physically close enough to them to be reassuring.

• The medical carers need to maintain reassuring physical contact with the dying. One American hospital renowned for its excellent palliative care was filmed looking after a dying woman who was rigged up to the most high tech equipment. She died with the medical team in full attendance and with a record kept of the exact time of her death. But nobody held her hand or had anything to do with her as a person or even said a word of blessing over her dead body.

• The nursing staff could show carers and visitors simple techniques such as scalp massage and Boerstler's breath relaxation method which can be helpful to the dying person and which give family and friends a feeling of involvement.

• Patients need to be allowed to acknowledge the deaths of fellow patients and to say goodbye in some way – rather than the drawing of ward curtains around each bed, so that no patient is disturbed by seeing the dead body moved away. Dr Elizabeth Lee, in her book *A Good Death*, describes, in contrast, a death in a small Kenyan hospital. The patient's mother stood and, raising one arm above her head, began to sing a hymn. All the other young women on the ward stood by their beds, faces turned to the dead woman, and singing with her mother. They faced her death and bade her goodbye.

• Where it suits their particular style, doctors and nurses in hospital could evolve a brief ritual (depending on their own belief systems and that of the patient) to say together over the body of someone who has just died.

• How to support the dying person and a knowledge of the various kinds of basic information in this handbook should become an integral and important part of the training of doctors and nurses. (Nurses should not be able to use their 'supernumerary status' to opt out of this subject in their training.) Medical staff need encouragement to recognise the difference between healing and curing, and to acknowledge that a peaceful death is an achievement rather than a failure on their part. All Accident and Emergency staff should be trained in dealing with those who are bereaved, and each such unit should have a counsellor on call (as suggested in the *Nursing Times*, January 8th 1992). Counselling help, discussion groups, talks by experts and other support must be available to all personnel caring for the dying (as suggested by Pam Williams, see the booklist).

• Some hospitals continue to incinerate miscarried foetuses with the hospital waste. A better approach is that of the Aberdeen Maternity Hospital where, since 1985, a service is held at the local crematorium every three months attended by the hospital and those families and friends who wish to come. The main point being that parents should have some choice about what happens to the body – and about visiting the body.

• Whilst mindful of the exceptions – Mother Teresa, for instance, with her great zest for life, who had a pacemaker fitted at the age of 82 – and whilst accepting that the patient's own wishes come first, we believe it would be helpful in some cases if doctors were to take any evidently frail and elderly patients (and their carers) through a detailed series of questions aimed at ascertaining the person's perceived quality of life, before pressurising the patient to accept a major operation and the subsequent stresses and strains of 'maximum recovery' treatment.

• A doctor seeing a very elderly person peacefully dying in a residential home may need to resist the temptation to rush the patient by ambulance to hospital, just so as to guard against claims of negligence.

• When dealing with those who are very elderly and dying, cardiopulmonary resuscitation given by emergency teams should be reserved for those patients who want it, or whose relatives request it on their behalf, or who stand a good chance of surviving and being discharged. This routine assault on those who are very elderly and dying should be something a patient has to be 'opted in' for, rather than 'opted out' from as at present. (See 'Whose Life Is It Anyway?' by nurse Pam Williams, an unpublished paper in the Centre library.)

• The legal standing of Advance Health Care Directives should be confirmed by an act of parliament, if only to give more secure legal protection to any medical carer who follows a patient's requests.

• All patients should be offered the opportunity of drawing up an Advance Directive (AD) before entering hospital for serious treatment. Indeed, GPs need to discuss the concept with all their patients who reach pension age. The US government in 1987 concluded that Advance Directives could save its health service $5 billion a year ('one out of every seven health care dollars are spent on the last six months of life'). Here then is a reform that would not only save the NHS money, but that would improve the quality of living and dying.

• The hospital should endeavour to leave the body undisturbed for a period after death, if so desired by the next-of-kin, for religious or other reasons.

• The Natural Death Centre backs the proposal made by the A.B. Welfare and Wildlife Trust that postmortems should be performed only in exceptional cases, so as to reduce the trauma for relatives. In cases where the coroner knows that death was natural, bodies should be swiftly released to the families. (In the wake of the Shipman inquiry, 122 recommendations for change were made to the coroner's system for England and Wales. These included fewer post-mortem examinations, that more inquests should be carried out in private, and a 'family charter' with rights for the bereaved to request a review of certain decisions made by the coroner. Implementation of these changes, however, will be hampered by a 'probable lack of resources', according to the Coroners' Society.)

• The Anatomy Act 1984 needs amending, to remove the right of hospitals and similar institutions to send unclaimed bodies for anatomical use, irrespective of whether these institutions at present make use of these powers. Under S.4(9) 'in the case of a body lying in a hospital, nursing home or other institution', any person acting on behalf of the management has legal powers to decide whether to send the body for anatomical use. This only applies when no friends or relatives take lawful possession of the body. (Information from *Green Burial* by John Bradfield, 1994; now out of print.)

• Hospitals need to make available leaflets for families explaining how they can organise funerals inexpensively and without funeral directors. All hospital staff need to know that the next-of-kin have the legal right to take possession of the body. (The National Funerals College has published a very basic but clear leaflet on arranging a funeral which could perhaps inspire a more detailed guide. The NFC also ran a pilot project in hospices and residential homes, where 'Funeral Advisors' – either existing staff members or trained volunteers – offered free and independent information on request. Resistance and avoidance around the subject of death seemed to be the major obstacle; as project trainer Jane Warman observed: 'Perhaps training should start with death awareness.')

Euthanasia and suicide

The word 'euthanasia' comes from the Greek for 'good death' and in the dictionary has the definition of 'a quiet and easy death or the means of procuring this or the action of inducing this'. With such a definition it seems hard to imagine who could be against it – even to enter a hospice could count as slow euthanasia. It may reassure relatives of those who have taken their own lives to know that our culture's present stand against suicide and euthanasia has not been shared at other times and in other cultures. For Christians it stems from a decision of the church council of Braga in AD 562 to refuse funeral rites to all suicides. This in turn came about because early Christians were killing themselves in worrying numbers – martyrs had all their transgressions wiped out and were glorified by the church, and Christian suicide was prevalent and acceptable in the fifth century. The Christians had inherited the Roman attitude to suicide. They saw it as a virtuous act if undertaken with dignity, just as the Greek stoics before them viewed death and suicide with equanimity. Plato too felt that if life became 'immoderate' through disease, then suicide was a justified and reasonable act.

The arguments in favour of doctor-assisted active euthanasia include the following: that a small percentage of terminal pain cannot be controlled by drugs; that some patients are either insufficiently mobile or conscious to take their own lives unassisted; that the drugs required for a swift and painless exit are unobtainable without a prescription; and that, as a democracy, we should accept the verdict of the overwhelming majority of people – 82 per cent of respondents to a recent UK survey agreed that 'doctors should be permitted to end a life when someone requests it'.

The arguments against euthanasia include: that pain relief as practised in hospices is an advanced art; that it is against the Hippocratic Oath for a doctor to kill a patient; that it is not for the doctor to play God and to decide that a patient's time is up; that the soul may have lessons to learn from the body's helplessness and suffering – the 'labour pains' of dying; and, most powerfully, that it is a slippery slope – once mercy killing is legalised, where will it end?

In nature, some animals who realise their time has come refuse all food, just as, traditionally, Native Americans who had decided that 'now is a good time to die' thereafter refused all food. Hindus who are taken to muktibhavans (hospices) in Benaras consider it appropriate and natural not to eat. The *slowness* of this kind of dying seems to be the crux of the matter. Rather than a possibly impulsive decision regretted in the event – a regret implied, for instance, by the positive and almost mystical transformations experienced by those few who survived suicide jumps from Golden Gate Bridge – fasting to death requires commitment and perseverance.

In an editorial for the *International Journal of Palliative Nursing* entitled 'Why not natural death?', Christi A. Holland argued that the 'natural process' of the body withdrawing and shutting down as death becomes imminent 'is often prolonged with artificial nutrition and hydration support that frequently creates misery for the family and undermines quality of life for the patient'. Furthermore, 'research supports that loss of appetite is an observed feature of the dying process and that lack of nutrition and hydration has been associated with euphoria and analgesia' (*IJPN*, 7;10;464). In its early stages, fasting can sometimes have a meditative effect, helping people to feel centred and spiritual. If they then change their mind when viewing their condition from this new perspective, they can simply start accepting food again. President Mitterrand, suffering from terminal cancer, called his wife to his bedside and told her that his end was near – he would take no more medicines and no more food. Such a death can be a slow, orderly and graceful process that allows the person time to come to terms with his or her exit.

As a way of dying, fasting is tough on the relatives, watching the patient become more and more skeletal. But perhaps the very fact that it is hard on the relatives is an additional safeguard against pressure on the elderly person from potential beneficiaries from the estate. Fasting is also a way that absolves doctors or nurses from ethically problematic involvement, as long as the terminally ill person makes clear his or her rejection of enforced feeding, preferably through filling in an Advance Directive.

Chris Docker of Exit writes that fasting has the distinction 'of being the only method at the present time in which all sides in the "right to die" debate may reach common agreement under the law' (Exit, 21;2;11). Exit's position, however, is that although a painless death is possible through fasting, it is by no means guaranteed and medical supervision is recommended.

The Natural Death Centre's tentative conclusions, therefore, are:

• Euthanasia actively assisted by doctor or relative should remain illegal, but judges should be given more scope for leniency in their sentencing, should such cases come to court. We support the recommendations of the Committee on the Penalty for Homicide, chaired by Lord Lane, which called for an end to compulsory life sentences for murder.

• The Natural Death Centre would like to see research into alternatives to active euthanasia, such as better relief of pain and anxiety in terminal care.

Funerals and procedures

• Given that our investigations show that few of the mainstream coffin manufacturers will sell a coffin directly to a member of the public and that most funeral directors do not see themselves as 'coffin shops' – if they grudgingly sell just a coffin they tend to add an extravagant mark-up – the Natural Death Centre recommends that the Office of Fair Trading issue a requirement that funeral suppliers and directors sell coffins to the general public without undue profit. The Office of Fair Trading has made a move in this direction, writing that 'consumers should be afforded the right to buy a coffin (independently of other funerary goods and services)'.

• Just as funeral directors are required by their associations to offer a basic or 'simple' funeral as one of their options, so they should also be obliged to offer a basic container for those not wanting a fancy coffin. This could be, as in the United States, either an unfinished wood box or a cardboard coffin or other rigid container (supported by a plank of wood if necessary).

• Given that 97 per cent of people are 'hooked' the moment they contact an undertaker, and do not shop around, the Natural Death Centre recommends the adoption of regulations similar to the 1984 funeral rules of the American Federal Trade Commission, whereby funeral directors are obliged:

(a) to give a price breakdown over the phone (whilst the funeral directors listed in Chapter 7 have said that they do so, several of those we surveyed refused. Unfortunately it is also our experience, and that of some of our readers, that even those funeral directors who say that they do give price breakdowns over the phone, can often be more than a little reticent to do so when the time comes).

(b) to give a written and itemised breakdown of prices to be displayed on the premises and to be readily available for visitors to take away. In 2002, the National Association of Funeral Directors inspected 259 member firms and found that 12 were still failing to display a price list, despite the fact that such display is required by the Association's Code. (In total, 28.8 per cent were in breach of their Code; 20 failed to have readily available a written price list; and 15 failed to provide information about a basic funeral.) The OFT has recommended that price lists should be prominently displayed (2001), but we further recommend that the OFT should seek a Price Marking Order, legislating as to the composition and distribution of price lists, and making noncompliance a criminal offence. Of the replies to our questionnaire to over 2,000 funeral directors, the most fully itemised price list came from George Brooke of Dewsbury, West Yorkshire (the average price list hides many of the funeral costs behind an inflated coffin price). Several others are also to be commended – in general we are pleased to note that there has been an improvement in recent years.

(c) to give an *itemised written estimate* before the funeral, so that you can add or subtract items to get what you want. (In addition, we ask all families to check this estimate in detail, and to immediately query anything with which they disagree or for which they require more information. It is vital to do this *before* the funeral takes place; you can always take your business elsewhere if things are not sorted to your satisfaction.)

(d) to charge a fee for embalming only if authorised by the family or required by law – eg when required for transport out of the country.

(e) to disclose in writing what service fee, if any, is being added by the funeral director to the cost of disbursements, and whether he or she is getting a refund, discount or rebate from the disbursement supplier.

• There should also be an enforcement of the requirement that funeral directors reveal clearly on their paperwork and premises if they are part of a larger firm. (The latter, unlike most chains in other businesses, have pushed up prices, and they will tend to bring about a bland uniformity of style.) One small firm complained in the *FSJ* that 'certain multinationals openly admit they do not display ownership on the premises or paperwork, which is against trading law. Even those that do, go under a pseudonym to fool the public.' Some chains claim to be 'family funeral directors', meaning only that they serve families, a fraudulent use of words which the National Association of Funeral Directors has nevertheless explicitly condoned. Other groups continue to use the word 'independent': 'This is affecting every true independent funeral director in the country', according to Joyce Dean from SAIF (*FSJ*, Nov 2002).

• The A. B. Welfare and Wildlife Trust reports that at present very small nature reserves (intended for burials or other purposes) cannot become wildlife charities, based on precedent court cases. The Charity Commission needs to press for the acceptance of such small nature reserves as charities.

• Even more local authorities should copy the pioneering efforts in Nottingham, Crewe and elsewhere whereby the councils work with local funeral directors to provide an inexpensive 'Local Funeral' package.

• Following the collapse of the Funeral Ombudsman Scheme, the various funeral directors' associations need to improve their self-policing and in particular their complaints procedure. All complaints should be acknowledged within ten days and dealt with within three months. (While the OFT has called for 'speedy' complaints procedures, the NAFD's recently launched three-stage funeral arbitration scheme allows a wait of at least six months before any dispute 'may' be referred to independent arbitration.)

• Members of the public do not shop around in the trauma of bereavement. We recommend in this book that they get a friend who is less involved do so on their behalf, so as to find a funeral director that suits their particular requirements. But it would also be of assistance to the public if there were regularly published comparative surveys of price and services, drawn up on a regional basis, naming particular establishments. This book is a step towards such a goal.

• Local authorities, church authorities or the government should offer financial incentives to churchyards to reopen their graveyards and any impeding legislation should be amended. At the moment it can be to a church's financial advantage to declare a graveyard closed, and to pass its maintenance over to the local authority. Cemeteries too, particularly in urban areas, are rapidly running out of space. Re-use of old graves (using the lift and deepen method common across Europe and widely used in Britain until the 18th century) is tentatively being re-introduced, for instance in the pioneering City of London Cemetery, and local authorities have begun to sell shorter Rights of Burial (usually 50, 75 or 100 years). However, we believe that if all Rights of Burial were for, say, a minimum period of 30 years (renewable), local burials would remain possible and graves would be well tended.

• All new crematoria buildings should be adaptable, with flexible seating arrangements.

• UK crematoria and cemeteries should offer biodegradable and other coffins and shrouds for sale to those who are not using funeral directors, and could consider having a vehicle available for hire for the collection of bodies and cold storage facilities. The OFT should take action against groupings of funeral directors threatening to boycott such places. Likewise, all coffin manufacturers should be willing to sell direct to the public, with the OFT investigating those which are threatened by funeral directors as a result.

• Crematoria, cemeteries and others in the funeral business are urged to adopt the Charter for the Bereaved (published by the Institute of Burial and Cremation Administration); it has already been officially adopted by 83 cemeteries or crematoria.

• Cemeteries should allow family and friends to help dig and fill the graves if they so wish, subject to any safeguards.

• Every local authority should encourage the development of natural burial grounds in its area. Every church, county wildlife trust and environmental charity should set one up and conscientious farmers could do so.

• The DIY superstores could offer flatpack coffins. Sainsbury's Homebase wrote to Jane Spottiswoode to say that they would not sell coffins, as their stores were intended for family shopping 'based on the future and therefore not associated with death', whereas of course death in the future is one certainty that every family faces! Argos wrote to say that the sale of coffins would require a 'truly personal service' – in fact all that is required is the assurance that the coffin is big enough: two or three standard sizes should suffice.

• Every town needs its funeral shop where inexpensive coffins can be bought, along with every other funeral item, from lowering webbing to urns.

• 'At present', writes K. A. Gilchrist to the Natural Death Centre, 'it is far easier to take time off for having a bad cold than for the death of a close relative.' The entitlement of those who are bereaved to adequate leave of absence needs recognition.

• Probate work should no longer remain an expensive monopoly of the banks and solicitors. Others should be able to offer their services, subject of course to effective safeguards against fraudulent practices.

• The rules about the styles of memorial permitted in churchyards, cemeteries and crematoria should be relaxed, with any design or type of stone allowed. The disliked Albert Memorial monstrosities of one era become the much-loved tourist attractions of the future. And as one vicar complained in the journal *Funerals*: 'I can't tell you how often I deal with clients who are deeply upset because they have set their heart on some appropriate memorial which has then been forbidden'. The Church of England court ruling in 1996 that bereaved families should be allowed to attach photographs of the deceased to their tombstones, and Calne (Wiltshire) town council's approval of photographs, etched pictures and even holograms, are both positive development.

• Everyone is entitled to an obituary. Even funerals paid for by the state should include a small fee so that the minister or presiding person can help assemble a brief life story of the deceased for publication – if nowhere else, then at least for putting online in one of the free and permanent 'Gardens of Remembrance' on the Internet (see the Resources chapter). All priests should follow the practice of celebrants and officiants, who talk before the funeral to relatives, a friend and a colleague, so that at the service they can recount the biography of the person who has died.

Perhaps the next millennium will see the emergence of the new profession described by the science fiction writer Orson Scott Card, that of Speaker for the Dead – memorial service orators who provide catharsis for the friends and relatives by painstakingly assembling the unvarnished truth about the deceased's motivations, intentions and achievements. It could be a suitable job for resting novelists.

• Birthdays are recognised social occasions. Deathdays could be recognised too. On the first anniversary of the death, it could become the accepted practice for there to be a meal for close friends and relatives, and at subsequent deathdays just the simple gesture at mealtime of a toast to the person's memory or those present telling a story or memory about the one whose anniversary it is – thus passing on family lore to the next generations.

This may be the appropriate moment to wish you, dear reader, a peaceful deathday. May death for you be as graceful as Walt Whitman imagined it could be:

Come, lovely and soothing Death,
Undulate round the world, serenely arriving, arriving,
In the day, in the night, to all, to each,
Sooner or later, delicate death.
    From Leaves of Grass *by Walt Whitman*.

Chapter 12

RESOURCES

Bookshops

• **Internet bookshops**. UK books may be researched at online stores such as **www.amazon.co.uk** (or www.amazon.com for American books) but it is kinder to your local small bookshop to then place the order with them.

• **The Natural Death Centre** (see under Organisations) sells its own publications, as listed below. It also has a small library.

• **St Christopher's Hospice** (51-59 Lawrie Park Road, London SE26 6DZ, ☎ 020 8768 4500) have a book service.

• **Watkins** (19 Cecil Court, Charing Cross Road, London WC2N 4EZ, ☎ 020 7836 2182, **f**: 020 7836 6700; **e**: service@watkinsbooks.com) is probably one of the best bookshops in London for books on dying.

Booklist

✪✪✪ = *HIGHLY RECOMMENDED by the Natural Death Centre (NDC).*

Preparing for Dying

• ✪✪✪ Speyer, Josefine & Wienrich, Stephanie (eds), **The Natural Death Handbook**, 4th edn (this present book), Rider, 2003, 384pp, £14.99 incl. p&p from NDC (see under Organisations below), ISBN 1844132269.

• ✪✪✪ Wienrich, Stephanie et al (eds), **After Life – Reports from the frontline of death**, NDC, 2002, 100pp, £6.50 incl. p&p from NDC (see under Organisations), ISBN 0952328097. The right to die at home; natural burial; surviving bereavement. Complements this Handbook.

• ✪✪✪ Albery, Nicholas et al (eds), **Progressive Endings – Changing attitudes to death and dying**, NDC, 2001, 104pp, £6.20 incl. p&p from NDC, ISBN 0952328089. Death as a process; words spoken to my dying love.

• ✪✪✪ Albery, Nicholas et al (eds), **Ways To Go – Naturally: For families and palliative care workers**, NDC, 2000, 80pp, £6.20 incl. p&p from NDC, ISBN 0952328070. Fear of death; woodland burial; befriending.

• Albom, Mitch, **Tuesdays with Morrie – An old man, a young man, and life's greatest lesson**, Little, Brown & Company, 1998, 192pp, £12.99, ISBN 0316648051. Mitch travels by plane every Tuesday to visit Morrie, his former college professor, dying of ALS, for poignant lessons on life and death.

• ✪✪✪ Anderson, Megory, **Sacred Dying: Creating rituals for embracing the end of life**, Prima, 2001, 364pp, £17.99, ISBN 0761534539.

• Berridge, Kate, **Vigor Mortis: The end of the death taboo**, Profile Books (58a Hatton Garden, London EC1N 8LX, UK, w: www.profilebooks.co.uk). 2001, 288pp, £7.99, ISBN 1861974116.

• Blackmore, Susan, **Dying to Live – Science and the Near-Death Experience**, Prometheus, 1994, 291pp, £19.99, ISBN 0879758708. Discusses the stages of dying, examines accounts of NDEs, and argues that brain chemistry best explains the sensations felt near death.

• Boerstler, Richard, **Letting Go: A holistic and meditative approach to living and dying**, Associates in Thanatology (115 Blue Rock Road, South Yarmouth, MA 02664, USA; w: www.gis.net/~hulenk), 1985, 60pp, $5.95 incl. p&p, ISBN 0960792805T.

• British Medical Association, **Advance Statements About Medical Treatments**, BMA Professional Division Publications, 1995, 39pp, £5.95, ISBN 0727909142.

• ✪✪✪ Department for Work and Pensions, **What To Do After A Death in England and Wales (D49)**, & **What To Do After A Death in Scotland (D49S)** available free from a registry office, CAB, social security office or from the DWP (☎ 020 7712 2171; w: www.dwp.gov.uk). D49S is also available from the Scottish Executive Justice Department, Spur VI, Saughton House, Broomhouse Drive, Edinburgh EH1 3XD (☎ 0131 244 3581).

• Dickenson, Donna and Johnson, Malcolm (eds), **Death, Dying and Bereavement**, Sage, 1993, 355pp, £12.95. The reader for the Open University course on death and dying (see under courses).

• Dunn, Michael, **The Good Death Guide – Everything you wanted to know but were afraid to ask**, Pathways (How to Books Ltd, 3 Newtec Place, Magdalen Road, Oxford OX4 1RE, ☎ 01865 793806; e: info@howto books.co.uk), 2000, 256pp, £12.95, ISBN 1857035593. Family reference dealing with practical issues using statistics and humour.

• Foos-Graber, Anya, **Deathing – An intelligent alternative for the final moments of life**, Nicolas-Hays, 1989, 397pp, £11.95 from Airlift (☎ 020 7607 5792; w: nowbooks.co.uk), ISBN 0892540168.

• Garsia, Marlene, **How to Write a Will and Gain Probate**, Kogan Page (☎ 020 7278 0433; w: www.kogan-page.co.uk), 2001, 208pp, £8.99, ISBN 0749436336. Covers consequences of dying intestate.

• Hjelmstad, Lois Tschetter, **Fine Black Lines – Reflections on facing cancer, fear and loneliness**, Mulberry Hill Press (2710 S. Washington, Englewood, CO 80113, USA, ☎ 001 800 294 4714; w: www.facingbreastcancer.com or www. mulberryhill.com), 1993, 2003, 184pp, $15.95, ISBN 0963713981. Includes some fine poems. NDC Award winner 1996.

• Huxley, Laura, **This Timeless Moment – A personal view of Aldous Huxley**, Celestial Arts, 2000, 280pp, $14.95, ISBN 0890879680. The story of his dying.

• Keizer, Bert, **Dancing with Mister D – Notes on life and death**, Black Swan, 1997, £6.99, ISBN 0552996912. A doctor's memoir of caring for the terminally ill in the Netherlands. Euthanasia is a recurring theme.

• Levine, Stephen, **A Gradual Awakening**, Gill & Macmillan (Goldenbridge, Dublin 8, Ireland), 1993, 192pp, £6.95, ISBN 0452271371.

• Levine, Stephen, **Who Dies? – An investigation of conscious living and conscious dying**, Gill & Macmillan (see above), 2000, 317pp, £12.99, ISBN 0717131211.

• Morgan, Ernest, **Dealing Creatively with Death: A manual of death education and simple burial**, Upper Access, 2001, 160pp, £11.95, ISBN 0942679245.

• Morris, Virginia, **Talking About Death Won't Kill You**, Workman Publishing, 2001, 294pp, £15.30, ISBN 0761112316. Confronting death as a means to get the most out of life.

• Morse, Melvyn, **Closer to the Light – Learning from children's Near-Death Experiences**, Souvenir Press, 1991, 237pp, £12.95, ISBN 028563030X.

• Nearing, Helen, **Loving and Leaving the Good Life**, Chelsea Green Publishing (Post Mills, Vermont, USA), 1995, 208pp, £10.95, ISBN 0930031636. The life and dying of Scott Nearing.

• Ring, Kenneth, **Heading Toward Omega – In search of the meaning of the Near-Death Experience**, Quill, 1985, 348pp, $8.95, ISBN 0688062687.

• Rinpoche, Sogyal, **The Tibetan Book of Living and Dying**, Rider, 2002, 427pp, £12.99, ISBN 0712615695. Adapted for the Westerner, it gives the background to the teachings (See also Rigpa under Organisations).

• Rose, Gillian, **Love's Work**, Vintage, 1997, 144pp, £7.99, ISBN 0099545810. Courageous and passionate memoirs of a philosopher facing cancer.

• Simpson, Ray, **Before We Say Goodbye – Preparing for a good death**, HarperCollins, 2001, £9.99, ISBN 0007119399.

• Taylor, Allegra, **Acquainted with the Night – A year on the frontier of death**, Fontana (HarperCollins), 1995, 191pp, £7.95, ISBN 0852072856.

• Terkel, Studs, **Will the Circle be Unbroken? Reflections on death and dignity**, Granta, 2/3 Hanover Yard, London N1 8BE, 2002, 407pp, £15, ISBN 1862075115. Features interviews with people from Terkel's home, Chicago.

• Volk, Tyler, **What is Death? A scientist looks at the cycle of life**, John Wiley & Sons, 2002, 255 pp, $27.95, ISBN 047137544 6. Leading developer of Gaia theory considers life and death, weaving in his own life-threatening experience.

• Weinholtz, Donn, **Longing to Live ... Learning to Die**, iUniverse (5220 S. 16th St, Suite 200, Lincoln NE68512, USA), 2002, 162pp, £11.99, ISBN 059521231X. Self-published book about how a family coped with a series of deaths from terminal illnesses.

• Which? Books, **Guide to Giving and Inheriting, Tax-efficient ways to pass on money, property and other valuables**, Which? Books (☎ 0800 252 100), 2003, 300pp, £10.99, ISBN 0852029462.

• Which? Books (see above), **Make Your Own Will: A step-by-step action pack for writing your own will (England and Wales)**, 2001, 28pp, £10.99 incl. p&p, ISBN 085202875X.

• Which? Books (see above), **What To Do When Someone Dies: How to deal with the practical arrangements that have to be made after a death**, 2002, 176pp, £9.99 incl. p&p, ISBN 0852028997.

• ✪✪✪ Which? Books (see above), **Wills and Probate**: **How to make a Will and how to administer the estate of someone who has died, without employing a solicitor**, 2001, 224pp, £10.99 incl. p&p, ISBN 085202858X.
• Young, Michael & Cullen, Lesley, **A Good Death – Conversations with East Londoners**, Routledge, 1996, 272pp, £19.99, ISBN 0415137977.
• Zaleski, Carol, **Otherworld Journeys – Accounts of Near-Death Experience in medieval and modern times**, OUP, 1989, 285pp, £12, ISBN 0195056655.

Care for the Dying

• Acorn Children's Hospice Trust, **Enhancing the Quality of Care for Hindu, Muslim & Sikh Families**. Three booklets (mailorder ☎ 0121 248 4817).
• Ainsworth-Smith, Ian & Speck, Peter, **Letting Go – Caring for the dying and bereaved**, SPCK, 1999, 176pp, £9.99, ISBN 0281052255
• Bell, Lesley, **Carefully – A guide for home care assistants**, ACE Books (Age Concern), 1999, 268pp, £12.99, ISBN 086242285X.
• Boerstler, Richard & Kornfeld, Hulen, **Life to Death: Harmonising the transition – A holistic and meditative approach for caregivers and the dying**, Inner Traditions International, 1996, 256pp, £12.99, ISBN 0892813296. Draws on the practice of Tibetan lamas, using special breathing techniques and shared meditation ('comeditation') to maintain calm and peace in the dying person.
• Buckman, Dr Robert, **I Don't Know What To Say – How to help and support someone who is dying**, Pan, 1996, 272pp, £8.99, ISBN 0330347543.
• Callanan, Maggie and Kelley, Patricia, **Final Gifts – Understanding the special awareness, needs, and communications of the dying**, Bantam Books (New York), 1997, 241pp, $12.95, ISBN 0553378767.
• CancerLink (see under Organisations), **Caring at Home – Caring at home when cancer cannot be cured**, 2001, 44pp, £5, ISBN 1870534670.
• Diamond, John, **C – Because cowards get cancer too**, Vermilion, 1999, 256pp, £6.99, ISBN 0091816653. Diamond's personal perspective on: 'How will cancer affect me? What is it like to deal with the pain, the fear and the anger?'
• Doyle, Derek, **Domiciliary Palliative Care: A handbook for family doctors and community nurses**, Oxford University Press, 1994, 160pp, £29.95, ISBN 019262489X. Covers pain, diet, equipment, and counselling.
• ✪✪✪ Duda, Deborah, **Coming Home – A guide to dying at home with dignity**, Aurora Press (☎ 001 505 989 9804; **e**: Aurorep@aol.com), 1987, 404pp, $14.95 from Airlift (☎ 020 7607 5792), ISBN 0943358310.
• Elkington, Gail & Harrison, Gill, **Caring for Someone at Home**, Chivers Press, 1998, 304pp, £14.99, ISBN 0754031055.
• Fremantle, Francesca & Trungpa, Chögyam (eds), **The Tibetan Book of the Dead**, Shambhala, 1991, 119pp, £7.99, ISBN 0877730741. Traditionally read aloud to the dying.
• Kessler, David, **The Rights of the Dying – A companion for life's final moments**, Vermilion, 1998, 224pp, £8.99, ISBN 0091864135.
• Kübler-Ross, Elisabeth, **On Death and Dying: What the dying have to teach doctors, nurses, clergy, and their own families**, Routledge, 1999, 272pp, £15.99, ISBN 0415040159.

• Lawton, Julia, **The Dying Process – Patients' experiences of palliative care**, Routledge, 2000, 229 pp, £15.99, ISBN 041522679. Academic look at palliative care from patients' viewpoint.
• Lee, Dr Elizabeth, **In Your own Time: A guide for patients and their carers facing a last illness at home**, OUP, 2002, 268pp, £10.99, ISBN 0198509758. Explains how dying at home can be managed in all but a few cases.
• ❂❂❂ LeShan, Lawrence, **Cancer as a Turning Point – A handbook for people with cancer, their families, and health professionals**, Gill & Macmillan, 1996, 256pp, £8.95, ISBN 1858600464.
• Levine, Stephen, **Guided Meditations, Explorations and Healings**, Gill & Macmillan, 2000, 336pp, £12.99, ISBN 0717130835. Used widely in meditation centres, hospices and hospitals.
• Longaker, Christina, **Facing Death & Finding Hope – A guide to the emotional and spiritual care of the dying**, Arrow, 1998, 256pp, £6.99, ISBN 0099176920.
• ❂❂❂ Lunn, Joanne, & Harrold, Joan, & The Centre to Improve Care of the Dying at George Washington University, **Handbook for Mortals – Guidance for people facing serious illness**, OUP (New York) 2001, 242pp, £14.99, ISBN 0195116623. Authoritative and fascinating book on preparing for dying.
• Neuberger, Julia, **Dying Well – A guide to enabling a good death**, Radcliffe Medical Press, 1999, 186pp, £17.95, ISBN 1898507260.
• Marie Curie Cancer Care, **Partners in Caring**, free booklet from Marie Curie (see under Organisations). Aimed at people caring for a relative at home.
• Pratt, Mandy, & Wood, Michele J. M., **Art Therapy in Palliative Care – The creative response**, Routledge, 1998, 202pp, £16.99, ISBN 0415161576.
• Reoch, Richard, **Dying Well – A holistic guide for the dying and their carers**, Gaia Books (66 Charlotte Street, London W1P 1LR), 1997, 192pp, £11.99, ISBN 1856750191.
• Shipman, Cathy, et al, **Psychosocial Support for Dying People: What can primary care trusts do?**, 2002, Kings Fund discussion paper (☎ 020 7307 2691; or download from: www.kingsfund.org.uk). Argues that dying people need better support from health services.
• Thorpe, Graham, **Enabling More Dying People to Remain at Home**, British Medical Journal, 1993, 307, 915-918.
• Todd, Jacquelyne, **Living with Lymphoedema – Your guide to treatment**, Marie Curie Cancer Care (see under Organisations), 1996, £6.49 incl. p&p, ISBN 0951645439.
• Williams, Pam, **Knowing About Caring for the Dying**, available from author (5 Penybryn Road, Gorseinon, Swansea SA4 4UJ, ☎ 01909 773507). How nurses' training is now and how it could be improved.

Funerals

• Astley, Neil (ed), **Do Not Go Gentle: Poems for funerals**, Bloodaxe Books, 2003, 96pp, £6.99, ISBN 1852246359. For people of all faiths or none.
• Baum, Rachel R. (ed), **Funeral and Memorial Service Readings, Poems and Tributes**, McFarland Publishers, 1999, 172pp, £26.95, ISBN 0786406992.

• Bentley, James, Best, Andrew & Hunt, Jackie, **Funerals: A Guide – Prayers, hymns and readings**, Hodder and Stoughton (338 Euston Road, London NW1 3BH), 1994, 319pp, £12.99, ISBN 0340612401. Drawn from a wide range of faiths and traditions.

• Carlson, Lisa, **Caring For Your Own Dead**, Upper Access, 1987, 344pp, $12.50, ISBN 0942679008. Carlson has become a national spokesperson for the 'do-it-yourself' funeral movement over the last few years, in the US.

• Collins, Nigel, **Seasons of Life: Prose and poetry for secular ceremonies and private reflection,** Rationalist Press Assoc., 2000, 246pp, £11.50, ISBN 0301000018. Includes poems for funeral use that do not mention God or religion.

• Gill, Sue & Fox, John, **The Dead Good Funerals Book**, 2004, 192pp, £9.50, ISBN 952715902.

• Gordon, Kate, **A Practical Guide to Alternative Funerals (Rites & ceremonies)**, Constable, 1999, 197pp, £6.99, ISBN 0094787700. Traditional, religious and secular ceremonies.

• Hockey, Jennifer, **Making the Most of a Funeral**, CRUSE (see under Organisations), 1992, 54pp, £0.95 plus p&p, ISBN 0900321040. Useful suggestions aimed at priests.

• Kirkpatrick, Bill, **Going Forth**, Darton, Longman & Todd, 1997, 224pp, £10.95, ISBN 0232522375. Hymns, music, readings and funeral service advice.

• Mill, Andrew, **Celebrating Life – A book of special services for use in the Unitarian and Free Christian tradition**, Lindsey Press (GA Mail Order Service, Information Dept, Unitarian HQ, Essex Hall, 1-6 Essex Street Strand, London WC2R 3HY, ☎ 020 7240 2384; f: 020 7240 3089; e: bookshop@unitarian.org.uk), 1999, 243pp, £15.50 incl. p&p, ISBN 0853190410.

• Smale, David A., **Davies' Law of Burial, Cremation and Exhumation**, Shaw and Sons, 2002, £39.95, ISBN 0721900658.

• Spottiswoode, Jane, **Undertaken with Love: The story of a DIY funeral**, Robert Hale, 1992, 176pp, ISBN 070904979X. Currently out of print.

• Walter, Dr Tony, **Funerals – And how to improve them**, Hodder & Stoughton, 1990, 352pp, ISBN 0340531258. Out of print.

• Waugh, Evelyn, **The Loved One**, Penguin, 2000, 128pp, £6.99, ISBN 0141184248. A satire on the funeral industry in the United States.

• ✪✪✪ Willson, Jane Wynne, **Funerals Without God – A practical guide to non-religious funerals**, British Humanist Association (see under Organisations and Officiants), 1995, 67pp, £5 incl. p&p, ISBN 090182514X.

Bereavement

• ✪✪✪ Becvar, Dorothy S, **In the Presence of Grief – Helping family members resolve death, dying and bereavement issues**, Guilford Press (72 Spring Street, New York, NY 10012 USA), 2001, 292pp, £27.50 (hb), ISBN 1572306971 (e: info@guilford.com). 'A goldmine', according to our reviewer.

• Brown, Erica. (ed), **The Death of a Child – Care for the child, support the family**, Acorns Children's Hospice Trust, 2002, £9 mail-order (☎ 0121 248 4817). Basic information and identification of holistic needs of families.

• Brown, Erica., **Loss, Change and Grief – An educational perspective**, Acorns Children's Hospice Trust, 1999, £16.20 mail-order from 0121 248 4817. How to help children come to terms with and be aware of loss, change and grief.
• Collick, Elizabeth, **Through Grief: The bereavement journey**, Darton, Longman & Todd Ltd; available from CRUSE (see under Organisations), £7.95 plus p&p, ISBN 0232516820.
• Cunningham, James, (ed), **All is Well – Poems and readings in remembrance of loved ones**, HarperCollins, 1997, 120pp, £6.99, ISBN 0002557975.
• Doka, Kenneth, **Living With Grief: After sudden loss**, Hospice Foundation of America (w: www.hospicefoundation.org), 1996, 261pp, $16.95, ISBN 156032578X.
• Elison, Jennifer, & McGonigle, Chris, **Liberating Losses: When death brings relief**, Perseus Publishing, 2003, 240pp, £16 (hb), ISBN 0738206377.
• Enright, D. J. (ed), **The Oxford Book of Death**, OUP, 2002, 351pp, £7.99, ISBN 0192803808. Prose and poetry.
• Harris, Jill Werman (ed), **Remembrances and Celebrations – A book of eulogies, elegies, letters, and epitaphs**, Pantheon Books (Random House, New York), 1999, 308pp, $25, ISBN 0375401237. From over 100 writers including Auden, Dickens, Wordsworth and Woolf.
• Kon, Andrea, **How to Survive Bereavement**, Hodder & Stoughton (338 Euston Road, London NW1 3BH) 2002, 194pp, £6.99, ISBN 0340786248. A practical and supportive guide, written from experience.
• Kupfermann, Jeannette, **When the Crying's Done**, Robson Books, 1996, £8.99, ISBN 086051904X. A moving account of widowhood.
• Lake, Dr Tony, **Living With Grief (Overcoming common problems)**, Sheldon Press, 1984, 154pp, £6.99, ISBN 0859694267. Self-help guide.
• ✪✪✪ LaGrand, Louis, **Messages & Miracles – Extraordinary experiences of the bereaved**, Llewellyn, 1999, 336pp, $12.95, ISBN 1567184065 (w: www.llewellyn.com/bookstore & w: www.anotherreality.com). Accounts of people's experiences of after-death communications. 'Groundbreaking!'
• Levine, Stephen, **Meetings at the Edge: Dialogues with the grieving and the dying, the healing and the healed**, Gateway, 1993, 264pp, £9.99, ISBN 0946551901. Basic meditation derived from the Buddhist Vipassana method.
• Lewis, C. S., **A Grief Observed**, Faber & Faber, 2001, 112pp, £5.40, ISBN 0060652381. On the death of his wife from cancer.
• ✪✪✪ Moody, Raymond & Arcangel, Dianne, **Life after Loss: Finding hope through life after life,** Rider, 2001, 228pp, £9.99, ISBN 071260272. Sensitive, insightful and inspiring, with personal stories from the authors and others, including visionary experiences at the moment of death.
• Picardie, Justine, **If the Spirit Moves You: Life and love after death**, Picador, 2002, 208pp, £7.99, ISBN 0330487868.
• Rando, Therese A., **How to Go on Living when Someone You Love Dies,** Bantam Doubleday Dell Publishing Group, 1991, 352pp, ISBN 0553352695.

• Rees, Dewi, **Death and Bereavement – The psychological, religious and cultural interfaces**, Whurr Publishers Ltd (19b Compton Terrace, London N1 2UN, ☎ 020 7359 5979), 2001, 258pp, £22.50, ISBN 1861562233.

• Sanders, Dr Catherine, **Surviving Grief and Learning to Live Again**, John Wiley, 1992, 240pp, £13.50, ISBN 0471534714.

• Schiff, Harriet Sarnoff, **The Bereaved Parent**, Souvenir Press, 1979, 160pp, £6.99, ISBN 0285648918.

• Staudacher, Carol, **Beyond Grief – A guide to recovering from the death of a loved one**, New Harbinger Publications, 1987, 244pp, £9, ISBN 0934986436.

• Steiner, Rudolf, **Living with the Dead – Meditations for maintaining a connection to those who have died**, Sophia Books, 2002, 62pp, £8.95, ISBN 1855841274. Inspiring writing and verse from the late spiritual philosopher.

• Stillbirth And Neo-Natal Death Society (SANDS, see Organisations), **Saying Goodbye to Your Baby**. A booklet for bereaved parents.

• Umberson, Debra, **Death of a Parent: Transition to a new adult identity**, Cambridge University Press, 2003, 264pp, £22.50, ISBN 0521813387 (w: uk.cambridge.org). Helping adults deal with the crisis of beliefs, goals, and sense of self triggered by a parent's death.

• Wallbank, Susan, **Facing Grief – Bereavement and the young adult 18-28**, from CRUSE (see Organisations), 1996, £12.99 plus p&p,. ISBN 0718828070.

• Walter, Tony, **On Bereavement: The culture of grief (facing death)**, Open University Press, 1999, 256pp, £19.99, ISBN 033520080X.

• Wertheimer, Alison, **A Special Scar: The experience of people bereaved through suicide**, Routledge, 2001, 288pp, £15.99, ISBN 0415220270.

• Whitaker, Agnes, **All in the End is Harvest: An anthology for those who grieve**, Darton, Longman & Todd Ltd, 1991, 144pp, £8.95, ISBN 0232516243. 'Popular anthology of prose and poetry'.

• ✪✪✪ Wilber, Ken, **Grace and Grit: Spiritual healing in the life and death of Treya Killam Wilber**, Gateway, 2001, 432pp, £12.99, ISBN 071713234X. About the death of his wife from cancer.

• Worden, William, **Grief Counselling and Grief Therapy: A handbook for the mental health practitioner**, Brunner-Routledge; 2003, 248pp, £15.99, ISBN 1583919414.

Perspectives

• Barley, Nigel, **Dancing on the Grave – Encounters with death**, Abacus, 1997, 250pp, £8.99, ISBN 0719552869. Looks at the variety of ways in which cultures around the world deal with death and give it meaning.

• Gold, E.J., **The American Book of the Dead**, Gateways Books and Tapes (PO Box 370, Nevada City, CA 95959, USA, ☎ 001 530 272 0180; e: info@gatewaysbooksandtapes.com), 1993, £12.99, ISBN 0895560518. Readings. For UK, see also 'Gold' under Music, Talks and Multimedia.

• Henley, Alix and Schott, Judith, **Culture, Religion and Patient Care in a Multi-Ethnic Society – A handbook for professionals**, Age Concern (see under Organisations), 1999, 602pp, £19.99, ISBN 0862422310.

• Justice, Christopher, **Dying the Good Death – The pilgrimage to die in India's holy city**, State University of New York Press, 1997, 224pp, £16.25, ISBN 0791432629.

• Kastenbaum, R. J., **Death, Society, and Human Experience**, Allyn & Brown, 2003, 464pp, £13.99, ISBN 0205381936. 'Landmark' reader drawing on social and psychological aspects of death and dying as well as the arts and humanities. This revised edition covers reaction to September 11th.

• Lamm, Maurice, **The Jewish Way in Death and Mourning**, Jonathan David Publishers, 2000, 266pp, £11, ISBN 0824604229.

• Jupp, Peter & Gittings, Clare (eds), **Death in England: An illustrated history**, Manchester University Press (Oxford Road, Manchester, M13 9NR) 1999, 290 pp, £19.99, ISBN 0719058112 (☎ 0161 273 5539; **w**: www.man.ac.uk/mup).

• Litten, Julian, **The English Way of Death – The common funeral since 1450**, Robert Hale, 2002, 265pp, £17.99, ISBN 0709070977.

• Magida, Arthur J. & Matlins, Stuart M., **How to be a Perfect Stranger – The essential religious etiquette handbook**, Skylight Paths, 2002, 423pp, £12.95, ISBN 1893361675.

• Starhawk, **The Pagan Book of Living and Dying – Practical rituals, prayers, blessings, and meditations on crossing over**, HarperSanFrancisco, 1998, 288pp, £11.99, ISBN 0062515160. An inspiring collection.

• Taylor, Richard P. **Death and the Afterlife: A cultural encyclopedia**, ABC-CLIO Inc, 2000, 448pp, £59.95 (hardback), ISBN 0874369398.

For Children

• Couldrick, Ann, **When Your Mum or Dad Has Cancer**, 2000, 21pp, ISBN 0951753738, available from OICPC for £2.35 incl. p&p (☎ 01865 225 896; **e**: courses@oicpc.demon.co.uk; **w**: www.oicpc.demon.co.uk).

• Grollman, E., **Talking About Death: A dialogue between parent and child**, Beacon Press (Boston), 1991, £12.99, ISBN 0807023639. Includes an illustrated, read-along story.

• Jackson, Maggie & Colwell, Jim, **A Teacher's Handbook of Death**, Jessica Kingsley (☎ 020 7833 2307; **e**: post@jkp.com), 2001, 176 pp, £13.95, ISBN 1843100150. Designed to help teachers explain the subject to children in the classroom environment; also suitable for parents.

• St Christopher's Hospice (see Bookshops above), **Someone Special Has Died**, £2. Illustrated booklet for children.

• St Christopher's Hospice (see Bookshops above), **Your Parent Has Died**, 1991, £2.

• Wells, Rosemary, **Helping Children Cope with Grief – Facing a death in the family**, Sheldon Press, 1988, 110pp, £6.99, ISBN 085969559X.

Music, Talks & Multimedia

• **British Holistic Medical Association** (see Organisations), tapes at £9.20 incl. p&p include: **Imagery for Relaxation**, **Coping with Persistent Pain**, **Coping with Stress**, **Introducing Meditation** and **The Breath of Life** (relaxation).

• **Buddhist Death Ritual for Dharmachari Ajita**, on Super VHS or Betacam SP, from Suryaprabha, Lights in the Sky (39a Lough Road, London N7 8RH, ☎ 020 7607 9480; **e**: surya@budacom.com; **w**: www.budacom.com).

• **CD-Rom: You Can Live With Cancer**, available from the Bristol Cancer Centre (Grove House, Cornwallis Grove, Bristol BS8 4PG, ☎ 0117 980 9500; **w**: www.bristolcancerhelp.org). In Dutch with English subtitles. £12.99.

• **Collick, Elizabeth**, **Through Grief**, tape available from CRUSE (see under Organisations), £5.50 plus p&p. Also available as a book (see above).

• **Levine, Stephen** tapes are available from Warm Rock Tapes, PO Box 100, Chamisal, NM 87521, USA. Send two international reply coupons for details.

• **Long, Barry**, **Seeing Through Death** audio cassette and **The Truth of Death** video talk by the spiritual teacher Barry Long. Barry Long Audio, BCM Box 876, London WC1N 3XX. Both supplied in UK by Prinz Publications (☎ 01736 751910; **e**: prinz@stampaccessories.net; **w**: www.barrylongbooks.com). Long shares his thoughts on his own dying at: www.barrylong.org

• **Portrait of Family Grief Pack – On the death of a child**, video plus training booklet, £16.50 from Acorns Children's Hospice Trust (☎ 0121 248 4817). Six sections: On the death of a child; Men and women grieving differently; Young people have feelings too; How other people react; When will it end?; Learning to live again. Includes poems and prose written by bereaved families.

• **Programme of music for those who are dying, Bedard, Gilles** (c/o Inerson 6727, 12e Av. Montreal, Quebec, Canada H1B 3X2, ☎ 001 514 727 3827, **e**: inerson@microtec.net, **w**: www.near-death.com/music). Upon hearing a 'majestic sound current' during an NDE, Bedard sought out the equivalent in man-made music. It is said to aid the dying. The website details specific artists.

Internet Resources

The Internet holds a vast amount of information on death and dying, including some of the **Natural Death Centre's books** (linked to www.naturaldeath.org.uk). Other places to start looking include: a site on the **sociology** of death and dying (www.trinity.edu/~mkearl/death.html); a free online journal on **end-of-life care** (www.lastacts.org; to join, send an email to: join-lastacts-discussion@lists.lyris); comprehensive information on **funerals** and **bereavement** plus useful links (www.ifishoulddie.co.uk); **USA funeral resources** (www.funerals.org); and free access to back issues of the British Medical Journal (bmj.com).

Gardens of Remembrance

On the Internet these are numerous. Some charge a great deal, some offer only temporary postings and some are free:

• **At-rest.co.uk** (Tyne Spirit Ltd, 52 Chirton Dene Quays, North Shields, Tyne & Wear NE29 6YW, ☎ 0191 258 7584; **e**: info@at-rest.co.uk; **w**: www.at-rest.co.uk). Tributes can include video, photographs, text, voice messages, audio, and a memory board. From £50 to £125. 'All information is safely and securely stored' (Jo Brain).

• **Jacob's Ladder** (**w**: www.jacobsladder.org.uk). Allows anyone, anywhere to

post or read a comment or condolence message for someone who has died. Free.
• **In-Memoriam-uk.com** (**w**: www.in-memoriam-uk.com). Online memorials
may comprise tributes, photographs and a life story. From £135 to £235.
• **In Memory Of...** (www.inmemoryof.co.uk). Free temporary obituaries.
Memorial space can be rented for £25 to £50 per year.
• **Net Memorials** (www.netmemorials.co.uk). Web tributes: £35.
• **Obituariesonline.net** (**f**: 0709 2001840; **e**: webmaster@obituariesonline.net;
w: www.obituariesonline.net). British obituary internet service. Obituaries can
be submitted online and by fax. £19: one-year obituary posted without photo;
£23 with photo. Further personal messages can then be added for £5 each.
• **Partingwishes.com** (**e**: support@partingwishes.com; **w**: www.parting
wishes.com/mymemorials.asp). Free online memorials, and other death-related
information.
• **Treasured Moments** (www.treasured-moments.co.uk). Online memorial:
£29.95, obituary submission: free.

Organisations & Individuals

Counselling, Support, Information & Advice

• **Advice UK**, 12th Floor, New London Bridge House, 25 London Bridge Street,
London SE1 9ST (☎ 020 7407 4070; **f**: 020 7407 4071; **e**: general@
adviceuk.gov.uk; **w**: www.advice.org.uk). Offers everyone, but particularly
'people in disadvantaged, vulnerable and marginalised circumstances', access
to help concerning rights, responsibilities and entitlements vital to individual
welfare and liberty.
• **Age Concern**, Astral House, 1268 London Road, London SW16 4ER (☎
Freephone: 0800 009 966; Wills: 020 8765 7527; **e**: supporterservices@
ace.org.uk [will writing service]; **w**: www.ageconcern.org.uk). Will-writing
service and free factsheet (No. 27) on arranging a funeral.
• **Alzheimer's Disease Society**, Gordon House, 10 Greencoat Place, London
SW1P 1PH (☎ 020 7306 0606; **f**: 020 7306 0808; **e**: enquiries@alzheimers.
org.uk; **w**: www.alzheimers.org.uk). Advice and information.
• **Ananda Network**, c/o Dennis Sibley, Flat 1, Laurel House, Trafalgar Road,
Newport, Isle of Wight PO30 1QN (☎ 01983 526 945; **e**: dsibley@
buddhisthospice.org.uk) or Peter Goble (☎ 01268 741419; **e**: pgoble@ buddhist
hospice.org.uk). Volunteer outreach arm of the Buddhist Hospice Trust.
• **Antenatal Results & Choices** (**ARC**; formerly **SAFTA**), 73 Charlotte Street
London W1T 4PN (☎ Helpline 020 7631 0285; General: 020 7631 0280; **e**:
arcsafta@aol.com; **w**: www.arc-uk.org). Support around antenatal testing and
decisions regarding foetal abnormalities.
• **Asian Family Counselling Service**, Suite 51, Windmill Place, 2/4 Windmill
Lane, Southall, Middlesex UB2 4NJ (☎ 020 8571 3933; **e**: afcs99@hotmail.com).
• **Association for Death Education and Counselling**, 342 North Main Street,
West Hertford, Connecticut 06117, USA (☎ 001 860 586 7503; **f**: 001 860 586
7550; **e**: info@adec.org; **w**: www.adec.org). Conferences and courses.

- **Association of InterFaith Ministers** (**AIMS**), Haslecombe House, Parsons Hill, Porlock, Somerset TA24 8QP (☎ 01643 862 621; **e**: haslecombe@aol.com; **w**: www.interfaithministers.org.uk).
- **The Befriending Network**, Claremont, 24-27 Lion Street, London N1 9PD (☎ 020 7689 2443; **e**: info@befriending.net; **w**: www.befriending.net). Oxfordshire BN, St Barnabus Community Centre, 33a Canal Street, Oxford OX2 6BQ (☎ 01865 316 200; **e**: oxford@befriending.net). Trained volunteers who offer support to people with a terminal or life-threatening illness at home, for 2-3 hours per week. The Network is currently active in North and West London, and Oxfordshire; and can provide referrals to other similar agencies nationwide.
- **Bristol Cancer Help Centre**, Grove House, Cornwallis Grove, Clifton, Bristol BS8 4PG (☎ 0117 980 9500; **f**: 0117 923 9184; **e**: info@bristolcancer help.org; **w**: www.bristolcancerhelp.org). Holistic treatment and publications. Grief, loss, death and dying workshops, and phone-in service.
- **British Association for Counselling**, 1 Regent Place, Rugby, Warwickshire CV21 2PJ (☎ 01788 578 328; Office: 01788 550 899; **e**: bacp@bacp.co.uk **w**: www.counselling.co.uk). Information on organisations, counsellors and therapists nationwide (some of whom are free).
- **British Complementary Medicine Association** (**BCMA**), P.O. Box 5122, Bournemouth BH8 0WG (☎ 0845 345 5977; **e**: web@bcma.co.uk; **w**: www.bcma.co.uk). Guides the public through the 'maze' of alternative therapies and therapists available, and represents vetted organisations.
- **British Holistic Medical Association**, 59 Landsdowne Place, Hove, East Sussex BN3 1FL (☎ /f: 01273 725 951; **e**: bhma@bhma.org; **w**: www.bhma.org). Self-help breathing, relaxation, meditation and tapes (see Music, Talks and Multimedia, above) and an informative quarterly, *Holistic Health*.
- **British Medical Association**, BMA House, Tavistock Square, London WC1H 9JP (☎ 020 7387 4499; **f**: 020 7383 6400; **e**: info.web@bma.org.uk; **w**: www.bma.org.uk). The governing body for the British medical profession.
- **British Organ Donor Society** (**BODY**), Balsham, Cambridge CB1 6DL (☎ 01223 893 636; **e**: body@argonet.co.uk; **w**: www.argonet.co.uk/body).
- **The Bryna Trust**, 8a The Drive, London NW11 9SR (☎ 020 8455 7661; **f**: 020 8381 4050; **e**: admin@thebrynatrust.org.uk; **w**: www.thebrynatrust.org.uk). For people facing life-threatening illness. Runs seminars and workshops which stress 'living life fully and joyfully'. E-mail for details of forthcoming events.
- **The Buddhist Hospice Trust** (see Ananda Network, above, for contact info). A particularly friendly nonsectarian organisation, 'it was established to explore Buddhist approaches to dying, death and bereavement and bring together the teachings of the Buddha and the philosophy of modern hospice care' (in fact it is at this stage just a network of people, 'a hospice of the heart' only). Publishes a biannual magazine, *Raft* (£5 subs), and holds meetings. Its Ananda Network volunteers (see above) are prepared to sit with and befriend the terminally ill.
- **Cancer Aid & Listening Centre** (**CALL**), (☎ Helpline 0161 205 7780 [7.30pm-10.30pm]; **w**: www.canceraid.co.uk). Helpline providing emotional support and advice to cancer patients and their families. Also provides a branch-

based support service in the Greater Manchester region. See website for details.
• **Cancer BACUP (British Association of Cancer United Patients)**, 3 Bath
Place, Rivington St, London EC2A 3JR (☎ Helpline 0800 800 1234 [Mon-Fri
9am-7pm]; General: 020 7696 9002; **f**: 020 7696 9002; **w**: www.cancerbackup.
org.uk). National charity offering information and counselling for people with
cancer, their families and friends. The helpline is staffed by specialist nurses who
can offer advice and send out free information booklets, incl. 'Coping at Home
– Caring for someone with advanced cancer' (which can also be viewed online).
Face-to-face counselling is available in London (☎ 020 7616 7628), Glasgow
(☎ 0141 553 1553) and at other drop-in locations across the UK (see website).
All their services are free and confidential. Donations welcome.
• **Care for the Carers Ltd**, Braemar House, 28 St Leonards Road, Eastbourne,
East Sussex BN21 3UT (☎ 01323 738 390; Careline: 01323 745777; **f**: 01323
745 770 **e**: info@cftc.org.uk; **w**: www.cftc.org.uk). Advice, information and
support, primarily for the East Sussex area. Also offers training for carers.
• **Carers UK**, 20-25 Glasshouse Yard, London EC1A 4JT (☎ 0808 808 7777
[10am-12pm & 2pm-4pm weekdays]; **f**: 020 7490 8824; **e**: info@ukgs.org; **w**:
www.carersonline.org.uk). Advice for carers & former carers. Support groups.
• **Chai-Lifeline, Jewish Cancer Support & Health Centre**, Shield House,
Harmony Way, off Victoria Road, Hendon, London NW4 2BZ (☎ 020 8202
2211; **e**: info@chaicancercare.org.uk; **w**: www.chaicancercare.org). Works
with youth and adults facing life-threatening illnesses, providing support groups,
visitors and complementary therapies.
• **The Cinnamon Trust**, Foundry House, Foundry Square, Hayle, Cornwall
TR27 4HE (☎ 01736 757 900; **f**: 01736 757010; **e**: admin@cinnamon.org.uk;
w: www.cinnamon.org.uk). Care for pets of the elderly and terminally ill.
• **Continence Foundation**, 307 Hatton Square, 16 Baldwins Gardens, London
EC1N 7RJ (☎ Helpline 0845 345 0165; General: 020 7404 6875; **f**: 020
7404 6876; **e**: continence-help@dial.pipex.com; **w**: www.continence-
foundation.org.uk). A continence advisory service.
• **Council for Music in Hospitals**, 74 Queens Road, Hersham, Surrey KT12
5LW (☎ 01932 252809; **f**: 01932 252966; **e**: info@music-in-hospitals.org.uk.
w: www.music-in-hospitals.org.uk). Puts on many concerts every year for
adults and children whose lives are restricted by long-term illness or disability.
• **Counsel and Care – Advice and help for older people**, Twyman House, 16
Bonny St, London NW1 9PG (Helpline 0845 300 7585 [Mon-Fri 10am-1pm];
admin: 020 7241 8555; **f**: 020 7267 6877; **e**: advice@counselandcare.org.uk; **w**:
www.counselandcare.org.uk). Advice on finding and paying for residential and
nursing care. Free factsheets.
• **Court of Protection**, Public Guardianship Office, Archway Tower, 2 Junction
Road, London N19 5SZ (☎ 0845 330 2900; **e**: custserve@guardianship.gov.uk;
w: www.publictrust.gov.uk). If you need to apply to manage the financial affairs
of someone who has become mentally incapacitated.
• **Crossroads – Caring for Carers**, Crossroads Association, 10 Regents Place,
Rugby, Warwickshire CV21 2PN (☎ 0845 450 0350; **f**: 01788 565 498;

e: communications@crossroads.org.uk; **w**: www.crossroads.org.uk).
Trained carers to give regular carers a break.
• **DIPEx**, Dept of Primary Health Care, Institute of Health Sciences, University
of Oxford, Old Road, Headington, Oxford OX3 7LF (☎ 01865 226672; **e**: info
@dipex.org; **w**: www.dipex.org). The website gives those recently diagnosed
with an illness access to personal experiences of others in the same situation.
• **Disability Information Trust**, Mary Marlborough Centre, Nuffield Ortho-
paedic Centre, Headington, Oxford OX3 7LD (☎ 01865 227 592; **e**:
news@abilityonline.org.uk; **w**: www.abilityonline.net/disability_information_
trust.htm). Their books range from 'Manual Wheelchairs – A practical guide' to
'Hoists, Lifts and Transfers'.
• **Disabled Living Foundation**, 380-384 Harrow Road, London W9 2HU
(☎ Helpline 0845 130 9177 [Mon-Fri 10am-1pm]; General: 020 7289 6111;
Textphone: 0870 603 9176; **f**: 020 7266 2922; **e**: advice@dlf.org.uk;
w: www.dlf.org.uk). National charity offering information and advice on daily
living equipment for people with a disability.
• **Edgework Ceremonies**, Plume Cottage, Tavernspite, Whitland, SA34 0NL
(☎ 01834 831 121). Counselling, dramatherapy, ceremonies and training.
• **Exit**, 17 Hart Street, Edinburgh EH1 3RN (☎ 0131 556 4404, **f**: 0131 557
4403; **e**: exit@euthanasia.cc). Advice on assisted suicide and voluntary euthanasia. Exit worker Chris Docker is well informed on the varieties of Living Will
texts worldwide and their shortcomings in practice. Email for best response.
• **Family Welfare Association**, 501-505 Kingsland Road, Dalston, London E8
4AU (☎ 020 7254 6251; **f**: 020 7249 5443; **e**: fwa.headoffice@fwa.org.uk; **w**:
www.fwa.org.uk). Gives grants to individuals and families.
• **Final Passages**, PO Box 1721, Sebastopol, CA 95473, USA (☎ 001 707 824
0268; **e**: info@finalpassages.org; **w**: www.finalpassages.org). An American
project with similarities to the Natural Death Centre.
• **Good Endings** (Donalyn Gross, PhD ☎ 001 413 733 8592; **w**: www.good
endings.net). Psycosocial and psychological death education for (US) nursing
homes and healthcare facilities. Also provides music for the dying.
• **Horizon Research Foundation**, Mailpoint 888, Southampton General Hospital,
Tremona Road, Southampton, Hampshire, SO16 6YD. (☎ 0870 333 3722; **f**:
0870 333 3721; **e**: horizonresearch@hotmail.com; **w**: www.horizon-research.
co.uk). End of life and NDE information. Supports scientific research and
understanding into the state of the human mind at the end of life.
• **Hospice Information Service**, St Christopher's Hospice, 51-59 Lawrie Park
Road, Sydenham, London SE26 6DZ (☎ 0870 903 3903 [Mon-Fri 9am-5pm];
e: online enquiry form; **w**: www.hospiceinformation.info). Publishes a UK
directory of hospices and palliative care services. International information for
anyone caring for people dying. Also helps patients, families and carers to
identify and access appropriate support and resources.
• **Ian Rennie Hospice at Home**, 52a Western Road, Tring, Herts HP23 4BB
(☎ 01442 890 222; **f**: 01442 891 276; **e**: info@irhh.org; **w**: www.irhh.org).
Provides specialist 24-hour nursing care in the Chilterns area of Hertfordshire
and Buckinghamshire. For patients with a terminal illness.

• **The Janki Foundation**, Global Co-operation House, 65 Pound Lane, London NW10 2HH (☎ 020-8727 3401). 'For Global Health Care'. Offers a training package addressing the psychological and spiritual needs of doctors and nurses.

• **Jessie's Fund**, 10 Bootham Terrace, York YO30 7DH (☎/f: 01904 658 189; e: info@jessiesfund.org.uk; w: www.jessiesfund.org.uk). A charity with music therapists helping children in hospices.

• **Jewish Bereavement Counselling Service**, PO Box 6748, London N3 3BX (☎ 020 8349 0839; e: jbcs@visit.org.uk; w: www.visit.org.uk/jbcs).

• **John Bell and Croyden**, 50–54 Wigmore St, London W1 (☎ 020 7935 5555 ext 212; f: 020 7935 9605; e: jbc@johnbellcroyden.co.uk; w: www.john bellcroyden.co.uk). Chemist for specialist medical requirements, everything from a sheepskin rug to a walking frame.

• **Last Rights**, c/o 45 Grenville Road, Falmouth, Cornwall TR11 2NP (☎ Lorely Lloyd 01326 317587; Diane 01326 211002). To encourage and support last human rights and rites.

• **Law Centres Federation**, Duchess House, 18-19 Warren Street, London W1T 5LR (☎ 020 7387 8570; f: 020 7387 8368; e: info@lawcentre.org.uk; w: www.lawcentres.org.uk). Can put you in touch with your local law centre which can provide free advice about wills etc.

• **Lymphoedema Support Network**, St Luke's Crypt, Sydney Street, London SW3 6NH (☎ Advice: 020 73514480; Admin: 020 73510990; f: 0171 3499809; e: adminlsn@lymphoedema.freeserve.co.uk; w: www.lymphoedema.org/lsn).

• **Macmillan Cancer Relief Fund & Cancer Line**, 89 Albert Embankment, London SE1 7UQ (☎ 0808 808 2020 [Mon-Fri 9am-6pm]; e: cancerline@ macmillan.org.uk [support]; w: www.macmillan.org.uk). The helpline is manned by Macmillan Nurses who can help with emotional support, and pain and symptom control. Financial assistance is on offer for some patients. The website links to a directory of complementary therapy services.

• **MAP Foundation**, Centre for Medical Humanities, Royal Free & University College Medical School, Holburn Union Building, 2-10 Highgate Hill, London N19 5LW (e: info@mapfoundation.org; w: www.mapfoundation.org). Founded by former cancer patient Michele Angelo Petrone. Uses art as the therapeutic expression of the experience of life-threatening illness. See website for details of workshops for cancer patients, carers and professionals.

• **Marie Curie Cancer Care**, 89 Albert Embankment, London SE1 7TP (☎ 0207 599 7777; e: info@mariecurie.org.uk; w: www.mariecurie.org.uk). Hospice centres and night nurses, who are free, but normally obtained through your health authority's community nursing manager.

• **Marsden: Web resources for cancer patients**, Royal Marsden, Fulham Road, London SW3 6JJ (☎ 020 7352 8171; w: www.royalmarsden.org/ patientinfo/booklets). The website connects cancer patients and their families to 'an authentic source of accurate information' about cancers and their treatment.

• **Maytree**, 72 Moray Road, London N4 3LG (☎ 020 7263 7070, f: 020 7561 1732; e: maytree@maytree.org.uk; w: www.maytree.org.uk). 'A sanctuary for the suicidal': offers temporary accommodation, solace and counselling.

• **Mortality Journal**, edited by David Field (**e**: df29@leicester.ac.uk). Academic journal on death and dying; socio-historical perspectives. Editorial ☎ 01235 828 600. Subs (£62 pa) ☎ 01256 813 000 (**e**: orders@tandf.co.uk; **w**: www.tandf.co.uk/journals/titles/13576275.html).

• **Motor Neurone Disease Association**, PO Box 246, Northampton NN1 2PR (☎ Helpline 08457 626262; General: 01604 250 505; **f**: 01604 638 289; **e**: enquiries@mndassociation.org; **w**: www.mndassociation.org). Advice, information, equipment loan, local groups, financial help and useful booklets.

• **National Federation of Spiritual Healers**, Old Manor Farm Studio, Church Street, Sunbury-on-Thames TW16 6RG (☎ 0845 123 2777; **f**: 01932 779 648; **e**: office@nfsh.org.uk; **w**: www.nfsh.org.uk).

• **Natural Death Centre**, 6 Blackstock Mews, Blackstock Road, London N4 2BT (☎ 020 7359 8391 [9.30am-5.30pm Mon-Fri]; **f**: 020 7354 3831; **e**: ndc@alberyfoundation.org; **w**: www.naturaldeath.org.uk). Edits this book. Advice and information on dying, funerals, and bereavement.

• **NHS Direct** (☎ 0845 608 4455 [free medical advice from an NHS nurse]; **w**: www.nhsdirect.nhs.uk [health information and links].

• **Office of Fair Trading**, Fleetbank House, 2-6 Salisbury Square, London EC4Y 8JX (☎ 020 7211 8000; **e**: enquiries@oft.gov.uk; **w**: www.oft.gov.uk). Aims to protect consumers and explain their rights.

• **OyezStraker Ltd** (☎ 020 7556 3200; **w**: www.oyezforms.co.uk) for various legal forms as mentioned in Chapters 2 & 4 of this book.

• **Pagan Federation**, BM Box 7097, London WC1N 3XX (☎ 01295 277 244; **e**: secretary@paganfed.demon.co.uk; **w**: www.paganfed.demon.co.uk). Defends paganism as a 'spiritual way of life rooted in the ancient nature religions of the world'. Publishes an info pack (£3) and a journal (£12). See also LifeRites.

• **Pain Relief Institute** Clinical Sciences Centre, University Hospital, Aintree, Lower Lane, Liverpool L9 7AL (☎ 0151 529 5820; **f**: 0151 529 5821; **e**: pri@liv.ac.uk; **w**: www.painrelieffoundation.org.uk).

• **Palliative Care Arts**, Sobell Study Centre, Sir Michael Sobell House, Churchill Hospital, Oxford, OX3 7LJ, UK (☎ 01865 225886; **f**: 01865 225599; **e**: ssc@orh.nhs.uk; **w**: www.palliativecourses.com). For research and courses for professionals regarding palliative care, with emphasis on the arts.

• **People's Dispensary for Sick Animals (PDSA)**, Whitechapel Way, Priorslee, Telford, Shropshire TF2 9DQ (☎ 0800 917 2509; **f**: 01952 291 035; **w**: www.pdsa.org.uk). They have a will-making advice pack and provide a re-homing service for the pets of the deceased (if they leave the PDSA money).

• **Pets As Therapy**, 17 Ambrook Road, Reading RG2 8SL (☎ 0870 240 1239; **e**: reception@petsastherapy.org; **w**: www.petsastherapy.org). Sends out dogs to visit the sick and elderly.

• **Positive Partners & Positively Children**, Unit M4, Shakespeare Commercial Centre, 245a Coldharbour Lane, London SW9 8RR (☎ 020 7738 7333; **e**: office@ppc.london.org.uk). Support for families affected by HIV/AIDS.

• **Positively Women**, 347-349 City Road, London EC1 1LR (☎ Helpline 020 7713 0222; General: 020 7713 044; **f**: 020 7713 1020; **e**: info@positively

women.org.uk; **w**: www.positivelywomen.org.uk). Supports women with HIV.
• **Probate Registry**, Principal Registry, Personal Applications Dept, First Avenue House, 42-49 High Holborn, London WC1V 6NP (☎ 0845 302 0900; **w**: www.courtservice.gov.uk). Or see the phone book for your nearest office.
• **Red Cross Medical Loans Service**, British Red Cross, 9 Grosvenor Crescent, London SW1X 7EJ (☎ 020 7235 5454; **f**: 020 7245 6315; **e**: information@red cross.org.uk; **w**: www.redcross.org.uk). Branches (see phone book for your nearest) can supply equipment (wheelchairs, commodes, etc) on short term loan.
• **Rigpa (Spiritual Care Education & Training Programme)**, 330 Caledonian Road, London N1 1BB (☎ 020 700 0185; **f**: 020 609 6068; **e**: enquiries@rigpauk.org; **w**: www.rigpauk.com). A Buddhist centre running courses on death and dying. Its Spiritual Care Programme, inspired by Rinpoche's *The Tibetan Book of Living and Dying*, is aimed at everyone.
• **Rosetta Life**, Hospice House, 33-44 Britannia Street, London WC1X 9JG (☎ 020 7520 8270; **f**: 020 7520 8288; **e**: info@rosettalife.org; **w**: www.rosettalife.org). Artist-led charity. Uses video, photography, drama, and other media to help patients come to terms with their individual diagnoses.
• **The Ruby Care Foundation**, PO Box 21, Llandysul, SA39 9WA Wales (☎ 0870 794 5353; **e**: info@rubycare.org; **w**: www.rubycare.org). Charity dedicated to care of the terminally ill, companionship of the dying, and support and counselling for the bereaved. There are currently affiliated organisations in the UK, USA, Australia, New Zealand, Ireland and Holland.
• **St Joseph's Hospice**, Mare Street, Hackney, London E8 4SA (☎ 020 8525 6000; **f**: 020 8533 0513; **e**: info@stjh.org.uk; **w**: www.stjh.org.uk).
• **Samaritans**, 10 The Grove, Slough, Berks SL1 1QP (☎ Helpline 08457 90 90 90; General: 020 8394 8300; **f**: 020 8394 8301; **e**: jo@samaritans.org; **w**: www.samaritans.org.uk). Or see phone book. For those in despair or suicidal.
• **Self-help groups**: Lists are maintained by the Patients Association, PO Box 935, Harrow, Middlesex HA1 3YJ (☎ 0845 608 4455; **f**: 020 8423 9119; **e**: mailbox@patients-association.com; **w**: www.patients-association.com); CancerLink and NHS Direct (see above). There are also 70-plus online cancer and information groups to be found at: www.medinfo.co.uk; and over 250 searchable health and medical newsgroups at: www.medexplorer.com
• **Terrence Higgins Trust** (incorporates **London Lighthouse**), 52-54 Grays Inn Road, London WC1X 8JU (☎ Helpline 0845 1221 200 [Mon-Fri 10am-10pm, weekends 12-6pm]; General: 020 7831 0330; **e**: info@tht.org.uk; **w**: www.tht.org.uk). Information, advice and help on AIDS and HIV infection.
• **Victim Support**, National Office, Cranmer House, 39 Brixton Road, London SW9 6DZ (☎ Helpline 0845 30 30 900; General: 020 7735 9166; **f**: 020 7582 5712; **e**: contact@victimsupport.org.uk; **w**: www.victimsupport.org.uk; **e-support**: supportline@victimsupport.org.uk). Trained staff and volunteers help victims of crime ranging from burglary to murder. Witness service offers support and information about court proceedings.
• **Voluntary Euthanasia Society** (**VES**), 13 Prince of Wales Terrace, London W8 5PG (☎ 020 7937 7770; **f**: 020 7376 2648; **e**: info@ves.org.uk; **w**:

www.ves.org.uk). Aims 'to make it legal for a competent adult, who is suffering unbearably from an incurable illness, to receive medical help to die at their own considered and persistent request'. Pioneered the Living Will (advance directive) in the UK – a Living Will pack costs £15 incl. p&p.

• **Welfare State International**, The Ellers, Ulverston, Cumbria LA12 0AA (☎ 01229 581 127; **f**: 01229 581 232; **e**: info@welfare-state.com; **w**: www.welfare-state.org). Run funeral workshops and courses on rites of passage. See in Publications above, under 'Gill' (for *The Dead Good Funerals Book*).

• **Wireless for the Bedridden**, 195a High Street, Hornchurch, Essex RM11 3YB (☎ 0800 0182 137 or 01708 621 101; **f**: 01708 620 816). National charity providing radios and televisions to elderly, disabled and housebound people unable to afford sets themselves. Sponsor-based application via local authorities.

• **Zen Hospice Project**, 273 Page Street, San Francisco CA94102 (☎ 001 415 8632910; **e**: mail@zenhospice.org; **w**: www.zenhospice.org). This first Buddhist hospice in America, founded by Frank Ostaseski , offers lectures, retreats and workshops, nationally and internationally, about the mindful practice of compassionate care for the dying.

Celebrants & Officiants

• **Alternative Ceremonies**, Laura Conyngham, 26 Old Tiverton Road, Crediton EX17 1EG (☎ 01363 773 000; **e**: laurac@eclipse.co.uk; **w**: www.alternative ceremonies.co.uk). 'Tailor-made ceremonies nationwide' from £180 to £230.

• **British Humanist Association**, 1 Gower Street, London WC1E 6HD (☎ 020 7430 0908; **e**: info@humanism.org.uk; **w**: www.humanism.org.uk). Offers meaningful and personal secular ceremonies throughout the UK, to those who would feel uncomfortable with a religious service. Variable charges (eg £85 in NW London). Search for officiants by postcode at the above website. See also Jane Wynne Willson under books.

• **British Liberal Free Church**, Rev Stephen Callander, Quaker Meeting House, 40 Spencer Hill Road, London SW19 1HL (☎ 07986 472065; **e**: libfree@blueyonder.co.uk; **w**: www.lfc.faithweb.com). Aims to assist those who feel marginalised by mainstream churches or seek the services of a church, but are secular in beliefs. Director of the pastoral ministry, Rev Callander offers to officiate free of charge, accepting donations. He covers London and the South East, but will travel further subject to travelling costs.

• **Choice Ceremonies**, Revd. Lesley Edwards, 107 Salisbury Rd, Totton, Southampton, SO40 3HZ (☎ 023 8086 1256; **e**: Lesley@choice ceremonies.co.uk; **w**: www.choiceceremonies.co.uk). 'Our personal and uniquely custom-made funerals or memorial ceremonies commemorate and celebrate life whilst saying a gentle farewell or adieu. The service includes appropriate poetry and prose written exclusively with your wishes in mind'. Ceremonies: £150 plus travel at 50p/mile. UK-wide, but mainly Hampshire, Dorset and Wiltshire.

• **Circles of Life**, 44 Staple Hill Road, Fishponds, Bristol BS16 5BS (☎ 0117 377 0346; **e**: info@circlesoflife.co.uk; **w**: www.circlesoflife.co.uk). Founded by Carol Pool. Provides a choice of non-religious, semi-religious and spiritual life-centred ceremonies as a 'beautiful and meaningful way' to mark death.

• **Civil Ceremonies Ltd**, (**w**: www.civilceremonies.co.uk). Formal non-religious ceremonies conducted by a professional celebrant for a fixed fee of £155. Scripted to reflect the beliefs and values of the deceased. Contact your local authority or visit the website for your nearest civil ceremony celebrant.

• **Funerals For Your Faith**, (Spiritual Funerals Minister Maggy Whitehouse, ☎ 020 8446 7655; **e**: maggywhitehouse@onetel.net.uk). 'Individual services to honour individual people.' From North London to Birmingham. From £90.

• **Green Fuse**, The Old Stables, Station Road, Totnes, Devon TQ9 5HW (☎ 01803 840 779; **f**: 01803 840 361; **e**: greenfuse@lineone.net; **w**: www.greenfuse.co.uk). 'We help a family focus on the type of funeral they really want and how to go about organising this'. Celebrants Jane Morrell and Oliver Hurd-Thomas conduct ceremonies for between £150 and £350 plus hourly charges for preparation. 'Travel costs are charged at 35p per mile and we work within a 70-mile radius of Totnes.' They run a drop-in advice centre in Totnes, which doubles as a florist.

• **Human Rites & Ceremonies**, 17 Wensley Gardens, Emsworth, Hants PO10 7RA (☎ 01243 374 870). This organisation say they will help you with the arrangement of the service – giving shape to the ceremony, finding suitable words and music and an appropriate tribute.

• **Humanist Society of Scotland** (☎ 07010 714775; **w**: www.humanism-scotland.org.uk). Officiants who can carry out personal secular ceremonies in Scotland. Call, or search the website, for the full list of officiants and prices.

• **LifeRites**, Gwndwn Mawr, Trelech, Carmarthenshire SA33 6SA (☎ 01994 484527; **e**: info@liferites.org; **w**: www.liferites.org). Pagan. Has a national network of registered celebrants who conduct and/or advise on specific or general ceremonies. Services draw on the personal and meaningful celebration of life, not the teachings of religions. Costs around £80 (see also Organisations).

• **McGrath, Judith**, (281 Court Lodge Road, Horley, Surrey, RH6 8RG, ☎ 0705 012 8305). Will help the bereaved to arrange a personal and meaningful funeral with tributes, poetry, readings, music and other special requirements.

• **Society of St Brigid**, (Mother Elizabeth ☎ 0238 032 974; **e**: Sboratory @aol.com). An order of Christian clergy (men and women) spread all over the UK. 'We are deeply committed to the philosophy of natural death. We are willing to officiate at funerals and to help construct meaningful services. We do not charge fees but ask for a donation and travel expenses.'

• **Unitarian Churches**, Essex Hall, 1-6 Essex St, Strand, London WC2R 3HY (☎ 020 7240 2384; **f**: 020 7240 3089; **e**: ga@unitarian.org.uk; **w**: www.unitarian.org.uk). A network of free spiritual ministers and lay officials across the UK who conduct personalised, non-religious or Humanist funerals reflecting the life and beliefs of the deceased, without dogma. Modest expenses may be requested if long distance travel is involved.

Funerals & Memorials

• **A. B. Welfare and Wildlife Trust**, 7 Knox Road, Harrogate, North Yorkshire HG1 3EF (☎ 01423 530 900/868 121). Advises dying and bereaved people on any type of funeral in any type of place, anywhere in the country. The Trust was set up by John Bradfield, a social worker, conservationist and author of *Green Burial – The DIY Guide to Law and Practice* (published by NDC but now out of print). This summarised the authoritative research undertaken for the Trust. Charity giving sound advice on emotional needs, the full extent of choices, all aspects of the law, environmental health and using burials to promote wildlife. 'Funds are desperately needed to provide the free advice service, train volunteers from all parts of the country and to buy land, so more burials can be arranged in nature reserves. Obtaining advice by telephone may continue to be difficult, unless the Trust is supported with donations and grants.'

• **Another Way** (Registered Charity SCO29726), Jean Pilborough, Secretary, 16 Midtown, Dalry, Castle Douglas, Dumfries DG7 3UT (☎ 01644 430324; **e**: jeanniep@bushinternet.com). Scottish natural death and green burial charity.

• **Association of Burial Authorities**, 155 Upper Street, London N1 1RA (☎ 020 7288 2522; **f**: 020 7288 2533; **e**: aba@swa-pr.co.uk). Represents the interests of organisations engaged in the management and operation of burial grounds.

• **Benefits Agency**: phone your local office, under Social Security or Benefits Agency in your local phone book, or phone the Public Enquiry Office (☎ 020 7712 2171). Potentially relevant leaflets to ask for include: 'Help when someone Dies' (FB29), 'National Insurance for widows' (CA 09), 'Rates of war pensions and allowances' (MPL 154), 'War widows and other dependants' (MPL 152), 'What to do after a death in England and Wales' (D49), 'What to do after a death in Scotland' (D49S) and 'Widow's benefits' (NP 45).

• **Celestis**, 2444 Times Blvd, Suite 260, Houston TX 77005-3253, USA (☎ 001 713 522 7282; **e**: info@celestis.com; **w**: www.celestis.com). Space 'burials'.

• **Cremation Society of Great Britain**, 2nd Floor, Brecon House, 16/16a Albion Place, Maidstone, Kent ME14 5DZ (☎ 01622 688 292/3; **f**: 01622 686 698; **e**: cremsoc@aol.com; **w**: www.cremation.org.uk). Can tell you the nearest crematorium. Their booklet 'What You Should Know About Cremation' can now be viewed online, and a directory of crematoria is available for £22 with binder, or £18 without (incl. p&p).

• **Eternal Reefs**, PO Box 2473, Decatur, GA 30031, USA (☎ 001 888 423 7333; **f**: 001 404 966 7337; **e**: info@eternalreefs.com; **w**: www.eternalreefs.com). Inserts cremated remains into man-made eco-reefs .

• **Federation of British Cremation Authorities**, 41 Salisbury Road, Carshalton, Surrey SM5 3HA (☎/**f**: 020 8669 4521; **e**: mchale@fbca.co.uk).

• **The Funeral Consumers Alliance** (**e**: info@funerals.org; **w**: www.funerals. org). Information on US alternatives to costly funerals.

• **Funeral Service Journal**, PO Box IW73, Leeds LS16 9XW (*Subs* ☎ 01903 602 120, **f**: 01903 537 321; **e**: info@fsj.co.uk; **w**: www.fsj.co.uk. *Editorial* ☎ 0113 284 1177; **f**: 0113 284 2152; **e**: editor@fsj.co.uk). The best of the industry journals (subs £18 pa).

• **LifeRites**, Gwndwn Mawr, Trelech, Carmarthenshire, Wales SA33 6SA (☎ 01994 484 527; **e**: info@liferites.org; **w**: www.liferites.org). A pagan organisation with information on rites of passage. Offers celebrants who will conduct services for about £80, people who work interactively with the terminally ill, and training (see also the Pagan Federation and the Celebrants section).

• **LifeScript**, PO Box 697, Watford, Herts WD25 9YU. £7.50 for a booklet helping you to record personal memories, requests and preferred style of burial.

• **Malik, Yvonne**, Sweet Briar, Wray, Nr. Lancaster LA2 8QN (☎ 0152 422 1767). Advice on creating memory or celebration boxes. Interest in NDEs.

• **Memorial Messages**, Thom Osborn, 1 Brecknock Road, London N7 0BL (☎ 020 7485 2076; **e**: thomosborn@onetel.net.uk). Thom Osborn is a film director who charges from £100 to help people make short videotape messages that can be shown after their death, whether for the funeral or for other times.

• **Memorials by Artists**, Snape Priory, Saxmundham, Suffolk, IP17 1SA (☎ 01728 688 934; **f**: 01728 688 411; **e**: enquiries@memorialsbyartists.co.uk; **w**: www.memorialsbyartists.co.uk). Nationwide service to put people in touch with designer-carvers who make individual memorials. Any profits go to their associated Memorial Arts Charity.

• **Motorcycle Funerals**, (☎ 01530 834 616; **e**: info@motorcyclefunerals.com; **w**: www.motorcyclefunerals.com). For a side-car hearse.

• **National Association of Funeral Directors**, 618 Warwick Road, Solihull, West Midlands B91 1AA (☎ 0845 230 1343; **f**: 0121 711 1351 **e**: info@ nafd.org.uk; **w**: www.nafd.org.uk). Its members' Code of Practice is available free. If complaining about a funeral director, you are supposed to write first to the funeral director, though there is nothing to prevent you going direct to NAFD or to the trading standards department (via your local council) or to a small claims court. The NAFD magazine is *The Funeral Director*.

• **National Association of Memorial Masons**, 27a Albert Street, Rugby, Warwickshire CV21 2SG (☎ 01788 542 264, **f**: 01788 542 276; **e**: enquiries@ namm.org.uk; **w**: www.namm.org.uk). Code of practice and ethics for members. Has a list of members who produce individually-crafted memorials.

• **National Funerals College**, run by Professor Malcolm Johnson, Leyton House, 6 Warwick Road, Bristol BS6 6HE (☎ 0117 9730 045, **f**: 0117 330 6162; **e**: malcolm.johnson@bristol.ac.uk). The NFC issued the Dead Citizens Charter. Organisation currently suspended with view to reconvening in 2004.

• **National Society of Allied and Independent Funeral Directors** (SAIF), SAIF Business Centre, 3 Bullfields, Sawbridgeworth, Hertfordshire CM21 9DB (☎ 0845 230 6777; **f**: 01279 726 300; **e**: info@saif.org.uk; **w**: www.saif.org.uk). Coordinating body for the smaller independent firms.

• **Paradise Preserved** (**w**: www.english-heritage.org.uk & www.english-nature.org.uk). A website for cemetery managers, conservation officers, and local people interested in getting involved in caring for their own cemetery.

• **Rituals for Remarkable Times**, Anja Saunders, 14 Neal's Yard, London WC2H 9DP (☎ 020 7497 0321; **e**: anja@ndirect.co.uk). Anja Saunders can advise a family to design extraordinary and imaginative funerals.

• **Safari Select**, Warren Farm, Main Road, Sundridge, Kent TN14 6EE (☎ 01959 562 193; **f**: 01959 561 591; **e**: sales@safariselect.co.uk; **w**: www.safariselect.co.uk). For the releasing of white doves at gravesides and memorials. One dove costs £65 + VAT, and deals are offered on up to 24 doves (£480 + VAT). When released, the birds return to their lofts in Kent.

• **The Stile Company**, The Leggett, Thatcher's Close, Epwell, Banbury, Oxfordshire OX15 6LJ. (☎   01295 780 372; **f**: 01295 780 972; **e**: info@the-stile.co.uk; **w**: www.the-stile.co.uk). Advice, planning and installation for celebratory and commemorative features in the countryside or garden.

• **The White Dove Company**, 9/11 High Beech Road, Loughton, Essex IG10 4BN. (☎ 020 8508 1414; **e**: thewhitedovecompany@lineone.net **w**: www. thewhitedovecompany.co.uk/memorialdoves.html). For doves at funerals.

Bereavement

• **Alder Centre**, Royal Liverpool Children's NHS Trust, Alder Hey, Eaton Road, Liverpool L12 2AP (☎ 0151 228 4811; **f**: 0151 228 0328; **w**: www.alderhey. org.uk/RLCH). For all those affected by a child's death. Counselling, groups, befriending. See Child Death Helpline for freephone helpline (see also The Compassionate Friends).

• **Child Death Helpline**, c/o Bereavement Services Department, Great Ormond Street Hospital, Great Ormond Street, London WC1N 3JH (☎ Helpline 0800 282 986 [Mon-Fri 10am-1pm & Sun-Sun 7pm-10pm]; Admin: 020 7813 8551; **w**: www.childdeathhelpline.org.uk). Trained volunteers, virtually all of whom are bereaved parents themselves, offer free telephone counselling and emotional support to anyone affected by the death of a child or young adult.

• **Commonwealth War Graves Commission**, 2 Marlow Road, Maidenhead, Berkshire SL6 7DX (☎ 01628 634 221; **e**: enq@cwgc.org; **w**: www.cwgc.org).

• **The Compassionate Friends**, 53 North Street, Bristol BS3 1EN (☎ Helpline 0117 953 9639; Admin: 0117 966 5202; **e**: info@tcf.org.uk; **w**: www.tcf.org.uk). Befriending bereaved parents and their families.

• **The Cot Death Helpline**, Artillery House, 11/19 Artillery Row, London SW1P 7 1RT (☎ Helpline 0870 787 0554, Mon-Fri 9am-1pm; Sat & Sun 6am-11pm). For other details see Foundation for Study of Infant Deaths below.

• **Cruse Bereavement Care**, Cruse House, 126 Sheen Road, Richmond, Surrey TW9 1UR (☎ 020 8939 9530; **f**: 020 8940 7638; **e**: info@cruse bereavementcare.org.uk; **w**: www.crusebereavementcare.org.uk). Helplines: *Day-by-Day*: 0870 1671677 [Mon-Fri, 9.30am-5pm]; *Young people* (12-18 yrs) 0808 8081677; **e**: helpline@crusebereavementcare.org.uk. For all who have suffered a bereavement: socials & advice, counselling, training and publications

• **Deceased Register** (☎ Active Media Ltd 0845 850 8833; **e**: info@ebiquita.com; **w**:www.ebiquita.com/mortality/deceased.html). Removes dead peoples' details from mailing lists. See also the **Bereavement Register** (☎ 0870 600 7222; **w**: www.the-bereavement-register.org.uk).

• **Disaster Action**, Holborn Studios, 49-50 Eagle Wharf Road, London N1 7ED (☎ /**f**: 01483 799 066; **e**: pamela_dix@daction.freeserve.co.uk; **w**: www. disasteraction.org.uk). Self-help group for those bereaved by a major disaster.

• **The Foundation for the Study of Infant Deaths (FSID)**, Artillery House, 11/19 Artillery Row, London SW1P 1RT (☎ 0870 787 0554; Cot Death Helpline 0870 787 0885; **f**: 0870 787 0725; **e**: fsid@sids.org.uk; **w**: www.sids.org.uk). Offers information and support to families and professionals. Information, fundraising for research, befriending service, local groups.

• **Invisible Community**, c/o the Cultural Freedom Trust, Mulberry House, Hoathly Hill, West Hoathly, West Sussex, RH19 4SJ (☎ 0870 321 0246; **f**: 0870 321 0247; **w**: www.theinvisiblecommunity.org). Quarterly newsletter 'Invisible News' looks at life after death and communication between the living and departed. (Send £12 cheque for 2-year subscription. Virtual version available.)

• **Lesbian and Gay Bereavement Project**, c/o The Healthy Gay Living Centre, 40 Borough High Street, London SE1 1XW (☎ Helpline 020 7403 5969 [Mon, Tue, Thur: 7pm-10.30pm]; Admin: 020 7407 3550). Counselling and support. Offers information on wills and funerals. See also Terrence Higgins Trust.

• **London Bereavement Network**, 356 Holloway Road, London N7 6PN (☎ 020 7700 8134, **f**: 020 7700 8146; **e**: info@bereavement.org.uk; **w**: www.bereavement.org.uk). Support and links to many bereavement services.

• **Merry Widow** (**e**: merrywidow@tiscali.co.uk; **w**: www.merrywidow.co.uk). Website dedicated to advising young widows. Kate Boydell provides a poignant yet frank and friendly online 'Survival Guide' for young bereaved women, based on her personal experience. Available in PDF format.

• **Miscarriage Association**, Clayton Hospital, Northgate, Wakefield WF1 3JF (☎ Helpline 01924 200 799; General: 01924 200 795; **f**: 01924 298 834; **e**: info@miscarriageassociation.org.uk; **w**: www.miscarriageassociation.org.uk). Support and information on all aspects of pregnancy loss.

• **National Association of Widows**, 3rd Floor, 48 Queens Road, Coventry CV1 3EH (☎/**f**: 024 7663 4848; **e**: office@nawidows.org.uk; **w**: www.widows.uk.net). Free info sheets, incl. one for widowed mothers (please send SAE), and local branch socials. A young widows' contact list is also available.

• **Pet Bereavement Support Group**, c/o The Blue Cross, Shilton Road, Burford, Oxfordshire, OX18 4PF (☎ 0800 096 6606). Helpline offering aid to grieving pet owners, run by the Society for Companion Animal Studies (www.scas.org.uk). Callers are linked to a telephone befriender.

• **RoadPeace**, PO Box 2579, London, NW10 3PW (☎ Helpline 0845 450 0355; General: 020 8838 5102; **e**: info@roadpeace.org; **w**: www.roadpeace.org). Supporting those bereaved or injured in a road crash. Memorial trees planted for those who died in road accidents in RoadPeace Wood.

• **The Stillbirth And Neonatal Death Society (SANDS)**, 28 Portland Place, London W1B 1LY (☎ Helpline 020 7436 5881; Admin: 020 7436 7940; **e**: support@uk-sands.org; **w**: www.uk-sands.org). Befriending and publications.

• **Support After Murder or Manslaughter (SAMM)**, Cranmer House, 39 Brixton Road, London SW9 6DZ (☎ 020 7735 3838; **e**: enquiries.samm.org.uk; **w**: samm.org.uk). Support groups around the UK.

• **Survivors of Bereavement by Suicide (SOBS)**, Centre 88, Saner Street, Hull HU3 2TR (☎ Helpline 0870 241 3337 [9am-9pm daily]; General: 01482

610728; **f**: 01482 210287; **e**: sobs.support@care4free.net; **w**: www.uk-sobs.org.uk). Offers support.

• **TAMBA Bereavement Support Group**, 2 The Willows, Gardner Road, Guildford, Surrey GU1 4PG (☎ Helpline 01732 868 000; General: 0870 770 3305; **f**: 0870 770 3303; **e**: enquiries@tamba.org.uk; **w**: www.tamba.org.uk). Subdivision of the Twins And Multiple Births Association providing support to those who have lost children to multiple birth.

• **War Widows' Association of Great Britain (WWA)**, c/o 48 Pall Mall, London SW1Y 3JY (☎ 0870 2411 305; **e**: info@warwidowsassociation.org.uk; **w**: www. warwidows association.org.uk). Advice on pensions. Support for all war widows.

• **The WAY Foundation**, PO Box 74, Penarth, Cardiff CF64 5ZD (☎ 0870 011 3450; **e**: info@wayfoundation.org.uk; **w**: www.wayfoundation.org.uk). Offers a self-help social and support network for men and women widowed under 50, and their children. When writing, enclose an SAE for information.

For Children

• **ACT**, Orchard House, Orchard Lane, Bristol BS1 5DT (☎ 0117 922 1556; **f**: 0117 930 4707; **e**: info@act.org.uk; **w**: www.act.org.uk). Association for children with life-threatening terminal conditions and their families.

• **The Centre for Attitudinal Healing**, 33 Buchanan Drive, Sausalito, California 94965, USA (☎ 001 415 331 6161; **e**: cah@well.com; **w**: healingcenter.org). Works with children facing serious illnesses, or whose parents have cancer.

• **The Child Bereavement Trust**, Aston House, West Wycombe, High Wycombe, Buckinghamshire HP14 3AG (☎ 01494 446 648; **f**: 01494 440 057; **e**: enquiries@childbereavement.org.uk; **w**: www.childbereavement.org). Provides support to children and young adults who have lost someone.

• **Helen House – A hospice for children**, 37 Leopold Street, Oxford OX4 1QT (☎ 01865 728 251; **f**: 01865 794 829; **e**: helen-house.org.uk; **w**: www.helen-house.org.uk). Offers terminally ill children and their families practical help and friendship. One of a number of such hospices across Britain (see www.helpthehospices.org.uk/links.html).

• **The Orchard Project** (Barnardos), Orchard House, Fenwick Terrace, Jesmond, Newcastle-Upon-Tyne NE2 2JQ (☎ 0191 240 4813; **f**: 0191 240 4833; **e**: orchard.project@barnardos.org.uk). Support and counselling for bereaved children and their families.

• **Papyrus,** Rossendale GH, Union Road, Rawtenstall, Lancs BB4 6NE (**w**: www.papyrus-uk.org). Aims to prevent suicide in the young.

• **Rainbow Trust**, Claire House, Bridge Street, Leatherhead, Surrey KT22 8BZ (☎ 01372 363 438; **f**: 01372 363 101; **w**: www.rainbowtrust.org.uk). Help and respite for children with life-threatening illnesses and their families.

• **React**, St Luke's House, 270 Sandycombe Road, Kew, Richmond, Surrey TW9 3NP (☎ 020 8940 2575; **f**: 020 8940 2050; **e**: react@reactcharity.org; **w**: www.reactcharity.org). Money and equipment for children with reduced life expectancy. Applications via GP or a professional worker.

• **St Christopher's Hospice**, St Christopher's Candle Project, 51-59 Lawrie Park Road, London SE26 6DZ (☎ 0181 778 9252; **f**: 0208 659 8680). Support for all children, young people and their families in South East London. They also offer a specialist training, advice and consultancy service to schools and other agencies working with children facing bereavement.

• **Starlight Children's Foundation**, Macmillan House, Paddington Stations, London W2 1HD (☎ 020 7262 2881; **f**: 020 7402 7403; **e**: info@starlight.org.uk; **w**: www.starlight.org.uk). Attempts to grant the wishes of critically, chronically and terminally ill children.

• **Teenage Cancer Trust**, 38 Warren Street, London W1T 6AE, (☎ 020 7387 1000; **f**: 020 7387 6000; **e**: tct@teencancer.bdx.co.uk; **w**: www.teencancer.org). For young people with leukaemia, Hodgkin's and similar malignant diseases.

• **Winston's Wish**, The Clara Burgess Centre, Gloucestershire Royal Hospital, Great Western Road, Gloucester GL1 3NN (☎ 01452 394 377; **e**: info@winstonwish.org.uk; **w**: www.winstonswish.org.uk). Supports bereaved children, young people and their families.

Training, Courses & Workshops

Independent

• **Accepting Death and Living Fully**. A 12-session course or individual tailor-made workshops with Josefine Speyer, founder-director of the Natural Death Centre (20 Heber Road, London NW2 6AA, ☎ 020 8208 0670). To explore issues surrounding loss and grief, terminal illness, caring for the dying, creating a funeral, for professional groups or the general public. The course draws on personal experiences and beliefs of the individual to facilitate a deeper understanding of the needs and concerns of the self and others in relation to dying.

• **'Live This Year as Though it were Your Last'**. 'Share your knowledge of death, write your own epitaph, design your ideal funeral and consider Living Wills and Wills. These retreats offer the opportunity to deeply recognise the implications of having no more time' (Caroline Sherwood, 11 Old Wells Road, Glastonbury BA6 8ED, ☎ 01458 832487; **e**: carosher@ukonline.co.uk).

• **Living with Dying**. A one- or two-day course with Christianne Heal (1 Petersfield, Cambridge CB1 1BB, ☎ 01223 319 310) held in Cambridge, regularly in London at the Mary Ward Centre (42 Queens Square WC1N 3AQ, ☎ 020 7831 7711), or elsewhere on request.

• **The Natural Death Centre** (see Organisations) offers a variety of educational events and workshops on various topics related to preparing for death, caring for the dying, how to organise a funeral and issues of loss and bereavement.

• **Spiritual Care Programme**. An education and training project of Rigpa (330 Caledonian Road, London N1 1BB; ☎ Paul Kimber 020 7609 7010; **w**: www.spcare.org). Based on the work of Sogyal Rinpoche and drawing on methods introduced in his book, *The Tibetan Book of Living and Dying*. One day or weekend seminars offered at places of work or at Rigpa.

• **Training for Cancer Self-Help and Support**. Courses designed to meet the needs of anyone affected by cancer. For details contact Heather Petty, Training Administrator, Macmillan Cancer Relief (see Organisations entry).

• **Where Two Worlds Meet: Letting go into life and death** with Archa Kate Robinson (40 Freshfield Street, Brighton BN2 9ZG, ☎ 01273 607374; **e**: archasans@onetel.net.uk). 'The workshop is mostly conducted in silence, allowing time for private reflection.' Some exercises incorporate the teachings of the Indian guru, Osho.

Academic

• **Death and Dying** (Department of Health & Social Care, The Open University, PO Box 724, Milton Keynes MK7 6ZS, ☎ 01908 653231; **f**: 01908 655072; **e**: general-enquiries@open.ac.uk; **w**: www.open.ac.uk/courses). Course module K260 in Death and Dying is related to BA/BSc Hons Health Studies, but can be studied separately, and is open to anyone. Covers ethics, law, cultural and practical perspectives on death, dying and bereavement. Price: £335. Start: February. Duration: 8-month tutor-assisted distance study.

• **MA in Death and Immortality** (Department of Theology, Religious Studies & Islamic Studies, University of Wales, Lampeter, Ceredigion, Wales SA48 7ED, ☎ 01570 424748; **f**: 01570 423 641; **e**: trs@lamp.ac.uk; **w**: www.religious-studies.net). Core modules in 'philosophy and life after death' and 'eternal life in Christian thought' plus optional units. F/T or P/T non-residential study.

• **MA in Death and Society** (Department of Sociology, Faculty of Letters & Social Sciences, University of Reading, Whiteknights, Reading, Berkshire RG6 6AH, ☎ 0118 987 5123; **f**: 0118 931 4404; **e**: info@reading.ac.uk; **w**: www.rdg.ac.uk/DeathSoc). From burial archaeology and martyrdom to bereavement and medical ethics. Currently suspended, but worth checking website for updates. Bath University is planning a similar MA for 2004; contact Glennys Howarth for details (**e**: G.Howarth@bath.ac.uk).

• **MA in Death Studies** (School of Anthropology, University of Wales, Lampeter, Ceredigion, Wales SA48 7ED, ☎ 01570 424748; **f**: 01570 423423; **e**: pg-office@lampeter.ac.uk; **w**: www.lamp.ac.uk). Multidisciplinary course covering philosophical and theological issues and historical perspectives. Introduction to training in bereavement counselling. Possibility of distance learning.

• **MA in Religion: The rhetoric and rituals of death** (King Alfred's College, Winchester SO22 4NR, ☎ 01962 841515; **f**: 01962 842280; **w**: www.wkac.ac.uk/trs) The Department of Theology and Religion offers this course which looks at the theology, philosophy and liturgies of death in different cultures and religions incl. Christianity and Hinduism. F/T or P/T. Available by distance learning.

• **Short course in Aspects of Death and Dying** (Birkbeck College, University of London, Malet Street, London WC1H 7HX, ☎ 020 7631 6669/6665; **e**: psychology@fce.bbk.ac.uk; **w**: www.bbk.ac.uk/study/fce). A 12-week course exploring ways of understanding the human response to death. Run by the Psychology and Psychotherapy Department, it is open to anyone regardless of educational background (for prospectus **e**: info@fce.bbk.ac.uk). Starts in September, runs for two hours each Thursday (6.30-8.30pm) and costs £70.

Index